★ **Musée du Louvre** ⑥
See pp122–9.

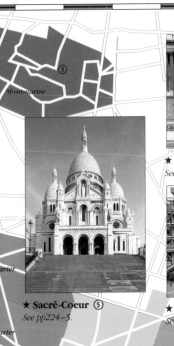

★ **Sacré-Coeur** ⑤
See pp224–5.

★ **Pompidou Centre** ⑦
See pp110–13.

Montmartre

The Marais

*Beaubourg and
Les Halles*

⑥

⑦

⑧

⑨

*St-Germain-
des-Prés*

⑩

Ile de la Cité

⑪

Ile St-Louis

⑫

*Latin
Quarter*

★ **Musée de Cluny** ⑫
See pp154–7.

★ **Musée Picasso** ⑧
See pp100–1.

*Luxembourg
Quarter*

⑬

*Jardin des Plantes
Quarter*

★ **Panthéon** ⑬
See pp158–9.

★ **Sainte-Chapelle** ⑩
See pp88–9.

★ **Notre-Dame** ⑪
See pp82–5.

University of **Chester**

LIS Library

Helpdesk 01244 511234
lis.helpdesk@chester.ac.uk

EYEWITNESS *TRAVEL GUIDES*

PARIS

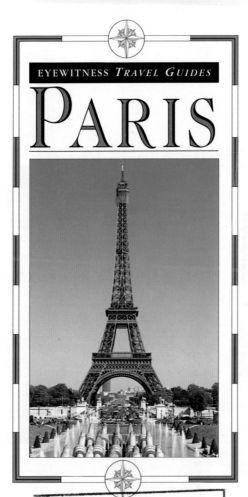

DK EYEWITNESS *TRAVEL GUIDES*

PARIS

Main Contributor: ALAN TILLIER

DORLING KINDERSLEY

LONDON • NEW YORK • MUNICH

MELBOURNE • DELHI

www.dk.com

A Dorling Kindersley Book

www.dk.com

Project Editor Heather Jones
Art Editor Janis Utton
Editor Alex Gray
Designer Vanessa Hamilton
Design Assistant Clare Sullivan

Contributors
Chris Boicos, Michael Gibson, Douglas Johnson

Photographers
Max Alexander, Neil Lukas, Robert O'Dea

Illustrators
Stephen Conlin, Stephen Gyapay,
Maltings Partnership

•

This book was produced with the assistance of
Websters International Publishers.

•

Reproduced by Colourscan, Singapore
Printed and bound by South China Printing Co. Ltd., China

First published in Great Britain in 1993
by Dorling Kindersley Limited
80 Strand, London WC2R 0RL

A Pearson Company

**Reprinted with revisions 1994, 1995, 1997 (twice),
1999, 2000, 2001, 2002**

Copyright 1993, 2002 © Dorling Kindersley Limited, London

A CIP catalogue record is available from the British Library.

ISBN 0-7513-4708-6

This DK Eyewitness Travel Guide is updated annually.
We value the views and suggestions of our readers very highly.
Please write to: Senior Publishing Manager, DK Eyewitness Travel
Guides, Dorling Kindersley, 80 Strand, London WC2R 0RL.
Or contact us via: travelguides@dk.com

Even though every effort has been made to ensure that this book
is as up-to-date as possible at the time of going to press, some
details are liable to change. The publishers cannot accept
responsibility for any consequences arising from the use of
this book, nor for any material on third-party websites, and
cannot guarantee that any website address in this book
will be a suitable source of travel information.

See our complete catalogue at:
www.dk.com/travel

Contents

Henri II (1547–59)

Introducing
Paris

Pont Alexandre III

Opéra de Paris Bastille

The Kiss by Rodin (1886)

Sacré-Coeur in Montmartre

An island in the Bois de Boulogne

TRAVELLERS' NEEDS

Noisettes of lamb

SURVIVAL GUIDE

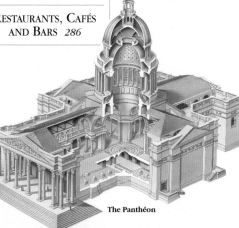

The Panthéon

HOW TO USE THIS GUIDE

THIS EYEWITNESS TRAVEL GUIDE helps you get the most from your stay in Paris with the minimum of practical difficulty. The opening section, *Introducing Paris*, locates the city geographically, sets modern Paris in its historical context and explains how Parisian life changes through the year. *Paris at a Glance* is an overview of the city's specialities. The main sightseeing section of the book is *Paris Area by Area*. It describes all the main sights with maps, photographs and detailed illustrations. In addition, five planned walks take you to parts of Paris you might otherwise miss.

Carefully researched tips for hotels, shops and markets, restaurants and bars, sports and entertainment are found in *Travellers' Needs*, and the *Survival Guide* has advice on everything from posting a letter to catching the metro.

PARIS AREA BY AREA

The city has been divided into 14 sightseeing areas. Each section opens with a portrait of the area, summing up its character and history, with a list of all the sights to be covered. These are clearly located by numbers on an *Area Map*. This is followed by a large-scale *Street-by-Street Map* focusing on the most interesting part of the area. Finding your way about the section is made simple by the numbering system used throughout for the sights. This refers to the order in which they are described on the pages that complete the section.

1 Area Map

For easy reference, the sights in each area are numbered and located on an area map. To help the visitor, the map also shows metro and mainline RER stations and car parks.

The Concergerie ❽ is shown on this map as well.

Colour-coding on each page makes the area easy to find in the book.

2 Street-by-Street Map

This gives a bird's-eye view of the heart of each sightseeing area. The most important buildings are picked out in stronger colour, to help you spot them as you walk around.

A locator map shows you where you are in relation to surrounding areas. The area of the *Street-by-Street Map* is shown in red.

Photographs of facades and distinctive details of buildings help you to locate the sights.

Sights at a Glance lists the sights in the area by category: Historic Streets and Buildings, Churches, Museums and Galleries, Monuments, and Squares, Parks and Gardens.

The area covered in greater detail on the *Street-by-Street Map* is shaded red.

Travel tips help you reach the area quickly.

Numbered circles pinpoint all the listed sights on the area map. The Concergerie, for example, is ❽

A suggested route for a walk takes in the most attractive and interesting streets in the area.

Red stars indicate the sights that no visitor should miss.

ILE DE LA CITÉ AND ILE ST-LOUIS

Street-by-Street: Ile de la Cité

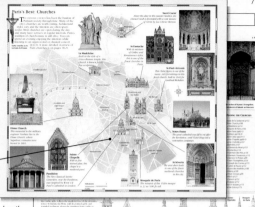

PARIS AT A GLANCE

Each map in this section concentrates on a specific theme: *Museums and Galleries, Churches, Squares, Parks and Gardens, Remarkable Parisians.* The top sights are shown on the map; other sights are described on the following two pages.

Each sightseeing area is colour-coded.

The theme is explored in greater detail on the pages following the map.

3 Detailed information on each sight

All important sights in each area are described in depth in this section. They are listed in order, following the numbering on the Area Map. Practical information is also provided.

PRACTICAL INFORMATION

Each entry provides all the information needed to plan a visit to the sight. The key to the symbols used is on the inside back cover.

Nearest metro station

Telephone number

Sight number

Opening hours

Conciergerie ⑧

1 Quai de l'Horloge 75001.
Map 13 A3. **℡** 01 53 73 78 50.
Ⓜ Cité. **⊙** Apr–Sep: 9.30am–6pm daily.

Map reference to *Street Finder* at back of book

Services and facilities available

Address

4 Paris's major sights

These are given two or more full pages in the sightseeing area in which they are found. Historic buildings are dissected to reveal their interiors; and museums and galleries have colour-coded floor plans to help you find important exhibits.

The Visitors' Checklist provides the practical information you will need to plan your visit.

The facade of each major sight is shown to help you spot it quickly.

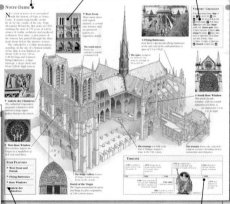

Red stars indicate the most interesting architectural details of the building, and the most important works of art or exhibits on view inside.

A timeline charts the key events in the history of the sight.

INTRODUCING
PARIS

Putting Paris on the Map

P ARIS, THE CAPITAL of France, is a city of over two million people covering 1,200 sq km (460 sq miles) of northern France. It is on the River Seine at the centre of the Ile-de-France, the region which is home to ten million people, around one-fifth of the French population. An important European business and cultural centre, it is the focus of activity in the north of France.

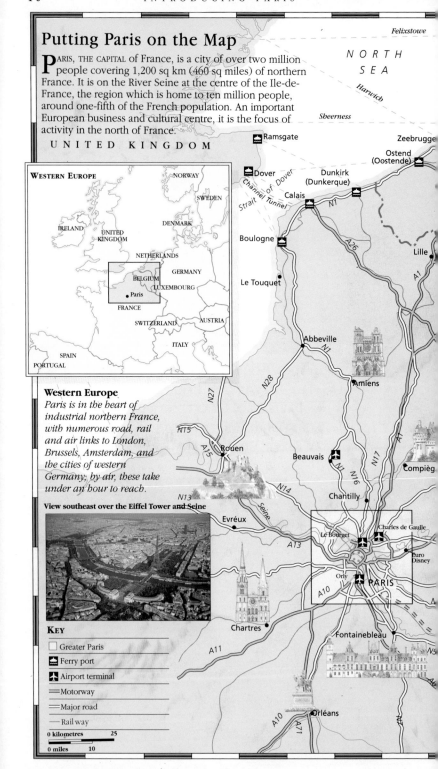

WESTERN EUROPE

NORWAY

SWEDEN

IRELAND

UNITED KINGDOM

DENMARK

NETHERLANDS

BELGIUM

GERMANY

LUXEMBOURG

• Paris

FRANCE

SWITZERLAND

AUSTRIA

ITALY

SPAIN

PORTUGAL

Western Europe

Paris is in the heart of industrial northern France, with numerous road, rail and air links to London, Brussels, Amsterdam, and the cities of western Germany; by air, these take under an hour to reach.

View southeast over the Eiffel Tower and Seine

KEY

☐ Greater Paris

⚓ Ferry port

✈ Airport terminal

═══ Motorway

══ Major road

— Railway

| 0 kilometres | 25 |
| 0 miles | 10 |

UNITED KINGDOM

NORTH SEA

Felixstowe

Harwich

Sheerness

Ramsgate

Zeebrugge

Ostend (Oostende)

Dover

Dunkirk (Dunkerque)

Channel of Dover

Strait of Dover

Channel Tunnel

Calais

N1

Boulogne

Lille

A26

A1

Le Touquet

Abbeville

N1

Amiens

N27

N28

Rouen

N15

A15

Beauvais

Chantilly

N1

N16

N17

Compièg.

N13

N14

Seine

Evréux

Le Bourget

Charles de Gaulle

A13

Euro Disney

Orly

PARIS

Chartres

A10

Fontainebleau

A11

A10

A71

Orléans

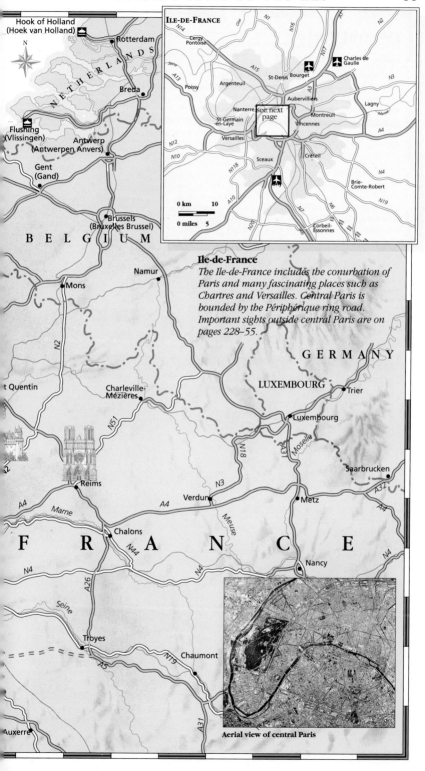

Ile-de-France

N14

Cergy
Pontoise

Oise N1 N16 N17 N2

Seine

A15

St-Denis
✈ Bourget ✈ Charles de
Gaulle

N3

A13 Poissy
Argenteuil

Nanterre Aubervilliers

Lagny

Marne

St-Germain
-en-Laye Montreuil
**see next
page** Vincennes

A4

N12 Versailles

N10 Créteil

N118 Sceaux

Brie-
Comte-Robert

A10 N7 N6 N4 N19

N20

Corbeil-
Essonnes

0 km   10

0 miles   5

Ile-de-France

*The Ile-de-France includes the conurbation of
Paris and many fascinating places such as
Chartres and Versailles. Central Paris is
bounded by the Périphérique ring road.
Important sights outside central Paris are on
pages 228–55.*

G E R M A N Y

LUXEMBOURG

Hook of Holland
(Hoek van Holland)

Rotterdam

N E T H E R L A N D S

Breda

Flushing
(Vlissingen)

Antwerp
(Antwerpen Anvers)

Gent
(Gand)

Brussels
(Bruxelles Brussel)

B E L G I U M

Namur

Mons

N2

t Quentin

Charleville-
Mézières

N51

Reims

A4 Marne

Chalons

N44

F   R   A   N   C   E

N4

A26

Seine

Troyes

A5 N19 Chaumont

Auxerre

A31

Verdun

A4

Meuse

N3

Trier

Luxembourg

N18 Moselle A31

Saarbrucken

A4

Metz

N4

Nancy

Aerial view of central Paris

Central Paris

THIS BOOK DIVIDES PARIS into 14 areas, comprising central Paris and the nearby area of Montmartre. Most of the sights covered in the book lie within these areas, each one of which has its own chapter. Each area contains a range of sights that convey some of its history and distinctive character. The sights of Montmartre, for example, reveal its village charm and its colourful history as a thriving artistic enclave. In contrast, Champs-Elysées is renowned for its wide avenues, expensive fashion houses and opulent mansions. Most of the city's famous sights are within reach of the heart of the city and are easy to reach on foot or by public transport.

PAGES 202–9
*Street Finder maps
3–4, 5, 11*

Champs-Elysées

Chaillot Quarter

0 kilometres 1

0 miles 0.5

R I V E R S E

Invalides and Eiffel Tower Quarter

PAGES 194–201
*Street Finder maps
3, 9–10*

PAGES 182–93
*Street Finder maps
9–10, 11*

PAGES 116–33
*Street Finder maps
6, 11–12*

PAGES 134–47
*Street Finder maps
11–12*

PAGES 174–81
*Street Finder maps
15–16*

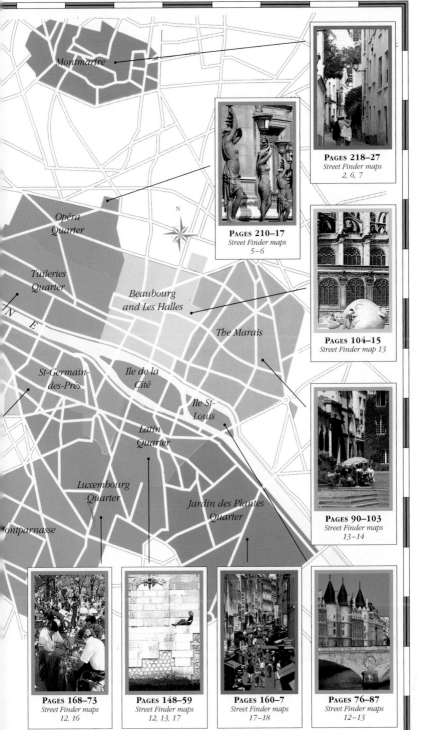

Montmartre

Opéra
Quarter

Tuileries
Quarter

Beaubourg
and Les Halles

The Marais

N

St-Germain-
des-Prés

Ile de la
Cité

Ile St-
Louis

Latin
Quarter

Luxembourg
Quarter

Jardin des Plantes
Quarter

Montparnasse

PAGES 218–27
*Street Finder maps
2, 6, 7*

PAGES 210–17
*Street Finder maps
5–6*

PAGES 104–15
Street Finder map 13

PAGES 90–103
*Street Finder maps
13–14*

PAGES 168–73
*Street Finder maps
12, 16*

PAGES 148–59
*Street Finder maps
12, 13, 17*

PAGES 160–7
*Street Finder maps
17–18*

PAGES 76–87
*Street Finder maps
12–13*

REPUBLIQUE FRANCAISE
LIBERTE EGALITE · FRATERNITE

THE HISTORY OF PARIS

THE PARIS CONQUERED by the Romans in 55 BC was a small flood-prone fishing village on the Ile de la Cité, inhabited by the Parisii tribe. A Roman settlement soon flourished and spread on to the Left Bank of the Seine. The Franks succeeded the Romans, named the city Paris and made it the centre of their kingdom.

During the Middle Ages the city flourished as a religious centre and architectural masterpieces such as Sainte-Chapelle were erected. It also thrived as a centre of learning, enticing European scholars to its great university, the Sorbonne.

Paris emerged during the Renaissance and the Enlightenment as a great centre of culture and ideas, and under the rule of Louis XIV it also became a city of immense wealth and power. But rule by the monarch gave way to rule by the people in the bloody Revolution of 1789. By

Fleur-de-lys, the royal emblem

the early years of the new century, revolutionary fervour had faded and the brilliant militarist Napoleon Bonaparte proclaimed himself Emperor of France and pursued his ambition to make Paris the centre of the world.

Soon after the Revolution of 1848 a radical transformation of the city began. Baron Haussmann's grand urban scheme replaced Paris's medieval slums with elegant avenues and boulevards. By the end of the century, the city was the driving force of Western culture. This continued well into the 20th century, interrupted only by the German military occupation of 1940–44. Since the war, the city has revived and expanded dramatically, as it strives to be at the heart of a unified Europe.

The following pages illustrate Paris's history by providing snapshots of the significant periods in the city's evolution.

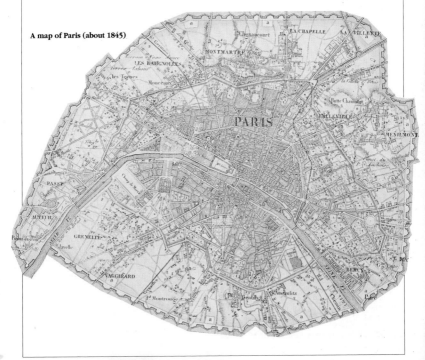

A map of Paris (about 1845)

Allegory of the Republic (1848) by Dominique Louis Papety

Kings and Emperors in Paris

PARIS BECAME the power base for the kings of France at the beginning of the Capetian dynasty, when Hugh Capet ascended the throne. Successive kings and emperors have left their mark and many of the places mentioned in this book have royal associations: Philippe-Auguste's fortress, the Louvre Palace, is now one of the world's great museums; Henri IV's Pont Neuf bridge links the Ile de la Cité with the two banks of the Seine; and Napoleon conceived the Arc de Triomphe to celebrate his military victories. The end of the long line of kings came with the overthrow of the monarchy in 1848, during the reign of Louis-Philippe.

768–814 Charlemagne

743–751 Childéric III

716–721 Chilpéric II

695–711 Childebert II

566–584 Chilpéric I

558–562 Clotaire I

447–458 Merovich

458–482 Childéric I

674–691 Thierri III

655–668 Clotaire III

628–637 Dagobert I

954–986 Lothaire

898–929 Charles III, the Simple

884–888 Charles II, the Fat

879–882 Louis III

840–877 Charles I, the Bald

1137–80 Louis VII

987–996 Hugh Capet

1031–60 Henri I

1060–1108 Philippe I

400	500	600	700	800	900	1000	1100
MEROVINGIAN DYNASTY				**CAROLINGIAN DYNASTY**		**CAPETIAN DYNASTY**	

400	500	600	700	800	900	1000	1100

751–768 Pépin the Short

721–737 Thierri IV

711–716 Dagobert III

691–695 Clovis III

668–674 Childéric II

637–655 Clovis II

584–628 Clotaire II

562–566 Caribert

511–558 Childebert I

996–1031 Robert II, the Pious

986–987 Louis V

936–954 Louis IV, the Foreigner

888–898 Odo, Count of Paris

882–884 Carloman

877–879 Louis II, the Stammerer

814–840 Louis I, the Debonair

482–511 Clovis I

1108–37 Louis VI, the Fat

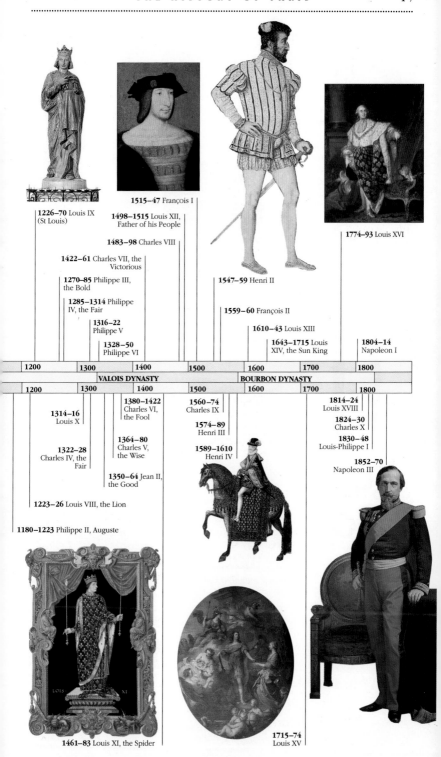

1515–47 François I

1226–70 Louis IX (St Louis)

1498–1515 Louis XII, Father of his People

1483–98 Charles VIII

1422–61 Charles VII, the Victorious

1270–85 Philippe III, the Bold

1285–1314 Philippe IV, the Fair

1316–22 Philippe V

1328–50 Philippe VI

1547–59 Henri II

1559–60 François II

1610–43 Louis XIII

1643–1715 Louis XIV, the Sun King

1774–93 Louis XVI

1804–14 Napoleon I

| 1200 | 1300 | 1400 | 1500 | 1600 | 1700 | 1800 |

VALOIS DYNASTY **BOURBON DYNASTY**

| 1200 | 1300 | 1400 | 1500 | 1600 | 1700 | 1800 |

1314–16 Louis X

1322–28 Charles IV, the Fair

1380–1422 Charles VI, the Fool

1364–80 Charles V, the Wise

1350–64 Jean II, the Good

1560–74 Charles IX

1574–89 Henri III

1589–1610 Henri IV

1814–24 Louis XVIII

1824–30 Charles X

1830–48 Louis-Philippe I

1852–70 Napoleon III

1223–26 Louis VIII, the Lion

1180–1223 Philippe II, Auguste

1461–83 Louis XI, the Spider

1715–74 Louis XV

Gallo-Roman Paris

PARIS WOULD NOT have existed without the Seine. The river provided early peoples with the means to exploit the land, forests, marshes and islands. Recent excavations have unearthed canoes dating back to 4,500 BC, well before a Celtic tribe, known as the Parisii, settled there in the 3rd century BC, in an area known as Lutetia. From 59 BC, the Romans undertook the conquest of Gaul (France). Seven years later Lutetia was sacked by the Romans. They fortified and rebuilt it, especially the main island (the Ile de la Cité) and the Left Bank of the Seine.

Roman enamel brooch

EXTENT OF THE CITY
☐ 200 BC   ☐ Today

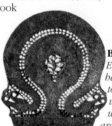

Bronze-Age Harness
Everyday objects like harnesses continued to be made of bronze well into the Iron Age, which began in Gaul around 900 BC.

Iron Daggers
From the 2nd century BC, short swords of iron replaced long swords and were sometimes decorated with human and animal shapes.

Baths

Theatre

Forum

Glass Beads
Iron-Age glass beads and bracelets have been found on the Ile de la Cité.

Fired-Clay Vase
Pale ceramics with coloured decoration were common in Gaul.

Present-day Rue Soufflot

Present-day Rue St-Jacques

TIMELINE

4500 BC Early boatmen operate from the banks of the Seine		*Helmet worn by Gaulish warriors*		**52 BC** Labienus, Caesar's lieutenant, defeats the Gauls under Camulogenes. The Parisii destroy their own city
4500	400	300	200	100 BC
Parisii gold coin minted on the Ile de la Cité **300 BC** Parisii tribe settle on the Ile de la Cité			**100 BC** Romans rebuild the Ile de la Cité, and create a new town on the Left Bank	

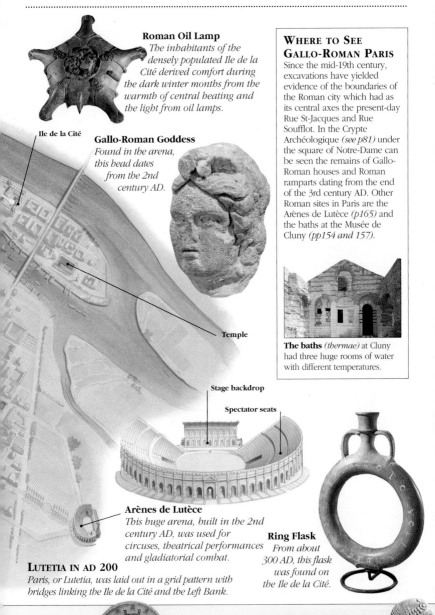

Roman Oil Lamp
The inhabitants of the densely populated Ile de la Cité derived comfort during the dark winter months from the warmth of central heating and the light from oil lamps.

Ile de la Cité

Gallo-Roman Goddess
Found in the arena, this head dates from the 2nd century AD.

Temple

WHERE TO SEE GALLO-ROMAN PARIS
Since the mid-19th century, excavations have yielded evidence of the boundaries of the Roman city which had as its central axes the present-day Rue St-Jacques and Rue Soufflot. In the Crypte Archéologique *(see p81)* under the square of Notre-Dame can be seen the remains of Gallo-Roman houses and Roman ramparts dating from the end of the 3rd century AD. Other Roman sites in Paris are the Arènes de Lutèce *(p165)* and the baths at the Musée de Cluny *(pp154 and 157).*

The baths *(thermae)* at Cluny had three huge rooms of water with different temperatures.

Stage backdrop

Spectator seats

Arènes de Lutèce
This huge arena, built in the 2nd century AD, was used for circuses, theatrical performances and gladiatorial combat.

Ring Flask
From about 300 AD, this flask was found on the Ile de la Cité.

LUTETIA IN AD 200
Paris, or Lutetia, was laid out in a grid pattern with bridges linking the Ile de la Cité and the Left Bank.

Roman floor mosaic from the Cluny baths

200 Romans add arena, baths and villas

285 Barbarians advance, Lutetia swept by fire

360 Julien, prefect of Gaul, is proclaimed Emperor. Lutetia changes its name to Paris

| 100 AD | 200 | 300 | 400 |

250 Early Christian martyr, St Denis, beheaded in Montmartre

451 Sainte Geneviève galvanizes the Parisians to repulse Attila the Hun

485–508 Clovis, leader of the Franks, defeats the Romans. Paris becomes Christian

Medieval Paris

Manuscript illumination

THROUGHOUT THE MIDDLE AGES, strategically placed towns like Paris, positioned at a river crossing, became important centres of political power and learning. The Church played a crucial part in intellectual and spiritual life. It provided the impetus for education and for technological advances such as the drainage of land and the digging of canals. The population was still confined mainly to the Ile de la Cité and the Left Bank. When the marshes *(marais)* were drained in the 12th century, the city was able to expand.

EXTENT OF THE CITY
☐ *1300*   ☐ *Today*

Sainte-Chapelle
The upper chapel of this medieval masterpiece (see pp88–9) *was reserved for the royal family.*

The Ile de la Cité, including the towers of the Conciergerie and Sainte-Chapelle, features in the pages for June.

Octagonal Table
Medieval manor houses had wooden furniture like this trestle table.

Drainage allowed more land to be cultivated.

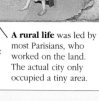

Weavers' Window
Medieval craftsmen formed guilds and many church windows were dedicated to their crafts.

A rural life was led by most Parisians, who worked on the land. The actual city only occupied a tiny area.

TIMELINE

512 Death of Sainte Geneviève. She is buried next to Clovis

725–732 Muslims attack Gaul

845–862 Normans attack Paris

| 500 | 700 | 800 | 900 |

543–556 Foundation of St-Germain-des-Prés

Golden hand reliquary of Charlemagne

800 Charlemagne crowned Emperor by the Pope

Notre-Dame
The great Gothic cathedrals took many years to build. Work continued on Notre-Dame from 1163 to 1334.

University Seal
The University of Paris was founded in 1215.

The Monasteries
Monks of many different orders lived in monasteries in Paris, especially on the Left Bank of the Seine.

The Louvre of Charles V
with its defensive wall is seen here from the Ile de la Cité.

The Nobility
From the mid-14th century, dress was considered to be a mark of class; noble ladies wore high, pointed hats.

A MEDIEVAL ROMANCE
It was in the cloisters of Notre-Dame that the romance between the monk Pierre Abélard and the young Héloïse began. Abélard was the most original theologian of the 12th century and was hired as a tutor to the 17-year-old niece of a canon. A love affair soon developed between the teacher and his pupil. In his wrath, Héloïse's uncle had the scholar castrated; Héloïse took refuge in a convent for the rest of her life.

THE MONTHS: JUNE AND OCTOBER
This illuminated prayer book and calendar, the Très Riches Heures (left and above), was made for the Duc de Berri in 1416. It shows many Paris buildings.

1010–22 Christians burn Jews and heretics

1167 Les Halles food market created on the Right Bank of the Seine

1253 The Sorbonne opens

Joan of Arc

1380 The Bastille fortress completed

1000	1100	1200	1300	1400

1079 Birth of Pierre Abélard

1163 Work starts on Notre-Dame cathedral

1245 Work starts on Sainte-Chapelle

1226–70 Reign of Louis IX, St Louis

1430 Henry VI of England crowned King of France after Joan of Arc fails to defend Paris

1215 Paris University founded

Renaissance Paris

Couple in fine courtly dress

AT THE END of the Hundred Years' War with England, Paris was in a terrible state. By the time the occupying English army had left in 1453, the city lay in ruins, with many houses and trees burned. Louis XI brought back prosperity and a new interest in art, architecture, decoration and clothes. During the course of the 16th century, French kings came under the spell of the Italian Renaissance. Their architects made the first attempts at town planning, creating elegant, uniform buildings and open urban spaces like the magnificent Place Royale.

EXTENT OF THE CITY
☐ *1590*   ☐ *Today*

A Knight Preparing to Joust
The Place Royale was the setting for jousting displays well into the 17th century.

Printing Press (1470)
Religious tracts, mainly in Latin, were printed on the first press at the Sorbonne.

Jewel-Encrusted Pendant
A sign of the new prosperity, jewels became an important part of dress.

Pont Notre-Dame
This bridge with its row of houses was built at the start of the 15th century. The Pont Neuf (1589) was the first bridge without houses.

PLACE ROYALE
Built by Henri IV in 1609, with grand symmetrical houses round an open, central space, this was Paris' first square. Home to the aristocracy, it was re-named Place des Vosges in 1800 (see p94).

TIMELINE

1453 End of the Hundred Years' War with England

François I

1516 François I invites Leonardo da Vinci to France. He brings the *Mona Lisa* with him

1450	1460	1470	1480	1490	1500	1510	1520

1469 First French printing works starts operating at the Sorbonne

1528 François I takes up residence in the Louvre

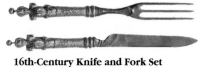

16th-Century Knife and Fork Set
Ornate knife and fork sets were used in the dining rooms of the wealthy to carve joints of meat. Diners used hands or spoons for eating.

WHERE TO SEE RENAISSANCE PARIS TODAY
Besides the Place des Vosges with its fine buildings, there are many examples of the Renaissance in Paris today. Churches include the Tour St-Jacques (*p115*), St-Etienne-du-Mont (*p153*) and St-Eustache (*p114*). Mansions such as the Hôtel Carnavalet (*pp96–7*) have recently been restored and the staircases, courtyard and turrets of the Hôtel de Cluny (*pp154–5*) date from 1485–96.

The rood screen of St-Etienne-du-Mont (about 1520) is of outstanding delicacy.

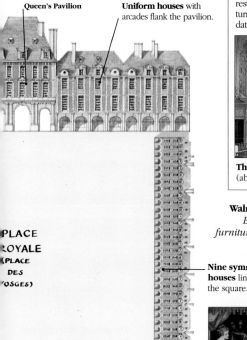

Queen's Pavilion

Uniform houses with arcades flank the pavilion.

PLACE ROYALE (PLACE DES VOSGES)

Walnut Dresser (about 1545)
Elegant carved wooden furniture decorated the homes of the wealthy.

Nine symmetrical houses line each side of the square.

King's Pavilion

Duels were fought in the centre of the square in the 17th century.

Hyante and Climente
Toussaint Dubreuil and other artists took up Renaissance mythological themes.

1534 Ignatius of Loyola founds the Society of Jesus

1546 Work starts on new Louvre palace; first stone quay built along Seine

1559 Primitive street lanterns introduced; Louvre completed

1572 St Bartholomew's Day massacre of Protestants

1589 Henri III assassinated at St-Cloud, near Paris

1609 Henri IV begins building Place des Vosges

| 1530 | 1540 | 1550 | 1560 | 1570 | 1580 | 1590 | 1600 |

1534 Founding of the Collège de France

1533 Hôtel de Ville rebuilt

1547 François I dies

1559 Henri II killed in a Paris tournament

1589 Protestant Henri of Navarre converts to Catholicism, crowned as Henri IV

1589 Henri IV completes Pont-Neuf and improves capital's water supply

1610 Henri IV is assassinated by Ravaillac, a religious fanatic

The assassin Ravaillac

The Sun King's Paris

**Emblem of
the Sun King**

THE 17TH CENTURY in France, which became known as *Le Grand Siècle* (the great century), is epitomized by the glittering extravagance of Louis XIV (the Sun King) and his court at Versailles. In Paris, imposing buildings, squares, theatres and aristocratic *hôtels* (mansions) were built. Beneath this brilliant surface lay the absolute power of the monarch. By the end of Louis' reign the cost of his extravagance and of waging almost continuous war with France's neighbours led to a decline in the monarchy.

EXTENT OF THE CITY

| 1657 | Today |

The mansard roof, with its slopes at both sides and both ends, came to typify French roofs of this period.

An open staircase rose from the internal courtyard.

Cross section of the living quarters

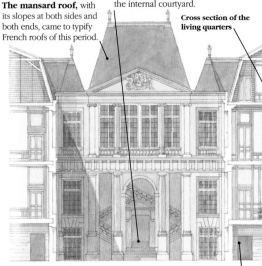

The Gardens of Versailles
Louis XIV devoted a lot of time to the gardens, which were designed by André Le Nôtre.

Louis XIV as Jupiter
On ascending the throne in 1661, Louis, depicted here as Jupiter triumphant, ended the civil wars that had been raging since his childhood.

The ground floor contained the servants' quarters.

Chest of Drawers
This gilded piece was made by André-Charles Boulle for the Grand Trianon at Versailles.

TIMELINE

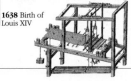

1610 Louis XIII's accession marks the start of *Le Grand Siècle*

Louis XIII

1624 Completion of Tuileries Palace

Cardinal Mazarin

1631 Launch of *La Gazette,* Paris's first newspaper

1643 Death of Louis XIII. Regency under control of Marie de Médicis and Cardinal Mazarin

1661 Louis XIV becomes absolute monarch. Enlargement of Château de Versailles begun

1610	1620	1630	1640	1650	1660

1614 Final meeting of the Estates Council (the main legislative assembly) before the Revolution

1622 Paris becomes an episcopal see

1627 Development of the Ile St-Louis

1629 Richelieu, Louis XIII's first minister, builds Palais Royal

1638 Birth of Louis XIV

1662 Colbert, Louis XIV's finance minister, founds Gobelins tapestry works

Weaving frame

Ceiling by Charles Le Brun
Court painter to Louis XIV, Le Brun decorated many ceilings like this one at the Hôtel Carnavalet (see p96).

Madame de Maintenon
When the queen died in 1683, Louis married Madame de Maintenon, shown here in a framed painting by Caspar Netscher.

Decorated Fan
For special court fêtes, Louis XIV often stipulated that women carry fans.

The Galerie d'Hercule with Le Brun ceiling

Formal Classical Garden

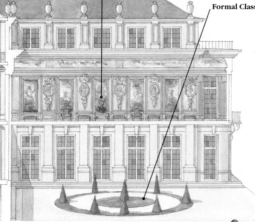

Dôme Church (1706)

HÔTEL LAMBERT (1640)
In the 17th century, the aristocracy built luxurious town houses with grand staircases, courtyards, formal gardens, coach houses and stables.

Neptune Cup
Made from lapis lazuli with a silver Neptune on top, this cup was part of Louis' vast collection of art objects.

WHERE TO SEE THE SUN KING'S PARIS
Many 17th-century mansions such as the Hôtel Lambert still exist in Paris, but not all are open to the public. However, the Hôtel des Invalides *(p184)*, the Dôme Church *(p188)*, the Palais du Luxembourg *(p172)* and Versailles *(p248)* all give a magnificent impression of the period.

1667 Louvre rebuilt and observatory established

1682 Court moves to Versailles where it stays until the Revolution

1686 Le Procope, Paris's first café

1702 Paris first divided into 20 arrondissements (districts)

1715 Louis XIV dies

| 1670 | 1680 | 1690 | 1700 | 1710 |

1670 Hôtel des Invalides built

1692 Great famines due to bad harvests and wars

1689 Pont Royal built

Statue of Louis XIV at Musée Carnavalet

Paris in the Age of Enlightenment

Bust of François Marie Arouet, known as Voltaire

THE ENLIGHTENMENT, with its emphasis on scientific reason and a critical approach to existing ideas and society, was centred on the city of Paris. In contrast, nepotism and corruption were rife at Louis XV's court at Versailles. Meanwhile the economy thrived, the arts flourished as never before and intellectuals, such as Voltaire and Rousseau, were renowned throughout Europe. In Paris, the population rose to about 650,000: town planning was developed, and the first accurate street map of the city appeared in 1787.

EXTENT OF THE CITY

☐ 1720   ☐ Today

Nautical Instruments
As the science of navigation advanced, scientists developed telescopes and trigonometric instruments (used for measuring longitude and latitude).

18th-Century Wigs
These were not only a mark of fashion but also a way of indicating the wearer's class and importance.

COMÉDIE FRANÇAISE
The Age of Enlightenment saw a burst of dramatic activity and new theatres opened, such as the Comédie Française (see p120). Today the Théâtre Français company is based here.

The auditorium, with 1,913 seats, was the largest in Paris.

TIMELINE

Fireman

1720	1730	1740	1750

1722 City's first fire brigade founded

1734 Fontaine des Quatre Saisons built

1748 Montesquieu's *L'Esprit des Lois* (an influential work about different forms of government) published

1751 First volume of Diderot's *Encyclopedia* published

Madame de Pompadour
Although generally remembered as the mistress of Louis XV, she was renowned as a patron of the arts and had great political influence.

Chocolate Pot
By the 18th century, bourgeois families could afford tobacco, tea, chocolate and coffee from Asia and the New World.

Vestibule with painted ceiling

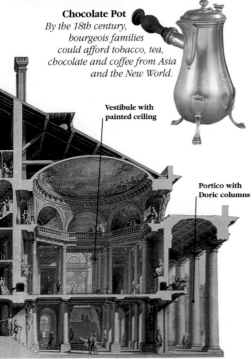

Portico with Doric columns

The Catacombs
These were set up in 1785 as a more hygienic alternative to Paris's cemeteries (see p179).

WHERE TO SEE ENLIGHTENMENT PARIS

The district around the Rue de Lille, the Rue de Varenne and the Rue de Grenelle *(pp182–3)* has many luxurious town houses, or *hôtels*, which were built by the aristocracy during the first half of the 18th century. Memorabilia from the lives of the great intellectuals Voltaire and Jean-Jacques Rousseau is in the Musée Carnavalet *(pp96–7)*, along with 18th-century interior designs and paintings.

Churches were built throughout the Enlightenment. St-Sulpice *(p172)* was completed in 1776.

Le Procope *(p140)* is the oldest café in Paris. It was frequented by Voltaire and Rousseau.

1757 First oil street lamps

c.1760 Place de la Concorde, Panthéon and Ecole Militaire built

1762 Rousseau's *Emile* and the *Social Contract*

1764 Madame de Pompadour dies

Rousseau, philosopher and writer, believed that humans were naturally good and had been corrupted by society.

1774 Louis XV, great grandson of Louis XIV, dies

1760	1770	1780

1778 France supports American independence

1782 First pavements built, in the Place du Théâtre Français

1783 Montgolfier brothers make the first hot-air balloon ascent

1785 David paints the *Oath of the Horatii*

Paris During the Revolution

A plate made in celebration of the Revolution

IN 1789 MOST PARISIANS were still living in squalor and poverty, as they had since the Middle Ages. Rising inflation and opposition to Louis XVI culminated in the storming of the Bastille, the king's prison; the Republic was founded three years later. However, the Terror soon followed, when those suspected of betraying the Revolution were executed without trial: more than 60,000 people lost their lives. The bloody excesses of Robespierre, the zealous revolutionary, led to his overthrow and a new government, the Directory, was set up in 1795.

EXTENT OF THE CITY

☐ 1796   ☐ Today

The prison turrets were set alight.

The French guards, who were on the side of the revolutionaries, arrived late in the afternoon with two cannons.

Declaration of the Rights of Man and the Citizen
The Enlightenment ideals of equality and human dignity were enshrined in the Declaration. This illustration is the preface to the 1791 Constitution.

REPUBLICAN CALENDAR
The revolutionaries believed that the world was starting again, so they abolished the existing church calendar and took 22 September 1792, the day the Republic was declared, as the first day of the new era. The Republican calendar had 12 equal months, each sub-divided into three ten-day periods, with the remaining five days of each year set aside for public holidays. All the months of the year were given poetic names which linked them to nature and the seasons, such as fog, snow, seed-time, flowers and harvest.

A coloured engraving by Tresca showing *Ventôse*, the windy month (19 Feb–20 Mar) from the new Republican calendar

Drawbridge

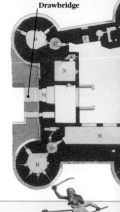

TIMELINE

1789	1790	1791	1792
14 Jul Fall of the Bastille	**4 Aug** Abolition of feudalism		**10 Aug** The storming of the Tuileries
	26 Aug Declaration of the Rights of Man and the Citizen		
	17 Sep Law of Suspects passed: the Terror begins		

Cartoon on the three Estates: the clergy, the nobility and the awakening populace

Lafayette, Commander of the National Guard, takes his oath to the Constitution

17 Jul Champ de Mars massacre

25 Apr *La Marseillaise* composed

5 May The Estates council meets

14 Jul Fête de la Fédération

Paper Money
Bonds, called assignats, *were used to fund the Revolution from 1790–3.*

La Marseillaise
The revolutionaries' marching song is now the national anthem.

The Sans Culottes
By 1792, the wearing of trousers instead of breeches (culottes) *was a political symbol of Paris's artisans and shopkeepers.*

"Patriotic" Chair
The back of this wooden chair is topped by red bonnets, symbol of revolutionary politics.

Wallpaper
Commemorative wallpaper was produced to celebrate the Revolution.

The dead and wounded totalled 171 by the end of the day.

Coin tower

Great court

Well court

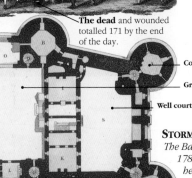

Guillotine
This was used for the first time in France in April 1792.

STORMING OF THE BASTILLE
The Bastille was overrun on 14 July 1789 and the seven prisoners held there released. The defenders (32 Swiss guards, 82 wounded soldiers and the governor) were massacred.

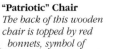

0 Jun Invasion of the Tuileries	**21 Jan** Execution of Louis XVI	**16 Oct** Execution of Marie-Antoinette	**5 Apr** Execution of Danton and supporters	**22 Aug** New constitution: the Directory
10 Aug Overthrow of Louis XVI	**Autumn** Robespierre in control of Committee of Public Safety	**24 Nov** Churches closed	**19 Nov** Jacobin Club (a revolutionary pressure group) closed	

1793   **1794**   **1795**

20 Sep Battle of Valmy	**13 Jul** Assassination of Marat, founder of *L'Ami du Peuple*, the revolutionary newspaper	*Robespierre, revolutionary and architect of the Terror*
2–6 Sep September massacres		**27 Jul** Execution of Robespierre

Napoleonic Paris

Napoleon's imperial crown

Napoleon Bonaparte was the most brilliant general in the French army. The instability of the new government after the Revolution gave him the chance to seize power, and in November 1799 he installed himself in the Tuileries Palace as First Consul. He crowned himself Emperor in May 1804. Napoleon established a centralized administration and a code of laws, reformed France's educational system and set out to make Paris the most beautiful city in the world. The city was endowed with grand monuments and embellished with the spoils of conquest. His power was always fragile and dependent on incessant wars. In March 1814 Prussian, Austrian and Russian armies invaded Paris and Napoleon fled to Elba. He returned to Paris in 1815 but was defeated at Waterloo and died in exile in 1821.

Extent of the City

☐ 1810   ☐ Today

Château Malmaison
This was the favourite home of Josephine, Napoleon's first wife.

Ladies-in-Waiting hold Josephine's train.

Opaline-Glass Clock
The decoration on this clock echoed the fashion for draperies.

Elephant Project
This monument was planned for the centre of the Place de la Bastille.

Eagle's Flight
Napoleon's flight to Elba in 1814 was satirized in this cartoon.

TIMELINE

1799 Napoleon seizes power	**1800** Banque de France founded			**1812** Russian campaign ends in defeat	**1815** Waterloo; second abdication of Napoleon. Restoration of the monarchy
1797 Battle of Rivoli	**1802** Legion of Honour established				
1800		**1805**	**1810**	**1815**	**1820**
1804 Napoleon crowned	**1806** Arc de Triomphe commissioned		**1814** Napoleon abdicates		**1821** Napoleon dies
1800 Napoleon returns from Egypt on his ship *L'Orient*			**1809** Napoleon divorces Josephine and marries Marie-Louise		*Napoleon's death mask*

Bronze Table Top
Inlaid with Napoleon's portrait, this table marks the victory at Austerlitz.

Josephine kneels before Napoleon.

Napoleon holds the crown for his Empress, Josephine.

Russian Cossacks in the Palais Royal
After Napoleon's defeat and flight in 1814, Paris suffered the humiliation of being occupied by foreign troops, including Austrians, Prussians and Russians.

The Pope makes the sign of the cross.

The **Arc de Triomphe du Carrousel** was erected in 1806 and crowned with the horses looted from St Mark's, Venice.

WHERE TO SEE NAPOLEONIC PARIS

Many of the grand monuments Napoleon planned for Paris were never built, but two triumphal arches, the Arc de Triomphe (pp208–9) and Arc de Triomphe du Carrousel (p122), were a major part of his legacy. La Madeleine church (p214) was also inaugurated in his reign and much of the Louvre was rebuilt (pp122–3). Examples of the Empire style can be seen at Malmaison (p255) and at the Carnavalet (pp96–7).

NAPOLEON'S CORONATION
Napoleon's rather dramatic crowning took place in 1804. In this recreation by J L David, the Pope, summoned to Notre-Dame, looks on as Napoleon crowns his Empress just before crowning himself.

The Empress
Josephine was divorced by Napoleon in 1809.

1842 First railway line between Paris and St-Germain-en-Laye opens

1825	1830	1835	1840	1845

1831 Victor Hugo's *Notre-Dame de Paris* published

Cholera epidemic hits Paris

1840 Reburial of Napoleon at Les Invalides

Napoleon's tomb

1830 Revolution in Paris and advent of constitutional monarchy

The Grand Transformation

IN 1848 PARIS SAW a second revolution which brought down the recently restored monarchy. In the uncertainties that followed, Napoleon's nephew assumed power in the same way as his uncle before him – by a *coup d'état*. He proclaimed himself Napoleon III in 1851. Under his rule Paris was transformed into the most magnificent city in Europe. He entrusted the task of modernization to Baron Haussmann. Haussmann demolished the crowded, unsanitary streets of the medieval city and created a well-ordered, well-ventilated capital within a geometrical grid of avenues and boulevards. Neighbouring districts such as Auteuil were annexed, creating the suburbs.

EXTENT OF THE CITY

☐ 1859　　☐ Today

Lamppost outside the Opéra

Arc de Triomphe

Boulevard des Italiens
This tree-lined avenue, painted by Edmond Georges Grandjean (1889), was one of the most fashionable of the new boulevards.

Twelve avenues
formed a star
(*étoile*).

AVE DE FRIEDLAN
AVE HOCHE
AVE DE WAGRAM
AVE MAC-MAHON
AVE CARNOT

Laying the Sewers
This engraving from 1861 shows the early work for laying the sewer system (see p190) *from La Villette to Les Halles. Most was the work of the engineer Belgrand.*

Circular Hoarding
Distinctive hoardings advertised opera and theatre performances.

Grand mansions were built around the Arc de Triomphe between 1860 and 1868.

TIMELINE

1851 Napoleon III declares the Second Empire

Viewing the exhibits at the World Exhibition

1852 Haussmann begins massive town-planning schemes

1855 World Exhibition

1850	1852	1854	1856	1858

20 centimes stamp showing Napoleon III

1857 The poet, Baudelaire, prosecuted for obscenity for *The Flowers of Evil*

PLACE DE L'ETOILE

The new scheme for the centre of Paris included redesigning the area at one end of the Champs-Elysées (Elysian Fields). Haussmann created a star of 12 broad avenues around the new Arc de Triomphe.
(The inset map shows the area as it was in 1790.)

Fields

Avenue des Champs-Elysées

Site of Arc de Triomphe

Drinking Fountain

In 1840, fifty fountains were erected in poor areas of Paris through the generosity of the English francophile, Richard Wallace.

AVE DES CHAMPS ELYSEES

AVE MARCEAU

AVE D'IENA

AVE KLEBER

L'ETOILE

DE

AVE DE LA GRANDE ARMEE

AVE VICTOR HUGO

AVE FOCH

Bois de Boulogne

Given to the city in 1852 by Napoleon III, this park became a popular place for walking and riding (see p254).

BARON HAUSSMANN

Lawyer by training and civil servant by profession, Georges-Eugène Haussmann (1809–91) was appointed Prefect of the Seine by Napoleon III. For 17 years he was in charge of urban planning. With the best architects and engineers of the day, he planned a new city, improved the water supply and sewerage, and created beautiful parks.

Some avenues were named after French generals.

1861 Garnier designs new Opera House

1863 The nudity in Manet's *Le Déjeuner sur l'Herbe* causes a scandal and is rejected by the Academy *(see pp144–5)*

1867 World Exhibition

1870 Napoleon's wife, Eugénie, flees Paris at threat of war

1860	1862	1864	1866	1868

1863 Credit Lyonnais bank established

1862 Victor Hugo's epic novel of Paris's poor, *Les Misérables*, published

1868 Press censorship relaxed

1870 Start of Franco-Prussian War

The Belle Epoque

THE FRANCO-PRUSSIAN war culminated in the terrible Siege of Paris. When peace came in 1871, it fell to the new government, the Third Republic, to bring about economic recovery. From about 1890 life was transformed: the motor-car, aeroplane, cinema, telephone and gramophone all contributed to the enjoyment of life and the *Belle Epoque* (beautiful age) was born. Paris became a glittering city where the new style, *Art Nouveau,* decorated buildings and objects. The paintings of the Impressionists, such as Renoir, reflected the *joie de vivre* of the times, while later those of Matisse, Braque and Picasso heralded the modern movement in art.

Art Nouveau pendant

EXTENT OF THE CITY

☐ *1895*   ☐ *Today*

The interior was arranged as tiers of galleries around a central grand staircase.

Cabaret Poster
Toulouse-Lautrec's posters immortalized the singers and dancers of the cafés and cabaret clubs of Montmartre, where artists and writers congregated in the 1890s.

Electricity illuminated the window displays.

Windows facing on to the Boulevard Haussmann displayed the goods on offer.

Central Hall of the Grand Palais
The Grand Palais (pp206–7) was built to house two huge exhibitions of French painting and sculpture at the World Exhibition of 1889.

Art Nouveau Cash Till
Even ordinary objects like this cash till were beautified by the new style.

TIMELINE

1871 Third Republic established

1874 Monet paints first Impressionist picture: *Impression: Soleil levant*

Louis Pasteur

1889 Eiffel Tower built

1870	1875	1880	1885	1890

Zoo animals were shot to feed the hungry (see p224)

1870 Siege of Paris

Entrance ticket to the exhibition

1891 First metro station opens

1885 Louis Pasteur discovers rabies vaccine

1889 Great Exhibition

Citroën 5CV
France led the world in the early development of the motor-car. By 1900 the Citroën began to be seen on the streets of Paris, and long-distance motor racing was popular.

The glass dome could be seen from all parts of the store.

Moulin Rouge (1890)
The old, redundant windmills of Montmartre became nightclubs, like the world-famous Moulin Rouge (red windmill) (see p226).

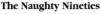

GALERIES LAFAYETTE (1906)
This beautiful department store , with its dome a riot of coloured glass and wrought ironwork, was a sign of the new prosperity.

The Naughty Nineties
The Lumière brothers captured the daring negligée fashions of the 1890s in the first moving images of the cinematograph.

WHERE TO SEE THE BELLE EPOQUE
Art Nouveau can be seen in monumental buildings like the Grand Palais and Petit Palais *(p206)*, while the Galeries Layfayette *(pp212–13)* and the Pharamond restaurant *(p300)* have beautiful Belle Epoque interiors. The Musée d'Orsay *(pp144–7)* has many objects from this period.

The entrance to the metro at Porte Dauphine was the work of leading Art Nouveau designer Hector Guimard *(p226)*.

The doorway of No. 29 Avenue Rapp *(p191)*, in the Eiffel Tower quarter, is a fine example of Art Nouveau.

Captain Dreyfus was publicly humiliated for selling secrets to the Prussians. He was later found innocent.

1894–1906 Dreyfus affair

1907 Picasso paints *Les Demoiselles d'Avignon*

1913 Proust publishes first volume of *Remembrance of Things Past*

1895	1900	1905	1910

1898 Pierre and Marie Curie discover radium

1909 Blériot flies across the English Channel

1911 Diaghilev brings the Russian ballet to Paris

1895 Lumière brothers introduce cinematography

Avant-Garde Paris

FROM THE 1920s TO THE 1940s, Paris became a mecca for artists, musicians, writers and film-makers. The city was alive with new movements such as Cubism and Surrealism represented by Cézanne, Picasso, Braque, Man Ray and Duchamp. Many new trends came from the USA, as writers and musicians including Ernest Hemingway, Gertrude Stein and Sidney Bechet took up residence in Paris. In architecture, the geometric shapes created by Le Corbusier changed the face of the modern building.

Office chair by Le Corbusier

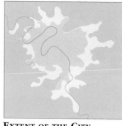

EXTENT OF THE CITY
☐ 1940   ☐ Today

Napoleon by Abel Gance
Paris has always been a city for film-makers. In 1927 Abel Gance made an innovative movie about Napoleon, using triple screens and wide-angle lenses.

Occupied Paris
Paris was under occupation for most of World War II. The Eiffel Tower was a favourite spot for German soldiers.

Josephine Baker
Arriving in Paris in 1925, the outlandish dancer catapulted to fame in "La Revue Nègre" wearing nothing but feathers.

Stilts
supported the concrete shell.

Living space was made into a picture gallery.

LA ROCHE VILLA BY LE CORBUSIER
Made from concrete and steel, with straight lines, horizontal windows and a flat roof, this house (1923) epitomized the new style.

Sidney Bechet
In the 1930s and 1940s the jazz clubs of Paris resounded to the swing music of black musicians such as the saxophonist Sidney Bechet.

TIMELINE

PARIS-1925

EXPOSITION INTERNATIONALE DES ARTS DÉCORATIFS ET INDUSTRIELS MODERNES AVRIL-OCTOBRE

1919 Treaty of Versailles signed in the Hall of Mirrors

1924 Olympic Games held in Paris

1924 André Breton publishes Surrealist Manifesto

1925 Art Deco style first seen at the Exposition des Arts Décoratifs

1914	1916	1918	1920	1922	1924	1926	192

1914–18 World War I. Paris is under threat of German attack, saved by the Battle of the Marne. A shell hits St-Gervais–St-Protais.

World War I soldier in uniform

1920 Interment of the Unknown Soldier

An eternal flame for the Unknown Soldier burns under the Arc de Triomphe.

Fashion in the 1940s
After World War II, the classic look for men and women was reminiscent of military uniforms.

The roof was designed as a garden terrace.

Airmail Poster
Airmail routes developed during the 1930s, especially to French North Africa.

The bedroom was above the dining room.

The kitchen was built at the back with a sloping glass roof.

The garage was built into the ground floor.

Windows were arranged in a horizontal strip.

Claudine in Paris by Colette
The Claudine series of novels, written by Colette Willy, known simply as "Colette", were extremely popular in the 1930s.

The old Trocadéro was changed to the Palais de Chaillot *(see p198)* for the World Exhibition.

WHERE TO SEE AVANT-GARDE PARIS

La Roche Villa is now part of the Fondation Le Corbusier *(p254)* and can be visited in the Paris suburb of Auteuil. Hemingway's haunt, the bar-brasserie Closerie des Lilas in Montparnasse *(p179)*, has retained much of its period decor. For fashion don't miss the Musée de la Mode et du Costume *(p201)*.

1931 Colonial Exhibition

A visitor to the exhibition in colonial dress

1937 Picasso paints *Guernica* in protest at the Spanish Civil War

1940 World War II: Paris bombed and occupied by Nazis

| 1930 | 1932 | 1934 | 1936 | 1938 | 1940 | 1942 |

1934 Riots and strikes in response to the Depression

1937 Palais de Chaillot built

Symbol of Free French superimposed on the victory sign

Aug 1944 Liberation of Paris

The Modern City

Late President, François Mitterrand

In 1962 a programme of renovation was started in Paris. Run-down districts like the Marais began to be restored. This work was continued by François Mitterrand's *Grand Travaux* (great works) scheme. Access was improved to historical monuments and art collections, such as the Grand Louvre *(see pp122–9)* and the Musée d'Orsay *(pp144–7)*. The scheme was responsible for the building of several monuments to the modern age, including the Opéra Bastille *(p98)*, the Cité des Sciences *(pp236–9)* and the Bibliothèque Nationale in Tolbiac *(p246)*. With these, and the magnificently modern Défense, Grande Arche and Stade de France, Paris prepared herself for the 21st century.

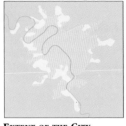

EXTENT OF THE CITY
☐ *1959*　　☐ *Today*

La Grande Arche is taller and wider than Notre-Dame and runs in an axis linking the Arc de Triomphe and the Louvre Pyramid.

Christo's Pont Neuf
To create a work of art, the Bulgarian-born artist Christo wrapped Paris's oldest bridge, the Pont Neuf, in fabric in 1985.

Simone de Beauvoir
Influential philosopher and life-long companion of J-P Sartre, de Beauvoir fought for the liberation of women in the 1950s.

Shopping centre

Citroën Goddess (1956)
With its ultra-modern lines, this became Paris's most prestigious car.

TIMELINE

1950 Construction of UNESCO, and the Musée de Radio-France	**1962** André Malraux, Minister of Culture, begins renovation programme of run-down districts and monuments	*Ducting at the Pompidou Centre*	**1977** Pompidou Centre opens. Jacques Chirac is installed as first elected Mayor of Paris since

1945	1950	1955	1960	1965	1970	1975

President de Gaulle

1958 Establishment of Fifth Republic with de Gaulle as President

1964 Reorganization of the Ile de France

1968 Student riots and workers strikes in the Latin

1969 Les Halles market transfers to Rungis

1973 Construction of Montparnasse Tower and the Périphérique (ring road)

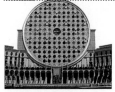

Marne La Vallée
Like a gigantic loud speaker, this residential complex is in one of Paris's dormitory towns near Disneyland Paris.

Chanel Designs
Paris is the centre of the fashion world with important shows each year.

The Pompidou Centre
The nation's collection of modern art is housed here in this popular building (see pp110–13).

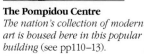

The Fiat Tower is one of Europe's tallest buildings.

Opéra de la Bastille
It was built in 1989 to mark the bicentenary of the fall of the Bastille.

STUDENTS AT THE BARRICADES
In May 1968 Paris saw a revolution of a kind. The Latin Quarter was taken over by students and workers. What began as a protest against the war in Vietnam spread to other issues and became an expression of discontent with the Government. President de Gaulle rode out the storm but his prestige was severely damaged.

Rioting students clash with police

The Défense Palace, housing the centre for industry, is the oldest tower.

LA DÉFENSE
This huge business centre was started on the edge of Paris in 1958. Today 30,000 people commute here from Paris's surrounding areas.

1985 Christo wraps Pont Neuf

Participant of the bicentenary wearing the French national colours

Victorious French football team holding aloft the World Cup trophy in Paris

1980	1985	1990	1995	2000	2005	2010

1980 Thousands greet Pope John-Paul on his official visit

1994 Eurostar inaugurated: Paris to London in 3 hrs

1989 Bicentenary celebrations to mark the French Revolution

2002 The Euro replaces the Franc as exclusive legal tender

1999 December hurricanes hit Paris: Versailles loses 10,000 trees

1998 France hosts – and wins – the 1998 football World Cup tournament

PARIS AT A GLANCE

THERE ARE NEARLY 300 places of interest described in the *Area by Area* section of this book. A broad range of sights is covered: from the ancient Conciergerie and its grisly associations with the guillotine *(see p81)*, to the modern opera house, the Opéra de la Bastille *(see p98)*; from No. 51 Rue de Montmorency *(see p114)*, the oldest houses in Paris, to the elegant Musée Picasso *(see pp100–1)*. To help make the most of your stay, the following 20 pages are a time-saving guide to the best Paris has to offer. Museums and galleries, historic churches, spacious parks, gardens and squares all have a section. There are also guides to Paris's famous personalities. Each sight has a cross reference to its own full entry. Below are the top tourist attractions to start you off.

PARIS'S TOP TOURIST ATTRACTIONS

La Défense
See p255.

Sainte-Chapelle
See pp88–9.

Palace of Versailles
See pp248–53.

Pompidou Centre
See pp110–13.

Musée d'Orsay
See pp144–7.

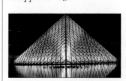

Musée du Louvre
See pp122–9.

Jardin du Luxembourg
See p172.

Eiffel Tower
See pp192–3.

Bois de Boulogne
See pp254–5.

Notre-Dame
See pp82–5.

Arc de Triomphe
See pp208–9.

The Dôme Church, adjoining the Hôtel des Invalides

Celebrated Visitors and Residents

THROUGHOUT ITS HISTORY Paris has lured the world's greatest talents. It has been a haven for those seeking a place to express themselves and live life to the full. Thomas Jefferson, before becoming president of the United States in 1801, lived near the Avenue des Champs-Elysées in the 1780s and called the city "everyone's second home". Over the centuries, Paris has been one of the creative centres of the Western world. It has accommodated kings and political exiles (Americans, Russians, Chinese and Vietnamese among them) who went on to achieve power, and painters, writers, poets and musicians who became household names. All succumbed to the pull of the city's beauty, its distinctive way of life, its sense of style and, of course, its superb gastronomy.

Marlene Dietrich *(1901–92)*
The German-born singer gave some of her best shows at the Olympia music hall (see p337).

Champs-Elysées

Chaillot Quarter

RIVER SEIN

Invalides and Eiffel Tower Quarter

Josephine Baker *(1906–75)*
The "Queen" of the Paris music halls hit the headlines in 1925 dancing the black bottom dressed in nothing but a string of bananas. Her early performances were at the Théâtre des Champs-Elysées (see p334).

Montparnas.

Richard Wagner *(1813–83)*
After fleeing his creditors in Germany, the composer lived at No.14 Rue Jacob.

Roman Polanski *(b. 1933)*
The Polish film-maker (left in the picture) can be seen frequently at the fashionable café, La Coupole (see p311).

0 kilometres 1

0 miles 0.5

Montmartre

Salvador Dali *(1904–89)*
*The Surrealist artist moved
to Paris in 1929. Later, he
was a regular at the Hôtel
Meurice at No. 228 Rue de
Rivoli (see p281). The
Espace Montmartre is
devoted to aspects of his
work (see p222).*

Pablo Picasso *(1881–1973)*
*The Spanish artist lived in
the artists' colony at the
Bateau-Lavoir (see p226).*

Vincent Van Gogh
(1853–90)
*The Dutch painter stayed
at No. 56 Rue Lepic
with his art dealer
brother, Theo.*

Opéra Quarter

Tuileries Quarter

N

*Beaubourg and Les
Halles*

The Marais

*St-Germain-
des-Prés*

Ile de la Cité

Ile St-Louis

Rudolf Nureyev *(1938–93)*
*The Russian ballet star was director
of the Ballet de l'Opéra (see p335).*

Latin Quarter

*Luxembourg
Quarter*

*Jardin des Plantes
Quarter*

Leon Trotsky
(1879–1940)
*Before the Russian
Revolution in 1917,
leading Bolshevik,
Trotsky, was often seen
with Lenin in the Dôme
Café (see p311).*

Oscar Wilde *(1854–1900)*
*After his release from Reading
jail, the exiled Irish writer
died in L'Hôtel (see p281).*

Remarkable Parisians

BY VIRTUE OF ITS STRATEGIC position on the Seine, Paris has always been the economic, political and artistic hub of France. Over the centuries, many prominent and influential figures from other parts of the country and abroad have come to the city to absorb her unique spirit. In return they have left their mark: artists have brought new movements, politicians new schools of thought, musicians and film-makers new trends, and architects a new environment.

Actress Catherine Deneuve

ARTISTS

Sacré-Coeur by Utrillo (1934)

IN THE EARLY 18TH-CENTURY, Jean-Antoine Watteau (1684–1721) took the inspiration for his paintings from the Paris theatre. Half a century later, Jean-Honoré Fragonard (1732–1806), popular painter of the Rococo, lived and died here, financially ruined by the Revolution. Later, Paris became the cradle of Impressionism. Its founders Claude Monet (1840–1926), Pierre-Auguste Renoir (1841–1919) and Alfred Sisley (1839–99) met in a Paris studio. In 1907, Pablo Picasso

(1881–1973) painted the seminal work *Les Demoiselles d'Avignon* at the Bateau-Lavoir, *(see p226)* where Georges Braque (1882–1963), Amedeo Modigliani (1884–1920) and Marc Chagall (1887–1985) also lived. Henri de Toulouse-Lautrec (1864–1901) drank and painted in Montmartre. So did Salvador Dali (1904–89) who frequented the Café Cyrano, centre of the Surrealists. The Paris School eventually moved to Montparnasse, home to sculptors Auguste Rodin (1840–1917), Constantin Brancusi (1876–1957) and Ossip Zadkine (1890–1967).

POLITICAL LEADERS

HUGH CAPET, Count of Paris, became King of France in 987. His palace was on the Ile de la Cité. Louis XIV, XV and XVI lived at Versailles *(see pp248–53)* but Napoleon *(see pp30–31)* preferred the Tuileries. Cardinal Richelieu (1585–1642), the power behind Louis XIII, created the Académie Française and the Palais-Royal *(see p120)*. Today the President lives in the Palais de l'Elysée *(p207)*.

Portrait of Cardinal Richelieu by Philippe de Champaigne (about 1635)

FILMS AND FILM-MAKERS

PARIS HAS ALWAYS been at the heart of French cinema. The prewar and immediate postwar classics were usually made on the sets of the Boulogne and Joinville studios, where whole areas of the city were reconstructed, such as the Canal St-Martin for Marcel Carné's *Hôtel du Nord*. Jean-Luc Godard and other New Wave directors preferred to shoot outdoors. Godard's *Au Bout du Souffle* (1960) with Jean-Paul Belmondo and Jean Seberg was filmed in and around the Champs-Elysées.

Simone Signoret (1921– 1985) and Yves Montand (1921–1991), the most celebrated couple of French cinema, were long associated with the Ile de la Cité. Actresses, such as Catherine Deneuve (b.1943) and Isabelle Adjani (b.1955), live in the city to be near their couturiers.

MUSICIANS

JEAN-PHILIPPE RAMEAU (1683–1764), organist and pioneer of harmony, is associated with St-Eustache *(see p114)*. Hector Berlioz (1803–69) had his *Te Deum* first performed there in 1855, and Franz Liszt (1811–86) his *Messe Solennelle* in 1866. A great dynasty of organists, the Couperins, gave recitals in St-Gervais–St-Protais *(see p99)*.

The stage of the Opéra *(see p215)* has seen many talents, but audiences have not always been appreciative. Richard Wagner (1813–83) had his *Tannhäuser* hooted down. George Bizet's *Carmen*

(1838–75) was booed, as was *Peléas et Mélisande* by Claude Debussy (1862–1918).

Soprano Maria Callas (1923–77) gave triumphal performances here. The composer and conductor Pierre Boulez (b.1925) has devoted his talent to experimental music at IRCAM near the Pompidou Centre *(see p333)*, which he helped to found.

The diminutive *chanteuse*, Edith Piàf (1915–63), known for her nostalgic love-songs, began singing in the streets of Paris and then went on to tour the world. There is now a museum devoted to her life and work *(see p233)*.

Renée Jeanmaire as Carmen (1948)

ARCHITECTS

GOTHIC, CLASSICAL, Baroque and Modernist – all co-exist in Paris. The most brilliant medieval architect was Pierre de Montreuil, who built Notre-Dame

The Grand Trianon at Versailles, built by Louis Le Vau in 1668

and Sainte-Chapelle. Louis Le Vau (1612–70) and Jules Hardouin-Mansart (1646–1708) designed Versailles *(see pp248–53)*. Jacques-Ange Gabriel (1698–1782) built the Petit Trianon *(see p249)* and Place de la Concorde *(see p131)*. Haussmann (1809–91) gave the city its boulevards *(see pp32–3)*. Gustave Eiffel (1832–1923) built his tower in 1889. A century later, I M Pei added the Louvre's glass pyramid *(see p129)*, Jean Nouvel created the Institut du Monde Arabe *(see p164)* and Dominique Perrault the new Bibliothèque Nationale de France *(see p246)*. The 21st century already has several new landmarks underway.

WRITERS

FRENCH HAS BEEN dubbed "the language of Molière", after playwright Jean-Baptiste Molière (1622–73), who helped create the Comédie-Française, now situated near his home in Rue Richelieu. On the Left Bank, the Théâtre de l'Odéon was home to playwright Jean Racine (1639–99). It is near the statue of Denis Diderot (1713–84), who published his *L'Encyclopédie*

between 1751 and 1776. Marcel Proust (1871–1922), author of the 13-volume *Remembrance of Things Past*, lived on the Boulevard Haussmann. To the existentialists, the district of St-Germain was the only place to be *(see pp142–3)*. Here Sylvia Beach welcomed James Joyce (1882–1941) to her bookshop on the Rue de l'Odéon. Ernest Hemingway (1899–1961) and F Scott Fitzgerald (1896–1940) wrote novels in Montparnasse.

Proust by J-E Blanche (about 1910)

SCIENTISTS

PARIS HAS a Quartier Pasteur, a Boulevard Pasteur, a Pasteur metro and the world-famous Institut Pasteur *(see p247)*, all in honour of Louis Pasteur (1822–95), the great French chemist and biologist. His apartment and laboratory are faithfully preserved. The Institut Pasteur is today home to Professor Luc Montagnier, who first isolated the AIDS virus in 1983. Discoverers of radium, Pierre (1859–1906) and Marie Curie (1867–1934), also worked in Paris. The Curies have been the subject of a long-running play in Paris, *Les Palmes de M. Schutz*.

EXILED IN PARIS
The Duke and Duchess of Windsor married in France after his abdication in 1936 as King Edward VIII. The city granted them a rent-free mansion in the Bois de Boulogne. Other famous exiles have included Chou En-Lai (1898–1976), Ho Chi Minh (1890–1969), Vladimir Ilyich Lenin (1870–1924), Oscar Wilde (1854–1900) and ballet danser Rudolf Nureyev (1938–93).

The Duke and Duchess of Windsor

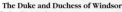

Paris's Best: Churches

THE CATHOLIC CHURCH has been the bastion of Parisian society through time. Many of the city's churches are worth visiting. Architectural styles vary and the interiors are often spectacular. Most churches are open during the day and many have services at regular intervals. Paris's tradition of church music is still alive. You can spend an evening enjoying the interiors while listening to an organ recital or classical concert *(p333)*. A more detailed overview of Paris churches is on pages 48–9.

Early crucifix in St-Gervais–St-Protais

La Madeleine
Built in the style of a Greco-Roman temple, this church is known for its fine sculptures.

Chaillot Quarter

Champs-Elysées

Tuileries Quar

RIVER SEINE

Invalides and Eiffel Tower Quarter

St-Germa des-Pré

Dôme Church
This memorial to the military engineer Vauban lies in the Dôme Church, where Napoleon's remains were buried in 1840.

Sainte-Chapelle
With its fine stained glass, this chapel is a medieval jewel.

Montparnasse

Panthéon
The Neo-Classical Sainte-Geneviève, now the Panthéon, was inspired by Wren's St Paul's Cathedral in London.

0 kilometres

0 miles   0.5

Montmartre

Sacré-Coeur
Above the altar in this massive basilica, the chancel vault is decorated with a vast mosaic of Christ by Luc-Olivier Merson.

St-Eustache
With its mixture of Gothic and Renaissance styles, this is one of the finest churches in Paris.

Opéra Quarter

St-Paul–St-Louis
This Christ figure is one of the many rich furnishings in this Jesuit church, built in 1641 for Cardinal Richelieu.

N

Beaubourg and Les Halles

The Marais

Ile de la Cité

Ile St-Louis

Notre-Dame
The great cathedral was left to rot after the Revolution, until Victor Hugo led a restoration campaign.

Latin Quarter

Luxembourg Quarter

Jardin des Plantes Quarter

St-Séverin
The west door leads to one of the finest medieval churches in the city.

Mosquée de Paris
The minaret of this 1920s mosque is 33 m (100 ft) tall.

Exploring Paris's Churches

SOME OF PARIS'S FINEST ARCHITECTURE is reflected in the churches. The great era of church building was the medieval period but examples survive from all ages. During the Revolution (see pp28–9) churches were used as grain or weapons stores but were later restored to their former glory. Many churches have superb interiors with fine paintings and sculptures.

MEDIEVAL

Tower of St-Germain-des-Prés

BOTH THE POINTED arch and the rose window were born in a suburb north of Paris at the Basilica de St-Denis, where most of the French kings and queens are buried. This was the first Gothic building, and it was from here that the Gothic style spread. The finest Gothic church in Paris is the city cathedral, **Notre-Dame**, tallest and most impressive of the early French cathedrals. Begun in 1163 by Bishop Maurice de Sully, it was completed in the next century by architects Jean de Chelles

and Pierre de Montreuil, who added the transepts with their fine translucent rose windows. Montreuil's masterpiece is Louis IX's medieval palace chapel, **Sainte-Chapelle**, with its two-tier structure. It was built to house Christ's Crown of Thorns. Other surviving churches are **St-Germain-des-Prés**, the oldest surviving abbey church in Paris (1050); the tiny, rustic Romanesque **St-Julien-le-Pauvre**; and the Flamboyant Gothic **St-Séverin**, **St-Germain l'Auxerrois** and **St-Merry**.

RENAISSANCE

THE EFFECT of the Italian Renaissance swept through Paris in the 16th century. It led to a unique architectural style in which fine Classical detail and immense Gothic proportions resulted in an impure, but attractive, cocktail known as "French Renaissance". The best example in Paris is **St-Etienne-du-Mont** whose interior has the feel of a wide and light basilica. Another is **St-Eustache**, the massive market church in Les Halles, and the nave of **St-Gervais–St-Protais** with its stained glass and carved choir stalls.

Facade of Eglise de la Sorbonne

BAROQUE AND CLASSICAL

CHURCHES and convents flourished in Paris during the 17th century, as the city expanded under Louis XIII and his son Louis XIV. The Italian Baroque style was first seen on the majestic front of **St-Gervais–St-Protais**, built by Salomon de Brosse in 1616. The style was toned down to suit French tastes and the rational temperament of the Age of Enlightenment (see pp26–7). The result was a harmonious and monumental Classicism in the form of columns and domes. One example is the **Eglise de la Sorbonne**, completed by Jacques Lemercier in 1642 for Cardinal Richelieu. Grander and more richly decorated, with a painted dome, is the church built by François Mansart to honour the birth of the Sun King at the **Val-de-Grâce** convent. The true gem of the period is Jules Hardouin-Mansart's **Dôme Church** with its enormous gilded

St-Gervais–St-Protais

TOWERS, DOMES AND SPIRES

The outlines of Paris's many churches have dominated her skyline since early Christian times. The Tour St-Jacques, in the Gothic style, reflects the medieval love of the defensive tower. St-Etienne-du-Mont, with its pointed gable and rounded pediment, shows the transition from Gothic to Renaissance. The dome, a much used feature of the French Baroque, was used to perfection in the Val-de-Grâce. By contrast, St-Sulpice with its severe arrangement of towers and portico is typical of the Neo-Classical style. With its ornate spires, Sainte-Clotilde is a Gothic Revival church. Modern landmarks include the mosque with its minaret.

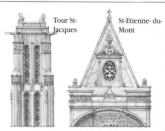

Tour St-Jacques

St-Etienne-du-Mont

Gothic

Renaissance

dome. Jesuit extravagance can be seen in **St-Paul–St-Louis** built in the style of Il Gesú in Rome. In contrast are Libéral Bruand's chapels, the **Salpêtrière** and **St-Louis-des-Invalides** with their severe geometry and unadorned simplicity. Other fine Classical churches are **St-Joseph-des-Carmes** and the 18th-century bankers' church, **St-Roch**, with its Baroque Marian chapel.

NEO-CLASSICAL

Interior of the Panthéon

An obsession with all things Greek and Roman swept France in the mid-18th century and well into the 19th century. The excavations at Pompeii (1738) and the influence of the Italian architect Andrea Palladio produced a generation of architects fascinated by the column, geometry and engineering. The best example of such churches is Jacques-Germain Soufflot's Sainte-Geneviève, now the **Panthéon**. Begun in 1773, its colonnaded dome was also inspired by Christopher Wren's St Paul's in London. The dome is supported by four pillars, built by Guillaume Rondelet, linking four great arches. The first colonnaded facade was Giovanni Niccolo Servandoni's **St-Sulpice**. Construction of this church began in 1733 and consisted of a two-storey portico, topped by a triangular pediment. **La Madeleine**, Napoleon's grand temple to his victorious army, was constructed on the ground plan of a Greco-Roman temple.

SECOND EMPIRE AND MODERN

Franz christian Gau's **Sainte-Clotilde** of the 1840s is the first and best example in Paris of the Gothic Revival or *style religieux*. Showy churches were built in the new districts created by Haussmann in the Second Empire *(pp32–3)*. One of the most lovely is Victor Baltard's St-Augustin, at the intersection of the Boulevard de Malesherbes and the Boulevard de la Madeleine. Here historic detail combines with modern iron columns and girders in a soaring interior space. The great basilica of the late 19th century, **Sacré-Coeur**, was built as a gesture of religious defiance. **St-Jean l'Evangéliste** by Anatole de Baudot is an interesting modern church combining the Art Nouveau style with Islamic arches. The modern gem of Islamic architecture, the **Mosquée de Paris**, is an attractive 1920s building in the Hispanic-Moorish style. It has a grand patio, inspired by the Alambra, woodwork in cedar and eucalyptus, and a fountain.

The arches of St-Jean L'Evangéliste, reminiscent of Islamic architecture

Val-de-Grâce

Baroque and Classical

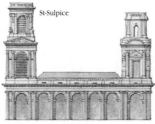

St-Sulpice

Neo-Classical

Sainte-Clotilde

Mosquée de Paris

Second Empire   **Modern**

Paris's Best: Gardens, Parks and Squares

FEW CITIES CAN BOAST the infinite variety of styles found in Parisian gardens, parks and squares today. They date from many different periods and have been central to Parisian life for the past 300 years. The Bois de Boulogne and the Bois de Vincennes enclose the city with their lush, green open spaces, while elegant squares and landscaped gardens, such as the Jardin du Luxembourg, brighten the inner city and provide a retreat for those craving a few moments peace from the bustling city.

Parc Monceau
This English-style park features many follies, grottoes, magnificent trees and rare plants.

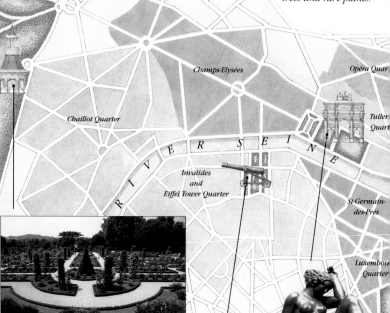

Champs-Elysées

Opéra Quar

Chaillot Quarter

Tuiler
Quart

RIVER SEINE

Invalides
and
Eiffel Tower Quarter

St-Germain-
des-Prés

Luxembou
Quarter

Bois de Boulogne
The Bagatelle gardens, set in this wooded park, have an amazing array of flowers including the spectacular rose garden.

Montparnasse

Esplanade des Invalides
From this huge square, lined with lime trees, are some brilliant views over the quays.

Jardin des Tuileries
These gardens are renowned for ornamental ponds, terraces and the collection of bronze figures by Aristide Maillol.

Parc des Buttes-Chaumont
Once a scraggy hilltop, this park was transformed to provide open spaces for the growing city. It is now beautifully landscaped with huge cliffs revealing caves.

0 kilometres   1

0 miles   0.5

Square du Vert-Galant
The square, named after Henri IV's nickname, forms the west point of the Ile de la Cité.

Place des Vosges
Considered one of the most beautiful squares in the world, it was finished in 1612 and is the oldest square in Paris.

Beaubourg and Les Halles

The Marais

Jardin des Plantes
The botanical garden has a vast collection of plants and flowers from around the world.

Ile de la Cité

Ile St-Louis

Latin Quarter

Jardin des Plantes Quarter

Jardin du Luxembourg
This park is a favourite with Parisians wanting to escape the bustle of the Latin Quarter.

Bois de Vincennes
The flower garden in this charming park is the perfect place to relax.

Exploring Gardens, Parks and Squares

PARIS IS DOTTED with many areas of parkland, intimate gardens and attractive tree-lined squares. Each is a reminder of the French capital's illustrious past. Many squares were formed during Napoleon III's transformation of the city, creating a pleasant environment for Parisians to live in (see pp32–3). This aim has been preserved right up to the present day. Paris's parks and gardens have their own character: some are ideal for a stroll, others for romance, while some provide space for sporting activities such as a game of *boules*.

Engraving of the Jardin du Palais Royal (1645)

HISTORIC GARDENS

THE OLDEST PUBLIC gardens in Paris were made for queens of France – the **Jardin des Tuileries** for Catherine de Médicis in the 16th century, and the **Jardin du Luxembourg** for Marie de Médicis in the 17th century. The Tuileries form the beginning of the axis running from the Arc du Triomphe du Carrousel through the Arc de Triomphe (pp208–9) to La Défense (p255). These gardens retain the formality devised by landscape architect André Le Nôtre, originally for the **Palace of Versailles**. Many of the Jardin des Tuileries's original sculptures survive, as well as modern pieces, notably the bronze nudes by Aristide Maillol (1861–1944).

The Jardin du Luxembourg also has the traditional formal plan – straight paths, clipped lawns, Classical sculpture and a superb 17th-century fountain. It is shadier and more intimate than the Tuileries, with lots of seats, pony rides and puppet shows to amuse the children.

The **Jardins des Champs-Elysées**, also by Le Nôtre, were reshaped in the English style in the 19th century. They have Belle Epoque pavilions, three theatres (L'Espace Pierre Cardin, Théâtre Marigny and the Théâtre Barrault), smart restaurants – and the ghost of the novelist Marcel Proust, who once played here as a child.

A haven of peace in a busy district is the **Jardin du**

Palais Royal built by Cardinal Richelieu in the 17th century. An elegant arcade encloses the garden. The 19th-century **Parc Monceau,** in the English picturesque style, has follies and grottoes. The flat **Jardins des Invalides** and the landscaped **Champ-de-Mars** were the grounds of the Hôtel des Invalides and the Ecole Militaire. They were the site of the Paris Universal Exhibition, whose reminder is the Eiffel Tower (pp192–3).

An attractive public garden is attached to the lovely Hôtel Biron, home of the **Musée Rodin**. The 17th-century **Jardin des Plantes** is famous for its ancient trees, flowers, alpine garden, hothouses and small zoo.

19TH-CENTURY PARKS AND SQUARES

Aquatic Garden, Bois de Vincennes

THE GREAT 19th-century parks and squares owe much to Napoleon III's long exile in London before he came to power. The unregimented planting and rolling lawns of Hyde Park and the leafy squares of Mayfair inspired him to bring trees,

FOLLIES AND ROTUNDAS

Dramatic features of Paris's parks and gardens are the many follies and rotundas. Every age of garden design has produced these ornaments. The huge Gloriette de Buffon in the Jardin des Plantes was erected as a memorial to the great naturalist (p166). It is the oldest metal structure in Paris. The pyramid in the Parc Monceau, the oriental temple in the Bois de Boulogne, and the recently restored 19th-century temple of love in the Bois de Vincennes reflect a more sentimental age. In contrast are the stark, painted-concrete follies that grace the Parc de la Villette.

Egyptian pyramid

Parc Monceau

Relaxing in Jardin du Luxembourg

fresh air and park benches to what was then Europe's most congested and dirty capital. Under his direction, landscape gardener Adolphe Alphand turned two woods at opposite ends of the city, the **Bois de Boulogne** (known as the "Bois") and the **Bois de Vincennes**, into English-style parks with duck ponds, lakes and flower gardens. He also added a race course to the "Bois". Today it is traversed by traffic and by prostitutes at night. Its most attractive feature is the Bagatelle rose garden.

Far more pleasant are the two smaller Alphand parks, **Parc Montsouris** in the south and the **Parc des Buttes-Chaumont** in the northeast. The "Buttes" (hills), a favourite with the Surrealists, was a quarry transformed into two craggy mini-mountains with overhanging vegetation, suspended bridge, temple of love and a lake below.

Part of the town-planning schemes for the old city included squares and avenues with fountains, sculptures, benches and greenery. One of the best is the **Square du Vert-Galant** on the Ile de la Cité. The Avenue de l'Observatoire in the **Jardin du Luxembourg** is rich in sculptures made by Jean-Baptiste Carpeaux.

Fountains and sculpture in the Jardins du Trocadéro

Parc Montsouris

MODERN PARKS AND GARDENS

THE SHADY **Jardins du Trocadéro** sloping down to the river from the Palais de Chaillot were planted after the 1937 Universal Exhibition. Here is the largest fountain in Paris and fine views of the river and the Eiffel Tower.

More recent Paris gardens eschew formality in favour of wilder planting, multiple levels, maze-like paths, children's gardens and modern sculpture. Typical are the gardens in front of the **Forum des Halles**, the **Parc André-Citroën**, the **Parc de la Villette** and the Jardins Atlantique above the Gare Montparnasse.

Pleasant strolls may be taken in Paris's waterside gardens: in the modern sculpture park behind Notre-Dame, at the Bassin de l'Arsenal at the Bastille, and along the quays of the Seine between the Louvre and the Place de la Concorde, or on the elegantly residential Ile St-Louis. The planted walkway above the **Viaduc des Arts** is a peaceful way to observe eastern Paris.

Jardin des Plantes — Gloriette de Buffon

Bois de Boulogne — Oriental temple

Bois de Vincennes — Temple of love

Parc de la Villette — Modern folly

Paris's Best: Museums and Galleries

SOME OF THE OLDEST, the newest, and certainly some of the finest museums and galleries are to be found in Paris – many are superb works of art in their own right. They house some of the greatest and strangest collections in the world. Some of the buildings complement their themes, such as the Roman baths and Gothic mansion which form the Musée de Cluny, or the Pompidou Centre, a modern masterpiece. Elsewhere there is pleasing contrast, such as the Picassos in their gracious 17th-century museum, and the Musée d'Orsay housed in its grand old railway station. Together they make an unrivalled feast for visitors.

Musée des Arts Decoratifs
Decorative and ornamental art like this Paris bathroom by Jeanne Lanvin is displayed here.

Champs-Elysées

Chaillot Quarter

RIVER SEINE

Invalides and Eiffel Tower Quarter

Petit Palais
A collection of works by the 19th-century sculptor Jean-Baptiste Carpeaux is housed here, including The Fisherman and Shell.

Musée Guimet
This 4th-century head of Buddha from India is part of a vast collection of Asian art and artefacts housed here.

Montparnass

Musée Rodin
The museum brings together works bequeathed to the nation by sculptor Auguste Rodin, like the magnificent Gates of Hell *doors.*

Musée d'Orsay
Carpeaux's Four Quarters of the World *(1867–72) can be found among this collection of 19th-century art.*

Musée du Louvre
The museum boasts one of the world's great collections of paintings and sculpture, from the ancient civilizations to the 19th century. This Babylonian monument, the Code of Hammurabi, *is the oldest set of laws in existence.*

Pompidou Centre
Paris's modern art collection from 1905 to the present day is housed here. The centre also has art libraries and an industrial design centre.

péra Quarter

←

Tuileries
Quarter

-Germain-
des-Prés

*Beaubourg
and
Les Halles*

The Marais

Ile de la
Cité

Ile St-Louis

Latin Quarter

Luxembourg
Quarter

Jardin des Plantes
Quarter

N

Musée Picasso
Sculptor and Model *(1931) is one of many paintings on display in Picasso's private collection, "inherited" in lieu of tax by the French government after his death in 1973.*

Musée Carnavalet
The museum is devoted to the history of Paris. Its historic buildings surround attractive garden courtyards.

Musée de Cluny
The remains of the old Gallo-Roman baths are part of this fine museum of ancient and medieval art.

0 kilometres	1
0 miles	0.5

Exploring Paris's Museums and Galleries

PARIS HOLDS great
treasures in its mus-
eums and art galleries.
The major national art
collection is to be found
at the **Musée du Louvre**,
which began collecting
400 years ago and is still
growing. Other important
museums, such as the
Musée d'Orsay, the
Musée Picasso and the
Pompidou Centre, have
their own treasures, but
there are scores of smaller,
specialized museums, each
with its own interest.

Dante and Virgil in the Underworld (1822) by Delacroix, Musée du Louvre

GREEK, ROMAN AND MEDIEVAL ART

Golden altar in the Musée de Cluny

SCULPTURE from Greek and
Roman times is well
represented in the **Musée du
Louvre**, which also has fine
medieval sculptures. The
major medieval collection is at
the **Musée de Cluny**, a
superb 15th-century mansion.
Among the highlights are the
Unicorn Tapestries, the Kings'
Heads from Notre-Dame and
the golden altar from Basel
Cathedral. Adjoining the
Cluny are the 3rd-century
Roman baths. Remains of
houses from Roman and
medieval Paris can be seen in
the **Crypte Archéologique**
near Notre-Dame cathedral.

OLD MASTERS

THE MONA LISA was one of
the **Musée du Louvre's**
first paintings, acquired 400
years ago. It also has other
fine Leonardos. They are to
be found along with superb

Titians, Raphaels and other
Italian masters. Other works
include Rembrandt's *Pilgrims
at Emmäus*, Watteau's *Gilles*
and Fragonard's *The
Bathers*. The **Musée
Cognacq-Jay** has a small,
but exquisite, collection of
paintings and drawings by
18th-century French
painters. The **Musée
Jacquemart-André** has
works by such masters as
Mantegna, Uccello,
Canaletto, Rembrandt
and Chardin.

IMPRESSIONIST AND POST-IMPRESSIONIST ART

INSTALLED IN A converted
19th-century railway station,
the **Musée d'Orsay** boasts
the world's largest collection
of art from the period
1848–1904. Admired for its
fine Impressionist and Post-
Impressionist collections, it
also devotes a lot of space to
the earlier Realists and the
formerly reviled 19th-century
academic and "Salon"
masters. There are superb
selections of Degas, Manet,
Courbet, Monet, Renoir,
Millet, Cézanne, Bonnard and
Vuillard, and some fine
Gauguins, Van Goghs and
Seurats, but these have to
contend with poor lighting
and an intrusive stone decor.
A great ensemble of late
Monets is to be found at the
Musée Marmottan and
another at the **Musée de**

l'Orangerie, including
Monet's last great waterlily
murals (1920–5). Here also is
a good collection of Cézannes
and late Renoirs.
Three artists' studios and
homes are now museums of
their life and work. The **Musée
Rodin**, in an attractive 18th-
century mansion and garden,
offers a complete survey of
the master's sculptures,
drawings and paintings. The
Musée Delacroix, set in a
garden near St-Germain-des-
Prés, has sketches, prints and
oils by the Romantic artist. The
Musée Gustave Moreau, in
an oppressive 19th-century
town house, has an extra-
ordinary collection of
intricately painted canvases
of legendary *femmes fatales*
and dying youths. The **Petit
Palais** has an interesting
collection of 19th-century
paintings with four major
Courbets, including *The Sleep*.

Dead Poet in Musée Gustave Moreau

MODERN AND CONTEMPORARY ART

A S THE INTERNATIONAL centre of the avant-garde from 1900 to 1940, Paris has a great concentration of modern painting and sculpture. The Pompidou Centre houses the **Musée National d'Art Moderne**, covering from 1905 to the present. It has a good selection of Fauvist and Cubist works, particularly by Matisse, Rouault, Braque, Delaunay, and Leger, as well as works by the 1960s' *Nouveaux Réalistes*.

The **Musée d'Art Moderne de la Ville de Paris**, in the elegant 1930s Palais de Tokyo also has an excellent collection, including Delaunays, Bonnards and Fauvist paintings. The highlight is Matisse's 1932 mural, *The Dance*.

Penelope by Bourdelle

The **Musée Picasso**, in a lovely 17th-century mansion, has the world's largest Picasso collection. It also has his own personal collection of the work of his contemporaries. Picasso, Matisse, Modigliani, Utrillo and late Derains make up the collection of 1920s art dealer Paul Guillaume on display at the **Musée de l'Orangerie**. For modern sculpture, the small **Musée Zadkine** has Cubist work by a minor school whose leading light was Ossip Zadkine. The **Musée Antoine Bourdelle** and the **Musée Maillol** house work by these two sculptors, who were both influenced by Rodin, in very different ways.

FURNITURE, DECORATIVE ARTS AND OBJETS D'ART

P RIDE OF PLACE after painting must go to furniture and the decorative arts, contained in a plethora of museums. Fine ensembles of French furnishings and decoration are in the **Louvre** (medieval to Napoleonic) and at the **Palace of Versailles** (17th–18th century). Furniture and *objets d'art* from the Middle Ages to the present century are arranged in period rooms at the **Musée des Arts Décoratifs**. The **Musée d'Orsay** has a large collection of 19th-century furniture, notably Art Nouveau. A superb example of Louis XV (1715–74) and Louis XVI (1774–93) furniture and decoration is in the **Musée Nissim de Camondo**, a mansion from 1910 facing the Parc Monceau. Other notable collections are the **Musée Cognacq-Jay**; the **Musée Carnavalet** (18th-century); the **Musée Jacquemart-André** (French furniture and earthenware); the **Musée Marmottan** (Empire) and **Musée d'Art Moderne de la Ville de Paris** (Art Deco).

Candelabra in the Galerie Royale

Jeweller's shop in the Carnavalet

SPECIALIST MUSEUMS

D EVOTEES OF antique sporting guns, muskets and hounds of the chase should make for the attractive Marais **Hôtel Guénégaud** (Musée de la Chasse et de la Nature). This museum also has some fine 18th-century animal paintings by Jean-Baptiste Oudry and Alexandre-François Desportes, as well as others by Rubens and Brueghel. The **Musée de la Contrefaçon** gives a fascinating insight into the world of counterfeit, whilst for locksmiths, and perhaps also for burglars, the Musée Bricard in the **Hôtel Libéral Bruand** houses a large collection of antique locks and keys. Numismatists will find a coin and medallion museum in luxurious surroundings at the 18th-century Paris Mint at the **Musée de la Monnaie**. French coins are no longer minted here, but the old Mint still makes medals which are on sale. Stamps are on show at the **Musée de la Poste**. The history of postal services is also covered, as are all aspects of philately old and new, with temporary shows on current philatelic design. Sumptuous silver dinner services and other silverware can be seen at the **Galerie Royale**. They were made over a period of 150 years by the Paris firm whose founder was Charles Bouilhet-Christofle, silversmith to King Louis-Philippe and Napoleon III. Antique glass-ware can also be seen here.

FASHION AND COSTUME

T HE TWO RIVAL fashion museums in Paris are the **Musée de la Mode et de la Costume** at the Palais Galliera and the more recent national museum within the **Musée des Arts Décoratifs**. Neither displays a permanent collection, but both hold shows devoted to the great Paris couturiers, such as Saint Laurent and Givenchy. They also display fashion accessories and – more rarely – historical costumes.

Poster for the Palais Galliera

ASIAN, AFRICAN AND OCEANIAN ART

THE MAJOR collection of Asian art in France is housed at the **Musée National des Arts Asiatiques Guimet**, covering China, Tibet, Japan, Korea, Indochina, Indonesia, India and Central Asia. It includes some of the best Khmer art outside Cambodia. The **Musée Cernuschi,** named after the banker, has a smaller but well-chosen Chinese collection, noted for its ancient bronzes and reliefs. France's premier showcase for African art and culture is the **Musée Dapper**, part of an important ethnographic research centre, housed in an elegant 1910 *hôtel particulier* with an African garden. Artefacts from the former French colonies (North and Sub-Saharan Africa, and the South Pacific) are displayed at the **Musée National des Arts d'Afrique et d'Océanie** in an Art Deco building near the Bois de Vincennes.

Sri Lankan theatrical mask

HISTORY AND SOCIAL HISTORY

Café in Musée de Montmartre

COVERING THE entire history of Paris, the **Musée Carnavalet** is housed in two historic Marais *hôtels*. It has period interiors, paintings

of the city and old shop signs, a fascinating section covering events and artefacts from the French Revolution, and even Marcel Proust's bedroom. Also in the Marais, the **Musée d'Art et d'Histoire du Judaisme** explores the culture of French Jewry. The **Musée de l'Armée,** in the Hôtel des Invalides, recounts French military history, and the Musée de l'Histoire de France, in the Rococo **Hôtel de Soubise,** has historical documents from the national archives on display. Famous *tableaux vivants* and characters, both current and historical, await the visitor at the **Musée Grévin** wax museum. The intriguing

Musée de Montmartre, overlooking Paris's last surviving vineyard, holds exhibitions on the history of Montmartre.

ARCHITECTURE AND DESIGN

THE CENTRE de la Création Industrielle holds modern and contemporary design and architecture exhibitions at the **Pompidou Centre**. Superb scale models of fortresses built for Louis XIV and later are on display at the **Musée des Plans-Reliefs**. The work of the celebrated Franco-Swiss architect forms the basis of the **Fondation Le Corbusier**. The showpiece is his 1920s villa for his friend, art collector Raoul La Roche. Some of his furniture is also on display.

THE FRENCH IMPRESSIONISTS

***Impression: Sunrise* by Monet**

IMPRESSIONISM, the great art revolution of the 19th century, began in Paris in the 1860s, when young painters, influenced in part by the new art of photography, started to break with the academic values of the past. They aimed to capture the "impression" of

Monet's sketchbooks

what the eye sees at a given moment and used brushwork designed to capture the fleeting effects of light falling on a scene. Their favourite subjects were landscapes and scenes from contemporary urban life.

The movement had no founder, though Edouard Manet (1832–83) and the radical Realist painter Gustave Courbet (1819–77) both inspired many of the

younger artists. Paintings of scenes of everyday life by Manet and Courbet often offended the academicians who legislated artistic taste. In 1863 Manet's *Le Déjeuner sur l'Herbe (see p144)* was exhibited at the Salon des Refusés, an exhibition set up for paintings rejected by the official Paris Salon of that year. The first time the term "Impressionist" was used to describe this new artistic movement was at another unofficial exhibition, in 1874. The name came from a painting by Claude Monet, *Impression: Sunrise,* a view of Le Havre in the mist from 1872. Monet was almost exclusively a landscape artist, influenced by the works of the English

***Harvesting* (1876) by Pissarro**

The living room of La Roche Villa by Le Corbusier (1923)

SCIENCE AND TECHNOLOGY

IN THE JARDIN des Plantes the **Muséum National d'Histoire Naturelle** has sections on palaeontology, minerology, entomology, anatomy and botany, plus a zoo and a botanical garden. In the Palais de Chaillot, the **Musée de l'Homme** is a major museum of anthropology, ethnology and prehistory with numerous African artefacts. Next door, the **Musée de la Marine** covers French naval history from the 17th century onwards, with fine 18th-century models of ships and sculpted figureheads. The **Musée des Arts et Métiers** imaginatively displays the world of science and industry, of invention and manufacturing. The **Palais de la Découverte** covers the history of science and has a good planetarium, somewhat overshadowed by the spectacular one at the **Cité des Sciences** in the Parc de la Villette. This vast museum is on several levels, with a spherical movie screen, the Géode.

Gabrielle (1910) by Renoir

artists, Constable and Turner. He always liked to paint out of doors and encouraged others to follow his example.

At the 1874 exhibition, a critic wrote that one should stand well back to see these "impressions" – the further back the better – and that members of the establishment should retreat altogether. Other exhibitors at the show were Pierre-Auguste Renoir, Edgar Degas, Camille Pissarro, Alfred Sisley and Paul Cézanne.

There were seven more Impressionist shows up to 1886. By then the power of the Salon had waned and the whole direction of art had changed. From then on, new movements were defined in terms of their relation to Impressionism. The leading Neo-Impressionist was Georges Seurat, who used thousands of minute dots of colour to build up his paintings. It took later generations to fully appreciate the work of the Impressionists. Cézanne was rejected all his life, Degas sold only one painting to a museum, and Sisley died unknown. Of the great artists whose genius is now universally recognized, only Renoir and Monet were ever acclaimed in their lifetimes.

Profile of a Model (1887) by Seurat

Artists in Paris

THE CITY FIRST attracted artists during the reign of Louis XIV (1643–1715), and Paris became the most sophisticated artistic centre in Europe; the magnetism has persisted. During the 18th century, all major French artists lived and worked in Paris. In the latter half of the 19th century and early part of this century, Paris was the European centre of modern and progressive art, and movements such as Impressionism and Post-Impressionism were founded and blossomed in the city.

Monet's palette

BAROQUE ARTISTS
Champaigne, Philippe de (1602–74)
Coysevox, Antoine (1640–1720)
Girardon, François (1628–1715)
Le Brun, Charles (1619–90)
Le Sueur, Eustache (1616–55)
Poussin, Nicolas (1594–1665)
Rigaud, Hyacinthe (1659–1743)
Vignon, Claude (1593–1670)
Vouet, Simon (1590–1649)

ROCOCO ARTISTS
Boucher, François (1703–70)
Chardin, Jean-Baptiste-Siméon (1699–1779)
Falconet, Etienne-Maurice (1716–91)
Fragonard, Jean-Honoré (1732–1806)
Greuze, Jean-Baptiste (1725–1805)
Houdon, Jean-Antoine (1741–1828)
Oudry, Jean-Baptiste (1686–1755)
Pigalle, Jean-Baptiste (1714–85)
Watteau, Jean-Antoine (1684–1721)

Boucher's Diana Bathing *(1742), typical of the Rococo style (Louvre)*

1600	1650	1700	1750
BAROQUE		ROCOCO	NEO-CLASSICISM
1600	1650	1700	1750

1627 Vouet returns from Italy and is made court painter by Louis XIII. Vouet revived a dismal period in the fortunes of French painting

1667 First Salon, France's official art exhibition; originally held annually, later every two years

Philippe de Champaigne's Last Supper *(about 1652). His style slowly became more Classical in his later years (Louvre)*

1648 Foundation of the Académie Royale de Peinture et de Sculpture, which had a virtual monopoly on art teaching

1793 Louvre opens as first national public gallery

Vouet's The Presentation in the Temple *(1641) with typically Baroque contrasts of light and shade (Louvre)*

David's The Oath of the Horatii *(1784), in the Neo-Classical style (Louvre)*

NEO-CLASSICAL ARTISTS
David, Jacques-Louis (1748–1825)
Gros, Antoine Jean (1771–1835)
Ingres, Jean-Auguste-Dominique (1780–1867)
Vigée-Lebrun, Elizabeth (1755–1842)

ROMANTIC AND REALIST ARTISTS

Courbet, Gustave (1819–77)
Daumier, Honoré (1808–79)
Delacroix, Eugène (1798–1863)
Géricault, Théodore (1791–1824)
Rude, Francois (1784–1855)

Courbet's The Burial at Ornans *(1850) which showed Courbet to be the foremost exponent of Realism (Musée d'Orsay)*

Rude's Departure of the Volunteers in 1792 *(1836), a tribute to the French Revolution (see p209)*

MODERN ARTISTS

Arp, Jean (1887–1966)
Balthus (1908–2001)
Brancusi, Constantin (1876–1957)
Braque, Georges (1882–1963)
Buffet, Bernard (1928–1999)
Chagall, Marc (1887–1985)
Delaunay, Robert (1885–1941)
Derain, André (1880–1954)
Dubuffet, Jean (1901–85)
Duchamp, Marcel (1887–1968)
Epstein, Jacob (1880–1959)
Ernst, Max (1891–1976)
Giacometti, Alberto (1901–66)
Gris, Juan (1887–1927)
Léger, Fernand (1881–1955)
Matisse, Henri (1869–1954)
Miró, Joan (1893–1983)
Modigliani, Amedeo (1884–1920)
Mondrian, Piet (1872–1944)
Picasso, Pablo (1881–1973)
Rouault, Georges (1871–1958)
Saint-Phalle, Niki de (1930–)
Soutine, Chaim (1893–1943)
Stael, Nicolas de (1914–55)
Tinguely, Jean (1925–91)
Utrillo, Maurice (1883–1955)
Zadkine, Ossip (1890–1967)

Giacometti's Standing Woman II *(1959), one of his many tall, thin bronze figures (see p113)*

1904 Picasso settles in Paris

1886 Van Gogh moves to Paris

1874 First Impressionist exhibition

1905 Birth of Fauvism, the first of the "isms" in modern art

800	1850	1900	1950
ROMANTICISM/REALISM		IMPRESSIONISM	MODERNISM
800	1850	1900	1950

1863 Manet's *Le Déjeuner sur l'Herbe* causes a scandalous sensation at the Salon des Refusés, both for "poor moral taste", and for its broad brushstrokes. The artist's *Olympia* was thought just as outrageous, but it was not exhibited until 1865 *(see p144)*

1938 International Surrealist exhibition in Paris

1977 Pompidou Centre opens

Monet's Impression: Sunrise *(1872), which led to the name Impressionism*

IMPRESSIONIST AND POST-IMPRESSIONIST ARTISTS

Bonnard, Pierre (1867–1947)
Carpeaux, Jean-Baptiste (1827–75)
Cézanne, Paul (1839–1906)
Degas, Edgar (1834–1917)
Gauguin, Paul (1848–1903)
Manet, Edouard (1832–83)
Monet, Claude (1840–1926)
Pissarro, Camille (1830–1903)
Renoir, Pierre-Auguste (1841–1919)
Rodin, Auguste (1840–1917)
Rousseau, Henri (1844–1910)
Seurat, Georges (1859–91)
Sisley, Alfred (1839–99)
Toulouse-Lautrec, Henri de (1864–1901)
Van Gogh, Vincent (1853–90)
Vuillard, Edouard (1868–1940)
Whistler, James Abbott McNeill (1834–1903)

Delacroix's Liberty Leading the People *(1830) romantically celebrates victory in war (Louvre)*

1819 Géricault paints *The Raft of the Medusa,* one of the greatest works of French Romanticism *(see p124)*

Tinguely and Saint-Phalle's Fontaine Igor Stravinsky *(1980), a modern kinetic sculpture (Pompidou Centre)*

PARIS THROUGH THE YEAR

ARIS'S PULLING POWER is strongest in spring – the season for chestnuts in blossom and tables under trees. From June Paris is slowly turned over to tourists; the city almost comes to a standstill for the French Tennis Open, and the major race tracks stage the big summer races. Next comes the 14 July Bastille Day parade down the Champs-Elysées; towards the end of the month the Tour de France ends here.

The end of July also sees the end of Paris' three-month Jazz Festival, after which most Parisians abandon the city to visitors until *la rentrée,* the return to school and work in September. Dates of events listed on the following pages may vary. For details consult the listings magazines, or contact Allo Sports *(see p343).* The Office du Tourisme *(see p351)* also produces an annual calendar of events.

SPRING

A GOOD MANY OF the city's annual 20-million visitors arrive in the spring. It is the season for fairs and concerts, when the marathon street race is held and the outdoor temperature is pleasant. Spring is also the time when hoteliers offer weekend packages, often with tickets for jazz concerts and with museum passes included.

French Tennis Open, Stade Roland Garros

MARCH

Collectionamania *(last weekend),* Espace Austerlitz, 30 Quai d'Austerlitz. Curio and object collectors' fair.
Foire du Trône *(late Mar–May),* Bois de Vincennes *(p246).* Large funfair.
Banlieues Bleues Festival *(Mar–early Apr),* Paris suburbs. Jazz, blues, soul & funk.
Jumping International de Paris *(3rd week),* Palais d'Omnisports de Paris-Bercy *(pp343–4).* International show jumping.
Salon International d'Agriculture *(1st week),*

Paris International Marathon

Parc des Expositions de Paris, Porte de Versailles. Vast farming fair.
Spring flower shows at the Bagatelle Gardens in the Bois de Boulogne *(p254)* and Parc Floral in the Bois de Vincennes *(p246).*

APRIL

Six Nations Trophy *(early Apr),* Stade de France*(p343).* International rugby.
Salon de la Musique à la Villette *(last week).* International music extravaganza.
Jeune Creation *(mid–end month).* Exhibition of contemporary young artists' work.
Shakespeare Garden Festival *(until Oct),* Bois de Boulogne *(p254).* Classic plays performed outdoors.
Paris International Marathon *(April),* from Place de la Concorde to Château de Vincennes.
Foire de Paris *(end-Apr–1st week May),* Paris Expo. Food, wine, homes and gardens and tourism show.

MAY

Carré Rive Gauche *(one week, mid-month).* Exhibits at antiques dealers in St-Germain-des-Prés *(p135).*
Football Cup Final *(second week),* Stade de France.

Spring colour, Jardin du Luxembourg

Grands Eaux Musicales *(Apr–mid-Oct: Sundays; Jul–Sep: Saturdays),* Versailles *(pp248–53).* Open-air concerts.
French Tennis Open *(last week May–first week Jun),* Stade Roland Garros *(p343).*

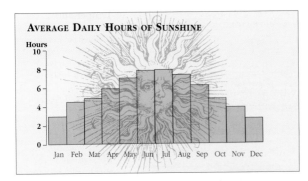

Average Daily Hours of Sunshine

Sunshine Hours
The northerly position of Paris gives it long and light summer evenings, but in winter the daylight recedes with few truly bright days.

SUMMER

SUMMER begins with the French Tennis Open, and there are many events and festivities until July. Thereafter the French begin thinking of their own annual holiday, but there are big celebrations on Bastille Day (14 July) with military displays for the president and his guests.

Final lap of the Champs-Elysées during the **Tour de France**

Jardin du Luxembourg in summer

JUNE

Festival St-Denis, Basilique St-Denis. Concerts with emphasis on large-scale choral works *(pp333–4)*.
Fête du Cinéma, films shown all over Paris for 1€ nominal entry fee *(p340)*.

Fête de la Musique
(21 Jun), all over Paris. Nightlong summer solstice celebrations with amateur and professional bands.
Flower show, Bois de Boulogne *(p254)*. Rose season in the Bagatelle Gardens.
Paris Jazz Festival
(May–Jul), Parc Floral de Paris. International jazz musicians come to play in Paris *(p337)*.
Paris Air and Space Technology Show *(mid-Jun)*, Le Bourget Airport.
Prix de Diane-Hermès
(2nd Sun), Chantilly. French equivalent of the British Ascot high society horse racing event.

JULY

Tournoi International de Pétanque *(2nd weekend)*, Porte de Montreuil. International bowls. Contact the Fédération Française de Pétanque *(p343)*.
Paris Quartier d'Eté *(mid-Jul–mid-Aug)*. Dance, music, theatre, ballet.
Tour de France *(late Jul)*. Last stage of the world's greatest cycle race finishes in the Champs-Elysées.
Fêtes de Nuit *(Jul–mid-Sep: Saturdays)*, Versailles. Son et lumiere with music, dance and theatre *(pp333–4)*.
La Villette Jazz Festival *(early July)*, Parc de la Villette *(pp234–5)*.

March past of troops on Bastille Day (14 July)

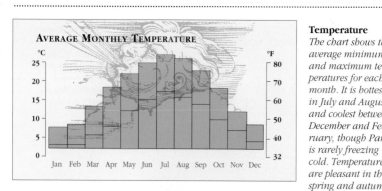

AVERAGE MONTHLY TEMPERATURE

Temperature
The chart shows the average minimum and maximum temperatures for each month. It is hottest in July and August and coolest between December and February, though Paris is rarely freezing cold. Temperatures are pleasant in the spring and autumn.

AUTUMN

SEPTEMBER SEES the start of the social season, with gala performances of new films, and parties in big houses on the Ile St-Louis. Paris is the world's largest congress centre and there are a rush of shows in September, ranging from children's clothes and gifts to leisure and music. The pace barely slackens in October and November when Parisians begin to indulge their great love for the cinema. French and Hollywood stars make appearances at premiers staged on the Champs-Elysées.

SEPTEMBER

Festival d'Automne à Paris *(mid-Sep–end Dec)*, throughout Paris. Music, dance, theatre *(pp333–4)*.
Journées du Patrimoine *(usually 3rd week)*. Three hundred historic buildings, monuments, museums and ministries are open free to the public for two days.

The Prix de l'Arc de Triomphe (October)

Garçons de Café race *(one Sun mid-Sep)*, from Place de la République to Place de la Bastille *(p98)*. Dozens of waiters race with a bottle and glass balanced on a tray.

OCTOBER

Foire Internationale d'Art Contemporain (FIAC) *(last week)*, Parc des Expositions, Porte de Versailles. The biggest international modern and contemporary art fair in Paris.
Prix de l'Arc de Triomphe *(1st week)*, Longchamp. An international field competes for the richest prize in European horse-racing.
Salon de l'Automobile *(1st*

2 weeks, every other year), Parc des Expositions, Porte de Versailles. Commercial motor show, which is alternated annually with a motorcycle show.

Jazz fusion guitarist Al di Meola playing in Paris

NOVEMBER

Paris Tennis Open *(usually Nov)*, Palais d'Omnisports de Paris-Bercy *(pp342–3)*.
Festival d'Art Sacré *(Nov–24 Dec)*, at St-Sulpice, St-Eustache and St-Germain-des-Prés churches. Religious art festival.
Mois de la Photo *(Oct–Dec, biennial)*. Numerous photography shows in museums and galleries.
Biennale Internationale du Film sur l'Art *(last week)*, Centre Georges Pompidou.

Autumn in the Bois de Vincennnes

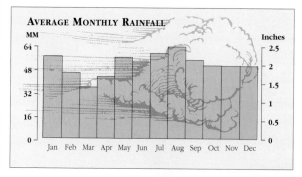

AVERAGE MONTHLY RAINFALL

Rainfall
August is the wettest month in Paris as well as the hottest. In August and September you risk getting caught in storms. Sudden showers, sometimes with hail, can occur between January and April – notoriously in March. There is occasional snow in winter.

WINTER

PARIS RARELY sees snow; winter days tend to be invigorating rather than chilly. There are jazz and dance festivals, candlelit Christmas church services and much celebrating in the streets over the New Year. After New Year, the streets seem to become slightly less congested and on bright days the riverside quays are used as the rendezvous point of strollers and lovers.

Snow in the Tuileries, a rare occurrence

DECEMBER

Christmas illuminations *(until Jan)* in the Grands Boulevards, Opéra, Ave Montaigne, Champs-Elysées and the Rue du Faubourg St-Honoré.
Crèche des Andes *(early Dec–early Jan)*, under a canopy in Place de l'Hôtel de Ville, Marais *(p91)*. Lifesize Christmas crib in the South American tradition.

January fashion show

Horse & Pony Show *(1st fortnight)*, Parc des Exposi-tions, Porte de Versailles.
Paris International Boat Show *(1st fortnight)*, venue: as above.

JANUARY

Commemorative mass for Louis XVI *(Sun nearest to 21 Jan)*, Chapelle Expia-toire, 29 Rue Pasquier 75008.
Fashion shows, summer collections. *(See Haute Couture p316.)*

FEBRUARY

Carnaval *(probably 10 Feb)*, Quartier de St-Fargeau.
Fête de l'Imaginaire *(last week, for 4 mths)*, Maison des Cultures du Monde, 101 Bvd Raspail, 75006. Ethnic exhibitions/performances from around the world.
Floraisons *(all month)*, Parc Floral de Paris, Bois de Vincennes *(p254)* and Parc de Bagatelle, Bois de Boulogne *(p246)*. Displays of crocuses and snowdrops.

PUBLIC HOLIDAYS
New Year's Day (1 Jan)
Easter Monday
Labour Day (1 May)
VE Day (8 May)
Ascension Day (6th Thu after Easter)
Whit Monday (2nd Mon after Ascension)
Bastille Day (14 Jul)
Assumption (15 Aug)
All Saints' Day (1 Nov)
Remembrance Day (11 Nov)
Christmas (25 Dec)

Eiffel Tower Christmas decorations

A RIVER VIEW OF PARIS

Sculpture on the Pont Alexandre III

THE REMARK-
ABLE French
music-hall
star Mistinguett
described the Seine
as a "pretty blonde
with laughing eyes".
The river most certainly has a beguiling quality, but the relationship that
exists between it and the city of Paris
is far more than one of flirtation.

No other European city defines
itself by its river in the same way as
Paris. The Seine is the essential point
of reference to the city: distances are
measured from it, street numbers
determined by it, and it divides the
capital into two distinct areas, with
the Right Bank on the north side of
the river and the Left Bank on the
south side. These are as well defined
as any of the supposedly official
boundaries. The city is also divided
historically, with the east more
closely linked to the city's ancient
roots and the west more closely
linked to the 19th and 20th centuries.

Practically every building of note in
Paris is either along the river or within a stone's throw. The quays are
lined by fine bourgeois apartments,
magnificent town houses, great
museums and striking monuments.

Above all, the river is very much
alive. For centuries fleets of small
boats used it, but motorized land
traffic stifled this once-bustling scene.
Today, the river is busy with commercial barges and massive *bateaux
mouches* pleasure boats cruising
sightseers up and down the river.

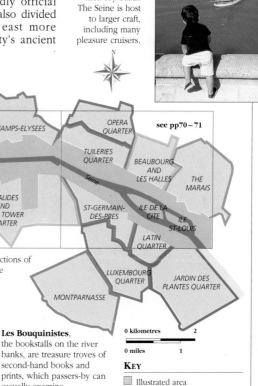

**The octagonal
lake,** in the Jardin
de Luxembourg, is
a favourite spot for
children to sail
their toy boats.
The Seine is host
to larger craft,
including many
pleasure cruisers.

see pp68–9

CHAILLOT
QUARTER

CHAMPS-ELYSEES

OPERA
QUARTER

see pp70–71

TUILERIES
QUARTER

BEAUBOURG
AND
LES HALLES

THE
MARAIS

INVALIDES
AND
EIFFEL TOWER
QUARTER

Seine

ST-GERMAIN-
DES-PRES

ILE DE LA
CITE

ILE
ST-LOUIS

LATIN
QUARTER

This map shows the sections of
the river depicted on the
following pages.

LUXEMBOURG
QUARTER

JARDIN DES
PLANTES QUARTER

MONTPARNASSE

Les Bouquinistes,
the bookstalls on the river
banks, are treasure troves of
second-hand books and
prints, which passers-by can
casually examine.

0 kilometres   2

0 miles   1

KEY

☐ Illustrated area

Pont Alexandre III, encrusted with exuberant statuary

From Pont de Grenelle to Pont de la Concorde

THE SOARING monuments and grand exhibition halls along this stretch of the river are remnants of the Napoleonic era and the Industrial Revolution with its great exhibitions. The exhilarating self-confidence of the Eiffel Tower, the Petit Palais and the Grand Palais is matched by more recent buildings, such as the Palais de Chaillot, the Maison de Radio France and the skyscrapers of the Left Bank.

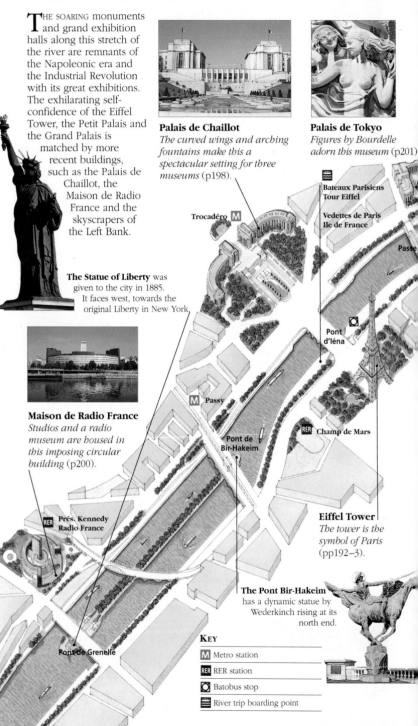

Palais de Chaillot
The curved wings and arching fountains make this a spectacular setting for three museums (p198).

Palais de Tokyo
Figures by Bourdelle adorn this museum (p201)

Bateaux Parisiens Tour Eiffel

Vedettes de Paris Ile de France

Passe

Trocadéro Ⓜ

The Statue of Liberty was given to the city in 1885. It faces west, towards the original Liberty in New York.

Pont d'Iéna

Ⓜ Passy

Maison de Radio France
Studios and a radio museum are housed in this imposing circular building (p200).

RER Champ de Mars

Pont de Bir-Hakeim

RER Prés. Kennedy Radio France

Eiffel Tower
The tower is the symbol of Paris (pp192–3).

The Pont Bir-Hakeim has a dynamic statue by Wederkinch rising at its north end.

Pont de Grenelle

KEY

Ⓜ	Metro station
RER	RER station
⬛	Batobus stop
▦	River trip boarding point

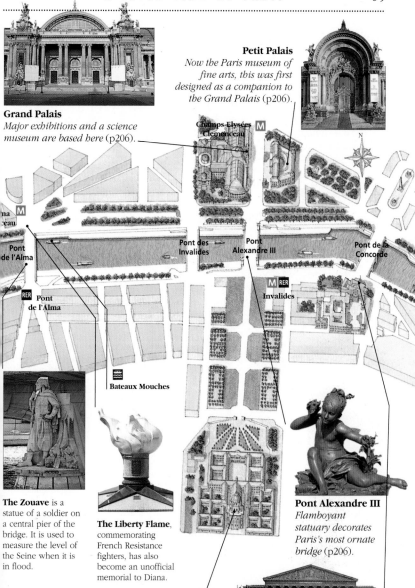

Grand Palais
Major exhibitions and a science museum are based here (p206).

Petit Palais
Now the Paris museum of fine arts, this was first designed as a companion to the Grand Palais (p206).

Champs-Elysées Clemenceau M

M
eau

Pont de l'Alma

RER Pont de l'Alma

Pont des Invalides

Pont Alexandre III

Pont de la Concorde

M RER Invalides

Bateaux Mouches

The Zouave is a statue of a soldier on a central pier of the bridge. It is used to measure the level of the Seine when it is in flood.

The Liberty Flame, commemorating French Resistance fighters, has also become an unofficial memorial to Diana.

Pont Alexandre III
Flamboyant statuary decorates Paris's most ornate bridge (p206).

Dôme Church
The majestic gilded dome (p188–9) is here seen from Pont Alexandre III.

Assemblée Nationale Palais-Bourbon
Louis XIV's daughter once owned this palace, which is now used by the Chambre des Députés as the national forum for political debate (p190).

From Pont de la Concorde to Pont de Sully

T HE HISTORIC heart of Paris lies on the banks and islands of the east river. At its centre is the Ile de la Cité, a natural stepping stone across the Seine and the cultural core of medieval Paris. Today it is still vital to Parisian life.

Jardin des Tuileries
These are in the formal style (p130).

Musée du Louvre
Before becoming the world's greatest museum and home to the Mona Lisa, this was Europe's largest royal palace (pp122–9).

Pont de la Concorde

Assemblée Nationale Ⓜ

Passerelle Solférino

RER **Quai d'Orsay**

Pont Royal

Pont du Carrousel

Passerelle des Arts

Musée de l'Orangerie
An important collection of 19th-century paintings are on display here (p131).

The Passerelle des Arts
is a steel reconstruction of Paris's first cast-iron bridge (1804), and was inaugurated in 1984.

Bâteaux Vedettes du Pont Neuf

Musée d'Orsay
Paris's most important collection of Impressionist art is housed in this converted railway station (pp144–7).

Hôtel des Monnaies
Built in 1768-85, this former Mint has a fine coin collection in its old milling halls (p141).

Ile de la Cité

The medieval identity of this small island was almost completely erased in the 19th century by Baron Haussmann's grand scheme. Sainte-Chapelle and parts of the Conciergerie are the only buildings of the period that remain today (pp76–89).

Conciergerie

During the Revolution this building, with its distinctive towers, became notorious as a prison (p81).

Ile St-Louis

This has been a desirable address since the 17th century (pp76–89).

The Tour de l'Horloge, a 14th-century clock tower, features the first public clock in Paris. Germain Pilon's fine carvings continue to adorn the clock face.

St-Gervais–St-Protais

The oldest organ in Paris, dating from the early 17th century, is in this church (p99).

Pont
Neuf
M

Neuf

M Châtelet
Hôtel de Ville
M

Pont au
Change

Pont Notre-
Dame

Cité

Pont d'Arcole

RER M
St-Michel

Petit Pont

Pont au
Double

Pont Louis
Philippe

M Pont Marie

Pont St Louis

Pont Marie

Pont de
Archevêché

M

Pont de la
Tournelle

Sully Morland

Pont de Sully

Notre-Dame

This towering cathedral surveys the river (pp82–5).

Bâteaux Parisiens

How to Take a River or Canal Trip

R IVER SEINE CRUISES on *bateaux mouches* and *vedettes* pleasure boats operate along the main sightseeing reaches of the river, taking in many of the city's famous monuments. The Batobus river service operates as a shuttle or bus service, allowing you to get on and off anywhere along the route. The main city canal trips operate along the old industrial canal at St-Martin in the city's east.

Pleasure-cruise boats passing under the Pont Alexandre III

Types of Boats

Bateaux mouches, *the largest of the pleasure-cruise boats, are a spectacular sight with their passenger areas enclosed in glass for excellent all round viewing. At night floodlights are used to pick out river bank buildings. A more luxurious version of these is used on the Bateaux Parisien cruises. The* vedettes *are smaller and more intimate boats, with viewing through glass walls. The Canauxrama canal boats are flat-bottomed.*

SEINE CRUISES AND CANAL SHUTTLE SERVICES

The Seine cruises and shuttle services information below includes the location of boarding points, the nearest metro and RER stations, and the nearest bus routes. Lunch and dinner cruises must be booked in advance, and passengers must board them 30 minutes before departure.

ILE de FRANCE

Vedettes de Paris Ile de France Seine Cruise

A fleet of six boats, each of which has the capacity to carry an average of up to 100 passengers in comfort and style. The boarding point is:

Pont d'Iena.
Map 10 D2. ☎ *01 47 05 71 29.* Ⓜ *Bir Hakeim.* RER *Champ de Mars.* 🚌 *22, 30, 32, 44, 63, 69, 72, 82, 87.* **Departures** *May–Oct: 10am–11pm daily (every hour); Nov–Apr: 11am–8pm daily (every hour).* **Duration** *1 hr.* **Dinner cruise** *8pm Thu– Sat.* **Duration** *2hr30min.*

CANAUXRAMA

Parc de la Villette Shuttle Service

This canal trip takes you from the Rotonde de Ledoux, in the Esplanade du Bassin de la Villette, to the Parc de la Villette *(see pp234–9).* The boarding points are:

13 Quai de la Loire.
Map 8 E1.
☎ *01 42 39 15 00.* Ⓜ *Jaures.*
Parc de la Villette.
Ⓜ *Porte de Pantin.*
Departures *Apr–Oct: 11am– noon, 1.30pm–6pm Sat, Sun & public hols (every 30 min).*
Duration *15 min.*

BATEAUX PARISIENS

Bateaux Parisiens Notre-Dame Seine Cruise

This is the company that also organizes the Tour Eiffel trip. This trip, however, only operates during the summer months, following the same route but in the opposite direction. The boarding point is:

Port de Montebello.
Map 13 B4. ☎ *01 43 26 92 55.* Ⓜ *Maubert– Mutualite, St- Michel.* RER *St-Michel.* 🚌 *24, 27, 47.*
Departures *May–Oct: 2.20– 6.20pm daily (every hour). Also 8.20pm & 9.20pm Fri, Sat.* **Duration** *1 hr.*

BATEAUX PARISIENS

Bateaux Parisiens Tour Eiffel Seine Cruise

This company has a fleet of seven boats with a carrying capacity of 100–400 passengers. A commentary is provided in English and French. The boarding point is:

Pont d'Iena.
Map 10 D2. ☎ *01 44 11 33 44.* Ⓜ *Trocadéro, Bir Hakeim.* RER *Champs de Mars.* 🚌 *42, 82, 72.*
Departures *Easter–Oct: 10am–10.30pm daily (every 30 min); Nov– Easter: 10am– 9pm Sun–Thu; 10am–10pm Fri–Sat (every hour).*
Duration *1 hr.* **Lunch cruise** *12.30pm daily.* **Duration** *1 hr 45 min.* **Dinner cruise** *8pm.* **Duration** *3hrs. Unsuitable for children. Jacket & tie required.*

Boarding Points

The boarding points for the river cruises and the Batobus services are easy to find

along the river. Here you can buy tickets, and there are amenities such as snack-bars. Major cruise companies also have foreign exchange booths. There is limited parking around the points, but none near the Pont Neuf.

River boarding point

BATOBUS

Batobus
Shuttle service. 1 or 2 day passes are available. ▊ 01 44 11 33 99. **Departures** Apr–Oct: 10am–7pm (9pm Jun–Aug) daily (every 25 min). Board at: **Eiffel Tower: Map** 10 D3. Ⓜ Bir Hakeim. **Musée d'Orsay: Map** 12 D2. Ⓜ Solferino. **Louvre: Map** 12 E2. Ⓜ Louvre. **St-Germain-de-Prés: Map** 12 E3. Ⓜ St-Germain-de-Prés. **Notre-Dame: Map** 13 B4. Ⓜ Cité. **Hôtel de Ville: Map** 13 B4. Ⓜ Hôtel de Ville.

BATEAUX-MOUCHES

Bateaux Mouches Seine Cruise
This well-known pleasure boat company's fleet of 11 boats carries between 600 and 1,400 passengers at a time. The boarding point is:

Pont de l'Alma.
Map 10 F1. ▊ 01 42 25 96 10. Ⓜ Alma-Marceau. 🚆 Pont de l'Alma. 🚌 28, 42, 49, 63, 72, 80, 83, 92.
Departures Mar–Nov: 10am–11.30pm daily (every 30 min); Nov– Mar: 11am, 2.30pm, 4pm, 9pm (with extra departures on Sat, Sun & public hols).
Duration 1 hr.
Lunch cruise Mar–Nov only. 1pm Tue–Sun.
Duration 1 hr 45 min.
Children under 12, half price. **Dinner cruise** 8.30pm daily. **Duration** 2 hr 15 min. Jacket and tie required.

Vedettes du Pont Neuf

Bateaux Vedettes Pont Neuf Seine Cruise
This company runs a fleet of six 80-passenger boats. The boats are of an older style and provide a quainter cruise. The boarding point is:

Square du Vert-Galant (Pont Neuf). **Map** 12 F3. ▊ 01 46 33 98 38. Ⓜ Pont Neuf. 🚆 Châtelet. 🚌 24, 27, 58, 67, 70, 72, 74, 75. **Departures** Mar–Oct: 10am, 11.15am, noon; 1.30–10.30pm daily (every 30 min); Nov–Feb: 10.30am, 11.15am, noon, 2–6.30pm (every 45 min), 8pm, 10pm Mon–Fri; 10.30am, 11.15am, noon, 2–6.30pm, 8pm, 9–10.30pm (every 30 min) Sat, Sun. **Duration** 1hr. Offer lunch/dinner cruises.

CANAL TRIPS
The Canauxrama company operates boat cruises along the city's Canal St-Martin and along the Canal de l'Ourcq. The St-Martin journey passes along the tree-lined canal, which has nine locks, two swing bridges and eight romantic footbridges. The Canal de l'Ourcq trip travels well into the French countryside as far as the Vignely lock. The **Paris Canal Company** (01 42 40 96 97) also has a St-Martin canal trip, but this one extends beyond the canal, passing into the River Seine and travelling up as far as the Musée d'Orsay.

CANAUXRAMA

Canal St-Martin
The Canauxrama company offers many different trips along this canal, but it has two 125-passenger boats that operate regularly between the Bassin de la Villette and the Porte de l'Arsenal. The boarding points are:
Bassin de la Villette. Map 8 E1. Ⓜ Jaures.
Porte de l'Arsenal. Map 14 E4. Ⓜ Bastille.
▊ 01 42 39 15 00. **Departures** Apr–Oct, times may vary so phone to check and to make a reservation: Bassin de la Villette 9.45 am and 2.45pm; Porte de l'Arsenal 9.45am and 2.30pm daily. On weekday mornings there are concessions for students, pensioners and children under 12. Children under six travel free. Concert cruises are available on chartered trips on the Canal St-Martin and the Seine.
Duration 3 hr.

Canal de l'Ourcq
This all-day cruise extends 108 km (67 miles) north-east of Canal St-Martin. Passengers stop for their own lunch at the charming village of Claye-Souilly. The boarding point is:**Bassin de la Villette. Map** 8 E1. Ⓜ Jaures. ▊ 01 42 39 15 00. **Departures** Apr–Oct: 8.30am Thu–Tue. Reservations necessary. Not suitable for children. **Duration** 8 hr 30 min.

Canal-cruise boat in the Bassin de la Villette

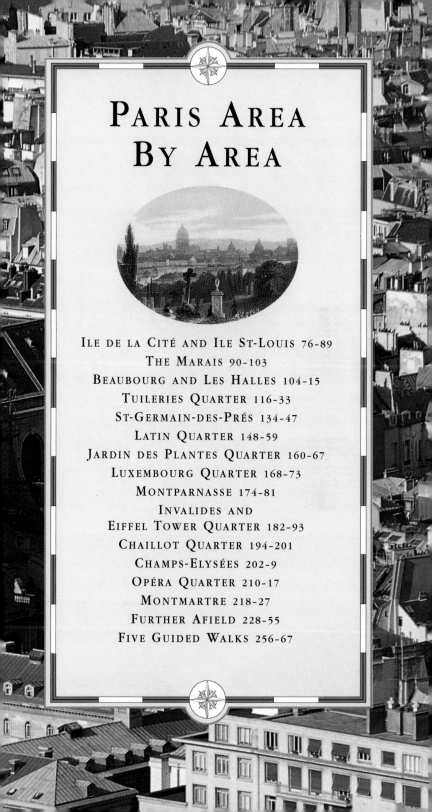

PARIS AREA BY AREA

ILE DE LA CITÉ AND ILE ST-LOUIS

THE HISTORY of the Ile de la Cité is the history of Paris. This island on the Seine was no more than a primitive village when the conquering Julius Caesar arrived in 53 BC. Ancient kings later made it the centre of political power and in medieval times it became the home of church and law. It no longer has its power, but church and law persist to animate the island, armies of tourists being drawn to the imposing Palais de Justice and to the brilliant Gothic masterpiece, Notre-Dame.

The medieval huddles of tiny houses and excruciatingly narrow streets that so characterized the island at one time were swept away by the spacious thoroughfares built in the 19th century. But there are still small areas of charm and relief, among them the colourful bird and flower market, the romantic Square du Vert-Galant and the ancient Place Dauphine.

At the eastern end of the island the St-Louis bridge connects it to the smaller Ile St-Louis. This former swampy pastureland was transformed into an elegant 17th-century residential area. More recently, rich artists, doctors, actresses and heiresses have lived there. Its tree-lined quays are the most enchanting aspect – intimate and picturesque.

The motto of the city of Paris

SIGHTS AT A GLANCE

Historic Buildings
Hôtel Dieu ⑥
Conciergerie ⑧
Palais de Justice ⑩
Hôtel de Lauzun ⑯

Bridges
Pont Neuf ⑫

Monuments
Mémorial des Martyrs de la Déportation ④

Markets
Marché aux Fleurs and Marché aux Oiseaux ⑦

Squares and Gardens
Square Jean XXIII ③
Place Dauphine ⑪
Square du Vert-Galant ⑬

Museums and Galleries
Musée de Notre-Dame de Paris ②
Crypte Archéologique ⑤
Musée Adam Mickiewicz ⑭

Churches and Cathedrals
Notre-Dame pp82–5 ①
Sainte-Chapelle pp88–9 ⑨
St-Louis-en-l'Ile ⑮

GETTING THERE

This area served by the metro station at Cité and the RER at St-Michel. The bus routes 21, 38, 47, 85 and 96 cross the Ile de la Cité, and 67, 86 and 87 cross the Ile St-Louis.

SEE ALSO

- *Street Finder*, map 12–13
- *St-Louis Walk* pp262–3
- *Where to Stay* pp278–9
- *Restaurants* pp296–8

KEY

▨	Street-by-Street map
M	Metro station
RER	RER station
P	Car park

0 metres 400
0 yards 400

View of the Conciergerie and the Pont au Change

Street-by-Street: Ile de la Cité

THE ORIGINS OF PARIS are here on the Ile de la Cité, the boat-shaped island on the Seine first inhabited over 2,000 years ago by Celtic tribes. One tribe, the Parisii, eventually gave its name to the city. The island offered a convenient river crossing on the route between northern and southern Gaul and was easily defended. In later centuries the settlement was expanded by the Romans, the Franks and the Capetian kings to form the nucleus of today's city.

There is no older place in Paris, and remains of the first buildings can still be seen today in the archaeological crypt under the square in front of Notre-Dame, the great medieval cathedral and place of pilgrimage for millions of visitors each year. At the other end of the island is another Gothic masterpiece, Sainte-Chapelle – a miracle of light.

★ **Conciergerie**
A grisly ante-chamber to the guillotine, this prison was much used in the Revolution ❽

The Cour du Mai
is the impressive main courtyard of the Palais de Justice.

Metro Cité

★ **Sainte-Chapelle**
A jewel of Gothic architecture and one of the most magical sights of Paris, Sainte-Chapelle is noted for the magnificence of its stained glass ❾

To Pont Neuf

The Quai des Orfèvres
owes its name to the goldsmiths *(orfèvres)* who frequented the area from medieval times onwards.

The Préfecture de Police
is the headquarters of the police and was the scene of intense battles during World War II.

Palais de Justice
With its ancient towers lining the quays, the old royal palace is today a massive complex of law courts. Its history extends back over 16 centuries ❿

| 0 metres | 100 |
| 0 yards | 100 |

The Statue of Charlemagne
commemorates the emperor who was crowned in 768. He united all the Christian peoples of the West.

★ **Marché aux Fleurs et Oiseaux**
The flower and bird market is a colourful, lively island sight. Paris was once famous for its flower markets but this is now one of the last ⑦

LOCATOR MAP
See Central Paris Map pp12–13

Hôtel Dieu
Once an orphanage, this is now a city hospital ⑥

CRYPTE DU PARVIS

★ **Crypte Archéologique**
Deep under the square, there are remains of houses from 2,000 years ago ⑤

STAR SIGHTS

★ **Notre-Dame**

★ **Sainte-Chapelle**

★ **Conciergerie**

★ **Marché aux Fleurs et Oiseaux**

★ **Crypte Archéologique**

KEY

– – – Suggested route

The Rue Chanoinesse has had many famous residents, such as the 17th-century playwright Racine.

Musée Notre-Dame
Many exhibits tracing the cathedral's history are in this museum ②

Point Zéro
is a mark from which all distances are measured in France.

The Square Jean XXIII
is a peaceful square close to the river ③

★ **Notre-Dame**
This cathedral is a superb example of French medieval architecture ①

To Latin Quarter

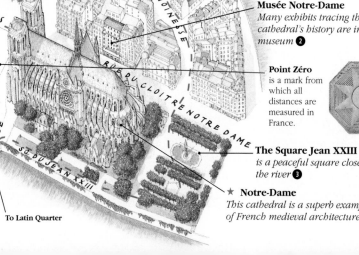

Notre-Dame from
the Left Bank

Notre-Dame ❶

See pp82–5.

Musée de Notre-Dame de Paris ❷

10 Rue du Cloître-Notre-Dame 75004.
Map 13 B4. 01 43 25 42 92. M
Cité. ◯ *2.30pm–6pm Wed, Sat, Sun
(last adm: 5.40pm).*

Founded in 1951, this
museum has exhibits and
documents that commemorate
and illustrate the great events
in Notre-Dame's history. The
displays include Gallo-Roman
objects, old engravings, works
of art and the city
of Paris's oldest
extant Christian
relic, a fine
4th-century
glass cup.

A Gallo-Roman coin

Square Jean XXIII ❸

75004. **Map** 13 B4. M *Cité.*

Notre-dame's St Stephen's
door opens on to this
pleasant garden square,
dedicated to Pope John XXIII.
The garden runs alongside
the river and is an excellent
place for enjoying the
sculptures, rose windows and
flying buttresses of the east
end of the cathedral.

From the 17th century, the
square was occupied by the
archbishop's palace, which
was ransacked by rioters in
1831 and later demolished.
A square was conceived
as a replacement by
the Prefect of Paris,
Rambuteau. The Gothic-
style fountain of the
Virgin standing in the
centre of the square has
been there since 1845.

Mémorial des Martyrs de la Déportation ❹

Sq de l'Île de France 75004. **Map** 13 B4.
01 46 33 87 56. M *Cité.* ◯
*Apr–Sep: 10am–noon, 2pm–7pm daily;
Oct–Mar: 10am–noon, 2pm–5pm daily.*

The simple, modern
memorial to the 200,000
French men, women and
children deported to Nazi
concentration camps in World
War II is covered with a roll-
call of names of the camps to
which they were deported.
Earth from these camps has
been used to form small
tombs. At the far end is the
tomb dedicated to the
Unknown Deportee.

**Inside the Mémorial des Martyrs
de la Déportation**

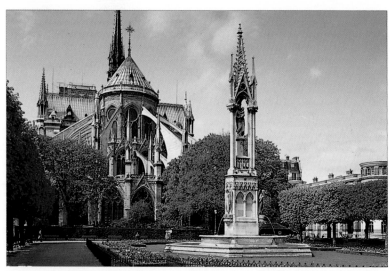

The Square Jean XXIII behind Notre-Dame

Gallo-Roman ruins in the Crypte Archéologique

Crypte Archéologique ❺

Pl du Parvis Notre-Dame 75004.
Map 13 A4. 01 44 59 58 78.
Cité. Tue–Sun 10am–6pm (last adm: 30 min before closing). 1 May, 1 & 11 Nov, 25 Dec, 1 Jan. w www.paris-france.org/musees

SITUATED ON the main square (the *parvis*) in front of Notre-Dame and stretching 120 m (393 ft) underground, this crypt exhibits the remains of foundations and walls that pre-date the cathedral by several hundred years. There are traces of a sophisticated underground heating system in a house from Lutèce, the settlement of the Parisii, the Celtic tribe who inhabited the island 2000 years ago, giving their name to the present city.

Hôtel Dieu ❻

1 Pl du Parvis Notre-Dame 75004.
Map 13 A4. to the public for visits. Cité.

ON THE NORTH side of the place du Parvis Notre-Dame is the Hôtel Dieu, the hospital serving central Paris. It was built on the site of an

Hôtel Dieu, central Paris's hospital

orphanage between 1866 and 1878. The original Hôtel Dieu, built in the 12th century and stretching across the island to both banks of the river, was demolished in the 19th century to make way for one of Baron Haussmann's urban-planning schemes.

It was here in 1944 that the Paris police courageously resisted the Germans; the battle is commemorated by a monument in Cour de 19-Août.

Paris's main flower market

Marché aux Fleurs and Marché aux Oiseaux ❼

Pl Louis-Lépine 75004. **Map** 13 A3.
Cité. 8am–7.30pm Mon–Sat; 8am–7pm Sun.

THE YEAR-ROUND flower market adds colour and scent to an area otherwise dominated by administrative buildings. It is the most famous and unfortunately one of the last remaining flower markets in the city of Paris, offering a wide range of specialist varieties such as orchids. Each Sunday it makes way for the cacophony of the caged bird market.

Conciergerie ❽

1 Quai de l'Horloge 75001. **Map** 13 A3. 01 53 73 78 50. Cité. Apr–Sep: 9.30am–6.30pm daily; Oct–Mar: 10am–5pm daily (last adm: 30 min before closing). 1 Jan, 1 May, 1 & 11 Nov, 25 Dec. 11am, 3pm daily.

OCCUPYING PART of the lower floor of the Palais de Justice, the historic Conciergerie was originally the residence of the Comte des Cierges (Count of the Candles), the palace superintendent in charge of taxes and lodgings. He became chief gaoler when the splendid Gothic halls were transformed into a prison. Henry IV's assassin, Ravaillac, was imprisoned and tortured here.

During the Revolution it housed over 4,000 prisoners, including Marie-Antoinette, who was held in a tiny cell until her execution, and Charlotte Corday, who stabbed Revolutionary leader Marat as he lay in his bath. Ironically, the Revolutionary judges Danton and Robespierre also became "tenants" before being sent to the guillotine.

The Conciergerie has a superb four-aisled Gothic Salle des Gens d'Armes (Hall of the Men-at-Arms), where guards of the royal household once lived. The building, renovated in the 19th century, retains the 11th-century torture chamber, the Bonbec Tower and the 14th-century public clock tower on the Tour de l'Horloge (Palais de Justice). It is the city's oldest and is still operating.

A portrait of Marie-Antoinette in the Conciergerie, awaiting her execution at the guillotine

Notre-Dame ❶

No OTHER BUILDING is so associated with the history of Paris as Notre-Dame. It stands majestically on the Ile de la Cité, cradle of the city. Pope Alexander III laid the first stone in 1163, marking the start of 170 years of toil by armies of Gothic architects and medieval craftsmen. Ever since, a procession of the famous has passed through the three main doors below the massive towers.

The cathedral is a Gothic masterpiece, standing on the site of a Roman temple. At the time it was finished, in about 1330, it was 130 m (430 ft) long and featured flying buttresses, a large transept, a deep choir and 69-m (228-ft) high towers.

★ **West Front**
Three main doors with superb statuary, a central rose window and an openwork gallery are important details.

The south tower houses the cathedral's famous Emmanuel bell.

★ **Galerie des Chimères**
The cathedral's legendary gargoyles (chimères) hide behind a large upper gallery between the towers.

★ **West Rose Window**
This window depicts the Virgin in a medallion of rich reds and blues.

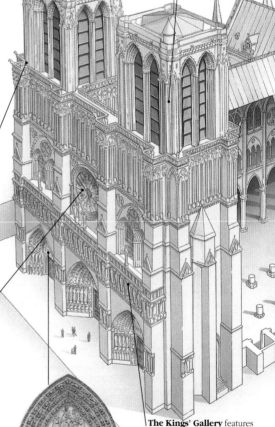

STAR FEATURES
★ **West Front and Portals**
★ **Flying Buttresses**
★ **Rose Windows**
★ **Galerie des Chimères**

The Kings' Gallery features 28 Kings of Judah gazing down on the crowds.

Portal of the Virgin
The Virgin surrounded by saints and kings is a fine composition of 13th-century statues.

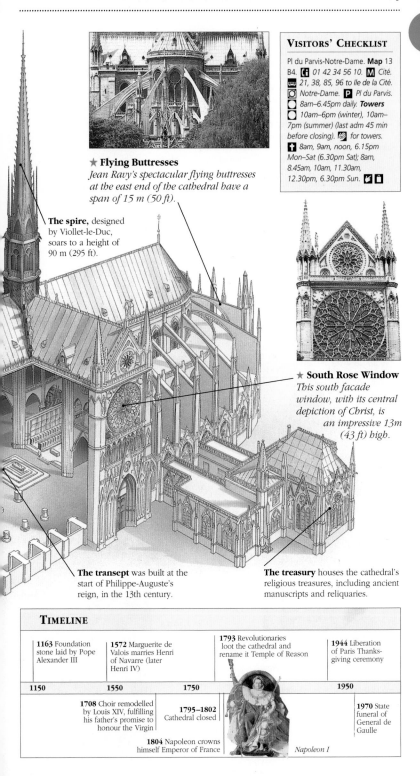

★ Flying Buttresses
*Jean Ravy's spectacular flying buttresses
at the east end of the cathedral have a
span of 15 m (50 ft).*

VISITORS' CHECKLIST

Pl du Parvis-Notre-Dame. **Map** 13
B4. ⓘ 01 42 34 56 10. Ⓜ *Cité.*
🚌 *21, 38, 85, 96 to Ile de la Cité.*
Ⓡ *Notre-Dame.* Ⓟ *Pl du Parvis.*
◯ *8am–6.45pm daily.* **Towers**
◯ *10am–6pm (winter), 10am–
7pm (summer) (last adm 45 min
before closing).* 💳 *for towers.*
✝ *8am, 9am, noon, 6.15pm
Mon–Sat (6.30pm Sat); 8am,
8.45am, 10am, 11.30am,
12.30pm, 6.30pm Sun.* 📷 🏛

The spire, designed
by Viollet-le-Duc,
soars to a height of
90 m (295 ft).

★ South Rose Window
*This south facade
window, with its central
depiction of Christ, is
an impressive 13m
(43 ft) high.*

The transept was built at the
start of Philippe-Auguste's
reign, in the 13th century.

The treasury houses the cathedral's
religious treasures, including ancient
manuscripts and reliquaries.

TIMELINE

1163 Foundation stone laid by Pope Alexander III	**1572** Marguerite de Valois marries Henri of Navarre (later Henri IV)	**1793** Revolutionaries loot the cathedral and rename it Temple of Reason	**1944** Liberation of Paris Thanksgiving ceremony

1150	1550	1750		1950

1708 Choir remodelled by Louis XIV, fulfilling his father's promise to honour the Virgin	**1795–1802** Cathedral closed		**1970** State funeral of General de Gaulle
	1804 Napoleon crowns himself Emperor of France	*Napoleon I*	

A Guided Tour of Notre-Dame

NOTRE-DAME'S INTERIOR grandeur is instantly apparent on seeing the high-vaulted central nave. This is bisected by a huge transept, at either end of which are medieval rose windows, 13 m (43 ft) in diameter. Works by major sculptors adorn the cathedral. Among them are Jean Ravy's old choir screen carvings, Nicolas Coustou's *Pietà* and Antoine Coysevox's Louis XIV statue. In this majestic setting kings and emperors were crowned and royal Crusaders were blessed. But Notre-Dame was also the scene of turmoil. Revolutionaries ransacked it, banished religion, changed it into a temple to the Cult of Reason, and then used it as a wine store. Napoleon restored religion in 1804 and architect Viollet-le-Duc later restored the buildings, replacing missing statues, as well as raising the spire and fixing the gargoyles.

A jewelled chalice of Notre-Dame

⑨ **North Rose Window**
This 13th-century stained-glass window, depicting the Virgin encircled by figures from the Old Testament, is 21 m (69 ft) high.

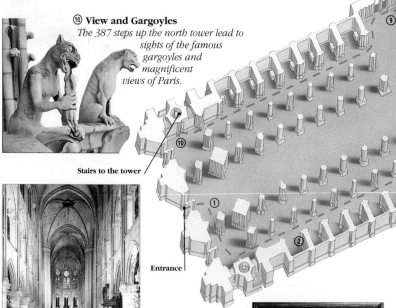

⑩ **View and Gargoyles**
The 387 steps up the north tower lead to sights of the famous gargoyles and magnificent views of Paris.

Stairs to the tower

Entrance

① **View of Interior**
From the main entrance, the view takes in the high-vaulted central nave looking down towards the huge transept, the choir and the high altar.

KEY

— — — Walk route

② **Le Brun's "May" Paintings**
These religious paintings by Charles Le Brun hang in the side chapels. In the 17th and 18th centuries, the Paris guilds presented a painting to the cathedral on May Day each year.

⑧ **Carved Choir Stalls**

Noted for their 18th-century carved woodwork, the choir stalls were commissioned by Louis XIV, whose statue stands behind the high altar. Among the details carved in bas-relief on the back of the high stalls are scenes from the life of the Virgin.

⑦ **Louis XIII Statue**

After many years of childless marriage, Louis XIII pledged to erect a high altar and to redecorate the east chancel to honour the Virgin if an heir was born to him. The future Louis XIV was born in 1638, but it took 60 years before the promises were made good. One of the surviving features from that time is the carved choir stalls.

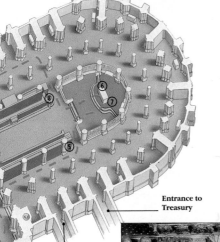

Entrance to Treasury

Entrance to Sacristy

⑥ **Pietà**

Behind the high altar is Nicolas Coustou's Pietà, *standing on a gilded base sculptured by François Girardon.*

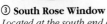

⑤ **Chancel Screen**

A 14th-century high stone screen enclosed the chancel and provided canons at prayer with peace and solitude from noisy congregations. Some of it has survived to screen the first three north and south bays.

③ **South Rose Window**

Located at the south end of the transept, this window retains some of its original 13th-century stained glass. The window depicts Christ in the centre, surrounded by virgins, saints and the 12 Apostles.

④ **Statue of the Virgin and Child**

Against the southeast pillar of the transept stands the 14th-century statue of the Virgin and Child. It was brought to the cathedral from the chapel of St Aignan, and is known as Notre-Dame de Paris (Our Lady of Paris).

The Pont Neuf, extending to the north and south of the Ile de la Cité

Sainte-Chapelle ❾

See pp88–9.

A Sainte-Chapelle decoration of angels with the Crown of Thorns

Palais de Justice ❿

4 Blvd du Palais (entrance by the Cour de Mai) 75001. **Map** 13 A3.
C 01 44 32 50 00. **M** Cité.
◯ 8.30am–6.30pm Mon–Fri.
⊘ ▢ ⓫

THIS HUGE BLOCK of build-ings making up the law courts stretches the entire width of the Ile de la Cité. It is a splendid sight with its old towers lining the quays. The site has been occupied since Roman times and was the seat of royal power until Charles V moved the court to the Marais in the 14th century. In April 1793 the Revolutionary Tribunal began dispensing justice from the Première Chambre (gilded chamber). Today the site embodies Napoleon's great legacy – the French judicial system.

Place Dauphine ⓫

75001 (enter by Rue Henri-Robert). **Map** 12 F3. **M** Pont Neuf, Cité.

EAST OF PONT NEUF is this ancient square, laid out in 1607 by Henri IV and named after the Dauphin, the future Louis XIII. No. 14 is one of the few buildings to have avoided any subsequent restoration. This haven of 17th-century charm is popular with *pétanque* (boules) players and employees of the adjoining Palais de Justice.

Pont Neuf ⓬

75001. **Map** 12 F3. **M** Pont Neuf, Cité.

DESPITE ITS name (New Bridge), this bridge is the oldest in Paris and has been immortalized by major literary and artistic figures since it was built. The first stone was laid by Henri III in 1578, but it was Henri IV who inaugurated it and gave it its name in 1607. The bridge has 12 arches and spans 275 m (912 ft). The first stone bridge to be built without houses, it heralded a new era in the relationship between the Cité and the river and has been popular ever since. Fittingly, Henri IV's statue stands in the central section.

A sculptured relief on the Palais de Justice

Henri IV in Square du Vert-Galant

Square du Vert-Galant ⑬

75001. **Map** 12 F3. Ⓜ *Pont Neuf, Cité.*

O NE OF THE magical spots of Paris, this square bears the nickname of Henri IV. This amorous and colourful monarch did much to beautify Paris in the early 17th century, and his popularity has lasted to this day. From here there are splendid views of the Louvre and the Right Bank of the river, where Henri was assassinated in 1610. This is also the point from which the Vedettes de Paris pleasure boats depart *(see pp72–3).*

Musée Adam Mickiewicz ⑭

6 Quai d'Orléans 75004. **Map** 13 C4. Ⓒ *01 55 42 83 83.* Ⓜ *Pont Marie.* Ⓞ *for renovation until 2003.* 🎫 Ⓕ *2pm, 3.30pm & 5pm.*

T HE POLISH Romantic poet Adam Mickiewicz, who lived in Paris in the 19th century, was a major force in Polish cultural and political life, devoting his writing to helping his countrymen who were oppressed at home and abroad. The museum was founded in 1903 by the poet's eldest son, Ladislas. Part of the famous Polish library has moved to 74 rue Lauriston, but the archives remain. Altogether

they form probably the finest Polish collection outside Poland: paintings, books, maps, emigration archives covering the 19th and 20th centuries and, above all, Frédéric Chopin memorabilia, including his death mask.

St-Louis-en-l'Ile ⑮

19 bis Rue St-Louis-en-l'Ile 75004. **Map** 13 C4. Ⓒ *01 46 34 11 60.* Ⓜ *Pont Marie.* Ⓞ *9am–noon, 3pm–7pm Tue–Sun.* Ⓦ *public hols.* **Concerts.**

T HE CONSTRUCTION of this church was begun in 1664 from plans by the royal architect Louis Le Vau, who lived on the island. It was completed and consecrated in 1726. Among its outstanding exterior features are the 1741 iron clock at the entrance and the pierced iron spire.

The interior, in the Baroque style, is richly decorated with gilding and marble. There is a statue of St Louis holding a crusader's sword. A plaque in the north aisle, given in 1926, bears the inscription "in grateful memory of St Louis in whose honour the City of St Louis, Missouri, USA is named". The church is also twinned with Carthage cathedral in Tunisia, where St Louis is buried.

A bust of Adam Mickiewicz

The interior of St-Louis-en-l'Ile

Hôtel de Lauzun ⑯

17 Quai d'Anjou 75004. **Map** 13 C4. Ⓜ *Pont Marie.* Ⓦ *but occasional very limited guided tours (01 44 54 19 30).*

T HIS SPLENDID mansion was built by Louis Le Vau in the mid-1650s for Charles Gruyn des Bordes, an arms dealer. It was sold in 1682 to the French military commander Duc de Lauzun, who was a favourite of Louis XIV. It later became a focus for Paris's Bohemian literary and artistic life. It now belongs to the city of Paris and, for those lucky enough to see inside, offers an unsurpassed insight into wealthy lifestyles in the 17th century. Charles Le Brun worked on the decoration of its magnificent panelling and painted ceilings before moving on to Versailles.

The poet Charles Baudelaire (1821–67) lived on the third floor and wrote the major part of his controversial masterpiece *Les Fleurs du Mal* here in a room packed with antiques and bric-a-brac. The celebrated French Romantic poet, traveller and critic, Théophile Gautier (1811–72), had apartments here in 1848. Meetings of the Club des Haschischines (the Hashish-Eaters' Club) took place on the premises.

Other famous residents were the Austrian poet Rainer Maria Rilke, the English artist Walter Sickert and the German composer Richard Wagner. Nowadays it is used for public receptions by the mayor of Paris.

Sainte-Chapelle ❾

ETHEREAL AND MAGICAL, Sainte-Chapelle has been hailed as one of the greatest architectural masterpieces of the Western world. In the Middle Ages the devout likened this church to "a gateway to heaven". Today no visitor can fail to be transported by the blaze of light created by the 15 magnificent stained-glass windows, separated by the narrowest of columns that soar 15 m (50 ft) to the star-studded, vaulted roof. The windows portray over 1,000 religious scenes in a kaleidoscope of red, gold, green, blue and mauve. The chapel was built in 1248 by Louis IX to house Christ's purported Crown of Thorns and other relics.

The spire
rises 75 m (245 ft) into the air. It was erected in 1853 after three previous spires burned down.

The Crown of Thorns
decorates the pinnacle as a symbol of the first relic bought by Louis IX.

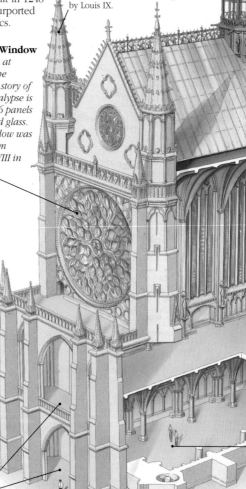

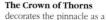

★ **Rose Window**
Best seen at sunset, the religious story of the Apocalypse is told in 86 panels of stained glass. The window was a gift from Charles VIII in 1485.

STAR FEATURES

★ **Rose Window**

★ **Window of Christ's Passion**

★ **Apostle Statues**

★ **Window of the Relics**

Main Portal
The two-tier structure of the portal, the lower half of which is shown here, echoes that of the chapel.

St Louis' Relics

Louis IX was so devout a king that he came to be known as Saint Louis. In 1239 he acquired the Crown of Thorns from the Emperor of Constantinople and then, in 1241, other relics, including a fragment of Christ's Cross. He built this beautiful chapel as a shrine to house them. Louis paid nearly three times more for the relics than he did for the whole of the construction of Sainte-Chapelle.

Visitors' Checklist

2 Blvd du Palais. **Map** 13 A3.
01 53 73 78 50. **M** Cité.
21, 38, 85, 96 to Ile de la
Cité. **RER** St-Michel. Notre-
Dame. **P** Palais de Justice.
Open Apr–Sep: 9.30am–6.30pm;
Oct–Mar: 10am–5pm daily. Last
adm 30 mins before closing.
Closed 1 Jan, 1 May, 1 Nov,
11 Nov, 25 Dec. **Adm charge.**

The angel
once revolved so that its cross could be seen from anywhere in Paris.

Upper Chapel
The windows are a pictorial Bible, showing scenes from the Old and New Testaments.

Upper Chapel Windows

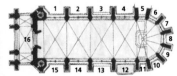

1 Genesis
2 Exodus
3 Numbers
4 Deuteronomy: Joshua
5 Judges
6 *left* Isaiah *right* Rod of Jesse
7 *left* St John the Evangelist *right* Childhood of Christ
8 Christ's Passion
9 *left* St John the Baptist *right* Story of Daniel
10 Ezekiel
11 *left* Jeremiah *right* Tobiah
12 Judith and Job
13 Esther
14 Book of Kings
15 Story of the Relics
16 Rose Window: The Apocalypse

★ **Window of Christ's Passion**
The Last Supper is shown here in one of the most beautiful windows in the upper chapel.

★ **Apostle Statues**
These magnificent examples of medieval wood carving adorn the 12 pillars of the upper chapel.

Lower Chapel
Servants and commoners worshipped here, while the chapel above was reserved for the use of the king and the royal family.

★ **Window of the Relics**
This shows the journey of the True Cross and the nails of the Crucifixion to Sainte-Chapelle.

THE MARAIS

THE MARAIS IS ARGUABLY the most fascinating area of Paris. A place of royal residence in the 17th century, it was mercilessly abandoned to the people during the Revolution, and descended into an architectural wasteland before being rescued in the 1960s. It was officially declared a historical monument by the Charles de Gaulle government in 1962 and its resurrection then began.

Buildings have come to life and the area is fashionable again with its new galleries and restaurants, chic fashion boutiques and cultural centres. The main streets and the narrow passageways are again bustling. Many of the traders have been driven out by high prices, but enough artisans, bakers and small cafés have survived, as has the ethnic mix of Jews, former Algerian settlers, Asians and others.

SIGHTS AT A GLANCE

Historic Buildings and Streets
Hôtel de Lamoignon ②
Rue des Francs-Bourgeois ③
Rue des Rosiers ⑧
Hôtel de Ville ⑲
Hôtel de Rohan ㉒

Churches
St-Paul–St-Louis ⑮
St-Gervais–St-Protais ⑱
Cloître des Billettes ⑳
Notre-Dame-des-Blancs-Manteaux ㉑

Museums and Galleries
Musée Carnavalet pp96–7 ①
Musée Cognacq-Jay ④
Maison de Victor Hugo ⑥
Hôtel de Sully ⑦
Hôtel de Coulanges ⑨
Hôtel Libéral Bruand (Musée Bricard) ⑩
Musée Picasso pp100–1 ⑪
Hôtel de Sens ⑯

Hôtel de Soubise ㉓
Hôtel Guénégaud (Musée de la Chasse et de la Nature) ㉔
Musée des Arts et Métiers ㉕
Musée d'Art et d'Histoire du Judaïsme ㉗

Monuments and Statues
Colonne de Juillet ⑬
Mémorial du Martyr Juif Inconnu ⑰

Opera Houses
Opéra de Paris Bastille ⑫

Squares
Place des Vosges ⑤
Place de la Bastille ⑭
Square du Temple ㉖

GETTING THERE
The metro stations in the area include Bastille, and Hôtel de Ville. Bus route 29 travels along Rue des Francs-Bourgeois, passing by the Rue de Sévigné, where the Musée Carnavalet is located, and by the Place des Vosges.

SEE ALSO

KEY
▮	Street-by-Street map
Ⓜ	Metro station
Ⓞ	Batobus boarding point
Ⓟ	Car park

0 metres 400
0 yards 400

Lunchtime at a Marais park café

Street by Street: The Marais

ONCE AN AREA of marshland as its name suggests (*marais* means swamp), the Marais grew steadily in importance from the 14th century, by virtue of its proximity to the Louvre, the preferred residence of Charles V. Its heyday was in the 17th century, when it became the fashionable area for the monied classes. They built many grand and sumptuous mansions (*hôtels*) that still dot the Marais today. Many of these *hôtels* have recently been restored and turned into museums. Once again fashionable with the monied classes, designer boutiques, trendy restaurants and cafés now line the streets.

To the Pompidou Centre

Rue des Francs-Bourgeois
This ancient street is lined with important museums ❸

Hôtel Libéral Bruand
Named after the architect who built it for his own use, this mansion now contains a museum devoted to locks ❿

Rue des Rosiers
The smell of hot pastrami and borscht wafts from restaurants and shops in the heart of the Jewish area ❽

Musée Cognacq-Jay
An exquisite collection of 18th-century paintings and furniture is shown in perfect period setting ❹

STAR SIGHTS

★ **Musée Picasso**

★ **Musée Carnavalet**

★ **Place des Vosges**

KEY

━ ━ ━ Suggested route

0 metres	100
0 yards	100

Hôtel de Lamoignon
Behind the ornate doorway of this fine mansion is Paris's historical library ❷

★ **Musée Picasso**
The palatial home of a 17th-century salt-tax collector is the setting for the largest collection of Picassos in the world, the result of a family bequest to the state ⓫

LOCATOR MAP
See Central Paris Map pp12–13

The Hôtel le Peletier de St-Fargeau adjoins the Hôtel Carnavalet to form the museum of Paris History.

★ **Musée Carnavalet**
The statue of Louis XIV in Roman dress by Coysevox is in the courtyard of the Hôtel Carnavalet ❶

Maison de Victor Hugo
Author of Les Misérables, *Victor Hugo lived at No. 6 Place des Vosges, where his house is now a museum of his life and work* ❻

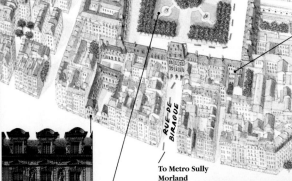

To Metro Sully Morland

★ **Place des Vosges**
Once the site of jousting and tournaments, the historic Place des Vosges, in the very heart of the Marais, is a square of perfect symmetry ❺

Hôtel de Sully
This Renaissance hôtel *was built for a notorious gambler* ❼

Musée Carnavalet ❶

See pp96–7.

Hôtel de Lamoignon ❷

24 Rue Pavée 75004. **Map** 14 D3.
☎ *01 44 59 29 40.* Ⓜ *St-Paul.*
◯ *9.30am–6pm Mon–Sat.*
⬤ *public hols & 1–15 Aug.* 🔓

THE IMPOSING Hôtel de Lamoignon is home to the historical library of the city of Paris. This mansion was built in 1584 for Diane de France, also known as the Duchesse d'Angoulême, daughter of Henri II. The building is noted for six high Corinthian pilasters topped by a triangular pediment and flourishes of dogs' heads, bows, arrows and quivers – recalling Diane's passion for hunting. The collection includes documents from the French Revolution and 80,000 prints covering the history of Paris.

Rue des Francs-Bourgeois ❸

75003, 75004. **Map** 14 D3.
Ⓜ *Rambuteau, Chemin-Vert.*

THIS STREET is an important thoroughfare in the heart of the Marais, linking the Rue des Archives and the Place

Courtyard of the Musée Carnavalet

des Vosges, with the imposing Hôtel de Soubise at one end and the Musée Carnavalet at the other. The street got its name from the *francs* (free from taxes) – almshouses built for the poor in 1334 at Nos. 34 and 36. These were later closed because of illegal financial activities, although the state kept its pawnshop nearby, still there today.

Musée Cognacq-Jay ❹

Hôtel de Donon, 8 Rue Elzévir 75004.
Map 14 D3. ☎ *01 40 27 07 21.* Ⓜ
St-Paul. ◯ *10am–5.40pm Tue–Sun).*
⬤ *public hols.* 📷 📹 *pre-book.* 🔓
Ⓦ *www.paris-france.org/musees*

THIS FINE small collection of French 18th-century works of art and furniture was

formed by Ernest Cognacq and his wife, Louise Jay, founder of La Samaritaine, Paris's largest department store *(see p115)*. The private collection was bequeathed to the city and is now housed in the heart of the Marais at the Hôtel de Donon – an elegant building dating from 1575 with an 18th-century extension and facade.

Place des Vosges ❺

75003, 75004. **Map** 14 D3.
Ⓜ *Bastille, St-Paul.*

THIS SQUARE is considered among the most beautiful in the world by Parisians and visitors alike *(see pp22–3)*. Its impressive symmetry – 36 houses, nine on each side, of brick and stone, with deep slate roofs and dormer windows over arcades – is still intact after 400 years. It has been the scene of many historic events over the centuries. A three-day tournament was held here to celebrate the marriage of Louis XIII to Anne of Austria in 1615. The famous literary hostess, Madame de Sévigné, was born here in 1626; Cardinal Richelieu, pillar of the monarchy, stayed here in 1615; and Victor Hugo, the writer, lived here for 16 years.

A 19th-century engraving of the Place des Vosges

Maison de Victor Hugo ❻

6 Pl des Vosges 75004. **Map** 14 D3.
【 *01 42 72 10 16*. Ⓜ *Bastille*.
○ *10am–5.40pm Tue–Sun*.
● *public hols*. ▨ ☑ **Library**.
Ⓦ *www.paris-france.org/musees*

THE FRENCH poet, dramatist and novelist lived on the second floor of the former Hôtel Rohan-Guéménée, the largest house on the square, from 1832 to 1848. It was here that he wrote most of *Les Misérables* and completed many other famous works. On display are some reconstructions of the rooms in which he lived, penand-ink drawings, books and mementos from the crucially important periods in his life, from his childhood to his exile between 1852 and 1870.

Marble bust of Victor Hugo by Auguste Rodin

Hôtel de Sully ❼

62 Rue St-Antoine 75004.
Map 14 D4. 【 *01 44 61 21 50*. Ⓜ
St-Paul. ○ *(courtyard only)*
9am–7pm daily. ● *public hols*.

THIS FINE 17th-century mansion on one of Paris's oldest streets has been extensively restored, using old engravings and drawings as reference. It was built in 1624 for a notorious gambler, Petit Thomas, who lost his whole fortune in one night. The Duc de Sully, Henri IV's chief minister, purchased the house in 1634 and added some of the interior decoration as well as the Petit Sully orangery in the gardens. Today it is the head office of the Centre des Monuments Nationaux. The exterior of the *hôtel* has a late-Renaissance facade. Inside there is a courtyard with carved pediments, dormer windows and statues of the four seasons and sphinxes.

Late-Renaissance facade of the Hôtel de Sully

Rue des Rosiers ❽

75004. **Map** 13 C3. Ⓜ *St-Paul*.

THE JEWISH quarter in and around this street is one of the most colourful areas of Paris. The street's name refers to the rosebushes within the old city wall. Jews first settled here in the 13th century, with a second wave in the 19th century from Russia, Poland and central Europe. Sephardic Jews arrived from Algeria, Tunisia, Morocco and Egypt in the 1950s and 1960s. Some 165 students were rounded up and deported from the old Jewish Boys' school nearby at 10 rue de Hospitalières-St-Gervais. *N'Oubliez pas* (Do not forget) is engraved on the wall. Today this area contains synagogues, bakeries and kosher restaurants, the most famous being Jo Goldenberg's (*see p322*).

Orthodox Jews in the Marais

Hôtel de Coulanges ❾

35 rue des Francs Bourgeois, 75004.
Map 13 C3. 【 *01 44 61 85 85*. Ⓜ
St-Paul. ○ *8.30am–6.30pm Mon–Fri*. ● *public hols*. **Concerts** ▨
phone for times (01 42 07 22 07).

THIS HOTEL IS a magnificent example of the architecture of the early 18th century. The right wing of the building, separating the courtyard from the garden, dates from the early 17th century. The hôtel was given in 1640 to Phillipe II de Coulanges, the King's counsellor. Renamed the "Petit hôtel Le Tellier" in 1662 by its new owner Le Tellier, this is where the children of Louis XIV and Madame de Montespan were raised in secrecy. It is now home to the Maison de L'Europe, with exhibitions on themes relating to Europe.

Musée Carnavalet ●

Carnavalet entrance

Devoted to the history of Paris, this vast museum occupies two adjoining mansions. They include entire decorated rooms with panelling, furniture and *objets d'art*; many works of art such as paintings and sculptures of prominent personalities; and engravings showing Paris being built. The main building is the Hôtel Carnavalet, built as a town house in 1548 and transformed in the mid-17th century by François Mansart. The neighbouring 17th-century mansion house, Hôtel le Peletier features superb interiors dating from the beginning of the 20th century.

Marie Antionette in Mourning *(1793)*
Alexandre Kucharski painted her at the Temple prison after the execution of Louis XVI.

Memorabilia in this room is dedicated to 18th-century philosophers, in particular Jean-Jacques Rousseau and Voltaire.

★ **Charles Le Brun Ceiling**
Magnificent works by the 17th-century artist decorate the former study and great hall from the Hôtel de la Rivière.

★ **Mme de Sévigné's Gallery**
The gallery includes this portrait of Mme de Sévigné, the celebrated letter-writer, whose beloved home this was for the 20 years up to her death.

STAR EXHIBITS

- ★ **Mme de Sévigné's Gallery**

- ★ **Charles Le Brun Ceiling**

- ★ **Hôtel d'Uzès Reception Room**

- ★ **Ballroom of the Hôtel de Wendel**

★ **Hotel d'Uzès Reception Room**
The room was created in 1761 by Claude Nicolas Ledoux. The gold-and-white panelling is from a Rue Montmartre mansion.

Entrance
the muse

Second floor

Convention Room
Georges Danton's portrait is among the memorabilia of the Revolution.

First floor

Fouquet Jewellery Boutique *(1900)*
The Art Nouveau decor of this shop from Rue Royale is by A Moucha.

Hôtel le Peletier

VISITORS' CHECKLIST

23 Rue de Sévigné 75003. **Map** 14 D3. 📞 *01 44 59 58 58.* Ⓜ *St-Paul.* 🚌 *29, 69, 76, 96 to St-Paul, Pl des Vosges.* 🅿 *Hôtel de Ville, Rue St-Antoine.* ⏰ *10am–5.40pm Tue–Sun (rooms open in rotas; phone to check).* ⬤ *public hols.* 💷 *free Sun am* 📷 📹 *phone for times.* 🚻 Ⓦ www.paris-france.org/musees

★ **Ballroom of the Hôtel de Wendel**
The early 20th-century ballroom interior has been reconstructed. This immense mural depicts the retinue of the Queen of Sheba and is by the Catalan designer and painter José María Sert y Badia.

Louis XV Lilas Room
This delightful room contains art from the Bouvier collection and panelling from the Hôtel de Broglie.

KEY TO FLOOR PLAN

- 🟫 Prehistory to Gallo-Roman
- ⬜ Medieval Paris
- ⬜ Renaissance Paris
- ⬜ 17th-Century Paris
- ⬜ Louis XV's Paris
- ⬜ Louis XVI's Paris
- 🟫 Revolutionary Paris
- ⬜ First Empire to Second Empire
- ⬜ Second Empire to Present
- ⬜ Temporary exhibitions
- ⬜ Non-exhibition space

GALLERY GUIDE
The collection is mainly arranged chronologically. It covers the history of Paris up to 1789. The Renaissance is on the ground floor, and the exhibits covering the 17th century to the Revolution are on the first floor. In the Hôtel le Peletier the ground floor covers the First–Second Empires, with the new Prehistory–Gallo-Roman departments in the Orangery; from the Second Empire to the present day is on the first floor, and the second floor is devoted to the Revolution.

Hôtel Libéral Bruand ⑩

1 Rue de la Perle 75003. **Map** 14 D3.
☎ 01 42 77 79 62. **M** St-Paul,
Chemin-Vert. **Museum** ◻ 10am–
noon Tue–Fri, 2pm–5pm Mon–Fri.
● Aug & public hols. 🖼

T**HIS SMALL** private house,
built by the architect
Libéral Bruand for himself in
1685, is far removed, with its
elegant Italianate touches,
from his most famous work,
the Invalides (see pp186–7).
The building has been
completely restored and now
contains the Musée Bricard,
one of the most intriguing
collections of its kind in the
world, with locks, door-knobs
and knockers from as long
ago as Roman times.

Musée Picasso ⑪

See pp100–1.

Opéra de Paris Bastille ⑫

120 Rue de Lyon 75012. **Map** 14 E4.
☎ 01 40 01 17 89. **🖷** 08 36 69 78 68.
M Bastille. ◻ phone for details.
● certain public hols. 🖼 ♿ ✔
See **Entertainment** pp334–5.

O**NE OF THE** most modern
and controversial opera
houses in Europe, the
"people's opera" was officially
opened on 14 July 1989 to

**The "genius of liberty" on top of
the Colonne de Juillet**

coincide with the bicentennial
celebrations of the fall of the
Bastille. Carlos Ott's imposing
building is a notable break
with 19th-century opera-
house design, epitomized by
Garnier's opulent Opéra in
the heart of the city (see
pp214–15). It is a massive,
curved, glass building. The
main auditorium seats an
audience of 2,700; its design
is functional and modern with
black upholstered seats
contrasting with the granite of
the walls and the impressive
glass ceiling. With its five
moveable stages, this opera
house is a masterpiece of
technological wizardry.

Colonne de Juillet ⑬

Pl de la Bastille 75004. **Map** 14 E4.
M Bastille. **Not open** to the public.

T**OPPED BY** the statue of the
"genius of liberty", this
column of hollow bronze
reaches 51.5 m (170 ft) into
the sky. It is a memorial to
those who died in the street
battles of July 1830 that led
to the overthrow of the
monarch (see pp30–31). The
crypt contains the remains of
504 victims of the violent
fighting and others who died
in the 1848 revolution.

Place de la Bastille ⑭

75004. **Map** 14 E4. **M** Bastille.

N**OTHING IS NOW** left of the
prison (see pp28–9)
stormed by the revolutionary
mob on 14 July 1789, an
event celebrated annually by
the French at home and
abroad. A line of paving
stones from No. 5 to No. 49
Boulevard Henri IV traces the
former towers and fortifications. A large, traffic-clogged
square is the site of the
prison's former stronghold.
The square still has its old
link between smart central
Paris and the eastern fau-
bourgs or working-class areas.
Gentrification, however, is
now underway with the
construction of attractive
cafés and a marina.

**The glass façade of the Bastille
Opéra**

St-Paul–St-Louis ⓯

99 Rue St-Antoine 75004. **Map** 14 D4. 🄲 01 42 72 30 32. Ⓜ St-Paul. ⭕ 8am–8pm daily. **Concerts**

A JESUIT CHURCH, St-Paul–St-Louis was an important symbol of the influence which the Jesuits held from 1627, when Louis XIII laid the first stone, to 1762 when they were expelled from France. The Gesù church in Rome served as the model for the nave, while the 60-m high (180-ft) dome was the forerunner of those of the Invalides and the Sorbonne. Most of the church's treasures were removed during periods of turmoil, but Delacroix's masterpiece, *Christ in the Garden of Olives,* can still be seen. The church stands on one of the main streets of the Marais, but can also be approached by the ancient Passage St-Paul.

Christ in the Garden of Olives **by Delacroix in St-Paul–St-Louis**

him to die of rage in 1594 on hearing that the Protestant Henri IV had entered Paris. Marguerite de Valois, lodged here by her ex-husband, Henri IV, led a life of breathtaking debauchery and scandal. This culminated in the beheading of an ex-lover, who had dared to assassinate her current favourite.

Hôtel de Sens ⓰

1 Rue du Figuier 75004. **Map** 13 C4. 🄲 01 42 78 14 60. Ⓜ Pont-Marie. ⭕ 1.30pm–8.30pm Tue–Fri; 10am–8.30pm Sat. ⬤ public hols. 🔲 for exhibitions. 🚫 by appointment only.

T HIS IS ONE of the few medieval buildings left in Paris. It now houses the Forney fine arts library. In the 16th century, at the time of the Catholic League, it was turned into a fortified mansion and occupied by the Bourbons, the Guises and Cardinal de Pellevé, whose religious fervour led

The memorial to the unknown Jewish martyr, dedicated in 1956

Mémorial du Martyr Juif Inconnu ⓱

17 Rue Geoffroy-l'Asnier 75004. **Map** 13 C4. 🄲 01 42 77 44 72. Ⓜ Pont-Marie. ⭕ 9am–1pm, 2pm–5.30pm Sun–Fri. 🔲 ♿ 🔲

T HE ETERNAL FLAME burning in the crypt is the memorial, built in 1956, to the unknown Jewish martyr of the Holocaust. It is situated at the edge of the Jewish quarter. Its striking feature, apart from its emotional impact, is a large cylinder with the names of the concentration camps. The marble-faced building behind the memorial at No. 17 contains the new Musée du Shoah, as well as the archives of the Jewish documentation centre and a library.

St-Gervais–St-Protais ⓲

Pl St-Gervais 75004. **Map** 13 B3. 🄲 01 48 87 32 02. Ⓜ Hôtel de Ville. ⭕ 5.30am–10pm daily.

N AMED AFTER Gervase and Protase, two Roman soldiers who were martyred by Nero, this remarkable church dates from the 6th century. It has the oldest Classical facade in Paris, which is formed of a three-tiered arrangement of columns: Doric, Ionic and Corinthian. Behind its facade lies a beautiful Gothic church renowned for its association with religious music. It was for the church's fine organ that François Couperin (1668–1733) composed his two masses. The church currently has a Roman Catholic monastic community whose liturgy attracts people from all over the world.

The Hôtel de Sens, now home to a fine arts library

The facade of St-Gervais–St-Protais with its Classical columns

Musée Picasso ⓫

ON THE DEATH of the Spanish-born artist Pablo Picasso (1881–1973), who lived most of his life in France, the French State inherited many of his works in lieu of death duties. It used them to establish the Musée Picasso, which opened in 1986. The museum is housed in a large 17th-century mansion, the Hôtel Salé, in the Marais. The original character of the Hôtel, which was built in 1656 for Aubert de Fontenay, a salt-tax collector (*salé* means "salty"), has been preserved. The breadth of the collection reflects both the full extent of Picasso's artistic development, including his Blue, Pink and Cubist periods, and his use of so many different materials.

★**Self-Portrait**
Poverty, loneliness and the onset of winter all made the end of 1901, when this picture was painted, a particularly difficult time for Picasso.

Violin and Sheet Music
This collage (1912) is from the artist's Synthetic Cubist period.

★ **The Two Brothers**
During the summer of 1906 Picasso returned to Catalonia in Spain, where he painted this picture.

★ **The Kiss** *(1969)*
Picasso married Jacqueline Roque in 1961, and at around the same time he returned to the familiar themes of the couple and of the artist and model.

GALLERY GUIDE
The collection is mainly presented in chronological order, starting on the first floor with the Blue and Pink periods, Cubist and Neo-Classical works. Exhibitions change regularly – not all paintings are on show at any one time. On the ground floor there is a sculpture garden and works from the late 1920s to late 1930s, and from the mid-1950s to 1973.

Basement

KEY TO FLOORPLAN

☐	Paintings
☐	Illustrations
☐	Sculpture garden
☐	Ceramics
☐	Non-exhibition space

Woman with a Mantilla *(1949)*
Picasso extended his range when he began working in ceramics in 1948.

First floor

Painter with Palette and Easel *(1928)*
This Post-Cubist portrait in oils was painted at a time when Picasso's work was verging on Surrealism.

★ **Two Women Running on the Beach** *(1922)*
In 1924 this was used for the stage curtain design for Diaghilev's ballet The Blue Train.

Ground floor

Woman Reading *(1932)*
Purples and yellows were often used by Picasso when painting his model Marie-Thérèse Walter.

STAR PAINTINGS

★ **Self-Portrait**

★ **The Two Brothers**

★ **Two Women Running on the Beach**

★ **The Kiss**

Entrance

Entrance

The Bathers *(1956)*
This group of sculptures is located in the garden at the back of the Hôtel.

PICASSO AND SPAIN
After 1934, Picasso never returned to his homeland due to his rejection of Franco's regime. However, throughout his life in France he used Spanish themes in his art, such as the bull (often in the form of a minotaur) and the guitar, associated with his Andalusian childhood.

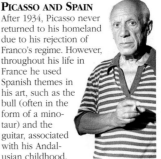

The town hall (Hôtel de Ville), overlooking a delightful square

Hôtel de Ville ⓳

Pl de l'Hôtel de Ville 75004. **Map** 13 B3. 🄲 *01 42 76 50 49.* Ⓜ *Hôtel-de-Ville.* ◯ *groups: phone to arrange.* ● *public hols, official functions.* ♿ ✉

HOME OF the city council, the town hall is a 19th-century reconstruction of the 17th-century town hall that was burned down in 1871. It is highly ornate, with elaborate stonework, turrets and statues overlooking a pedestrianized square which is a delight to stroll in, especially at night when the fountains are illuminated.

The square was once the main site for hangings, burnings and other horrific executions. It was here that Ravaillac, who assassinated Henri IV in 1610, was quartered alive, his body ripped to pieces by four strong horses.

Inside the Hôtel de Ville, a notable feature is the long Salles des Fêtes (ballroom), with adjoining salons devoted to science, the arts and literature. The impressive staircase, the decorated coffered ceilings with their chandeliers and the numerous statues and caryatids all add to the air of ceremony and pomp – a fitting power base for mayors of the city to hold elaborate banquets and receptions for foreign dignitaries in the building's grand halls.

Cloître des Billettes ⓴

24 Rue des Archives 75004. **Map** 13 B3. 🄲 *01 42 72 38 79.* Ⓜ *Hôtel-de-Ville.* ◯ **Cloister** *2–6pm daily;* **church** *6.30–7.45pm Thu, 9.30am–4pm Sun.*

THIS IS THE only remaining medieval cloister in Paris. It was built in 1427 for the Brothers of Charity, or *Billettes*, and three of its four original galleries are still standing. The adjoining church is a simple Classical building which replaced the monastic original in 1756.

The oldest cloister in Paris

Notre-Dame-des-Blancs-Manteaux ㉑

12 Rue des Blancs-Manteaux 75004. **Map** 13 C3. 🄲 *01 42 72 09 37.* Ⓜ *Rambuteau.* ◯ *10am–noon, 4pm–7pm daily.* **Concerts**.

THIS CHURCH, built in 1685, takes its name from the white habits worn by the Augustinian friars who founded a convent on the site in 1258. It has a magnificent 18th-century Rococo Flemish pulpit, and its famous organ is best appreciated at one of its regular concerts of religious music.

Hôtel de Rohan ㉒

87 Rue Vieille-du-Temple 75003. **Map** 13 C2. 🄲 *01 40 27 60 09.* Ⓜ *Rambuteau.* ◯ *for temporary exhibitions only.*

ALTHOUGH NOT resembling it in appearance, the Hôtel de Rohan forms a pair with the Hôtel de Soubise. It was built by the same architect, Delamair, for Armand de Rohan-Soubise, a cardinal and Bishop of Strasbourg. The *hôtel* has been home to a part of the national archives since 1927. In the courtyard over the doorway of the stables is the 18th-century sculpture *Horses of Apollo* by Robert Le Lorrain.

***Horses of Apollo* by Le Lorrain**

Hôtel de Soubise ❷❸

60 Rue des Francs-Bourgeois 75003.
Map 13 C2. 🕿 01 40 27 60 96.
Ⓜ Rambuteau. ◯ 10am–5.45pm
Mon, Wed–Fri; 2–5.45pm Sat–Sun.
⬤ public hols. 📷 🎥 🚻

The Hôtel de Soubise

THIS IMPOSING mansion, built
from 1705 to 1709 for the
Princesse de Rohan, is one of
two main buildings housing
the national archives. (The
other is the Hôtel de Rohan.)
The Hôtel de Soubise displays
a majestic courtyard and a
magnificent interior decoration dating from 1735 to 1740
by some of the most gifted
painters of the day: Carl Van
Loo, Jean Restout, Natoire
and François Boucher.

Natoire's *rocaille* work on
the Princess's bedroom, the
Oval Salon, can still be enjoyed
by many today because it
forms part of the museum of
French history that is now
housed here. Other exhibits
include Napoleon's will, in
which he asks for his remains
to be returned to France.

Hôtel Guénégaud ❷❹

60 Rue des Archives 75003.
Map 13 C2. 🕿 01 42 72 86 43.
Ⓜ Hôtel de Ville. ◯ 11am–6pm
Tue–Sun. ⬤ public hols.
📷 🚻 🎥

THE CELEBRATED architect
François Mansart built this
superb mansion in the mid
17th century for Henri de
Guénégaud des Brosses, who
was Secretary of State and
Keeper of the Seals. One wing

now contains the Musée de la
Chasse et de la Nature
(Hunting Museum) inaugur-
ated by André Malraux in
1967. The exhibits include a
fine collection of hunting
weapons from the 16th to the
19th centuries, many from
Germany and Central Europe.
There are also animal trophies
from around the world, along
with drawings and paintings
by Oudry, Rubens, Rembrandt,
Monet and other artists.

Musée des Arts et Métiers ❷❺

60 Rue Réaumur 75003. **Map** 13 B1-
C1. 🕿 01 53 01 82 00. Ⓜ Arts et
Métiers. ◯ 10am–6pm Tue–Sun
(9.30pm Thu). ⬤ public hols. 📷 🎥
♿ 🚻 🚻 Ⓦ www.cnam.fr/museum

HOUSED WITHIN the old
Abbey of Saint-Martin-
des-Champs, the Arts and
Crafts museum was founded
in 1794 and closed down two
centuries later for interior
restructuring and renovation.
It reopened in 2000 as a high-
quality museum of science
and industry displaying 5,000
items (it has 75,000 other items
in store available to academics
and researchers). The theme
is man's ingenuity and the
world of invention and
manufacturing, covering such
topics as textiles, photography
and machines. Among the most
entertaining displays are ones
of musical clocks, mechanical
music instruments and
automata (mechanical figures),
one of which, the "Joueuse de
Tympanon", is said to
represent Marie-Antoinette.

Square du Temple ❷❻

75003. **Map** 13 C1. Ⓜ Temple.

A QUIET AND pleasant square
today, this was once a
fortified centre of the medieval
Knights Templars. A state within a state, the area contained a
palace, a church and shops
behind high walls and a drawbridge, making it a haven for
those who were seeking to
escape from royal jurisdiction.
Louis XVI and Marie-Antoinette
were held here after their
arrest in 1792 *(see pp28–9)*.
The king left from here for his
execution on the guillotine.

Musée d'Art et d'Histoire du Judaïsme ❷❼

Hôtel de St-Aignan, 71 rue du Temple
75003. **Map** 13 B2. 🕿 01 53 01 86
53. Ⓜ Rambuteau. ◯ 11am–6pm
Mon–Fri, 10am–6pm Sun.
🎥 ♿ 🚻 🚻 🚻

THIS MUSEUM in a Marais
mansion brings together
collections formerly scattered
around the city, and commemorates the culture of French
Jewry from medieval times to
the present. There has been a
sizeable Jewish community in
France since Roman times, and
some of the world's greatest
Jewish scholars were French.
Much exquisite craftsmanship
is displayed, with elaborate
silverware, Torah covers,
fabrics, and items of fine
Judaica and religious objects.
There are also photographs,
paintings and cartoons and
historical documents.

"Being a Jew in Paris in 1939", a display in the Jewish Museum

BEAUBOURG AND LES HALLES

THIS RIGHT BANK AREA is dominated by the modernistic Forum des Halles and the Pompidou Centre. These two spectacular undertakings are now the city's most thriving public areas of contact for shoppers, art lovers, students and tourists. Literally millions flow between the two squares. The Halles is for street fashion, with most of the shops underground, and the clientele strolling under the new concrete and glass bubbles is young. The surrounding streets are coloured by popular cheap shops

and bars. But there are still enough specialist food shops, butchers and small markets to recall what Les Halles must have been like in its prime as the city's thriving market. All roads round Les Halles lead to the Beaubourg area and the Pompidou Centre, a no-compromise avant-garde assembly of vast pipes, ducts and cables, re-opened after a much-needed facelift to cope with its 20,000 daily visitors. The adjoining streets, such as Rues St-Martin and Beaubourg, house small contemporary art galleries in crooked, gabled buildings.

Fountain in the Place Igor Stravinsky

SIGHTS AT A GLANCE

Historic Buildings and Streets
No. 51 Rue de Montmorency ⑪
Tour de Jean Sans Peur ⑫
Bourse du Commerce ⑭
Tour St-Jacques ⑰

Churches
St-Merry ②
St-Eustache ⑬
St-Germain l'Auxerrois ⑮

Museums and Galleries
Pompidou Centre pp110–13 ①
Pavillon des Arts ⑤
Forum des Images ⑦
Musée de la Poupée ⑩

Modern Architecture
Forum des Halles ⑧
Le Défenseur du Temps ⑨

Cafés
Café Beaubourg ④
Bistrot d'Eustache ⑥

Fountains
Fontaine des Innocents ③

Shops
La Samaritaine ⑯

GETTING THERE

Among the metro stations serving the area are Rambuteau, Hôtel de Ville, Châtelet and Les Halles. Among the bus routes passing through the area, 47 goes along Rue Beaubourg past the Pompidou Centre and along Boulevard Sebastopol.

SEE ALSO

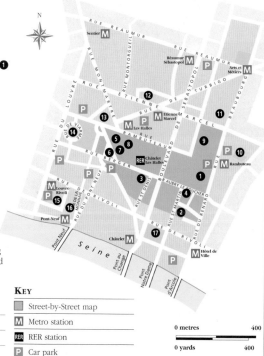

KEY

▦	Street-by-Street map
Ⓜ	Metro station
RER	RER station
℗	Car park

0 metres   400
0 yards   400

St-Eustache and sculptured head, *l'Ecoute*, by Henri de Miller

Street-by-Street: Beaubourg and Les Halles

WHEN EMILE ZOLA described Les Halles as the "belly of Paris" he was referring to the meat, vegetable and fruit market that had thrived here since 1183. Traffic congestion in the 1960s forced the market to move to the suburbs and Baltard's giant umbrella-like market pavilions were pulled down, despite howls of protest, and replaced by a shopping and leisure complex, the Forum. The conversion worked: today, Les Halles and the Pompidou Centre, which lies in the Beaubourg quarter and has been Paris's main tourist attraction ever since it opened in 1977, draw the most mixed crowds in Paris.

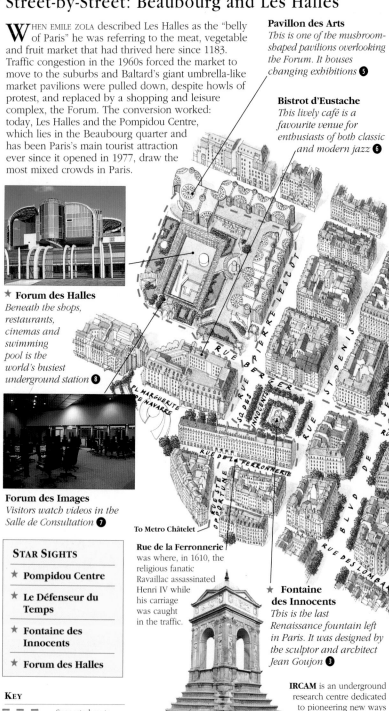

Pavillon des Arts
This is one of the mushroom-shaped pavilions overlooking the Forum. It houses changing exhibitions **⑤**

Bistrot d'Eustache
This lively café is a favourite venue for enthusiasts of both classic and modern jazz **⑥**

★ **Forum des Halles**
Beneath the shops, restaurants, cinemas and swimming pool is the world's busiest underground station **⑧**

Forum des Images
Visitors watch videos in the Salle de Consultation **⑦**

STAR SIGHTS

★ Pompidou Centre

★ Le Défenseur du Temps

★ Fontaine des Innocents

★ Forum des Halles

KEY

– – – Suggested route

To Metro Châtelet

Rue de la Ferronnerie
was where, in 1610, the religious fanatic Ravaillac assassinated Henri IV while his carriage was caught in the traffic.

★ **Fontaine des Innocents**
This is the last Renaissance fountain left in Paris. It was designed by the sculptor and architect Jean Goujon **③**

IRCAM is an underground research centre dedicated to pioneering new ways of making music.

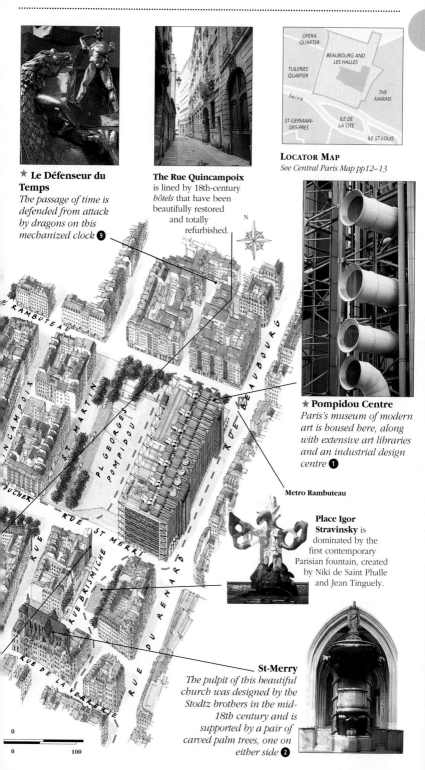

★ **Le Défenseur du Temps**
The passage of time is defended from attack by dragons on this mechanized clock **9**

The Rue Quincampoix is lined by 18th-century *hôtels* that have been beautifully restored and totally refurbished.

LOCATOR MAP
See Central Paris Map pp12–13

OPERA QUARTER

BEAUBOURG AND LES HALLES

TUILERIES QUARTER

THE MARAIS

Seine

ST-GERMAIN-DES-PRÉS

ILE DE LA CITE

ILE ST-LOUIS

N

★ **Pompidou Centre**
Paris's museum of modern art is housed here, along with extensive art libraries and an industrial design centre **1**

Metro Rambuteau

Place Igor Stravinsky is dominated by the first contemporary Parisian fountain, created by Niki de Saint Phalle and Jean Tinguely.

St-Merry
The pulpit of this beautiful church was designed by the Stodtz brothers in the mid-18th century and is supported by a pair of carved palm trees, one on either side **2**

0

0   100

Pompidou Centre ❶

See pp110–13.

A Nativity scene from the stained-glass windows in St-Merry

St-Merry ❷

76 Rue de la Verrerie 75004. **Map** 13 B3. **⦗** *01 42 71 93 93.* **Ⓜ** *Hôtel-de-Ville.* **◯** *3pm–7pm daily.* **⦗** *1st & 3rd Sun, pm.* **Concerts**.

THE SITE of this church dates back to the 7th century. St Médéric, the abbot of St-Martin d'Autun, was buried here at the beginning of the 8th century. The saint's name, which was eventually corrupted to Merry, was given to a chapel built nearby. The building of the church – in the Flamboyant Gothic style – was not completed until 1552. The west front is particularly rich in decoration, and the northwest turret contains the oldest bell in Paris, dating from 1331. It was the wealthy parish church of the Lombard moneylenders, who gave their name to the nearby Rue des Lombards.

Fontaine des Innocents ❸

Sq des Innocents 75001. **Map** 13 A2. **Ⓜ** *Les Halles.* **RER** *Châtelet-Les-Halles.*

THIS CAREFULLY-restored Renaissance fountain stands in the Square des Innocents, the area's main crossroads. Erected in 1549 on the Rue St-Denis, it was moved to its present location in the 18th century, when the square was constructed on the site of a former graveyard. Popular with the city's youth as a meeting place, the fountain is one of the landmarks of Les Halles.

Decoration on the Fontaine des Innocents

Café Beaubourg ❹

100 Rue St-Martin, 75004. **Map** 13 B2. **⦗** *01 48 87 63 96.* **Ⓜ** *Les Halles.* **RER** *Châtelet-Les-Halles.* **◯** *8am–1am Sun–Thu; 8am–2am Fri, Sat.*

Interior of the Café Beaubourg

OPENED BY Gilbert Costes in 1987, this stylish café was designed and decorated by one of France's star architects, Christian de Portzamparc, who created the impressive Cité de la Musique in the Parc de la Villette *(see p234).* Its vast terrace is lined with comfortable red and black wicker chairs. The spacious and coolly elegant interior is decorated with rows of books which soften its severely Art Deco ambience. The café is a favourite meeting point for art dealers from the surrounding galleries and Pompidou Centre staff. It serves light meals and brunch. If the crush gets too much around Les Halles, the Café Beaubourg is the ideal place to soothe the nerves.

Pavillon des Arts ❺

101 Rue Rambuteau, Terrasse Lautréamont 75001. **Map** 13 A2. **⦗** *01 42 33 82 50.* **Ⓜ** *Les Halles.* **RER** *Châtelet-Les-Halles.* **◯** *11.30am–6.30pm Tue–Sun.* **●** *public hols.*

IN CREATING this exhibition centre in 1983, Paris opened up the newly revitalized quarter of Les Halles to the arts. Housed in the futuristic glass and steel of the Baltard Pavilion, its programme of changing exhibitions often focuses on unusual or rarely-seen subjects and works, drawn together from French and foreign museums. For example, past exhibitions have included Russian history as portrayed by Soviet photographers, Surrealists recalled through their collections of Indian dolls, or the Seine through the eyes of Turner.

Exterior of the Pavillon des Arts

Bistrot d'Eustache ⑥

37 Rue Berger, 75001. **Map** 13 A2.
01 40 26 23 20. M *Les Halles.*
RER *Châtelet-Les-Halles.* ⏰ *Tue–Sat:
9am–6am, Sun–Mon: 9am– 2am.* **Live
jazz** Thu, **Flamenco/gypsy** Fri–Sat.

THIS COMPACT café, decorated
with old wood panelling
and attractive mirrors, retains
a feeling of Paris as it was in
the 1930s and 1940s – a period
when jazz venues flourished
throughout the city. It is
always packed on Thursday
nights, when musicians
squeeze into a handkerchief-
sized space to play racy
guitar-led gypsy jazz. The
café serves a variety of traditional French food, at all
times throughout the day
and at very reasonable prices.

Terrace of the Bistrot d'Eustache

Forum des Images ⑦

2 Grande Galerie, Forum des Halles
75001. **Map** 13 A2. **01 44 76 62 00.**
M *Les Halles.* **RER** *Châtelet-Les-Halles.*
⏰ *1pm–9pm Tue, Wed, Fri–Sun; 1pm–
10pm Thu.* ⬛ *public hols.* 🎬 ♿ 💻
W www.forumdesimages.net

AT THE FORUM you can
choose from thousands of
cinema, television, and
amateur films. All feature the
city of Paris. There is footage
on the history of Paris since
1895 including a remarkable
newsreel of General de Gaulle
avoiding sniper fire during the
Liberation of Paris in 1944.
There are countless movies
such as Truffaut's *Baisers Volés.*
Admission includes two hours'
viewing of your chosen film in
the Salle de Consultation *(see
p106)* and entry to two
auditoriums showing films
linked by a theme.

François Truffaut's *Baisers Volés*

Forum des Halles ⑧

75001. **Map** 13 A2. **M** *Les Halles.*
RER *Châtelet-Les-Halles.*

THE PRESENT Forum des
Halles, which is simply
known as Les Halles, was
built in 1979, amid much
controversy, on the site of the
famous old fruit and vegetable market. The present
complex occupies 7 ha
(750,000 sq ft), partly above
and partly below ground. The
underground levels 2 and 3
are occupied by a varied
array of shops, from chic
boutiques to megastores.
Above ground there are well-
tended gardens, pergolas and
mini-pavilions. Also outside
are the palm-shaped buildings
of metal and glass which
house the Pavillon des Arts
and the Maison de la Poésie.
The Pavillon des Arts and the
Maison de la Poésie are cultural centres for contemporary
art and poetry respectively.

Le Défenseur du Temps ⑨

Rue Bernard-de-Clairvaux 75003.
Map 13 B2. **M** *Rambuteau.*

THE MODERN Quartier de
l'Horloge (Clock Quarter)
is the location of Paris's
newest public clock, "The
Defender of Time" by Jacques
Monastier. An impressive
brass-and-steel mechanical
sculpture, it stands 4 m (13 ft)
high and weighs 1 tonne. The
defender battles against the
elements: air, earth and water.
In the shape of savage beasts,
they attack him at the approach
of each hour, to the
accompanying sound of
earthquakes, hurricanes and
rough seas. At 2pm and 6pm
he overcomes
all three, as
watching
children cheer.

Pygmalion by
Julio Silva in
the Forum des
Halles

Pompidou Centre ❶

THE POMPIDOU IS LIKE a building turned inside out: escalators, lifts, air and water ducts and even the massive steel struts that are the building's skeleton have all been placed on the outside. This allowed the architects, Richard Rogers, Renzo Piano and Gianfranco Franchini, to create an uncluttered and flexible space within it for the Musée National d'Art Moderne and for the Pompidou's other activities. Among the schools represented in the museum are Fauvism, Cubism and Surrealism. Outside in the piazza, large crowds gather to watch the street performers. The Pompidou has been completely renovated for the new millennium.

The escalator that rises step by step up the facade overlooking the piazza runs through a glass conduit. From the top there is a spectacular view over Paris that includes Montmartre, La Défense and the Eiffel Tower.

KEY

☐ Exhibition space

☐ Non-exhibition space

GALLERY GUIDE

The permanent collections are on Levels 5 & 4: works from 1905 to 1960 are on the former, with the latter reserved for contemporary art. Levels 1 & 6 are for major exhibitions, while Levels 1, 2 & 3 house an information library. The lower levels make up "The Forum", the focal public area, which include a performance centre for dance, theatre and music, a cinema and children's workshop.

Portrait of the Journalist Sylvia von Harden *(1926)*
The surgical precision of Dix's style makes this a harsh caricature.

Le Cheval Majeur
This bronze horse (1914–16) by Duchamp-Villon is one of the finest examples of Cubist sculpture.

To Russia, the Asses and the Others *(1911)*
Throughout his life Chagall drew inspiration from the small Russian town of Vitebsk, where he was born.

VISITORS' CHECKLIST

Pl Georges Pompidou. **Map** 13
B2. **C** *01 44 78 12 33.* **M**
*Rambuteau, Châtelet, Hôtel de
Ville.* 🚌 *21, 29, 38, 47, 58, 69,
70, 72, 74, 75, 76, 81, 85, 96.*
RER *Châtelet-Les-Halles.* ⭕
*MNAM & temp. exhibs: 11am–
9pm Wed– Mon; Library: noon–
10pm Mon– Fri; 11am–10pm Sat–
Sun; Atelier Brancusi: 1pm–6.45pm
Wed–Sun.* 🚫 ♿ 🖼 🎬 🍴 🛍
📷 🔲 *www.centrepompidou.fr*

Basin and
Sculpture
Terrace

Sorrow of the King *(1952)*
*Towards the end of his life, Matisse produced a
number of collages using gouache-painted
paper cut-outs.*

Le Duo *(1937)*
*Georges Braque, like
Picasso, developed the
Cubist technique of repre-
senting different views of a
subject in a single picture.*

Basin and
Sculpture
Terrace

COLOUR-CODING

The coloured pipes that are the most striking
feature at the back of the Pompidou, on the rue
de Renard, moved one critic to compare the
building to an oil refinery. Far from being merely
decorative, the colours serve to distinguish the
pipes' various functions: air-conditioning ducts
are blue, water pipes green and electricity lines
are painted yellow. The areas through which
people move vertically (such as escalators) are
red. The white funnels are ventilation shafts for
the underground areas, and structural beams are
clad in stainless steel. The architects' idea was to
help the public understand the way the
dynamics of a building function.

Exploring the Pompidou's Modern Art Collection

WITH A COLLECTION OF OVER 50,000 works of art from more than 42,000 artists, the Pompidou encompasses all of the fine arts. Since its renovation, classic disciplines – painting, sculpture, drawing and photography – have been integrated with other media such as cinema, architecture, design, and visual and sound archives. The collections now represent a complete overview of modern and contemporary creation.

The Two Barges (1906) by André Derain

ART FROM 1905–60

THE "HISTORICAL" collections bring together the great artistic movements of the first half of the 20th century, from Fauvism to Abstract Expressionism to the changing currents of the 1950s. The rich collection of Cubist sculptures, of which the *Cheval Majeur* by Duchamp-Villon (1914–1916) is a fine example, is displayed, as well as examples of the great masters of the 20th century. Matisse, Picasso, Braque, Duchamp, Kandinsky, Léger, Miro, Giacometti and Dubuffet command large

areas at the heart of the collection. Towards the end of his life, Matisse made several collages from cut up large sheets of paper. Among others, the museum possesses *La Tristesse du Roi* (Sorrow of the King) which he created in 1952. With *Homme à la Guitare* (Man with a Guitar), Braque demonstrates his command of the Cubist technique which he pioneered along with Picasso. Considered as one of the first, if not

the first, Abstract painter, Kandinsky transformed works inspired by nature into constructions of colour and form. The museum has a large collection of the Russian painter's works, of which the Impressions (*Impressions V, Parc*, 1911) mark the end of his Expressionist period before his plunge into Abstract art with *Improvisations XIV* or *Avec l'Arc Noir* (With the Black Arc) both dating from 1912 compositions.

The collection also shows the groups and the movements on which the history of modern art is based, or by which it has been affected, including Dada, Abstract Art and Informal. A pioneer of Informal art, Jean Fautrier is represented in the collections with *Otages* (Hostages), a commemoration of the suffering of the resistance fighters.

At the heart of this chronological progression, some newly opened spaces are a revelation. One set shows the Union des Artistes Modernes (Modern Artists Union) where architects, visual artists and designers met in the 1920s. Another room recreates the atmosphere of André Breton's workshop in which the works of his Surrealist friends are also shown. Silent pauses have also been allowed for: the room reserved for Miro's three huge *Bleus* (Blues) gives time and space for visitors to meditate on the explosion and revolutions of modern art.

BRANCUSI'S STUDIO
The Atelier Brancusi, on the rue Rambuteau side of the piazza, is a reconstruction of the workshop of the Romanian born artist Constantin Brancusi (1876-1957), who lived and worked in Paris. He bequeathed his entire collection of works to the French state on condition that his workshop be rebuilt as it was. The collection includes more than 200 sculptures and plinths, 1600 photographs and a selection of his tools. Also featured are some of his more personal items such as documents, pieces of furniture and his book collection.

Miss Pogany (1919–20) by Constantin Brancusi

With the Black Arc (1912) by
Vassily Kandinsky

The Good-bye Door (1980) by Joan Mitchell

ART SINCE 1960

THE CONTEMPORARY depart-
ment opens with the
1960s and pays homage to
Jean Tinguely. This sculptor/
engineer was creator of the
Stravinsky fountain situated
near the Centre, along with
Niki de Saint-Phalle. The
display is organized around a
central aisle from which the
rooms holding the museum's
collections lead off.

The 1960s saw the rise of
Pop Art in America, which
introduced advertising and
mass-media images, along
with objects from the
consumer society, into art.
Works by Jasper Johns, Andy
Warhol and Claes Oldenburg
are in the collection. In the
Rauschenberg *Oracle*, for
example, products become
abstract shapes. Among other
works of importance are
Ghost Drums Set by Claes
Oldenburg and *Electric Chair*
by Andy Warhol.

In France, the New Realists,
a heterogenous group
including Yves Klein, César,
Arman and others, were also
interested in contemporary
objects. They believed that by
choosing mundane things
from everyday life the artist
could imbue them with
artistic significance. Arman
makes "accumulations",

Mobile on Two Planes (1955) by
Alexander Calder

Raymond Hains collects wall
posters in order to make
abstract canvases while Jean
Tinguely builds machines
using materials collected.

The subtle eroticism of
Balthus (Count Balthasar
Klossowski de Rola) glows
through *The Painter and His
Model* (1980 – 81). In another
area are ink drawings by
poet-painter Henri Michaux.

Homogenous Infiltration (1966)
by Joseph Beuys

The work of Herbin, who
founded the Abstraction-
Création group, a loosely-
based association of non-
figurative painters, is the
focus for the work of the
Geometric Abstractionists,
while the Hard Edge
Abstraction movement in
America, which specializes in
flat-coloured, well-defined
shapes, is represented by
Ellsworth Kelly and Frank
Stella, among others. Richard
Serra's *Corner Prop No. 7
(For Natalie)* (1983) and Carl
André's *144 Tin Square*
(1975) are just two of the
several Minimalist sculp-
tures in the collection.

The museum has a
selection of figurative art
by Georg Baselitz, Gilbert
and George, and Anselm
Kiefer, as well as art from
the abstract landscape
painter Joan Mitchell.

Kinetic Art, Poor Art
and Conceptual Art, and
new trends in figurative and

abstract painting, punctuate
the route of the contemporary
department's galleries.

Since the Pompidou's
reopening, certain areas have
been designated to bring
together different disciplines
around a theme and no
longer around a school or
movement. For example, the
use of plastic materials in
contemporary art is shown in
the works of Jean Dubuffet,
César or Claes Oldenburg
and compared against the
work of architects such as
Richard Buckminster or Hans
Hollein and designers such
as Ettore Sottsass.

In its new arrangement the
fourth floor offers areas allowing different aspects of the
museum's collections to be
discovered. They often reflect
the museum's preference for
the more ironic and
conceptual forms.
One display offered
such works as
Joseph Beuys's
Plight (1985), which
included a grand
piano and wall and
ceiling covered with about 7
tonnes of thick felt, and the
video artist Nam June Paik's
Video Fish (1979 – 85), in
which video screens flashed
manic sequences of images
from behind aquaria pop-
ulated by indifferent fish.

The museum gallery allows
temporary exhibitions to be
mounted from works held in
reserve. A graphic arts exhibition room and a video area
complete the arrangement.
A screening room gives
access to the museums' entire
collection of videotapes and
audio recordings of a wide
range of modern artists.

Ben's Store (1973) by Ben (Vautier Benjamin)

Musée de la Poupée ⑩

Impasse Berthaud 75003. **Map** 13 B2.
C *01 42 72 73 11.* **M** *Rambuteau.*
◐ *10am–6pm Tue–Sun.* 🚫
🎟 *for groups, by appt.*

AN IMPRESSIVE collection of hand-made dolls, from the mid-19th century to the present day, are on show in this charming museum. Thirty-six of the displays contain French dolls with porcelain heads ranging from 1850 to 1950. Another 24 display windows are devoted to themed exhibitions of dolls from around the world.

Father and son, Guido and Samy Odin, who own the museum, are at your service if your doll needs medical care. The museum shop stocks everything you need to preserve and maintain these unique works of art in pristine condition. The Odins also offer comprehensive classes on doll-making for both adults and children.

A 19th-century French doll with porcelain head

No. 51 Rue de Montmorency ⑪

75003. **Map** 13 B1. **M** *Réaumur-Sébastopol.* **Not open** to the public.

THIS HOUSE is considered to be the oldest in Paris, followed by No. 3 Rue Volta in the Marais quarter. No. 51 was built in 1407 by Nicolas Flamel, a writer and teacher. His house was always open to poor labourers, from whom he demanded nothing more than that they should pray for those who were dead.

The interior of St-Eustache in the 1830s

Tour de Jean Sans Peur ⑫

20 Rue Etienne-Marcel 75002.**Map** 13 A1. **C** *01 40 26 20 28.* **M** *Etienne-Marcel.* ◐ *1.30–6pm Wed, Sat, Sun.* 🚫 🎟

AFTER THE Duc d'Orléans had been assassinated on his orders in 1408, the Duc de Bourgogne feared reprisals. To protect himself, he had this 27-m (88-ft) tower built on to his home, the Hôtel de Bourgogne. He moved his bedroom up to the fourth floor of the tower (which was reached by climbing a flight of 140 steps) to sleep safe from the plots of his enemies.

No. 51 Rue de Montmorency, the oldest house in Paris

St-Eustache ⑬

Pl du Jour 75001. **Map** 13 A1.
C *01 42 36 31 05.* **M** *Les Halles.* **RER** *Châtelet-Les-Halles.* ◐ *9am–8pm (7pm winter) daily.* **P** 🚻 *10am, 6pm Tue–Fri; 6pm Mon & Sat; 9.30am, 11am, 6pm Sun.* **Organ recitals Sun pm.**

WITH ITS GOTHIC plan and Renaissance decoration, St-Eustache is one of the most beautiful churches in Paris. Its interior plan is modelled on Notre-Dame, with five naves and side and radial chapels. The 105 years (1532–1637) it took to complete the church saw the flowering of the Renaissance style, which is evident in the magnificent arches, pillars and columns. The stained-glass windows in the chancel are created from cartoons by Philippe de Champaigne.

The church has associations with many famous figures: Molière was buried here; the Marquise de Pompadour, official mistress of Louis XV, was baptized here, as was Cardinal Richelieu.

Entrance to the Bourse du
Commerce, the old corn exchange

Bourse du Commerce ⑭

2 Rue de Viarmes 75001. **Map** 12 F2.
[01 55 65 55 65. **M** Les Halles.
RER Châtelet-Les-Halles. **○** 9am–1pm,
2–5pm Mon–Fri. **✔** groups only.

COMPARED BY Victor Hugo to
a jockey's cap without a
peak, the old corn exchange
building was built in the 18th
century and remodelled in
1889. Today its huge, domed
hall is filled with the hustle
and bustle of the commodities
market for coffee and sugar. It
houses a World Trade Centre
and the offices of the
Chambre de Commerce et
d'Industrie de Paris.

St-Germain l'Auxerrois ⑮

2 Pl du Louvre 75001. **Map** 12 F2.
[01 42 60 13 96. **M** Louvre, Pont-
Neuf. **○** 8am–7pm daily (closed
1–3pm Sun). **Organ recitals** Sun pm.
Concerts

AFTER THE Valois Court
decamped to the Louvre
from the Ile de la Cité in the
14th century, this became the
favoured church of kings,
who attended mass here.
  Its many historical associations include the horrific St
Bartholomew's Day Massacre
on 24 August 1572, the eve of
the royal wedding of Henri of
Navarre and Marguerite de
Valois. Thousands of
Huguenots who had been
lured to Paris for the wedding

were murdered as the church
bell tolled. Later, after the
Revolution, the church was
used as a barn. Despite many
restorations, it is a jewel of
Gothic architecture.

La Samaritaine ⑯

19 Rue de la Monnaie 75001.
Map 12 F2. **[** 01 40 41 20 20.
M Pont-Neuf. **○** 9.30am–7pm
Mon–Wed, Fri, Sat; 9.30am–10pm
Thu. **⑪** **⬚** **P** See p313.

THIS FASHIONABLE department
store was founded in 1900
by Ernest Cognacq, a former
street trader. Built in 1926
with a framework of iron and
wide expanses of glass, La
Samaritaine is an outstanding
example of the Art Deco
style. The renovated interior
now has a fine Art Nouveau
ironwork staircase and
hanging galleries under a
large dome. The roof-top
restaurant offers some of the
most spectacular views of
Paris. Cognacq was also a
leading collector of 18th-
century art, and his collection
is now on display in the
Musée Cognacq-Jay in the
Marais quarter (see p94).

The stylish Art Deco interior of
La Samaritaine

The Tour St-Jacques with its
ornate decoration

Tour St-Jacques ⑰

Square de la Tour St-Jacques 75004.
Map 13 A3. **M** Châtelet. **Not open**
to the public.

THIS IMPOSING late Gothic
tower, dating from 1523, is
all that remains of an ancient
church that was a rendezvous
for pilgrims setting out on
long journeys. The church
was destroyed after the
Revolution. Earlier, Blaise
Pascal, the 17th-century
mathematician, physicist,
philosopher and writer, used
the tower for barometrical
experiments. There is a
memorial statue to him on
the ground floor of the tower.
Queen Victoria passed by on
her state visit in 1854, giving
her name to the nearby
Avenue Victoria.

The St Bartholomew's Day Massacre (c. 1572–84) by François Dubois

TUILERIES QUARTER

THE TUILERIES AREA is bounded by the vast and harmonious expanse of the Concorde square at one end and the Grand Louvre at the other. This was a place for kings and palaces. The Sun King (Louis XIV) lives on in the Place des Victoires, which was designed solely to show off his statue. But fashion kings are today's objects of admiration. In Place Vendôme, royal glitter has been replaced by the precious stones of Cartier, Boucheron and Chaumet,

and the fine cut of Arab, German and Japanese bankers, not to mention the chic ladies visiting the luxurious Ritz. The area is crossed by two of Paris's most magnificent shopping streets. Parallel to the Jardin des Tuileries is the long Rue de Rivoli, with its arcades, expensive boutiques, bookshops and five-star hotels. And just north beyond the Rivoli is the Rue St-Honoré, another extensive street, bringing together the richest and humblest in people and commerce.

Ornate lamppost on Place de la Concorde

SIGHTS AT A GLANCE

Historic Buildings
Palais Royal ❸
Banque de France ⓴

Museums and Galleries
Musée du Louvre pp122–9 ❶
Musée de la Mode et des Textiles ❾
Musée de la Publicité ❿
Musée des Arts Décoratifs ⓫
Galerie National du Jeu de Paume ⓯
Musée de l'Orangerie ⓰
Village Royale ⓲

Monuments and Fountains
Fontaine Molière ❻
Arc de Triomphe du Carrousel ⓬

Squares, Parks and Gardens
Jardin du Palais Royal ❺
Place des Pyramides ❽
Jardin des Tuileries ⓮

Place de la Concorde ⓱
Place Vendôme ⓳
Place des Victoires ㉑

Theatres
Comédie Française ❹

Shops
Louvre des Antiquaires ❷
Rue de Rivoli ⓭

Churches
St-Roch ❼

GETTING THERE
This area is well served by the metro system, with stations at Tuileries, Pyramides, Palais Royal and Louvre. There are frequent buses through the area. Routes 24 and 72 travel along the quayside passing the Jardin des Tuileries and the Musée du Louvre.

KEY

▓	Street-by-Street map
M	Metro station
P	Car park

View of the Place de la Concorde and the Obelisk

Street by Street: Tuileries Quarter

Elegant squares, formal gardens, street arcades and courtyards give this part of Paris its special character. Monuments to monarchy and the arts coexist with contemporary luxury: five-star hotels, world-famous restaurants, fashion emporiums and jewellers of international renown. Sandblasting and washing have given a new glow to the façades of the Louvre and the Palais Royal square, where Cardinal Richelieu's creation, the royal palace, is now occupied by government offices. From here the Ministry of Culture surveys the cleaning and restoration of the city's great buildings. The other former royal palace, the Louvre, is now one of the great museums of the world.

The Normandy is an elegant hotel in the Belle Epoque style, a form of graceful living that prevailed in Paris at the turn of the century.

★ **Jardin des Tuileries**
Donkey rides are a popular attraction in these formal gardens, which were designed by the royal gardener André Le Nôtre in the 17th century ⓮

St-Roch
The papal statue stands in this remarkably long 17th-century church, unusually set on a north–south axis. St-Roch is a treasure house of religious art ❼

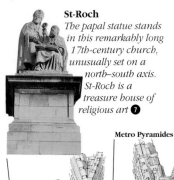

Metro Pyramides

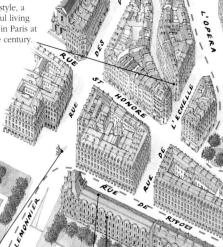

Place des Pyramides
Frémiet's gilded statue of Joan of Arc is the focus of pilgrimage for royalists ❽

To the Quai du Louvre

Musée de la Mode et des Textiles
The haute couture collections that are kept in this museum have given the Louvre a new role ❾

Musée des Arts Décoratifs
A highlight of the museum's displays of art and design is the Art Nouveau collection ⓫

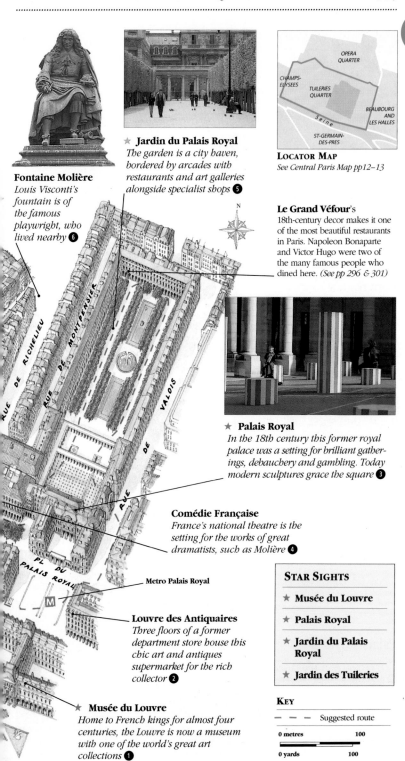

Fontaine Molière
Louis Visconti's fountain is of the famous playwright, who lived nearby ⑥

★ **Jardin du Palais Royal**
The garden is a city haven, bordered by arcades with restaurants and art galleries alongside specialist shops ⑤

LOCATOR MAP
See Central Paris Map pp12–13

Le Grand Véfour's
18th-century decor makes it one of the most beautiful restaurants in Paris. Napoleon Bonaparte and Victor Hugo were two of the many famous people who dined here. *(See pp 296 & 301)*

★ **Palais Royal**
In the 18th century this former royal palace was a setting for brilliant gatherings, debauchery and gambling. Today modern sculptures grace the square ❸

Comédie Française
France's national theatre is the setting for the works of great dramatists, such as Molière ❹

Metro Palais Royal

Louvre des Antiquaires
Three floors of a former department store house this chic art and antiques supermarket for the rich collector ❷

★ **Musée du Louvre**
Home to French kings for almost four centuries, the Louvre is now a museum with one of the world's great art collections ❶

STAR SIGHTS

★ **Musée du Louvre**

★ **Palais Royal**

★ **Jardin du Palais Royal**

★ **Jardin des Tuileries**

KEY

– – – Suggested route

0 metres   100

0 yards   100

The five-arched Pont Royal linking the Louvre with the Left Bank

Musée du Louvre ❶

See pp122–9.

Louvre des Antiquaires ❷

2 Pl du Palais Royal 75001. **Map** 12 E2. 01 42 97 27 00. ☐ 11am–7pm Tue–Sun (Jul & Aug: Tue–Sat). ● 1 Jan, 25 Dec. 🍴 ☐ See pp322–3.

One of the shops in the Louvre des Antiquaires market

A LARGE DEPARTMENT store – the Grands Magasins du Louvre – was converted at the end of the 1970s into this three-floor collection of art galleries and antique shops. Few bargains are found here, but the 250 shops of this chic market provide clues about what *nouveaux riches* collectors are seeking.

Palais Royal ❸

Pl du Palais Royal 75001. **Map** 12 E1. Ⓜ Palais Royal. **Buildings not open to public.**

T HIS FORMER royal palace has had a turbulent history. Starting out in the early 17th century as Richelieu's Palais Cardinale, it passed to the Crown on his death and became the childhood home of Louis XIV. Under the control of the 18th-century royal dukes of Orléans it was the scene of brilliant gatherings, interspersed with periods of debauchery and gambling. The cardinal's theatre, where Molière had performed, burned down in 1763, but was replaced by the Comédie Française. After the Revolution, the palace became a gambling house. It was reclaimed in 1815 by the future King Louis-Philippe, one of whose librarians was Alexandre Dumas. The building narrowly escaped the flames of the 1871 uprising.

After being restored again, between 1872 and 1876, the palace reverted to the state, and it now houses both the Council of State, the supreme legal body for administrative matters, and its more recent "partner", the Constitutional Council. Another wing of the palace is occupied by the Ministry of Culture.

Comédie Française ❹

2 Rue de Richelieu 75001. **Map** 12 E1. 01 44 58 15 15. Ⓜ Palais Royal. ☐ for performances. 🕙 10.15am, 10.30am Sun (01 44 58 13 16). See **Entertainment** pp330–33.

A stone plaque to Pierre Corneille

O VERLOOKING TWO charming, if traffic-choked squares named after the writers Colette and André Malraux, sits France's national theatre. The company has its roots partly in Molière's 17th-century players. In the foyer is the armchair in which Molière collapsed, dying, on stage in 1673 (ironically while he was performing *Le Malade Imaginaire – The Hypochondriac*). Since the company's founding in 1680 by Louis XIV, the theatre has enjoyed state patronage as a centre of national culture, and it has been based in the present building since 1799. The repertoire includes works of Corneille, Racine, Molière and Shakespeare, as well as those of modern playwrights.

Daniel Buren's stone columns (1980s) in the Palais Royal courtyard

Jardin du Palais Royal ❺

Pl du Palais Royal 75001. **Map** 12 F1.
Ⓜ *Palais Royal.*

THE PRESENT garden is about a third smaller than the original one, laid out by the royal gardener for Cardinal Richelieu in the 1630s. This is due to the construction, between 1781 and 1784, of 60 uniform houses bordering three sides of the square. Today restaurants, art galleries and specialist shops line the square, which maintains a strong literary history – Jean Cocteau, Colette and Jean Marais are among its famous recent residents.

Statue in the Jardin du Palais Royal

Fontaine Molière ❻

Rue de Richelieu 75001. **Map** 12 F1.
Ⓜ *Palais Royal.*

FRANCE'S MOST famous playwright lived near here, in a house on the site of No. 40 Rue de Richelieu. The 19th-century fountain is by Louis Visconti, who also designed Napoleon's tomb at Les Invalides *(see pp188–9).*

St-Roch ❼

296 Rue St-Honoré 75001. **Map** 12 E1.
📞 01 42 44 13 20. Ⓜ *Tuileries.*
🕐 8am–7pm daily. ● *non-religious public hols.* ✝ *Daily, times vary.*
Concerts. 📷

THIS HUGE church was designed by Lemercier, architect of the Louvre, and its foundation stone was laid

Vien's *St Denis Preaching to the Gauls* (1767) in St-Roch

by Louis XIV in 1653. Jules Hardouin-Mansart added the large Lady Chapel with its richly decorated dome and ceiling in the 18th century and two further chapels extended the church to 126 m (413 ft), just short of Notre-Dame. It is a treasure house of religious art, much of it from now-vanished churches and monasteries. It also contains the tombs of the playwright Pierre Corneille, the royal gardener André Le Nôtre and the philosopher Denis Diderot. The facades reveal marks of Napoleon's attack, in 1795, on royalist troops who were defending the church steps.

Place des Pyramides ❽

75001. **Map** 12 E1. Ⓜ *Tuileries, Pyramides.*

JOAN OF ARC, wounded nearby fighting the English in 1429, is commemorated by a 19th-century equestrian statue by the sculptor Emmanuel Frémiet. The statue is a rallying point for royalists.

Musée de la Mode et des Textiles ❾

107 Rue de Rivoli 75001. **Map** 12 E1.
📞 01 44 55 57 50. Ⓜ *Palais Royal, Tuileries.* 🕐 *11am–6pm Tue–Fri (9pm Wed); 10am–6pm Sat, Sun.* 🅷 🅿
Ⓦ www.ucad.fr

SET IN THE LOUVRE'S Pavillon de Marsan, this museum promotes one of the city's oldest and most famous industries – fashion.
It houses an impressive collection of *haute couture* costumes and accessories and has become an important venue of temporary exhibitions of costumes.

Schiaparelli jacket in the museum

Musée du Louvre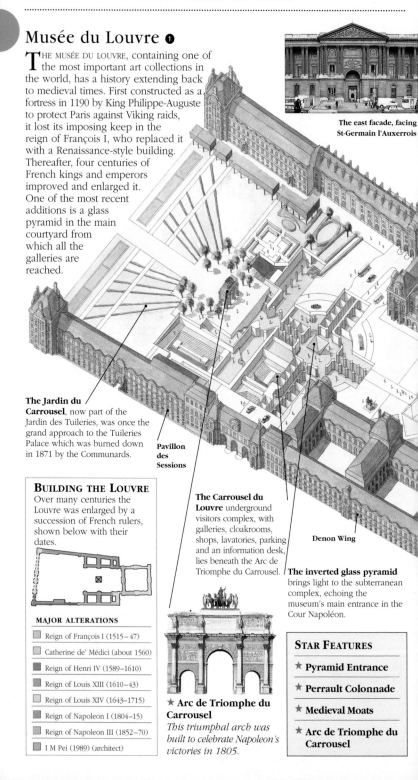

THE MUSÉE DU LOUVRE, containing one of the most important art collections in the world, has a history extending back to medieval times. First constructed as a fortress in 1190 by King Philippe-Auguste to protect Paris against Viking raids, it lost its imposing keep in the reign of François I, who replaced it with a Renaissance-style building. Thereafter, four centuries of French kings and emperors improved and enlarged it. One of the most recent additions is a glass pyramid in the main courtyard from which all the galleries are reached.

The east facade, facing St-Germain l'Auxerrois

The Jardin du Carrousel, now part of the Jardin des Tuileries, was once the grand approach to the Tuileries Palace which was burned down in 1871 by the Communards.

Pavillon des Sessions

BUILDING THE LOUVRE

Over many centuries the Louvre was enlarged by a succession of French rulers, shown below with their dates.

The Carrousel du Louvre underground visitors complex, with galleries, cloakrooms, shops, lavatories, parking and an information desk, lies beneath the Arc de Triomphe du Carrousel.

Denon Wing

The inverted glass pyramid brings light to the subterranean complex, echoing the museum's main entrance in the Cour Napoléon.

MAJOR ALTERATIONS

- Reign of François I (1515 – 47)
- Catherine de' Médici (about 1560)
- Reign of Henri IV (1589–1610)
- Reign of Louis XIII (1610–43)
- Reign of Louis XIV (1643–1715)
- Reign of Napoleon I (1804–15)
- Reign of Napoleon III (1852–70)
- I M Pei (1989) (architect)

★ **Arc de Triomphe du Carrousel**
This triumphal arch was built to celebrate Napoleon's victories in 1805.

STAR FEATURES

★ **Pyramid Entrance**

★ **Perrault Colonnade**

★ **Medieval Moats**

★ **Arc de Triomphe du Carrousel**

Pavillon Richelieu
This imposing 19th-century pavilion is part of the Richelieu Wing, once home to the Ministry of Finance but now converted into magnificent galleries.

VISITORS' CHECKLIST

Map 12 E2. 01 40 20 53 17. 01 40 20 51 51. **M** *Palais Royal, Musée du Louvre.* 21, 24, 27, 39, 48, 68, 69, 72, 81, 95. **RER** *Châtelet-Les-Halles.* Louvre. **P** *Carrousel du Louvre (entrance via Ave du General Lemmonier); Pl du Louvre, Rue St-Honoré.* 9am–6pm Wed–Mon (9.45pm Mon & Wed), History of the Louvre rooms only open Mon & Fri, same hrs as above. (Not all departments are open daily - check rota.) some public hols. (reduced price after 3pm & all day Sun; free 1st Sun of each month and for under 18). partial (01 40 20 53 17). phone 01 40 20 52 09. **Lectures, films, concerts** (01 40 20 67 89). **W** www.louvre.fr

Cour Marly is the glass-roofed courtyard that now houses the Marly Horses *(see p125).*

Richelieu Wing

★ **Pyramid Entrance**
The popular new main entrance, designed by the architect I M Pei, was opened in 1989.

Cour Puget

Cour Khorsabad

Sully Wing

Cour Carrée

★ **Perrault's Colonnade**
The east facade with its majestic rows of columns was built by Claude Perrault, who worked on the Louvre with Louis Le Vau in the mid-17th century.

Cour Napoléon

The Salle des Caryatides
takes its name from the statues of women created by Jean Goujon in 1550 to support the upper gallery.

The Louvre of Charles V
In about 1360, Charles V transformed Philippe-Auguste's robust old fortress into a royal residence.

★ **Medieval Moats**
The base of the twin towers and the drawbridge support of Philippe-Auguste's fortress can be seen in the excavated area.

The Louvre's Collection

THE LOUVRE'S TREASURES can be traced back to the collection of François I (1515–47) who purchased many Italian paintings including the *Mona Lisa (La Gioconda)*. In Louis XIV's reign (1643–1715) there were a mere 200 works, but donations and purchases augmented the collection. The Louvre was first opened to the public in 1793 after the Revolution, and has been continually enriched ever since.

The Lacemaker
In this exquisite picture from about 1665, Jan Vermeer gives us a glimpse into everyday domestic life in Holland. The painting came to the Louvre in 1870.

The Raft of the Medusa *(1819)*
Théodore Géricault derived his inspiration for this gigantic and moving work from the shipwreck of a French frigate in 1816. The painting shows the moment when the few survivors sight a sail on the horizon.

GALLERY GUIDE

The main entrance is beneath the glass pyramid. From here corridors radiate out to the museum's wings. The works are displayed on four floors: the painting and sculpture collections are arranged by country of origin. There are separate departments for Oriental, Egyptian, Greek, Etruscan and Roman antiquities, objets d'art and prints and drawings. Arts from Africa, Asia, Oceania & the Americas are in the Pavillon des Sessions until 2004.

Cour Marly

Richelieu Wing

Main entrance

Underground
visitors' complex

Pavillon
des Sessions

Denon Wing

★ **Venus de Milo**
Found in 1820 on the island of Milo in Greece, this ideal of feminine beauty was made in the Hellenistic Age at the end of the 2nd century BC.

KEY TO FLOORPLAN

- ▢ Painting
- ▢ Objets d'art
- ▢ Sculpture
- ▢ Antiquities
- ▢ Non-exhibition space

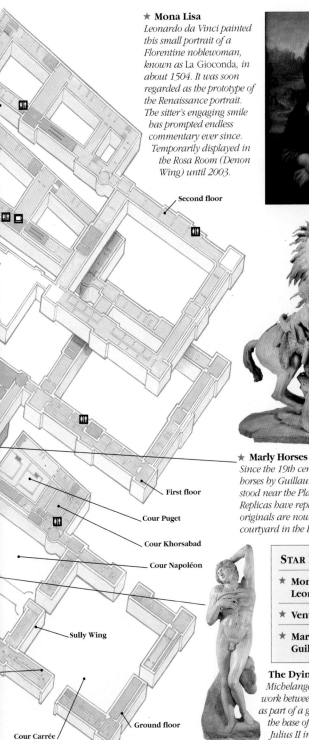

★ Mona Lisa

Leonardo da Vinci painted this small portrait of a Florentine noblewoman, known as La Gioconda, *in about 1504. It was soon regarded as the prototype of the Renaissance portrait. The sitter's engaging smile has prompted endless commentary ever since. Temporarily displayed in the Rosa Room (Denon Wing) until 2003.*

Second floor

First floor

Cour Puget

Cour Khorsabad

Cour Napoléon

★ Marly Horses

Since the 19th century, these wild horses by Guillaume Coustou have stood near the Place de la Concorde. Replicas have replaced them – the originals are now in a glass-covered courtyard in the Louvre.

Sully Wing

Cour Carrée

Ground floor

STAR EXHIBITS
★ **Mona Lisa by Leonardo da Vinci**
★ **Venus de Milo**
★ **Marly Horses by Guillaume Coustou**

The Dying Slave
Michelangelo sculpted this work between 1513 and 1520 as part of a group of statues for the base of the tomb of Pope Julius II in Rome.

Exploring the Louvre's Collections

IT IS IMPORTANT NOT TO UNDERESTIMATE the size of these vast collections and useful to set a few viewing priorities before starting. The collection of European paintings (1400–1850) is comprehensive and 40 per cent of the works are by French artists, while the selection of sculptures is less complete. The museum's antiquities – Oriental, Egyptian, Greek, Etruscan and Roman – are of world renown and offer the visitor an unrivalled range of objects. The *objets d'art* on display are very varied and include furniture and jewellery.

The Fortune Teller (about 1594) by Caravaggio

EUROPEAN PAINTING: 1200 TO 1850

PAINTING FROM northern Europe (Flemish, Dutch, German and English) is well covered. One of the earliest Flemish works is Jan van Eyck's *Madonna of Chancellor Rolin* (about 1435) which shows the Chancellor of Burgundy kneeling in prayer before the Virgin and Child.

Portrait of Erasmus (1523) by Hans Holbein

Hieronymus Bosch's *Ship of Fools* (1500) is a fine, satirical account of the futility of human existence. In the Dutch collection, Anthony van Dyck's portrait *King Charles out Hunting* (1635) shows Charles I of England in all his refined elegance. Jacob Jordaens, best known for scenes of gluttony and lust, reveals unusual sensitivity in his *Four Evangelists*. The saucy smile of the *Gipsy Girl* (1628) displays Frans Hals's effortless virtuosity. Rembrandt's *Self-portrait*, his *Disciples at Emmaus* (1648) and his *Bathsheba* (1654) are examples of the artist's genius.

There is relatively little German painting, but the three major German painters of the 15th and 16th centuries are represented by important works. There is a *Self-portrait* from 1493 by Albrecht Dürer as a young artist of 22, a *Venus* by Lucas Cranach from 1529 and a portrait of the great humanist scholar Erasmus by Hans Holbein. English artists include Thomas Gainsborough (*Conversation in a Park*, about

1746), Sir Joshua Reynolds (*Master Hare*, 1788) and J M W Turner (*Landscape with a River and Bay in the Distance*, about 1835–40).

Many of the master works in the Spanish collection depict the tragic side of life: El Greco's *Christ on the Cross Adored by Donors* (1576) and Francisco de Zurbarán's *Lying-in-State of St Bonaventura* (about 1629) with its dark-faced corpse are two of the Louvre's prize pieces. The subject of José de Ribera's *Club-Footed Boy* (1642) is a poor mute, who carries a scrap of paper requesting alms. In a lighter vein, there are several portraits by Goya from the 19th century.

The museum's collection of Italian paintings is large, covering the period 1200 to 1800. The father figures of the early Renaissance, Cimabue and Giotto, are here, as is Fra Angelico, with his *Coronation of the Virgin* (1435), and Pisanello, with his delightful *Portrait of Ginevra d'Este* (about 1435). There is also a fine portrait in profile of Sigismondo Malatesta by Piero della Francesca (about 1450) and an action-packed battle scene by Paolo Uccello. Several paintings by Leonardo da Vinci, for instance the *Virgin with the Infant Jesus and St Anne*, are as enchanting as his *Mona Lisa*.

The Louvre's fine collection of French painting ranges from the 14th century to 1848. Paintings after this date are housed in the Musée d'Orsay (*see pp144–7*). An outstanding

Gilles or *Pierrot* (about 1717) by Jean Antoine Watteau

LEONARDO DA VINCI IN FRANCE

Leonardo, artist, engineer and scientist, was born in 1452 and became a leading figure in the Italian Renaissance. François I met Leonardo in 1515 and invited him to live and work in France. The painter brought the *Mona Lisa* with him. Already in poor health, he died three years later in the arms of the king.

Self-portrait (early 16th century)

early work is Enguerrand Quarton's *Villeneuve-les-Avignon Pietà* (1455). Another early painting shows *Gabrielle d'Estrée*, mistress of Henri IV, in her bathtub. From the 16th and 17th centuries there are several splendid works by Georges de la Tour with the dramatic torch-light effect so typical of his work.

That great 18th-century painter of melancholy, Jean Watteau, is represented, as is J H Fragonard, master of the Rococo. His delightfully frivolous subjects are evident in *The Bathers* from 1770. In stark contrast is the Classicism of Nicolas Poussin and the history painting of J L David. Most of J D Ingres's work is in the Musée d'Orsay, but the Louvre kept the erotic *Turkish Bath* of 1862.

EUROPEAN SCULPTURE: 1100 TO 1850

EARLY FLEMISH and German sculpture in the collection has many masterpieces such as Tilman Riemenschneider's *Virgin of the Annunciation* from the end of the 15th century and an unusual life-size, nude figure of the penitent Mary Magdalen by Gregor Erhart (early 16th century). An ornate gilded-wood altarpiece of the same period exemplifies Flemish church art. Another important work of Flemish sculpture is Adrian de Vries's long-limbed *Mercury and Psyche* from 1593, which was originally made for the court of Rudolph II in Prague.

The French section opens with early Romanesque works, such as the figure of Christ by a 12th-century Burgundian sculptor and a head of St Peter. With its eight black-hooded mourners, the tomb of Philippe Pot (a high-ranking official in Burgundy) is one of the more unusual pieces. Diane de Poitiers, mistress of Henri II, had a large figure of her namesake Diana, goddess of the hunt, installed in the courtyard of her castle west of Paris. It is now in the Louvre. The works of Pierre Puget (1620–94), the great sculptor from Marseilles, have been assembled inside a glass-covered courtyard, Cour Puget. They include a figure of Milo of Crotona, the Greek athlete who got his hands caught in the cleft of a tree stump and was eaten by a lion. The wild horses of Marly now stand in the glass-roofed Cour Marly, surrounded by other masterpieces of French sculpture, including Jean-Antoine Houdon's early 19th-century busts of such famous men as Diderot and Voltaire.

The collection of Italian sculpture includes such splendid exhibits as Michelangelo's *Slaves* and Benvenuto Cellini's Fontainebleau *Nymph*.

Tomb of Philippe Pot (late 15th century) by Antoine le Moiturier

ORIENTAL, EGYPTIAN, GREEK, ETRUSCAN AND ROMAN ANTIQUITIES ·

THE RANGE of antiquities in the Louvre is impressive. There are objects from the Neolithic period (about 6000 BC) to the fall of the Roman Empire. Important works of Mesopotamian art include the seated figure of Ebih-iI, from 2400 BC, and several portraits of Gudea, Prince of Lagash, from about 2255 BC. A black basalt block bearing the code of the Babylonian King Hammurabi, from about 1700 BC, is one of the world's oldest legal documents.

The warlike Assyrians are represented by delicate carvings and a spectacular reconstruction of part of Sargon II's (722–705 BC) palace with its huge, winged bulls. A fine example of Persian art is the enamelled brickwork depicting the king of Persia's personal guard of archers (5th century BC). It decorated his palace at Susa.

Most Egyptian art was made for the dead, who were provided with the things that they needed for the after-life. It often included vivid images of daily life in ancient Egypt. One example is the tiny funeral chapel built for a high official in about 2500 BC. It is covered with exquisite carvings: men in sailing ships, catching fish, tending cattle and fowl.

It is also possible to gain insights into family life in ancient Egypt through a number of life-like funeral portraits, like the squatting scribe, and several sculptures

of married couples. The earliest sculpture dates from 2500 BC, the latest from 1400 BC.

From the New Kingdom (1555–1080 BC) a special crypt dedicated to the god Osiris contains some colossal sarcophagi, and a large number of mummified animals.

Some smaller objects of considerable charm include a 29-cm (11-inch) headless body of a woman, sensually outlined by the transparent veil of her dress and thought to be Queen Nefertiti (about 1365–1349 BC).

Winged Bull with Human Head **from 8th century BC, found in Khorsabad, Assyria**

The department of Greek, Roman and Etruscan antiquities contains a vast array of fragments, among them some exceptional pieces. There is a large, geometric head from the Cyclades (2700 BC) and an elegant, swan-necked bowl, quite modern in its unadorned simplicity. It is hammered out of a single gold sheet and dates from about 2500 BC. The Archaic Greek period, from the 7th to the 5th century BC, is represented by the *Auxerre Goddess*, one of the earliest-known pieces of Greek sculpture, and the *Hera of Samos* from the Ionian Islands. From the height of the Classical Greek period (about the 5th century

Winged Victory of Samothrace **(Greece, late 3rd–early 2nd century BC)**

BC) there are several fine male torsos and heads such as the *Laborde Head*. This head has been identified as part of the sculpture that once decorated the west pediment of the Parthenon in Athens.

The two most famous Greek statues in the Louvre, the *Winged Victory of Samothrace* and the *Venus de Milo*, belong to the Hellenistic period (late 3rd to 2nd century BC) when more natural-looking human forms were produced.

The undisputed star of the Etruscan collection is the terracotta sarcophagus of a married couple who appear

Etruscan Sarcophagus (6th century BC)

as though they are attending an eternal banquet.

The sculptures in the Roman section demonstrate the great debt owed to the art of ancient Greece. There are many fine pieces: a bust of Agrippa, a basalt head of Livia, the wife of Augustus, and a splendid, powerful bronze head of Emperor Hadrian from the 2nd century AD. This has the look of a true portrait, unlike so many Imperial heads which are uninspired and impersonal.

Squatting Scribe (Egyptian, about 2500 BC)

OBJETS D'ART

THE TERM *objets d'art* (art objects) covers a vast range of 'decorative art' objects: jewellery, furniture, clocks, watches, sundials, tapestries, miniatures, silver and glassware, cutlery, small French and Italian bronzes, Byzantine and Parisian carved ivory, Limoges enamels, porcelain, French and Italian stoneware, rugs, snuffboxes, scientific instruments and armour. The Louvre has well over 8,000 items, from many ages and regions.

Many of these precious objects were in the Abbey of St-Denis, where the kings of France were crowned. Long before the Revolution, a regular flow of visitors had made it something of a museum. After the Revolution all the objects were removed and presented to the nation. Much was lost or stolen during the move but what remains is still outstanding.

The treasures include a serpentine stone plate from the 1st century AD with a 9th-century border of gold and precious stones. (The plate itself is inlaid with eight golden dolphins.) There is also a porphyry vase which Suger, Abbot of St-Denis, had mounted in gold in the shape of an eagle, and the golden sceptre made for King Charles V in about 1380.

The French crown jewels include the coronation crowns of Louis XV and Napoleon, sceptres, swords and other accessories of the coronation ceremonies. On view is also the Regent, one of the purest diamonds in the world. It was bought in 1717 and worn by Louis XV at his coronation in 1722.

One whole room is taken up with a series of tapestries called the *Hunts of Maximilian,* which were originally executed for Emperor Charles V

The Eagle of Suger (mid-12th century)

in 1530 after drawings by Bernard Van Orley.

The large collection of French furniture ranges from the 16th to the 19th centuries and is assembled by period, or in rooms devoted to donations by distinguished collectors such as Isaac de Camondo. On display are important pieces by exceptionally prominent furniture-makers such as André-Charles Boulle, cabinet-maker to Louis XIV, who worked at the Louvre in the late 17th to mid-18th centuries. He is noted for his technique of inlaying copper and tortoiseshell. From a later date, the curious inlaid steel and bronze writing desk, created by Adam Weisweiler for Queen Marie-Antoinette in 1784, is one of the more unusual pieces in the museum's collection.

THE GLASS PYRAMID

Plans for the modernization and expansion of the Louvre were first conceived in 1981. They included the transfer of the Ministry of Finance from the Richelieu wing of the Louvre to new offices elsewhere, and a new main entrance to the museum. A Chinese-American architect, I M Pei, was chosen to design the changes. He designed the pyramid as both the focal point and new entrance to the Louvre. Made out of glass, it enables the visitor to see the historic buildings that surround it while allowing light down into the underground visitors' reception area.

Musée de la Publicité ⑩

Palais du Louvre, 107 rue de Rivoli 75001. **Map** 12 E2. 📞 01 44 55 57 50. Ⓜ *Palais Royal, Tuileries.* 🕐 11am–6pm Tue, Thu, Fri; 11am–9pm Wed; 10am–6pm Sat–Sun. 📷 🌐 www.ucad.fr

THE MUSEUM OF advertising, open from the end of 1999, brings together a superb collection of over 40,000 historic posters dating from the 18th century to 1949, plus around 45,000 more recent posters, and modern, multimedia advertising ranging from videos to promotional items. There is also a good reference library.

Musée des Arts Décoratifs ⑪

Palais du Louvre, 107 Rue de Rivoli 75001. **Map** 12 E2. 📞 01 44 55 57 50. Ⓜ *Palais Royal, Tuileries.* 🕐 11am– 6pm Tue, Thu, Fri; 11am–9pm Wed; 10am– 6pm Sat & Sun. *Library* 🕐 until 2003. 📷 🌐 www.ucad.fr

WITH FIVE FLOORS and over 100 rooms, this museum offers an eclectic display of decorative and ornamental art and design from the Middle Ages to the present.

Among the highlights are Art Nouveau and Art Deco rooms, including a reconstruction of the Left Bank home of couturier Jeanne Lanvin, the inter-war queen of the Parisian fashion world. Art Deco jewellery and Gallé glass are prominently featured.

Other floors show Louis XIV, XV and XVI styles of artistic decoration and furniture. The doll collection is remarkable.

Lemot's Restoration group of statues with the gilded figure of Victory

Arc de Triomphe du Carrousel ⑫

Pl du Carrousel 75001. **Map** 12 E2. Ⓜ *Palais Royal.*

BUILT BY NAPOLEON in 1806– 1808 as an entrance to the former Palais des Tuileries, its marble columns are topped by soldiers of the Grande Armée. They replaced the Horses of St Mark's which he was forced to return in 1815, after Waterloo.

Arcades along the Rue de Rivoli

Rue de Rivoli ⑬

75001. **Map** 11 C1 & 13 A2. Ⓜ *Louvre, Palais Royal, Tuileries, Concorde.*

THE LONG ARCADES with their shops, topped by Neo-Classical apartments, date back to the early 18th century,

though they were only finished in the 1850s. Commissioned by Napoleon after his victory at Rivoli, in 1797, the street completed the link between the Louvre and the Champs-Elysées, and became an important artery as well as an elegant centre for commerce. The Tuileries walls were replaced by railings and the whole area opened up.

Today along the Rue de Rivoli there are makers of expensive men's shirts and bookshops towards the Place de la Concorde, and popular department stores near the Châtelet and Hôtel de Ville. Angélina's, at No. 226, is said to serve the best hot chocolate in Paris (*see p287*).

Jardin des Tuileries ⑭

75001. **Map** 12 D1. 📞 01 40 20 90 43. Ⓜ *Tuileries, Concorde.* 🕐 7.30am–7.30pm daily

THESE FORMAL gardens were once the gardens of the old Palais des Tuileries. They are an integral part of the landscaped area running parallel to the Seine from the Louvre to the Champs-Elysées and the Arc de Triomphe.

The gardens were laid out in the 17th century by André Le Nôtre, royal gardener to Louis XIV. Recent restoration has created a new garden with chestnut and lime trees, as well as filling the entire gardens with striking modern and contemporary sculpture.

A 17th-century engraving of the Jardin des Tuileries by G Perelle

Galerie Nationale du Jeu de Paume 🄯

Jardin des Tuileries, Pl de la Concorde 75008. **Map** 11 C1. 🅃 01 47 03 12 50. 🄵 01 42 60 69 69. Ⓜ Concorde. ◐ noon–9.30pm Tue; noon–7pm Wed–Fri; 10am–7pm Sat, Sun. ● 1 Jan, 1 May, 25 Dec. 🄯 🄿
🚻 🄿 📷 🄿 📷

THE JEU DE PAUME – or *réal* tennis court – was built by Napoleon III in 1851. When *réal* (royal) tennis was replaced in popularity by lawn tennis, the court was used to exhibit art. Eventually the Impressionist museum was founded on the site. In 1986, the collection was moved to the new Musée d'Orsay (in the former Orsay railway station, see pp144–7) across the river. The Jeu de Paume now shows exhibitions of contemporary art.

Entrance to the Jeu de Paume

Musée de l'Orangerie 🄯

Jardin des Tuileries, Pl de la Concorde 75008. **Map** 11 C1.
🅃 01 42 97 48 16. Ⓜ Concorde. ◐ until late 2002/early 2003.
🄯 📷 🚻 🄿 by appointment. 🄿

CLAUDE MONET'S crowning work, the water lily series, fills the oval ground floor rooms of this museum. Known as the *Nymphéas*, the series was painted in his garden at Giverny, near Paris, and presented to the public in 1927. This superb work is complemented well by the outstanding Walter-Guillaume collection of artists of the Ecole de Paris, from the late Impressionist era to the inter-war period. This is a remark-

Monet's water lilies, on display in the Musée de l'Orangerie

able concentration of masterpieces, including a room of dramatic works by Soutine and some 14 works by Cézanne – still lifes, portraits *(Madame Cézanne)* and landscapes, such as *Dans le Parc du Château Noir*.

Renoir is represented by 27 canvases, including *Les Fillettes au Piano (Young Girls at the Piano)*. There are early Picassos, works by Henri Rousseau – notably *Le Carriole du Père Junier (Old Junier's Cart)* – Matisse and a portrait of Paul Guillaume by Modigliani. All are bathed in the natural light which flows through the window.

Place de la Concorde 🄯

75008. **Map** 11 C1. Ⓜ Concorde.

THIS IS ONE of Europe's most magnificent and historic squares, covering more than 8 ha (20 acres) in the middle of Paris. Starting out as Place Louis XV, for displaying a statue of the king, it was built in the mid-18th century by architect Jacques-Ange Gabriel, who chose to make it an open octagon with only the north side containing mansions.

The 3,200-year-old obelisk from Luxor

In the square's next incarnation, as the Place de la Révolution, the statue was replaced by the guillotine. The death toll in the square in two and a half years was 1,119, including Louis XVI, Marie-Antoinette (who died in view of the small, secret apartment she kept at No. 2 Rue Royale) and the revolutionary leaders Danton and Robespierre.

Renamed Concorde (originally by chastened Revolutionaries) in a spirit of reconciliation, the grandeur of the square was enhanced in the 19th century by the 3,200-year-old Luxor obelisk, two fountains and eight statues personifying French cities. It has become the culminating point of triumphal parades down the Champs-Elysées each 14 July, most notably on the memorable Bastille Day of 1989 when the Revolution's bicentenary was celebrated by a million people, and many world leaders.

Colonnaded entrance to the Village Royale

Village Royale ⓲

75008. **Map** 5 C5. **M** *Madeleine.*
Galerie Royale ⓞ *10am–6pm*
Tue–Sat. ⓞ *public hols.*

THIS DELIGHTFUL enclave of 18th-century town houses sits discreetly between the Rue Royale and the Rue Boissy d'Anglas. The Galerie Royale is the former home of the Duchess d'Abrantès. It was converted in 1994 by architect Laurent Bourgois who has combined classical and modern in superb style, reflecting both the antique glass- and silverware on display and the contemporary glassworkers and goldsmiths who occupy the vaults. Beneath the original glass roof in the central courtyard, a statue of the goddess Pomona is lit by fibre-optics and coloured with blue cabochons of Bohemian crystal. There is also a quiet, elegant Bernardaud Porcelain tearoom.

Place Vendôme ⓳

75001. **Map** 6 D5. **M** *Tuileries.*

PERHAPS THE best example of 18th-century elegance in the city, the architect Jules Hardouin-Mansart's royal square was begun in 1698. The original plan was to house academies and embassies behind the arcaded facades. However, bankers moved in and created opulent homes. Miraculously the square has remained virtually intact, and is home to jewellers and bankers. Among the famous, Frederic Chopin died here in 1848 at No. 12 and César Ritz established his famous hotel at the turn of the century at No. 15.

Banque de France ⓴

39 Rue Croix des Petits Champs 75001.
Map 12 F1. **M** *Palais Royal.*

FOUNDED BY Napoleon in 1800, France's central bank is housed in a building intended for quite different purposes. The 17th-century architect François Mansart designed this mansion for Louis XIII's wealthy Secretary of State, Louis de la Vrillière,

Napoleon's statue in Place Vendôme

FORMAL GARDENS IN PARIS

The South Parterre at Versailles (see pp248–9)

FOR THE PAST 300 years the main formal gardens in Paris have been open to the public and are a firm fixture in the city's life. Today the Jardin des Tuileries (see p130) has recently undergone extensive renovation and replanting; the Jardin du Luxembourg (see p172), the private garden of the French Senate, is still beloved of Left Bankers; and the Jardin du Palais Royal (see p121) is enjoyed by those who seek peace and privacy.

French landscaping was raised to an art form in the 17th century, thanks to Louis XIV's talented landscaper André Le Nôtre, who created the gardens of Versailles (see pp248–9). He achieved a brilliant marriage between the traditional Italian Renaissance garden and the French love of rational design.

The role of the French garden architect was not to tend nature but to transform it, pruning and planting to

The long Galerie Dorée in the Banque de France

with the sumptuous 50-m (164-ft) long Galerie Dorée specially created for hanging his great collection of historical paintings. The house was later sold to the Comte de Toulouse, son of Louis XIV and Madame de Montespan. The building was extensively reconstructed in the 19th century after the ravages of the Revolution. The bank's most famous modern alumnus is Jacques Delors, ex-president of the European Commission.

Place des Victoires ㉑

75002. **Map** 12 F1. Ⓜ *Palais Royal.*

THIS CIRCLE of elegant mansions was built in 1685 solely to set off the statue of Louis XIV, which was placed in the middle, with torches burning day and night. The proportions of the buildings and even the arrangement of the surrounding streets were designed by the architect and courtier Jules Hardouin-Mansart to display the statue to its best advantage.

Unfortunately, the 1792 mobs were less sycophantic and tore down the statue. A replacement, of a different style, was erected in 1822, to the detriment of the whole system of proportions of buildings to statue. Yet the square retains much of the original design, and today it is the address of major names in the fashion business, most notably Thierry Mugler, Cacharel and Kenzo.

Louis XIV on Place des Victoires

A Bagatelle garden with floral colour *(see p255)*

create leafy sculptures out of trees, bushes and hedges. Complicated geometrical designs that were created in beds and paths were interspersed with pebbles and carefully thought-out splashes of floral colour. Symmetry and harmony were the land-scaper's passwords, a sense of grandeur and magnificence his ultimate goal.

In the 17th century, as now, French formal gardens served two purposes: as a setting or backdrop for a château or palace, and for enjoyment. The best view of a formal garden was from the first floor of the château, from which the combination of boxwood hedges, flowers and gravel came together in an intricate, abstract pattern, a blossoming tapestry which complemented the château's interior. Paths of trees drew the eye into infinity, reminding the onlooker of how much land belonged to his host, and therefore establishing his undoubted wealth. So, early on the formal garden became a status symbol, and it still is. This is obvious in both private gardens and in grand public projects. Napoleon Bonaparte com-pleted his vista from the Jardin des Tuileries with a triumphal arch. The late President Mitterrand applied the principle in building his Grand Arc de la Défense *(see pp38–9, 255)* along the same axis as the Tuileries and Arc de Triomphe.

But formal gardens were also made to be enjoyed. People in the 17th century believed that walking in the fresh air kept them in good health. What more perfect spot than a formal garden bedecked with statues and fountains for additional entertainment. The old and infirm could be pushed around in sedan chairs and people could meet one another around a boxwood hedge or on a stone bench under the marbly gaze of the goddess Diana.

St-Germain-des-Prés

THIS LEFT BANK AREA is fuller and livelier, its streets and cafés more crowded than when it was at the forefront of the city's intellectual life in the 1950s. The leading figures of the time have now gone, and the rebellious disciples have retreated to their bourgeois backgrounds. But the new philosophers are there, the radical young thinkers who emerged from the 1960s upheavals, and the area still has its major publishing

Musée d'Orsay clock

houses, whose executives entertain treasured writers and agents at the celebrated cafés. But they now share the area with the smart set, those who patronize Yves St-Laurent's opulent premises and the elegant Rue Jacob's smart interior designers. On the south side of Boulevard St-Germain the streets are quiet and quaint, with lots of good restaurants, and at the Odéon end there are brassy cafés and a profusion of cinemas.

Sights at a Glance

Historic Buildings and Streets
Palais Abbatial ❷
Boulevard St-Germain ❼
Rue du Dragon ❽
Rue de l'Odéon ❿
Cour de Rohan ⓬
Cour du Commerce St-André ⓭
Institut de France ⓯
Ecole Nationale Supérieure des Beaux-Arts ⓰
Ecole Nationale d'Administration ⓱
Quai Voltaire ⓲

Churches
St-Germain-des-Prés ❶

Museums and Galleries
Musée Eugène Delacroix ❸
Musée de la Monnaie ⓮
Musée d'Orsay pp144–7 ⓳
Musée Nationale de la Légion d'Honneur ⓴

Theatres
Théâtre National de l'Odéon ⓫

Cafés and Restaurants
Les Deux Magots ❹
Café de Flore ❺
Brasserie Lipp ❻
Le Procope ❾

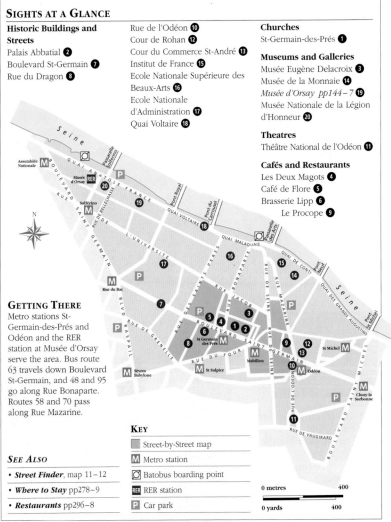

Getting There
Metro stations St-Germain-des-Prés and Odéon and the RER station at Musée d'Orsay serve the area. Bus route 63 travels down Boulevard St-Germain, and 48 and 95 go along Rue Bonaparte. Routes 58 and 70 pass along Rue Mazarine.

See Also
• *Street Finder*, map 11–12
• *Where to Stay* pp278–9
• *Restaurants* pp296–8

Key
▪ Street-by-Street map
Ⓜ Metro station
⊘ Batobus boarding point
RER RER station
P Car park

| 0 metres | 400 |
| 0 yards | 400 |

Les Deux Magots café beside the church of St-Germain-des-Prés

Street-by-Street: St-Germain-des-Prés

Organ grinder in St-Germain

AFTER WORLD WAR II, St-Germain-des-Prés became synonymous with intellectual life centred around bars and cafés. Philosophers, writers, actors and musicians mingled in the cellar nightspots and brasseries, where existentialist philosophy co-existed with American jazz. The area is now smarter than in the heyday of Jean-Paul Sartre and Simone de Beauvoir, the haunting singer Juliette Greco and the New Wave film-makers. The writers are still around, enjoying the pleasures of sitting in Les Deux Magots, Café de Flore and other haunts. The 17th-century buildings have survived, but signs of change are evident in the affluent shops dealing in antiques, books and fashion.

Les Deux Magots
The café is famous for the patronage of celebrities such as Hemingway ❹

Café de Flore
In the 1950s, French intellectuals wrestled with new philoso-phical ideas in the Art Deco interior of the café ❺

RUE DU DRAGON

RUE DU SABOT

RUE DE RENNES

RUE BONAPARTE

RUE DU FOUR

BLVD

RUE BONAPARTE

Metro St-Germain-des-Prés

Brasserie Lipp
Colourful ceramics decorate this famous brasserie frequented by politicians ❻

★ **St-Germain-des-Prés**
Descartes and the king of Poland are among the notables buried here in Paris's oldest church ❶

★ **Boulevard St-Germain**
Café terraces, boutiques, cinemas, restaurants and bookshops characterize the central section of the Left Bank's main street ❼

Picasso's sculpture *Homage to Apollinaire* is a tribute to the artist's friend, the poet Guillaume Apollinaire. It was erected in 1959, near the Café de Flore, where the poet held court.

★ **Musée Delacroix**
Here, Delacroix created the splendid mural, Jacob Wrestling, *for St-Sulpice.* (see p172.) ❸

Rue de Fürstenberg is a tiny square with old-fashioned street lamps and shady trees. It is often used as a film setting.

LOCATOR MAP
See Central Paris Map pp12–13

STAR SIGHTS

★ **St-Germain-des-Prés**

★ **Boulevard St-Germain**

★ **Musée Delacroix**

KEY

– – – Suggested route

| 0 metres | 100 |
| 0 yards | 100 |

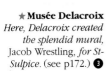

Rue de Buci was for centuries an important Left Bank street and the site of some Real Tennis courts. It now holds a lively market every day.

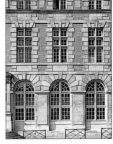

Palais Abbatial
This was the residence of abbots from 1586 till the 1789 Revolution ❷

Metro Odéon

Metro Mabillon

Marché St-Germain is an old covered food market which was opened in 1818, taking over the site of a former fairground. *(See p326.)*

Danton's statue (1889), by Auguste Paris, is a tribute to the Revolutionary leader.

St-Germain-des-Prés ❶

3 Pl St-Germain-des-Prés 75006.
Map 12 E4. 📞 *01 43 25 41 71.*
Ⓜ *St-Germain-des-Prés.* 🕐 *8am–7pm daily.* **Concerts.** 🎫 🅿

THIS IS THE OLDEST CHURCH in Paris, originating in 542 when King Childebert built a basilica to house holy relics. This became an immensely powerful Benedictine abbey, which was suppressed during the Revolution, when most of the buildings were destroyed by a fire in 1794. One of the Revolution's most horrific episodes took place in a nearby monastery when 318 priests were hacked to death by the mob on 3 September 1792. The present church dates from about the 11th century and was heavily restored in the 19th century. One of the three original towers survives, housing one of the oldest belfries in France. The interior of the church is an interesting mix of architectural styles, with some 6th-century marble columns, Gothic vaulting and Romanesque arches. Famous tombs include those of the 17th-century philosopher René Descartes, the poet Nicolas Boileau and John Casimir, king of Poland, who later became abbot of St-Germain-des-Prés in 1669.

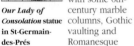
Our Lady of Consolation statue in St-Germain-des-Prés

Palais Abbatial ❷

1–5 Rue de l'Abbaye 75006.
Map 12 E4. Ⓜ *St-Germain-des-Prés.*
Not open to the public.

THIS BRICK and stone palace was built in 1586 for Charles of Bourbon who was cardinal-abbot of St-Germain and, very briefly, king of France. Ten more abbots lived there until the Revolution, when the building was

An ironwork detail from the facade of the Palais Abbatial

sold. James Pradier, the 19th-century sculptor who was famous for his female figures, established a studio here. The palace is now noted for its mixture of building materials and its splendid vertical windows.

Musée Eugène Delacroix ❸

6 Rue de Fürstenberg 75006.
Map 12 E4. 📞 *01 44 41 86 50.*
Ⓜ *St-Germain-des-Prés.* 🕐 *9.30am–5pm Wed–Mon (last adm: 4.30pm).*
📷 🅿 🅦 *www.museedelacroix.fr*

Eugène Delacroix

THE LEADING non-conformist Romantic painter, Eugène Delacroix, known for his passionate and highly-coloured canvases, lived and worked here from 1857 to his death in 1863. Here he painted *The Entombment of Christ* and *The Way to Calvary* (which now hang in the museum). He also created superb murals for the Chapel of the Holy Angels in the nearby St-Sulpice church, which is part of the reason why he moved to this area.

The first-floor apartment and garden studio now form a national museum, where regular exhibitions of Delacroix's work are held. The apartment has a portrait of George Sand, self-portraits, studies for future works and artistic memorabilia.

The charm of Delacroix's garden is reflected in the tiny Fürstenberg square. With its pair of rare catalpa trees and old-fashioned street lamps, the square is one of Paris's most romantic corners.

Les Deux Magots ❹

6 Pl St-Germain-des-Prés 75006.
Map 12 E4. 📞 *01 45 48 55 25.*
Ⓜ *St-Germain-des-Prés.*
🕐 *7.30am–1.30am daily.*
⬤ *for one week in Jan.*

THE CAFÉ STILL trades on its self-styled reputation as the rendezvous of the literary and intellectual elite of the city. This derives from the patronage of Surrealist artists and young writers including Ernest Hemingway in the 1920s and 1930s, and existentialist philosophers and writers in the 1950s.

The present clientele is more likely to be publishers or people-watchers than the new Hemingway. The café's name comes from the two wooden statues of Chinese commercial agents (*magots*) that adorn one of the pillars. This is a good place for enjoying an old-fashioned hot chocolate and watching the world go by.

The interior of Les Deux Magots

Façade of the Café de Flore, former meeting-place of existentialists

Café de Flore **❺**

172 Blvd St-Germain 75006.
Map 12 D4. **☎** 01 45 48 55 26.
Ⓜ St-Germain-des-Prés. **☐** 7am–
1.30am daily. **♿** restricted.

THE CLASSIC Art Deco interior of all-red seating, mahogany and mirrors has changed little since the war. Like its rival Les Deux Magots, it has hosted most of the French intellectuals during the postwar years. Jean-Paul Sartre and Simone de Beauvoir would meet "the Family" (their cronies) here and develop their philosophy of existentialism over a drink.

A waiter at the Brasserie Lipp

Brasserie Lipp **❻**

151 Blvd St-Germain 75006.
Map 12 E4. **☎** 01 45 48 53 91.
Ⓜ St-Germain-des-Prés.
☐ noon–1am daily. (See p302.)

THIRD OF THE famous cafés clustered around St-Germain-des-Prés, Brasserie Lipp combines Alsatian beer, sauerkraut and sausages (it was founded by a refugee from Alsace) with excellent coffee to produce a Left Bank fixture popular with French politicians and fashion gurus as well as visitors. Originally opened in the late 19th century, it is regarded by many as the quintessential Parisian brasserie, although the experience is more atmospheric than culinary these days. The interior is bright with ceramic tiles of parrots and cranes.

Boulevard St-Germain **❼**

75006, 75007. **Map** 11 C2 & 13 C5.
Ⓜ Solférino, Rue du Bac,
St-Germain-des-Prés, Mabillon, Odéon.

THE LEFT BANK'S most celebrated thoroughfare, over 3 km (2 miles) long, curves across three districts from the Ile St-Louis to the Pont de la Concorde. The architecture is homogeneous because the boulevard was another of Baron Haussmann's bold strokes of 19th-century urban planning, but it encompasses a wide range of different lifestyles as well as a number of religious and cultural institutions.

From the east (the low street numbers) the boulevard passes the late François Mitterrand's private town residence in the Rue de Bièvre, the Maubert-Mutualité market square, the Musée de Cluny and the Sorbonne university before crossing the lively Boulevard St-Michel.

It continues past the Ecole de Médecine and the Place de l'Odéon to St-Germain-des-Prés, with its historic church and café terraces. Fashion boutiques, cinemas, restaurants and bookshops give this central portion its distinctive character. It is also here that one is most likely to see a celebrity. The area is active from midday to the early morning hours.

Beyond this section the boulevard becomes more exclusively residential and then distinctly political with the Ministry of Defence and the National Assembly.

Rue du Dragon **❽**

75006. **Map** 12 D4.
Ⓜ St-Germain-des-Prés.

THIS SHORT street, between the Boulevard St-Germain and the Carrefour de la Croix Rouge, dates back to the Middle Ages and still has houses from the 17th and 18th centuries. Notice their large doors, tall windows and ironwork balconies. A group of Flemish painters lived at No. 37 before the Revolution. The novelist Victor Hugo rented a garret at No. 30 when a 19-year-old bachelor.

A plaque at No. 30 Rue du Dragon commemorating Victor Hugo's house

Le Procope ❾

13 Rue de l'Ancienne-Comédie 75006.
Map 12 F4. 01 40 46 79 00 Odéon.
7am–1am daily (midnight Sun–Wed).
See *The History of Paris* pp26–7.

The rear facade of Le Procope restaurant

FOUNDED IN 1686 by the
Sicilian Francesco Procopio
dei Coltelli, this claims to be
the world's first coffee house.
It quickly became popular
with the city's political and
literary elite and with actors
from the Comédie-Française .

Its patrons have included
Benjamin Franklin and the
philosopher Voltaire – who
supposedly drank 40 cups of
his favourite mixture of coffee
and chocolate every day. The
young Napoleon would leave
his hat as security while he
went searching for the money
to pay the bill. Now a
restaurant, Le Procope was
revamped in 1989 in the style
of the 18th century.

The Théâtre de l'Odéon, former
home of the Comédie-Française

Rue de l'Odéon ❿

75006. **Map** 12 F5. Odéon.

SYLVIA BEACH'S bookshop
Shakespeare & Company
(see pp320–21) stood at No. 12
from 1921 to 1940. She
befriended many struggling
American and British writers,
such as Ezra Pound, T S Eliot,
Scott Fitzgerald and Ernest
Hemingway. It was largely
due to her support – as
secretary, editor, agent and
banker – that James Joyce's
Ulysses was first published in
English. Adrianne Monnier's
French equivalent at No. 7
opposite, Les Amis des Livres,
was frequented by André
Gide and Paul Valéry.

Opened in 1779 to improve
access to the Odéon theatre,
this was the first street in
Paris to have pavements with
gutters and it still has many
attractive houses and shops,
most of them dating from the
18th century.

Théâtre National de l'Odéon ⓫

1 Pl Paul-Claudel 75006. **Map** 12 F5.
01 44 41 36 00. Odéon,
Luxembourg. for performances
only. See *Entertainment* pp332–3.
www.theatre-odeon.fr

THIS NEO-CLASSICAL theatre
was built in 1779 by
Marie-Josephe Peyre and
Charles de Wailly in the
grounds of the former Hôtel
de Condé. The site had been
purchased by the king and
given to the city to house the
Comédie Française. The
premiere of *The Marriage of
Figaro*, by Beaumarchais,
took place here in 1784. With
the arrival of a new company
in 1797 the name of the
theatre was changed to Odéon.
In 1807 the theatre was
consumed by fire. It was rebuilt in the same year by the
architect Jean-François Chalgrin.

Following World War II, the
theatre specialized in 20th-
century drama and was the
best attended in Paris. It was
badly damaged during the
1968 student riots, a political
rather than aesthetic gesture,
but has since been restored.

A young Hemingway in the 1920s

Cour de Rohan ⓬

75006. **Map** 12 F4. Odéon.
Access from the Rue du Jardinet until
8pm; 8pm–8am access from the Blvd
St-Germain.

The unusual middle courtyard in
the Cour de Rohan

THIS PICTURESQUE series of
three courtyards was
originally part of the 15th-
century pied-à-terre of the
archbishops of Rouen
(corrupted to "Rohan"). The
middle courtyard is the most
unusual. Its three-legged
wrought-iron mounting block,
known as a *pas-de-mule*, was
used at one time by elderly
women and overweight
prelates to mount their mules.
It is probably the last
mounting block left in Paris.
Overlooking the yard is the
facade of a fine Renaissance
building, dating from the
beginning of the 17th century.
One of its important former
residents was Henri II's
mistress, Diane de Poitiers.

The third courtyard opens
on to the tiny Rue du
Jardinet, where the composer
Saint-Saëns was born in 1835.

Cour du Commerce St-André ⑬

75006. **Map** 12 F4. **M** *Odéon.*

THE GRISLY spectre of the guillotine hangs over No. 9, since it was here that Dr Guillotin is supposed to have perfected his "philanthropic decapitating machine". In fact, although the idea was Guillotin's, it was Dr Louis, a Parisian surgeon, who was responsible for putting the "humane" plan into action. When the guillotine was first used for execution in 1792 it was known as a *Louisette.*

A print of a Revolutionary mob at a guillotine execution

Musée de la Monnaie ⑭

11 Quai de Conti 75006. **Map** 12 F3. **C** *01 40 46 55 35.* **M** *Pont-Neuf, Odéon.* ◯ *11am–5.30pm Tue–Fri, noon–5.30pm Sat–Sun.* **📷 📹** *Films.*

WHEN LOUIS XV decided to rehouse the Mint in the late 18th century, he hit upon the idea of launching a design competition for the new building. The present Hôtel des Monnaies is the result of this competition. It was completed in 1777, and the architect, Jacques Antoine, was so pleased with the building that he lived there until his death in 1801.

Coins were minted in the mansion until 1973, when the process was moved to Pessac in the Gironde. The minting and milling halls now contain the coin and medallion museum. The extensive collection is displayed in vertical glass stands so that both sides of the coins are visible, and everything is presented in the context of the history of the day. The final room of the museum shows a production cycle with late 19th-century and early 20th-century tools and machines on display.

Instead of minting coins, the building's workshops are now devoted to the creation of medallions, a selection of which are on sale.

Institut de France ⑮

23 Quai de Conti 75006. **Map** 12 E3. **C** *01 44 41 44 41.* **M** *Pont-Neuf, St-Germain-des-Prés.* ◯ *Sat & Sun by appointment only.* **📷 📹**

NOW HOME TO the illustrious Académie Française, this Baroque building was built as a palace in 1688 and was given over to the Institut de France in 1805. Its distinctive cupola was designed by the palace's architect, Louis Le Vau, to harmonize with the Palais du Louvre.

The Académie Française is the most famous of the five academies within the institute. It was founded in 1635 by

A sign to the former Mint, which is now a museum

Cardinal Richelieu and charged with the compilation of an official dictionary of the French language. From the beginning, membership has been limited to 40, who are entrusted with working on the dictionary.

Ecole Nationale Supérieure des Beaux-Arts ⑯

14 Rue Bonaparte 75006. **Map** 12 E3. **C** *01 47 03 50 00.* **M** *St-Germain-des-Prés.* ◯ *groups by appt only (phone 01 47 03 52 15 to arrange).* **📖** *Library.*

THE MAIN FRENCH school of fine arts occupies an enviable position at the corner of the Rue Bonaparte and the riverside Quai Malaquais. It is housed in several buildings, the most imposing being the 19th-century Palais des Etudes.

A host of budding French and foreign painters and architects have crossed the large courtyard to study in the ateliers of the school. Young American architects, in particular, have studied there over the past century.

The façade of the Ecole Nationale Supérieure des Beaux-Arts

THE CELEBRATED CAFÉS OF PARIS

ONE OF THE most enduring images of Paris is the café scene. For the visitor it is the romantic vision of great artists, writers or eminent intellectuals consorting in one of the Left Bank's celebrated cafés. For the Parisian the café is one of life's constants, an everyday experience, providing people with a place to tryst, drink and meet friends, or to conclude business deals, or to simply watch the world go by.

The first café anywhere can be traced back to 1686, when the café Le Procope (*see p140*) was opened. In the following century cafés became a vital part of Paris's social life. And with the widening of the city's streets, particularly during the 19th century and the building of Haussmann's Grands Boulevards, the cafés spread out on to the pavements, evoking Emile Zola's comment as to the "great silent crowds watching the street live".

The nature of a café was sometimes determined by the interests of its patrons. Some were the gathering places for those interested in playing chess, dominoes or billiards. Literary gents gathered in Le Procope during Molière's time in the 17th century. In the 19th century, First Empire Imperial guards officers were drawn to the Café d'Orsay and Second Empire financiers gathered in the cafés along the Rue de la Chaussée d'Antim. The smart set patronized the Café de Paris and Café Tortini, and theatre-goers met at the cafés around the Opéra, including the Café de la Paix (*see p213*).

Newspaper reading is still a typical café pastime

Ecole Nationale d'Administration ⑰

13 Rue de l'Université 75007. **Map** 12 D3. ☐ *01 49 26 45 45.* Ⓜ *Rue du Bac.* **Not open** to the public.

THIS FINE 18th-century mansion was originally built as two houses in 1643 by Briçonnet. In 1713 they were replaced by a *hôtel*, built by Thomas Gobert for the widow of Denis Feydeau de Brou. It was passed on to her son, Paul-Espirit Feydeau de Brou, until his death in 1767. The *hôtel* then became the residence of the Venetian ambassador. It was occupied by Belzunce in 1787 and became a munitions depot during the Revolution until the restoration of the monarchy. Until recently it housed the Ecole Nationale d'Administration, where the elite in politics, economics and science, such as France's current President, Jacques Chirac, once studied.

Plaque marking the house in Quai Voltaire where Voltaire died

Quai Voltaire ⑱

75006 and 75007. **Map** 12 D3. Ⓜ *Rue du Bac.*

FORMERLY PART of the Quai Malaquais, then later known as the Quai des Théatins, the Quai Voltaire is now home to some of the most important antiques dealers in Paris. It is also noted for its attractive 18th-century houses and for the famous people who lived in many of them, making it an especially interesting and pleasant street to walk along.

The 18th-century Swedish ambassador Count Tessin lived at No. 1, as did the sculptor James Pradier, famed for his statues and for his wife, who swam naked across the Seine. Louise de Kéroualle, spy for Louis XIV and created Duchess of Portsmouth by the infatuated Charles II of England, lived at Nos. 3–5.

Famous residents of No. 19 included the composers Richard Wagner and Jean Sibelius, the novelist Charles Baudelaire and the disgraced exile Oscar Wilde.

The French philosopher Voltaire died at No. 27, the Hôtel de la Villette. St-Sulpice, the local church, refused to accept his corpse (on the grounds of his atheism) and his body was rushed into the country to avoid a pauper's grave.

Entertainment in the Claude Alain café in the Rue de Seine during the 1950s

The most famous cafés are on the Left Bank, in St-Germain and Montparnasse, where the literati of old used to gather and where the glitterati of today love to be seen. Before World War I, Montparnasse was haunted by hordes of Russian revolutionaries, most eminently Lenin and Trotsky, who whiled away their days in the cafés, grappling with the problems of Russia and the world over a *petit café*. Cultural life flourished in the 1920s, when Surrealists, like Salvador Dali and Jean Cocteau, dominated café life, and later when American writers led by Ernest Hemingway and Scott Fitzgerald talked, drank and worked in various cafés, among them La Coupole *(see p178)*, Le Sélect and La Closerie des Lilas *(see p179)*.

After the end of World War II, the cultural scene shifted northwards to St-Germain. Existentialism had become the dominant creed and Jean-Paul Sartre its tiny charismatic leader.

Sartre and his intellectual peers and followers, among them the writers Simone de Beauvoir and Albert Camus, the poet Boris Vian and the enigmatic singer Juliette Greco, gathered to work and discuss their ideas in Les Deux Magots *(see p138)* and the nearby rival Café de Flore *(see p139)*. The traditional habitué of these cafés is still to be seen, albeit mixing with the international jet-set and with self-publicizing intellectuals hunched over their notebooks.

Works by one of St-Germain's elite, Albert Camus (1913–60)

Musée d'Orsay **⑲**

See pp144–7.

Musée Nationale de la Légion d'Honneur **⑳**

2 Rue de Bellechasse (Place de la Légion d'Honneur) 75007. **Map** 11 C2.
C *01 40 62 84 00.* **M** *Solférino.*
RER *Musée d'Orsay.* **◯** *11am–5pm Tue-Sun.* 🖾 📷 ⬚

The Musée d'Orsay, converted from a railway station into a museum

Nᴇxᴛ ᴛᴏ ᴛʜᴇ Musée d'Orsay is the truly massive Hôtel de Salm. It was one of the last great mansions to be built in the area (1782). The first owner was a German count, Prince de Salm-Kyrbourg, who was guillotined in 1794.

Today the building contains a museum where one can learn all about the Legion of Honour, a decoration launched by Napoleon I and so cherished by the French (and foreigners). Those

Napoleon III's Great Cross of the Legion of Honour

awarded the honour wear a small red rosette in their buttonhole. The impressive displays of medals and insignia are complemented by paintings. In one of the rooms, Napoleon's Legion of Honour is on display with his sword and breastplate.

The museum also covers decorations from most parts of the world, among them the British Victoria Cross and the American Purple Heart.

Musée d'Orsay ⑲

IN 1986, 47 YEARS AFTER it had closed as a mainline railway station, Victor Laloux's superb turn-of-the-century building was reopened as the Musée d'Orsay. Originally commissioned by the Orléans railway company to be its terminus in the heart of Paris, it narrowly avoided demolition in the 1970s following the outcry over the destruction of Baltard's pavilions at Les Halles food market. During the conversion much of the original architecture was retained. The new museum was set up to present each of the arts of the period from 1848 to 1914 in the context of the contemporary society and all the various forms of creative activity happening at the time.

The Museum, from the Right Bank
Victor Laloux designed the building for the Universal Exhibition in 1900.

Chair by Charles Rennie Mackintosh
The style developed by Mackintosh was an attempt to express ideas in a framework of vertical and horizontal forms, as in this tearoom chair (1900).

★ **The Gates of Hell** *(1880–1917)*
Rodin included figures that he had already created, such as The Thinker *and* The Kiss, *in this famous gateway.*

★ **Le Déjeuner sur l'Herbe** *(1863)*
Manet's painting, first exhibited in Napoleon III's Salon des Refusés, is presently on display in the first area of the upper level.

KEY TO FLOORPLAN

- ☐ Architecture & Decorative Arts
- ☐ Sculpture
- ☐ Painting before 1870
- ☐ Impressionism
- ☐ Neo-Impressionism
- ☐ Naturalism and Symbolism
- ☐ Art Nouveau
- ☐ Temporary exhibitions
- ☐ Non-exhibition space

GALLERY GUIDE

The collection occupies three levels. On the ground floor there are works from the mid to late 19th century. The middle level features Art Nouveau decorative art and a range of paintings and sculptures from the second half of the 19th century to the early 20th century. The upper level has an outstanding collection of Impressionist and Neo-Impressionist art.

The Dance *(1867–8)*
Carpeaux's sculpture caused a scandal when first exhibited.

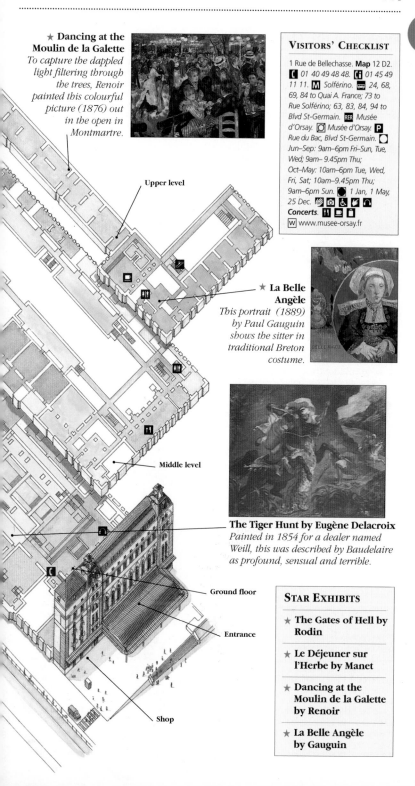

★ **Dancing at the Moulin de la Galette**
To capture the dappled light filtering through the trees, Renoir painted this colourful picture (1876) out in the open in Montmartre.

Upper level

VISITORS' CHECKLIST

1 Rue de Bellechasse. **Map** 12 D2.
📞 *01 40 49 48 48.* 📠 *01 45 49 11 11.* Ⓜ *Solférino.* 🚌 *24, 68, 69, 84 to Quai A. France; 73 to Rue Solférino; 63, 83, 84, 94 to Blvd St-Germain.* Ⓡ *Musée d'Orsay.* Ⓟ *Musée d'Orsay.* Ⓟ *Rue du Bac, Blvd St-Germain.* 🕐 *Jun–Sep: 9am–6pm Fri–Sun, Tue, Wed; 9am–9.45pm Thu; Oct–May: 10am–6pm Tue, Wed, Fri, Sat; 10am–9.45pm Thu; 9am–6pm Sun.* ⬤ *1 Jan, 1 May, 25 Dec.* 📷 ⬛ ♿ 🎁 ♫ **Concerts.** 🍴 ⬛ ⬛
Ⓦ *www.musee-orsay.fr*

★ **La Belle Angèle**
This portrait (1889) by Paul Gauguin shows the sitter in traditional Breton costume.

Middle level

The Tiger Hunt by Eugène Delacroix
Painted in 1854 for a dealer named Weill, this was described by Baudelaire as profound, sensual and terrible.

Ground floor

Entrance

STAR EXHIBITS

★ **The Gates of Hell by Rodin**

★ **Le Déjeuner sur l'Herbe by Manet**

★ **Dancing at the Moulin de la Galette by Renoir**

★ **La Belle Angèle by Gauguin**

Shop

Exploring the Orsay

MANY OF THE EXHIBITS now in the Musée d'Orsay originally came from the Louvre, and the superb collection of Impressionist art that was housed in the cramped Jeu de Paume until it closed in 1986 has been rehung here. In addition to the main exhibition, there are displays that explain the social, political and technological context in which the art was created, including exhibits on the history of cinematography.

Ceiling design (1911) by the artist and designer Maurice Denis

ART NOUVEAU

THE BELGIAN architect and designer Victor Horta was among the first to give free rein to the sinuous line that gave Art Nouveau its French sobriquet of *Style Nouille* (noodle style). Taking its name from a gallery of modern design that opened in Paris in 1895, Art Nouveau flourished throughout Europe until World War I.

In Vienna, Otto Wagner, Koloman Moser and Josef Hoffmann combined high craft with the new design, while the School of Glasgow, under the impetus of Charles Rennie Mackintosh, developed a more rectilinear approach which anticipated the work of Frank Lloyd Wright in the United States.

René Lalique introduced the aesthetics of Art Nouveau into jewellery and glassware, while Hector Guimard, inspired by Horta, is most famous today for his once-ubiquitous Art Nouveau entrances to the Paris metro.

One exhibit not to be missed is the carved wooden bookcase by Rupert Carabin (1890), with its proliferation of allegorical seated female nudes, bronze palm fronds and severed bearded heads.

SCULPTURE

THE MUSEUM'S CENTRAL aisle overflows with an oddly-assorted selection of sculptures. These illustrate the eclectic mood around the middle of the 19th century when the Classicism of Eugène Guillaume's *Cenotaph of the Gracchi* (1848–53) co-existed with the Romanticism of François Rude. Rude created the relief on the Arc de Triomphe (1836), often referred to as *La Marseillaise (see p209).*

There is a wonderful series of 36 busts of members of parliament (1832) – bloated, ugly, unscrupulous and self-important – by the satirist Honoré Daumier, and work by the vital but short-lived genius Jean-Baptiste Carpeaux, whose first major bronze, *Count Ugolino* (1862), was a character from Dante. In 1868 he produced his Dionysian delight, *The Dance,* which caused a storm of protest: it was "an insult to public morals". This contrasts with the derivative and mannered work of such sculptors as Alexandre Falguière and Hyppolyte Moulin.

Edgar Degas' famous *Young Dancer of Fourteen* (1881) was displayed during his lifetime, but the many bronzes on show were made from wax sculptures found in his

studio after his death. In contrast, the sculpture of Auguste Rodin was very much in the public eye, and his sensuous and forceful work makes him pre-eminent among 19th-century sculptors. The museum contains many of his works, including the original plaster of *Balzac* (1897). Rodin's talented companion, Camille Claudel, who spent much of her life in an asylum, is represented by a grim allegory of mortality, *Maturity* (1899 –1903).

The turn of the century is marked by the work of Emile-Antoine Bourdelle and Aristide Maillol.

PAINTING BEFORE 1870

THE SURPRISING diversity of styles in 19th-century painting is emphasized by the close juxtaposition on the ground floor of all paintings prior to 1870 – the crucial year in which Impressionism first made a name for itself. The raging colour and almost Expressionistic vigour of Eugène Delacroix's *Lion Hunt* (1854) stands next to Jean-Dominiques Ingres' cool Classical *The Spring* (1820–56). As a reminder of the academic manner that dominated the century up to that point, the uninspired waxwork style of Thomas Couture's monumental *The Romans in the Age of Decadence* (1847) dominates the central aisle. In a class of their own are Edouard Manet's provocative *Olympia* and *Le Déjeuner sur l'Herbe* (1863), while works painted around the same time by his friends, Claude Monet, Pierre-Auguste Renoir, Frédéric Bazille and Alfred Sisley, give a glimpse of the Impressionists before the Impressionist movement began.

Young Dancer of Fourteen (1881) by Edgar Degas

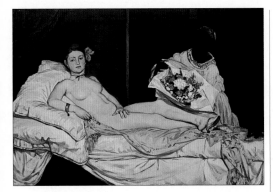

Olympia (1863) by Edouard Manet

IMPRESSIONISM

ROUEN CATHEDRAL caught at various moments of the day (1892–3) is one of the many works on show by Claude Monet, the leading figure of the Impressionist movement. Pierre-Auguste Renoir's plump nudes and his young people *Dancing at the Moulin de la Galette* (1876) were painted at the high point of his Impressionist period. Other artists on display include Camille Pissarro, Alfred Sisley and Mary Cassatt.

Edgar Degas, Paul Cézanne and Vincent Van Gogh are included here although their techniques differed from those of the Impressionists. Degas often favoured crisp Realism, though he was quite capable of using the sketchy manner of the Impressionists, as, for instance, in *L'Absinthe* (1876). Cézanne was more concerned with substance than light, as can be seen in his *Apples and Oranges* (1895–1900). Van Gogh was momentarily influenced by the movement but then went his own way, illustrated here by works from the collection of Dr Gachet.

Breton Peasant Women (1894) by Paul Gauguin

NEO-IMPRESSIONISM

ALTHOUGH LABELLED Neo-Impressionism, the work of Georges Seurat (which includes *The Circus* from 1891) was quite unrelated to the older movement. He, along with Maximilien Luce and Paul Signac, painted by applying small dots of colour that blended together when viewed from a distance. *Jane Avril Dancing* (1892) is just one of many pictures by Henri de Toulouse-Lautrec on display. The work Paul Gauguin did at Pont-Aven in Brittany is shown next to that of younger

Blue Waterlilies (1919) by Claude Monet

artists who knew him at the time, such as Emile Bernard and the Nabis group. There are also a number of paintings from his Tahitian period.

The Nabis (which included Pierre Bonnard) tended to treat the canvas as a flat surface out of which a sense of depth emerged as the viewer gazed upon it.

The dream-like visions of Odilon Redon are in the Symbolist vein, while the naïve art of Henri (Douanier) Rousseau is represented by *War* (1894) and *The Snake Charmer* (1907).

NATURALISM AND SYMBOLISM

THREE LARGE ROOMS are devoted to paintings that filled the Salons from 1880 to 1900. The work of the Naturalists was sanctioned by the Third Republic and widely reproduced at the time. Fernand Cormon's figure of *Cain* was highly acclaimed when it first appeared in the 1880 Salon. Jules Bastien-Lepage's interest lay in illustrating peasant life, and in 1877 he painted *Haymaking*, which established him as one of the leading Naturalists. His fairly free handling of paint was influenced by what he had learned from Manet and his friends. More somberly (and effectively) naturalistic is Lionel Walden's view of *The Docks of Cardiff* (1894).

Symbolism developed as a reaction against Realism and Impressionism and tended to be dominated by images of dreams and thoughts. This resulted in a wide variety of subjects and modes of expression. There is the over-sweet vision of levitating harpists, *Serenity* by Henri Martin (1899), Edward Burne-Jones' monumental work *Wheel of Fortune* (1883) and Jean Delville's *School of Plato* (1898). One of the most evocative paintings in this section is Winslow Homer's lyrical *Summer Night* (1890).

LATIN QUARTER

15th-century stained glass in Musée de Cluny

STUDENT BOOK SHOPS, cafés, cinemas and jazz clubs fill this ancient, riverside quarter between the Seine and the Luxembourg Gardens. Famous institutes of learning abound, among them the two most prestigious *lycées*, Henri IV and Louis le Grand, through which passes a large percentage of the future French elite.

As the leaders of the 1968 revolt *(see pp38–9)* disappeared into the mainstream of French life, so the Boulevard St-Michel, the area's spine, turned increasingly to commerce, not demonstrations. Today, there are cheap shops and fast-food outlets, and the maze of narrow, cobbled streets off the boulevard are full of inexpensive ethnic shops, quirky

boutiques and avant-garde theatres and cinemas. But the area's 800 years of history are difficult to efface. The Sorbonne retains much of its old character and the eastern half of the area has streets dating back to the 13th century. And the Rue St-Jacques still remains, the long Roman road stretching out of the city, and the forerunner of all the city's streets.

A young musician playing music under the Pont St-Michel is part of the Latin Quarter's long tradition as a focus for the young from all walks of life.

SIGHTS AT A GLANCE

Historic Buildings and Streets
Boulevard St-Michel **2**
La Sorbonne **7**
Collège de France **8**

Museums and Galleries
Musée de Cluny pp154–7 **1**
Musée de la Préfecture de la Police **6**

Churches and Temples
St-Séverin **3**
St-Julien-le-Pauvre **4**

Squares
Place Maubert **5**

Eglise de la Sorbonne **9**
St-Etienne-du-Mont **10**
Panthéon pp158–9 **11**

GETTING THERE
Metro stations in the area include those at St-Michel and Cluny La Sorbonne. The Balabus and routes 24 and 87 travel along Boulevard St-Germain, and 38 travels along Boulevard St-Michel, passing the Sorbonne and the Musée de Cluny.

0 metres 400
0 yards 400

KEY

	Street-by-Street map
M	Metro station
	Batobus boarding point
RER	RER station
P	Car park

A peaceful spot along a Latin Quarter quay

Street-by-Street: Latin Quarter

S INCE THE MIDDLE AGES this riverside quarter
has been dominated by the Sorbonne, and
acquired its name from the early Latin-
speaking students. It dates back to the
Roman town across from the Ile de
la Cité; at that time the Rue St-
Jacques was one of the main roads
out of Paris. The area is generally
associated with artists, intellectuals and
the bohemian way of life; it also has a
history of political unrest. In 1871, the Place St-Michel
became the centre of the Paris Commune, and in May
1968 it was the site of the student uprisings. Today the
eastern half has become sufficiently chic, however,
to contain the homes of some of the Establishment.

Place St-Michel
contains a fountain
by Davioud. The
bronze statue by
Duret shows St
Michael killing
the dragon.

Metro St-Michel

Little Athens is a lively place in the evening,
especially at the weekend, when the Greek
restaurants situated in the picturesque streets
around St-Séverin are at their busiest.

**Metro Cluny
La Sorbonne**

★ **Boulevard St-Michel**
*The northern end of the Boul'Mich, as
it is affectionately known, is a lively
mélange of cafés, book and clothes
shops, with nightclubs and
experimental cinemas nearby* ❷

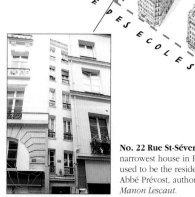

★ **Musée de Cluny**
*One of the finest collections of
medieval art in the world is
kept here in a superb late
15th-century building, which
includes the ruins of some
Gallo-Roman baths* ❶

No. 22 Rue St-Séverin is the
narrowest house in Paris and
used to be the residence of
Abbé Prévost, author of
Manon Lescaut.

★ **St-Séverin**

Begun in the 13th century, this beautiful church took three centuries to build and is a fine example of the flamboyant Gothic style ❸

Rue du Chat qui Pêche is a narrow pedestrianized street which has changed little in its 200-year history.

LOCATOR MAP
See Central Paris Map pp12–13

Shakespeare & Co
(see pp320 & 321) at No.37 Rue de la Bûcherie is a delightful, if chaotic, bookshop. Any books purchased here are stamped with *Shakespeare & Co Kilometre Zéro Paris*.

RUE DU PETIT PONT
PETIT PONT
LA HUCHETTE
CHEL
QUAI DE MONTEBELLO
RUE ST-JULIEN-LE-PAUVRE
PONT AU DOUBLE
RUE GALANDE
RUE LAGRANGE
RMAIN

N

★ **St-Julien-le-Pauvre**
Rebuilt in the 17th century, this church was used to store animal feed during the Revolution ❹

Rue de Fouarre used to host lectures in the Middle Ages. The students sat on straw *(fouarre)* in the street.

STAR SIGHTS

★ **Musée de Cluny**

★ **St-Séverin**

★ **St-Julien-le-Pauvre**

★ **Boulevard St-Michel**

Ⓜ Metro
Maubert
Mutualité

Rue Galande was home to the rich and chic in the 17th century, but subsequently became notorious for its taverns.

KEY

– – – Suggested route

0 metres	100
0 yards	100

Musée de Cluny **❶**

See pp154–7.

Boulevard St-Michel **❷**

75005 & 75006. **Map** 12 F5 & 16 F2.
M *St-Michel, Cluny-La Sorbonne.*
RER *Luxembourg.*

CUT THROUGH the area in
1869, the boulevard
gained fame initially from the
literary cafés that have existed
along it from its earliest days.
Much of the boulevard is now
lined with clothes shops but
the Café Cluny remains a
cosmopolitan meeting place
at the junction of Boulevard
St-Germain. In the Place St-
Michel, marble plaques
commemorate the many
students who died here in
1944 fighting the Nazis.

Gargoyles adorning St-Séverin

St-Séverin **❸**

1 Rue-des-Prêtres-St-Séverin 75005.
Map 13 A4. **C** 01 42 34 93 50. **M**
St-Michel. ○ *11am–7.30pm Mon–Fri;*
11am–7.40pm Sat; 9am–
8.30pm Sun. 🔲 *Concerts.*

ONE OF THE most beautiful
churches in Paris, St-
Séverin is a perfect example
of the Flamboyant Gothic
style. It is named after a 6th-
century hermit who lived in
the area and persuaded the
future St Cloud, grandson of
King Clovis, to take holy
orders. Construction finished
in the early 16th century and
included a remarkable double
ambulatory circling the

Inside St-Julien-le-Pauvre

chancel. In 1684 the Grande
Mademoiselle, cousin to Louis
XIV, adopted St-Séverin after
breaking with her parish
church of St-Sulpice and had
the chancel modernized.

The burial ground, now a
garden, was the site of the
first operation for gall stones
in 1474. An archer, condemned
to death, was offered his
freedom by Louis XI if he
consented to the operation
and lived. (It was a success,
and the archer went free.) In
the garden stands the
church's medieval gable-
roofed charnel house.

St-Julien-le-Pauvre **❹**

1 Rue St-Julien-le-Pauvre 75005.
Map 13 A4. **C** 01 43 29 09 09.
M *St-Michel.* **RER** *St-Michel.*
○ *9.30am–1.30pm, 3pm–6pm daily.*
Concerts. See **Entertainment** p336.

AT LEAST THREE saints can
claim to be patron of this
church, but the most likely is
St Julian the Hospitaller. The
church, together with St-
Germain-des-Prés, is one of
the oldest in Paris, dating
from between 1165 and 1220.
The university held its official
meetings in the church until
1524, when a student protest
created so much damage that
university meetings were
barred from the church by
parliament. Since 1889 it has
belonged to the Melchite sect
of the Greek Orthodox
Church, and it is now the
setting for chamber and
religious music concerts.

Place Maubert **❺**

75005. **Map** 13 A5.
M *Maubert-Mutualité.*

FROM THE 12TH to the middle
of the 13th century, "La
Maub" was one of Paris's
scholastic centres, with
lectures given in the open air.
After the scholars moved to
the new colleges of the
Montagne St-Geneviève, the
square became a place of
torture and execution,
including that of the
philosopher Etienne Dolet,
who was burned alive at the
stake as a heretic in 1546. So
many Protestants were burnt
here in the 16th century
that it became a place of
pilgrimage for the followers
of the new faith. Today, its
infamous reputation has been
replaced by respectability and
a notable street market.

Musée de la Préfecture de la Police **❻**

4 Rue de la Montagne Ste-Geneviève
75005. **Map** 13 A5. **C** 01 44 41 52
50. **M** *Maubert-Mutualité.* ○ *9am–*
5pm Mon–Fri; 10am–5pm Sat (last
adm: 4.30pm). ● *public hols.*

Weapons in the police museum

A DARKER SIDE to Paris's
history is illustrated in
this small museum. Created in
1909, the museum traces the
development of the police in
Paris from the Middle Ages to
the 20th century. Curiosities
on show here include arrest
warrants for figures such as
the famous revolutionary
Danton, and a rather sobering
display of weapons and tools
used by famous criminals.
There is also a section on the
part the police played in the
Resistance and subsequent
liberation of Paris.

La Sorbonne ❼

47 Rue des Ecoles 75005.
Map 13 A5. 🚇 *01 40 46 22 11.*
Ⓜ *Cluny-La Sorbonne, Maubert-Mutualité.* ⏰ *9am–5pm Mon–Fri.*
⬤ *public hols.* ✔ *only, by appt: write to* Service des Visites.

T HE SORBONNE, seat of the University of Paris, was established in 1253 by Robert de Sorbon, confessor to Louis IX, for 16 poor students to study theology. From these modest beginnings the college soon became the centre of scholastic theology. In 1469, the rector had three printing machines brought over from Mainz, thereby founding the first printing house in France. The college's opposition to liberal 18th-century philosophy led to its suppression during the Revolution. It was re-established by Napoleon in 1806. The buildings built by Richelieu in the early 17th century were replaced by the ones seen today.

Statues outside the college

Collège de France ❽

11 Pl Marcelin-Berthelot 75005.
Map 13 A5. 🚇 *01 44 27 12 11.*
Ⓜ *Maubert-Mutualité.* ⏰ *Oct– Jun: 9am–6.30pm Mon–Fri.*

O NE OF PARIS'S great institutes of research and learning, the college was established in 1530 by François I. Guided by the great humanist Guillaume Budé, the king aimed to counteract the intolerance and dogmatism of the Sorbonne. A statue of Budé stands in the west courtyard, and the unbiased approach to learning is reflected in the inscription on the entrance to the old college: *docet omnia* (all are taught here). Lectures are free and open to the public.

ST-ETIENNE-DU-MONT

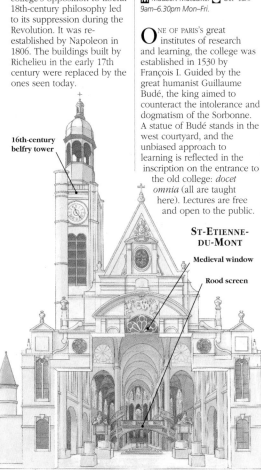

16th-century belfry tower

Medieval window

Rood screen

Chapelle de la Sorbonne ❾

Pl de la Sorbonne 75005.
Map 13 A5. 🚇 *01 40 46 22 11.*
Ⓜ *Cluny-La Sorbonne, Maubert-Mutualité.* 🚆 *Luxembourg.*
⏰ *for temporary exhibitions only.*
♿

E RECTED BY Lemercier between 1635 and 1642, this chapel is, in effect, a monument to Richelieu, with his coat of arms on the dome supports and his white marble tomb, carved by Girardon in 1694, in the chancel. The chapel's attractive lateral facade looks on to the main courtyard of the Sorbonne.

Eglise de la Sorbonne clock

St-Etienne-du-Mont ❿

Pl Ste-Geneviève 75005. **Map** 17 A1.
🚇 *01 43 54 11 79.* Ⓜ *Cardinal Lemoine.* ⏰ *8am–7.30pm Mon–Fri; w/e closed noon–2.30pm (noon–4pm on hols).* ⬤ *Mon in Jul–Aug.* 📷 🚹

T HIS REMARKABLE church houses not only the shrine of Sainte Geneviève, patron saint of Paris, but also the remains of the great literary figures Racine and Pascal. Some parts are in the Gothic style and others date from the Renaissance, including a magnificent rood screen. The stained glass windows are also of note.

Panthéon ⓫

See pp158–9.

Musée de Cluny ●

Head of St John the Baptist

Now KNOWN AS THE Musée National du Moyen Age – Thermes de Cluny, its original owner was Pierre de Chalus, Abbot of Cluny, who bought the ruins in 1330. Surrounded by imaginative newly-created medieval gardens, it is a unique combination of Gallo-Roman ruins, incorporated into a medieval mansion, and one of the world's finest collections of medieval art.

Medieval Mansion
The museum building, completed in 1500, was erected by Jacques d'Amboise, Abbot of Cluny.

Medieval chapel

★ Lady with the Unicorn
This outstanding series of tapestries is a fine example of the millefleurs style, which was developed in the 15th and early 16th centuries. The style is noted for its graceful depiction of plants, animals and people.

★ Golden Rose of Basel *(1330)*
The goldsmith Minucchio da Siena made this rose for the Avignon Pope John XXII.

Gallo-Roman Baths
Built in AD 200, the baths lasted for about 100 years before being sacked by the barbarians.

Caldarium (hot bath room)

STAR EXHIBITS

- ★ Gallery of the Kings
- ★ Lady with the Unicorn
- ★ Golden Rose of Basel

Gallo-Roman Frigidarium
The arches of this cold bath room, dating from the late 2nd and early 3rd centuries, were once decorated with pairs of carved ship prows, the symbol of the association of Paris boatmen (nautes).

Books of Hours

The museum possesses two Books of Hours from the first half of the 15th century. The illuminated pages include scenes showing the Labours of the Months, accompanied by the relevant sign of the zodiac.

VISITORS' CHECKLIST

6 Pl Paul-Painlevé. **Map** 13 A5.
🆔 01 53 73 78 00. Ⓜ Cluny, St-Michel, Odéon. 🚌 63, 86, 87, 21, 27, 85, 38 to Rue Soufflot, Rue des Ecoles. 🚉 St-Michel, Cluny-La Sorbonne. 🅿 Blvd St-Germain, Pl Edmond Rostand.
◯ 9.15am–5.45pm Wed–Mon (last adm: 5.05pm). ● 1 Jan, 25 Dec. 🈺 ◙ ☑ 🎫 **Concerts**. **Medieval poetry readings**.
🆆 www.musee-moyenage.fr

Octagonal tower

★ Gallery of the Kings

In 1977, 21 of the 28 stone heads of the Kings of Judah (carved around 1220 during the reign of Philippe Auguste) were unearthed during excavations in the Rue de la Chaussée-d'Antin behind the Opéra.

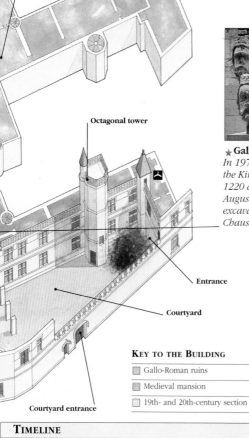

Entrance

Courtyard

GALLERY GUIDE

The collection is spread throughout the two floors of the building. It is mainly medieval and covers a wide range of items, including illuminated manuscripts, tapestries, textiles, precious metals, alabaster, ceramics, sculpture and church furnishings. A number of Gallo-Roman artefacts are displayed around the sides of the frigidarium, and the small circular room nearby contains some capitals.

KEY TO THE BUILDING

▨	Gallo-Roman ruins
▨	Medieval mansion
☐	19th- and 20th-century section

Courtyard entrance

TIMELINE

200	1450	1750	1800	1850
c. 200 Public baths built	**1747** Octagonal tower used as observatory		**1789** Seized in the Revolution and sold by the State	**1833** Acquired by Alexandre du Sommerard, collector of medieval artefacts
1500 Building of mansion by Jacques d'Amboise completed				**1844** Opened as a museum
c. 300 Baths sacked and burned by barbarians		**1819** Baths excavated on the orders of Louis XVIII		
1600 Hôtel becomes residence of papal nuncios		*Louis XVIII at his desk*		**1842** House and collection bought by State

Exploring the Cluny's Collection

Alexandre du Sommerard took over the Hôtel de Cluny in 1833 and installed his art collection with great sensitivity to the surroundings and a strong sense of the dramatic. After his death the Hôtel and its contents were sold to the State and turned into a museum.

The Grape Harvest tapestry

TAPESTRIES

The museum's tapestries are remarkable for their quality, age and state of preservation. The images present a surprising mixture of the naive with more complex notions. One of the earliest, *The Offering of the Heart* (early 15th century), shows a man who is literally proffering his heart to a seated medieval beauty. More everyday scenes are shown in the magnificent series *The Noble Life* (about 1500). Upstairs is the mysterious *Lady with the Unicorn* series.

CARVINGS

The diverse techniques of medieval European woodcarvers are well represented. From the Nottingham workshops in England, there are wood as well as alabaster works which were widely used as altarpieces all over Europe. Smaller works include *The School*, which is touchingly realistic and dates from the early 16th century. Upstairs there are some fine Flemish and south German woodcarvings. The multi-coloured figure of St John is typical. Two notable altarpieces are the intricately carved and painted *Lamentation of Christ* (about 1485) from the Duchy of Clèves, and the Averbode altarpiece, made in 1523 in Antwerp, which depicts three scenes including the Last Supper. Not to be missed is the full-length figure of Mary Magdalene.

STAINED GLASS

Most of the cluny's glass from the 12th and 13th centuries is French. The oldest examples were originally installed in the Basilique St-Denis in 1144. There are also three fragments from the Troyes Cathedral, destroyed by fire, two of which illustrate the life of St Nicholas while the third depicts that of Christ. Numerous panels came to the Cluny from Sainte-Chapelle *(see pp88–9)*, during its mid-19th-century restoration, and were never returned, including five scenes from the story of Samson dating from 1248.

The technique of contrasting coloured glass with surrounding grisaille (grey-and-white panels) developed in the latter half of the 13th century. Four panels from the royal château at Rouen illustrate this.

Stained-glass scenes from Brittany (1400)

The School woodcarving (English, early 16th century)

Head of a queen from St-Denis from before 1120

SCULPTURE

THE HIGHLIGHT HERE is the Gallery of the Kings, a display of heads and decapitated figures from Notre-Dame. There is also an very graceful statue of Adam, sculped in the 1260s.

In the vaulted room opposite are displays of fine Romanesque sculpture retrieved from French churches. Among the earliest are the 12 capitals from the nave of St-Germain-des-Prés, from the early 11th century. Retrieved from the portal of St-Denis is a boldly sculpted head of a queen (c.1140) which, though badly mutilated, is still compelling.

Other Romanesque and early Gothic capitals include six finely sculpted works from Catalonia and four of the museum's most famous statues, early 13th-century apostles made for Sainte-Chapelle.

EVERYDAY OBJECTS

HOUSEHOLD GOODS show another side to medieval life, and this large collection is grouped in a sensitive way to illustrate their use – from wallhangings and caskets to kitchenware and clothing. Children's toys bring a very human aspect to the display, while travel cases and religious emblems evoke journies of exploration and pilgrimage.

PRECIOUS METALWORK

THE CLUNY HAS a fine collection of jewellery, coins, metal and enamelwork from Gallic times to the Middle Ages. The showcase of Gallic jewellery includes gold torques, bracelets and rings, all of a simple design. In between these is one of the Cluny's most precious exhibits, the Golden Rose of Basel, a delicately wrought piece from 1330 and the oldest known of its kind.

The earliest enamelwork on display is the late Roman and Byzantine *cloisonné* pieces, culminating in the remarkable Limoges enamels, which flourished in the late 12th century. There are also two exceptional altarpieces, the Golden Altar of Basel and the Stavelot altarpiece.

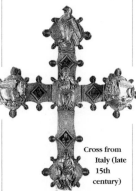

Cross from Italy (late 15th century)

The Pillar of the Nautes

GALLO-ROMAN RUINS

ONE OF THE MAIN reasons for visiting the Musée de Cluny is to see the scale and layout of its earliest function, the Gallo-Roman baths. The vaulted *frigidarium* (cold bath room) was the largest of its kind in France. Here there is another of the Cluny's highlights, the Pillar of the Nautes (boatmen), unearthed during excavations beneath Notre-Dame in 1711.

Composed of five carved stone blocks representing Gallic and Roman divinities, its crowning element is presumed to depict the Seine's boatmen. There are also the ruins of the *caldarium* and *tepidarium* (hot and tepid baths), and visitors can tour the underground vaults.

LADY WITH THE UNICORN TAPESTRIES

This series of six tapestries was woven in the late 15th century in the southern Netherlands. It is valued for its fresh harmonious colours and the poetic elegance of the central figure. Allegories of the senses are illustrated in the first five: sight (gazing into a mirror), hearing (playing a portable organ), taste (sampling sweets), smell (sniffing carnations) and touch (the lady holding the unicorn's horn). The enigmatic sixth tapestry (showing jewels being placed in a box) includes the words "to my only desire" and is now thought to represent the principle of free choice.

Unicorn on the sixth tapestry

Panthéon ⓫

WHEN LOUIS XV recovered from desperate illness in 1744, he was so grateful to be alive that he conceived a magnificent church to honour Sainte Geneviève. The design was entrusted to the French architect Jacques-Germain Soufflot, who planned the church in Neo-Classical style. Work began in 1764 and was completed in 1790, ten years after Soufflot's death, under the control of Guillaume Rondelet. But with the Revolution underway the church was soon turned into a pantheon – a location for the tombs of France's good and great. Napoleon returned it to the Church in 1806, but it was secularized and then desecularized once more before finally being made a civic building in 1885.

The Façade
Inspired by the Rome Pantheon, the temple portico has 22 Corinthian columns.

The arches of the dome show a renewed interest in the lightness of Gothic architecture and were designed by Rondelet. They link four pillars supporting the dome, which weighs 10,000 tonnes and is 83 m (272 ft) high.

Pediment Relief
David d'Angers' pediment bas-relief depicts the mother country (France) granting laurels to her great men.

The Panthéon Interior
The interior has four aisles arranged in the shape of a Greek cross, from the centre of which the great dome rises.

Entrance

STAR FEATURES

★ **Iron-Framed Dome**

★ **Frescoes of Sainte Geneviève**

★ **Crypt**

★ **Frescoes of Sainte Geneviève**
Murals along the south wall of the nave depict the life of Sainte Geneviève. They are by Pierre Puvis de Chavannes, the 19th-century fresco painter.

The dome lantern allows only a little light to filter into the church's centre. Intense light was thought inappropriate for the place where France's heroes rested.

VISITORS' CHECKLIST

Pl du Panthéon. **Map** 17 A1.
📞 01 44 32 18 00. Ⓜ Jussieu,
Cardinal-Lemoine. 🚌 84 to
Panthéon; 21, 27, 38, 85 to Gare
du Luxembourg. RER St-Michel.
🅿 Pl Edmond Rostand.
Crypt ◻ Apr–Sep: 9.30am–
6.30pm daily; Oct–Mar: 10am–
6.15pm daily (last adm 45 mins
before closing.) ● 1 Jan, 1 May,
11 Nov, 25 Dec.

★ **Iron-Framed Dome**
The tall dome, with its stone cupolas and three layers of shells, was inspired by St Paul's in London and the Dôme Church (see p188).

The dome galleries afford a magnificent panoramic view of France's capital.

Colonnade
The colonnade encircling the dome is both decorative and part of an ingenious supporting system.

Monument to Diderot
This is Alphonse Terroir's statue (1925) to the political writer Denis Diderot.

★ **Crypt**
Covering the entire area under the building, the crypt divides into galleries flanked by Doric columns. Many French notables rest here.

THE PANTHÉON'S ENSHRINED

The first of France's great men to be entombed was the popular orator Honoré Mirabeau. (Later, under the revolutionary leadership of Maximilien Robespierre, he fell from grace and his body was removed.) Voltaire followed. He died in 1788 and was buried outside Paris, so his remains were removed to the city in a funerary procession. A statue of Voltaire by Jean-Antoine Houdon stands in front of his tomb. In the 1970s the remains of the wartime Resistance leader Jean Moulin were reburied here. Others here include Jean-Jacques Rousseau, Victor Hugo and Emile Zola.

JARDIN DES PLANTES QUARTER

THIS AREA, TRADITIONALLY, has been one of the most tranquil corners of Paris. It takes its character from the 17th-century botanical gardens where the kings of the *ancien régime* grew their medicinal herbs and where the National Natural History Institute stands today. The many hospitals in the area, notably Paris's largest, Pitié Salpêtrière, add to the atmosphere. Bustle is very much a feature of the colourful market that takes over much of Rue Mouffetard every day. And the streets off Mouffetard are redolent of life in medieval times.

SIGHTS AT A GLANCE

Museums and Galleries
Musée de la Sculpture en Plein Air **2**
Collection des Minéraux de l'Université **4**
Muséum National d'Histoire Naturelle **10**
La Manufacture des Gobelins **13**

Modern Architecture
Institut du Monde Arabe **1**

Churches and Temples
St-Médard **8**
Mosquée de Paris/Institut Musulman **9**

Squares, Parks and Gardens
Ménagerie **3**
Place de la Contrescarpe **6**
Jardin des Plantes **11**

Historic Buildings and Streets
Arènes de Lutèce **5**
Rue Mouffetard **7**
Groupe Hospitalier Pitié-Salpêtrière **12**

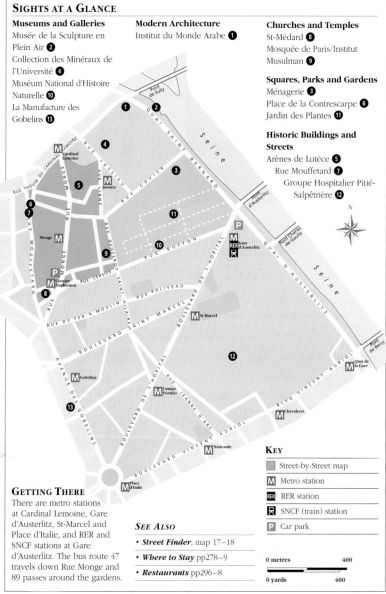

GETTING THERE
There are metro stations at Cardinal Lemoine, Gare d'Austerlitz, St-Marcel and Place d'Italie, and RER and SNCF stations at Gare d'Austerlitz. The bus route 47 travels down Rue Monge and 89 passes around the gardens.

KEY

▨	Street-by-Street map
M	Metro station
RER	RER station
🚆	SNCF (train) station
P	Car park

0 metres		400
0 yards		400

Market scene on the Rue Mouffetard

Street-by-Street: Jardin des Plantes Quarter

Two PHYSICIANS TO Louis XIII, Jean Hérouard and Guy de la Brosse, obtained permission to establish the royal medicinal herb garden in the sparsely populated St-Victor suburb in 1626. The herb garden and gardens of various religious houses gave the region a rural character. In the 19th century the population and thus the area expanded and it became more built up, until it gradually assumed the character it has today: a well-to-do residential patchwork of 19th- and early 20th-century buildings interspersed with much older and some more recent buildings.

Metro
Cardinal
Lemoine

Place de la Contrescarpe
This village-like square filled with restaurants and cafés buzzes with student life after dusk **6**

★ Rue Mouffetard
Locals flock to the daily open-air market here which is one of the oldest Paris street markets. A board of louis d'or *gold coins from the 18th century were found at No. 53 during its demolition in 1938* **7**

Pot de Fer fountain is one of 14 that Marie de Médicis had built on the Left Bank in 1624 as a source of water for her palace in the Jardin du Luxembourg. The fountain was rebuilt in 1671.

Metro
Monge

Passage des Postes is an ancient alley which was opened in 1830. Its entrance is in the Rue Mouffetard.

St-Médard
This church was started in the mid-15th century and completed by 1655. In 1784 the choir was made Classical in style, and the nave's 16th-century windows were replaced with contemporary stained glass **8**

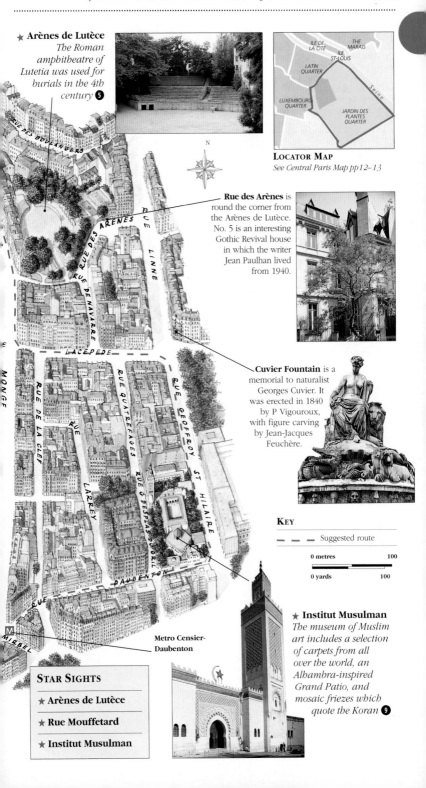

★ **Arènes de Lutèce**
The Roman amphitheatre of Lutetia was used for burials in the 4th century ❺

LOCATOR MAP
See Central Paris Map pp12–13

Rue des Arènes is round the corner from the Arènes de Lutèce. No. 5 is an interesting Gothic Revival house in which the writer Jean Paulhan lived from 1940.

Cuvier Fountain is a memorial to naturalist Georges Cuvier. It was erected in 1840 by P Vigouroux, with figure carving by Jean-Jacques Feuchère.

KEY

– – – Suggested route

| 0 metres | 100 |
| 0 yards | 100 |

Metro Censier-Daubenton

★ **Institut Musulman**
The museum of Muslim art includes a selection of carpets from all over the world, an Alhambra-inspired Grand Patio, and mosaic friezes which quote the Koran ❾

STAR SIGHTS

★ Arènes de Lutèce

★ Rue Mouffetard

★ Institut Musulman

Institut du Monde Arabe ❶

1 Rue des Fossées St-Bernard 75005. **Map** 13 C5. ☎ *01 40 51 38 38.* Ⓜ *Jussieu, Cardinal-Lemoine.* ◯ ***Museum & temp exhibs:*** *10am–6pm Tue–Sun.* ***Library:*** *1pm–8pm Tue–Sat.* ***Lectures.*** www.imarabe.org

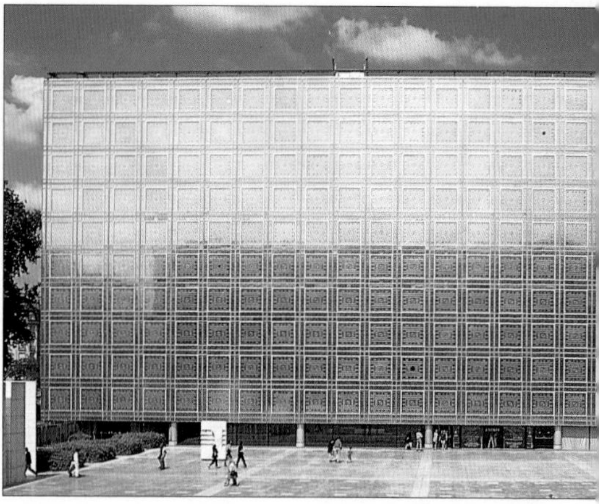

THIS CULTURAL INSTITUTE was founded in 1980 by France and 20 Arab countries with the intention of fostering cultural links between the Islamic world and the West. It is housed in a magnificent modern building, designed by the French architect Jean Nouvel, that combines modern materials with the spirit of traditional Arab architecture. The white marble book tower, which can be seen through the glass of the west wall, spirals upwards bringing to mind the minaret of a mosque. The emphasis that is traditionally placed on interior space in Arab architecture has been used here to create an enclosed courtyard reached by a narrow gap splitting the building in two.

On the seventh floor there is a fascinating display of Islamic works of art from the 9th to the 19th centuries, including glassware, ceramics, sculpture, carpets and a fine collection of astrolabes, so prized by ancient Arabic astronomers. There is also a library and media archive.

Musée de la Sculpture en Plein Air ❷

75004/ 75005. **Map** 13 C5. Ⓜ *Gare d'Austerlitz, Sully-Morland.*

BUTTING UP to the left hand corner of the Institut du Monde Arabe, the Pont de Sully links the Ile St Louis with both banks of the Seine. Opened in 1877 and built of cast iron, the Pont de Sully is not an especially beautiful structure. Despite this, it is well worth pausing for a moment on the bridge for a fabulous view of Notre-Dame rising dramatically behind the wonderfully graceful Pont Marie.

Running along the river from the Pont de Sully as far as the Pont d'Austerlitz is the peaceful Quai St-Bernard. Not always so sedate, Quai St-Bernard was famous during the 17th century as a spot for nude bathing, until scandalized public opinion made it illegal. The grassy slopes adjoining the quai make a perfect spot to enjoy a picnic. Opened in 1975, they are known as the Jardin Tino Rossi in honour of the celebrated Corsican singer. The garden has a display of open-air sculpture known as the Musée de la Sculpture en Plein Air. Vandalism and other problems have unfortunately necessitated the removal of some of the exhibits.

Ménagerie ❸

57 Rue Cuvier 75005. **Map** 17 C1. ☎ *01 40 79 37 94.* Ⓜ *Jussieu, Austerlitz.* ◯ *Oct–Mar: 10am–5pm daily; Apr–Sep: 10am–6pm Mon–Sat (6.30pm Sun & public hols).*

FRANCE'S OLDEST public zoo is situated in the lovely surroundings of the Jardin des Plantes. It was set up during the Revolution to house survivors from the Royal menagerie at Versailles – all four of them. The state then rounded up animals from circuses and exotic creatures were sent from abroad. During the Prussian siege of Paris (1870–71) most of them were slaughtered to feed the hungry citizens *(see pp224–5)*. Today the zoo specializes in small mammals, insects, birds, primates and reptiles, and it is a great favourite with children as it is possible for them to get quite close to the animals. The lion house contains a number of large cats, including panthers from China. Other attractions include a large monkey house, bear pits, a large waterfowl aviary and wild sheep and goats.

The displays in the vivarium (enclosures of live animals in natural habitat) are changed at regular intervals throughout the year and there is a permanent exhibition of micro-arthropods (creepy-crawlies).

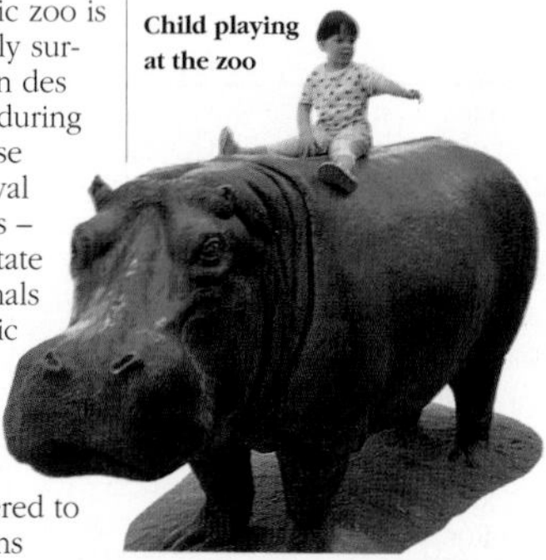

Child playing at the zoo

Light Screens

The south elevation is made up of 1,600 high-tech metal screens which filter the light entering the building. Their design is based on moucharabiyahs *(carved wooden screens found on the outsides of buildings from Morocco to Southeast Asia).*

Each screen contains 21 irises which are controlled electronically, opening and closing in response to the amount of sunlight falling on photosensitive screens.

The central iris is made up of interlocking metal blades which move to adjust the size of the central opening.

The peripheral irises are linked to one another and to the central iris. They open and close in unison forming a delicate pattern of light and shade inside the institute.

Collection des Minéraux de l'Université ❹

Université Pierre et Marie Curie, 34 Rue Jussieu 75005. **Map** 13 C5. 【 01 44 27 52 88. 🅜 *Jussieu.* ☐ *1pm–6pm Wed–Mon.* ● *1 Jan, Easter, 1 May, 14 Jul, 1 Nov, 25 Dec.* 🚫 🚻 ♿ ▨ *groups Tue pm.*

THIS FASCINATING small museum is housed in the basement of the main university building, named after the distinguished scientists. The collection comprises cut and uncut gemstones and rock crystal from all over the world, shown to maximum advantage through the expert use of specialized lighting.

Arènes de Lutèce ❺

Rue de Navarre 75005. **Map** 17 B1. 🅜 *Jussieu. See p19.*

THE REMAINS of this vast Roman arena (Lutetia was the Roman name for Paris)

date from the late 2nd century. Its destruction began towards the end of the 3rd century at the hands of the Barbarians, and later, parts of it were used to build the walls of the Ile de la Cité. The arena was then gradually buried and its exact location preserved only in old documents and the local name Clos des Arènes. It was rediscovered in 1869 during the construc-tion of the Rue Monge and the allocation of building

Topaz

plots nearby. Action towards its restoration began with the campaigning of Victor Hugo (among others) in the 19th century but work did not get really underway until 1918.

With a seating capacity of 15,000, arranged in 35 tiers, the original arena was used both for theatrical perfor-mances and as an amphitheatre for the more gruesome spectacle of gladiator fights. This type of combined use was peculiar to Gaul (France), and the arena is similar to the other French ones in Nîmes and Arles.

The public park at the Arènes de Lutèce

BUFFON AND THE JARDIN DES PLANTES

At the age of 32 Georges Louis Leclerc, Comte de Buffon (1707–88), became the curator of the Jardin des Plantes at a time when the study of natural history was at the forefront of contemporary thought – Charles Darwin's *The Origin of Species* was to be published 120 years later. Buffon masterminded the reorganization of the Jardin, propelling it to a pre-eminent position within the scientific world. He was elected to the Académie Française in 1752 following the publication of his two main works, *Natural History* and *The Epoques of Nature*. He died in his house in the Jardin.

Illustration of a primate from Buffon's *Natural History*

Place de la Contrescarpe ❻

75005. **Map** 17 A1. **M** *Place Monge.*

AT ONE TIME this site lay outside the city walls. It gets its name from the backfilling of the moat that ran along Philippe-Auguste's wall. The present square was laid out in 1852. At No. 1 there is a memorial plaque to the old "pine-cone club" immortalized in the writings of Rabelais; here a group of writers known as *La Pléiade* (named after the constellation of The Pleiades) used to meet in the 16th century.

The area has always been used for meetings and festivals. Today it is extremely lively at weekends, and on Bastille Day *(see pp64–5)* a delightful ball is held here.

Part of the medieval city wall

Cheese in the Mouffetard market

Rue Mouffetard ❼

75005. **Map** 17 B2. **M** *Censier-Daubenton, Place Monge.*
⬤ **Market** 8am–1pm Tue–Sun.
See **Shops and Markets** p326.

A MAJOR THOROUGHFARE since Roman times, when it ran between Lutetia (Paris) and Rome, this street is one of the oldest in the city. In the 17th and 18th centuries it was known as the Grande Rue du Faubourg St-Marcel, and many of its buildings date from this period. Some of the small shops still have ancient painted signs, and some of the houses have mansard roofs. No. 125 has an attractive, restored Louis XIII facade, and the entire front of No. 134 has beautiful decoration of wild beasts, flowers and plants.

The whole area is well known for its open-air markets, especially those in Place Maubert, Place Monge, and Rue Daubenton, a side street where a lively African market takes place.

St-Médard ❽

141 Rue Mouffetard 75005.
Map 17 B2. **☎** *01 44 08 87 00.*
M *Censier-Daubenton.*
⬤ *8.30am–noon Tue–Sat; 2.30–7pm Mon–Sat; 4–7pm Sun.* 📷 ♿

THE ORIGINS OF this charming church go back to the 9th century. St Médard, counsellor to the Merovingian kings, was known for his custom of giving a wreath of white roses to young girls noted for their virtue. The churchyard, now a garden, became notorious in the 18th century as the centre of the cult of the Convulsionnaires, whose hysterical fits were brought on by the contemplation of miracle cures. The interior has many fine paintings, including the 17th-century *St Joseph Walking with the Christ Child* by Francisco de Zurbarán.

Mosquée de Paris/Institut Musulman ❾

Pl du Puits de l'Ermite 75005.
Map 17 C2. **☎** *01 45 35 97 33.*
M *Place Monge.* ⬤ *9am–noon, 2pm–6pm Sat–Thu.* ⬤ *Muslim hols.*
⬤ 📷 🍴 ⬤ 🛍 **Library.**
W www.mosquee.de.paris.com

BUILT IN THE 1920s in the Hispano-Moorish style, this group of buildings is the spiritual centre for Paris's Muslim community and the home of the Grand Imam. The complex comprises religious, educational and commercial sections; at its

Decoration inside the mosque

heart is a mosque. Each of the mosque's domes is decorated differently and the minaret stands nearly 33 m (100 ft) high. Inside is a grand patio inspired by the Alhambra, with mosaics on the walls and tracery on the arches.

Once used only by scholars, the mosque's place in Parisian life has grown over the years. The Turkish baths there can be enjoyed by both men and women but on alternate days.

Muséum National d'Histoire Naturelle ⑩

2 Rue Buffon 75005. **Map** 17 C2.
📞 01 40 79 30 00. Ⓜ *Jussieu, Austerlitz.*
🕐 10am–5pm Wed–Mon (last adm: 4.30pm). 📷 ♿ restricted. 🔲 🚻
Library. 🅦 www.mnhn.fr

Skull of the reptile dimetrodon

THE HIGHLIGHT OF the museum is the Grande Galerie de l'Evolution. There are also four other departments: palaeontology, featuring skeletons, casts of various animals and an exhibition showing the evolution of the vertebrate skeleton; palaeobotany, devoted to plant fossils; mineralogy, including gemstones; and entomology, with some of the oldest fossilized insects on earth. The bookshop is in the house that was occupied by the naturalist Buffon, from 1772 until his death in 1788.

Jardin des Plantes ⑪

57 Rue Cuvier 75005. **Map** 17 C1.
Ⓜ *Jussieu, Austerlitz.* 🕐 9am–6pm (5pm winter) daily.

THE BOTANICAL gardens were established in 1626 when Jean Hérouard and Guy de la Brosse, Louis XIII's physicians, obtained permission to found

a royal medicinal herb garden here and then a school of botany, natural history and pharmacy. The garden was opened to the public in 1640 and flourished under the inspired direction of Buffon. Now one of Paris's great parks, it includes a natural history museum, botanical school and zoo.

As well as beautiful vistas and walkways flanked by ancient trees and punctuated with statues, the park has a remarkable alpine garden with plants from Corsica, Morocco, the Alps and the Himalayas and an unrivalled display of herbaceous and wild plants. It also has the first Cedar of Lebanon to be planted in France, originally from Britain's Kew Gardens.

Groupe Hospitalier Pitié-Salpêtrière ⑫

47 Blvd de l'Hôpital 75013. **Map** 18 D3. Ⓜ *St-Marcel, Austerlitz.* 🚉 *Gare d'Austerlitz.* 🕐 ***Chapel*** 8.30am–6.30pm daily. 🕂 3.30pm. daily. 📷 ♿

THE VAST Salpêtrière hospital stands on the site of an old gunpowder factory and derives its name from the saltpetre used in the making of explosives. It was founded by Louis XIV in 1656 to help sick or socially-disadvantaged women and children and later became renowned for its pioneering humane treatment of the insane. The main architectural feature is the domed chapel designed by Libéral Bruand in about 1670.

The Cedar of Lebanon in the Jardin

Outside the Hôpital Salpêtrière

La Manufacture des Gobelins ⑬

42 Ave des Gobelins 75013.
Map 17 B3. 📞 01 44 54 19 30.
Ⓜ *Gobelins.* 🕐 ***guided tours only*** 2pm, 2.45pm Tue–Thu (arrive 15 mins earlier). Groups by appt.
📷 ● public hols.

Versailles tapestry by Le Brun

ORIGINALLY A dyeing workshop set up in about 1440 by the Gobelin brothers, the building became a tapestry factory early in the 17th century. Louis XIV took it over in 1662 and gathered together the greatest craftsmen of the day – carpet weavers, cabinet makers and silversmiths – to furnish his new palace at Versailles (*see pp248–53*). Working under the direction of court painter Charles Le Brun, 250 Flemish weavers laid the foundations for the factory's international reputation. Today weavers continue to work in the traditional way but with modern designs, including those of Picasso and Matisse.

LUXEMBOURG QUARTER

Many a parisian dreams of living in the vicinity of the Luxembourg Gardens, a quieter, greener and somehow more reflective place than its neighbouring areas. Luxembourg is one of the most captivating places in the capital. Its charm is in its old gateways and streets, its bookshops, and in the sumptuous yet intimate gardens. Though writers of the eminence of Paul Verlaine and André Gide no longer stroll in its groves, the paths, lawns and avenues are still full of charm, drawing to them the numerous students from the nearby *grandes écoles* and *lycées*. And on

warm days old men meet under the chestnut trees to play chess or the traditional game of *boules*.

To the west the buildings are public and official, and on the east the houses are shaded by the tall chestnut trees of the Boulevard St-Michel.

Sailing boats are hired by children and adults to sail in the *grand bassin* (ornamental pond) in the Luxembourg Gardens.

SIGHTS AT A GLANCE

Museums
Musée du Service de Santé des Armées ❿
Ecole Nationale Supérieure des Mines ⓫

Historic Buildings
Palais du Luxembourg ❸
Institut Catholique de Paris ❻

Churches
St-Sulpice ❷
St-Joseph-des-Carmes ❼
Val-de-Grâce ❾

Squares and Gardens
Place St-Sulpice ❶
Jardin du Luxembourg ❺

Fountains
Fontaine de Médicis ❹
Fontaine de l'Observatoire ❽

GETTING THERE
The area is served by the metro, with stations at Mabillon and St-Sulpice, and by the RER, with a station at Luxembourg. Several bus routes pass through the area. Route 38 travels along Boulevard St-Michel on the east side of the Gardens and 58 and 89 pass along the Rue de Rennes on the north side. Route 82 passes along the southern end.

KEY

	Street-by-Street map
M	Metro station
RER	RER station
P	Car park

0 metres   400
0 yards   400

SEE ALSO
- **Street Finder**, map 12, 16
- **Where to Stay** pp278–9
- **Restaurants** pp296–8

Playing chess in the Jardin du Luxembourg

Street-by-Street: Luxembourg Quarter

SITUATED ONLY A FEW steps from the bustle of St-Germain-des-Prés, this graceful and historic area offers a peaceful haven in the heart of a modern city. The Jardin du Luxembourg and Palais du Luxembourg dominate the vicinity. The gardens became fully open to the public in the 19th century under the ownership of the Comte de Provence (later Louis XVIII), when for a small fee visitors could come in and feast on fruit from the orchard. Today the gardens, palace and old houses on the streets to the north remain unspoilt and attract many visitors.

★ St-Sulpice
This Classical church was built over 134 years to Daniel Gittard's plans. It has a facade by the Italian architect Giovanni Servandoni ❷

To St-Germain-des-Prés

Place St-Sulpice
The Fontaine des Quatre Points Cardinaux depicts four church leaders at the cardinal points of the compass. Point also means "never": the leaders were never made cardinals ❶

The Monument to Delacroix
(1890) by Jules Dalou is situated near the private gardens of the French Senate. Beneath the bust of the leading Romantic painter Eugène Delacroix are the allegorical figures of Art, Time and Glory.

STAR SIGHTS

★ St-Sulpice

★ Jardin du Luxembourg

★ Palais du Luxembourg

★ Fontaine de Médicis

★ Jardin du Luxembourg
Many fine statues were erected in the Luxembourg gardens in the 19th century during the reign of Louis-Philippe ❺

The Rue de Tournon is full of elegant architecture, boutiques and old bookshops. At No. 12 is the Grand Hôtel d'Entragues, reconstructed by Neveu in the 18th century during Louis XVI's reign.

LOCATOR MAP
See Central Paris Map pp12–13

KEY

— — — Suggested route

0 metres 100

0 yards 100

★ **Palais du Luxembourg**
In 1794, during the Revolution, the painter Jacques-Louis David was imprisoned here and made sketches for the Intervention of the Sabine Women ❸

★ **Fontaine de Médicis**
The 17th-century fountain is in the style of an Italian grotto and is thought to have been designed by Salomon de Brosse ❹

RUE DE TOURNON

N

RUE DE MÉDICIS

Sainte Geneviève, the patron saint of Paris, was a wealthy 5th-century Gallo-Roman landowner. When Paris was invaded by the Huns in AD 451, she prayed with women friends that the city would be spared – their prayers were answered. This statue by Michel-Louis Victor (1845) pays homage to her.

The Octagonal Lake (Grand Bassin), attributed to Jean-François Chalgrin, is surrounded by formal terraces where visitors to the gardens often sunbathe.

Place St-Sulpice ❶

75006. **Map** 12 E4. Ⓜ *St-Sulpice.*

THIS LARGE SQUARE, which is dominated on the east side by the enormous church from which it takes its name, was built in the last half of the 18th century.

Two main features of the square are the Fountain of the Four Bishops by Joachim Visconti (1844) and the pink-flowering chestnut trees. There is also the Café de la Mairie, a rendezvous of writers and students, which is often featured in French films.

Stained-glass window of St-Sulpice

St-Sulpice ❷

Pl St-Sulpice 75006. **Map** 12 E5.
Ⓒ 01 46 33 21 78. Ⓜ *St-Sulpice.*
Ⓞ 8.30am–7.30pm daily.
✝ frequent. ◎

IT TOOK more than a century, from 1646, for this huge and imposing church to be built. The result is a simple two-storey west front with two tiers of elegant columns. The overall harmony of the

building is marred only by the towers, one at each end, which do not match.

Large arched windows fill the vast interior with light. By the front door are two enormous shells given to François I by the Venetian Republic – they rest on rock-like bases sculpted by Jean-Baptiste Pigalle.

In the side chapel to the right of the main door are some magnificent murals by Eugène Delacroix, including his famous *Jacob Wrestling with the Angel (see p137)* and *Heliodorus Driven from the Temple*. Visitors can often enjoy recitals which are given on the splendid organ.

Palais du Luxembourg ❸

15 Rue de Vaugirard 75006.
Map 12 E5. Ⓒ 01 42 34 20 00.
Ⓜ *Odéon.* Ⓡ *Luxembourg.*
📷 Groups only, by appt: Mon, Fri, Sat.
Apply 3 months in advance. Ⓒ 01 42
34 20 60. 🚫 Ⓦ www.senat.fr

NOW THE HOME of the French Senate, this palace was built to remind Marie de Médicis, widow of Henri IV, of her native Florence. It was designed by Salomon de Brosse, who built it in the style of the Pitti Palace in Florence. By the time it was finished (1631) she had been banished, but it remained a royal palace until the Revolution. Since then the palace has been used (briefly) as a prison, and in World War II it was the headquarters of the Luftwaffe, with numerous air-raid shelters built underneath its famous gardens.

Figures on the Fontaine de Médicis

Fontaine de Médicis ❹

15 Rue de Vaugirard 75006.
Map 12 F5. Ⓡ *Luxembourg.*

BUILT IN 1624 for Marie de Médicis by an unknown architect, this vigorous Baroque fountain stands at the end of a long pond filled with goldfish and shaded by trees. The mythological figures were added much later by Auguste Ottin (1866).

Jardin du Luxembourg ❺

Blvd St-Michel 75006. **Map** 12 E5.
Ⓒ 01 42 34 20 00. Ⓡ *Luxembourg.*
Ⓞ Apr–Oct: 7.30am–9.30pm daily;
Nov–Mar: 8.15am–5pm daily (times
may vary slightly). ▣

A GREEN OASIS covering 25 ha (60 acres) in the heart of the Left Bank, this is the most popular park in the whole of Paris. The layout of the gardens is centred around the Luxembourg Palace and is dominated by a splendid octagonal pool – usually full of toy sailing boats.

Apart from the attraction of its formal terraces, broad avenues and many statues, the park also includes an open-air café, a puppet theatre, numerous tennis courts, a bandstand and a bee-keeping school. There is also a riding school nearby.

Sculptures on Palais du Luxembourg

Institut Catholique de Paris ⑥

21 Rue d'Assas 75006. **Map** 12 D5.
Ⓜ *St-Placide, Rennes.* **Musée Biblique** ◯ *Sat: 3–6pm or by appt.*
☎ *01 45 48 09 15.* **Musée Branly**
◯ *by appt.* ☎ *01 45 38 98 57.*
Ⓦ *www.icp.fr*

FOUNDED IN 1875, this is one of the most distinguished teaching institutions in France. It also houses two small museums: the Musée Biblique which displays objects excavated in the Holy Land, and the Musée Branly, devoted to the physicist Edouard Branly, inventor of the radio conductor (which made the wireless possible).

Courtyard statue at the Institut Catholique

St-Joseph-des-Carmes ⑦

70 Rue de Vaugirard 75006.
Map 12 D5. ☎ *01 44 39 52 00.*
Ⓜ *St-Placide.* ◯ *7am–7pm Mon–Sat; 9am–7pm Sun.*
◆ *Easter Mon, Pentecost.*
♿ *restricted.* ◙ *3pm Sat.*

COMPLETED IN 1620, this church was built as the chapel for a Carmelite convent but was used as a prison during the Revolution. In 1792 more than a hundred priests met a grisly end in the church's courtyard as part of the September Massacres *(see pp28–9)*. Their remains are now in the crypt.

Carpeaux's fountain sculpture

Fontaine de l'Observatoire ⑧

Pl Ernest Denis, in Ave de l'Observatoire. **Map** 16 E2.
RER *Port Royal.*

SITUATED AT THE southern tip of the Jardin du Luxembourg, this is one of the liveliest fountains in Paris. Made of bronze, it has four women holding aloft a globe representing four continents – the fifth, Oceania, was left out for reasons of symmetry. There are some subsidiary figures, including dolphins, horses and a turtle. The sculpture was erected in 1873 by Jean-Baptiste Carpeaux.

Val-de-Grâce ⑨

1 Pl Alphonse-Laveran 75005. **Map** 16 F2. ☎ *01 40 51 51 92.* Ⓜ *Gobelins.*
RER *Port Royal.* ◯ *noon–6pm Tue, Wed, Sat & Sun.* ◙ *(except for nave).*
✝ *frequent, pm.* ◙ *appt.*

ONE OF THE MOST beautiful churches in France, It was built for Anne of Austria (wife of Louis XIII) in thanks for the birth of her son. Young Louis XIV himself laid the first stone in 1645. The design is in the style of the great architect François Mansart.

The church is noted for its beautiful lead-and-gilt dome. In the cupola is Pierre Mignard's enormous fresco, with over 200 triple-life-size figures. The six huge, twisted marble columns that frame the altar are similar to those made by Bernini for St Peter's in Rome.

Musée du Service de Santé des Armées ⑩

1 Pl Alphonse-Laveran 75005. **Map** 16 F2. ☎ *01 40 51 51 92.* RER *Port Royal.* ◯ *Tue, Wed noon–5pm; Sat 1–5pm; Sun 1.30–5pm.* ◙
◙ *phone to arrange.*

FOUNDED DURING World War I and run by the army medical corps, this museum is also known as the Musée du Val-de-Grâce. It is in the west wing of the Val-de-Grâce church, where it became a military hospital in 1795.

The exhibits cover the history of medicine with gruesome memorabilia such as artificial limbs and surgical instruments. There are even reconstructions of military hospital trains that took wounded soldiers to hospital.

Engraving of the interior of a hospital train from 1887

Ecole Nationale Supérieure des Mines ⑪

60 Blvd St-Michel. **Map** 16 F1. ☎ *01 40 51 91 45.* RER *Luxembourg.*
◯ *1.30–6pm Tue–Fri; 10am–12.30pm, 2–5pm Sat.* ◙ ◙ ◙

LOUIS XIV set up the School of Mines in 1783 to train mining engineers. Today, it is one of the most prestigious *grandes écoles* – schools that provide the élite for the civil service and professions. It also houses the national collection of minerals – the Musée de Minéralogie.

Facade of St-Joseph-des-Carmes

MONTPARNASSE

I N THE FIRST three decades of this century Montparnasse was a thriving artistic and literary centre. So many modern painters and sculptors, new novelists and poets, the great and the young were drawn to this area. Its ateliers, conviviality and renowned Bohemian lifestyle made it a magnet for genius, some of it French, much of it foreign. The great epoch ended with World War II, and change continued with the destruction of many of the ateliers and the construction of the soaring Tour Montparnasse, Paris's tallest office tower, which heralded the more modern *quartier*. But the area has not lost its appeal. The great cafés remain very much in business and attract a lively international crowd. Small café-theatres have opened and the area springs to life at the weekends with cinema crowds.

Monument to Charles Augustin Ste-Beauve in the Cimetière du Montparnasse

SIGHTS AT A GLANCE

Historic Buildings and Streets
Rue Campagne-Première ❸
Catacombs ❿
Observatoire de Paris ⓫

Cemeteries
Cimetière du
Montparnasse pp180–1 ❹

Museums and Galleries
Musée Zadkine ❷

Musée Antoine Bourdelle ❻
Musée de la Poste ❼
Musée Montparnasse ❽
Fondation Cartier ❾

Modern Architecture
Tour Montparnasse ❺

Cafés and Restaurants
La Coupole ❶
La Closerie des Lilas ⓬

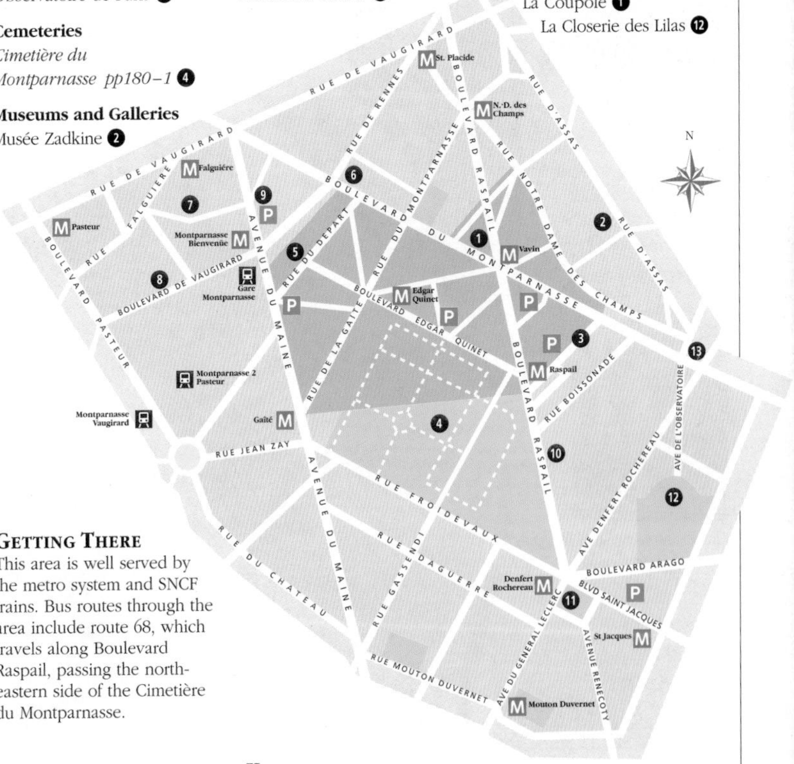

GETTING THERE
This area is well served by the metro system and SNCF trains. Bus routes through the area include route 68, which travels along Boulevard Raspail, passing the north-eastern side of the Cimetière du Montparnasse.

SEE ALSO
- *Street Finder*, map 15–16
- *Where to Stay* pp278–9
- *Restaurants* pp296–8

KEY
▨	Street-by-Street map
Ⓜ	Metro station
🚇	SNCF (train) station
🅿	Car park

0 metres	400
0 yards	400

View of Tour Montparnasse from the Cimetière du Montparnasse

Street-by-Street: Montparnasse

Renowned for its mix of art and high living, Montparnasse continues to live up to its name: Mount Parnassus was the mountain dedicated by the ancient Greeks to Apollo, god of poetry, music and beauty. That mix was especially potent in the 1920s and 1930s, when such artists and writers as Picasso, Hemingway, Cocteau, Giacometti, Matisse and Modigliani were to be seen in the local bars, cafés and cabarets.

★**La Coupole**
This traditional brasserie-style café, with its large enclosed terrace, opened in 1927 and became a famous meeting place for artists and writers ❶

★**Cimetière du Montparnasse**
This fine sculpture, The Separation of a Couple *by de Max, stands in the smallest of the city's major cemeteries* ❹

★**Tour Montparnasse**
Europe's second-tallest tower block rests on 56 piles that extend 62 m (203 ft) below the surface ❺

Metro Edgar Quinet

RUE DU DEPART

BLVD

RUE D'ODESSA

RUE DU MONTPARNASSE

BLVD EDGAR QUINE

RUE DE LA GAÎTE

The Théâtre Montparnasse
at No. 31, with its fully-restored original 1880's decor.

Star Sights
★ La Coupole
★ Tour Montparnasse
★ Rue Campagne-Première
★ Cimetière du Montparnasse

To Metro Gaîté

Rue Bréa has a variety of shops, including two restaurants and even a nightclub, all within 90 m (300 ft). A small square and two cinemas lie just across the street.

No. 14, Rue de la Grande Chaumière offers tuition in painting and sculpture.

LOCATOR MAP
See Central Paris Map pp12–13

The statue of Balzac by Auguste Rodin was erected in 1939, and stands 3 m (10 ft) tall.

Metro Vavin

★ **Rue Campagne-Première**
The block of artists' studios at No. 31 was built in 1911, and the facade was decorated by the ceramicist Paul Bigot

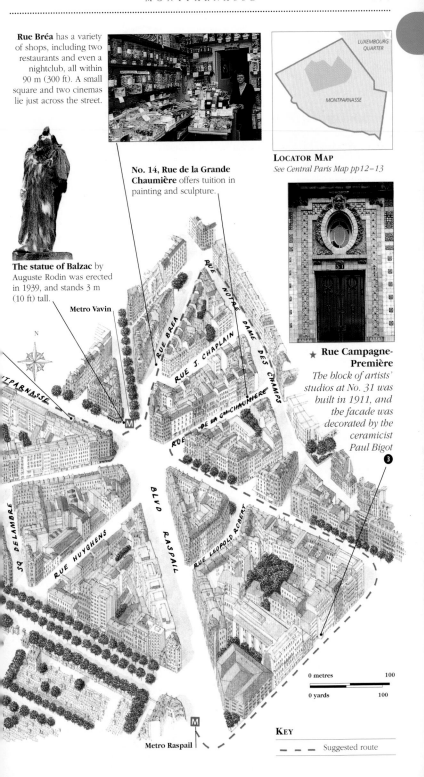

N

RUE BRÉA

RUE J. CHAPLAIN

RUE NOTRE DAME DES CHAMPS

RUE DE LA Gde CHAUMIÈRE

MONTPARNASSE

M

BLVD RASPAIL

SQ DELAMBRE

RUE HUYGHENS

RUE LEOPOLD ROBERT

❸

0 metres   100

0 yards   100

M

Metro Raspail

KEY

— — — Suggested route

The interior of La Coupole

La Coupole ❶

102 Blvd du Montparnasse 75014.
Map 16 D2. **[** 01 43 20 14 20. **M**
Vavin, Montparnasse. **◯** 7.30am–
1am (1.30 Fri–Sat) Sun–Thu. See
Restaurants and Cafés p303.

E STABLISHED IN 1927, this
historic café-restaurant and
dance hall underwent a facelift in the late 1980s. Its red
velvet seats and famous
columns, decorated by various
local artists, have survived.
Among its clientele have been
Jean-Paul Sartre, Josephine
Baker and Roman Polanski.

**The museum's Les Trois Belles
(1950) by Ossip Zadkine**

Musée Zadkine ❷

100 bis Rue d'Assas 75116. **Map** 16 E1.
[01 43 26 91 90. **M** Notre-Dame-Les
Champs. **◯** (check not closed for renovation) 10am–5.30pm Tue–Sun. **●** public
hols. **▨ ◉ ◪** by appt. **&** limited.

T HE RUSSIAN-BORN sculptor
Ossip Zadkine lived here
from 1928 until his death in

1967. The small house, studio
and daffodil-filled garden
contain his often tormented-
looking works. Here he
produced his great commemorative sculpture, *Ville Détruite*,
commissioned by Rotter-
dam after World War II,
and two monuments to
Vincent Van Gogh, one for
Holland and one for Auvers-
sur-Oise, where Van Gogh
died. The museum's works
span the development of
Zadkine's style, from his Cubist beginnings to Expressionism and Abstractionism.

Rue Campagne-
Première ❸

75014. **Map** 16 E2. **M** Raspail.

T HIS STREET HAS some
interesting Art Deco
buildings and a long artistic
tradition. Modigliani, ravaged
by opium and tuberculosis,
lived at No. 3. Between the
wars many artists resided
here, including Picasso, Joan
Miró and Kandinsky.

Cimetière du
Montparnasse ❹

See pp180–1.

Tour
Montparnasse ❺

Pl Raoul Dautry 75014. **Map** 15 C2.
M Montparnasse-Bienvenüe. **[** 01
45 38 52 56. **◯** 9.30am–10pm daily.
▨ ❚❚ ▣ & by appt.

T HIS WAS EUROPE'S largest
office block when it was
built in 1973 as the focal
point of a new business
sector intended to revitalize a
run-down inner-city
area. It stands 209 m
(690 ft) high, is made
of curved steel and
smoked glass, and
totally dominates the
quarter's skyline.
The bar, restaurant
and observatory on
the 56th floor offer
excellent panoramic
views of the city – up
to 40 km (25 miles)
on a clear day.

**The Archer (1909) by Antoine
Bourdelle**

Musée Antoine
Bourdelle ❻

18 Rue Antoine Bourdelle 75015.
Map 15 B1. **[** 01 49 54 73 73.
M Montparnasse-Bienvenüe.
◯ 10am–5.40pm Tue–Sun
● public hols. **▨ &** limited.
W www.paris-france.org/musees

T HE PROLIFIC sculptor,
Antoine Bourdelle, lived
and worked in the studio
here from 1884 until his death
in 1929. The house, studio
and garden are now a
museum devoted to his life
and work. Among the 900
sculptures on display are the
original plaster casts of his
monumental works planned
for wide public squares. They
are housed in the Great Hall
in an extension and include
the group of sculptures for
the relief decoration of the
Théatre des Champs-Elysées.

Musée de la
Poste ❼

34 Blvd de Vaugirard 75015.
Map 15 B2. **[** 01 42 79 23 45.
M Montparnasse-Bienvenüe.
◯ 10am–6pm Mon–
Sat. **●** public hols.
▨ ❚ & Library.

E VERY CONCEIVABLE
aspect of the
history of the
French postal
service and methods
of transportation is
covered in this well
laid out collection.
There is even a
room devoted to

A view of the tower

mail delivery in times of war – carrier pigeons were used during the Franco-Prussian War with postmarks stamped on their wings. Postage stamp art is displayed in the gallery.

A Miró-designed postage stamp

Musée du Montparnasse ⓼

21 Ave du Maine 75015. **Map** 15 C1. ⚊ 01 42 22 91 96. Ⓜ *Montparnasse Bienvenüe-Falguière*. ◯ *1pm–7pm Wed–Sun.* 🖼

DURING WORLD WAR I, this was a canteen for needy artists which, by its status as a private club, was not subject to curfew, and so the likes of Picasso, Braque, Modigliani and Léger could eat for 65 centimes and then party until late at night. This symbolic place is now a museum that recalls, through paintings and photos, how at the Vavin crossroads Western art turned some of the most beautiful pages of its modern history.

Fondation Cartier ⓽

261 Blvd Raspail 75014. **Map** 11 A2. ⚊ 01 42 18 56 50. Ⓜ *Raspail*. ◯ *noon–8pm Tue–Sun.* ● *1 Jan, 25 Dec.* 🖼 🚻 📷 Ⓦ www.fondation.cartier.fr

THIS FOUNDATION for contemporary art is housed in a building designed by architect Jean Nouvel. He has created an air of transparency and light, as well as incorporating a cedar of Lebanon planted in 1823 by François-René de Chateaubriand. The structure complements the nature of the exhibitions of progressive art, which showcase personal, group or thematic displays, often with works by young unknowns.

Catacombs ⓾

1 Pl Denfert-Rochereau 75014. **Map** 16 E3. ⚊ 01 43 22 47 63. Ⓜ *Denfert-Rochereau*. ◯ *2pm–4pm Tue–Fri; 9am–11am, 2pm–4pm Sat, Sun.* ● *public hols.* 🖼 📷 📹 Ⓦ www.paris-france.org/musees

IN 1786 A MONUMENTAL project began here: the removal of the millions of skulls and bones from the unsanitary city cemetery in Les Halles to the ancient quarries formed by excavations at the base of the three "mountains": Montparnasse, Montrouge and Montsouris. It took 15 months to transport the bones and rotting corpses at night across the city in huge carts to their new resting place.

Just before the Revolution, the Comte d'Artois (later Charles X) threw wild parties in the catacombs, and during World War II the French Resistance set up its headquarters here. Above the door outside are the words "Stop! This is the empire of death."

Observatoire de Paris ⓫

61 Ave de l'Observatoire 75014. **Map** 16 E3. ⚊ 01 40 51 22 21. 🖾 01 40 51 21 74. Ⓜ *Denfert-Rochereau*. **Visits** *(2 hrs) apply 2 mths ahead: 1st Sat of mth: 2.30pm; grps by appt.* ● *Aug.* 🖼 📹 Ⓦ www.obspm.fr

IN 1667 Louis XIV was persuaded by his scientists and astronomers that France needed a royal observatory. Building began on 21 June,

the day of the summer solstice, and took five years to reach completion.

Astronomical research undertaken here included the calculation of the exact dimensions of the solar system in 1672, calculations of the dimensions of longitude, the mapping of the moon in 1679 and the discovery of the planet Neptune in 1846.

The façade of the Observatoire

La Closerie des Lilas ⓬

171 Blvd du Montparnasse 75014. **Map** 16 E2. ⚊ 01 40 51 34 50. Ⓜ *Vavin*. 🆁🅴🆁 *Port Royal*. ◯ *Bar: 11–1am, brasserie: noon–11.30pm daily.*

LENIN, TROTSKY, Hemingway and Scott Fitzgerald all frequented the numerous bars and cafés of Montparnasse, but the Closerie was their favourite. Much of Hemingway's novel *The Sun Also Rises* takes place here. Hemingway wrote it on the terrace in just six weeks. Today the terrace is ringed with trees and the whole place is more elegant in appearance, but much of the original decor remains (*see p37*).

Skulls and bones stored in the catacombs

Cimetière du Montparnasse 4

THE MONTPARNASSE CEMETERY was planned by Napoleon outside the city walls to replace the numerous, congested small cemeteries within the old city, viewed as a health hazard at the turn of the 19th century. It was opened in 1824 and became the resting place of many illustrious Parisians, particularly Left Bank personalities. Like all French cemeteries it is divided into rigidly aligned paths forming blocks or divisions. The Rue Emile Richard cuts it into two parts, the Grand Cimetière and the Petit Cimetière.

★ **Charles Baudelaire Cenotaph**
This is a monument to the great poet and critic (1821–67), author of The Flowers of Evil.

Samuel Beckett, the great Irish playwright renowned for *Waiting for Godot*, spent most of his life in Paris. He died in 1989.

The Pétain tomb contains the family of the marshal who collaborated with the Germans during World War II. Pétain himself is buried near Nantes, where he was imprisoned.

Guy de Maupassant was a 19th-century novelist.

Alfred Dreyfus was a Jewish army officer whose unjust trial for treason in 1894 provoked a political and social scandal.

Frédéric Auguste Bartholdi was the sculptor of the Statue of Liberty (1886) in New York.

André Citroën, an engineer and industrialist who died in 1935, founded the famous French car firm.

★ **Charles Pigeon Family Tomb**
This wonderfully pompous Belle Époque tomb depicts the French industrialist and inventor in bed with his wife.

Charles-Augustin Sainte-Beuve was a critic of the French Romantic generation, and is generally described as the "father of modern criticism".

Camille Saint-Saëns, the pianist, organist and composer who died in 1921, was one of France's great post-Romantic musicians.

STAR FEATURES

★ **Charles Baudelaire Cenotaph**

★ **Charles Pigeon Family Tomb**

★ **Jean-Paul Sartre and Simone de Beauvoir**

★ **Serge Gainsbourg**

The Kiss by Brancusi
This is the famous Primitivo-Cubist sculpture (a response to Rodin's Kiss) *by the great Romanian artist, who died in 1957 and is buried just off the Rue Emile Richard.*

★ Serge Gainsbourg
The French singer, composer and pop icon of the 1970s and 1980s is known for his wistful and irreverent songs. He was married to the actress Jane Birkin.

VISITORS' CHECKLIST

3 Blvd Edgar Quinet. **Map** 16 D3. 01 44 10 86 50. M *Edgar Quinet.* 38, 83, 91 to *Port Royal.* RER *Port Royal.* P *Rue Campagne-Première, Blvd St-Jacques.* Mid-Mar–Oct: 8am–6pm Mon–Fri, 8.30am–6pm Sat, 9am–6pm Sun; Nov–mid-Mar closes 5.30pm. **Adm free.**

The Tower is all that remains of a 17th-century windmill. It was part of the old property of the Brothers of Charity on which the cemetery was built.

Génie du Sommeil Eternel
Horace Daillion's wistful bronze angel of Eternal Sleep (1902) is the cemetery's centrepiece.

Tristen Tzara, the Romanian writer, was leader of the literary and artistic Dada movement in Paris in the 1920s.

Henri Laurens
The French sculptor (1885–1954) was a leading figure in the Cubist movement.

Man Ray was an American photographer who immortalized the Montparnasse artistic and café scene in the 1920s and 1930s.

Charles Baudelaire, the 19th-century poet, is buried here in his detested step-father's family tomb, along with his beloved mother.

Chaim Soutine, a poor Jewish Ukranian, was a Montparnasse Bohemian painter of the 1920s. He was adopted by the Italian artist Modigliani.

JEAN PAUL SARTRE
1905 - 1980
SIMONE DE BEAUVOIR
1908 - 1986

Jean Seberg
The Hollywood actress, adopted by the French New Wave film-makers of the 1960s, was the epitome of American blonde beauty, youth and candour.

★ Jean-Paul Sartre and Simone de Beauvoir
The famous existentialist couple, undisputed leaders of the post-war literary scene, lie here close to their Left Bank haunts.

INVALIDES AND EIFFEL TOWER QUARTER

Musée de l'Armée cannon

EVERYTHING in the area of Invalides is on a monumental scale. Starting from the sprawling 18th-century buildings of the Ecole Militaire on the corner of the Avenue de la Motte Piquet, the Parc du Champs de Mars stretches down to the Eiffel Tower and the Seine. The avenues around the Tower are lined with luxurious buildings, some in the Art Nouveau style, and numerous embassies. The area was already highly prized between the World Wars when the noted actor Sacha Guitry lived there. Even earlier, in the 18th century, wealthy residents of the Marais moved to this part of the city, building the aristocratic town houses that line the Rue de Varenne and Rue de Grenelle.

SIGHTS AT A GLANCE

Historic Buildings and Streets
Hôtel des Invalides **6**
Hôtel Matignon **8**
Assemblée Nationale Palais-Bourbon **11**
Rue Cler **12**
Les Egouts **13**
Champ-de-Mars **14**
No. 29 Avenue Rapp **16**
Ecole Militaire **18**

Museums and Galleries
Musée de l'Ordre de la Libération **3**
Musée de l'Armée **4**
Musée des Plans-Reliefs **5**
Musée Rodin **7**
Musée Maillol **9**

Churches and Temples
Dôme Church pp188–9 **1**
St-Louis-des-Invalides **2**
Sainte-Clotilde **10**

Monuments and Fountains
Eiffel Tower pp192–3 **15**

Modern Architecture
Village Suisse **17**
UNESCO **19**

GETTING THERE
The metro system serves this area well, with stations at Invalides, Solferino, Sèvres Babylone, Varenne, Latour Maubourg and Ecole Militaire. There are also several bus routes through the area. Route 69 passes along Rue St-Dominique heading east and along Rue de Grenelle on the way back. Route 87 travels along the Avenue de Suffren and 28 along Avenue de la Motte Picquet.

SEE ALSO

0 metres 400
0 yards 400

KEY
Street-by-Street map
M Metro station
RER RER station
Batobus boarding point
P Car park

View of the Eiffel Tower

Street-by-Street: Invalides

Mounted military policeman

The IMPOSING HOTEL DES INVALIDES, from which the area takes its name, was built from 1671 to 1676 by Louis XIV for his wounded and homeless veterans and as a monument to his own glory. At its centre lies the glittering golden roof of the Sun King's Dôme Church, which marks the final resting place of Napoleon Bonaparte. The emperor's body was brought here from St Helena in 1840, 19 years after he died, and placed inside the majestic red sarcophagus, designed by Joachim Visconti, that lies at the centre of the Dôme's circular glass-topped crypt. Just to the east of the Hôtel on the corner of the Boulevard des Invalides, the superb Musée Rodin offers artistic relief from the pomp and circumstance of the surrounding area.

Metro La Tour Maubourg

The facade of the Hôtel is 196 m (645 ft) long and is topped by dormer windows, each decorated in the shape of a different trophy. A head of Hercules sits above the central entrance.

★ Musée de l'Armée
This museum covers military history from the Stone Age to World War II. It includes an exhibition on the development of the French flag, from the various standards of the ancien régime *to the Tricolour* ❹

AVE DE TOURVILLE

STAR SIGHTS
- ★ Dôme Church and Napoleon's Tomb
- ★ St-Louis-des-Invalides
- ★ Musée de l'Armée
- ★ Musée Rodin

Musée de l'Ordre de la Libération
The Order was set up to honour feats of heroism during World War II ❸

Musée de Plans-Relief
This museum contain military models of forts and towns, as well as a displa on model-making ❺

KEY
– – – Suggested route

0 metres   100
0 yards   100

General de Gaulle's Liberation Order and compass

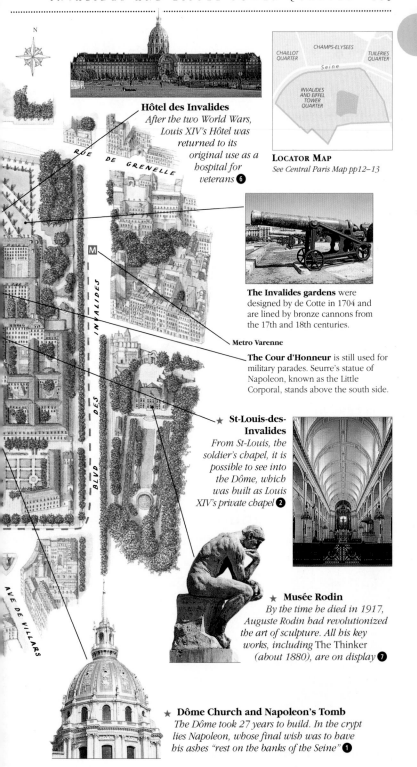

LOCATOR MAP
See Central Paris Map pp12–13

Hôtel des Invalides
After the two World Wars, Louis XIV's Hôtel was returned to its original use as a hospital for veterans ❻

The Invalides gardens were designed by de Cotte in 1704 and are lined by bronze cannons from the 17th and 18th centuries.

Metro Varenne

The Cour d'Honneur is still used for military parades. Seurre's statue of Napoleon, known as the Little Corporal, stands above the south side.

★ **St-Louis-des-Invalides**
From St-Louis, the soldier's chapel, it is possible to see into the Dôme, which was built as Louis XIV's private chapel ❷

★ **Musée Rodin**
By the time he died in 1917, Auguste Rodin had revolutionized the art of sculpture. All his key works, including The Thinker *(about 1880), are on display* ❼

★ **Dôme Church and Napoleon's Tomb**
The Dôme took 27 years to build. In the crypt lies Napoleon, whose final wish was to have his ashes "rest on the banks of the Seine" ❶

Dôme Church ❶

See pp188–9.

St-Louis-des-Invalides ❷

Hôtel des Invalides 75007. **Map** 11 A3. **M** *Varenne Latour-Maubourg.* **C** *01 44 42 37 65.* ◯ *Apr–Sep: 10am–6pm daily; Oct–Mar: 10am–5pm daily.*

ALSO KNOWN AS the "soldiers' church", this is the chapel of the Hôtel des Invalides. It was built from 1679 to 1708 by Jules Hardouin-Mansart from the original designs by Libéral Bruand, architect of the Hôtel des Invalides. The imposing, but stark, interior is decorated with banners seized in battle.

The fine 17th-century organ was built by Alexandre Thierry. The first performance of Berlioz's *Requiem* was given on it in 1837, with an orchestra accompanied by a battery of outside artillery.

Musée de l'Ordre de la Libération ❸

51 bis Blvd de Latour-Maubourg 75007. **Map** 11 A4. **C** *01 47 05 04 10.* **M** *Latour-Maubourg.* ◯ *10am–6pm (5pm in winter) daily.* ● *public hols.* 🎦 📷 🎫 *apply 1 mth before.*

THIS MUSEUM is devoted to the wartime Free French and their leader, General Charles de Gaulle. The Order

The altar of St-Louis-des-Invalides

The facade of the Musée de l'Ordre de la Libération

of Liberation was created by de Gaulle at Brazzaville in 1940. It is France's highest honour and was eventually bestowed on those who made an outstanding contribution to the final victory of the Allies in World War II. The *companions* who received the honour were French civilians and members of the armed forces, plus a handful of overseas leaders, including King George VI, Winston Churchill and General Dwight Eisenhower.

Cannons at the Musée de l'Armée

Musée de l'Armée ❹

Hôtel des Invalides 75007. **Map** 11 A3. **C** *01 44 42 37 72.* **M** *Latour-Maubourg, Varenne.* **RER** *Invalides.* ◯ *10am–6pm (5pm winter) daily.* ● *1 Jan, 1 May, 1 Nov, 25 Dec.* 🎦 🖴 🔘 *grd floor only.* 🎫 🖪 🎞 *Film.*

THIS IS ONE of the most comprehensive museums of military history in the world, with exhibits ranging from the Stone Age to the final days of World War II. The museum is housed in galleries occupying two of the former four refectories on either side of the magnificent courtyard of the 17th-century Hôtel des Invalides, and in the newly opened "Priests' Wing" with the enlarged World War II galleries.

In the Turenne gallery on the east side there is an impressive array of banners from 1619 to 1945, including Napoleon's flag of farewell flown at Fontainebleau in

1814, after his first abdication. The Restoration gallery on the second floor recalls the emperor's imprisonment on Elba, the Hundred Days War, Waterloo and his final exile on St Helena, with a reconstruction of the room where he died in 1821.

On the west side, the Oriental gallery has a rich display of arms and armour from China, Japan, India and Turkey; the Pauillac gallery has Renaissance swords and daggers; and the Arsenal has suits of armour, 1,000 helmets and hundreds of spears, swords and firearms.

Musée des Plans-Reliefs ❺

Hôtel des Invalides 75007. **Map** 11 B3. **C** *01 45 51 95 05.* **M** *Latour-Maubourg, Varenne.* **RER** *Invalides.* ◯ *10am–6pm (5pm in winter) daily.* ● *1 Jan, 1 May, 1 & 11 Nov, 25 Dec.* 🎦 📷 🎫

A map of Alessandria, Italy (1813)

THE DETAILED models of French forts and fortified towns, some dating back to Louis XIV's reign, were considered top secret until the 1950s, when they were put on public display. The oldest model is that of Perpignan, dating to 1686. It shows the fortifications drawn up by the legendary 17th-century military architect Vauban, who built the defences around several French towns, including Briançon.

Hôtel des Invalides ⑥

75007. **Map** 11 A3. 🔴 01 44 42 37 70.
🅼 Latour-Maubourg, Varenne.
⭘ 10am–6pm daily (5pm winter).
⬤ public hols.

The Invalides main entrance

FOUNDED BY Louis XIV, this was the first military hospital and home for French war veterans and disabled soldiers who had hitherto been reduced to begging. The decree for building this vast complex was signed in 1670, and construction, following the designs of Libéral Bruand, was finished five years later.

Today the harmonious Classical facade is one of the most impressive sights in Paris, with its four storeys, cannon in the forecourt, garden and tree-lined esplanade stretching to the Seine. The south side leads to St-Louis-des-Invalides, the soldiers' church, which backs on to the magnificent Dôme church of Jules Hardouin-Mansart. The dome was re-gilded in 1989 and now glitters anew.

Musée Rodin ⑦

77 Rue de Varenne 75007. **Map** 11 B3. 🔴 01 44 18 61 10. 🅼 Varenne.
⭘ Apr–Sep: 9.30am–5.45pm Tue–Sun; Oct–Mar: 10am–4.45pm (gdn 1 hr later) Tue–Sun. ⬤ 1 Jan, 1 May, 25 Dec. 🈺 📷 🔵 restricted. 🔲 🔲 occasional.

AUGUSTE RODIN, widely regarded as the greatest 19th-century French sculptor, lived and worked in the Hôtel

Biron, an elegant 18th-century mansion, from 1908 until his death in 1917. In return for a state-owned flat and studio, Rodin left his work to the nation, and it is now exhibited here. Some of his most celebrated sculptures are on display in the garden: *The Burghers of Calais, The Thinker, The Gates of Hell* and *Balzac.* The garden has a stunning array of 2,000 rose bushes.

The indoor exhibits are arranged in chronological order, spanning the whole of Rodin's career, with highlights such as *The Kiss* and *Eve.*

Hôtel Matignon ⑧

57 Rue de Varenne 75007.
Map 11 C4. 🅼 Solférino, Rue du Bac. **Not open** to the public.

ONE OF THE MOST beautiful mansions in the Faubourg area, this was built by Jean Courtonne in 1721 and has been substantially remodelled since. Former owners include Talleyrand, the statesman and diplomat who held legendary parties and receptions here, and several members of the nobility. It has been the official residence of the French Prime Minister since 1958 and has the largest private garden in Paris.

Rodin's *The Kiss* (1886) at the Musée Rodin

Musée Maillol ⑨

59 Rue de Grenelle 75007.
Map 11 C4. 🔴 01 42 22 59 58.
🅼 Sèvres-Babylone, Rue du Bac.
⭘ 11am–6pm Wed–Mon. 🔵 🔲 🔲
🔗 www.musee-maillol.com

ONCE LIVED IN by novelist Alfred de Musset, this museum was created by Dina Vierny, former model and muse to Aristide Maillol. All aspects of the artist's work are here: drawings, engravings, paintings, sculpture and decorative objects. Also displayed is Dina Vierny's private collection, in which naïve art sits alongside works by Matisse, Dufy, Picasso and Rodin.

Large allegorical figures of the city of Paris and the four seasons decorate Bouchardon's fountain in front of the house.

Sculptured figures at Ste-Clotilde

Sainte-Clotilde ⑩

23bis Rue Las Cases 75007.
Map 11 B3. 🔴 01 44 18 62 60.
🅼 Solférino, Varenne, Invalides.
⭘ 8.30am–7.30pm daily. ⬤ non-religious public hols. 🔲 🔲

DESIGNED BY the German-born architect Christian Gau and the first of its kind to be built in Paris, this Neo-Gothic church was inspired by the mid-19th-century enthusiasm for the Middle Ages, made fashionable by such writers as Victor Hugo. The church is noted for its imposing twin towers, visible from across the Seine. The interior decoration includes wall paintings by James Pradier and stained-glass windows with scenes relating to the patron saint of the church. The composer César Franck was the church organist here for 32 years.

Dôme Church ●

JULES HARDOUIN-MANSART was asked in 1676 by the Sun King, Louis XIV, to build the Dôme Church among the existing buildings of the Invalides military refuge. A soldiers' church had already been built, but the Dôme was to be reserved for the exclusive use of the Sun King and for the location of royal tombs. The resulting masterpiece complements the surrounding buildings and is one of the greatest examples of 17th-century French architecture.

After Louis XIV's death, plans to bury the royal family in the church were abandoned, and it became a monument to Bourbon glory. In 1840 Louis-Philippe decided to install Napoleon's remains in the crypt, and the addition of the tombs of Vauban, Marshal Foch and other figures of military prominence have since turned this church into a French military memorial.

Gilded Dome
The cupola was first gilded in 1715.

① **Tomb of Joseph Bonaparte**
The sarcophagus of Napoleon's older brother, the King of Naples and later of Spain, is in the side chapel to the right as visitors enter.

Main entrance

② **Memorial to Vauban**
Commissioned by Napoleon I in 1808, this contains an urn with Sébastien le Prestre de Vauban's heart. He was Louis XIV's great military architect and engineer who died in 1707. His long military career culminated in his appointment as Marshal of France in 1703. He revolutionized siege warfare when he introduced his ricochet-batteries. His reclining figure by Antoine Etex lies on top of the memorial, mourned by Science and War.

⑥ **Glass Gallery**
Access to the glass-topped crypt containing Napoleon's tomb is by the curved stairs in front of the altar. The glass partition behind the altar separates the Dôme from the older Invalides chapel beyond.

KEY

— — — Tour route

⑤ **St Jérôme's Chapel**
Passing across the centre of the church, the side chapel to the right of the main entrance contains the tomb of Napoleon's younger brother, Jérôme, King of Westphalia.

Stairs to crypt

③

④ **Dôme Ceiling**
Looking upwards, Charles de la Fosse's circular painting (1692) on the ceiling shows the Glory of Paradise, *with Saint Louis presenting his sword to Christ.*

③ **Tomb of Marshal Foch**
Ferdinand Foch's imposing bronze tomb was built by Paul Landowski in 1937.

NAPOLEON'S RETURN
King Louis-Philippe decided to bring the Emperor Napoleon's body back from St Helena *(see pp30–31)* as a gesture of reconciliation to the Republican and Bonapartist parties contesting his regime. The Dôme Church, with its historical and military associations, was an obvious choice for Napoleon's final resting place. His body was encased in six coffins and finally placed in the crypt in 1861, in the culmination of a grand ceremony which was attended by Napoleon III.

Neo-Classical façade of the Assemblée Nationale Palais-Bourbon

Assemblée Nationale Palais-Bourbon ⓫

126 Rue de l'Université 75007.
Map 11 B2. 📞 *01 40 63 60 00.* Ⓜ
Assemblée- Nationale. **RER** *Invalides.*
🕐 *10am, 2pm, 3pm Sat. Enter at 33
Quai d'Orsay. ID necessary.* 📷
📹 *for groups phone 01 40 63 64 08*

BUILT IN 1722 for the
Duchesse de Bourbon,
daughter of Louis XIV, the
Palais-Bourbon was confiscated during the Revolution.
It has been home to the lower
house of the French Parliament since 1830.

During World War II, the
palace became the Nazi
administration's seat of
government. The public can
enter to watch parliament in
action. The grand neo-
Classical façade with its fine

columns was added to the
palace in 1806, partly to
mirror the façade of La
Madeleine church facing it
across the Seine. The adjacent
Hôtel de Lassay, built by the
Prince de Condé, is now the
official residence of the
president of the National
Assembly.

Rue Cler ⓬

75007. **Map** 10 F3.
Ⓜ *Ecole-Militaire, Latour-Maubourg.*
Market 🕐 *Tue–Sat. See **Shops and
Markets** pp326–7.*

THIS IS THE STREET market of
the seventh arrondisse-
ment, the richest in Paris, for
here live the bulk of senior
civil servants, captains of
industry and many diplomats.
The market area occupies a

pedestrian precinct stretching
south from the Rue de
Grenelle. It is colourful, but
very much an exclusive
market, with the best-dressed
shoppers in town. As one
would expect, the produce is
excellent, the pâtisserie and
cheese shops in particular.

Of architectural interest are
the Art Nouveau buildings at
No. 33 and No. 151.

Les Egouts ⓭

In front of 93 Quai d'Orsay 75007.
Map 10 F2. 📞 *01 53 68 27 81.*
Ⓜ *Alma-Marceau.* **RER** *Pont de l'Alma.*
🕐 *11am–5pm (4pm in winter) Sat–
Wed.* 🌑 *last 3 wks Jan.* 🈂 📷 📹

ONE OF Baron Haussmann's
finest achievements, the
majority of Paris's sewers
(*égouts*) date from the Second
Empire (*see pp32–3*). If laid
end to end the 2,100 km (1,300
miles) of sewers would stretch
from Paris to Istanbul. This
century the sewers became a
popular attraction with tourists.
All tours have been limited to
a small area around the Quai
d'Orsay entrance and are now
on foot. A sewer museum has
now been established here
where visitors can discover
the mysteries of underground
Paris. There are also displays
of machinery used in the past
and in the sewers of today.

The interior of a wine shop in the Rue Cler

Doorway at No. 29 Avenue Rapp

Champ-de-Mars ⓮

75007. **Map** 10 E3. Ⓜ *Ecole-Militaire.*
Ⓡ *Champ-de-Mars–Tour-Eiffel.*

THE GARDENS stretching from the Eiffel Tower to the Ecole Militaire were originally a parade ground for the officer cadets of the Ecole Militaire (Military School). The area has since been used for horse-racing, balloon ascents and the mass ceremonies to celebrate the anniversary of the Revolution on 14 July. The first ceremony was held in 1790 in the presence of a glum, captive Louis XVI.

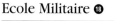

A Paris balloon ascent

Mammoth exhibitions were held here in the late 19th century, among them the 1889 World Fair for which the Eiffel Tower was erected.

Eiffel Tower ⓯

See pp192–3.

No. 29 Avenue Rapp ⓰

75007. **Map** 10 E2. Ⓜ *Pont-de-l'Alma.*

A PRIME EXAMPLE OF Art Nouveau architecture is No. 29 and it won its designer, Jules Lavirotte, first prize at the Concours des Facades de la Ville de Paris in 1901. Its ceramics and brickwork are decorated with animal and flower motifs intermingling with female figures. These are superimposed on a multi-coloured sandstone base to produce a facade that is deliberately erotic, and was certainly subversive in its day. Also worth visiting is Lavirotte's building, complete with watchtower, which can be found in the Square Rapp.

Village Suisse ⓱

Ave de Suffren 75015. **Map** 10 E4.
Ⓜ *Dupleix.* ◯ *10.30am–7pm Thu–Mon.*

THE SWISS government built a mock-Alpine village for the 1900 Universal Exhibition held in the Champ-de-Mars nearby. It was later used as a centre for dealing in secondhand goods. In the 1950s and 1960s antique dealers moved in, and everything became more fashionable and expensive. The village was renovated in the late 1960s.

Ecole Militaire ⓲

1 Pl Joffre 75007. **Map** 10 F4.
Ⓜ *Ecole-Militaire.* **Visits** *by special permission only – contact the Commandant in writing.* 📷

THE ROYAL MILITARY academy of Louis XV was founded in 1751 to educate 500 sons of impoverished officers. It was designed by architect Jacques-Ange Gabriel, and one of the features is the central pavilion. This is a magnificent example of the French Classical style, with eight Corinthian pillars and a quadrangular dome. The interior is decorated in Louis XVI style; of main interest are the chapel and a superb Gabriel-designed wrought-iron banister on the main staircase.

An early cadet at the academy was Napoleon, whose passing-out report stated that "he could go far if the circumstances are right".

A 1751 engraving showing the planning of the Ecole Militaire

UNESCO ⓳

7 Pl de Fontenoy 75007. **Map** 10 F5.
📞 *01 45 68 10 00.* 📠 *01 45 68 10 60 (in English).* Ⓜ *Ségur, Cambronne.* ◯ *9.30am–12.30pm, 2.30pm–5pm Mon–Fri.* ⬤ *public hols & during conference sessions.* 📷 ♿ 📹 🎥
🎭 **Exhibitions, films.**

THIS IS THE headquarters of the United Nations Educational, Scientific and Cultural Organization (UNESCO). The organization's aim is to contribute to international peace and security through education, science and culture.

UNESCO is a treasure-trove of modern art, notably an enormous mural by Pablo Picasso, ceramics designed by Joan Miró and sculptures by Henry Moore.

Moore's *Reclining Figure* at UNESCO (erected 1958)

Eiffel Tower ⑮

ORIGINALLY BUILT to impress visitors to the Universal Exhibition of 1889, the Eiffel Tower (Tour Eiffel) was meant to be a temporary addition to the Paris skyline. Designed by the engineer Gustave Eiffel, it was fiercely decried by 19th-century aesthetes. The author Guy de Maupassant lunched there to avoid seeing it. The world's tallest building until 1931, when New York's Empire State Building was completed, the tower is now the symbol of Paris. Since its recent renovation and installation of new lighting it has never looked better.

Eiffel Tower from the Trocadéro

Ironwork Pattern
According to Eiffel, the complex pattern of pig-iron girders came from the need to stabilize the tower in strong winds. But Eiffel's design quickly won admirers for its pleasing symmetry.

Lift Engine Room
Eiffel emphasized safety over speed when choosing the lifts for the tower.

STAR FEATURES

★ **Eiffel Bust**

★ **Cinémax**

★ **Hydraulic Lift Mechanism**

★ **Viewing Gallery**

★ Cinémax
This small museum tells the history of the tower through a short film. It includes footage of famous personalities who have visited the tower, including Charlie Chaplin, Josephine Baker and Adolf Hitler.

THE DARING AND THE DELUDED

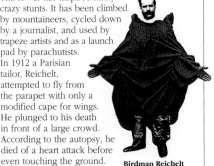

The tower has inspired many crazy stunts. It has been climbed by mountaineers, cycled down by a journalist, and used by trapeze artists and as a launch pad by parachutists.
In 1912 a Parisian tailor, Reichelt, attempted to fly from the parapet with only a modified cape for wings. He plunged to his death in front of a large crowd. According to the autopsy, he died of a heart attack before even touching the ground.

Birdman Reichelt

★ Hydraulic Lift Mechanism
Still in working order, this part of the original 1900 mechanism was automated in 1986.

The third level, 276 m (905 ft) above the ground, can hold 800 people at a time.

VISITORS' CHECKLIST

Champ de Mars. **Map** 10 D3. **C**
01 44 11 23 11. **M** Bir Hakeim.
▦ 42, 69, 72, 82, 87, 91 to
Champ de Mars. **RER** Champ de
Mars. **🅾** Tour Eiffel. **P** on site.
🕐 Sep–Jun: 9.30am–11.30pm; Jul
& Aug 9am–midnight (last adm
1hr before). **🎫 📷 ♿**
limited. **🍴 🎬** **Films, videos.**
W www.eiffel-tower.com

★ **Viewing Gallery**
*On a clear day it is possible to see
for 72 km (45 miles), including a
distant view of Chartres Cathedral.*

Double-Decker Lifts
*During the tourist season, the
limited capacity of the lifts means
that it can take up to a couple of
hours to reach the top. Queuing for
the lifts requires patience and a
good head for heights.*

THE TOWER IN FIGURES
• the top (including the
antennae) is 324 m
(1,063 ft) high
• the top can move in
a curve of 18 cm (7 in)
under the effect of heat
• 1,652 steps to the
third level
• 2.5 million rivets
hold the tower
together
• never sways more
than 7 cm (2.5 in)
• 10,100 tonnes in weight
• 40 tonnes of
paint are
used every
four years

A workman building the tower

The second level is at 115 m
(376 ft), separated from the
first level by 359 steps, or a
few minutes in the lift.

Jules Verne Restaurant is
one of the best restaurants
in Paris, offering superb
food and panoramic views
(see p304).

The first level, at 57 m
(187 ft) high, can be
reached by lift or by
360 steps. There is a
post office here.

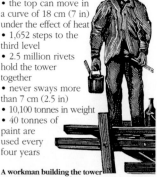

★ **Eiffel Bust**
*Eiffel's (1832–1923)
achievement was
crowned with the Légion
d'Honneur in 1889.
Another honour was the
bust by Antoine
Bourdelle, placed
beneath the tower
in 1929.*

Gilded bronze statues by a number of sculptors decorating the central square of the Palais de Chaillot

CHAILLOT QUARTER

THE VILLAGE of Chaillot was absorbed into Paris in the 19th century and transformed into an area rich in grand Second Empire avenues *(see pp32–3)*, opulent mansions and fascinating museums. Some of the avenues converge on the Place du Trocadéro, renowned for its elegant cafés, which leads on to the Avenue du Président Wilson, with a greater concentration of museums

Sculptures at the base of the Chaillot pool

than any other street in Paris. Many of the area's sumptuous private mansions are occupied by embassies, including the imposing Vatican embassy, and by major company headquarters. Others are celebrated for their once glittering gatherings of distinguished Parisians. To the west is the territory of the *haute bourgeoisie*, one of Paris's most exclusive, if staid, residential neighbourhoods.

SIGHTS AT A GLANCE

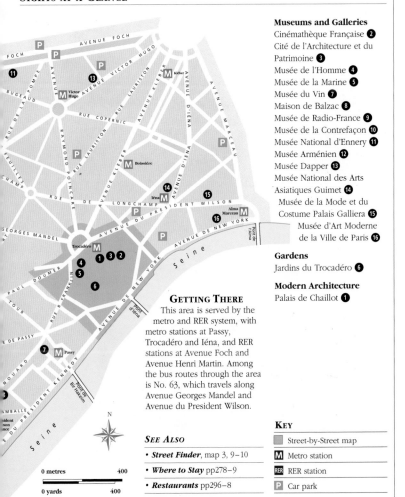

Museums and Galleries
Cinémathèque Française **2**
Cité de l'Architecture et du
Patrimoine **3**
Musée de l'Homme **4**
Musée de la Marine **5**
Musée du Vin **7**
Maison de Balzac **8**
Musée de Radio-France **9**
Musée de la Contrefaçon **10**
Musée National d'Ennery **11**
Musée Arménien **12**
Musée Dapper **13**
Musée National des Arts
Asiatiques Guimet **14**
Musée de la Mode et du
Costume Palais Galliera **15**
Musée d'Art Moderne
de la Ville de Paris **16**

Gardens
Jardins du Trocadéro **6**

Modern Architecture
Palais de Chaillot **1**

GETTING THERE
This area is served by the metro and RER system, with metro stations at Passy, Trocadéro and Iéna, and RER stations at Avenue Foch and Avenue Henri Martin. Among the bus routes through the area is No. 63, which travels along Avenue Georges Mandel and Avenue du President Wilson.

SEE ALSO

KEY
	Street-by-Street map
M	Metro station
RER	RER station
P	Car park

Street-by-Street: Chaillot

THE CHAILLOT HILL, with its superb position overlooking the Seine, was the site chosen by Napoleon for "the biggest and most extraordinary" palace that was to be built for his son – but by the time of his downfall only a few ramparts had been completed. Today, the monumental Palais de Chaillot, with its two massive curved wings, stands on the site. From the terrace in front of the Palais there is a magnificent view over the Trocadéro gardens and the Seine to the Eiffel Tower.

The statue of Marshal Ferdinand Foch, who led the Allies to victory in 1918, was unveiled on 11 November 1951. It was built by Robert Wlérick and Raymond Martin to commemorate the centenary of Foch's birth and the 33rd anniversary of the 1918 Armistice.

Metro Trocadéro

The Place du Trocadéro was created for the Universal Exhibition of 1878. Initially it was known as the Place du Roi-de-Rome, in honour of Napoleon's son.

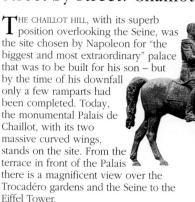

★ **Musée de la Marine**
While concentrating on France's maritime history, this museum also has exhibits of navigational instruments ❺

Palais de Chaillot
This Neo-Classical building was constructed for the World Fair of 1937. It replaced the Palais du Trocadéro, which was built in 1878 ❶

★ **Musée de l'Homme**
This chair from Benin is just one of the many artefacts from Africa that the museum possesses ❹

Cité de l'Architecture et du Patrimoine
This vast complex will soon house an Architecture Museum, a school and various heritage organisations. ❸

The Théâtre National de Chaillot, beneath the terrace, includes a multi-purpose cultural centre and a modern 1,200-seat theatre. *(See pp330–1.)*

LOCATOR MAP
See Central Paris Map pp12–13

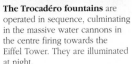

★ **Cinémathèque Française**
Paris's main film institute screens old movies, such as the 1956 classic The Red Balloon, *directed by Albert Lamorisse* ❷

The Trocadéro fountains are operated in sequence, culminating in the massive water cannons in the centre firing towards the Eiffel Tower. They are illuminated at night.

The Pont d'Iéna was built by Napoleon to celebrate his victory in 1806 over the Prussians at Jena (Iéna) in Prussia. It was widened in 1937 to complement the building of the Palais de Chaillot.

Jardins du Trocadéro
The present layout of the gardens was created by R Lardat after the World Fair of 1937 ❻

KEY

— — — Suggested route

0 metres	100
0 yards	100

STAR SIGHTS

★ Cinémathèque

★ Musée de l'Homme

★ Musée de la Marine

Trocadéro fountains in front of the Palais de Chaillot

Palais de Chaillot ❶

17 Pl du Trocadéro 75016.
Map 9 C2. **M** *Trocadéro.*
🕒 *9.45am–5.15pm Wed–Mon.*
🍴 🛒 🚻

Tʜᴇ ᴘᴀʟᴀɪꜱ, with its huge, curved colonnaded wings each culminating in an immense pavilion, houses four museums, a theatre and the Cinémathèque. Designed in Neo-Classical style for the 1937 Paris Exhibition by Azéma, Louis-Auguste Boileau and Jacques Carlu, it is adorned with sculptures and bas-reliefs. On the walls of the pavilions there are gold inscriptions by the poet and essayist Paul Valéry.

The *parvis*, or square, situated between the two pavilions is decorated with large bronze sculptures and ornamental pools. On the terrace in front of the *parvis*

stand two bronzes, *Apollo* by Henri Bouchard and *Hercules* by Pommier. Stairways lead from the terrace to the Théâtre National de Chaillot *(see pp330–31)*, which, after World War II, enjoyed huge fame for its avant-garde productions.

Cinémathèque Française ❷

Palais de Chaillot, 7 Ave Albert de Mun 75016. **Map** 10 D2. **C** 01 40 22 09 79. 🎬 01 56 26 01 01 for screenings. **M** *Trocadéro, Iéna.* 🎭 *See* ***Entertainment*** *pp340-341.*

Dᴇᴠᴀꜱᴛᴀᴛᴇᴅ ʙʏ ꜰɪʀᴇ in 1997, this magnificent film library has now been restored and reopened. Its archive contains the world's largest selection of film classics. Frequent retrospectives offer an opportunity to catch some

of the all-time screen greats (see p341 for address of one of its two cinemas). The Cinémathèque and the Musée du Cinéma are due to move to the Maison du Cinema in Rue de Bercy by 2003.

Church model from Bagneux, Cité de l'Architecture et du Patrimoine

Cité de l'Architecture et du Patrimoine ❸

Palais de Chaillot, Pl du Trocadéro 75016. **Map** 9 C2. **C** 01 44 05 39 10. **M** *Trocadéro.* 🕒 *temporary exhibitions only; permanent collections not till 2003.* 🎭 📷 🍴 🚻

Vɪᴏʟʟᴇᴛ-ʟᴇ-Dᴜᴄ's inspired Musée des Monuments Français (1789) which was formerly housed here, will soon be visible again as part of the vast new architecture complex currently under creation. It will include an enlarged Architecture Museum, with extended exhibition spaces, the famous Ecole de Chaillot "heritage" school, a governmental architectural agency, a library and archive centre and various heritage organizations.

Sequence from the film *Journey to the Moon* directed by Méliés in 1902

Musée de l'Homme ④

Palais de Chaillot, 17 Pl du Trocadéro 75016. **Map** 9 C2. **[** 01 44 05 72 72. **M** Trocadéro. ◯ 9.45am–5.15pm Wed–Mon. ● public hols. 🖼 📹 2.30pm Sat. *Exhibitions*, *films*. 🍴 🛍 🚻

SITUATED IN THE west wing of the Chaillot palace, this museum traces human evolution through a series of anthropological, archaeological and ethnological displays. The anthropology section covers subjects as diverse as tattooing, mummification and head-shrinking.

The African exhibits are particularly striking, with frescoes from the Sahara, Central African sculpture, magical figures and musical instruments. Other highlights include Asian costumes, and a gigantic Easter Island head in the Oceania section.

Gabon mask at Musée de l'Homme

Musée de la Marine ⑤

Palais de Chaillot, 17 Pl du Trocadéro 75016. **Map** 9 C2. **[** 01 53 65 69 69. **M** Trocadéro. ◯ 10am–6pm Wed–Mon. ● 1 Jan, 1 May, 25 Dec. 🖼 🚻 *Films, videos*. *Reference library*: appointment only.

FRENCH MARITIME history from the days of the royal wooden warships to today's aircraft carriers and nuclear submarines is told through wonderfully exact scale models (most of them two centuries old), mementoes of naval heroes, paintings and navigational instruments. The museum was set up by Charles X in

Relief outside the Maritime Museum

1827, and was then moved to the Chaillot palace in 1943. Exhibits include Napoleon's barge, models of the fleet he assembled at Boulogne-sur-Mer in 1805 for his planned invasion of Britain, and displays on underwater exploration and fishing vessels.

Jardins du Trocadéro ⑥

75016. **Map** 10 D2. **M** Trocadéro.

THESE LOVELY gardens cover 10 ha (25 acres). Their centrepiece is a long rectangular ornamental pool, bordered by stone and bronze-gilt statues, which look spectacular at night when the fountains are illuminated. The statues include *Man* by P Traverse and *Woman* by G Braque, *Bull* by P Jouve and *Horse* by G Guyot. On either side of the pool, the slopes of the Chaillot hill gently lead down to the Seine and the Pont d'Iéna. There is a freshwater aquarium in the northeast corner of the gardens, which are richly laid out with trees, walkways, small streams and bridges.

Musée du Vin – Caveau des Echansons ⑦

Rue des Eaux, 5 Sq Charles Dickens 75016. **Map** 9 C3. **[** 01 45 25 63 26. **M** Passy. ◯ 10am–6pm. Tue–Sun. ● 24 Dec–1 Jan. 🚫 🛍 🚻 🖼 groups only. 🍴 lunchtime only.

WAXWORK FIGURES illustrate the history of winemaking in these vaulted medieval cellars, once used by the monks of Passy. The exhibits include a collection of old wine bottles and glasses, as well as an array of scientific instruments that were used in the wine-making and bottling processes. There is also a wine bar, wine for sale and tours which include a wine-tasting session.

Bridge in the Trocadéro gardens

Maison de Balzac ⑧

47 Rue Raynouard 75016. **Map** 9 B3. **[** 01 55 74 41 80. **M** Passy, La Muette. ◯ 10am–5.40pm Tue–Sun (last adm: 5.30pm). ● public hols. 🖼 📷 🛍 🚻

THE AUTHOR Honoré de Balzac lived here from 1840 to 1847 under a false name, Monsieur de Brugnol, to avoid his numerous creditors. During this time he wrote many of his most famous novels, among them *La Cousine Bette* (1846).

The house now contains a reference library, with some of his original works, and a museum with memorabilia from his life. Many of the rooms have drawings and paintings portraying Balzac's family and close friends. The Madame Hanska room is devoted to the memory of the Russian woman who corresponded with Balzac for 18 years and was his wife for the five months before his death in 1850.

The house has a back entrance leading into the Rue Berton, which was used to evade unwelcome callers. Rue Berton, with its ivy-covered walls, has retained much of its old, country-like charm.

Plaque marking Balzac's house

Radio (1955) in radio museum

Musée de Radio-France ❾

116 Ave du Président-Kennedy 75016. **Map** 9 B4. 📞 *01 56 40 15 16.* Ⓜ *Ranelagh.* ⬤ *for tours only, Mon–Sat.* ⬤ *public hols.* 🚫 ⬤ 📷 *10.30–11.30am, 2.30–4.30pm.* ⓦ *www.radio-france.fr*

RADIO-FRANCE HOUSE is an impressive building designed by Henri Bernard in 1963 as the headquarters of the state-run Radio-France. The largest single structure in France, it is made up of three incomplete concentric circular constructions with a rectangular tower. The building covers an area of 2 ha (5 acres).

Here, in the 70-odd studios and main public auditorium, French radio programmes are produced. The museum traces the history of communications from the first Chappe telegraph of 1793 to the latest multimedia developments in radio-listening via the internet. It also gives a fascinating insight into how radio programmes are made.

Musée de la Contrefaçon ❿

16 Rue de la Faisanderie 75016. **Map** 3 A5. 📞 *01 56 26 14 00.* Ⓜ *Porte Dauphine.* ⬤ *2–5.30pm Tue–Sun.* ⬤ *public hols.* 📷 ▣ ⓦ *www.unifab.com*

FRENCH COGNAC and perfume producers, and the luxury trade in general, have been plagued for years by counterfeiters operating around the world. This museum was set up by the manufacturers' union and illustrates the history of this type of fraud, which has been going on since Roman times. Among the impressive display of forgeries are copies of Louis Vuitton luggage, Cartier watches and fake wine from the Narbonne region. The museum also has a display on the fate awaiting anyone who may be tempted to imitate a product.

Musée National d'Ennery ⓫

59 Ave Foch 75016. **Map** 3 B5. 📞 *01 45 53 57 96.* Ⓜ *Porte Dauphine.* ⬤ *for renovation until further notice.* ▣

THIS MANSION, which dates from the Second Empire period, houses two highly personal museums of precious *objets d'art*, the Musée d'Ennery and the Musée Arménien (see below), both currently closed for renovation. The former contains the huge collection of Chinese and Japanese items assembled by Adolphe d'Ennery, the 19th-century dramatist. Dating from the 17th to 19th centuries, the display includes human and animal figures, Japanese ceramic boxes, furniture and hundreds of *netsuke* – small, carved belt ornaments made of bone, wood or ivory.

Chinese vase (circa 18th century), Musée d'Ennery

Musée Arménien ⓬

59 Ave Foch 75016. **Map** 3 B5. 📞 *01 45 53 57 96.* Ⓜ *Porte Dauphine.* ⬤ *for renovation until further notice.*

THE GROUND FLOOR of No. 59 Avenue Foch houses the Armenian museum, founded after World War II. Despite its small size the collection has many fascinating treasures, including church plates, exquisite miniatures, silverware, ceramics, carpets and contemporary paintings.

Khmer art in the Musée National des Arts Asiatiques Guimet

Musée Dapper ⓭

50, avenue Victor Hugo, 75116. 📞 *01 45 00 01 50.* Ⓜ *Victor-Hugo.* ⬤ *11am-7pm daily.* 📷 *(free Wed).*

NOT JUST A MUSEUM, but a world-class ethnographic research centre called the Dapper Foundation, this is France's premier showcase of African art and culture. Located in an attractive building with an "African" garden, it is a treasure house of vibrant colour and powerful, evocative work from the black nations. The emphasis is on pre-colonial folk arts, with sculpture, carvings, and tribal work, but there is later art too. The highlight is tribal masks, with a dazzling, extraordinary array of richly carved religious, ritual and funerary masks, as well as theatrical ones used for comic, magical or symbolic performances, some dating back to the 12th century. Anthropologists, locals and tourists mingle here for the themed exhibitions and events.

Armenian crown (19th century)

Musée National des Arts Asiatiques Guimet ⑭

6 Pl d'Iéna 75116. **Map** 10 D1.
📞 01 56 52 53 00. M Iéna.
🕐 10am–6pm Wed–Mon. 🖼 🚫
♿ 🛍 🍴 🎧 🛍 Panthéon
Bouddhique (additional galleries) at
19 Ave d'Iéna 📞 01 40 73 88 00.
W www.museeguimet.fr

ONE OF THE world's leading museums of Asian art, the Musée Guimet has the finest collection of Khmer (Cambodian) art in the West. It was originally set up in Lyon in 1879 by the industrialist and orientalist Emile Guimet, to house his collection of Chinese and Japanese art.

Moved to Paris in 1884, it has just re-opened after extensive renovation, and now meticulously represents every artistic tradition from Afghanistan to India, to China and Japan, to Korea and Vietnam and the rest of southeast Asia. With over 45,000 artworks, the museum is acclaimed for some especially unusual collections, including the Cambodian Angkor Wat sculptures and 1600 displays of Himalayan Art. Other highlights include Chinese bronzes and lacquerware, and many statues of Buddha from Japan, India, Vietnam and Indonesia. It also houses an Asian research centre.

Gabriel Forestier's sculpted doors, Musée d'Art Moderne

Musée de la Mode et du Costume Palais Galliera ⑮

10 Ave Pierre 1er de Serbie 75116.
Map 10 E1. 📞 01 56 52 86 00.
M Iéna, Alma Marceau. 🕐 for
exhibitions only, 10am–6pm Tue–Sun.
🖼 **Children's room**.
W www.paris-france.org/musées

DEVOTED TO THE evolution of fashion, this museum is housed in the Renaissance-style palace built for the Duchesse Maria de Ferrari Galliera in 1892. The collection has more than 100,000 outfits, from the 18th century to the present day. Some, from more recent times, have been donated by such fashionable women as Baronne Hélène de Rothschild and Princess Grace of Monaco. Eminent couturiers such as Balmain and Balenciaga have donated their designs to the museum. Owing to the fragility of the garments, they are displayed in rotation in two exhibitions per year. These highlight a particular couturier's career or explore a single theme.

Musée d'Art Moderne de la Ville de Paris ⑯

Palais de Tokyo, 11 Ave du Président-Wilson 75016. **Map** 10 E1. 📞 01 53 67 40 00. M Iéna. 🕐 10am–5.30pm (noon–midnight for the Site de Création Contemporaine) Tue–Sun.
🖼 ♿ 🛍 🛍 🍴 Films.
W www.palaisdetokyo.com

THIS LARGE, lively museum is the municipality's own renowned collection of modern art, covering all major 20th century trends (the 21st century will be included). The museum occupies the vast east wing of the Palais de Tokyo, built for the 1937 World Fair. One of the highlights is Raoul Dufy's gigantic mural *La Fée Electricité*. Also notable are the Cubists, Amadeo Modigliani, Georges Rouault and The Fauves, especially Henri Matisse, whose *La Danse* is here in both versions. Much interesting and innovative contemporary work is shown here, as in the new **Site de Création Contemporaine** in the west wing opposite.

Garden and rear facade of the Palais Galliera

CHAMPS-ELYSÉES

TWO GREAT STREETS dominate this area: the Avenue des Champs-Elysées and the Rue St-Honoré. The former is the capital's most famous thoroughfare. Its breadth is spectacular. The pavements are wide and their cafés, cinemas and shops attract throngs of people, who come to eat and shop, but also to see and to be seen. Rond Point des Champs-Elysées is the pretty end, with shady chestnut trees and pavements colourfully bordered by flower beds. The avenue is a place of great parades, but also of stunning street fashion and a hedonistic lifestyle. Luxury and political power are nearby. Five-star hotels, fine restaurants and upmarket shops line the streets and avenues radiating off the Champs-Elysées. And along the Rue St-Honoré are the impressive, heavily guarded Palais de l'Elysée, the sumptuous town mansions of business chiefs, and the many embassies and consulates.

Ornate lamp-post on Pont Alexandre III

SIGHTS AT A GLANCE

Historic Buildings and Streets
Palais de l'Elysée **5**
Avenue Montaigne **6**
Avenue des Champs-Elysées **8**
Place Charles de Gaulle (l'Etoile) **9**

Monuments
Arc de Triomphe pp208 – 9 **10**

Bridges
Pont Alexandre III **1**

Museums and Galleries
Grand Palais **2**
Palais de la Découverte **3**
Petit Palais **4**
Musée Jacquemart-André **7**

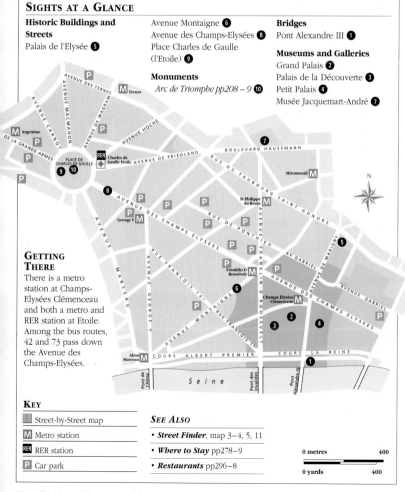

GETTING THERE

There is a metro station at Champs-Elysées Clémenceau and both a metro and RER station at Etoile. Among the bus routes, 42 and 73 pass down the Avenue des Champs-Elysées.

KEY

▢ Street-by-Street map
Ⓜ Metro station
RER RER station
Ⓟ Car park

SEE ALSO

• *Street Finder*, map 3–4, 5, 11
• *Where to Stay* pp278–9
• *Restaurants* pp296–8

| 0 metres | | 400 |
| 0 yards | | 400 |

View of the Arc de Triomphe at night

Street-by-Street: Champs-Elysées

THE FORMAL GARDENS that line the Champs-Elysées from the Place de la Concorde to the Rond-Point have changed little since they were laid out by the architect Jacques Hittorff in 1838. They were used as the setting for the World Fair of 1855, which included the Palais de l'Industrie, Paris's response to London's Crystal Palace. The Palais was later replaced by the Grand Palais and Petit Palais, which were created as a showpiece of the Third Republic for the Universal Exhibition of 1900. They sit on either side of an impressive vista that stretches from the Place Clémenceau across the elegant curve of the Pont Alexandre III to the Invalides.

The Théâtre du Rond-Point is the home of the Renaud-Barrault Company. There are plaques on the back door of the theatre representing Napoleon's campaigns.

Metro Franklin D Roosevelt Ⓜ

Avenue Montaigne
Christian Dior and other haute couture houses are based in this chic avenue **❻**

★ Grand Palais
Designed by Charles Girault, this grand 19th-century exhibition hall is still used for major exhibitions **❷**

The Lasserre restaurant is decorated in the style of a luxurious ocean liner from the 1930s.

LASSERRE

STAR SIGHTS

- ★ **Avenue des Champs-Elysées**
- ★ **Grand Palais**
- ★ **Petit Palais**
- ★ **Pont Alexandre III**

Palais de la Découverte
Outside this museum of scientific discoveries is a pair of equestrian statues **❸**

KEY

– – – Suggested route

0 metres   100
0 yards   100

★ **Avenue des Champs-Elysées**
This was the setting for the victory parades following the two World Wars, and for the bicentennial parade in 1989 ❽

LOCATOR MAP
See Central Paris Map pp12–13

Metro Champs-Elysées-Clémenceau

To the Place de la Concorde

The Jardins des Champs-Elysées, with their fountains, flowerbeds, paths and pleasure pavilions, became very popular towards the end of the 19th century. Fashionable Parisians, including Marcel Proust, often came here.

★ **Petit Palais**
The art collections of the city of Paris are housed here. They contain a range of objects from antique sculptures to Impressionist paintings ❹

To the Invalides

★ **Pont Alexandre III**
The bridge's four columns help to anchor the piers that absorb the immense forces generated by such a large single-span structure ❶

Pont Alexandre III ❶

75008. **Map** 11 A1. Ⓜ *Champs-Elysées-Clémenceau.*

THIS IS PARIS's prettiest bridge with its exuberant Art Nouveau decoration of lamps, cherubs, nymphs and winged horses at either end. It was built between 1896 and 1900, in time for the Universal Exhibition and it was named after Tsar Alexander III (father of Nicholas II) who laid the foundation stone in October 1896.

The style of the bridge reflects that of the Grand Palais, to which it leads on the Right Bank. The construction of the bridge is a marvel of 19th-century engineering, consisting of a 6-m (18-ft) high single-span steel arch across the Seine. The design was subject to strict controls that prevented the bridge from obscuring the view of the Champs-Elysées or the Invalides. So today you can still enjoy magnificent views from here.

Pont Alexandre III

Grand Palais ❷

Porte A, Ave Eisenhower 75008. **Map** 11 A1. ☎ *01 44 13 17 30.* Ⓜ *Champs-Elysées-Clémenceau.* ◯ *1pm–8pm (10pm Wed) Wed–Mon (mornings by appt).* ⬛ Ⓓ ♿ ▯ *Wed pm & Sat pm* ▯ ▯ ▯

BUILT AT THE SAME time as the Petit Palais and the Pont Alexandre III, the exterior of this massive palace combines an imposing Classical stone facade with a riot of Art Nouveau ironwork. It has a splendid glass roof,

and Récipon's colossal bronze statues of flying horses and chariots at its four corners. The building looks best at night, when the glass roof glows with the lights from inside and the statues are silhouetted against the sky. Sadly, this has not occurred since 1993, when the great hall was closed for renovation awaiting transformation into nobody quite knows what. Temporary exhibitions are however still held in the Galeries Nationales du Grand Palais. The basement houses a major police station.

Palais de la Découverte

Palais de la Découverte ❸

Ave Franklin D Roosevelt 75008. **Map** 11 A1. ☎ *01 56 43 20 21.* Ⓜ *Franklin D Roosevelt.* ◯ *9.30am–6pm Tue–Sat; 10am–7pm Sun.* ⬤ *1 Jan, 1 May, 14 Jul, 15 Aug, 25 Dec.* ⬛ Ⓞ *by permission.* ▯ ▯ Ⓦ *www.palais-decouverte.fr*

OPENED IN A WING of the Grand Palais for the World Fair of 1937, this museum of scientific discoveries was an immediate success and has continued to be popular ever since. The displays explain the basics of all the sciences.

Entrance to the Petit Palais

Petit Palais ❹

Ave Winston Churchill 75008. **Map** 11 B1. ☎ *01 42 65 12 73.* Ⓜ *Champs-Elysées-Clémenceau.* ⬤ *for renovation until 2003.* ⬛ Ⓞ Ⓥ *for exhibitions.*

BUILT FOR the Universal Exhibition in 1900, to stage a major display of French art, this jewel of a building now houses the Musée des Beaux-Arts de la Ville de Paris. Arranged around a pretty semi-circular courtyard and garden, the palace is similar in style to the Grand Palais, and has Ionic columns, a grand porch and a dome which echoes that of the Invalides across the river.

The exhibits are divided into sections: the Dutuit Collection of medieval and Renaissance *objets d'art*, paintings and drawings; the Tuck Collection of 18th-century furniture and *objets d'art*; and the City of Paris collections of works by the French artists Jean Ingres, Eugène Delacroix and Gustave Courbet, the landscape painters of the Barbizon School and the Impressionists.

GRAND PALAIS

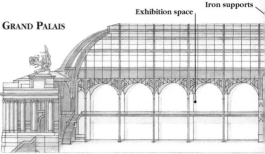

Exhibition space   Iron supports

Palais de l'Elysée ❺

55 Rue du Faubourg-St-Honoré
75008. **Map** 5 B5. Ⓜ St-Philippe-du-
Roule. **Not open** to the public.

S ET AMID SPLENDID English-
style gardens, the Elysée
Palace was built in 1718 and
has been the official
residence of the President of
the Republic since 1873.
In the 19th century it
was occupied by
Napoleon's sister,
Caroline, and her
husband, Murat.
Two charming
rooms have been
preserved from this
period: the Salon
Murat and the Salon
d'Argent. General de
Gaulle used to give
press conferences in
the Hall of Mirrors.
Today, the
President's
modernized
apartments can be found on
the first floor opposite the
Rue de l'Elysée.

Elysée guard

Avenue Montaigne ❻

75008. **Map** 10 F1. Ⓜ Franklin D
Roosevelt.

I N THE 19TH century this
avenue was famous for its
dance halls and its Winter
Garden, where Parisians went
to hear Adolphe Sax play his
newly-invented saxophone.
Today it is still one of Paris's
most fashionable
streets, bustling with
restaurants, cafés,
hotels and smart
boutiques.

Inside the Musée Jacquemart-André

Musée Jacquemart-André ❼

158 Blvd Haussmann 75008. **Map** 5
A4. ☎ 01 45 62 39 94. Ⓜ Miromesnil,
St-Philippe-du-Roule. ◷ 10am– 6pm
daily. 🅿 ⊘ 🛈 📷 🛒
Ⓦ www.musee-jacquemart-andre.com

T HIS MUSEUM is known for
its fine collection of Italian
Renaissance and French 18th-
century works of art, as well
as its beautiful frescoes by
Tiepolo. Highlights include
works by Mantegna, Uccello's
masterpiece *St George and
the Dragon* (about 1435),
paintings by Boucher and
Fragonard and 18th-century
tapestries and furniture.

Avenue des Champs-Elysées ❽

75008. **Map** 5 A5. Ⓜ Franklin D
Roosevelt, George V.

P ARIS'S MOST famous and
popular thoroughfare had
its beginnings in about 1667,
when the landscape garden

designer, André Le Nôtre,
extended the royal view from
the Tuileries by creating a
tree-lined avenue which
eventually became known as
the Champs-Elysées (Elysian
Fields). It has been the
"triumphal way" (as the
French call it) ever since the
home-coming of Napoleon's
body from St Helena in 1840.
With the addition of cafés and
restaurants in the second half
of the 19th century, the
Champs-Elysées became the
place in which to be seen.

Place Charles de Gaulle (l'Etoile) ❾

75008. **Map** 4 D4. Ⓜ Charles de
Gaulle-Etoile.

K NOWN AS the Place de
l'Etoile until the death of
Charles de Gaulle in 1969, the
area is still referred to simply
as l'Etoile, the star. The
present *place* was laid out in
accordance with Baron
Haussmann's plans of 1854
(see pp 32–3). For motorists, it
is the ultimate challenge.

Arc de Triomphe from the west

Arc de Triomphe ❿

See pp208–9.

Glass cupola

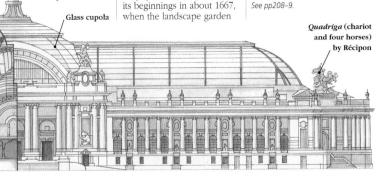

Quadriga (chariot
and four horses)
by Récipon

Arc de Triomphe ⑩

The east facade of the Arc de Triomphe

AFTER HIS greatest victory, the Battle of Austerlitz in 1805, Napoleon promised his men, "You shall go home beneath triumphal arches." The first stone of what was to become the world's most famous triumphal arch was laid the following year. But disruptions to architect Jean Chalgrin's plans and the demise of Napoleonic power delayed the completion of this monumental building until 1836. Standing 50 m (164 ft) high, the Arc is now the customary starting point for victory celebrations and parades.

Thirty shields just below the Arc's roof each bear the name of a victorious Napoleonic battle fought in either Europe or Africa.

East facade

The frieze was executed by Rude, Brun, Jacquet, Laitié, Caillouette and Seurre the Elder. This east facade shows the departure of the French armies for new campaigns. The west side shows their return.

The Battle of Aboukir, a bas-relief by Seurre the Elder, depicts a scene of Napoleon's victory over the Turkish army in 1799.

Triumph of Napoleon
J P Cortot's high-relief celebrates the Treaty of Vienna peace agreement of 1810.

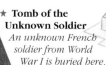

STAR FEATURES

★ **Departure of the Volunteers in 1792**

★ **Tomb of the Unknown Soldier**

★ **Tomb of the Unknown Soldier**
An unknown French soldier from World War I is buried here.

TIMELINE

1806 Napoleon commissions Chalgrin to build triumphal Arc

1836 Louis-Philippe completes the Arc

1885 Victor Hugo's body lies in state under the Arc

1944 Liberation of Paris. De Gaulle leads the crowd from the Arc

1800	1850	1900	1950

1840 Napoleon's cortège passes under the Arc

1815 Downfall of Napoleon. Work on Arc ceases

1919 Victory parade of Allied armies through the Arc

NAPOLEON'S NUPTIAL PARADE

Napoleon divorced Josephine in 1809 because she was unable to bear him children. A diplomatic marriage was arranged in 1810 with Marie-Louise, daughter of the Austrian emperor. Napoleon was determined to impress his bride by going through the Arc on their way to the wedding at the Louvre, but work had barely been started. So Chalgrin built a full-scale mock-up of the arch on the site for the couple to pass beneath.

VISITORS' CHECKLIST

Pl Charles de Gaulle. **Map** 4 D4.
01 55 37 73 77. M RER *Charles de Gaulle–Etoile.* 22, 30, 31, 73, 92 to Pl C de Gaulle.
P *off Pl C de Gaulle.*
Museum Apr–Sep: 9.30am–11pm daily; Oct–Mar: 10am–10.30pm daily (last adm 30 mins earlier). 1 Jan, 1 May, 14 Jul, 11 Nov, 25 Dec.

The viewing platform affords one of the best views in Paris, overlooking the grand Champs-Elysées on one side. Beyond the other side is La Défense.

General Marceau's Funeral
Marceau defeated the Austrians in 1795, only to be killed the following year, still fighting them.

The Battle of Austerlitz by Gechter shows Napoleon's army breaking up the ice on the Satschan lake in Austria to drown thousands of enemy troops.

Officers of the Imperial Army are listed on the walls of the smaller arches.

Entrance to museum

★ **Departure of the Volunteers in 1792**
François Rude's work shows citizens leaving to defend the nation.

Place Charles de Gaulle
Twelve avenues radiate from the Arc at the centre. Some bear the names of important French military leaders, such as Avenues Marceau and Foch.
(See pp32–3.)

OPÉRA QUARTER

THE OPERA QUARTER bustles with bankers and stockbrokers, newspapermen and shoppers, theatre-goers and sightseers. Much of its 19th-century grandeur survives in the Grands Boulevards of Baron Haussmann's urban design. These are still a favourite with thousands of Parisian and foreign promenaders, drawn by the profusion of shops and department stores, which range from the exclusively expensive to the popular.

Les Coulisses de l'Opéra (1889) by J Beraud

Much more of the area's older character is found in the many *passages*, delightful narrow shopping arcades with steel and glass roofs, remnants of another age. Fashion's bad boy, Jean-Paul Gaultier, has a shop in the smartest one, Galerie Vivienne. But more authentically old-style Parisian are the Passage des Panoramas and the Passage Jouffroy, the Passage Verdeau, with its old cameras and comics, and the tiny Passage des Princes, a pipe-smoker's dream. Two of the city's finest food shops are in the area. Fauchon and Hédiard are noted for their mouthwatering displays of costly mustards, jams, spices, pâtés and sauces. The area still has a reputation as an important press centre, although *Le Monde* has recently moved out, and it has a history of cinema and theatre. It was here in 1895 that the Lumière brothers held the world's first public film show and where the Opéra de Paris Garnier provided the setting for grand theatrical events.

SIGHTS AT A GLANCE

Historic Buildings and Streets
Place de la Madeleine ❷
Les Grands Boulevards ❸
Palais de la Bourse ❾
Avenue de l'Opéra ⓬

Churches
La Madeleine ❶

Opera Houses
Opéra de Paris Garnier ❹

Museums and Galleries
Musée de l'Opéra ❺
Musée Grévin ❼

Musée du Cabinet des Médailles et des Antiques ❿
Bibliothèque Nationale ⓫

Shops
Drouot (Hôtel des Ventes) ❻
Les Galeries ❽

GETTING THERE
This area is served by the metro and RER systems. Metro lines 3, 7 and 8 serve the station at the Opéra, line 14 stops at Madeleine and the RER Line A stops at Auber. Among the bus routes passing through the area, 42 and 52 travel along Boulevard Madeleine, and 21, 27 and 29 along Avenue de l'Opéra.

SEE ALSO
• *Street Finder*, map 5–6
• *Where to Stay* pp278–9
• *Restaurants* pp296–8

KEY
▭	Street-by-Street map
Ⓜ	Metro station
RER	RER station
Ⓟ	Car park

0 metres 400
0 yards 400

Lamppost statues of the vestal virgins outside the Opéra de Paris Garnier

Street-by-Street: Opéra Quarter

IT HAS BEEN SAID that if you sit for long enough at the Café de la Paix (opposite the Opéra de Paris Garnier) the whole world will pass by. During the day, the area is a mixture of commerce – France's top three banks are based here – and tourism. The shops range from the chic, in the elegant Place de l'Opéra, to the more popular, such as the Marks & Spencer store just off Place Diaghilev. In the evening, the theatres and cinemas attract a totally different crowd, and the cafés along the Boulevard des Capucines throb with life.

Statue by Gurnery on the Opéra

Place de la Madeleine
On the north side of the square, the windows of the Fauchon shop are filled with food from around the world ❷

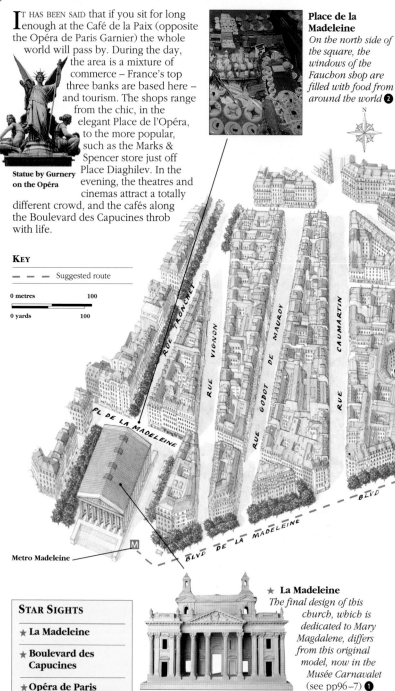

KEY

– – – Suggested route

0 metres 100
0 yards 100

Metro Madeleine

RUE TRONCHET
RUE VIGNON
RUE GODOT DE MAUROY
RUE CAUMARTIN
PL DE LA MADELEINE
BLVD DE LA MADELEINE
BLVD D

★ La Madeleine
The final design of this church, which is dedicated to Mary Magdalene, differs from this original model, now in the Musée Carnavalet (see pp96–7) ❶

★ **Opéra de Paris Garnier**
With a mixture of styles ranging from Classical to Baroque, this building from 1875 has come to symbolize the opulence of the Second Empire ❹

LOCATOR MAP
See Central Paris Map pp12–13

Metro Chaussée d'Antin

Musée de l'Opéra
Famous artists' work is often shown in temporary exhibition rooms ❺

The Place de l'Opéra
was designed by Baron Haussmann and is one of Paris's busiest intersections.

Metro Opéra

The Café de la Paix maintains its old-fashioned ways and still has its 19th-century decor, designed by Garnier. *(See p311.)*

Harry's Bar was named after Harry MacElhone, a bartender who bought the bar in 1913. Past regulars have included F Scott Fitzgerald and Ernest Hemingway.

★ **Boulevard des Capucines**
At No. 14 a plaque tells of the world's first public screening of a movie, by the Lumière brothers in 1895; it took place in the Salon Indien, a room in the Grand Café ❸

Charles Marochetti's *Mary Magdalene Ascending to Heaven* (1837) behind the high altar of La Madeleine

La Madeleine ❶

Pl de la Madeleine 75008. **Map** 5 C5.
📞 *01 44 51 69 00.* Ⓜ *Madeleine.*
🕐 *7.30am–7pm daily (9am Sat).*
✝ *frequent.* **Concerts.** 📷 📱
See **Entertainment** *pp333–4.*

THIS CHURCH, which is dedicated to Mary Magdalene, is one of the best-known buildings in Paris because of its prominent location and great size. It stands at one end of the curve of the Grands Boulevards and is the architectural counterpoint of the Palais-Bourbon (home of the Assemblée Nationale, the French parliament) across the river. It was started in 1764 but not consecrated until 1845. There were proposals to convert it into a parliament, a bank and a Temple of Glory to Napoleon's army.

The building that stands today is based on Barthélemy Vignon's design for Napoleon's Temple of Glory commissioned in 1806 after the Battle of Jena (Iéna). A colonnade of 64 ft high (20 m) Corinthian columns encircles the building and supports a sculptured frieze. The bas-reliefs on the bronze doors are by Henri de Triqueti and show the Ten Commandments.

The inside is decorated with marble and gilt, and has some fine sculpture, notably François Rude's *Baptism of Christ*.

Place de la Madeleine ❷

75008. **Map** 5 C5.
Ⓜ *Madeleine.* **Flower market** 🕐 *8am–7.30pm Tue–Sun.*

THE PLACE de la Madeleine was created at the same time as the Madeleine church. It is a food lover's paradise, with many shops specializing in luxuries such

Fauchon tin

as truffles, champagne, caviar and hand-made chocolates. Fauchon, the millionaires' supermarket, is situated at No. 26 and stocks more than 20,000 items *(see pp322–3).* The large house at No. 9 is where Marcel Proust spent his childhood. To the east of La Madeleine is a small flower market *(see p326).*

Scenery backdrop operated by pulley

OPÉRA DE PARIS GARNIER

Backstage area   **Stage**

Les Grands Boulevards ❸

75002 & 75009. **Map** 6 D5–7C5.
Ⓜ *Madeleine, Opéra, Richelieu-Drouot, Grands Boulevards.*

EIGHT BROAD boulevards – Madeleine, Capucines, Italiens, Montmartre, Poissonière, Bonne Nouvelle, St-Denis and St-Martin – run from La Madeleine to the Place de la République. They were constructed in the 17th century to turn obsolete city fortifications into fashionable promenades – *boulevard* came from the Middle Dutch *bulwerc*, which means bulwark or rampart. The boulevards became so famous in the 19th century that the name *boulevardier* was coined for one who cuts a figure on the boulevards.

Around the Madeleine church and the Opéra it is still possible to gain an impression of what the Grands Boulevards looked like in their heyday, lined with cafés and chic shops. Elsewhere, most of the cafés and restaurants have long since gone, and the old facades are now hidden by neon

advertising. However, the Grands Boulevards and the nearby department stores on the Boulevard Haussmann still attract large crowds.

Boulevard des Italiens

Opéra de Paris Garnier ❹

Pl de l'Opéra 75009. **Map** 6 E4.
🆔 *01 40 01 22 63.* Ⓜ *Opéra.*
⭕ *10am–5pm daily.* ⬤ *public hols.*
📷 ⭢ See *Entertainment pp334–6.*

SOMETIMES COMPARED to a giant wedding cake, this sumptuous building was designed by Charles Garnier for Napoleon III; construction started in 1862. Its unique appearance is due to a mixture of materials (including stone, marble and bronze) and styles, ranging from Classical to Baroque, with a multitude of columns, friezes and sculptures

on the exterior. The building took 13 years to complete, with interruptions during the Prussian War and the uprising of 1871, finally opening in 1875.

In 1858 Orsini had attempted to assassinate the emperor outside the old opera house. This prompted Garnier to include a pavilion on the east side of the new building, with a curved ramp leading up to it so that the sovereign could safely step out of his carriage into the suite of rooms adjoining the royal box.

The functions performed by each part of the building are reflected in the structure. Behind the flat-topped foyer, the cupola sits above the auditorium, while the triangular pediment that rises up behind the cupola marks the front of the stage. Underneath the building is a small lake, which provided inspiration for the phantom's hiding place in Paul Leroux's *Phantom of the Opera.*

Both the interior and the exterior have been recently refurbished. Inside, don't miss the magnificent Grand Staircase, made of white marble with a balustrade of red and green marble, and the Grand Foyer, with its domed ceiling covered with mosaics. The five-tiered auditorium is a riot of red velvet, plaster cherubs and gold leaf, which contrast with the false ceiling painted by Marc Chagall in 1964.

Most operas are now performed in the new Opéra Bastille *(see p98),* but the ballet remains here.

Statue by Millet

Copper-green roofed cupola

Emperor's pavilion

Grand Foyer with mosaic ceiling

Auditorium with seating for about 2,000

Grand Staircase

Sign outside the Musée Grévin

Musée de l'Opéra ❺

Pl de l'Opéra 75009. **Map** 6 E5. ◖ *01 40 01 17 89.* Ⓜ *Opéra.* ◗ *10am–5pm daily (Jul–Aug: 10am–6pm).* ◗ *1 Jan, 1 May.* 📷 ◪ *01 40 01 22 63.* ◫

T HE ENTRANCE TO this small, charming museum was originally the emperor's private entrance to the Opéra. The museum relates the history of opera through a large collection of musical scores, manuscripts, photographs and artists' memorabilia, such as the Russian dancer Waslaw Nijinsky's ballet slippers and tarot cards. Other exhibits include models of stage sets and busts of major composers. The museum also houses a superb library, containing books and manuscripts on theatre, dance and music, as well as more memorabilia.

Drouot (Hôtel des Ventes) ❻

9 Rue Drouot 75009. **Map** 6 F4. ◖ *01 48 00 20 20.* Ⓜ *Richelieu Drouot.* ◗ *11am–6pm Mon–Sat.* 📷 ◪ ◫ *See Shops and Markets pp324–5.* ⓦ *www.gazette-drouot.com*

T HIS IS THE leading French auction house (Hôtel des Ventes) and it takes its name from the Comte de Drouot who was Napoleon's aide-de-camp. There has been an auction house on the site since 1858, and in 1860 Napoleon III visited the Hôtel and purchased a couple of earthenware pots. It has been known as the Nouveau Drouot ever since the 1970s, when the existing building was demolished and replaced with today's rather dull structure.

Although overshadowed internationally by Christie's and Sotheby's, auctions at the Nouveau Drouot nevertheless provide a lively spectacle and involve a fascinating range of rare objects. Its presence in the area has attracted many antique and stamp shops, which are located in the nearby Galeries.

Musée Grévin ❼

10 Blvd Montmartre 75009. **Map** 6 F4. ◖ *01 47 70 85 05.* Ⓜ *Grands Boulevards* ◗ *10am–6pm daily.* 📷 ◫ ⓦ *www.musee-grevin.com*

T HIS WAXWORK MUSEUM was founded in 1882 and is now a Paris landmark, on a par with Madame Tussauds in London. It contains tableaux of vivid historical scenes (such as Louis XIV at Versailles and the arrest of Louis XVI), distorting mirrors and the Cabinet Fantastique, which includes regular conjuring shows given by a live magician. Famous figures from the worlds of art, sport and politics are also on show, with new celebrities replacing faded and forgotten stars.

Galerie Vivienne

Les Galeries ❽

75002. **Map** 6 F5. Ⓜ *Bourse.*

T HE EARLY 19th-century Parisian shopping arcades (known as *galeries* or *passages)* are located between the Boulevard Montmartre and the Rue St-Marc (the extensive Passage des Panoramas). Other arcades are found between the Rue du Quatre Septembre and the Rue des Petits Champs.

At the time of their construction, the Galeries represented a new traffic-free area for commerce, workshops and apartments. They fell into disuse, but were dramatically revamped in the 1970s and now house an eclectic mixture of small shops selling anything from designer jewellery to rare books. They have high, vaulted roofs of iron and glass. One of the most charming is the Galerie Vivienne (off the Rue Vivienne or the Rue des Petits Champs) with its mosaic floor and excellent tearoom.

Model of a set for *Les Huguenots* (1875) in the Musée de l'Opéra

The colonnaded Neo-Classical facade of the Palais de la Bourse

Palais de la Bourse ❾

(Bourse des Valeurs) 4 Pl de la Bourse 75002. **Map** 6 F5. 🄲 01 49 27 55 54 (tours). Ⓜ Bourse. ⭘ by appt only. 🚫 ♿ 🄲 compulsory. **Films**.

THIS NEO-CLASSICAL temple of commerce was commissioned by Napoleon and was home to the French Stock Exchange from 1826 to 1987. Today the French stock market, located at 29 rue Cambon (not open to visits), is fully computerized. The hectic floor trading of the Palais de la Bourse has been considerably reduced and is limited to the Matif (the futures market) and the Monep (the traded options market).

Sainte-Chapelle cameo in Musée du Cabinet

Musée du Cabinet des Médailles et des Antiques ❿

58 Rue de Richelieu 75002. **Map** 6 F5. 🄲 01 53 79 83 34. Ⓜ Bourse. ⭘ 1–6pm Mon–Sat (5pm Sat); noon–6pm Sun. ● public hols. ♿ 🚫 🄲 🅆 www.bnf.fr

THIS VALUABLE collection of coins, medals, jewels and Classical objects is part of the Bibliothèque Nationale. Exhibits include the Berthouville Treasure (1st-century Gallo-Roman silver- ware) and the Grand Camée (cameo) from Sainte-Chapelle.

Bibliothèque Nationale ⓫

58 Rue de Richelieu 75002. **Map** 6 F5. 🄲 01 47 03 81 26. Ⓜ Bourse. **Not open** to the public. 🅆 www.bnf.fr

THE BIBLIOTHEQUE Nationale (National Library) originated with the manuscript collections of medieval kings, to which a copy of every French book printed since 1537, has, by law, been added. The collection, which includes two Gutenberg bibles, is partially housed in this complex, created in the

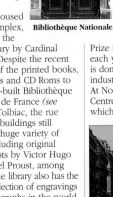

Bibliothèque Nationale

17th century by Cardinal Mazarin. Despite the recent removal of the printed books, periodicals and CD Roms to the newly-built Bibliothèque Nationale de France *(see p246)* at Tolbiac, the rue Richelieu buildings still contain a huge variety of items, including original manuscripts by Victor Hugo and Marcel Proust, among others. The library also has the richest collection of engravings and photographs in the world, and departments for maps and plans, theatrical arts, and musical scores. Sadly, the 19th-century reading room is not open to the public.

Avenue de l'Opéra ⓬

75001 & 75002. **Map** 6 E5. Ⓜ Opéra, Pyramides.

THIS BROAD avenue is a notable example of Baron Haussmann's dramatic modernization of Paris in the 1860s and 1870s *(see pp32–3)*. Much of the medieval city was swept away to make way for the wide thoroughfares of today. The Avenue de l'Opéra, which runs from the Louvre to the Opéra de Paris Garnier, was completed in 1876. The imposing uniformity of the five-storey buildings that line it contrast with those found in nearby streets, which date from the 17th and 18th centuries. Just off the avenue, in the Place Gaillon, is the Café and Restaurant Drouant where the prestigious Goncourt Prize for literature is decided each year. Today, the avenue is dominated by the travel industry and luxurious shops. At No. 27 there is the National Centre for the Visual Arts, which has a false entrance.

Avenue de l'Opéra

MONTMARTRE

ONTMARTRE AND ART are insep-
arable. By the end of the
19th century, the area
was a mecca for artists, writers,
poets and their disciples, who
gathered to sample the bor-
dellos, cabarets, revues and
other exotica that contributed
to Montmartre's reputation as
a place of depravity, in the
eyes of the city's more up-
standing citizens. Many of the
artists and writers have long
since left the area, and the lively night
life no longer has the same charm.

But the hill of Montmartre (the
Butte) still has its physical charms,
and the village atmosphere remains
remarkably intact. Mobs of eager
tourists ascend the hill, most of them

**Street theater in
Montmartre**

gathering in the most spacious parts,
alive with talented quick portrait
artists and souvenir sellers, as
in the old village square, the
Place du Tertre. Elsewhere there
are charming and exquisite
squares, winding streets,
small terraces and long stairways, plus the Butte's famous
vineyard, where the few
grapes are harvested in an
atmosphere of revelry in early
autumn. And there are spectacular views of the city from various
points, most especially from the
monumental Sacré-Coeur. The Butte
has long been a place to have fun,
and this tradition continues with lat-
ter-day, would-be Edith Piafs singing
in the restaurants and cafés.

SIGHTS AT A GLANCE

Historic Buildings and Streets
Bateau-Lavoir **11**
Moulin de la Galette **14**
Avenue Junot **15**

Churches
Sacré-Coeur pp224–5 **1**
St-Pierre de Montmartre **2**

Chapelle du Martyre **8**
St-Jean l'Evangéliste de
Montmartre **10**

Museums and Galleries
Espace Montmartre **4**
Musée de Montmartre **5**
Musée d'Art Naïf Max
Fourny **7**

Squares
Place du Tertre **3**
Place des Abbesses **9**

Cemeteries
Cimetière de Montmartre **13**

Theaters and Nightclubs
Au Lapin Agile **6**
Moulin Rouge **12**

SEE ALSO
• **Street Finder**, map 2, 6, 7
• **Montmartre Walk** pp266–7
• **Where to Stay** pp278–9
• **Restaurants** pp296–8

GETTING THERE
This area is served by several
metro stations, including
Abbesses and Pigalle. The
Montmartrobus leaves Pigalle
for the village area and bus
route 80 passes Montmartre's
cemetery. Route 85 passes
along Rue de Clignancourt.

KEY
■ Street-by-Street map
Ⓜ Metro station
Ⓟ Parking

0 meters   400
0 yards   400

The narrow Rue St-Rustique winding up the hill to Sacré-Coeur

Street-by-Street: Montmartre

THE STEEP *butte* (hill) of Montmartre has been associated with artists for 200 years. Théodore Géricault and Camille Corot came here at the start of the 19th century, and in the 20th century Maurice Utrillo immortalized the streets in his works. Today street painters thrive on a lively tourist trade as travellers flock to this picturesque district which in places still preserves the atmosphere of prewar Paris. The name of the area is ascribed to local martyrs tortured in Paris around AD 250, hence *mons martyrium*.

Streetside painter

Montmartre vineyard is the the last surviving vineyard in Paris. On the first Saturday in October the start of the grape harvest is celebrated.

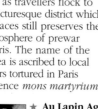

Metro Lamarck Caulaincourt

★ **Au Lapin Agile**
Literary meetings have been held in this rustic nightclub ("The Agile Rabbit") since 1910 ❻

A La Mère Catherine was a favourite eating place of Russian Cossacks in 1814. They would bang on the table and shout *"Bistro!"* (Russian for "quick") – hence the bistro was named.

Espace Montmartre Salvador Dali
The exhibition pays homage to the eclectic artist Dali. Some of the works are on public display for the first time in France ❹

★ **Place du Tertre**
The square is the tourist centre of Montmartre and is full of portraitists. No. 3 commemorates local children, as popularized in the artist Poulbot's drawings ❸

STAR SIGHTS

- ★ Sacré-Coeur
- ★ Place du Tertre
- ★ Musée de Montmartre
- ★ Au Lapin Agile

KEY

– – – Suggested route

0 metres	100
0 yards	100

Map labels: RUE ST-, RUE DE L'ABREUVOIR, RUE DES SAULES, RUE, RUE ST-, NORVINS, RUE LEPIC, PL. J. B. CLEMENT, RUE POULBOT, RUE DE LA MIRE, RAVIGNAN, PL. E. GOUDEAU, RUE, RUE, RUE DES TROIS FRERES, RUE

★ **Musée de Montmartre**
The museum includes the work of artists who lived in the area: this Portrait of a Woman *(1918) is by the Italian painter and sculptor Amedeo Modigliani* ❺

LOCATOR MAP
See Central Paris Map pp12–13

★ **Sacré-Coeur**
This Romano-Byzantine church, started in the 1870s and completed in 1914, has many treasures, such as this figure of Christ by Eugène Benet (1911) ❶

St-Pierre de Montmartre
This church became the Temple of Reason during the Revolution ❷

The funiculaire, or cable railway, at the end of the Rue Foyatier takes you to the foot of the basilica of the Sacré-Coeur. Metro tickets are valid on it.

To metro Anvers

Square Willette lies below the forecourt of the Sacré-Coeur. It is laid out on the side of the hill in a series of descending terraces with lawns, shrubs, trees and flowerbeds.

Musée d'Art Naïf Max Fourny
The museum houses 580 examples of naïve art. This oil painting, L'Opéra de Paris *(1986), is by L Milinkov* ❼

Montmartre streetside paintings

Sacré-Coeur ❶

See pp224–5.

St-Pierre de Montmartre ❷

2 Rue du Mont-Cenis 75018. **Map** 6 F1.
[☎] *01 46 06 57 63.* [M] *Abbesses.*
[◷] *8.30am–7pm daily.* [✝] *frequent.*
[📷] [♿] *Concerts.*

S ITUATED IN the shadow of
Sacré-Coeur, St-Pierre de
Montmartre is one of the
oldest churches in Paris. It is
all that remains of the great
Benedictine Abbey of
Montmartre, founded in 1133
by Louis VI and his wife,
Adelaide of Savoy, who, as its
first abbess, is buried here.

Inside are four marble
columns supposedly from a
Roman temple which
originally stood on the site.
The vaulted choir dates from
the 12th century, the nave
was remodelled in the 15th
century and the
west front in the
18th. During the
Revolution the
abbess was
guillotined, and the
church fell into
disuse. It was
reconsecrated in
1908. Gothic-style
stained-glass
windows replace
those destroyed by
a stray bomb in
World War II. The
church also has a
tiny cemetery
which is open to the public
only on 1 November.

Place du Tertre ❸

75018. **Map** 6 F1. [M] *Abbesses.*

T ERTRE MEANS "hillock", or
mound, and this
picturesque square is the
highest point in Paris at some
130 m (430 ft). It was once
the site of the abbey gallows
but is associated with artists,
who began exhibiting
paintings here in the 19th
century. It is lined with
colourful restaurants – La
Mère Catherine dates back to
1793. No. 21 was formerly the
home of the irreverent "Free
Commune", founded in 1920
to perpetuate the Bohemian
spirit of the area, and now the
site of the Old Montmartre
information office.

The Spanish artist Salvador Dali

Espace Montmartre Salvador Dali ❹

11 Rue Poulbot 75018.
Map 6 F1. [☎] *01 42 64
40 10.* [M] *Abbesses.*
[◷] *10am–6.30pm daily.*
[📷] [🎫] *groups by appt.*

A PERMANENT
exhibition of
330 works of the
painter and sculptor
Salvador Dali is
on display here
at the heart of
Montmartre. Inside,
Doors to St-Pierre church the vast, dark
setting reflects the
dramatic character of this
20th-century genius as moving

lights grace first one, then
another, of his Surrealist works.
This in turn is counterpointed
with the regular rhythm of
Dali's voice. There is an
additional art gallery as well
as a library housed in this
original museum.

Musée de Montmartre ❺

12 Rue Cortot 75018. **Map** 2 F5.
[☎] *01 46 06 61 11.* [M] *Lamarck-
Caulaincourt.* [◷] *11am–6pm Tue–Sun.*
[📷] [Ø] [🔲]

D URING THE 17th century
this charming home
belonged to the actor Roze de
Rosimond (Claude de la
Rose), a member of Molière's
theatre company who, like
his mentor Molière, died
during a performance of
Molière's play *Le Malade
Imaginaire.* From 1875 the
big white house, undoubtedly
the finest in Montmartre,
provided living and studio
space for numerous artists,
including Maurice Utrillo
and his mother, Suzanne
Valadon, a former acrobat
and model who became a
talented painter, as well as
Dufy and Renoir.

The museum recounts the
history of Montmartre from
the days of the abbesses to
the present, through artefacts,
documents, drawings and
photographs. It is particularly
rich in memorabilia of
Bohemian life, and even has
a reconstruction of the Café
de l'Abreuvoir, Utrillo's
favourite watering hole.

Café de l'Abreuvoir reconstructed

The deceptively rustic exterior of Au Lapin Agile, one of the best-known nightspots in Paris

Au Lapin Agile 6

22 Rue des Saules 75018.
Map 2 F5. [C] *01 46 06 85 87.*
[M] *Lamarck-Caulaincourt.*
[O] *9pm–2am Tue–Sun.*
See *Entertainment* pp330–1.

THE FORMER Cabaret des Assassins derived its current name from a sign painted by the humorist André Gill. His picture of a rabbit escaping from a pot (*Le Lapin à Gill*) became known as the nimble rabbit (*Lapin Agile*). The club enjoyed popularity with intellectuals and artists at the turn of the century. Here in 1911 the novelist Roland Dorgelès' hatred for modern art, as practised by Picasso and the other painters at the "Bateau-Lavoir" (No. 13 Place Emile-Goudeau), led him to play an illuminating practical joke on one of the customers, Guillaume Apollinaire – poet, art critic and champion of Cubism. He tied a paintbrush to the tail of the café-owner's donkey, and the resulting daub was shown at a Salon des Indépendents exhibition under the enlightening title *Sunset over the Adriatic*.

In 1903 the premises were bought by the cabaret entrepreneur Aristide Bruand (painted in a series of posters by Toulouse-Lautrec). Today it manages to retain much of its original atmosphere.

Musée d'Art Naïf Max Fourny 7

Halle St-Pierre, 2 Rue Ronsard 75018.
Map 7 A1. [C] *01 42 58 72 89.*
[M] *Anvers.* [O] *10am–6pm (last adm: 5.30pm) daily.* [symbols]
[W] *www.hallesaintpierre.org*

NAIVE ART is usually characterized by simple themes, bright, flat colours and a disregard for perspective. Max Fourny's publishing activities brought him into contact with many naïve-style painters and this unusual museum, located in the Halle St-Pierre, contains his collection of paintings and sculptures from more than 30 countries,

The Wall by F Tremblot (1944)

with exhibitions on selected themes. Many of the paintings are rarely seen in museums.

The museum also organises temporary exhibitions of outsider art, folk art and work by self-taught artists, as well as conducting children's workshops. The building itself is a 19th-century iron-and-glass structure which was once part of the St-Pierre fabrics market.

Chapelle du Martyre 8

9 Rue Yvonne-Le-Tac 75018.
Map 6 F1. [M] *Pigalle.*
[O] *10am–noon, 3pm–5pm Fri–Wed.*

THIS 19TH-CENTURY chapel stands on the site of a medieval convent's chapel, which was said to mark the place where the early Christ-ian martyr and first bishop of Paris, Saint Denis, was beheaded by the Romans in AD 250. It remained a major pilgrimage site throughout the Middle Ages. In the crypt of the original chapel in 1534 Ignatius de Loyola, founder of the Society of Jesus (the mighty Jesuit order designed to save the Catholic Church from the onslaught of the Protestant Reformation), took his Jesuit vows with six companions.

Sacré-Coeur ❶

South-east rose window (1960)

A T THE OUTBREAK of the Franco Prussian War in 1870, two Catholic businessmen made a private religious vow. It was to build a church dedicated to the Sacred Heart of Christ should France be spared the impending Prussian onslaught. The two men, Alexandre Legentil and Rohault de Fleury, lived to see Paris saved from invasion despite the war and a lengthy siege – and the start of what is the Sacré-Coeur basilica. The project was taken up by Archbishop Guibert of Paris. Work began in 1875 to Paul Abadie's designs. They were inspired by the Romano-Byzantine church of St-Front in Périgueux. The basilica was completed in 1914, but the German invasion forestalled its consecration until 1919, when France was victorious.

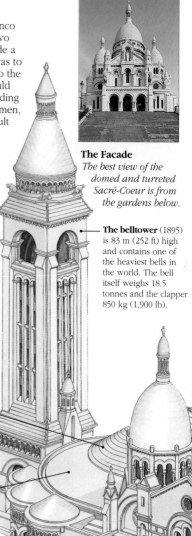

The Facade
The best view of the domed and turreted Sacré-Coeur is from the gardens below.

The belltower (1895) is 83 m (252 ft) high and contains one of the heaviest bells in the world. The bell itself weighs 18.5 tonnes and the clapper 850 kg (1,900 lb).

★ **Great Mosaic of Christ**
The colossal Byzantine mosaic of Christ (1912–22) dominating the chancel vault is by Luc Olivier Merson.

Virgin Mary and Child (1896)
This Renaissance-style silver statue is one of two in the ambulatory by P Brunet.

THE SIEGE OF PARIS

Prussia invaded France in 1870. During the four-month siege of Paris, instigated by the Prusso-German statesman Otto von Bismarck, Parisians became so hungry that they ate all the animals in the city.

★ **Crypt Vaults**
A chapel in the basilica's crypt contains Legentil's heart in a stone urn.

STAR FEATURES

★ **Great Mosaic of Christ**

★ **Bronze Doors**

★ **Ovoid Dome**

★ **Crypt Vaults**

VISITORS' CHECKLIST

35 Rue de Chevalier 75018.
Map 6 F1. **[** 01 53 41 89 00.
M Abbesses (then take the
funiculaire to the steps of the
Sacré-Coeur), Anvers, Barbès-
Rochechouart, Château-Rouge,
Lamarck-Caulaincourt.
▥ 30, 54, 80, 85.
P Blvd de Clichy, Rue Custine.
Basilica ◯ 6.15am–10pm daily.
Dome and crypt ◯ 9am–7pm
daily (6pm winter). **▨ for crypt
and dome**. **✝** 10.30am,
12.15pm, 6.30pm, 10pm
Mon–Fri (& 3pm Fri); 10.30am,
12.15pm, 6pm, 10pm Sat;
9.30am, 11am, 6pm, 10pm
Sun. **Ø &** restricted. **▣**

★ **Ovoid Dome**
This is the second-highest point in Paris, after the Eiffel Tower.

Spiral staircase

The inner structure supporting the dome is made from stone.

The stained-glass gallery affords a view of the whole of the interior.

Statue of Christ
The basilica's most important statue is symbolically placed above the two bronze saints.

Equestrian Statues
The statue of Joan of Arc is one of a pair by H Lefèbvre. The other is of Saint Louis.

★ **Bronze Doors**
Relief sculptures on the doors in the portico entrance illustrate scenes from the life of Christ, such as the Last Supper.

Main entrance

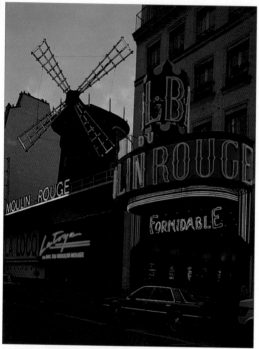

The famous silhouette of the Moulin Rouge nightclub

Place des Abbesses 🟢

75018. **Map** 6 F1. **M** *Abbesses*.

THIS IS ONE OF PARIS'S most picturesque squares. It is sandwiched between the rather dubious attractions of the Place Pigalle with its strip clubs and the Place du Tertre which is mobbed with hundreds of tourists. Be sure not to miss the Abbesses metro station with its unusual green wrought-iron arches

Entrance to the Abbesses metro

and amber lights. Designed by the architect Hector Guimard, it is one of the few original Art Nouveau stations.

St-Jean l'Evangéliste de Montmartre 🔟

19 Rue des Abbesses 75018. **Map** 6 F1. **C** *01 46 06 43 96*. **M** *Abbesses*. **O** *9am–noon, 3pm–7pm Mon–Sat; 2pm–7pm Sun.* **↑** *frequent.* **O** **C** *once a month.*

DESIGNED BY Anatole de Baudot and completed in 1904, this church was the first to be built from reinforced concrete. The flower motifs on the interior are typical of Art Nouveau, while its interlocking arches suggest Islamic architecture. The red-brick facing has earned it the nickname St-Jean-des-Briques.

Detail of St-Jean l'Evangéliste facade

Bateau-Lavoir 🕚

13 Pl Emile-Goudeau 75018. **Map** 6 F1. **M** *Abbesses*. **Not open** to public.

THIS ARTISTIC and literary mecca was an old piano factory. Its name comes from its resemblance to the laundry boats that used to travel along the River Seine. Between 1890 and 1920 it was home to some of the most talented artists and poets of the day. They lived in squalid conditions with only one tap and took it in turns to sleep in the beds. The artists Picasso, Van Dongen, Marie Laurencin, Juan Gris and Modigliani were just a few of the residents. It was here that Picasso painted *Les Demoiselles d'Avignon* in 1907, usually regarded as the painting that inspired Cubism. The shabby building burned down in 1970, but a concrete replica has been built – with studio space for up-and-coming artists.

Moulin Rouge 🕛

82 Blvd de Clichy 75018. **Map** 6 E1. **C** *01 53 09 82 82.* **M** *Blanche.* **O** *Dinner: 7pm; 1st show: 9pm (daily); 2nd show: 11pm (Sat–Sun).* **△** *See* **Entertainment** *p339.* **W** *www.moulin-rouge.com*

BUILT IN 1885, it was turned into a dance hall as early as 1900. The cancan originated in Montparnasse, in the polka gardens of the Rue de la Grande-Chaumière, but it will always be associated with the Moulin Rouge where the wild and colourful dance shows were immortalized in the posters and drawings of Henri de Toulouse-Lautrec. The high-kicking routines of famous dancers such as Yvette Guilbert and Jane Avril continue today in a glittering, Las Vegas-style revue that includes computerized lights and displays of magic.

Waslaw Nijinsky lies in Montmartre

Cimetière de Montmartre ⑬

20 Ave Rachel 75018.
Map 2 D5. 🕿 *01 43 87 64 24.*
Ⓜ *Place de Clichy, Blanche.*
🕐 *8am–5.30pm Mon–Sat; 9am–
5.30pm Sun (last adm: 5.15pm).* ♿

THIS HAS been the resting place for many artistic luminaries since the beginning of the 19th century. The composers Hector Berlioz and Jacques Offenbach (who wrote the famous cancan tune), are buried here, alongside many other celebrities such as La Goulue (stage name of Louise Weber, the high-kicking danceuse who was the can-can's first star performer and Toulouse-Lautrec's model), the painter Edgar Degas, writer Alexandre Dumas, German poet Heinrich Heine, Russian dancer Waslaw Nijinsky, and film director François Truffaut. It's an evocative, atmospheric place, conveying some of the heated energy and artistic creativity of Montmartre a century ago.

Nearby, close to Square Roland Dorgeles, there is another, smaller, often overlooked Montmartre cemetery – **Cimetière St-Vincent**. Here lie more of the great artistic names of the district, including the Swiss composer Arthur Honegger and the writer Marcel Aymé. Most notable of all at St-Vincent is the grave of the great French painter Maurice Utrillo, the quintessential Montmartre artist, many of whose works are now some of the most enduring images of the area.

Moulin de la Galette ⑭

T-junction at Rue Tholoze and Rue Lepic 75018. **Map** 2 E5. Ⓜ *Lamarck-Caulaincourt.* **Not open** to public.

ONCE MORE THAN 30 windmills dotted the Montmartre skyline and were used for grinding wheat and pressing grapes. Now only two remain: the Moulin du Radet, which stands further along the Rue Lepic, and the rebuilt Moulin de la Galette, now converted into a restaurant. The latter was built in 1622 and is also known as the Blute-fin; one of its mill owners, Debray, was supposedly crucified on the windmill's sails during the 1814 Siege of Paris. He had been trying to repulse the invading Cossacks. At the turn of the century the mill became a famous dance hall and provided inspiration for many artists, notably Auguste Renoir and Vincent Van Gogh.

The steep Rue Lepic is a busy shopping area with a good market *(see p327).* The Impressionist industrial and seascape painter Armand Guillaumin once lived on the first floor of No. 54, and Van Gogh inhabited its third floor.

Moulin de la Galette

Avenue Junot ⑮

75018. **Map** 2 E5. Ⓜ *Lamarck-Caulaincourt.*

OPENED IN 1910, this broad, peaceful street includes many painters' studios and family houses. No. 13 has mosaics designed by its former illustrator resident Francisque Poulbot, famous for his drawings of urchins. He is credited with having invented a bar billiards game. At No. 15 is Maison Tristan Tzara, named after its previous owner, the Romanian Dadaist poet. Its eccentric design by the Austrian architect Adolf Loos aimed to complement the poet's character. No. 25 is the Villa Léandre, a group of perfect Art Deco houses.

Just off the Avenue Junot up the steps of the Allée des Brouillards is an 18th-century architectural folly, the Château des Brouillards. In the 19th century it was the home of the mad French symbolist writer Gérard de Nerval, who committed suicide in 1855.

Sacré-Coeur, Montmartre, **by Maurice Utrillo**

FURTHER AFIELD

MANY OF THE GREAT châteaux outside Paris originally built as country retreats for the aristocracy and post-revolutionary bourgeoisie are now preserved as museums. Versailles is one of the finest, but if your tastes are Modernist, there's also Le Corbusier architecture to see. There are two theme parks – Disneyland Paris and Parc de la Villette – to amuse adults and children alike, and excellent parks to relax in when the bustle of the city gets too much.

SIGHTS AT A GLANCE

Museums and Galleries
Musée Nissim de Camondo ❸
Musée Cernuschi ❹
Musée Gustave Moreau ❺
Musée de Cristal de Baccarat ❽
Musée Edith Piaf ⓭
Musée National des Arts
d'Afrique et d'Océanie ⓱
Musée Marmottan ㉙
Musée des Années 30 ㉛

Churches
St-Alexandre-Nevsky
Cathédral ❶
Basilique Saint-Denis ❼
Notre-Dame du Travail ㉓

Historic Buildings and Streets
Bercy ⓳
Bibliotheque Nationale de
France ⓴
Cité Universitaire ㉒
Institut Pasteur ㉔
Versailles pp248–53 ㉖
Rue de la Fontaine ㉗
Fondation Le Corbusier ㉘
La Défense ㉜
Château de Malmaison ㉝

Markets
Marché aux Puces
de St-Ouen ❻
Portes St-Denis et St-Martin ❾
Marché d'Aligre ⓰

Parks, Gardens and Canals
Parc Monceau ❷
Canal St-Martin ❿
Parc des Buttes-Chaumont ⓫
Château et Bois de
Vincennes ⓲
Parc Montsouris ㉑
Parc André Citroën ㉕
Bois de Boulogne ㉚

Cemeteries
*Cimetière du Père Lachaise
pp240–41* ⓮

Theme Parks
Parc de la Villette pp234–9 ⓬
Disneyland Paris pp242–5 ⓯

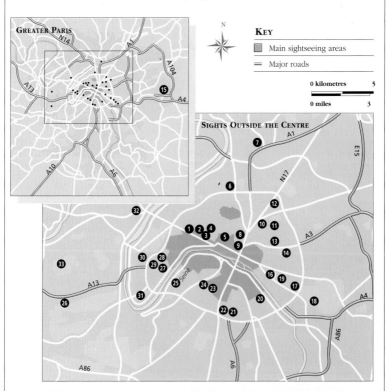

GREATER PARIS

KEY

Main sightseeing areas

Major roads

| 0 kilometres | 5 |
| 0 miles | 3 |

SIGHTS OUTSIDE THE CENTRE

A landscaped island in the Bois de Boulogne

North of the City

St-Alexandre-Nevsky Cathédral

St-Alexandre-Nevsky Cathédral ❶

12 Rue Daru 75008. **Map** 4 F3.
📞 *01 42 27 37 34.* Ⓜ *Courcelle.*
🕐 *3pm–5pm Tue, Fri, Sun.*
✝ *6pm Sat, 10.30am Sun.* 🚫 ♿

THIS IMPOSING Russian Orthodox cathedral with its five golden-copper domes signals the presence of a large Russian community in Paris. Designed by members of the St Petersburg Fine Arts Academy and financed jointly by Tzar Alexander II and the local Russian community, the cathedral was completed in 1861. Inside, a wall of icons divides the church in two. The Greek-cross plan and the rich interior mosaics and frescoes are Neo-Byzantine in style, while the exterior and gilt domes are traditional Russian Orthodox in design.

The Russian population in the city increased dramatically following the Bolshevik Revolution of 1917, when thousands of Russians fled to Paris for safety. The Rue Daru, in which the cathedral stands, and the surrounding area form "Little Russia", with its Russian schools and the many dance academies, and delightful tea shops and bookshops where visitors can browse around.

Parc Monceau ❷

Blvd de Courcelles 75017. **Map** 5 A3.
📞 *01 42 27 08 64.* Ⓜ *Monceau.*
🕐 *7am–8pm daily (10pm summer).*
See **Five Guided Walks** pp258–9.

THIS GREEN HAVEN dates back to 1778 when the Duc de Chartres (later Duc d'Orléans) commissioned the painter-writer and amateur landscape designer Louis Carmontelle to create a magnificent garden. Also a theatre designer, Carmontelle created a "garden of dreams", an exotic landscape full of architectural follies in imitation of English and German fashion of the time. In 1783 the Scottish landscape gardener Thomas Blaikie laid out an area of the garden in English style. The park was the scene of the first recorded parachute landing, made by André-Jacques Garnerin on 22 October 1797.

Over the years it changed hands and in 1852 was acquired by the state and half the land sold off for property development. The remaining 9 ha (22 acres) were made into public gardens. These were restored and new buildings were erected by Adolphe Alphand, architect of the Bois de Boulogne and the Bois de Vincennes.

Today the park remains one of the most chic in the capital but has lost many of its early features. A *naumachia* basin flanked by Corinthian columns remains. This is an ornamental version of a Roman pool used for simulating naval battles. There are also a Renaissance arcade, pyramids, a river and the Pavillon de Chartres, a charming rotunda which was once used as a tollhouse.

Musée Nissim de Camondo

Musée Nissim de Camondo ❸

63 Rue de Monceau 75008.
Map 5 A3. 📞 *01 53 89 06 40.*
Ⓜ *Monceau, Villiers.*
🕐 *10am–5pm Wed–Sun*
(last adm: 4.30pm). ● *public hols.*
📷 📷 *(01 44 55 59 26).* 📷

COMTE MOISE de Camondo, a leading Jewish financier, commissioned this mansion in 1914 in the style of the Petit Trianon, at Versailles *(see pp248–9)* to house a rare collection of 18th-century furniture, tapestries, paintings and other precious objects. The museum has been faithfully restored to recreate an aristocratic town house of the Louis XV and XVI eras. In the museum are Savonnerie carpets, Beauvais tapestries, and the Buffon service (Sèvres porcelain).

The very latest gadgets, for the period, are now displayed in the restored kitchen and service quarters, equipped with the utmost efficiency and forethought by their owner.

Colonnade beside the *naumachia* basin in Parc Monceau

Musée Cernuschi ❹

7 Ave Vélasquez 75008. **Map** 5 A3.
📞 01 45 63 50 75. Ⓜ Villiers, Monceau.
🕐 10am–5.40pm Tue–Sun. ⬤ public
hols. ♿ 📷 🎫 🚪
🌐 www.paris-france.org/musees

THIS MANSION near Parc
Monceau contains an
intriguing private collection of
late East Asian art which was
amassed by the politician and
banker Enrico Cernuschi
(1821–96). The wide-ranging
collection includes such treats
as the 5th-century seated
Bodhisattva (Buddhist divine
being) from Yunkang; *La
Tigresse* (a 12th-century BC
bronze vase); and *Horses and
Grooms*, an 8th-century T'ang
painting on silk attributed to
the era's greatest horse painter,
the court artist Han Kan.

Bodhisattva in the Musée Cernuschi

Musée Gustave Moreau ❺

14 Rue de la Rochefoucauld 75009.
Map 6 E3. 📞 01 48 74 38 50. Ⓜ
Trinité. 🕐 11am–5.15pm Mon, Wed;
10am–12.45pm, 2pm–5.15pm Thu–
Sun. ⬤ 1 Jan, 1 May, 25 Dec (phone
to check). ♿ 📷 🚪

THE SYMBOLIST painter
Gustave Moreau (1826–
98), known for his vivid,
imaginative works depicting
biblical and mythological
fantasies, left to the state a
vast collection of more than
1,000 oils, watercolours and
some 7,000 drawings in his
town house. One of
Moreau's best-known and
most outstanding works,
Jupiter and Semele, can be
seen here.

***Angel Traveller* by Gustave Moreau,
in the Musée Gustave Moreau**

Marché aux Puces de St-Ouen ❻

Rue des Rosiers, St-Ouen 75018.
Map 2 F2. Ⓜ Porte-de-
Clignancourt. 🕐 9am–6pm
Sat–Mon. See **Markets** p327.

THIS IS THE OLDEST and largest
of the Paris flea markets,
covering 6 ha (15 acres). In
the 19th century, rag merchants
and tramps would gather
outside the city limits and offer
their wares for sale. By the
1920s there was a proper
market here, where masterpieces could sometimes be
purchased cheaply from the
then-unknowing sellers.
    Today it is divided into
specialist markets. It is known
especially for its profusion of
furniture and ornaments from
the Second Empire (1852–
70). Few bargains are to be
found these days, yet some
150,000 weekend bargain-
hunters, tourists and dealers
still flock here to browse
among more than 2,000 open
or covered market stalls.

Basilique Saint-Denis ❼

2 Rue de Strasbourg, 93200 St-Denis.
📞 01 48 09 83 54. Ⓜ St-Denis-Bas-
ilique. ⓇⒺⓇ St-Denis. 🕐 Apr–Sep:
10am–7pm Mon–Sat, noon–6.30pm
Sun; Oct–Mar: 10am–5pm Mon–
Sat, noon–5pm Sun. 🕐 8.30am,
10am Sun. ♿ 📷 🎫 🚪

CONSTRUCTED BETWEEN 1137
and 1281, the Basilica is
on the site of the tomb of St
Denis, the first bishop of Paris,
who was beheaded in Mont-
martre in AD 250. The building
was the original influence for
Gothic art in Europe. From
Merovingian times it was a
burial place for rulers of France.
During the Revolution many
tombs were desecrated and
scattered, but the best were
stored, and now represent a
fine collection of funerary art.
Memorials include those of
Dagobert (died 638), François I
(died 1547), Henri II (died
1559) and Catherine de'Medici
(died 1589), and Louis XVI and
Marie-Antoinette (died 1793).

**Le Vase d'Abyssinie, made of
Baccarat crystal and bronze**

Musée de Cristal de Baccarat ❽

30 bis Rue de Paradis 75010. **Map** 7
B4. 📞 01 47 70 64 30. Ⓜ Château
d'Eau. 🕐 10am–6pm Mon–Sat.
⬤ public hols. ♿ 📷 🎫 🚪
🌐 www.baccarat.fr

THE RUE DE PARADIS is home
to many glass and ceramics
retailers, including the Baccarat
company, founded in 1764 in
Lorraine. The Musée de Cristal,
also known as the Musée
Baccarat, is beside the Baccarat
showroom and has on display
over 1,200 articles made by
the company. These include
services created for the royal
and imperial courts of Europe
and the finest pieces created
in the workshops.

Western arch of the Porte St-Denis, once the entrance to the city

Portes St-Denis et St-Martin ❾

Blvds St-Denis & St-Martin 75010.
Map 7 B5. Ⓜ *St-Martin, Strasbourg-St-Denis.*

THESE GATES give access to the two ancient and important north–south thoroughfares whose names they bear. They once marked the entrance to the city. The Porte St-Denis is 23 m (76 ft) high and was built in 1672 by François Blondel. It is decorated with figures by Louis XIV's sculptor, François Girardon. They commemorate victories of the king's armies in Flanders and the Rhine that year. Porte St-Martin is 17 m (56 ft) tall and was built in 1674 by Pierre Bullet. It celebrates Besançon's capture and the defeat of the Triple Alliance of Spain, Holland and Germany.

Boats berthed at Port de l'Arsenal

East of the City

Canal St-Martin ❿

Map 8 E2. Ⓜ *Jaurès, J Bonsergent, Goncourt. See* **Five Guided Walks** *pp260–61.*

THE FIVE-KILOMETRE (3 mile) canal, opened in 1825, provides a short-cut for river traffic between loops of the Seine. It has long been loved by novelists, film directors and tourists alike. It is dotted with barges and pleasure boats that leave from the Arsenal. At the north end of the canal is the Bassin de la Villette waterway and the elegant Neo-Classical Rotonde de la Villette, spectacularly floodlit at night.

Parc des Buttes-Chaumont ⓫

Rue Manin 75019 (main access from Rue Armand Carrel). Ⓒ *01 53 35 89 35.* Ⓜ *Botzaris, Buttes-Chaumont.* ◯ *Oct–Apr: 7am–9pm daily; May–Sep: 7am–11pm daily.* ⑪

FOR MANY THIS is the most pleasant and unexpected park in Paris. The panoramic hilly site was converted in the 1860s by Baron Haussmann from a rubbish dump and quarry with a gallows below. Haussmann worked with the landscape architect/designer Adolphe Alphand, who organized a vast 1860s programme to furnish the new pavement-lined avenues with benches and lampposts. Others involved in the creation of what was then a highly praised park were the engineer Darcel and the landscape gardener Barillet-Deschamps. They created a lake, made an island with real and artificial rocks, gave it a Roman-style temple and added a waterfall, streams, foot-bridges leading to the island, and beaches and firs. Today visitors will also find boating facilities and donkey rides.

Parc de la Villette ⓬

See pp234–9.

Musée Edith Piaf ⓭

5 Rue Crespin du Gast 75011.
Ⓒ *01 43 55 52 72.* Ⓜ *Ménilmontant.* ◯ *1pm–6pm Mon–Thu (last adm: 5.30pm), by appointment only.* ◯ *public hols.* 🖼 🚫 🎦 🛗

Edith Piaf – "the little sparrow" (1915–63)

BORN EDITH GASSION in the working-class east end of Paris in 1915, Edith Piaf took her stage name from her nickname meaning "the little sparrow". She started her career as a torch singer in local cafés and bars before becoming an international star in the late 1930s.

She never lived at the address of this museum, which was founded in 1967 by an association of fans, Les Amis d'Edith Piaf. Since then, they have collected a host of memorabilia and squeezed it into this small apartment. It contains many photographs and portraits, lithographs by Charles Kiffer, intimate letters, clothes and books – gifts from Piaf's parents-in-law or bequests from other singers. Records by the singer, who died in 1963 and lies in Père Lachaise cemetery *(see pp240–41)*, are played in the museum on request (visits are by appointment only).

Cimetière du Père Lachaise ⑭

See pp240–41.

Disneyland Paris ⑮

See pp242–5.

Marché d'Aligre ⑯

Place d'Aligre 75012. **Map** 14 F5.
Ⓜ *Ledru-Rollin.* ⬜ *7.30am–12.30pm daily.*

ON SUNDAY mornings this lively market offers one of the most colourful sights in Paris. French, Arab and African traders hawk fruit, vegetables, flowers and clothing on the streets, while the adjoining covered market, the Beauveau St-Antoine, offers meats, cheeses, pâtés and many intriguing international delicacies.

Aligre is where old and new Paris meet. Here the established community of this old artisan quarter coexists with a more

Exterior relief on Musée National des Arts d'Afrique et d'Océanie

recently established group of up-and-coming young people. They have been lured here to live and work by the recent transformation of the nearby Bastille area *(see p98)*.

Musée National des Arts d'Afrique et d'Océanie ⑰

293 Ave Daumesnil 75012.
Ⓒ *01 44 74 84 80.* Ⓜ *Porte Dorée.*
⬜ *10am–5.30pm Wed–Mon (last adm: 4.50pm).* **Aquarium** ⬜ *10am–5.30pm Wed–Mon.*
⬛ *1 May.* 🗒 🗒 *grps only, by appt.*
🚫 ♿ *restricted.* 🏠

THIS MUSEUM IS housed in a beautiful Art Deco building which was designed by the architects Albert Laprade and Léon Jaussely especially for the 1931 Colonial Exhibition. The impressive facade has a vast frieze by A Janniot, depicting the contributions of France's overseas territories.

Inside is a remarkable display of primitive and tribal art covering West, Central and North Africa, as well as Oceania and Australasia. The exhibits include antelope masks from Mali; finely carved ivory tusks from Benin; Moroccan jewellery; Aboriginal bark paintings; plus West and Central African masks and carved wooden and copper figures.

In the basement there is a tropical aquarium filled with vivid fish, as well as terrariums containing tortoises and crocodiles.

The imposing Château de Vincennes

Château et Bois de Vincennes ⑱

Ⓜ *Château de Vincennes.* Ⓡⓔⓡ *Vincennes.* **Château** Ave de Paris 94300 Vincennes. Ⓒ *01 48 08 31 20.*
⬜ *10am–6pm (5pm winter) daily.* 🗒
📷 📹 *compulsory in keep & chapel.*
🏠 **Bois de Vincennes** ⬜ *dawn to dusk daily.* **Zoological Park** Ⓕ *01 44 75 20 10.* ⬜ *9am–6pm (5pm winter) daily (last adm 30 min before).*
🗒 🗒 ♿

THE CHÂTEAU de Vincennes, enclosed by a defensive wall and a moat, was once a royal residence. It was here that Henry V of England died painfully of dysentery in 1422. His body was boiled in the Château's kitchen to prepare it for shipping back to England. Abandoned when Versailles was completed, the château was converted into an arsenal by Napoleon and in 1840 became a fortress.

The 14th-century keep is a fine example of medieval military architecture and houses the Château's museum. The Gothic chapel was finished around 1550, with beautiful stone rose windows and a magnificent single aisle. Two 17th-century pavilions house a museum of army insignia.

Once a royal hunting ground, the forest of Vincennes was given to the City of Paris by Napoleon III in 1860 as a public park. Baron Haussman's landscape architect added ornamental lakes and cascades. Among its main attractions are the zoo and the largest funfair in France (held from Palm Sunday to the end of May).

Parc de la Villette ⑫

THE OLD SLAUGHTERHOUSES and livestock market of Paris have been transformed into this massive urban park, designed by Bernard Tschumi. Its vast and ambitious facilities stretch across 55 ha (136 acres) of a previously run-down part of the city. The great plan is to revive the tradition of parks for meetings and activities and to stimulate interest in the arts and sciences. Work began in 1984 and the park has grown to include a huge science museum, a pop concert hall, an exhibition pavilion, a spherical cinema and a music centre. Linking them all is the park itself, with its follies, walkways, gardens and playgrounds.

The Follies
These red cubes punctuate the park and provide a variety of services, such as a day-care centre, café and a children's workshop.

Children's Playground
A dragon slide, sand pits and colourful play equipment in a maze-like setting make the playground a paradise for young children.

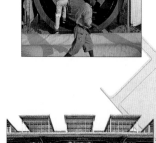

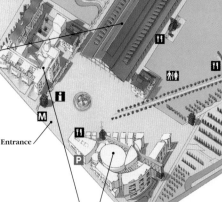

★ Grande Halle
The old cattle hall has been transformed into a flexible exhibition space with mobile floors and auditorium.

Entrance

★ Cité de la Musique
This quirky but elegant all-white complex holds the music conservatory, a concert hall, library, studios and a museum.

STAR BUILDINGS

★ Cité des Sciences

★ Grande Halle

★ Cité de la Musique

★ Zénith Theatre

Maison de la Villette is a history centre with documents and displays on the history of the site and area.

ntrance

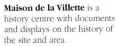

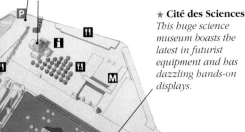

★ **Cité des Sciences**
This huge science museum boasts the latest in futurist equipment and has dazzling hands-on displays.

La Géode
The cinema's gigantic 360° movie screen combines visual and sound effects to create fantastic experiences, such as the sense of travelling in space.

★ **Zénith Theatre**
This vast polyester tent was built as a venue for pop concerts with a capacity to seat more than 6,000 spectators.

L'Argonaute
The exhibit consists of a 1950s submarine and a nearby navigation museum.

Musicians from Guadeloupe performing outside the Museum

LE MUSÉE DE LA MUSIQUE

This museum brings together a collection of over 4,500 instruments, objects, tools and works of art covering the history of music since the Renaissance. The permanent collection of over 900 items is displayed chronologically and can be traced using infrared audio headphones.

La Villette: Cité des Sciences

THIS IMMENSE science and technology museum occupies the largest of the old Villette slaughterhouses. The building soars 40 m (133 ft) high and stretches over 3 ha (7 acres). Architect Adrien Fainsilber has created an imaginative interplay between the building and three natural themes: water surrounds the structure; vegetation penetrates through the greenhouses; and light flows in through the cupolas. The museum is on five levels. Its heart is the Explora exhibits on levels 1 and 2, where lively and entertaining displays of equipment and activities promote an interest in science and technology. Visitors can actively engage in computerized games on space, computers and sound. On other levels there are cinemas, a science newsroom, conference centre, library and shops.

Statue of Atlas

Cupolas
The two glazed domes, 17 m (56 ft) in diameter, filter the flow of natural light into the main hall.

★ Planetarium
In this 260-seat auditorium, special effects projectors and the latest sound systems create exciting images of the stars and planets.

Main Hall
A soaring network of shafts, bridges escalators and balconies creates a cathedral-like atmosphere here.

Entrance from the west

STAR EXHIBITS

★ Planetarium

★ Ariane Rocket

★ La Géode

★ Ariane Rocket
The fascinating displays of rockets explain how astronauts are launched into outer space, and include an example of the European rocket Ariane.

The moat was designed by Fainsilber at 13 m (43 ft) below the level of the park, so that natural light could penetrate into the lower levels of the building. The sense of the building's massiveness is enhanced by reflections in the water.

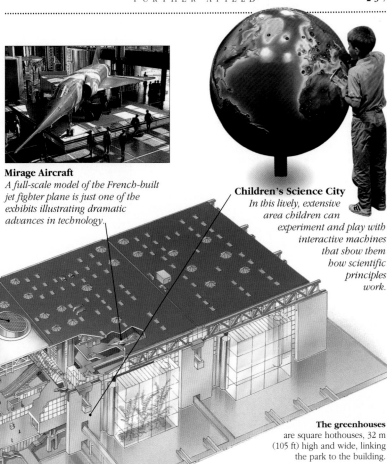

Mirage Aircraft
A full-scale model of the French-built jet fighter plane is just one of the exhibits illustrating dramatic advances in technology.

Children's Science City
In this lively, extensive area children can experiment and play with interactive machines that show them how scientific principles work.

The greenhouses
are square hothouses, 32 m (105 ft) high and wide, linking the park to the building.

To the Géode

Walkways
The walkways cross the encircling moat to link the various floors of the museum to the Géode and the park.

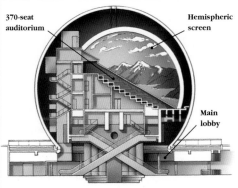

370-seat auditorium

Hemispheric screen

Main lobby

LA GÉODE

This giant entertainment sphere, 36 m (116 ft) in diameter, has a "skin" composed of 6,500 stainless-steel triangles, which reflect the surroundings and the sky. Inside, a huge hemispherical cinema screen, 1,000 sq m (11,000 sq ft), shows films on nature, travel and space.

Cité des Sciences: Explora

THE EXPLORA exhibits on levels 1 and 2 of the Cité are a fascinating guide to the worlds of science and technology. Our understanding of computers, space, ocean, earth, sound and film is heightened by bold, imaginative presentations of multimedia displays, interactive computer exhibits and informative models. Children and adults can learn while playing with light, space and sound. Young children can walk through the sound sponge, experience optical illusions, see how astronauts live in outer space, whisper to one another through the parabolic sound screen, and listen to talking walls. Older children can learn more about how man lives and works under water, how special effects are made in films, listen to the story of a star, and see the birth of a mountain.

Sound Dishes
These parabolic sound screens transmit a conversation between people standing 15m (48ft) apart.

Monory's frescoes are Jacques Monory's painted aluminium plates, linked by neon tubes, which decorate the Planetarium's external walls.

★ Star Display
Ten thousand stars are projected on to the dome of the Planetarium by the astronomic simulator. The visual and sound effects simulate breathtaking voyages through space.

Level 2

Starball
The Planetarium's 10,000-lens sphere reproduces images of what the sky looks like to astronauts travelling beyond the earth's atmosphere.

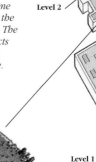

Level 1

Tele-X is a full-scale model of a satellite with interactive exhibits.

KEY TO FLOORPLAN

☐	Permanent exhibitions
☐	Temporary exhibitions
☐	Planetarium
☐	Future exhibition space
☐	Non-exhibition space

STAR EXHIBITS

★ **Star Display**

★ **Roussi's Robot**

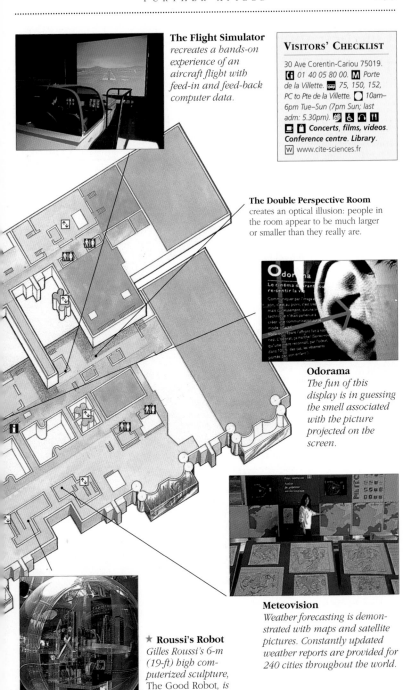

The Flight Simulator *recreates a hands-on experience of an aircraft flight with feed-in and feed-back computer data.*

The Double Perspective Room
creates an optical illusion: people in
the room appear to be much larger
or smaller than they really are.

Odorama
The fun of this display is in guessing the smell associated with the picture projected on the screen.

Meteovision
Weather forecasting is demonstrated with maps and satellite pictures. Constantly updated weather reports are provided for 240 cities throughout the world.

★ **Roussi's Robot**
Gilles Roussi's 6-m (19-ft) high computerized sculpture, The Good Robot, is highly sensitive. It reacts to the slightest movement of people nearby by lighting up and speaking in its own voice.

Cimetière du Père Lachaise ⑭

PARIS'S MOST PRESTIGIOUS cemetery is set on a wooded hill overlooking the city. The land was once owned by Père de la Chaise, Louis XIV's confessor, but it was bought by order of Napoleon in 1803 to create a new cemetery. The cemetery became so popular with the Paris bourgeoisie that it was expanded six times during the century. Here were buried celebrities such as the writer Honoré de Balzac and the composer Frédéric Chopin, and more recently, the singer Jim Morrison and the actor Yves Montand. Famous graves and striking funerary sculpture make this a pleasant place for a leisurely, nostalgic stroll.

The Columbarium was built at the end of the 19th century. The American dancer Isadora Duncan is one of the many celebrities whose ashes are housed here.

Marcel Proust
Proust brilliantly chronicled the Belle Epoque in his novel Remembrance of Things Past.

★ Simone Signoret and Yves Montand
France's most famous post-war cinema couple were renowned for their left-wing views and long turbulent relationship.

Allan Kardec was the founder of a 19th-century spiritual cult, which still has a strong following. His tomb is forever covered in pilgrims' flowers.

Sarah Bernhardt
The great French tragedienne, who died in 1923 aged 78, was famous for her portrayal of Racine heroines.

Monument aux Morts
by Paul Albert Bartholmé is one of the best monumental sculptures in the cemetery. It dominates the central avenue.

Entrance

Frédéric Chopin, the great Polish composer, belonged to the French Romantic generation.

Théodore Géricault
The French Romantic painter's masterpiece, The Raft of Medusa *(see p124), is depicted on his tomb.*

★ **Oscar Wilde**
The Irish dramatist, aesthete and great wit was cast away from virtuous Britain to die of drink and dissipation in Paris in 1900. Jacob Epstein sculpted the monument.

The remains of Molière, the great 17th-century actor and dramatist, were transferred here in 1817 to add historic glamour to the new cemetery.

Mur des Fédérés is the wall against which the last Communard rebels were shot by government forces in 1871. It is now a place of pilgrimage for left-wing sympathizers.

★ **Edith Piaf**
Known as "the little sparrow" because of her size, Piaf was this century's greatest French popular singer. In her tragic voice she sang of the sorrows and love woes of the Paris working class.

Victor Noir
The life-size statue of this 19th-century journalist shot by Pierre Bonaparte, a cousin of Napoleon III, is said to have fertility powers.

George Rodenbach, the 19th-century poet, is depicted as rising out of his tomb with a rose in the hand of his outstretched arm.

Elizabeth Demidoff, a Russian princess who died in 1818, is honoured by a three-storey Classical temple by Quaglia.

★ **Jim Morrison**
The death of The Doors' lead singer in Paris in 1971 is still a mystery.

François Raspail
The tomb of this much-imprisoned partisan of the 1830 and 1840 revolutions is in the form of a prison.

Disneyland Paris ⓑ

Dᴵsɴᴇʏʟᴀɴᴅ ᴘᴀʀɪs is built on a 200ha (5,000 acre) site – about one fifth the size of Paris. It comprises two theme parks; six hotels (the largest in Europe); a shopping, dining and entertainment village; a campsite; ice skating rink; lakes; two convention centres; a golf course; and several swimming pools. One stop down the line from their very own train station lies Val d'Europe, a huge new shopping mall with more than 180 discount shopping outlets and a Sea World centre.

Unbeatable for complete escapism, combined with vibrant excitement and sheer energy, the park offers extreme rides and gentle experiences, all accompanied by phenomenal visual effects.

The Queen of Hearts' Castle, in Alice's Curious Labyrinth

The Parks

Dᴵsɴᴇʏʟᴀɴᴅ ᴘᴀʀɪs consists of Disneyland Park and Walt Disney Studios. Disneyland Park is based on the Magic Kingdom of California and has 42 rides or attractions. The newest park is the Walt Disney Studios, based on Disney MGM in Florida and only the second in the world to build on Disney's relationship with the legendary Metro Goldwyn Mayer film studios. Find out more at www.2000. disneylandparis.com

Getting There

By Car
Disneyland Paris lies 32 km (20 miles) to the east of Paris, and has its own link (exit 14) from the A4 westbound from Paris and eastbound A4, from Strasbourg. If you get confused, simply follow the signs to Marne la Vallée (Val d'Europe) until you see the Disneyland signs. (The Davy Crockett ranch is exit 13.)

By Air
Both Orly and Charles de Gaulle Airports have a shuttle bus which runs every 30 minutes (45 in the low season). No booking is necessary. The fare is about 12 per person.

By Train
The Paris RER runs directly to the Park, as does the TGV which has connections throughout Europe.

Parking

There is space for over 12,000 vehicles, and an efficient moving sidewalk conveys you to the exit. Parking costs 6 per day for cars, and 10 for campers and coaches. Parking at Disneyland Paris hotels is free to guests, and the Disneyland and New York hotels offer valet parking.

Opening hours

Gᴇɴᴇʀᴀʟʟʏ, the Park opens at 9am in high season and 10am otherwise. Closing times are usually 10pm in high season and between 7pm and 9pm in the low on weekdays and 8–10pm on Saturdays. Times change at short notice and special events, such as Hallowe'en, can mean extended hours.

When to visit

Tʜᴇ ʙᴜsɪᴇsᴛ ᴛɪᴍᴇs are Christmas and New Year, mid-February to early April and July to early September, and mid-October. Busiest days are Saturday–Monday, Tuesday and Wednesday are quietest.

Length of visit

Tᴏ ᴇxᴘᴇʀɪᴇɴᴄᴇ everything Disneyland Paris has to offer you really need to spend three or four days at the resort. Although it is possible to tour the parks in one day each (just), to enjoy them at less than breakneck pace you need at least two days for Disneyland Park alone, and if you want to include the Wild

Eating and Drinking

There's no need to leave the park to eat during the day. **Au Chalet de la Marionette** (Fantasyland) is excellent for kids (and almost deserted at 3pm) as is the **Cowboy Cookout** (Frontierland), which tends to be rather more crowded. **Colonel Hathi's Pizza Place** (Adventureland) is worth a visit just to see the authentic colonial gear, whilst **Café Hyperion – Videopolis** (Discoveryland) offers good food plus excellent entertainment, but service is very slow.

You pay a premium for full-service restaurants but the experience of eating in the **Blue Lagoon** (Adventureland) is one you will remember. You dine on the "shore" of a Caribbean Pirate hideaway while the boats from Pirates of the Caribbean glide past. **Walt's**, on Main Street, is also a good but pricey restaurant offering American fare. If you're lucky, they'll seat you so that you can watch the afternoon Main Street parade in comfort from an upstairs window..

In Disney Village **Annette's Diner** is staffed by roller-skating waitresses against a background of '50s records. **Planet Hollywood** is another good option, and the **Rainforest Cafe** provides an interestingly animated meal. The **Steakhouse** is excellent, although a little pricey, while a giant **McDonald's** serves the usual fare. The hotel restaurants are more expensive the nearer they are to the park.

West show or visit some of the nightclubs in Disney Village, then you'll be pushed to manage it all in under four days. Locals turn up on a daily basis from Paris, which is only 35 minutes away on the RER, but most guests from further afield will stay in hotels. Disney offer several packages for those who wish to savour the delights of staying on site. These include passes for the parks, and accommodation with continental breakfast included. All inclusive packages can also be booked.

TICKETS AND PASSES

IF YOU BOOK a package, Passports (Disney-speak for tickets) will be included in the price. Disneyland Park Passports can be bought from any Disney Store before you leave home, or at the Park upon arrival – although this means wasting good riding time waiting at a ticket booth. 1,2 or 3 day Passports are available, and prices vary according to season.

GETTING AROUND

DISNEY PROVIDE an efficient transport system between the Parks and the hotels (excluding Davy Crockett Ranch) with buses on the half hour. In summer, one delight is the fleet of little open-top buses which drive slowly around Lake Disney, ferrying guests between the three lakeside hotels and Disney Village. However, if you're staying at any of the on-site hotels it's only a short walk (20 minutes at most) to the park gates.

Sleeping Beauty's Castle, the centrepiece of of the Park

WHICH HOTEL?

There are six hotels on site, and one campsite 2km (3 miles) away. The best hotels are the closest to the Parks.
Santa Fe: basic, small and reasonably inexpensive. The only hotel which offers parking immediately outside your room.
Hotel Cheyenne: a Wild West theme hotel, about 17 minutes walk from the park. Small rooms (with bunks for the kids), a Native American village play area and use of the Sequoia Lodge swimming pool. Inexpensive and a great experience. Kids love this hotel.
Sequoia Lodge: a lakeside "hunter's lodge", moderately priced with more than 1,000 rooms. Ask for a room in the main building. Rooms at the front have great views.
Newport Bay: a huge, nautically-themed hotel on the lakeside. Moderately priced, this massive hotel has a huge convention centre, magnificent swimming pool and three floors offering extra services for a supplement.
New York: expensive and business-oriented; not a lot for the kids. This hotel also has a large convention centre, and there's an ice-skating rink from October to March.
Disneyland Hotel: the Jewel in the crown. Expensive, but right at the entrance to the Park. Full of delightful touches, such as grandfather clocks that run backwards, and ever-present Disney characters. The Castle Club is a 50-room hotel-within-a-hotel. If you can afford it, a week of decadent fawning and unrestrained hedonism can be yours!
Davy Crockett Ranch: the relatively-expensive campsite. The price includes all electrical hook-ups, and dedicated water and drainage connections. Some excellent facilities: the pool ranks as one of the best in Disneyland Paris.

MONEY

CREDIT CARDS are accepted everywhere within the resort. ATMs and commission-free foreign exchange are available immediately inside the Park entrances and at reception in all the hotels.

DISABLED TRAVELLERS

CITY HALL (immediately within Disneyland Park) has a brochure outlining the facilities for the disabled, and a Disabled Guest Guide can be pre-ordered (free) from the Disneyland Paris website. The complex is designed very much with the disabled in mind, but note that cast members are not allowed to assist with lifting people or moving wheelchairs.

STAYING IN A DISNEY HOTEL

THE ON-SITE HOTELS offer rooms at a wide range of prices, with the rule of thumb being that those closest to the Parks are the most expensive. Advantages include virtually

The runaway mine-train track of Big Thunder Mountain

no travelling to reach the Parks, and "early bird" entry to the parks on selected dates (usually at peak times).

If you stay at a Disney Hotel you will be given a hotel ID card. This unprepossessing little item is very important. As well as being used to charge anything you buy back to your hotel room (and have it delivered there), it also allows you entry to the Disneyland hotel grounds early in the morning while they're still shut to day trippers (the grounds also act as an entrance to the Park).

For children (of any age), one of the most exciting bonuses of staying in an on-site hotel is the chance to dine with Disney characters.

Exploring Disneyland Paris

T HE PARK'S 56 ha (138 acres) are divided into five Lands: each one nostalgically celebrates a legendary past strongly coloured by Hollywood folklore. The entire concept, with its imitation exotic buildings, novel forms of transport and technological wonders, owes much to the great 19th-century World Fairs.

MAIN STREET, USA

M AIN STREET is Walt Disney's idea of a small-town America that never was. The traffic includes horse-drawn rail cars, a Keystone-cops-style paddy wagon and other vintage transport. They're actually a transport system that runs between the Town Square and Central Plaza, the main hub of the Park, from where paths radiate to the other lands.

The Victorian façades offer a wealth of authentic detail, and hide several interesting stores. The Emporium is the place for gifts. Further along, a genuine, if pricey, Barber's will cut your hair while the rest of the family have a snack at Casey's or succumb to the lure of the aromas from Cookie Kitchen or the Cable Car Bake Shop. Either side of the shops are the Discovery and Liberty Arcades, offering a covered route to the Central Plaza and hosting displays and small stalls. They are also the quickest route to Frontierland in the morning at "rope drop" when the park opens.

At night, thousands of tiny lights bring a warm glow to Main Street's spotless paving.

The Electrical Parade, a shimmering fantasy of music, live action and illuminated floats, begins at Town Square. It's the last place to fill with guests waiting to see the Parade and thus an excellent place from which to watch. Standing in the Town Square also allows you to leave the Park straight afterwards, before thousands of others try to do likewise.

From Main Street you can ride a 19th century "steam" engine around the park (departures every 10 mins). It stops in each of the other lands, but boarding at other than Main Street is not always possible before noon.

FRONTIERLAND

T HIS IS Disney's recreation of America's Wild West. Entry is through Fort Comstock's imposing wooden gate and fort grounds.

Frontierland hosts some of the most popular attractions in the Park. Big Thunder Mountain, a rollercoaster ride through a midwest landscape, is circled by the Mark Twain and Molly Brown paddle steamers, taking a musical cruise around re-creations of some of America's finest natural monuments. Phantom Manor is a gentle and ultimately amusing ghost ride. The queuing is almost as fascinating as the ride itself. As you leave, read the gravestones, some of which are very witty.

At the outdoor Chaparral Theatre, you can see some of the amazing stage performances for which Disney is renowned. If there's time, Pocahontas Indian Village and Critter Corral are both popular with younger children.

ADVENTURELAND

I NSPIRED BY TALES of swashbuckling pirates and adventurers, enjoy the wild rides and amazing audioanimatronics of Adventure Island. Indiana Jones™ and the Temple of Peril hurtles you through a derelict mine at high speed – in reverse! Based on the Spielberg movies, the ride is replete with flaming torches, steep drops and tight 360° loops. The queues are also an experience.

Pirates of the Caribbean is a dark boat ride, through dank underground prisons and past 16th-century fighting galleons. Every special effect possible is used, even the smell of the Caribbean is introduced, partly by the Blue Lagoon restaurant nearby. At the exit, one of the Park's most interesting shops sells accessories for the aspiring privateer. *La Cabane des Robinson*, based on Jonathan Wyss's *Swiss Family Robinson*, starts with a shaky climb up a 27-m (88-ft) Banyan Tree. From here you explore the rest of the island, including the caves of Ben Gunn from *Treasure Island*; and the superb suspension bridge near Eyeglass Hill. The children's playground, Pirate's Beach, is also worth a visit if you have kids in tow.

FANTASYLAND

D ISNEY'S "IMAGINEERS" have modelled the buildings here on the animated movies. The Castle, *Le Chateau de la Belle au Bois Dormant*, is just as it looks in *Sleeping Beauty*.

WALT DISNEY STUDIOS

The new Studio's shows and rides are all based on films and entertainment. The Backlot Tour tram ferries guests round the sets (this is a working studio) and Catastrophe Canyon takes you through a "live" set which then undergoes some alarming changes. The Rock 'n' Roller Coaster is a multi-loop enclosed ride that bombards you with loud music and bright neon signs. The fun part here is the catapult launch, which accelerates the car to over 72kph (45 mph) in a little under 2 seconds. On the Animation Tour, you can match your artistic efforts against some of Disney's best animators, at work on upcoming productions. The Great Movie Ride takes visitors through a montage from the past 100 years of European and American screen gems, combining live action with state of the art special effects. Last but not least is a professional stunt show.

Beneath it a huge, smoke-breathing dragon stirs restlessly, enrapturing older children while scaring the young.

Many attractions here appeal to younger children, such as Snow White and the Seven Dwarfs, a gentle ride complete with wicked witch, and Pinocchio's Travels. The very young love Dumbo the Flying Elephant which quickly builds up long queues. Other rides, like the Mad Hatter's Teacups, also develop queues early. Peter Pan, one of the most popular attractions in the Park, is a triumph of imagination and technology, flying you over the streets of London. A popular diversion is Alice's Curious Labyrinth, leading to the Queen of Hearts' castle.

Hourly, there's a musical parade of clockwork figures at It's a Small World, one of the earliest rides conceived by Walt Disney himself. Aboard a boat, you meander through lands of animated models to the strains of the eponymous song. Le Pays des Contes des Fées (the Land of Fairytales) is another boat ride, passing miniature scenes from many of the greatest Disney movies. The haunting music accompanying this voyage makes it the ultimate antidote to stress. Next, hop aboard Casey Jr – le Petit Train du Cirque – for a gentle train ride circling the boats and giving a close view of the lovely castle miniature from Beauty and the Beast.

DISCOVERYLAND

SPACE MOUNTAIN dominates, looking just as it does in Jules Verne's From the Earth to the Moon. This fast, multi-loop ride draws crowds from the outset, but at the end of the day you can often walk straight on. Les Mysteres du Nautilus takes you into the submarine from Verne's 20,000 Leagues Under the Sea. Autopia, where you can drive a petrol-engined car round a railed track, is a magnet for youngsters. Orbitron features spaceships and soon gets crowded, but is worth experiencing. In a Land of amazing experiences, Star Tours is one of the greatest. You're a passenger in a star shuttle on a nightmare journey of near misses and narrow escapes. This Disney–Lucas collaboration is breathtaking.

The best shows are in Videopolis, a cavernous café showing cartoons between shows, and capacity crowds pack each performance. Le Visionarium is a stand-up, 360° experience that whisks you through time and space.

Finally, in Honey, I Shrunk the Audience, Disney have produced a masterpiece of total experience, that combines every sensory stimulus to create an overwhelming and very funny experience.

RIDES AND TOURS CHECKLIST

This chart is designed to help you make the best use of your time at Disneyland Paris, decide on which rides and tours are best for you, and choose when to visit them.

	Queues	Height / Age Restriction	Best Time to Ride	Fastpass	Scary Rating	May Cause Motion Sickness	Rating Overall
PHANTOM MANOR	◗		Any		❷		★
PADDLE STEAMERS	○		Any		❶		▼
BIG THUNDER MOUNTAN	●	1.2m	FT	✔	❷		★
POCOHANTAS INDIAN VILLAGE	○		Any		❶		▼
INDIANA JONES & THE TEMPLE OF PERIL	●	1.4m	LT	✔	❸	✔	★
ADVENTURE ISLAND	○		Any		❶		▼
LA CABANE DES ROBINSON	○		Any		❶		▼
PIRATES OF THE CARIBBEAN	○		Any		❶		★
PETER PAN	●		FT	✔	❶		◆
SNOW WHITE & THE SEVEN DWARFS	●		▸11		❶		◆
PINOCCHIO'S TRAVELS	●		▸11		❶		▼
DUMBO THE FLYING ELEPHANT	●		FT		❶		▼
MAD HATTER'S TEACUPS	◗		▸12		❶		▼
ALICE'S CURIOUS LABYRINTH	○		Any		❶		▼
IT'S A SMALL WORLD	○		Any		❶		◆
CASEY JR	○		▸11		❶		◆
LE PAYS DES CONTES DES FEES	○		Any		❶		◆
STAR TOURS	○	1.3m	Any	✔	❶		★
SPACE MOUNTAIN	●	1.4m	LT	✔	❸	✔	★
HONEY, I SHRUNK THE AUDIENCE	○		Any		❶		★
AUTOPIA	●		FT		❶		▼
ORBITRON	●	1.2m	FT		❶		▼

Short - ○   Medium - ◗   Long - ●   Anytime - Any   Before 11 - ▸11   First thing - FT   Last thing - LT
Not Scary - ❶   Slightly - ❷   Very - ❸   Quite good - ▼   Very good - ◆   Outstanding - ★

Bercy ⑲

75012. **Map** 18 F3. Ⓜ *Bercy,*
Cour St-Emilion. 🚤 *Port de Bercy (01*
43 43 40 30).

THIS FORMER wine-trading
quarter just east of the city
centre, with its once-grim
riverside warehouses and
pavilions and slum housing,
has been transformed into an
ultra-modern district beside
the Seine. A new automatic
metro line (Line 14) links it to
the heart of the city.

Centrepiece of the new
district is the Palais
d'Omnisports de Paris-Bercy,
known as POPB or simply
Bercy, now the city centre's
principal venue for major
concerts, as well as its premier
sports stadium. The vast
pyramid structure, its steep
sides clad with real lawns, has
become a contemporary landmark for the eastern part of
central Paris. A wide variety
of championship sports events
is held here, as well as classical
operas and, especially, rock
concerts (*see pp337 & 343*).

Other architecturally adventurous administrative and
commercial buildings dominate
the new Bercy skyline, notably
Chemetov's massive building
for the Ministry of Finance,
moved here from the Louvre;
and Frank Gehry's American
Center (intended to house a
new Maison du Cinema and
the Cinémathèque Française
by the year 2003).

At the foot of these struc-
tures, the imaginative 70-ha
(173-acre) Parc de Bercy
provides a welcome green

Bibliothèque Nationale de France

space for this section of the
city. Brick – in an echo of the
former warehouses – has
been used to lay out paths
between lawns, roses and
vegetables, while mature plane
trees and water are punctuated
with modern sculpture. The
park's attractions for children
include a traditional carousel.

Former wine stores and
cellars along Cours St Emilion
have been restored as bars,
restaurants and shops. Some
of the warehouses have been
restructured as the Pavillons
de Bercy, one of which
contains the Musée des Arts
Forains (Fairground Museum).

The Marina de Bercy is the
starting and finishing point for
cruises along the Seine as far
as the Eiffel Tower.

Nearby is the Promenade
Plantée, a pleasant landscaped
walkway and cycle path, part
of which runs along a disused
viaduct known as the Viaduc
des Arts, whose arches house
artists' workshops, boutiques
and restaurants.

Bibliothèque Nationale de France ⑳

Quai François-Mauriac 75013.
Map 18 F4. 🛈 *01 53 79 59 59.*
Ⓜ *Bibliothèque François Mitterrand,*
Quai de la Gare. ◻ *10am–7pm Tue–*
Sat; noon–7pm Sun. ⬤ *public hols &*
2 wks mid-Sep. 🛈 ♿ ⬛ ⬜
ⓦ *www.bnf.fr*

DOMINIQUE PERRAULT'S 1996
landmark national library
is the most striking and controversial of the *Grands Projets*
with which President Mitterand
revitalized this eastern part of
the city. Four great towers
house 12,000,000 volumes,
with reference and research
libraries in the central podium.
Other resources include over
50,000 digitized illustrations,
sound archives and CD-ROMs.

South of the City

Parc Montsouris ㉑

Blvd Jourdan 75014. 🛈 *01 45 88 28*
60. Ⓜ *Porte d'Orléans.* Ⓡ *Cité Univer-*
sitaire. ◻ *summer: 7.30am– 7pm*
daily; winter: 7.30am–5.30pm daily. ⬛

THIS ENGLISH-STYLE park was
laid out by the landscape
architect Adophe Alphand,
between 1865 and 1878. It has
a pleasant restaurant, lawns,
slopes, elegant tall trees and a
lake which is home to many
different species of birds. This
park is the second largest in
central Paris and is also home
to the municipal meteorological
weather station.

Bercy's striking American Center, designed by Frank Gehry

Cité Universitaire ②

19–21 Blvd Jourdan 75014. ☎ 01 44 16 64 00. RER Cité Universitaire.

THIS IS AN INTERNATIONAL city in miniature for more than 5,000 foreign students attending the University of Paris. Created orginally in the 1920s by benefactors from all over the world, it now contains 37 houses, each in a different architectural style linked to different countries. The Swiss House and the Franco-Brazilian House were designed by the Modernist architect Le Corbusier. The International House, donated by John D Rockefeller in 1936, has a library, restaurant, swimming pool and theatre. The student community makes this a lively and stimulating area of the city.

Japan House at Cité Universitaire

Notre-Dame du Travail ②

59 Rue Vercingetorix 75014. **Map** 15 B3. ☎ 01 44 10 72 92. M Pernety. ◻ 8am–noon Tue–Sun, 2.30pm– 6.30pm daily. ✝ 9am, 7pm Mon–Fri, 6.30pm Sat, 9am, 11am Sun.

THIS CHURCH DATES from 1902 and is made of an unusual mix of materials: stone, rubble and bricks over a riveted steel and iron framework. It was the creation of Father Soulange-Boudin, a priest who organized cooperatives and sought to reconcile labour and capitalism. Local parishioners

The Sebastopol Bell in Notre-Dame du Travail

raised the money for its construction, but lack of funds meant that many features, such as the bell towers, were never built. On the façade hangs the Sebastopol Bell, a trophy from the Crimean War given to the people of the Plaisance district by Napoleon III. The Art Nouveau interior has been completely restored, and features paintings of patron saints.

Institut Pasteur ②

25 Rue du Docteur Roux 75015. **Map** 15 A2. ☎ 01 45 68 82 83. M Pasteur. ◻ 2pm–5.30pm daily (last adm: 4.45pm). ● Aug, public hols. ♿ ⊘ **Films**, **videos**. ⚑ compulsory. 🖥 ⓦ www.pasteur.fr

THE INSTITUT PASTEUR is France's leading medical research centre and was founded by the world-renowned scientist Louis Pasteur in 1888–9. He discovered the process of milk pasteurization as well as vaccines against rabies and anthrax. The centre houses a museum which includes a reconstruction of Pasteur's apartment and laboratory. It was designed by his grandchildren (also scientists) and is faithful to the original down to the last detail. Pasteur's tomb is in a basement crypt built in the style of a small Byzantine chapel. The tomb of Dr Emile Roux, the inventor of the

Louis Pasteur

treatment of diphtheria by serum injection, lies in the garden. The institute has laboratories for pure and applied research, lecture theatres, a reference section, and a hospital founded to apply Pasteur's theories.

There is also a library – the institute's original building from 1888 – where research into AIDS is carried out, led by pioneering Professor Luc Montagnier who discovered the HIV virus in 1983.

Garden in the Parc André Citroën

Parc André Citroën ②

Rue Balard 75015. ☎ 01 40 71 74 03. M Javel, Balard. ◻ 7:30am–dusk Mon–Fri (9am Sat, Sun & public hols).

OPENED IN 1992, this park is the third large-scale vista on the Seine, along with Les Invalides and the Champ-de-Mars. Designed by both landscapers and architects, it is a fascinating blend of styles, ranging from wildflower meadow in the north to the sophisticated monochrome mineral and sculpture gardens of the southern section. Numerous modern water sculptures dot the park, and huge glasshouses nurture a range of environments from a Mediterranean garden and a southern hemisphere zone to an Orangery which is used for horticultural shows in summer.

Versailles ②

See pp248–53.

The Palace and Gardens of Versailles ❷⑥

VISITORS passing through the rich interior of this colossal palace, or strolling in its vast gardens, will understand why it was the glory of the Sun King's reign. Starting in 1668 with his father's modest hunting lodge, Louis XIV built the largest palace in Europe, housing 20,000 people at a time. Architects Louis Le Vau and Jules Hardouin-Mansart designed the

Garden statue of a flautist

buildings, Charles Le Brun did the interiors, and André Le Nôtre, the great landscaper, redesigned the gardens. The gardens are formally styled into regular patterns of paths and groves, hedges and flowerbeds, pools of water and fountains.

★ **Formal Gardens**
Geometric paths and shrubberies are features of the formal gardens.

The Orangery was built beneath the Parterre du Midi to house exotic plants in winter.

The South Parterre's shrubbery and ornate flowerbeds overlook the Swiss pond.

★ **The Château**
Louis XIV made the château into the centre of political power in France.

The Water Parterre's vast pools of water are decorated with superb bronze statues.

Fountain of Latona
Marble basins rise to Balthazar Marsy's statue of the goddess Latona.

Dragon Fountain
The fountain's centrepiece is a winged monster.

The King's Garden with Mirror Pool are a 19th-century English garden and pool created by Louis XVIII.

Colonnade
Mansart designed this circle of marble arches in 1685.

VISITORS' CHECKLIST

Versailles. 🛈 01 30 83 77 88
📠 01 30 83 77 77 🚌 171 to
Versailles. **RER** Versailles Rive
Gauche. **Château** ◻ Oct–Apr:
9am–5.30pm Tue–Sun; May–Sep:
9am–6.30pm Tue–Sun. ♿
Grand Trianon & Petit Trianon
◻ Apr–Oct: noon–6.30pm daily;
Nov–Mar: noon–5.30 daily. ♿
♿🚻🛍️🖼️📷 Les Fêtes
de Nuit (Jul–Sep); Les Grandes
Eaux Musicales (Apr–Oct).
🌐 www.chateauversailles.com

The Grand Canal was the setting for Louis XIV's many boating parties.

Petit Trianon
Built in 1762 as a retreat for Louis XV, this small château became a favourite of Marie-Antoinette.

Fountain of Neptune
Groups of sculptures spray spectacular jets of water in Le Nôtre and Mansart's 17th-century fountain.

STAR SIGHTS

★ **The Château**

★ **Formal Gardens**

★ **Grand Trianon**

★**Grand Trianon**
Louis XIV built this small palace of stone and pink marble in 1687 to escape the rigours of court life, and to enjoy the company of his mistress, Madame de Maintenon.

The Main Palace Buildings of Versailles

Gold crest from the Petit Trianon

THE PRESENT palace grew as a series of envelopes enfolding the original hunting lodge, whose low brick front is still visible in the centre. In the 1660s, Louis Le Vau built the first envelope, a series of wings which expanded into an enlarged courtyard. It was decorated with marble busts, antique trophies and gilded roofs. On the garden side, columns were added to the west facade and a great terrace was created on the first floor. Mansart took over in 1678 and added the two immense north and south wings and filled Le Vau's terrace to form the Hall of Mirrors, which was finished in 1710. The Opera House (*L'Opéra*) was added by Louis XV in 1770.

South Wing
The wing's original apartments for great nobles were replaced by Louis-Philippe's museum of French history.

The Royal Courtyard
was separated from the Ministers' Courtyard by elaborate grillwork during Louis XIV's reign. It was accessible only to royal carriages.

Louis XIV's statue, erected by Louis Philippe in 1837, stands where a gilded gateway once marked the beginning of the Royal Courtyard.

STAR SIGHTS

★ **Marble Courtyard**

★ **L'Opéra**

★ **Chapelle Royale**

Ministers' Courtyard

Main Gate
Mansart's original gateway grille, surmounted by the royal arms, is the entrance to the Ministers' Courtyard.

TIMELINE

1650	1700	1750	1800	1850

Louis XV

1667 Grand Canal begun

1668 Construction of new château by Le Vau

1671 Interior decoration by Le Brun begun

1661 Louis XIV enlarges château

1722 12-year-old Louis XV occupies Versailles

1715 Death of Louis XIV. Versailles abandoned by court

1682 Louis XIV and Marie-Thérèse move to Versailles

1793 Louis XVI and Marie-Antoinette executed

1789 King and queen forced to leave Versailles for Paris

1774 Louis XVI and Marie-Antoinette live at Versailles

1833 Louis-Philippe turns the château into a museum

1919 Treaty of Versailles signed on 28 June

The Clock
Hercules and Mars flank the clock overlooking the Marble Courtyard.

★ **Marble Courtyard**
The courtyard is decorated with marble paving, urns, busts and a gilded balcony.

North Wing
The chapel, Opéra and picture galleries occupy this wing, which originally housed royal apartments.

★ **L'Opéra**
The Opéra was completed in 1770, in time for the marriage of the future Louis XVI and Marie-Antoinette.

★ **Chapelle Royale**
Mansart's last great work, this two-storey, Baroque chapel, was Louis XIV's last addition to Versailles.

Inside the Château of Versailles

THE SUMPTUOUS main apartments are on the first floor of the vast château complex. Around the Marble Courtyard are the private apartments of the king and the queen. On the garden side are the state apartments where official court life took place. These were richly decorated by Charles Le Brun with coloured marbles, stone and wood carvings, murals, velvet, silver and gilded furniture. Beginning with the Salon d'Hercule, each state room is dedicated to an Olympian deity. The climax is the Hall of Mirrors, where 17 great mirrors face tall arched windows.

★ **Queen's Bedroom**
In this room the queens of France gave birth to the royal children in full public view.

STAR SIGHTS
★ **Chapelle Royale**
★ **Salon de Venus**
★ **Hall of Mirrors**
★ **Queen's Bedroom**

KEY

	South wing
	Coronation room
	Madame de Maintenon's apartments
	Queen's apartments and private suite
	State apartments
	King's apartments and private suite
	North wing
	Non-exhibition space

Entrance

Louis XVI's library features Neo-Classical panelling and the king's terrestrial globe.

The Salon du Sacre   **Entrance** is adorned with huge paintings of Napoleon by Jacques-Louis David.

★ **Salon de Venus**
A Louis XIV statue stands amidst the rich marble decor of this room.

★ **Chapelle Royale**
The chapel's first floor was reserved for the royal family and the ground floor for the court. The interior is richly decorated in white marble, gilding and Baroque murals.

★ Hall of Mirrors

Great state occasions were held in this multi-mirrored room stretching 70 m (233 ft) along the west facade. Here in 1919 the Treaty of Versailles was ratified, ending World War I.

Oeil-de-Boeuf

The King's Bedroom
is where Louis XIV died
in 1715, aged 77.

Salon de la Guerre
The room's theme of war is dramatically reinforced by Antoine Coysevox's stuccoed relief of Louis XIV riding to victory.

The Cabinet du Conseil is where the king received his ministers and his family.

Salon d'Apollon
Designed by Le Brun and dedicated to the god Apollo, this was Louis XIV's throne room. A copy of Hyacinthe Rigaud's famous portrait of the king (1701) hangs here.

Salon d'Hercule

Stairs to ground floor reception area

PURSUIT OF THE QUEEN

On 6 October 1789, a Parisian mob invaded the palace seeking the despised Marie-Antoinette. The queen, roused in alarm from her bed, fled towards the king's rooms through the anteroom known as the Oeil-de-Boeuf. As the mob tried to break into the room, the queen beat on the door of the king's bedroom. Once admitted she was safe, at least until morning, when she and the king were removed to Paris by the cheering and triumphant mob.

West of the City

An Art Nouveau window in the Rue la Fontaine

Rue la Fontaine ②⑦

75016. **Map** 9 A4. **M** *Jasmin, Michel-Ange Auteuil.*

T HE RUE LA FONTAINE and surrounding streets act as a showcase for some of the most exciting architecture of the early 20th century. At No. 14 stands the Castel Béranger, a stunning apartment block made from cheap building materials to keep costs low, yet featuring stained glass, convoluted ironwork, balconies and mosaics. It established the reputation of Art Nouveau architect Hector Guimard, who went on to design the entrances for the Paris metro. Several more examples of his work can be seen further along the street, such as the Hôtel Mezzara at No. 60.

Fondation Le Corbusier ②⑧

8–10 Square du Docteur Blanche 75016.
C *01 42 88 41 53.* **M** *Jasmin.*
○ *10am–12.30pm, 1.30pm–6pm (5pm Fri) Mon–Fri.* **●** *public hols, Aug, 24 Dec–2 Jan.* **⌘ ○** *Films, videos.*
⃣ See *History of Paris pp36–7.*
W *www.fondationlecorbusier.asso.fr*

I N A QUIET CORNER of Auteuil stand the villas La Roche *(see p265)* and Jeanneret, the first two Parisian houses built by the brilliant and influential 20th-century architect Charles-Edouard Jeanneret, known as Le Corbusier. Built at the start of the 1920s, they demonstrate his revolutionary use of white concrete in Cubist forms. Rooms flow into each other allowing maximum light and volume, and the houses stand on stilts with windows along their entire length.

Villa La Roche was owned by the art patron Raoul La Roche (admission is limited to 20, so you may have to wait). Today both villas serve as a documentation centre on Le Corbusier.

Musée Marmottan ②⑨

2 Rue Louis Boilly 75016.
C *01 44 96 50 33.* **M** *Muette.*
○ *10am–6pm Tue–Sun (last adm: 5.30pm).* **●** *1 May, 25 Dec.* **⌘**
○ W *www.marmottan.com*

T HE MUSEUM WAS created in the 19th-century mansion of the art historian Paul Marmottan in 1932, when he bequeathed his house and his Renaissance, Consular and

First Empire collections of paintings and furniture to the Institut de France. The focus of the museum changed in 1971 after the bequest by Michel Monet of 65 paintings by his father, the Impressionist painter Claude Monet. Some of Monet's most famous paintings are here, including *Impression – Sunrise* (from which the term Impressionist was derived), a painting of Rouen Cathedral and several *Water Lilies*.

Part of Monet's personal art collection also passed to the museum, including paintings by Camille Pissarro and the Impressionists Pierre Auguste Renoir and Alfred Sisley. The museum also displays medieval illuminated manuscripts.

La Barque **(1887) by Claude Monet, in the Musée Marmottan**

Bois de Boulogne ③⓪

75016. **M** *Porte Maillot, Porte Dauphine, Porte d'Auteuil, Sablons.*
○ *24 hrs daily.* **⌘** *to specialist gardens and museum.*
⛨ Shakespeare garden ⃣
Open-air theatre **C** *01 40 19 95 33/01 42 76 55 06.* **○** *May–Sep.*
Bagatelle & Rose gardens **C** *01 40 67 97 00.* **○** *8.30am. Closing times vary from 4.30pm to 8pm according to season.* **Jardin d'Acclimatation**
C *01 40 67 90 82.* **○** *10am–7pm daily (Oct–May: 6pm).* **▣ ▮▮**
Musée en Herbe **C** *01 40 67 97 66.*
○ *10am–6pm Mon–Fri, 2pm–6pm Sat.* **⌘ ⛨ Musée des Arts et Traditions Populaires** **C** *01 44 17 60 00.* **○** *9.30am–5.15pm Wed–Mon.*
⌘ ⛨ *by appt.*

B ETWEEN THE western edges of Paris and the River Seine this 865-ha (2,137-acre) park offers a vast belt of greenery for strolling, cycling, riding, boating, picnicking or

Villa La Roche, home of the Fondation Le Corbusier

Kiosque de l'Empereur, on an island in the Grand Lac, Bois de Boulogne

spending a day at the races. The Bois de Boulogne is all that remains of the vast Forêt du Rouvre. In the mid-19th century Napoleon III had it redesigned and landscaped by Haussmann along the lines of London's Hyde Park.

There are many beautiful areas within the Bois. The Pré Catelan is a self-contained park with the widest beech tree in Paris, and the charming Bagatelle gardens feature architectural follies and an 18th-century villa famous for its rose garden, where an international rose competition is held in June. The villa was built in 64 days as a bet between the Comte d'Artois and Marie-Antoinette. The Bois has a reputation as a seedy area after dark so is best avoided at night.

Musée des années 30 **31**

28 Ave André Morizet, Boulogne-Billancourt 92100. **(** 01 55 18 46 42. **M** Marcel Sembat. **⏱** 11am–5.45pm Tue–Sun. **&** ☒ ☐ ☐ **W** www.boulognebillancourt.com

La Grande Arche in La Défense

INAUGURATED IN 1998, this museum of the 1930s forms part of an arts complex, the Espace Landowski, named after Paul Landowski, a sculptor who lived in Boulogne-Billancourt from 1905 until his death in 1961, and his musician brother, Marcel. Several of Paul's works are on show in the museum. The complex also includes a library, a gallery of video directors and a cinema, and will soon have a multimedia centre with artists studios.

Through paintings, drawings, sculpture and artifacts, the museum gives a vivid impression of the aesthetic mood of the era. The museum also organizes temporary thematic exhibitions relating to the period. Themed tours of the architectural and industrial heritage of Boulogne-Billancourt are also run.

La Défense **32**

La Grande Arche. **(** 01 49 07 27 57. **RER** La Défense. **⏱** 10am–7pm daily (last adm: 1 hr before closing). ☒ ☐ **H** See **History of Paris** pp38–9. **W** www.grandearche.com

THIS SKYSCRAPER business city on the western edge of Paris is the largest new office development in Europe and covers 80 ha (198 acres). It was launched

in the 1960s to create a new home for leading French and multi-national companies. A major artistic scheme has transformed many of the squares into fascinating open-air museums.

In 1989 La Grande Arche was added to the complex, an enormous hollow cube large enough to contain Notre-Dame cathedral. This was designed by Danish architect Otto von Spreckelsen as part of major construction works, or *Grands Travaux*, which were initiated by (and are now a memorial to) the late President François Mitterrand.

The arch now houses an exhibition gallery and a conference centre, and commands a superb view over the city of Paris.

Château de Malmaison **33**

Ave du Château 92500 Rueil-Malmaison. **(** 01 41 29 05 55. **RER** La Défense then bus 258. **⏱** 10 am Wed–Mon; closing times vary according to season; phone for details. ☒ ☐ See **History of Paris** pp30–31. **W** www.napoleon.org

THIS 17TH-CENTURY château was bought in 1799 by Josephine de Beauharnais, wife of Napoleon I. A magnificent veranda, Classical statues and a small theatre were added. After his campaigns, Napoleon and his entourage would come here to relax.

The Empress Josephine's bed in the Château de Malmaison

The château became Josephine's main residence after their divorce. Today, it is an important Napoleonic museum, together with the nearby Château de Bois-Préau.

Furniture, portraits, artefacts and mementoes of the imperial family are displayed in rooms reconstructed in the style of the First Empire.

Part of the original grounds still exists, including Josephine's famous rose garden.

FIVE GUIDED WALKS

Paris is a city for walking. It is more compact and easier to get around than many other great capitals. Most of its great sights are within walking distance of one another and they are close to the heart of the city, the Ile de la Cité.

There are 14 classic tourist areas described in the *Area by Area* section of this book, each with a short walk marked on its *Street-by-Street* map, taking you past many of the most interesting sights. Yet Paris offers a wealth of lesser known but equally remarkable areas, whose special history, architecture and local customs reveal to the visitor other facets of the city.

The five walks around the following neighbourhoods not only take in their main sights, they also introduce visitors to the subtle details and contrasts that contribute to the special character of each district. These include cafés, street markets, quirky churches, canals, gardens, old village streets and bridges. And the literary,

Parc Monceau statue

artistic and historical associations make it possible for the past and present to blend into the changing and vibrant life of the modern city.

The walks contrast the smart areas of Auteuil, Monceau and Ile St-Louis with the old working-class areas of Montmartre and St-Martin. Auteuil is renowned for its luxury modern residential architecture, Monceau for its sumptuous Second Empire mansions and St-Louis for its *ancien régime* town houses, tree-lined river quays, narrow streets and film star and literati residents. Old village streets that were once home to famous artists and bohemians still enrich Montmartre, and the old-fashioned charm of the iron foot-bridges survives along the old industrial Canal St-Martin.

All the walk areas are readily accessible by public transport and the nearest metro stations and bus routes are listed in the *Tips for Walkers* boxes. For each of the walks there are suggestions on convenient resting points, such as cafés, restaurants, gardens and squares, along the route.

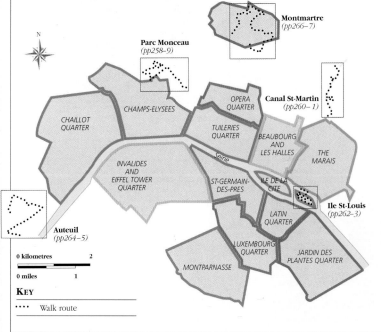

Montmartre
(pp266–7)

Parc Monceau
(pp258–9)

Canal St-Martin
(pp260–1)

OPERA QUARTER

CHAMPS-ELYSEES

CHAILLOT QUARTER

TUILERIES QUARTER

BEAUBOURG AND LES HALLES

THE MARAIS

Seine

INVALIDES AND EIFFEL TOWER QUARTER

ST-GERMAIN-DES-PRES

ILE DE LA CITE

Ile St-Louis
(pp262–3)

Auteuil
(pp264–5)

LATIN QUARTER

LUXEMBOURG QUARTER

JARDIN DES PLANTES QUARTER

MONTPARNASSE

N

0 kilometres   2

0 miles   1

KEY

•••• Walk route

Bridge over the canal St-Martin

A 90-Minute Walk around Parc Monceau

THIS LEISURELY WALK passes through the exquisite late-
18th-century Parc Monceau, the centrepiece of a
smart Second Empire district. It then follows a route
along surrounding streets, where groups of opulent
mansions stunningly convey the magnificence in which
some Parisians live, before ending at Place St-Augustin.
For details on Monceau sights, see pages 230–31.

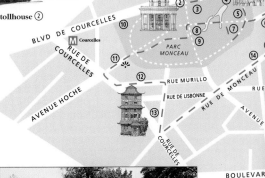

Ruysdaël gate

Parc Monceau to Avenue Velasquez

The walk starts at the Monceau metro station ① on the Boulevard de Courcelles. Enter the park where Nicolas Ledoux's 18th-century tollhouse ② stands. On either side are sumptuously gilded 19th-century wrought-iron gates which support ornate lampposts.

wide tree-lined street with 19th-century Neo-Classical mansions. At No. 7 is the splendid Cernuschi museum ⑥, which houses a collection of Far Eastern art.

Parc Monceau's tollhouse ②

Take the second path on the left past the monument to Guy de Maupassant ③ (1897). This is only one of a series of six Belle Epoque monuments of prominent French writers and musicians which are picturesquely scattered throughout the park. Most of them feature a solemn bust of a great man who is accompanied by a swooning muse.

Straight ahead is the most important remaining folly, a moss-covered Corinthian colonnade ④ running around the edge of a charming tiny lake with the requisite island in the centre. Walk around the colonnade and under a 16th-century arch ⑤ trans-planted from the old Paris Hôtel de Ville *(see p102)*, which burned down in 1871.

Turn left on the Allée de la Comtesse de Ségur and go into Avenue Velasquez, a

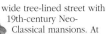

Colonnade in Parc Monceau ④

Avenue Velasquez to Avenue Van Dyck

Re-enter the park and turn left into the second small winding path, which is bordered by an 18th-century mossy pyramid ⑦, antique tombs, a stone arcade, an obelisk and a small Chinese stone pagoda. The romantically melancholy tone of these false ruins suits the spirit of the late 18th century.

Turn right on the first path past the pyramid and walk back to the central avenue. Straight ahead a Renaissance bridge fords the little stream running from the lake. Turn left and walk past the

monument (1902) to the musician Ambroise Thomas ⑧. Immediately behind there is a lovely artificial mountain with cascade. Turn left on the next avenue and walk to the monument (1897) to the composer Charles Gounod ⑨ on the left. From here follow the first winding path to the right towards the Avenue Van Dyck exit. Ahead to the right, in the corner of the park, is the Chopin monument ⑩ (1906), and looking along the Allée de la Comtesse de Ségur, the monument to the 19th-century French poet Alfred de Musset.

Ambroise Thomas statue ⑧

Avenue Van Dyck to Rue de Monceau

Leave the park and pass into Avenue Van Dyck. No. 5 on the right is a most impressive Parc Monceau mansion ⑪, a Neo-Baroque structure built by chocolate manufacturer Emile Menier; No. 6 is in the French Renaissance style that came back into favour in the 1860s. Straight ahead, beyond the ornate grille, there is a fine view of Avenue Hoche and in the distance the Arc de Triomphe. Walk past the

The mountain cascade ⑧

gate and turn left into Rue de Courcelles and left again into Rue Murillo, bordered by more elaborate town houses in 18th-century and French Renaissance styles ⑫. At the crossing of Rue Rembrandt, on the left, is another gate into the park and on the right a massive apartment building from 1900 (No. 7) and an elegant French Renaissance house with elaborately carved wooden front door (No. 1). At the corner of the Rue Rembrandt and the Rue de Courcelles stands the oddest of all the neighbourhood buildings, a striking five-storey red Chinese pagoda ⑬. It is an exclusive emporium of Chinese art.

Turn left on to the Rue de Monceau, walk past Avenue Ruysdaël and continue to the Musée Nissim de Camondo at No. 63 Rue de Monceau ⑭. Some nearby buildings worth having a look at are Nos. 52, 60 and 61 ⑮.

Boulevard Malesherbes

At the junction of Rue de Monceau and Boulevard Malesherbes turn right. This long boulevard with dignified six-storey apartment buildings is typical of the great avenues cut through Paris by Baron Haussmann, Prefect of the Seine during the Second Empire (see pp32–3). They

greatly pleased the Industrial Age bourgeoisie, but horrified sensitive souls and writers who compared them with the buildings of New York.

No. 75 is the posh marble front of Benneton, the most fashionable Paris card and stationery engraver ⑯. On the left, approaching the Boulevard Haussmann, looms the greatest 19th-century Paris church, St-Augustin ⑰, built by Victor-Louis Baltard. Enter the church through the back door on Rue de la Bienfaisance. Walk through the church and leave by the main door. On the left is the massive stone building of the French Officers' club, the Cercle Militaire ⑱. Straight ahead is a bronze statue of Joan of Arc ⑲. Continue on to Place St-Augustin to St-Augustin metro station.

Joan of Arc statue ⑲

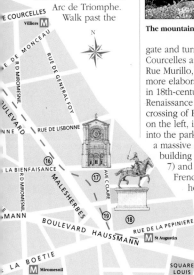

KEY

— Walk route

∴ Good viewing point

Ⓜ Metro station

| 0 metres | 250 |
| 0 yards | 250 |

Chinese pagoda emporium ⑬

TIPS FOR WALKERS

Starting point: Blvd de Courcelles.

Length: 3 km (2 miles).

Getting there: The nearest metro is Monceau, reached by bus No. 30; No. 84 goes to metro Courcelles and No. 94 stops between Monceau & Villiers metros.

St Augustin church: Open 8.30am –7pm daily (closed 12–4.30pm w/e).

Stopping-off points: Near the Renaissance bridge in the Parc Monceau there is a kiosk serving coffee and sandwiches. There are two cafés at Place de Rio de Janeiro and several brasseries around Place St-Augustin. The Square M Pagnol is a pleasant place to relax and take in the beauty of the park at the end of the walk.

A 90-Minute Walk along the Canal St-Martin

THE WALK ALONG the quays on either side of the Canal St-Martin is an experience of Paris very different from that of smarter districts. Here, the older surviving landmarks of the neighbourhood – the factories, warehouses, dwellings, taverns and cafés – hint at life in a thriving 19th-century industrial, working-class world. But there are also the softer charms of the old iron footbridges, the tree-lined quays, the inevitable fishermen, the river barges, and the still waters of the broad canal basins. A walk along the canal, which connects the Bassin de la Villette with the Seine, will evoke images of the Pernod-drinking, working-class Paris of Jean Gabin and Edith Piaf.

The 18th-century
Barrière de la Villette ②

Bassin de la Villette looking north ③

Place de Stalingrad to Avenue Jean-Jaurès

From the Stalingrad metro station ①, follow Boulevard de la Villette to the new square in front of the Barrière de la Villette ②. This is one of the few remaining 18th-century tollhouses in Paris, designed by the celebrated Neo-Classical architect Nicolas Ledoux in the 1780s. The fountains, square and terraces were designed in the 1980s to provide an attractive setting and fine views of the Bassin de la Villette ③ to the north.

Walk towards Avenue Jean-Jaurès. On the left is the first lock ④ leading down to the canal.

Quai de Valmy to Rue Bichat

Cross over to the Quai de Jemmapes, which runs the whole length of the east side

View from Rue E Varlin bridge ⑦

KEY

— Walk route

❀ Good viewing point

Ⓜ Metro station

0 metres	500
0 yards	500

Courtyard garden of Hôpital St-Louis ⑭

ENUE JEAN JAURÈS

AVE SECRETAN

Iron footbridges over the canal ⑤

French Communist Party headquarters ⑨ on Place du Colonel Fabien. The building can be recognized by its curving glazed tower.

Return to the Quai de Jemmapes, where at No. 134 ⑩ stands one of the few surviving brick-and-iron industrial buildings that used to line the canal in the 19th century. At No. 126 ⑪ is another notable modern building, a residence for the aged, with monumental concrete arches and glazed bay windows. Further along, at No. 112 ⑫, is an Art Deco apartment building with bay windows, decorative iron balconies and tiles. On the ground floor there is a typical 1930s proletarian café. Here the canal curves gracefully into the third lock, spanned by a charming transparent iron footbridge ⑬.

Hôpital St-Louis to Rue Léon Jouhaux

Turn left into Rue Bichat, which leads to the remarkable 17th-century Hôpital St-Louis ⑭. Enter through the hospital's old main gate with its high-pitched roof and massive stone arch. Pass into the courtyard. The hospital was founded in 1607 by Henri IV, the first Bourbon king, to care for the victims of the plague. Leave the courtyard from the central gate on the wing on your left. Here you pass by the 17th-century hospital chapel ⑮ and out into the Rue de la Grange aux Belles.

Turn left and walk back to the canal. At the junction of

of the canal and down to the first bridge on Rue Louis Blanc ⑤. Cross the bridge to the Quai de Valmy. From the corner there is a glimpse of the oblique granite and glass front of the new Paris Industrial Tribunal ⑥ on the Rue Louis Blanc.

Continue along Quai de Valmy. At Rue E Varlin cross the bridge ⑦, from where there is an attractive view of the second canal lock, lock-keeper's house, public gardens and old lampposts. At the other side of the bridge and slightly to the left, go along the pedestrianized Rue Haendel, which provides a good view of the towering, terraced buildings of a social housing estate ⑧. Nearby is the

Rue de la Grange and the Quai de Jemmapes stood, until 1627, the notorious Montfaucon gallows ⑯, one of the chief public execution spots of medieval Paris. Turn into the Quai de Jemmapes. At No. 101 ⑰ is the original front of the Hôtel du Nord, which was made famous in the eponymous 1930s film. In front is another iron footbridge and a drawbridge ⑱ for traffic, providing a charming setting with views of the canal on either side. Cross over and continue down the Quai de Valmy until the last footbridge ⑲ at the corner of the Rue Léon Jouhaux. From here the canal can be seen disappearing under the surface of Paris, to continue its journey, through a great stone arch.

Entrance to Hôpital St-Louis ⑭

Square Frédéric Lemaître to Place de la République

Walk along Square Frédéric Lemaître ⑳ to the start of Boulevard Jules Ferry, which has a public garden stretching down its centre. The garden was built over the canal in the 1860s. At its head stands a charmingly nostalgic statue of a flower girl of the 1830s, *La Grisette* ㉑. On the left is a busy working-class street, Rue du Faubourg du Temple ㉒, with flourishing ethnic shops and restaurants. Follow the street to the right and on to the metro station in the Place de la République.

A shop front in Rue du Temple ㉒

A 90-Minute Walk around the Ile St-Louis

T HE WALK AROUND this charming tiny
island passes along the enchanting,
picturesque tree-lined quays from Pont
Louis-Philippe to Quai d'Anjou, taking in
the sumptuous 17th-century *hôtels* that
infuse the area with such a powerful sense
of period. It then penetrates into the heart
of the island along the main street, Rue St-
Louis-en-l'Ile, enlivened by chic restaurants,
cafés, art galleries and boutiques, before
returning to the north side of the island and
back to Pont Marie. For more information on
the main sights, see pages 77 and 87.

Left Bank view of the Ile St-Louis

Fishing on a St-Louis quayside

Metro Pont Marie to Rue Jean du Bellay

From the Pont Marie metro
station ① walk down Quai
des Celestins and Quai de
l'Hôtel de Ville, lined with
traditional bookstands, from
where there is a good view of
Ile St-Louis. Turn left at Pont
Louis-Philippe ② and, having
crossed it, take the steps down
to the lower quay immediately
to the right. Walk around the
tree-shaded west point of the
island ③, then up the other

side to the Pont St-Louis
④. Opposite the bridge,
on the corner of Rue
Jean du Bellay, is the
Flore en l'Ile ⑤, the
smartest café-cum-tea
salon on the island.

Quai d'Orléans

From the corner
of the Quai
d'Orléans and
the Rue Jean
du Bellay
there are
fine views
of the
Panthéon's
dome and Notre-
Dame. Along the
quay, Nos. 18–20,
the Hôtel Rolland,
has unusual
Hispano-
Moorish
windows.
No. 12 ⑥ is
one of
several stately
17th-century
houses with handsome
wrought-iron balconies. At
No. 6 the former Polish library,

KEY

— Walk route

✢ Good viewing point

Ⓜ Metro station

0 metres	250
0 yards	250

founded in 1838, has a small
museum devoted to the Polish
poet Adam Mickiewicz (closed
for renovation until 2003) ⑦; it
also contains some Chopin
scores and autographs by
George Sand and Victor Hugo.
On the right, the Pont de la
Tournelle ⑧ links the island to
the Left Bank.

Seine barge passing a St-Louis quay

Quai de Béthune to Pont Marie

Continue beyond the bridge and into Quai de Béthune, where the Nobel-laureate Marie Curie lived at No. 36 ⑨, and where beautiful wrought-iron balconies gracefully decorate Nos. 34 and 30. The Hôtel Richelieu ⑩ at No. 18 is one of the island's most beautiful houses.

St-Louis church door ⑰

It features a fine garden where it has retained its original Classical blind arcades.

If you turn left down Rue Bretonvilliers there is an imposing 17th-century house ⑪, with a high-pitched roof resting on a great Classical arch spanning the street. Back on the Quai de Béthune, proceed to the Pont de Sully ⑫, a late 19th-century bridge joining the river banks. Ahead is the charming 19th-century Square Barye ⑬, a shady public garden at the east point of the island, from where there are fine river views. From here travel towards the Quai d'Anjou as far as the corner of Rue St-Louis-en-l'Ile to see the most famous house on

Gargoyle at No. 51 Rue St-Louis-en-l'Ile ⑳

small, chic, bistro-style restaurants with pleasantly old-fashioned decors. No. 31 is the original Berthillon shop ⑱, No. 60 an art gallery ⑲ with an original 19th-century window front, and at No. 51 is one of the few 18th-century *hôtels* on the island, Hôtel Chernizot ⑳, with a superb Rococo balcony which rests on leering gargoyles.

Turn right into Rue Jean du Bellay and along to Pont Louis-Philippe. Turn right again into the Quai de Bourbon, which is lined by one of the island's finest rows of *hôtels*, the most notable being Hôtel Jassaud at No. 19 ㉑. Continue to the 17th-century Pont Marie ㉒ and cross it to the Pont Marie metro on the other side.

The 17th-century Pont Marie ㉒

the island, the Hôtel Lambert ⑭ *(see pp24–5)*. Continue into the Quai d'Anjou where Hôtel de Lauzun ⑮ at No. 17 has a severe Classical front and a beautiful gilded balcony and drain-pipes. Now turn left into Rue Poulletier and note the convent of the Daughters of Charity ⑯ at No. 5 bis. Further on, at the corner of Rue Poulletier and Rue St-Louis-en-l'Ile, is the island church, St-Louis ⑰, with its unusual tower, projecting clock and carved main door.

Proceed along Rue St-Louis-en-l'Ile, which abounds in

Windows of the Hôtel Rolland

TIPS FOR WALKERS

Starting point: Pont Marie metro.
Length: 2.6 km (1.6 miles).
Getting there: The walk starts from the Pont Marie metro. However, bus route 67 takes you to Rue du Pont Louis-Philippe and also crosses the island along Rue des Deux Ponts and Blvd Pont de Sully; routes 86 and 87 also cross the island along Blvd Pont de Sully.
Stopping-off points: There are cafés, such as Flore en l'Ile and the Berthillon shops for ice cream (see p311). Restaurants on the Rue St-Louis-en-l'Ile include Auberge de la Reine Blanche (No. 30) and Au Gourmet de l'Isle (No. 42), as well as a pâtisserie and a cheese shop. Good resting-points are the tree-shaded quays and Square Barye to the eastern end of the island.

A 90-Minute Walk in Auteuil

PART OF THE FASCINATION of the walk around this bastion of bourgeois life in westernmost Paris lies in the contrasting nature of the area's streets. The old village provincialism of Rue d'Auteuil, where the walk begins, leads on to the masterpieces of luxurious modern architecture along Rue La Fontaine and Rue du Docteur Blanche. The walk ends at the Jasmin metro station. For more on the sights of Auteuil, see page 254.

Obelisk, Place d'Auteuil ①

Rue d'Auteuil

The walk begins at Place d'Auteuil ①, a leafy village square with a striking Guimard-designed metro station entrance, an 18th-century funerary obelisk, and the 19th-century Neo-Romanesque Notre Dame d'Auteuil. Walk down Rue d'Auteuil, the main street of the old village, and take in the sense of a past provincial world. The Auberge du Mouton Blanc brasserie ② now occupies the premises of the area's oldest tavern, favoured by Molière and his actors in the 17th century. The house at Nos. 45–47 ③ was the residence of American presidents John Adams and his son John Quincy Adams. Move on to the pleasantly shaded Place Jean Lorrain ④, the site of the local market. Here there is a Wallace drinking fountain,

Wallace fountain ④

donated by the English millionaire, Richard Wallace in the 19th century. On the right, down Rue Donizetti, is the Villa Montmorency ⑤, a private enclave of luxury villas, built on the former country estate of the Comtesse de Boufflers.

Rue La Fontaine

Continue the walk along Rue La Fontaine, renowned for its many Hector Guimard buildings. Marcel Proust was born at No.96. Henri Sauvage's ensemble of artists' studios at No. 65 ⑥ is one of the most original Art Deco buildings in Paris. No. 60 is a Guimard Art Nouveau house ⑦ with elegant cast-iron balconies. Further along there is a small Neo-Gothic chapel at No. 40 ⑧ and Art Nouveau apartment buildings at Nos. 19 and 21 ⑨. No. 14 is Guimard's most spectacular building, the Castel Béranger ⑩, with a superb iron gate.

TIPS FOR WALKERS

Starting point: Place d'Auteuil.
Length: 3 km (2 miles).
Getting there: The nearest metro station to the starting point is Eglise d'Auteuil, and buses that take you there are Nos. 22, 52 and 62.
Stopping-off points: Along Rue d'Auteuil is the inexpensive trendy brasserie, L'Auberge du Mouton Blanc, with 1930s decor. No. 17 Rue La Fontaine is a tiny 1900 Art Nouveau café with old tiled floors and original zinc-covered bar. Place Jean Lorrain is a pleasantly shaded square where walkers can rest, and on Rue La Fontaine there is a small park in front of the Neo-Gothic chapel at No. 40. Further on at Place Rodin there is a pleasant public garden.

Doorway of No. 28 Rue d'Auteuil.

⑯

⑦

⑱

Villa Montmorency

RUE DU DOCTEUR BLANCHE

RUE DE L'YVE

RUE RAFFET

RUE DE LA SOURCE

AVENUE M

RUE POUSSIN

RUE LA FONT

RUE D'AUTEUIL

④ RUE ② D'AUTE

Ⓜ③
Michel Ange Auteuil

RUE MICHEL ANGE

RUE BOILEAU

KEY

— Walk route

Good viewing point

Ⓜ Metro station

| 0 metres | 250 |
| 0 yards | 250 |

Rue de l'Assomption to Rue Mallet Stevens

At the corner of Rue de l'Assomption there is a view of the massive Maison de Radio-France ⑪ built in 1963 to house French radio and television *(see p200)*. It was one of the first modern postwar buildings in the city. Turn left into Rue de l'Assomption and walk to the fine 1920s apartment building at No. 18 ⑫. Turn left into Rue du Général Dubail and follow the street to Place Rodin, where the great sculptor's bronze

Shuttered bay window at No. 3 Square Jasmin ⑲

nude, *The Age of Bronze* (1877) ⑬, occupies the centre of the roundabout.

Take the Avenue Théodore Rousseau back to Rue de l'Assomption and turn left

Courtyard of No. 14 Rue La Fontaine

towards Avenue Mozart. Cut through in the 1880s, this is the principal artery of the 16th arrondissement, linking north and south and lined with typical bourgeois apartment buildings of the late 19th century. Cross the avenue and continue to the Avenue des Chalets where there is a typical collection of weekend villas ⑭ recalling the quieter suburban Auteuil of the mid-19th century. Further along Rue de l'Assomption, Notre-Dame de l'Assomption ⑮ is a Neo-Renaissance 19th-century church. Turn left into Rue du Docteur Blanche. At No. 9 and down the adjoining Rue Mallet Stevens ⑯ there is a row of celebrated modern houses in the International Modern style by the architect Robert Mallet Stevens. In this expensive, once avant-garde enclave lived architects, designers, artists and their modern-minded clients. The original proportions, however,

were altered dramatically by the addition of an extra three storeys in the 1960s.

Continue on Rue du Docteur Blanche until coming to Villa du Docteur Blanche on the left. At the end of this small cul de sac is the most celebrated modern house in Auteuil, Le Corbusier's Villa Roche ⑰. Together with the adjoining Villa Jeanneret, it is now part of the Corbusier Foundation *(see pp36–7)*. Built for an art collector in 1924 using the new technique of reinforced concrete, the house, with its geometric forms and lack of ornamentation, is a model of early Modernism.

No. 18 Rue de l'Assomption, detail ⑫

Rue du Docteur Blanche to Rue Jasmin

Walk back to Rue du Docteur Blanche and turn right into Rue Henri Heine. No. 18 bis ⑱ is a very elegant Neo-Classical 1920s apartment building offering a good contrast to one of Guimard's last creations from 1926 next door – an Art Nouveau facade much tamer than that at Castel Béranger but still employing brick, and with projecting bay windows and a terraced roof. Turn left on Rue Jasmin. In the second cul de sac on the left there is another Guimard house at No. 3 Square Jasmin ⑲. Towards the end of Rue Jasmin is the metro station.

The Age of Bronze ⑬

A 90-Minute Walk in Montmartre

THE WALK BEGINS at the base of the sand-stone *butte* (hill), where old theatres and dance halls, once frequented and depicted by painters from Renoir to Picasso, have now been taken over by rock clubs. It continues steeply uphill to the original village, along streets which still retain the atmosphere caught by artists like Van Gogh, before winding downhill to end at Place Blanche. For more on the main sights of Montmartre and the Sacré-Coeur, see pages 218–27.

Montmartre seen from a distance

Place Pigalle to Rue Ravignan

The walk starts at the lively Place Pigalle ① and follows Rue Frochot to the Rue Victor Massé. At the corner is the ornate entrance to an exclusive private street bordered by turn-of-the-century chalets ②. Opposite, at No. 27 Rue Victor Massé, is an ornate mid-19th century apartment building, and No. 25 is where Vincent Van Gogh and his

brother Theo lived in 1886 ③. The famous Chat Noir ④, Montmartre's most renowned artistic cabaret in the 1890s, flourished at No. 12. At the end of the street begins the wide tree-lined Avenue Trudaine. Take Rue Lallier on the left to Boulevard de Rochechouart. Continue east. No. 84 is the first address of the Chat Noir and No. 82 was the Grand Trianon ⑤, Paris' oldest-surviving cinema, from

Entrance gate to Avenue Frochot

TIPS FOR WALKERS

Starting point: Place Pigalle.
Length: 2.3 km (1.4 miles). The walk goes up some very steep streets to the top; if you do not feel like the climb, consider taking the Montmartrobus, which covers most of the walk and starts at Place Pigalle.
Getting there: The nearest metro is Pigalle; buses that take you there are Nos. 30, 54 and 67.
Stopping-off points: There are many cafés and shops in Rue Lepic and the Rue des Abbesses. Rayons de la Santé, to the right of the theatre in Place Charles Dullin, is one of the city's best vegetarian restaurants. For shade and a rest, Place Jean-Baptiste Clément and Square S Buisson at Avenue Junot are charming public squares.

the early 1890s. Further along, No. 74 is the original front of Montmartre's first great cancan dance hall, the Elysée-Montmartre ⑥.

Turn left on to Rue Steinkerque, which leads to Sacré-Coeur gardens, and then left into Rue d'Orsel, which leads to the leafy square, Place Charles Dullin, where the small early 19th-century Théâtre de l'Atelier ⑦ stands. Continue up the hill on Rue des Trois Frères and turn left on Rue Yvonne le Tac, which leads to Place des Abbesses ⑧. This is one of the most pleasant and liveliest squares in the area. It has conserved its entire canopied Art Nouveau metro entrance by Hector Guimard. Opposite is St-Jean l'Evangéliste ⑨, an unusual brick and mosaic Art

Rue André Antoine ⑩

Nouveau church. To the right of the church a flight of steep steps leads to the tiny Rue André Antoine where the Pointillist painter Georges Seurat lived at No. 39 ⑩. Continue along Rue des Abbesses and turn right at Rue Ravignan.

Rue Ravignan
From here there is a sweeping view of Paris. Climb the steps straight ahead to the deeply shaded Place Emile Goudeau ⑪. To the left, at No. 13, is the original entrance to the Bateau-Lavoir, the most important cluster of artists' studios

Artist selling his work at Place du Tertre ⑮

St-Jean l'Evangéliste, detail ⑨

in Montmartre. Here Picasso lived and worked in the early 1900s. Further up, at the corner of Rue Orchampt and Rue Ravignan, there is a row of picturesque 19th-century artists' studios ⑫.

Rue Ravignan to Rue Lepic
Continue up the hill along the small public garden, Place Jean-Baptiste Clément ⑬. At the top, cross Rue Norvins. Opposite is an old Monmartois restaurant, Auberge de la Bonne Franquette ⑭, which, as Aux Billards en Bois, used to be a favourite gathering place for 19th-century artists. Continue along the narrow Rue St-Rustique, from where Sacré-Coeur can be seen. At the end and to the right is Place du Tertre ⑮, the main village square. From here go north on Rue du Mont Cenis and turn left to Rue Cortot. Erik Satie, the eccentric composer, lived in No. 6 ⑯, and at No. 12 is the Musée de Montmartre ⑰. Turn right on Rue des Saules and walk past the very pretty Montmartre vineyard ⑱ to the Au Lapin Agile ⑲ at the

corner of Rue St-Vincent. Go back down Rue des Saules and right on Rue de l'Abreuvoir, an attractive street of turn-of-the-century villas and gardens. Continue into l'Allée des Brouillards, a leafy pedestrian alley. No. 6 ⑳ was Renoir's last house in Montmartre. Take the steps down into the Rue Simon Dereure and immediately turn left into a small park, which can be crossed to reach Avenue Junot. Here, No. 15 ㉑ was the house of Dadaist Tristan Tzara in the early 1920s. Continue up Avenue Junot, turn right on Rue Girardon and right again on Rue Lepic.

Au Lapin Agile nightclub ⑲

Rue Lepic to Place Blanche
At the corner is one of Montmartre's few surviving windmills, the Moulin du Radet ㉒. Continue along Rue Lepic: to the right at the top of a slope is another windmill survivor, the Moulin de la Galette ㉓. Turn left on Rue de l'Armée d'Orient, with its picturesque artists' studios ㉔, and left again into Rue Lepic. Van Gogh lived at No. 54 ㉕ in June 1886. Continue to Place Blanche, and on Boulevard de Clichy to the right is one of the area's great landmarks, the Moulin Rouge ㉖.

Moulin Rouge nightclub near the Place Blanche ㉖

TRAVELLERS'
NEEDS

WHERE TO STAY

Paris has more guest rooms than any other city in Europe. Hotels vary from magnificent luxurious places like the Ritz (the French call them *palaces*) and exclusive establishments like L'Hôtel, where Oscar Wilde died beyond his means, to much simpler hotels in charming older parts of Paris.

We have inspected hotels in all price brackets and have selected a broad range, all of which are good value for money. The choosing chart on pages 278–9 will help narrow down your choice of hotel; for more details on each one turn to the listings on pages 280–85. The listings and the choosing chart are organized by area according to hotel price. Information on other types of accommodation can be found on pages 272–4.

It is worth noting that *hôtel* does not always mean "hotel". It can also mean a town hall (*hôtel de ville*), hospital (*Hôtel-Dieu*) or a mansion.

WHERE TO LOOK

Hotels in Paris tend to cluster by type in particular areas, with the river separating the business and leisure districts. Luxury hotels tend to be on the north side and *hôtels de charme* on the south side.

In the fashionable districts near the Champs-Elysées lie many of the grandest hotels in Paris, including the Royal Monceau, the Bristol, the Four Seasons George V, the Meurice and the Plaza Athénée. Several less well known but elegant hotels can be found in the residential and ambassadorial quarter near the Palais de Chaillot.

To the east, still on the Right Bank, in the regenerated Marais, a number of the old mansions and palaces have been converted into exceptionally attractive small hotels at reasonable prices. The nearby areas around Les Halles and the Rue St-Denis, however, attract prostitutes and drug addicts. Just south of the Marais across the Seine, the Ile St-Louis and Ile de la Cité have several charming hotels.

The Left Bank covers some of the most popular tourist areas and has an excellent range of small hotels of great character. The atmosphere subtly changes from the much upgraded Latin Quarter and the chic and arty areas north and south of Boulevard St-Germain, to the rather tatty Boulevard itself and the staid institutional area towards Les Invalides and the Eiffel Tower. The hotels tend to reflect this.

Further from the centre, Montparnasse has several large business hotels in high-rise blocks, and the Porte de Versailles area to the south is usually packed with trade fair participants. The station areas around Gare du Nord and Gare de Lyon offer a number

Hôtel de Crillon *(see p280)*

of basic hotels (choose carefully). Montmartre has one or two pleasant hotels if you don't mind the hilly location, but beware of hotels allegedly in Montmartre but actually in the red-light, sex-show district of Pigalle. If you are looking for a hotel in person, the best times for inspecting are late morning or mid-afternoon. If the hotels are fully booked, try again after 6pm, when unclaimed provisional bookings become free. Don't rely on the impression of a hotel given by reception: ask to see the room offered, and if it isn't acceptable, ask to be shown another, if available. (For airport hotels *see pp360–65*.)

HOTEL PRICES

Hotel prices aren't always cheaper in low season (mid-November to March or July and August) because fashion shows and other major

The Hôtel du Louvre *(see p280)*, between the Louvre and the Palais Royal

events throughout the year can pack rooms, raising prices. However, in the older hotels differences in the size and position of rooms can have a marked effect on cost. Small rooms tend to be cheapest.

Twin rooms are slightly more expensive than doubles; single occupancy rates are as high or nearly as high as for two people sharing (tariffs are nearly always quoted per room, not per person). Single rooms are rare and many are extremely poky or poorly equipped. Rooms without a bath tend to be about 20% cheaper than those with. You might find a half-board arrangement unnecessary with such a wide choice of good restaurants around.

It's always worth asking for a discount: you may get a corporate rate, for instance. In some hotels special deals are offered for students, families or senior citizens.

HIDDEN EXTRAS

BY LAW, TAX and service must be included in the price quoted or displayed at the reception desk or in the rooms. Tips are unnecessary other than for exceptional service – if the concierge books you a show, for instance, or if the maid does some washing for you. However, before you make a reservation you should always establish whether breakfast is included in the price or not. Beware of extras such as drinks or snacks from

Four Seasons George V *(see p285)*

a mini-bar, which will probably be pricy, as will laundry services, garage parking or telephone calls from your room – especially telephone calls made through the switchboard.

Exchange rates in hotels invariably tend to be lower than in a bank, so make sure you have enough cash to pay your bill unless you are paying by credit card or using traveller's cheques.

HOTEL GRADINGS

FRENCH HOTELS are classified by the tourist authorities into five broad categories: one to four stars, plus a four-star deluxe rating. Some very simple places are unclassified. Star ratings indicate something about the level of facilities you can expect (for example, any hotel with more than three stars should have a lift). But the French rating system is no reliable guide to friendliness, cleanliness or tastefulness of the decor.

The Hôtel Meurice *(see p281)* **in the Tuileries Quarter**

FACILITIES

FEW PARISIAN hotels below a four-star rating have a restaurant, although there is nearly always a breakfast room. Quite a few hotel restaurants close in August. Many of the older hotels also lack a public lounge area. More modern or expensive hotels have correspondingly better facilities and generally some kind of bar. Inexpensive hotels may not have a lift – significant when you are dragging suitcases upstairs. Usually only the more expensive hotels have parking facilities. For exceptions to this rule, see the listings on pages 280–85. If you are driving you may prefer to stay in one of the peripheral motel-style chain hotels *(see pp273–4)*.

All but the very simplest of city hotels will have a telephone in the bedroom; many also have television. Business facilities (fax and internet) are now available in the grander hotels. Double beds *(grands lits)* are common, but you must specify whether or not you want one.

Statue in the Hôtel Relais Christine *(see p282)*

The Plaza Athénée *(see p284)* in Champs-Elysées

WHAT TO EXPECT

MANY HOTEL beds still stick to the time-honoured French bolster, a sausage-shaped headrest that can be uncomfortable if you are unused to it. If you prefer pillows, ask for *oreillers*. If you want to make sure you get a toilet, specify a *WC*, and if you want a bath, ask for a *bain*. Otherwise, a *cabinet de toilette* is just a basin and bidet, and *eau courante* means simply a basin with hot and cold running water. A duplex room is a suite on two floors.

The traditional French hotel breakfast of fresh coffee, croissants, jam and orange juice is in Paris gradually changing into an elaborate buffet breakfast with cold meats and cheeses. Whatever the type, insist on an *orange pressée* (freshly-squeezed orange juice) and not a *jus d'orange* which will usually be from a can. Some of the luxury hotels are now such popular venues for breakfast that it is worth reserving a place in the breakfast area if you don't want to eat in your room. A pleasant alternative is to head for the nearest café where French workers are enjoying breakfast over a newspaper.

Check-out time is usually noon and if you stay longer you will pay for an extra day.

SPECIAL BREAKS

AS PARIS IS such a popular destination with leisure as well as business travellers, weekend packages are rare. Providing there are no major events taking place, you can reduce costs by visiting in low season and negotiating a discount, or by seeking out an all-inclusive package.

TRAVELLING WITH CHILDREN

FAMILIES with young children will often find they can share a room at no or very little extra cost, and some operators offer packages with this in mind. Few hotels refuse to accept children, though facilities specifically for children are not universal.

DISABLED TRAVELLERS

OUR INFORMATION about wheelchair access to hotels was gathered by questionnaire and therefore relies on the hotels' own assessment of their suitability. Not many are well geared for use by disabled visitors. The **Association des Paralysés de France** and the **Comité Nationale pour la Réadaptation des Handicapés** both publish useful leaflets. *(For addresses see* Directory *p351.)*

SELF-CATERING

A SCHEME called **Résidences de Tourisme** provides apartments in specially-run self-catering blocks. Some hotel-type facilities are available, but you pay extra for them. Prices vary from around 90€ a night for a small studio to over 300€ a night for an apartment for

The quiet Hôtel des Grands Hommes *(see p282)*

several people. Either contact **Paris-Séjour-Réservation** or get in touch with each *résidence* directly. The Paris **Office du Tourisme** provides a full list of *résidences*.

Self-catering accommodation is an increasingly popular alternative for staying in Paris. The better known agencies include **Allo Logement Temporaire**, **At Home In Paris**, **ASLOM**, **Paris Appartements Services** and **3,2,1: International**. **Good Morning Paris** and **France-Lodge** also arrange self-catering apartments, as well as being B&B agencies (*see* Directory *p274*). All provide high-quality furnished apartments for stays from one week to six months, sometimes in the apartment of a Parisian who is abroad. Prices are comparable to the Résidences de Tourisme, sometimes slightly cheaper for the larger apartments.

STAYING IN PRIVATE HOMES

BED AND BREAKFAST, that typically-British phenomenon, is known as *chambre d'hôte* or *café-couette* ("coffee and a quilt"). B&B accommodation is available at moderate prices, between 35€ and 75€ for a double room per night. Agencies with rooms all over Paris include: **Alcôve & Agapes**, **Good Morning Paris**, **Mondialoca** and **France-Lodge**.

CHAIN HOTELS

A MUSHROOM CROP of motel-style establishments on the outskirts of Paris now take large numbers of both business and leisure visitors. The very cheapest chains such as Formule 1, Première Class and Fast Hotel, really have nothing except price to recommend them. Further up the ladder are **Campanile**, **Ibis** and **Primevère**. These places are practical, relatively inexpensive and useful if you have a car, but lack any real Parisian atmosphere or character. Many are in charmless locations on busy roads and may suffer from traffic noise. The newer motels of these chains are

The Hôtel Atala terrace (*see p284*)

The garden of the Relais Christine (*see p282*)

better equipped and more smartly decorated than the older ones. Several chains (**Sofitel**, **Novotel** and **Mercure**) are especially geared to business travellers, providing better facilities at higher prices; indeed some of the more central ones are positively luxurious. Reductions

The Hôtel Prince de Galles Sheraton (*see p284*)

can make these hotels good value at weekends. Many of the hotels have restaurants attached. Most of the chains produce their own brochures, often with useful maps detailing the motel's precise location (*see* Directory *p274*).

HOSTELS AND DORMITORY ACCOMMODATION

THERE ARE SEVERAL hostel networks in Paris. **Maisons Internationales de la Jeunesse et des Etudiants (MIJE)** provides dormitory accommodation for the 18–30s

in three splendid mansions in the Marais. There is no advance booking (except for groups) – you have to call at the central offices on the day.

The **Bureau Voyage Jeunesse (BVJ)** has double rooms and dormitory accommodation at affordable prices (from 20€ and 25€ with breakfast and private bathroom). Bookings can be made one week in advance.

La Maison de l'UCRIF (Union des Centres de Rencontres Internationales de France) has nine centres around Paris with individual, shared and dormitory rooms. No age limit is imposed. Cultural and sporting activities are available at some centres.

Fédération Unie des Auberges de Jeunesse (FUAJ) is a member of the International Youth Hostels Federation. There is no age limit at their two Paris hostels. (*For addresses see* Directory *p274*.)

CAMPING

THE ONLY campsite in Paris itself is the **Camping du Bois de Boulogne/Ile de France** (around 9€–25€ per night). This well-equipped site next to the Seine is usually fully booked during the summer. There are many more campsites in the surrounding region however, some of which are close to an RER line. Details can be obtained from the Paris Office du Tourisme or from a booklet produced by the **Fédération Française de Camping-Caravaning (FFCC)** (*see* Directory *p274*).

DIRECTORY

OFFICE DU TOURISME

127 Ave des Champs-Elysées 75008.
📞 08 36 68 31 12.
Branches at Gare de Lyon & Tour Eiffel (summer).
W www.paris-touristoffice.com

AGENCIES

Paris-Séjour-Réservation
90 Ave des Champs-Elysées 75008.
📞 01 53 89 10 50.
FAX 01 53 89 10 59.

Ely 12 12
9 Rue d'Artois 75008.
📞 01 43 59 12 12.
W www.ely1212.com

SELF-CATERING

Allo Logement Temporaire
64 Rue du Temple 75003.
📞 01 42 72 00 06.
FAX 01 42 72 03 11.

At Home in Paris
16 Rue Médéric 75017.
📞 01 42 12 40 40.
FAX 01 42 12 40 48.

ASLOM
75 Ave Parmentier 75011
📞 01 43 49 67 79.
W www.aslom.com

Paris Appartements Services
69 Rue d'Argout 75002.
📞 01 40 28 01 28.
FAX 01 40 28 92 01.

3,2,1: International
BP 60, 95472 Fosses.
📞 01 34 31 10 23.
W www.mondialoca.net

RÉSIDENCES DE TOURISME

Résidences in Paris
35 Rue de Berri 75008.
📞 01 53 77 56 00.
FAX 01 42 56 52 75.

Les Citadines
27 Rue Esquirol 75013.
📞 08 25 01 03 29.
W www.citadines.com

Flatotel
14 Rue du Théâtre 75015.
📞 01 45 75 62 20.
FAX 01 45 79 73 30.

Pierre et Vacances
10 Pl Charles-Dullin 75018.
📞 01 45 58 87 00.
FAX 01 42 54 48 87.

Résidence du Roy
8 Rue François-1er 75008.
📞 01 42 89 59 59.
W www.hroy.com

BED & BREAKFAST

Alcôve & Agapes
8bis Rue Coysevox 75018.
📞 01 44 85 06 05.
FAX 01 44 85 06 14

France-Lodge
41, Rue La Fayette 75009.
📞 01 53 20 09 09.
W www.apartments-in-paris.com

Mondialoca
BP 60, 95472 Fosses.
📞 01 34 31 10 23.
W www.mondialoca.net

Good Morning Paris
43 Rue Lacépède 75005.
📞 01 47 07 28 29.
FAX 01 47 07 44 45.

CHAIN HOTELS

Campanile
📞 01 64 62 46 46 (central reservations).
W www.campanile.fr

Ibis
📞 08 03 88 22 22 (central reservations).
W www.ibishotels.com

Primevère
📞 08 00 12 12 12 (central reservations).
W www.choicehotels.com

Golden Tulip St-Honoré
218 Rue du Faubourg St-Honoré 75008.
📞 01 49 53 03 03.
W www.gtshparis.com

Hilton
18 Ave de Suffren 75015.
📞 01 44 38 56 00.
W www.hilton.com

Holiday Inn
92 Rue de Vaugirard 75006.
📞 01 49 54 87 00.
W www.holiday-inn.com

Holiday Inn République
10 Pl de la République 75011.
📞 01 43 55 44 34.
W www.holiday-inn.com

Mercure Paris Bercy
77 Rue de Bercy 75012.
📞 01 53 46 50 50.
W www.mercure.com

Mercure Pont Bercy
6 Blvd Vincent Auriol 75013.
📞 01 45 82 48 00.
W www.mercure.com

Mercure Paris Montparnasse
20 Rue de la Gaîté 75014.
📞 01 43 35 28 28.
W www.mercure.com

Mercure Paris Tour-Eiffel Suffren
20 Rue Jean Rey 75015.
📞 01 45 78 50 00.
W www.mercure.com

Mercure Paris Porte de Versailles
69 Blvd Victor 75015.
📞 01 44 19 03 03.
W www.mercure.com

Méridien Montparnasse
19 Rue du Commandant René Mouchotte 75014.
📞 01 44 36 44 36.
W www.lemeridien-montparnasse.com

Nikko
61 Quai de Grenelle 75015.
📞 01 40 58 20 00.
W www.nikkohotels.com

Novotel Paris Bercy
85 Rue de Bercy 75012.
📞 01 43 42 30 00.
W www.novotel.com

Novotel Paris Les Halles
8 Pl Marguerite de Navarre 75001.
📞 01 42 21 31 31.
W www.novotel.com

Sofitel Paris Forum Rive Gauche
17 Blvd St-Jacques 75014.
📞 01 40 78 79 80.
W www.sofitel.com

Sofitel Paris CNIT
2 Pl de la Défense, 92053.
📞 01 46 92 10 10.
W www.sofitel.com

Sofitel Paris Arc de Triomphe
(see p285)

Sofitel Le Faubourg
15 Rue Boissy d'Anglas 75008.
📞 01 44 94 14 14.
W www.sofitel.com

Hotel Sofitel Scribe
1 Rue Scribe 75009.
📞 01 44 71 24 24.
W www.sofitel.com

Warwick
5 Rue de Berri 75008.
📞 01 45 63 14 11.
W www.warwick hotel.com

HOSTELS

FUAJ – Centre National
27 Rue Pajol 75018.
📞 01 44 89 87 27.
FAX 01 44 89 87 49.

MIJE
Head Office: 11 Rue du Fauconnier 75004.
📞 01 42 74 23 45.
FAX 01 40 27 81 64.

BVJ
44 Rue des Bernardins 75005.
📞 01 53 00 90 90.
FAX 01 53 00 90 91.`

La Maison de l'UCRIF
27 Rue de Turbigo 75002.
📞 01 40 26 57 64.
FAX 01 40 26 58 20.

CAMPING

Camping du Bois de Boulogne/Ile de France
Allée du Bord de l'Eau 75016.
📞 01 45 24 30 00.
FAX 01 45 24 51 85.

FFCC
78 Rue de Rivoli 75004.
📞 01 42 72 84 08.
FAX 01 42 72 70 21.

HOW TO BOOK

THE BUSIEST Paris tourist seasons are May, June, September and October, but special events such as fashion shows, trade fairs or major exhibitions can fill most rooms in Paris throughout the year. Disneyland Paris has further increased the pressure to find accommodation, as many visitors choose to stay in the capital and commute to the park on the RER. July and August are quieter, as many Parisians are on their annual holiday. But the August shutdown of old is no longer the case – around half the hotels, restaurants and shops remain open.

If you have decided on a hotel, it is vital to book ahead by at least a month as Paris is a popular destination. The hotels in the listings are among the best in their category and will fill particularly fast. Make a reservation six weeks in advance between May and October. The best way is to book directly with the hotel. If you make your initial inquiry by telephone, ring during the day if possible – you are more likely to find staff authorized to take bookings. During busy periods you will usually have to send written confirmation of your reservation (websites or email addresses are provided where available).

If you prefer to use an agency, **Ely 12 12** and **Paris-Séjour-Réservation** can book hotels and other kinds of accommodation, sometimes even a barge along the Seine.

If you aren't too fussy about where you stay, or if all the hotels are reportedly full, you can book via the Paris **Office du Tourisme**, which offers an on-the-spot booking service for a reasonable fee.

DEPOSITS

IF YOU MAKE a reservation by telephone you will be asked for either your credit card number (from which any cancellation fee may be deducted) or a deposit (*arrhes*). These *arrhes* can be as much as the price of a night's stay,

Tourist information desk, Charles de Gaulle airport

but usually cost only about 15% of this. Pay your deposit by credit card or by sending an international money order. You can sometimes send an ordinary cheque for an amount equivalent to the deposit as evidence of your intention to keep the booking. Usually the hotel will simply keep your foreign cheque as security until you arrive, then return it to you and give you one total bill when you leave. But do check with the hotel before sending an ordinary cheque. It's also quite acceptable in France to specify your choice of room when you book.

Try to arrive at your hotel by 6pm on the day you have booked, or at least telephone to say you will be late, otherwise you may well lose the room. A hotel that breaks a confirmed, prepaid booking is breaking a contract and the client is entitled to compensation of at least twice your deposit paid. If you have any problems, consult the Office du Tourisme.

TOURIST INFORMATION DESKS

YOU CAN BOOK hotels at all airport information desks but only in person and for the same day. The Gare de Lyon and the Tour Eiffel (seasonal) information desks provide a similar booking arrangement for all forms of accommodation. Many Paris information desks also keep a complete list of city hotels and some book entertainment, excursions etc (*see* Practical Information *p350*).

USING THE LISTINGS

The hotels on pages 280–85 are organized according to area and price. All are centrally situated. The symbols after the hotel's address summarize the facilities it offers.

⬤ annual closure
🛁 all rooms with bath and/or shower unless otherwise stated
1️⃣ single-rate rooms available
🛏 rooms for more than two people available or an extra bed can be put in a double room
🕐 24-hour room service
📺 television in all rooms
🍸 minibar in all rooms
🚭 non-smoking rooms available
🌸 good views from hotel
🌡 air-conditioning in all rooms
🏋 gym/fitness facilities
🏊 swimming pool in hotel
🗊 business facilities: message-taking service, fax machine for guests, desk and telephone in each room and a meeting room within the hotel
👶 children's facilities: child cots and babysitting service
♿ wheelchair access
🛗 lift
🐕 pets allowed in the bedrooms if confirmed. Most hotels accept guide dogs regardless.
🅿 hotel parking available
🌳 garden/terrace
🍸 bar
🍴 restaurant
ℹ tourist information desk
💳 credit cards accepted:
AE American Express
DC Diners Club
MC Mastercard/Access
V Visa
JCB Japanese Credit Bureau

Price categories for a double room for one night including breakfast, tax and service:
€ under 90€
€€ 90€–140€
€€€ 141€–180€
€€€€ 181€–260€
€€€€€ over 260€

Paris's Best: Hotels

Paris is famous for its hotels. It excels in all categories from the glittering opulent *palaces* (the top luxury hotels) to the *hôtels de charme*, full of character and romantic appeal, to the simpler good-value family hotels in quiet back streets. As a centre of culture and fashion, the city has long been a mecca for the rich and famous, great and good from all walks of life. Not surprisingly, therefore, it can boast some of the most magnificent hotels in the world and has more than a thousand hotels in the inner city alone. Whatever the price level, however, the hotels in our listings *(see pp280–85)* all show that inimitable style and taste that Parisians bring to everything they do. These are a selection of the very best.

Bristol
In the chic heart of Paris, this epitomizes luxury. (See p284.)

Champs-Elysées

Chaillot Quarter

Invalides and Eiffel Tower Quarter

Balzac
Small but stylish, this hotel exudes period charm. The restaurant, Pierre Gagnaire, is highly rated. (See p285.)

Hôtel de Crillon
One of the great palace *hotels, this was built for Louis XV.* (See p280.)

Plaza Athénée
In the heart of haute couture *Paris, this is the favourite haunt of the fashion world. Magnificent decor and a superb restaurant are the main attractions.* (See p284.)

Duc de St-Simon
Bedrooms overlook a leafy garden in this comfortable and peaceful hôtel de charme *situated in an 18th-century mansion south of the Seine.* (See p283.)

Le Grand Hôtel International
Built for Napoleon III in 1862, this historic hotel has been patronized by the rich and famous from Mata Hari to Winston Churchill. (See p285.)

L'Hôtel
Best known as the last home of Oscar Wilde, this stylish hotel boasts rooms both impressive and slightly bizarre. One room was furnished and occupied by the music hall star Mistinguett.
(See p281.)

Relais Christine
An oasis of calm in the hub of the city, this charming hotel offers traditional comforts such as a welcoming open fire in the drawing room. (See p282.)

Opéra Quarter

Beaubourg and Les Halles

ries Quarter

Germain-des-Prés

The Marais

Ile de la Cité

Ile St-Louis

Luxembourg Quarter

Latin Quarter

Jardin des Plantes Quarter

Hôtel du Jeu de Paume
This cleverly converted hotel was once a court for playing real tennis – jeu de paume. (See p280.)

| 0 kilometres | 1 |
| 0 miles | 0.5 |

Lutétia
This was decorated by top designer Sonia Rykiel. (See p282.)

Hotel de l'Abbaye
A pleasant garden and courtyard and attractive rooms are features of this small secluded hotel near the Jardins du Luxembourg. (See p282.)

Choosing a Hotel

THE HOTELS LISTED in the following pages have all been individually inspected and assessed specially for this guide. This choosing chart shows a selection of factors which may influence your choice. For more information on each hotel see the listings on pages 280–85.

	Price	NUMBER OF ROOMS	LARGE ROOMS	BUSINESS FACILITIES	CHILDREN'S FACILITIES	RECOMMENDED RESTAURANT	CLOSE TO SHOPS AND RESTAURANTS	QUIET LOCATION	24-HOUR ROOM SERVICE
ILE ST-LOUIS, THE MARAIS *(see p280)*									
Hôtel des Deux-Iles	€€	17						●	
St-Merry	€€	11							
St-Paul-le-Marais	€€	27		●			●		
Hôtel de la Bretonnerie	€€€	30	●		●		●		
Hôtel du Jeu de Paume	€€€€	31						●	
Pavillon de la Reine	€€€€€	55			●		●	●	
TUILERIES QUARTER *(see pp280–81)*									
Brighton	€€	70			●		●		
Clarion St-James et Albany	€€€€€	203		●	●		●		
Hôtel du Louvre	€€€€€	199			●		●		●
Regina	€€€€€	130	●	●	●		●		●
Hôtel de Crillon	€€€€€	160	●	●	●	●	●		●
Intercontinental	€€€€€	450		●	●	●	●		●
Lotti	€€€€€	130		●			●		
Meurice	€€€€€	160	●	●		●	●		●
Ritz	€€€€€	175	●	●	●	●	●		●
ST-GERMAIN-DES-PRÉS *(see pp281–2)*									
Hôtel du Quai Voltaire	€€	33			●				●
Hôtel d'Angleterre	€€	27					●	●	
Hôtel de Lille	€€	20					●		
Hôtel des Marronniers	€€	37					●	●	
Hôtel des Sts-Pères	€€	39					●	●	
Senateur	€€	40		●	●		●		
Lenox St-Germain	€€€	34					●	●	
Hôtel de Fleurie	€€€	29			●		●		
L'Hôtel	€€€€	27			●	●	●		●
La Villa St-Germain des Prés	€€€€	32			●		●	●	●
Lutétia	€€€€€	250	●	●	●	●	●		●
Montalembert	€€€€€	56		●		●	●	●	●
Relais Christine	€€€€€	51		●	●		●	●	●
LATIN QUARTER *(see p282)*									
Esmeralda	€	19						●	●
Hôtel des Grandes Ecoles	€	51			●			●	
Hôtel des Grands Hommes	€€	32			●			●	
Hôtel de Notre-Dame	€€	34					●	●	
Hôtel du Panthéon	€€€	34			●			●	
LUXEMBOURG QUARTER *(see p282)*									
Perreyve	€€	30						●	●
Récamier	€€	30					●	●	
Hôtel de l'Abbaye	€€€	46			●		●	●	

Price categories for a standard double room per night including breakfast and necessary charges:
€ under 90€
€€ 90–140€
€€€ 141–180€
€€€€ 181–260€
€€€€€ over 260€

CLOSE TO SHOPS AND RESTAURANTS
Within a 5-minute walk of a good centre for shops and restaurants.

CHILDREN'S FACILITIES
Indicates child cots and a baby sitting service available. A few hotels also provide children's portions and high-chairs in the dining areas.

BUSINESS FACILITIES
Message-taking service, fax machine for guests, desk and telephone in each room and a meeting room within the hotel.

	NUMBER OF ROOMS	LARGE ROOMS	BUSINESS FACILITIES	CHILDREN'S FACILITIES	RECOMMENDED RESTAURANT	CLOSE TO SHOPS AND RESTAURANTS	QUIET LOCATION	24-HOUR ROOM SERVICE
MONTPARNASSE (see p283)								
Lenox Montparnasse €€	52			●			■	
Ferrandi €€	42						■	
Villa des Artistes €€	59			●			■	
Ste-Beuve €€	22			●			■	
Le St-Grégoire €€€	20			●		●	■	
INVALIDES (see p283)								
Hôtel de Suède St-Germain €€	39			●				
Hôtel de Varenne €€	24			●				
Hôtel Bourgogne et Montana €€€€	32						■	
Duc de St-Simon €€€€	34					●	■	
CHAILLOT QUARTER, PORTE MAILLOT (see pp283–4)								
Hôtel de Banville €€€	38			●				●
Concorde La Fayette €€€€	968		■	●	■			●
Le Méridien €€€€	1,025		■	●	■			●
Square €€€€	22		■			●		
Melia-Alexander €€€€€	62	●		●		●		
Villa Maillot €€€€€	42	●	■					
Raphaël €€€€€	90	●	■		■	●	■	
St-James €€€€€	48		■		■	●	■	●
CHAMPS-ELYSÉES (see pp284–5)								
Résidence Lord Byron €€	31		●			●	■	
Atala €€€€	48				■	●		
Claridge-Bellman €€€€	42	●				●		
Bristol €€€€€	192	●	■	●	■	●		●
Plaza Athénée €€€€€	188	●	■		■	●		●
Four Seasons George V €€€€€	245	●	■	●	■	●		●
Balzac €€€€€	70	●			■	●	■	●
Prince de Galles Sheraton €€€€€	168	●	■	●	■	●		●
Royal Monceau €€€€€	219		■		■			●
San Regis €€€€€	44			●		●	■	●
Sofitel Paris Arc de Triomphe €€€€€	135	●	■	●		●		●
Hôtel de la Trémoille €€€€€	107	●	■	●	■	●	■	
Vernet €€€€€	51			●		●		●
OPÉRA QUARTER (see p285)								
Ambassador €€€€	288	●	■	●	■	●		●
Le Grand Hôtel Intercontinental €€€€€	514		■	●	■	●		●
MONTMARTRE (see p285)								
Terrass' Hôtel €€€€	101		■	●				

ILE ST-LOUIS
THE MARAIS

Hôtel des Deux-Iles

59 Rue St-Louis-en-l'Ile 75004.
Map 13 C4. **[** 01 43 26 13 35.
FAX 01 43 29 60 25. **Rooms:** 17.
TV AE, MC, V. €€
W www.hotel-ile-stlouis.com

It's a privilege to be able to stay
on the Ile St-Louis, and this converted 17th-century mansion offers
an affordable way to do so. Here
the atmosphere is peaceful, the
small bedrooms attractive and well
insulated, and the lounge in the
vaulted cellar has a real fire. The
rooms, however, are small.

St-Merry

78 Rue de la Verrerie 75004.
Map 13 B3. **[** 01 42 78 14 15.
FAX 01 40 29 06 82. **Rooms:** 11.
AE, MC, V. €€
W www.francehotelguide.com

Close to the Pompidou Centre, the
hotel was the presbytery of the
adjoining church in the 17th
century. Furnished in appropriately
Gothic style, this hotel is worth a
visit if only to glance at room 9,
built into the side of the church with
flying buttresses crossing the room.

St-Paul-le-Marais

8 Rue de Sévigné 75004. **Map** 14 D3.
[01 48 04 97 27. **FAX** 01 48 87 37 04.
W www.hotel-paris-marais.com
Rooms: 27. TV
AE, DC, MC, V, JCB. €€

Close to the Place des Vosges, in
the heart of the Marais, this hotel
with its wooden beams and old
stone will suit those who like a
rustic environment, although the
furnishings are simple, stylish and
modern. Ask for bedrooms facing
the courtyard to avoid the noise of
traffic coming from the narrow
Rue de Sévigné. Guests are
welcomed with a smile and made
to feel immediately at ease, a
splendid start to their stay.

Hôtel de la Bretonnerie

22 Rue Ste-Croix de la Bretonnerie
75004. **Map** 13 C3. **[** 01 48 87 77
63. **FAX** 01 42 77 26 78.
W www.labretonnerie.com
Aug. **Rooms:** 30. TV
MC, V. €€

The 17th-century Hôtel de la
Bretonnerie, situated on the
charming Rue Ste-Croix de la
Bretonnerie, is one of the
most comfortable hotels in the
Marais. The spacious bedrooms
have wooden beams and antique
furniture. The welcome is kind.

Hôtel du Jeu de Paume

54 Rue St-Louis-en-l'Ile 75004. **Map** 13
C4. **[** 01 43 26 14 18. **FAX** 01 40 46
02 76. **W** www.hoteljeudepaume.com
Rooms: 31.
AE, DC, MC, V, JCB.
€€€€

Standing on the site of a former
real tennis court, this hotel has
been skilfully converted into an
exemplary family hotel. Features
include a glass-walled lift, wooden
beams, old terracotta paving, a
sauna and several charming duplex
rooms. The welcome is warm.

Pavillon de la Reine

28 Pl des Vosges 75003. **Map** 14 D3.
[01 40 29 19 19. **FAX** 01 40 29 19 20.
W www.pavillon-de-la-reine.com
Rooms: 55. TV P AE, DC, MC, V,
JCB. €€€€€

This hotel, set back from the
marvellous Place des Vosges, is
the luxury hotel of the Marais. The
courtyard is a haven of peace and
the bedrooms are sumptuously
renovated and furnished with
excellent reproduction antiques.

TUILERIES QUARTER

Brighton

218 Rue de Rivoli 75001. **Map** 12 D1.
[01 47 03 61 61. **FAX** 01 42 60 41 78.
W www.esprit-de-france.com
Rooms: 70.
AE, DC, MC, V, JCB. €€

The Hôtel Brighton, once the
glory of the Rue de Rivoli, has
been rescued from decline by a
Japanese company. The bedrooms
have high moulded ceilings and
large windows looking either on
to the Jardin des Tuileries or on
to the courtyard. Courtyard rooms
are quieter but less attractive.
Some rooms have balconies.

Clarion St-James
et Albany

202 Rue de Rivoli 75001. **Map** 12 E1.
[01 44 58 43 21. **FAX** 01 44 58 43 11.
W www.clarionstjames.com
Rooms: 203. TV P AE,
DC, MC, V, JCB. €€€€€

This ill-matched group of buildings
includes the Hôtel Noailles with its
fine facade (listed). The hotel is
quiet and tidy but in need of
restoration. It is perfectly situated
opposite the Tuileries gardens,
however with all the traffic on the
Rue de Rivoli, it's best to ask for a
room overlooking the courtyard.

Hôtel du Louvre

Pl André Malraux 75001. **Map** 12 E1.
W www.hoteldulouvre.com **Rooms:**
200. TV AE,
DC, MC, V, JCB. €€€€€

In a prime location between the
Louvre and the Palais Royal. The
luxurious rooms have spectacular
views: the Pissarro Suite is where
the artist painted his view of *Place
du Théâtre Français*, while if you
book room 551 you can admire
the opera house from your bath!

Regina

2 Pl des Pyramides 75001. **Map** 12 E1.
[01 42 60 31 10. **FAX** 01 40 15 95 16.
W www.regina-hotel.com
Rooms: 130. TV AE,
DC, MC, V, JCB. €€€€€

Surprisingly the Hôtel Regina is
not known to many tourists. The
wood detail in the lounge is
stunning Art Nouveau and many
films have been shot here. There
are superb views from rooms on
the Rue de Rivoli, which are
furnished with antiques.

Hôtel de Crillon

10 Pl de la Concorde 75008. **Map**
11 C1. **[** 01 44 71 15 00. **FAX** 01 44 71
71 15 02. **W** www.crillon-paris.com
Rooms: 160. TV AE,
DC, MC, V, JCB. €€€€€

Occupying an unrivalled position
on the Place de la Concorde, the
Hôtel de Crillon offers elegance.
Features include the marble
lounge, gilded oak gallery and
magnificent dining room in the
Ambassadors Salon. The hotel is
used by foreign statesmen during
official visits. Bedrooms overlooking the Place de la Concorde
are best. The hotel has a
magnificent Royal Suite and terrace.

Intercontinental

3 Rue de Castiglione 75001. **Map** 12
D1. **[** 01 44 77 11 11. **FAX** 01 44 77
14 60. **W** www.paris.interconti.com
Rooms: 450. TV
AE, DC, MC, V, JCB. €€€€€

This elegant late 19th-century
hotel is ideally situated between
the Jardin des Tuileries and the
Place Vendôme. It was designed
by Charles Garnier, architect of the
Paris Opéra, and its historic salons
are often used for *haute couture*
fashion shows. Breakfast is served
in the sunny courtyard in summer.
Bedrooms are quiet – the best
overlook one of the courtyards.

...otti

...Rue de Castiglione 75001. **Map** 12
...1. [C] 01 42 60 37 34. [FAX] 01 40 15
...3 56. [W] www.jollihotels.com
...ooms: 130. ▦ 🔟 [TV] ▤ ▤
... 🔟 [Y] [Y] [Ⅱ] ▤ AE, DC, MC,
...JCB. €€€€€

...subdued atmosphere of quiet
...ecay surrounds this once-
...elebrated hotel, creating something
... a feeling of *temps perdu*.
...owever, some of the bedrooms
...e quite large and the attic rooms
... the sixth floor are still charming.

...eurice

...28 Rue de Rivoli 75001. **Map** 12 D1.
... 01 44 58 10 10. [FAX] 01 44 58 10 15.
...] www.meuricehotel.com
...ooms: 160. ▦ 🔟 [24] [TV] [Y] ▤
...▤ 🔟 [Y] [Y] [Ⅱ] 🔟 ▤ AE,
...C, MC, V, JCB. €€€€€

...he Hôtel Meurice is a perfect
...xample of successful restoration,
...ith excellent replicas of the
...riginal plasterwork and
...arnishings. Delightful musical
...ternoons are held in the
...ompadour Salon where a roaring
...re is often lit during the winter
...onths. Luxurious and spacious
...edrooms on the first and second
...oors overlook the Jardin des
...uileries so be sure to book these
...ooms well in advance.

...itz

...5 Pl Vendôme 75001. **Map** 6 D5.
... 01 43 16 30 30. [FAX] 01 43 16 31
...8. [W] www.ritzparis.com **Rooms:**
...75. ▦ 🔟 [##] [24] [TV] [Y] ▤ ▤
...▤ 🔟 [Y] [Y] [Ⅱ] ▤ ▤ ▤
...E, DC, MC, JCB. €€€€€

...fter a century, the Ritz still lives
...p to its discreet, high reputation,
...ombining elegance and comfort.
...he Louis XVI furniture, marble
...replaces and chandeliers are all
...he originals. The Duke of Windsor
...as a guest in the Windsor suite.
...Hemingway regularly frequented
...he Hemingway Bar (used only for
...pecial occasions). Autographed
...hotographs testify to his visits.
...he Ritz still equates to glamour,
... don't be surprised if you end
...p breakfasting next to the likes
... Kissinger or Madonna.

...T-GERMAIN-DES-PRÉS

...ôtel du Quai Voltaire

...9 Quai Voltaire 75007. **Map** 12 D2.
... 01 42 61 50 91. [FAX] 01 42 61 62
...5. [W] www.hotelduquaivoltaire.com
...ooms: 33. ▦ [Y] 30. 🔟 [##] [24]
[TV]
... request. ▦ 🔟 [Y] [Ⅱ] ▤ AE,
...C, MC, V, JCB. €€

Overlooking the river, this hotel
was once the favourite of Blondin,
Baudelaire and Pissarro. There is
no double glazing, so bedrooms
on the quay suffer from traffic
noise. However the views are
superb, the rooms are charmingly
decorated and the place has soul.

Hôtel d'Angleterre

44 Rue Jacob 75006. **Map** 12 E3.
[C] 01 42 60 34 72. [FAX] 01 42 60 16
93. [@] anglotel@wanadoo.fr **Rooms:**
27. ▦ 🔟 [TV] [Y] 🔟 [Y] 🔟 ▤
AE, DC, MC, V, JCB. €€

Once the British Embassy, the
Hôtel d'Angleterre has retained
many of the original features,
including the fine old staircase
(listed), the exquisite garden and
the salon mantelpiece. Similarly
impressive mantelpieces can be
seen in the stylish bedrooms, all
of which are different, and many
of which have beams and four-
poster beds. This is a charming,
utterly civilized hotel.

Hôtel de Lille

40 Rue de Lille 75007. **Map** 12 D2.
[C] 01 42 61 29 09. [FAX] 01 42 61 53
97. [W] www.hotel-de-lille.com
Rooms: 20. ▦ [TV] 🔟 [Y] ▤ AE,
DC, MC, V, JCB. €€

The Hôtel de Lille is situated near
the Orsay and Louvre museums in
the heart of the smart Faubourg
St-Germain. The modern, standard
bedrooms are small and the bar is
minute.There is a small, charming
lounge in the arched basement.

Hôtel des Marronniers

21 Rue Jacob 75006. **Map** 12 E3.
[C] 01 43 25 30 60. [FAX] 01 40 46 83
56. [W] www.hotel-marronniers.com
Rooms: 37. ▦ 🔟 [##] 🔟 🔟 🔟
▤ MC, V. €€

Situated between a courtyard and
a garden, this hotel provides total
quiet. The decor is unremarkable,
but bedrooms on the fourth floor,
on the garden side, overlook the
roofs of Paris and the St-Germain-
des-Prés church steeple. Book
well in advance, as the hotel is in
demand with regular customers.

Hôtel des Sts-Pères

65 Rue des Sts-Pères 75006. **Map** 12
E3. [C] 01 45 44 50 00. [FAX] 01 45 44
90 83. [W] www.esprit-de-france.com
Rooms: 39. ▦ 🔟 [TV] [Y] 🔟 🔟
[Y] ▤ AE, MC, V. €€

The hotel occupies one of the old
aristocratic mansions of St-Germain-
des-Prés. It has kept its inner
garden and original staircase with
a 17th-century wooden banister. If

the lounge seems cold, the bedrooms are quiet and roomy – the
best has a ceiling fresco and a bathroom separated only by a screen.

Senateur

10 Rue de Vaugirard 75006. **Map** 12
F5. [C] 01 43 26 08 83. [FAX] 01 46 34
04 66. **Rooms:** 40. ▦ 🔟 [##] [TV] [Y]
🔟 🔟 🔟 [Ⅱ] 🔟 ▤ AE, DC,
MC, V, JCB. €€

Ideally situated near the Senate
and the Jardins du Luxembourg,
most of the rooms are decorated
in a Classical and functional style
although the lounge has a tropical
note.The bathrooms are gleaming.

Lenox St-Germain

9 Rue de l'Université 75007.
Map 12 D3. [C] 01 42 96 10 95.
[FAX] 01 42 61 52 83.
[W] www.lenoxstgermain.com
Rooms: 34. ▦ 🔟 ▤ 🔟 🔟 ▤
AE, DC, MC, JCB, V. €€€

Located in the heart of Faubourg
St-Germain, the charm of this
hotel lies in its simplicity. The
welcome is often casual. The
rooms are impeccably decorated;
duplex rooms have balconies with
plants, corner fireplaces, and
wooden beams.

Hôtel de Fleurie

32 Rue Grégoire de Tours 75006.
Map 12 F4. [C] 01 53 73 70 00. [FAX] 01
53 73 70 20. [W] www.hotel-de-
fleurie.com **Rooms:** 29. ▦ 🔟 [TV]
[Y] ▤ 🔟 [Ⅱ] ▤ AE, DC, MC, V,
🔟 €€€

The facade alone is enough to
make one want to stay in this
welcoming, family-run hotel.
Inside, the woodwork and white
stone create the same light feel, as
do the bedrooms, all of which are
beautifully decorated, with well-
equipped bathrooms.

L'Hôtel

13 Rue des Beaux-Arts 75006. **Map**
12 E3. [C] 01 43 25 27 22. [FAX] 01 43
25 64 81. [W] www.l-hotel.com
Rooms: 27. ▦ [TV] ▤ 🔟 🔟
[Y] ▤ AE, DC, MC, V. €€€€€

Nowhere else will you find a domed
stairwell, a basement with vaulted
ceilings in the style of a harem, a
tree trunk across the dining room,
a metallic, golden-fleeced lamb, and
a parrot in a gigantic cage. Here it
is possible to stay in the room
where Oscar Wilde died beyond his
means, sleep in Mistinguett's bed or
in the Cardinal's Chamber. L'Hôtel
is also impressive for its quality and
style and is an oasis of calm in the
heart of St-Germain-des-Prés.

For key to symbols see p275

La Villa St-Germain des Prés

29 Rue Jacob 75006. **Map** 12 E3.
【 01 43 26 60 00. FAX 01 46 34 63 63. W www.villa-saintgermain.com
Rooms: 32. ▨ ▥ 📺 ▤ ▤
⛐ ▥ ▦ ▤ *AE, DC, MC, V, JCB.*
€€€€

Close to St-Germain-des-Prés, La Villa is a striking modern hotel. Its stark, stylized simplicity may not appeal to everyone, but the ground-floor lounge is distinctly elegant.

Lutétia

45 Blvd Raspail 75006. **Map** 12 D4.
【 01 49 54 46 46. FAX 01 49 54 46 00. W www.lutetia-paris.com
Rooms: 250. ▨ ▥ 24 📺 ▤ ▤
⛐ ▥ ▦ ▤ ▥ ▦ ▤ ▤ ▥ ▤
AE, DC, MC, V, JCB. €€€€€

The Lutétia, the only *palace hôtel* (luxury hotel) on the south side of the river, has long been visited by regular provincial customers. The building is partly Art Nouveau and partly Art Deco, and has been restored throughout. Publishers in the neighbourhood are regular customers of its restaurant and its literary bar. The Lutétia is a fashionable place to be and the French sculptor César Baldiaccini lives here permanently.

Montalembert

3 Rue de Montalembert 75007. **Map** 12 D3. 【 01 45 49 68 68. FAX 01 45 49 69 49. W www.montalembert.com
Rooms: 56. ▨ ▥ 24 📺 ▤ ▤
⛐ ▥ ▦ ▥ ▦ ▤ ▤ *AE, DC, MC, V.* €€€€€

Situated in the heart of the publishing district, this hotel has been sumptuously restored. The bar has become an increasingly fashionable meeting place, and the bedrooms boast fine wood and designer fabrics and are equipped with video recorders. The eighth-floor suites have good views.

Relais Christine

3 Rue Christine 75006. **Map** 12 F4.
【 01 40 51 60 80. FAX 01 40 51 60 81. W www.relais-christine.com **Rooms:** 51. ▨ ▥ 24 📺 ▤ ▤
▦ ▥ ▦ P ▤ ▤ ▤ *AE, DC, MC, V, JCB.* €€€€€

Always full, the Relais Christine is the epitome of the *hôtel de charme.* It is part of the cloister of a 16th-century abbey and is a romantic haven of peace in the heart of St-Germain-des-Prés. Breakfast is served in an old chapel. The bedrooms are bright and spacious, especially the duplex rooms.

LATIN QUARTER

Esmeralda

4 Rue St-Julien-le-Pauvre 75005.
Map 13 A4. 【 01 43 54 19 20.
FAX 01 40 51 00 68. **Rooms:** 19.
16. ▯ ▤ ▤ ⛐ ▥ ▦ *AE, V.* €

The bohemian Esmeralda lies in the heart of the Latin Quarter. The decor reflects contrasting ages and styles behind old stone walls and under beamed ceilings. Its irresistible charm has, in the past, seduced the likes of Chet Baker, Terence Stamp and Serge Gainsbourg into staying here. The best rooms overlook Notre-Dame.

Hôtel des Grandes Ecoles

75 Rue Cardinal Lemoine 75005.
Map 13 B5. 【 01 43 26 79 23.
FAX 01 43 25 28 15. W www.hotel-grandes-ecoles.com **Rooms:** 51. ▨
▤ ▤ ▥ ▦ ▤ ▤ ▤ *MC, V.* €

Situated between the Panthéon and the Place de la Contrescarpe, this hotel is an astonishing cluster of three small houses with a garden. Although the university has moved, the hotel still remains on the Montagne Ste-Geneviève site. The main building has been competently renovated but the other two houses have retained their old-fashioned charm.

Hôtel des Grands Hommes

17 Pl du Panthéon 75005. **Map** 17
A1. 【 01 46 34 19 60. FAX 01 43 26 67 32. @ hotel-grands-hommes @wanadoo.fr **Rooms:** 32. ▨ ▯ ▤ ▤
📺 ▤ ▥ ▦ ▥ ▦ ▤ ▤ *AE, DC, MC, V, JCB.* €€

Teachers at the Sorbonne frequent this quiet family hotel in the heart of the Latin Quarter close to the Jardins du Luxembourg. It boasts an unrivalled view of the Panthéon from the attic rooms on the upper floor. The bedrooms are comfortable with pleasant bathrooms but are otherwise unexceptional.

Hôtel de Notre-Dame

19 Rue Maître Albert 75006.
Map 13 B5. 【 01 43 26 79 00.
FAX 01 43 26 61 75. W www.france-hotel-guide.com **Rooms:** 34. ▨ 📺
▤ ▥ ▦ ▤ *AE, DC, MC, V, JCB.* €€

The Hôtel de Notre-Dame, not to be mistaken for the hotel of the same name on the Quai St-Michel, overlooks Notre-Dame cathedral on one side and the Panthéon on the other. It is the ideal base from which to discover old Paris.

Hôtel du Panthéon

19 Pl du Panthéon 75005. **Map** 17
A1. 【 01 43 54 32 95. FAX 01 43 26 64 65. W www.france-hotel-guide.com **Rooms:** 34. ▨ 📺 ▤ ▤
▥ ▦ ▤ *AE, DC, MC, V.* €€€

This hotel is managed by the same family as the Hôtel des Grands Hommes: the welcome is equally warm and the decor similarly Classical. There is a four-poster bed in room 33.

LUXEMBOURG QUARTER

Perreyve

63 Rue Madame 75006. **Map** 12 E5.
【 01 45 48 35 01. FAX 01 42 84 03 30. @ perreyvehotel@gofornet.com
Rooms: 30. ▨ ▯ 📺 ▥ ▦
▤ *AE, DC, MC, V.* €€

The Hôtel Perreyve is situated in a quiet street between Montparnasse and St-Germain-des-Prés. It has 30 sober, simple, clean bedrooms and is frequented by many doctors and university members, who are welcomed as friends. The corner bedrooms or sixth-floor attic rooms are best.

Récamier

3 bis Pl St-Sulpice 75006.
Map 12 E4. 【 01 43 26 04 89.
FAX 01 46 33 27 73. **Rooms:** 30. ▨
23. ▤ ▥ ▦ *MC, V.* €€

The Hôtel Récamier, situated on the Place St-Sulpice within walking distance of St-Germain-des-Prés, is a family hotel with no television sets or restaurant. With its air of old-fashioned charm, it is well known to writers and Left Bank tourists. Try to get a bedroom which looks out onto the square, for the view.

Hôtel de l'Abbaye

10 Rue Cassette 75006. **Map** 12 D5.
【 01 45 44 38 11. FAX 01 45 48 07 86. W www.hotel-abbaye.com
Rooms: 46. ▨ ▥ ▤
▥ ▦ ▤ *AE, MC, V.* €€€

Once an abbey, this is an elegant hotel with a tranquil atmosphere. The bedrooms are small but are impeccably furnished, and some retain their original beams. Breakfast is served in the pretty courtyard whenever possible. If not, the real fire in the salon helps to make you feel at home. The ground-floor bedrooms overlook the garden, and the comfortable duplex rooms are recommended.

MONTPARNASSE

Lenox Montparnasse

15 Rue Delambre 75014.
Map 16 D2. **[** 01 43 35 34 50.
FAX 01 43 20 46 64. **Rooms:** 52.
TV ♦ ♦ **Y** ♦ **ⓔ** AE, DC, MC, V,
JCB. €€ **w** www.parishotels.com

With less style than the Lenox St-
Germain, the Montparnasse hotel
is nevertheless centrally located in
a district which has few hotels of
charm. The bar is decorated in Art
Deco style, and the overall
atmosphere is one of restrained
elegance. The six large suites on
the upper floor each have a
fireplace. You can order light
meals in your room until 2am –
unusual for an hotel of this size.

Ferrandi

92 Rue du Cherche-Midi 75006. **Map**
15 C1. **[** 01 42 22 97 40. **FAX** 01 45
44 89 97. **w** www.123france.com
Rooms: 42. ♦ **TV** ♦ ♦ **ⓔ** AE,
DC, MC, V, JCB €€

The Rue du Cherche-Midi is known
to lovers of antiques and bistros,
as well as being the heart of the
publishing world. The Hôtel
Ferrandi is a quiet hotel with a
fireplace in the lounge and with
comfortable bedrooms, many with
four-poster or canopied beds.

Villa des Artistes

9 Rue de la Grande Chaumière 75006.
Map 16 D2. **[** 01 43 26 60 86.
FAX 01 43 54 73 70. **w** www.villa-
artistes.com **Rooms:** 59. ♦ ♦ **TV**
Y ♦ **0** **ⓔ** AE, DC, MC, V,
JCB. €€

The Villa des Artistes aims to
recreate the Belle Epoque era to
which the Montparnasse painters
were so attached. The bedrooms
are clean with good bathrooms,
but the main charm of the hotel is
its large patio garden and fountain,
where you can breakfast in peace.
Some rooms overlook the courtyard.
Children over 5 are catered for.

Ste-Beuve

9 Rue Ste Beuve 75006. **Map** 16 D1.
[01 45 48 20 07. **FAX** 01 45 48 67
52. **w** www.paris-hotel-charme.com
Rooms: 22. ♦ ♦ **TV** **Y** ♦ ♦
ⓔ AE, DC, MC, V. €€

The Ste-Beuve is a small carefully
restored hotel for aesthetes and
habitués of the Rive Gauche galleries.
Here you will receive an attentive
welcome in charming surroundings
(the decor was conceived by the
British interior designer David
Hicks). There is a fireplace in the

hall, the rooms are pleasantly
decorated in pastel shades and
there are a number of classic
contemporary paintings. For
breakfast, croissants and speciality
teas are bought in from top
suppliers and served at bridge
tables or at sofas in the salon. The
atmosphere is warm and cosy.

Le St-Grégoire

43 Rue de l'Abbé Grégoire 75006.
Map 11 C5. **[** 01 45 48 23 23. **FAX**
01 45 48 33 95. **Rooms:** 20. ♦ **1**
TV ♦ ♦ **ⓔ** AE, DC, MC, V, JCB.
€€€ **w** www.hotelstgregoire.com

Le St-Grégoire is a fashionable
town-house hotel with immacu-
lately-decorated bedrooms with
19th-century furnishings. At the
centre of the drawing room is a
charming fireplace with a real fire.
The excellent breakfast is served
in the vaulted cellar. Some rooms
have their own private terrace.

INVALIDES

Hôtel de Suède
St-Germain

31 Rue Vaneau 75007. **Map** 11 B4.
[01 47 05 00 08. **FAX** 01 47 05 69
27. **w** www.hoteldesuede.com
Rooms: 39. ♦ **1** ♦ ♦ **TV** ♦
AE, DC, MC, V, JCB. €€

The Hôtel de Suède look directly
over the park of the Hôtel
Matignon, home of the Prime
Minister. The elegant rooms are
decorated in late 18th-century
styles in pale tones and the
welcome is of rare warmth. Top
floor rooms have park views.

Hôtel de Varenne

44 Rue de Bourgogne 75007.
Map 11 B2. **[** 01 45 51 45 55.
FAX 01 45 51 86 63. **Rooms:** 24. ♦
♦ **TV** ♦ ♦ ♦ **0** **ⓔ** AE, MC, V.
€€ **@** hotel.varenne@wanadoo.fr

Beyond its severe facade, this
hotel conceals a narrow courtyard
garden where guests breakfast in
the summer. Double glazing in the
bedrooms minimizes street noise,
but rooms overlooking the courtyard
are the most quiet and cheerful.

Hôtel Bourgogne et
Montana

3 Rue de Bourgogne 75007. **Map** 11
B2. **[** 01 45 51 20 22. **FAX** 01 45 56
11 98. **w** www.bourgogne-
montana.com **Rooms:** 32. ♦ **TV**
♦ ♦ ♦ ♦ **ⓔ** AE, DC, MC, V.
JCB. €€€€

Situated in front of the Assemblée
Nationale, the hotel has an air of
sobriety. Features include a
mahogany bar, old lift and circular
hall with pink marble columns.
The bedrooms are more ordinary,
except for those on the fourth
floor which allow a glimpse of the
Place de la Concorde. This is a
relaxing, intimate hotel.

Duc de St-Simon

14 Rue de St-Simon 75007. **Map** 11 C3.
[01 44 39 20 20. **FAX** 01 45 48 68
25. **@** duc.de.st.simon@wanadoo.fr
Rooms: 34. ♦ **TV** ♦ **Y**
ⓔ AE, MC, V. €€€€

The Hôtel Duc de St-Simon is
among the most sought-after
hotels on the south side of the
river and popular with Americans.
A charming 18th-century mansion
furnished with antiques, it lives up
to its aristocratic pretensions and
is a match for the most famous
houses in the Faubourg St-
Germain. The bedrooms overlooking the large terrace are a
rare treat.

CHAILLOT QUARTER
PORTE MAILLOT

Hôtel de Banville

166 Blvd Berthier 75017. **Map** 4 D1.
[01 42 67 70 16. **FAX** 01 44 40 42
77. **w** www.hotelbanville.com
Rooms: 38. ♦ **1** **24** **TV** ♦
♦ ♦ **Y** **1** ♦ **ⓔ** AE, DC, MC,
V, JCB. €€€

This 1930s hotel was a family
house but has retained the original
iron gate, stone staircase and lift.
The salons are opulent and the
bedrooms comfortable.

Concorde La Fayette

3 Pl du Général Koenig 75017.
Map 3 C2. **[** 01 40 68 50 68.
FAX 01 40 68 50 43.
w www.concorde-lafayette.com
Rooms: 968. ♦ ♦ **24** **TV**
Y ♦ ♦ **1** ♦ ♦ ♦ ♦
Y **11** **ⓔ** AE, DC, MC, V, JCB.
€€€€

The formulaic Concorde La
Fayette with its egg-shaped tower
overlooks the Palais des Congrès
on the Porte Maillot and is
thoroughly high-tech. It has
numerous facilities, including a
fitness club, an amazing bar on
the 33rd floor, several restaurants,
a shopping gallery, and identical
bedrooms with splendid views –
the higher you are, the better the
views.

For key to symbols see p275

Le Méridien

81 Blvd Gouvion St-Cyr 75017. **Map** 3 C2. 📞 01 40 68 34 34. **FAX** 01 40 68 31 31. 🌐 www.lemeridien-hotels.com *Rooms: 1,025.* 🛏 📶 📺 📢 🎛 🍴 🐾 🔒 🛗 🏋 🛎 🎾 🍴 🅿 ⬛ *AE, DC, MC, V, JCB.* €€€€

Despite its lack of charm, the Hôtel Le Méridien is one of the most popular hotels in Paris. It is conveniently located opposite the Palais des Congrès and the Air France terminal for Roissy, and its restaurant is one of the best in Parisian hotels. Its Lionel Hampton Club has built a reliable reputation in the world of jazz and hosts a jazz brunch on winter Sundays.

Square

3 Rue de Boulainvilliers 75016. **Map** 9 A4. 📞 01 44 14 91 90. **FAX** 01 44 14 91 99. 🌐 www.bermuda-onion.com *Rooms: 22.* 📶 🎛 📺 📢 🅿 🐾 🍴 🐾 🎾 🛎 ⬛ *AE, DC, MC, V.* €€€€

Close to the Seine and with some great views over the river to the Eiffel Tower, this is a hotel which manages to be both stylishly modern and luxuriously welcoming. The 22 rooms and suites, some of which are designed for use by disabled guests, are furnished with sumptuous fabrics and exotic woods and each has its own marble bathroom, as well as full business facilities. There are contemporary art exhibitions in the atrium.

Villa Maillot

143 Ave de Malakoff 75016. **Map** 3 C4. 📞 01 53 64 52 52. **FAX** 01 45 00 60 61. 🌐 www.lavillamaillot.fr *Rooms: 42.* 🛏 📢 📺 📶 🛎 🐾 🔒 🐾 🍴 📢 ⬛ *AE, DC, MC, V, JCB.* €€€€€

Conveniently situated for Porte Maillot and La Défense, the Villa Maillot is a modern creation which harks back to the 1930s with its Art Deco-inspired furnishings. The rooms have large beds, concealed kitchenettes and marble bathrooms. On the eighth floor are suites, each one devoted to a different painter.

Melia-Alexander

102 Ave Victor Hugo 75016. **Map** 3 B5. 📞 01 45 53 64 65. **FAX** 01 45 53 12 51. 🌐 www.solmelia.com *Rooms: 62.* 🛏 📢 🎛 📺 🛎 🏋 📶 🐾 🍴 🛎 ⬛ *AE, DC, MC, V, JCB.* €€€€€

This comfortable, traditional hotel reflects the bourgeois self-confidence of the Avenue Victor

Hugo. The small, quiet public rooms convey a sense of warmth and intimacy and are perfect for meeting up with friends. The well-equipped bedrooms are large, with spacious bathrooms. Ask for a room on the courtyard.

Raphaël

17 Ave Kléber 75016. **Map** 4 D4. 📞 01 53 64 32 00. **FAX** 01 53 64 32 01. 🌐 www.raphael-hotel.com *Rooms: 90.* 🛏 📶 📺 🛎 🐾 🛎 🔒 🐾 🍴 📢 🅿 🎾 🍴 🛎 ⬛ *AE, DC, MC, V, JCB.* €€€€€

Many films are shot in the Neo-Gothic bar of this timeless hotel. Here no one asks questions, Italian film stars are sheltered from the paparazzi and the Turner hanging in the hall doesn't even attract a passing glance.

St-James

43 Ave Bugeaud 75016. **Map** 3 B5. 📞 01 44 05 81 81. **FAX** 01 44 05 81 82. 🌐 www.saint-james-paris.com *Rooms: 48.* 🛏 📢 📶 📺 📢 🛎 🐾 🔒 🐾 📢 🅿 🍴 🎾 🍴 🛎 ⬛ *AE, DC, MC, V, JCB.* €€€€€

The St-James occupies a mansion with a small park near the Avenue Foch and the Bois de Boulogne. Visitors are entitled "temporary members" (of the hotel club), and a token fee is included in the room price. The hotel has a princely atmosphere, with English-style salons, wood-panelled libraries, billiard rooms and large bedrooms opening onto the park.

CHAMPS-ELYSÉES

Résidence Lord Byron

5 Rue Chateaubriand 75008. **Map** 4 E4. 📞 01 43 59 89 98. **FAX** 01 42 89 46 04. *Rooms: 31.* 🛏 📢 🏋 📺 📢 🐾 📶 🛎 🍴 📢 ⬛ *AE, DC, MC, V, JCB.* €€€ 🌐 www.escapade-paris-.com

Close to the Etoile, the Résidence Lord Byron is a discreet, small hotel with a courtyard garden where you can take breakfast in summer. Its bright bedrooms are relatively quiet but small; if you want more space, ask for one of the few salon bedrooms or for a ground-floor room in the pavilion between the two gardens.

Atala

10 Rue Chateaubriand 75008. **Map** 4 E4. 📞 01 45 62 01 62. **FAX** 01 42 25 66 38. 🌐 www.france-hotel-guide.com *Rooms: 48.* 🛏 📢 📺 📢 🎾 🛎 📶 🐾 🔒 📢 🍴 🛎 ⬛ *AE, DC, MC, V, JCB.* €€€€

Situated in a quiet street yet within a few minutes' walk to the busy Champs-Elysées, the Atala's rooms overlook a tranquil garden with tall trees. The terrace restaurant is surrounded by hydrangeas, and the eighth-floor bedroom views of the Eiffel Tower are spectacular. The bedrooms have all been re-decorated, but the reception and restaurant remain ordinary.

Claridge-Bellman

37 Rue François-1er 75008. **Map** 4 F5. 📞 01 47 23 54 42. **FAX** 01 47 23 08 84. 🌐 www.france-infotourism.com *Rooms: 42.* 🛏 📢 📺 📢 🛎 🐾 📢 🍴 📢 ⬛ *AE, DC, MC, V.* €€€€

The Claridge-Bellman is a miniature version of the old Claridge Hotel and is managed by its former directors. The hotel has a truly traditional feel. It is quiet, sober and efficiently run, and is furnished throughout with tapestries and antiques. The sixth-floor attic rooms are charming.

Bristol

112 Rue du Faubourg-St-Honoré 75008. **Map** 5 A4. 📞 01 53 43 43 00. **FAX** 01 53 43 43 01. 🌐 www.hotel-bristol.com *Rooms: 192.* 🛏 📢 📶 📺 📢 🎾 🛎 🔒 🐾 📢 🅿 🛎 🍴 📢 ⬛ *AE, DC, MC, V, JCB.* €€€€€

One of Paris's finest hotels, its large rooms are sumptuously decorated with antiques and have magnificent marble bathrooms. The period dining room is decorated with Flemish tapestries and glittering crystal chandeliers. In summer, lunch is taken under an awning.

Plaza Athénée

25 Ave Montaigne 75008. **Map** 10 F1. 📞 01 53 67 66 65. **FAX** 01 53 67 66 66. 🌐 www.plaza-athenee-paris.com *Rooms: 204.* 🛏 📢 📶 📺 📢 🎾 🛎 🐾 🔒 🐾 📢 🍴 📢 🛎 ⬛ *AE, DC, MC, V, JCB.* €€€€€

The legendary Plaza Athénée has stood on the glamorous Avenue Montaigne for over 80 years. It is a hotel for honeymooners, old aristocracy and for *haute couture*. Its three-Michelin-starred restaurant of the same name, is wonderfully romantic, especially in summer on the ivy-decked terrace, while Le Relais has a reputation as being the most snobbish grill in Paris. The hotel's bedrooms conform to the very highest contemporary standards of luxury, as well as to the timeless dictates of comfort.

Four Seasons George V

31 Ave George V 75008. **Map** 4 E5.
(01 49 52 70 00. **FAX** 01 49 52 70 10. **W** www.fourseasons.com
Rooms: 245.

AE, DC, MC, V, JCB.
€€€€€

This legendary hotel, dotted with secret salons, old furniture and art, has lost a little of its charm during renovation, but has gained two Michelin stars for its restaurant, Le Cinq. The service remains excellent. Breakfast amongst the media.

Balzac

6 Rue Balzac 75008. **Map** 4 F4.
(01 44 35 18 00. **FAX** 01 44 35 18 05.
@ hotelbalzac@wanadoo.fr
Rooms: 70.

AE, DC, MC, V, JCB. €€€€€

The Balzac is known mainly for its restaurant, Pierre Gagnaire (Michelin 3-star). But this small luxury hotel deserves to be visited for its own sake. Behind the *fin-de-siècle* façade is an impressive columned lounge, and Philip Starck's 'Bar à Cigares'.

Prince de Galles Sheraton

33 Ave George V 75008. **Map** 4 E5.
(01 53 23 77 77. **FAX** 01 53 23 78 78.
Rooms: 168.

AE, DC, MC, V, JCB. €€€€€
W www.luxurycollection.com

The Prince de Galles Sheraton suffers from being seen as a second choice after its neighbour, the Four Seasons George V. The hotel is less prestigious and the bedrooms are certainly overdue for restoration. Only the comfortably British bar and the restaurant bear any true comparison.

Royal Monceau

37 Ave Hoche 75008. **Map** 4 F3.
(01 42 99 88 00. **FAX** 01 42 99 89 90. **W** www.royalmonceau.com
Rooms: 219.

AE, DC, MC, V, JCB.
€€€€€

Lying majestically between the Place de l'Etoile and the Parc Monceau, the Royal Monceau has been splendidly restored to its former glory. Its health club is now one of the most luxurious in Paris and its Le Carpaccio restaurant is one of the city's best Italian eateries. Judicious use of the former might even undo some of the damage incurred through over-indulgence at the latter. The breakfast room is unusual in its design – a striking glass gazebo with curved walls. The bedrooms are elegant – pamper yourself and pick a room overlooking the courtyard if possible or one of the prestigious suites.

San Regis

12 Rue Jean Goujon 75008. **Map** 11 A1. **(** 01 44 95 16 16. **FAX** 01 45 61 05 48. **W** www.hotel-sanregis.com **Rooms:** 44.

AE, DC, MC, V, .JCB. €€€€€

Since it opened in 1923 the San Regis has been the haunt of masters of *haute couture* and film actors, who enjoy its quiet but central location. This particularly welcoming, intimate luxury hotel is undeniably British in style – this is especially true of the famous bar. The suites on the upper-floors overlook a pleasant terrace.

Sofitel Arc de Triomphe

14 Rue Beaujon 75008. **Map** 4 E4.
(01 53 89 50 50. **FAX** 01 53 89 50 51. **W** www.sofitel.com **Rooms:** 135.

AE, DC, MC, V, JCB. €€€€€

The Sofitel Arc de Triomphe, situated in the business area near the Etoile, is a quiet hotel. The bedrooms have been restored in Pullman style and Neo-Art Deco furniture. The Clovis restaurant is astonishingly good and the junior suites particularly comfortable.

Hôtel de la Trémoille

14 Rue de la Trémoille 75008. **Map** 10 F1. **(** 01 56 52 14 00. **FAX** 01 40 70 01 08. **W** www.hotel-tremoille.com
Rooms: 107.

AE, DC, MC, V. €€€€€

The Hôtel de la Trémoille is impressive but at the same time relaxed. Housemaids customarily cast a ray of sunshine through residents' days by responding with a smile to the first ring; a fire burns in the restaurant fireplace; rooms are furnished with comfortable antiques; and the bathrooms are divine in their luxury.

Vernet

25 Rue Vernet 75008. **Map** 4 E4.
(01 44 31 98 00. **FAX** 01 44 31 85 69. **W** www.hotelvernet.com
Rooms: 51.

AE, DC, MC, V, JCB. €€€€€

The Hôtel Vernet is still relatively unknown to the general public. Gustave Eiffel, architect of the Eiffel Tower, created the dazzling glass roof of the dining room. The large, quiet bedrooms are pleasantly furnished and guests have free use of the Royal Monceau's fitness club.

OPÉRA QUARTER

Ambassador

16 Blvd Haussmann 75009. **Map** 6 E4. **(** 01 44 83 40 40. **FAX** 01 40 22 08 74. **W** www.hotelambassador-paris.com **Rooms:** 288.

AE, DC, MC, V, JCB.
€€€€

One of the best of Paris's Art Deco hotels, the Ambassador has been restored to its former glory and has deep carpeting and antique furniture. The ground floor has pink marble columns, Baccarat crystal chandeliers and Aubusson tapestries. The food is outstanding – the chef formerly managed the kitchen at the Grand Véfour restaurant (see p301).

Le Grand Hôtel International

2 Rue Scribe 75009. **Map** 6 D5.
(01 40 07 32 32. **FAX** 01 42 66 12 51. **W** www.paris.interconti.com
Rooms: 514.

AE, DC, MC, V, JCB.
€€€€€

The Intercontinental chain has invested a lot here, with a top-floor health club and the utmost in contemporary comfort in all the bedrooms. The hotel has a sumptuous Opera Salon beneath an Art Deco cupola.

MONTMARTRE

Terrass' Hôtel

12 Rue Joseph-de-Maistre 75018.
Map 6 E1. **(** 01 46 06 72 85. **FAX** 01 42 52 29 11. **W** www.terrass-hotel.com **Rooms:** 101.

AE, DC, MC, V, JCB.
€€€€

The Terrass Hôtel has a panoramic view over the rooftops of Paris from the upper floors and from the breakfast terrace. All the rooms are comfortably, if unremarkably, furnished. A few bedrooms retain the original Art Deco woodwork.

For key to symbols see p275

RESTAURANTS, CAFÉS AND BARS

THE FRENCH NATIONAL passion for good cuisine makes eating out one of the greatest pleasures of a visit to Paris. Everywhere in the city you see people eating – in restaurants, bistros, tea salons, cafés and wine bars.

Most restaurants serve French food but there is a range of Chinese, Vietnamese and North African eateries in many areas as well as Italian, Greek, Lebanese and Indian places. The restaurants in the listings (see pp299–309) have been selected from the best that Paris can offer across all price ranges. The listings and Choosing a Restaurant on pages 296–8 are organized by area and price. Most places will serve lunch from noon until around 2pm, and the menu often includes fixed-price meals. Parisians usually start to fill restaurants for dinner around 8.30pm and most places serve from around 7.30pm until 11pm. (See also Light Meals and Snacks pp310–11.)

WHAT TO EAT

A TREMENDOUS RANGE of food is available in Paris, from the rich meat dishes and perfect pâtisserie for which France is most famous to simpler French regional cuisines (see pp290–91). The latter are available in brasseries and bistros – the type usually depends on the birthplace of the chef. At any time of day simple, tasty meals can be had in cafés, wine and beer bars, and brasseries, bistros and cake shops – or pâtisseries – abound. Some cafés, like the Bar du Marché (see p311) in St-Germain-des-Prés, are known for their excellent cold food and don't offer hot meals at lunchtime.

The best ethnic food comes from France's former colonies: Vietnam or North Africa. North African places are known as couscous restaurants and serve filling, somewhat spicy, inexpensive food that varies in quality. Vietnamese restaurants are also good value and provide a light alternative to rich French food. Paris also has a number of good Japanese restaurants, notably around Rue Monsieur le Prince (6th arrondissement), while Rue de la Roquette (11th) and Rue de Belleville (19th) have others.

WHERE TO FIND GOOD RESTAURANTS AND CAFÉS

YOU CAN EAT well in almost any part of Paris. Wherever you are, as a rule of thumb you will find that the most outstanding restaurants and cafés are those that cater predominantly to a French clientele.

The Left Bank probably has the greatest concentration of restaurants, especially in tourist areas like St-Germain-des-Prés and the Latin Quarter. The quality of food varies, but there are some commendable bistros,

Beauvilliers restaurant (see p306)

outdoor cafés and wine bars. (For bistros, brasseries and restaurants with outdoor tables, see Choosing a Restaurant on pages 296–8.) The Latin Quarter also has a high concentration of Greek restaurants centred chiefly around Rue de la Huchette.

In the Marais and Bastille areas, small bistros, tea salons and cafés are plentiful, some new and fashionable. There are also many good, traditional long-established bistros and brasseries.

In the Champs-Elysées and Madeleine area it is difficult to find inexpensive good food. It is overrun with fast food joints and pricy but not very good cafés. There are, however, some very good expensive restaurants here.

Some great cafés of the 1920s are in Montparnasse on the Boulevard Montparnasse, including Le Sélect and La Rotonde (see p311). Sensitive renovation has recaptured

The prim Mariage Frères shop and tea room (see p311)

much of their old splendour.
There are excellent bistros in
this area as well.

There are many noteworthy
restaurants, bistros and cafés
in the Louvre-Rivoli area,
competing with tourist-
oriented, overpriced cafés. Just
to the east, Les Halles is choc-
a-bloc with fast food joints
and mediocre restaurants but
there are few places of note.

Good Japanese food can be
found near the Opéra together
with some fine brasseries, but
otherwise the area around the
Opéra and Grands Boulevards
is not the best for restaurants.
Near the Bourse are a number
of reputable restaurants and
bistros frequented by
stockbrokers.

Montmartre has a predictable
number of tourist restaurants,
but it also has a few very
pleasant small bistros. More
expensive are the luxurious
Beauvilliers (see p306), and
the Italian-influenced La Table
d'Anvers (see p306) near the
Butte Montmartre.

Quiet neighbourhoods in
the evening, the Invalides,
Eiffel Tower and Palais de
Chaillot tend to have less
noisy, more serious restaurants
than areas with lively nightlife.
Prices can be high.

Two Chinatowns, one in the
area south of the Place d'Italie,
the other in the traditionally
working-class, hill-top area of
Belleville, have concentrations
of ethnic food but few French
restaurants of note. There are a
number of Vietnamese eating
places as well as large,
inexpensive Chinese ones,
and Belleville is packed with
small North African restaurants.

Tour d'Argent decoration *(see p302)*

Le Grand Véfour in the Tuileries *(see p301)*

TYPES OF RESTAURANTS AND CAFÉS

O NE OF THE MOST enjoyable
aspects of eating in Paris
is the diversity of places to eat.
Bistros are small, often moder-
ately-priced restaurants with a
limited selection of dishes.
Those from the Belle Epoque
era are particularly beautiful,
with zinc bars, mirrors and
attractive tiles. The food is
generally, but not always,
regional and traditional. Many
chefs from the smartest
restaurants have now
also opened bistros
and these can be
very good value.

Brasseries are
generally large
bustling eateries,
many with an
Alsatian character
serving carafes of
Alsatian wine and
platters of sauerkraut
and sausage. They
have immense menus, and
most serve food throughout
the day and are open late.
Outside you may well see
impressive pavement displays
of shellfish, with apron-clad
oyster shuckers working late
into the night.

Cafés open early in the
morning, and apart from the
large tourist cafés, the majority
close by around 10pm. They
serve drinks and food all day
long from a short menu of
salads, sandwiches and eggs.
At lunch most also offer a
small choice of hot daily

**Menu at
Le Bistrot du Dôme**

specials. Café prices vary
from area to area, in direct
proportion to the number of
tourists. Smarter cafés, like
Café de Flore and Les Deux
Magots serve food until late at
night. Those cafés specializing
in beer almost always include
onion tarts, French fries and
hearty bowls of steamed
mussels on the menu. Brunch
is now served in many places
at weekends, from around 15€.

Wine bars are informal. They
usually have a moderately-
priced, simple lunch menu
and serve wine by
the glass. They serve
snacks at any time of
day – such as
marvellous open
sandwiches *(tartines)*
made with sourdough
Poilâne bread topped
with cheese, sausage
or pâté – until around
10pm, but a few stay
open for dinner.

Tea salons open
for breakfast or mid-morning
until the early evening. Many
offer lunch, as well as a
selection of sweet pastries for
afternoon tea. They are at
their best in the middle of the
afternoon and offer coffee
and hot chocolate as well as
fine teas. Some, like Le Loir
dans la Théière, are casual
with sofas and big tables,
while Mariage Frères is more
formal. Angélina on the Rue
de Rivoli is famous for its hot
chocolate, and Ladurée has
excellent chocolate macaroons.
(For addresses see p311.)

VEGETARIAN FOOD

VEGETARIAN RESTAURANTS in Paris are few, and non-vegetarian restaurant menus are usually firmly oriented towards meat and fish. However, you can get a good salad almost anywhere and you can often fare well by ordering two courses from the list of *entrées* (first courses). The North African restaurants will serve you *couscous nature* – which doesn't have meat.

Never be timid about asking for a change in a dish. If you see a salad with ham, bacon or *foie gras*, ask the waiter for it without the meat. If you are going to a smart restaurant, telephone ahead and ask the manager if it is possible to prepare a special meal for you. Most restaurants will be happy to oblige.

Organic produce is starting to be used in French cuisine.

HOW MUCH TO PAY

PRICES FOR MEALS in Paris range from extremely economic to astronomical. You can still enjoy a hearty restaurant or café lunch for 12€, but a typical good bistro, brasserie or restaurant meal in central Paris will average 30€–38€ with wine. (Remember that the better French wines will increase the size of your bill significantly.) More expensive restaurants begin at about 45€ with wine and go up to 150€ for the top places. Many places offer a *formule* or *prix-fixe* (fixed price) menu, especially at

Le Carré des Feuillants *(see p301)*

lunch, and this will almost always offer the best value. Some restaurants feature menus for under 15€ – a few at this price include wine. Coffee usually carries an extra charge.

All French restaurants are obliged by law to display their menu outside. The posted rates include service but a tip for particularly good service will always be appreciated (any amount from one Euro to 5% of the total).

The most widely accepted credit card is Visa. Few restaurants accept American Express, and some bistros do not accept credit cards at all, so it is wise to enquire when you book. Traveller's cheques are not widely accepted either, and cafés require cash.

MAKING RESERVATIONS

IT IS BEST TO reserve a table in all restaurants, brasseries and bistros. Although you can usually get into a brasserie without a reservation, you may have to wait for a table.

DRESS CODE

EXCEPT FOR SOME three-star restaurants which can be rather formal, you can dress up or down in Parisian restaurants – within reason. The restaurant listings *(see pp299–309)* indicate which places require formal dress.

READING THE MENU AND ORDERING

MENUS IN SMALL restaurants and bistros, and even in big brasseries, are often handwritten and can be difficult to decipher, so ask for help if necessary.

The waiter usually takes your choice of *entrée* (first course), then the *plat* (main course). Dessert is ordered after you have finished your main course, unless there are some hot desserts which have to be ordered at the start of

The Angélina restaurant, also known for its tea room *(see p311)*

the meal. The waiter will tell you this, or the dessert section of the menu will be marked *à commander avant le repas*.

The first course generally includes a choice of seasonal salads or vegetables, pâté and small hot or cold vegetable dishes or tarts. Small fish dishes like smoked salmon, grilled sardines, herring, fish salads and tartares are also offered. Brasseries have shell-fish such as oysters, which can also be eaten as a main course. (The French tend to eat shellfish only when the month ends in 're'!) Main dishes usually include a selection of meat, poultry and fish and upmarket restaurants offer game in autumn. Most

Le Pavillon Montsouris near the Parc Montsouris *(see p309)*

Le Train Bleu station restaurant in the Gare de Lyon *(see p309)*

restaurants also offer daily specials *(plats du jour)*. These dishes will incorporate fresh, seasonal produce and are usually good value.

Cheese is eaten either as a dessert or as a pre-dessert course. Some people have a green salad with their cheese. Coffee is served after, not with, dessert. You will need to ask specifically if you want it *au lait* (with milk). Decaffinated coffee *(décaffiné)* and herbal teas *(tisanes)* are also popular after-dinner beverages.

In most restaurants you will be asked if you would like a drink before ordering food. A typical apéritif is *kir* (white wine with a drop of crème de cassis, a blackcurrant liqueur) or *kir royal* (champagne with crème de cassis). Spirits, how-ever, are rarely drunk before a meal in France *(see* What to Drink in Paris *pp292–3).*

Bistros and brasseries usually include the wine list with the menu. The more expensive restaurants have separate wine lists, which are generally brought to the table by the wine waiter after you have seen the meal menu.

SERVICE

As EATING IS a leisurely pas-time in France, although the general standard of service in Paris restaurants is high, it is not always fast. In small restaurants in particular don't expect rapid attention: there may be only one waiter, and dishes are cooked to order.

CHILDREN

CHILDREN ARE usually very welcome, but there may be little room in a busy restaurant for push-chairs or prams. Nor are special facilities like high-chairs or baby seats commonly provided in eating places.

SMOKING

FRANCE HAS passed strict legislation forcing restau-rants to provide no-smoking tables. While most restaurants abide by this, cheaper eating places, especially cafés, still tend to be very smoky.

WHEELCHAIR ACCESS

WHEELCHAIR access may be restricted. A word when you are booking should ensure that you are given a more conveniently situated table and help when you arrive.

USING THE LISTINGS
Key to symbols in the listings on pp299–309.

🌑 annual closure
🍴 fixed-price menu
V vegetarian specialities
👶 children's portions
♿ wheelchair access
👔 jacket and tie required
🎵 live music
🪑 outdoor tables
🍷 particularly good wine list
★ highly recommended
💳 credit cards accepted:
AE American Express
DC Diners Club
MC Mastercard/Access
V Visa
JCB Japanese Credit Bureau

Price categories for a three-course meal including a half-bottle of house wine, tax and service:
€ under 25€
€€ 25€–35€
€€€ 36€–50€
€€€€ 51€–75€
€€€€€ over 75€

Lucas Carton restaurant *(see p306)*

What to Eat in Paris

Goat's cheese

FRENCH CUISINE is a still-evolving art. Classical French cooking is butter-based and centres on meat, poultry and fish. However, it is no longer all super-rich, nor is it the "nouvelle cuisine" of the 1980s. Today the chefs of many Parisian restaurants are interested in regional food and in simple home-style cooking. This relies on fresh, seasonal ingredients as in the shellfish dishes *coquilles Saint-Jacques* and *moules marinières* shown here. French cooking tends not to be highly spiced, although fresh herbs like chives, parsley and tarragon are essential ingredients in the sauces and stocks. The most popular regional cooking in Paris is from Lyon, Burgundy and the Southwest. Provençal traditions with scents of garlic and olive oil are also gaining in popularity. Lyonnais cooking is characterized by copious salads and hearty meat-based main dishes like *andouillettes*. Burgundian and Southwestern food is rich; typical dishes are: *foie gras* (fattened liver), *jambon* or *homard persillé* (ham or lobster with parsley) and *cassoulet*, a hearty main course with pork and beans.

Croissants
These flaky pastry crescents are eaten for breakfast.

Pains au Chocolat
These chocolate-filled pastries are an alternative to croissants.

Brioches
Doughy buns, they are torn and dipped in coffee.

Baguette
This characteristic long crusty loaf is wonderful as a sandwich or simply buttered fresh from a bakery.

Foie Gras
This is the liver of specially-fattened geese or ducks.

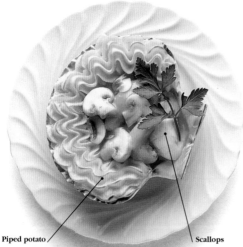

Piped potato   Scallops

Coquilles Saint-Jacques
Scallops can be prepared and garnished in many ways, but are classically cooked with sliced mushrooms in white wine, lemon juice and butter and then served on one half of the scallop shell. A piping of mashed potato is often used to keep the scallops and their sauce in the shell.

Moules Marinières
Mussels are steamed in garlicky wine stock.

Escargots à la Bourguignonne
Cooked snails are replaced in their shells and garnished.

Homard Persillé
This lobster terrine is cooked in a flavoured stock with parsley, shallots and herbs.

Oeufs en Cocotte à l'Estragon
A tarragon-flavoured sauce is poured over baked eggs.

Andouillettes à la Lyonnaise
These sausages made from pork intestines are grilled or fried and served with onions.

Noisettes d'Agneau
Small, tender lamb cutlets are fried in butter and served with a variety of garnishes.

Chèvre Tiede sur un Lit de Salade
Grilled goat's cheese sits on a classic mixed-leaf salad.

Slice of Brie de Meaux   **Crottins de Chavignol**

Cheeses (*Fromages*)

Cheese is one of the glories of France. Many varieties are made – from cow's, sheep's and goat's milk. The soft and semi-soft mild cheeses such as Brie and Camembert are available in all Parisian restaurants.

Slice of Pont l'Evêque

Whole Camembert

Crêpes Suzettes
Pancakes are served with tangerine and Curaçao sauce.

Tarte Tatin
This upside-down apple tart is a Parisian speciality.

Tarte Alsacienne
Classic Alsatian tarts contain confectioner's custard and fruit.

What to Drink in Paris

PARIS IS THE BEST place in France to sample a wide range of the country's many different wines. It's cheapest to order wine by the carafe, normally referred to by size: 25cl (*quart*), 33cl (*fillette*), 50cl (*demi*) or 75cl (*pichet*, equivalent to a bottle). Cafés and wine bars always offer wine by the glass – *un petit blanc* is a small glass of white, a larger glass of red, *un ballon rouge*. House wine is nearly always reliable.

Paris's last vineyard, near Sacré-Coeur (see p220)

RED WINE

SOME OF THE world's finest and most expensive red wines come from the Bordeaux and Burgundy regions, but for everyday drinking choose from the enormous range of basic Bordeaux or Côtes du Rhône wines. Alternatively try Beaujolais, which comes from the southern end of Burgundy and is light enough to serve chilled.

Distinctive bottle shapes for Bordeaux and Burgundy

Bordeaux châteaux include Margaux, which makes some of the world's most elegant red wines.

Burgundy includes some big, strong red wines from the village of Gevrey-Chambertin in the Côte de Nuits.

Beaujolais Nouveau, the fruity first taste of the year's new wine, is released on the third Thursday of November.

The Loire has very good red wines from the area around Chinon. They are usually quite light and very dry.

Southern Rhône is famous for its dark, rich red wines from Châteauneuf-du-Pape, north of Avignon.

Northern Rhône has some dark, fragrant red wines, best aged for at least 10 years, from Côte-Rôtie near Vienne.

FINE WINE VINTAGE CHART

	2000	1999	1998	1997	1996	1995	1994	1993	1992
BORDEAUX									
Margaux, St-Julien, Pauillac, St-Estèphe	8	7	7	7	8	8	6	5	5
Graves, Pessac-Léognan (red)	8	7	8	7	8	8	6	5	5
Graves, Pessac-Léognan (white)	8	8	7	8	7	7	7	7	6
St-Emilion, Pomerol	8	7	7	7	8	8	6	5	5
BURGUNDY									
Chablis	8	8	8	9	8	9	6	6	9
Côte de Nuits (red)	7	7	7	8	7	8	5	7	7
Côte de Beaune (white)	7	7	8	8	9	6	6	7	
LOIRE									
Bourgueil, Chinon	8	8	7	9	9	8	6	6	4
Sancerre (white)	8	8	7	9	8	8	7	6	6
RHONE									
Hermitage (red)	7	8	8	7	9	8	7	5	6
Hermitage (white)	9	7	8	8	8	7	7	5	6
Côte-Rôtie	8	9	8	7	9	8	7	5	6
Châteauneuf-du-Pape	8	7	8	7	8	8	7	6	5

The quality scale from 1 to 10 represents an overall rating for the year and is only a guideline.

WHITE WINE

THE FINEST white Bordeaux and Burgundy are best with food, but for everyday drinking try a light dry wine such as Entre-Deux-Mers from Bordeaux, or Anjou Blanc or Sauvignon de Touraine from the Loire. Alsace makes some reliable white wines. Sweet wines such as Sauternes, Barsac or Coteaux du Layon are delicious with *foie gras*.

Alsace Riesling and Burgundy

SPARKLING WINE

IN FRANCE champagne is the first choice for a celebration drink, and styles range from non-vintage to deluxe. Many other wine regions make sparkling wines by the champagne method which tend to be a lot cheaper. Look out for Crémant de Loire, Crémant de Bourgogne, Vouvray Mousseux, Saumur Mousseux and Blanquette de Limoux.

Champagne

Alsace wines are usually labelled by grape variety. Gewürz-traminer is one of the most distinctive.

Loire wines include Pouilly-Fumé, from the east of the region. It is very dry, often with a slightly smoky perfume.

Burgundy wines include Chablis, a fresh, full-flavoured dry wine from the northernmost vineyards.

The Loire has the perfect partner to seafood dishes in Muscadet, a dry white wine from the Atlantic Coast.

Champagne vineyards east of Paris produce the famous sparkling wine. Billecart-Salmon is a light, pink Champagne.

Sweet Bordeaux are luscious, golden-coloured dessert wines, the most famous being Barsac and Sauternes.

APÉRITIFS AND DIGESTIFS

KIR, WHITE WINE mixed with a small amount of blackcurrant liqueur or *crème de cassis*, is the ubiquitous apéritif. Also common is aniseed-flavoured *pastis* which is served with ice and a pitcher of water and can be very refreshing. Vermouths, especially Noilly-Prat, are also common apéritifs. *Digestifs*, or after-dinner drinks, are often ordered with coffee and include *eaux-de-vie*, the strong colourless spirits infused with fruit, and brandies such as Cognac, Armagnac and Calvados.

Kir: white wine with *cassis*

BEERS

BEER IN FRANCE is sold either by the bottle or, more cheaply, on tap by the glass – *un demi*. The cheapest is lager-style *bière française*, and the best brands are Meteor and Mutzig, followed by "33", "1664" and Kronenbourg. A maltier beer is Leffe, which comes as *blonde* (lager) or *brune* (darker, more fully-flavoured). Pelforth makes very good dark beer and lager. Some bars and cafés specialize in foreign beers, especially from Belgium, and these are very malty and strong; others brew their own beer. (For beer bars see pp310–11.)

OTHER DRINKS

THE BRIGHTLY-COLOURED drinks consumed in cafés all over Paris are mixtures of flavoured syrups and mineral waters, called *sirops à l'eau*. The emerald-green drinks use mint syrup, the red ones grenadine. Fruit juices and tomato juice are sold in bottles unless you specify *citron pressé* or *orange pressée* (freshly-squeezed lemon or orange), which is served with a pitcher of water and with sugar or sugar syrup for you to dilute and sweeten to taste. If you ask for water, you will be served mineral water, sparkling (*gazeuse*) or still (*naturelle*); if you don't want to be charged, ask for tap water (*eau de robinet*).

Fresh lemon juice is served with water and sugar.

Paris's Best: Restaurants

PARIS HAS A GREATER WEALTH of eating places than any other city of comparable size. From the simplest of zinc bars to the grandest of elegant restaurants it has something for everybody. Even in the humblest bistro the bread and pastries will be fresh from the bakery and the cheese will be perfectly ripe. The restaurants here are just a few of Paris's most memorable, chosen from the listings on pages 299–309 as much for the beauty of their decor as the excellence of their food.

Le Grand Colbert
This pretty brasserie is in a historic building and serves classic fare until late.
(See p306.)

Champs-Elysées

Chaillot Quarter

Opéra Quarter

Tuileries Quarter

R I V E R   S E I N E

Invalides and Eiffel Tower Quarter

St-Germain-des-Prés

L'Astrance
Just across the river from the Eiffel Tower, this restaurant is a surprise, not least for its skilfully inventive dishes.
(See p304.)

Luxembourg Quarter

Montparnasse

Taillevent
The discreetly luxurious surroundings, exquisite modern classic cuisine, extraordinary wine list and impeccable service make this a top restaurant. (See p305.)

0 kilometres   1

0 miles   0.5

L'Arpège
This starkly modern restaurant near the Musée Rodin offers wonderfully elegant haute cuisine. (See p303.)

Brasserie Flo
It's worth the trip to this brasserie for the authentic Alsatian cuisine. Sauerkraut platters, seafood and excellent regional wines and beers draw customers. (See p307.)

Chartier
The bustling atmosphere and inexpensive basic French food make this turn-of-the-century soup kitchen with listed decor a popular choice. (See p305.)

Au Pied de Cochon
This colourfully restored landmark of old Les Halles serves authentic brasserie fare. (See p300.)

eaubourg and Les Halles

Benoît
Classic French cuisine is served in this archetypal bistro with its 1912 mirrored interior. (See p300.)

The Marais

Ile de la Cité

Ile St-Louis

in Quarter

Brasserie Bofinger
Dating from 1864, the oldest and one of the most popular brasseries in Paris is known for its marvellous decor, excellent shellfish and reliable menu. (See p299.)

Jardin des Plantes Quarter

Pharamond
Mosaics and coloured tiles make this old bistro an Art Nouveau gem. (See p300.)

La Tour d'Argent
This famous restaurant with a panoramic view is the ultimate in luxury – and expense. (See p302.)

Choosing a Restaurant

THE RESTAURANTS LISTED on the following pages have been selected for their good value or exceptional food. This choosing chart highlights some of the main factors which may influence your choice. For more information on each restaurant see pages 299–309. Details of snack and sandwich bars are in Light Meals and Snacks on pages 310–11.

		Seafood Restaurant	Fixed-Price Menu	Late Opening (after 11.30pm)	Children's Facilities	Outdoor Eating	Quiet Restaurant	Vegetarian Specialities
ILE DE LA CITÉ *(see p299)*								
Vieux Bistrot	€€€€					●		
THE MARAIS *(see p299)*								
Galerie 88	€		■			●		●
Le Baracane	€		■					
Le Passage	€				■		■	
Aux Vins des Pyrénées	€			●			■	●
Le Repaire de Cartouche	€€							
Chez Jenny	€€		■	●		●		●
Le Bar à Huîtres	€€	●	■	●		●		
Brasserie Bofinger	€€€		■	●				
La Guirlande de Julie	€€€			●		●		
L'Ambroisie ★	€€€€€						■	
BEAUBOURG AND LES HALLES *(see p300)*								
Le Grizzli	€		■			●		
Le Loubechem	€		■					
Bleu Marine	€	●	■				●	■
Le Bistrot Beaubourg	€		■			●		
Aux Tonneaux des Halles	€			●		●		
Saudade	€€							
Le 404 ★	€€			●				●
Pharamond	€€€		■				●	■
Au Pied de Cochon	€€€		■	●		●		
Benoît ★	€€€€€							
TUILERIES QUARTER *(see pp300–1)*								
Gaya	€€	●	■					
Le Grand Louvre	€€		■		■			
L'Espadon ★	€€€€		■		■	●		
Goumard	€€€€	●						
Les Ambassadeurs ★	€€€€€		■					
Le Carré des Feuillants ★	€€€€€		■					
Le Grand Véfour ★	€€€€€		■					
ST-GERMAIN-DES-PRÉS *(see pp301–2)*								
Aux Charpentiers	€		■			●		
Rôtisserie d'en Face	€		■					
Le Petit St-Benoît	€							
Alcazar	€		■	●	■			●
Le Procope	€€		■	●				
Yugaraj	€€		■					●
Aux Fins Gourmets	€€€							
Brasserie Lipp	€€€			●				
Tan Dinh	€€€€						■	
Lapérouse	€€€€€		■					
Restaurant Jacques Cagna ★	€€€€€		■					
LATIN QUARTER *(see p302)*								
Restaurant Perraudin	€		■				■	
Loubnane	€€		■	●	■			

Price categories per person for a three-course meal with a half-bottle of house wine, including tax and service:
€ under 25€
€€ 25–35€
€€€ 36–50€
€€€€ 51–75€
€€€€€ over 75€

★ Means highly recommended.

FIXED-PRICE MENU
Fixed-price menu available at lunch, dinner or both.

CHILDREN'S FACILITIES
Children's portions provided. (Children are welcome in most restaurants in Paris even if special arrangements are not made for them.)

QUIET RESTAURANT
Restaurant has a quiet, intimate atmosphere. No piped music.

	Price	SEAFOOD RESTAURANT	FIXED-PRICE MENU	LATE OPENING (AFTER 11.30PM)	CHILDREN'S FACILITIES	OUTDOOR EATING	QUIET RESTAURANT	VEGETARIAN SPECIALITIES
Le Balzar	€€			●		●		
Restaurant Moissonnier	€€€		●					
Rôtisserie du Beaujolais	€€€					●		
La Tour d'Argent ★	€€€€€		●		●		●	
JARDIN DES PLANTES QUARTER *(see pp302–3)*								
Au Petit Marguéry	€€		●			●		
MONTPARNASSE *(see p303)*								
La Coupole	€		●	●				
La Cagouille ★	€€€	●	●		●	●		
Contre-Allée	€€€		●			●		
INVALIDES AND EIFFEL TOWER QUARTER *(see p303)*								
L'Oeillade	€€		●					
La Serre	€€				●			
Thoumieux	€€		●					
Vin sur Vin	€€€€							
L'Arpège ★	€€€€€		●					
Le Jules Verne	€€€€€		●					
CHAILLOT QUARTER, PORTE MAILLOT *(see pp303–4)*								
La Plage	€		●			●		
L'Huîtrier	€	●						
La Butte Chaillot	€€€		●	●		●		
Chez Géraud	€€€		●					
Oum El Banine	€€€						●	
Le Timgad	€€€							
L'Astrance	€€€		●				●	
Alain Ducasse ★	€€€€€		●		●			
Amphyclès ★	€€€€€		●		●			
CHAMPS-ELYSÉES *(see pp304–5)*								
La Fermette Marbeuf 1900	€€		●			●		
Savy	€€		●				●	
Sébillon	€€		●	●				
Le Cercle Ledoyen	€€€		●			●		
Spoon	€€€							●
L'Avenue	€€€€			●				
La Maison Blanche/15 Avenue Montaigne	€€€€					●		
Lasserre	€€€€€							
Taillevent ★	€€€€€							
Guy Savoy ★	€€€€€							
Laurent ★	€€€€€		●			●		
OPÉRA QUARTER *(see pp305–6)*								
Chartier	€		●					
La Ferme St-Hubert	€						●	●
Chez Clément	€		●	●				
Au Petit Riche	€€		●	●				
Café Runtz	€€							
Le Vaudeville	€€		●	●	●	●		

Price categories per person for a three-course meal with a half-bottle of house wine, including tax and service:
€ under €25
€€ €25–35
€€€ €36–50
€€€€ €51–75
€€€€€ over €75

★ Means highly recommended.

FIXED-PRICE MENU
Fixed-price menu available at lunch, dinner or both.

CHILDREN'S FACILITIES
Children's portions provided. (Children are welcome in most restaurants in Paris even if special arrangements are not made for them.)

QUIET RESTAURANT
Restaurant has a quiet, intimate atmosphere. No piped music.

	SEAFOOD RESTAURANT	FIXED-PRICE MENU	LATE OPENING (AFTER 11.30PM)	CHILDREN'S FACILITIES	OUTDOOR EATING	QUIET RESTAURANT	VEGETARIAN SPECIALITIES
Les Noces de Jeannette €€		■		■		■	
Café Drouant €€		■	●				
Le Grand Colbert €€€		■	●				
A.G. Le Poète €€€		■					
Chez Georges €€€€							
Lucas Carton ★ €€€€€		■					
MONTMARTRE (see pp306–7)							
La Table d'Anvers €€€		■					
Beauvilliers €€€€		■				●	
FURTHER AFIELD (see pp307–9)							
Dao Vien (75013) €		■					
Le Volant (75015) €		■					
Astier (75011) €		■		■			
Chez Fernand (75011) €		■					
Brasserie Flo (75010) €		■	●				●
Julien (75010) €			●				
Le Baron Rouge (75012) €	●	■		■			●
Le Petit Keller (75011) €							
Pause Café Bastille (75011) €		■	●		●		●
L'Occitanie (75011) €		■					
Favela Chic (75011) €			●				●
Les Allobroges (75020) €€		■					
Le Bistro des Deux Théâtres (75009) €€		■	●				
La Perle des Antilles (75014) €€		■		■			
Les Amognes (75011) €€		■					
L'Oulette (75012) €€		■			●		
La Marine (75010) €€	●				●		
Aux Senteurs de Provence (75015) €€		■			●		
La Maison du Cantal (75015) €€		■					
Le Clos Morillons (75015) €€		■				■	
Le Bistrot d'à Côté Flaubert (75017) €€€					●		
L'Auberge du Bonheur (75016) €€€		■		■	●		
Le Chardenoux (75011) €€€				■			
Le Pavillon Montsouris (75014) €€€		■			●		
La Table de Pierre (75017) €€€				■	●		
Au Trou Gascon (75012) €€€		■					
Le Train Bleu (75012) €€€		■					
Augusta (75017) €€€	●			■		■	
Pavillon Puebla (75019) €€€		■		■	●		●
Le Villaret (75011) ★ €€€		■					
Au Pressoir (75012) €€€€		■		■			
Le Pré Catelan (75016) €€€€		■		■	●		
Faucher (75017) €€€€€		■					
Apicius (75017) ★ €€€€€							

ILE DE LA CITÉ

Vieux Bistrot

14 Rue du Cloître-Notre-Dame 75004. **Map** 13 B4. 01 43 54 18 95. noon–2pm, 7.30pm–10.30pm daily. 24–25 Dec. AE, MC, V. €€€€

Despite the obvious name and touristy location next to Notre-Dame, this is an authentic, honest bistro, popular with many Paris restaurateurs and entertainment stars. The slightly rundown decor suits the place and the rendition of favourites like beef fillet with marrow, *boeuf bourguignon*, *gratin dauphinois* (sliced potatoes baked in cream), *tarte tatin* (upside-down apple tart) and profiteroles are very good.

THE MARAIS

Galerie 88

88 Quai de l'Hotel de Ville 75004. **Map** 13 B4. 01 42 72 17 58. noon–3pm, 7pm–11pm (10.30 Sun) daily. €

The bare walled decor in this tiny restaurant situated on the banks of the River Seine, appeals to students and people on a budget. Prices are low, service is very friendly if slow, and you really know you are in Paris. The food is straightforward and old-fashioned, and includes terrines and a selection of truly delicious home-made tarts, but also offers a few vegetarian dishes.

Le Baracane

38 Rue des Tournelles 75004. **Map** 14 E3. 01 42 71 43 33. noon–2.30pm, 7pm–midnight Mon–Fri; 7pm–midnight Sat. MC, V. €

In the tourist-intensive, pricy Marais district, this tiny restaurant has very good quality food at reasonable prices. The fixed-price menu is particularly good value: an aperitif, a 3-course meal, a bottle of wine (you select from the wine list) and coffee. It serves excellent Southwestern cuisine such as a delicious rabbit *confit* (cooked and potted), braised oxtail, pears poached in Madeira and Cassis (blackcurrant liqueur), and superb home-made chestnut bread.

Le Passage

18 Passage de la Bonne Graine 75011. **Map** 14 F4. 01 47 00 73 30. noon–2.30pm, 7.30pm–11.30pm Mon–Fri, 7.30pm–11.30pm Sat. AE, DC, MC, V. €

Hidden in the Passage de la Bonne Graine, a short walk from the Place de la Bastille, you may well be personally greeted by the proprietor Soizik. Although it calls itself a wine bar (and the selection of wines by the glass and bottle is excellent), it offers a full menu including five styles of *andouillette* (tripe sausage) and a variety of daily specials, frequently served with a delicious potato gratin. The cheeses are excellent and desserts include a vast chocolate éclair.

Aux Vins des Pyrénées

25 Rue Beautreillis 75004. **Map** 13 C3. 01 42 72 64 94. noon–3pm, 7.30–11.30pm Mon–Sat. DC, MC, V. €

A very old bistro whose friendly and typically Parisian atmosphere continue to make it as popular as ever. The day's menu, written up on a blackboard, typically offers a selection of grilled meats. There is an excellent selection of wines by the glass (particularly good value Bordeaux and lesser-known wines from southwest France).

Le Repaire de Cartouche

8 Blvd Filles du Calvaire 75011. **Map** 14 D2. 01 47 00 25 86. noon–2pm, 7.30pm–11pm Tue–Sat. Aug. DC, MC, V. €€

Like its "sister" establishment, Le Villaret, this restaurant is run by former employees of Astier, to the same excellent standards. It too has a constantly changing seasonal menu, which includes roast pigeon with leeks in a vinegar sauce and rabbit terrine with chocolate. The decor, like the cuisine, is reassuringly traditional without being oppressively heavy.

Chez Jenny

39 Blvd du Temple 75003. **Map** 14 D1. 01 42 74 75 75. 11.30am–1am daily. DC, MC, V. €€

This huge brasserie on the Place de la République has been a bastion of Alsatian cooking since it was founded over 60 years ago. Service by women in Alsatian dress adds to the convivial atmosphere. The basic *choucroute* (sauerkraut) *spéciale Jenny* makes a hearty meal with a fruit tart or sorbet served with a corresponding fruit liqueur for dessert.

Le Bar à Huîtres

33 Blvd Beaumarchais 75003. **Map** 14 E3. 01 48 87 98 92. noon–1am Mon–Thu, noon–2am Fri & Sat, noon–12.30am Sun. AE, MC, V. €€

Oysters predominate in Paris's two Bars à Huîtres (the other bar is in Montparnasse). You can compose your own seafood platter to start, followed by a choice of hot fish dishes, with meat available for the hopeless carnivore. This is an upbeat place convenient for the ever-buzzing Place de la Bastille and the Marais.

Brasserie Bofinger

5 Rue de la Bastille 75004. **Map** 14 E4. 01 42 72 87 82. noon–3pm, 6.30pm–1am daily. AE, DC, MC, V. €€€

Bofinger claims to be the oldest brasserie in Paris, established in 1864. It is certainly one of the prettiest, with turn-of-the-century stained glass, leather banquettes, brass decorations and murals by the Alsatian artist Hansi. It serves good shellfish, as well as respectable *choucroute* (sauerkraut), and grilled meats. This is a very popular place, frequented by politians, businessmen and opera-goers, as it is situated just across the Place de la Bastille from the opera house. You may have to wait for a table (even with a reservation).

La Guirlande de Julie

25 Pl des Vosges 75003. **Map** 14 D3. 01 48 87 94 07. noon–2.30pm, 7pm–10.30pm Tue–Sun. MC, V. €€€

This is a fine restaurant on the fabulous 17th-century Place des Vosges. Consumate restaurant professional Claude Terrail of the Tour d'Argent *(see p302)* has employed a good chef at the Guirlande de Julie, and the decor is feminine, fresh and appealing. For the best views, ask for a table near the window in the first dining room. In good weather meals are served under the vaulted stone arcades.

L'Ambroisie

9 Pl des Vosges 75004. **Map** 14 D3. 01 42 78 51 45. noon–1.30pm, 8pm–10pm Tue–Sat. ★ AE, MC, V. €€€€€

This discreet, romantic spot is one of only seven Michelin three-star restaurants in Paris. Reservations for the forty seats are accepted one month ahead (not a day earlier or later). The chef Monsieur Pacaud has restored this former jewellery shop, giving it a handsome stone floor and subtle lighting. The cuisine includes a mousse of sweet red peppers, truffle *feuilleté* (layered pastry), langoustines with sesame and *croustillant* of lamb.

BEAUBOURG AND LES HALLES

Le Grizzli

7 Rue St-Martin 75004. **Map** 13 B3.
[01 48 87 77 56. **□** noon–
2.30pm, 7.30pm–11pm Mon–Sat.
¶@¶ 🖬 🖨 AE, MC, V, JCB. **€**

A change of ownership has
breathed new life into the Grizzli –
founded in 1903 when it was one
of the last Parisian places to have
dancing bears! The owner orders
much produce from his native
southwest including local ham, lamb
chops, cooked on a sizzling slate,
cheeses and wines made by his
family. The decor is warm and there
is a dumbwaiter in frequent use.

Le Loubechem

31 Rue Berger 75001. **Map** 12 F2.
[01 42 33 12 99. **□** 11am–3pm
Mon–Sat. **¶@¶ 🖨** AE, DC, MC, V. **€**

A former butcher's shop back in
the 1950s when the wholesale meat
market was still in central Paris,
"Loubechem" means butcher in
their slang. Indeed, meat is what
this no-nonsense restaurant is all
about, with portions designed
more for rugby players than ballet
dancers. L'assiette du rôtisseur is a
classic (3-meat roast platter, each
with its own sauce), and the
aiguillette à la ficelle are still
prepared in the traditional manner.

Bleu Marine

28 Rue Léopold Bellan 75002.
Map 13 A1. **[** 01 42 36 92 44.
□ noon–3pm, 8pm–11pm Mon–Sat.
¶@¶ 🖬 🖨 MC, V. **€**

The limited menu of this
welcoming neighbourhood
restaurant is seasonal, with dishes
such as marinated sardines,
salmon profiteroles and sea trout
with basil. The varnished ivory-
coloured ash wood decor with
abundant flowers is refreshing.

Le Bistrot Beaubourg

25 Rue Quincampoix 75004. **Map** 13
B2. **[** 01 42 77 48 02. **□**
noon–2pm, 7.45pm–10pm daily. **¶@¶**
lunch only. **🖬 🖨** DC, MC, V. **€**

This arty but chic establishment
serves classic French food at
surprisingly affordable prices.
Skate with 'black' butter sauce and
rib steak with green pepper sauce
are typical of their excellent
menus, changed daily. Lingering
over one's meal is no sin here, and
is equally pleasurable inside, among
the unusual collection of posters,
or outside on the sunny terrace.

Aux Tonneaux des Halles

28 Rue Montorgueil 75001.
Map 13 A1. **[** 01 42 33 36 19.
□ 8am–midnight Mon–Sat. **🖬**
🖨 DC, MC, V. **€**

This genuine Parisian bistro is one
of the last of its kind, with its real
zinc bar, smoky interior and one
of the tiniest kitchens in Paris.
Service is not quick, but when the
food is this good, who cares! The
wines are original and good value.

Saudade

34 Rue des Bourdonnais 75001.
Map 13 A2. **[** 01 42 36 30 71.
□ noon–2pm Mon–Sat, 7.30pm–
10.30pm Mon–Thu, 7.30pm–11pm
Fri, Sat. **🖨** AE, MC, V. **€€**

This is probably the finest
Portuguese restaurant in Paris, and
with all the pretty tiles you expect
to find the Tajo and not the Seine
nearby. The Portuguese staple salt
cod is prepared in various ways:
in fritters, with tomato and onion
or with potatoes and eggs. Roast
suckling pig and cozido (Portugal's
national stew) are other typical,
tasty dishes. There is a good selection of Portuguese wines and ports.

Le 404

69 Rue Gravilliers 75003. **Map** 13 B1.
[01 42 74 57 81. **□** 8pm–2am daily.
🖨 V ★ 🖨 AEC, MC, V. **€€**

Magnificently located in the hôtel
particulier built for Gabrielle
d'Estrées (Henri IV's mistress) in
1737, the 404 is impeccably run by
the actor Smaïn, who also owns
Momo in London. The food here is
deeply rooted in native Morocco:
genuine-tasting couscous, tajine
and vegetarian delicacies. The
decor gives one the impression of
being in a bedouin tent. It is
crowded every night, so do book.

Pharamond

24 Rue de la Grand-Truanderie 75001.
Map 13 B2. **[** 01 40 28 03 00.
□ noon–3pm, 7.30pm–11.30pm
daily. **●** Sun eve winter. **¶@¶**
lunchtime. **🖬 🖨** AE, DC, MC, V.
€€€

Founded in 1870, this solid bistro
has survived the transfer of the Les
Halles market out of the city and
remains a charming remnant of the
19th century, with coloured tiles
and mosaics, handsome woodwork
and mirrors. Specialities include
tripes à la mode de Caen (tripe
cooked with onions, leeks, cider
and Calvados) and boeuf en daube
(beef stew). The Normandy cider
is strongly recommended.

Au Pied de Cochon

6 Rue Coquillière 75001. **Map** 12 F1.
[01 40 13 77 00. **□** 24 hrs daily.
¶@¶ 🖬 🖬 🖨 AE, DC, MC, V.
€€€

This colourfully-restored brasserie
was once popular with high
society, who came to pass a few
bourgeois minutes observing the
workers toiling in the old market
of Les Halles, and to relish the
onion soup, while discussing
matters of pith and moment.
Although touristy, this gigantic
place is fun, and has a menu with
something for everyone (including
excellent shellfish), and is still
considered to be one of the best
places to mop up a heavy night
on the town.

Benoît

20 Rue St-Martin 75004. **Map** 13 B2.
[01 42 72 25 76. **□** noon–2pm,
8pm–10pm daily. **🖬 ¶@¶** lunch
only. **★ 🖨** AE. **€€€€€€**

This is a gem of a Parisian bistro,
combining classic dependability
with a non-prohibitive price tag.
The owner has retained the faux-
marbre, polished-brass and lace-
curtain decor created by his
grandfather in 1912. The excellent
bistro cuisine includes saladiers
(assorted cold salads), house foie
gras, boeuf à la mode and cassoulet
(white bean and meat stew). The
wine list is outstanding.

TUILERIES QUARTER

Gaya

17 Rue Duphot 75001. **Map** 5 C5.
[01 42 60 43 03. **□** noon–
2.30pm, 7pm–11pm Mon–Fri. **¶@¶**
🖨 AE, MC, V. **€€**

Monsieur Goumard's bistrot de la
mer (seafood bistro) was once his
up-market fish restaurant before he
restored the 19th-century Goumard
Prunier. The menu consists of
simply-prepared fish dishes; the
dining area on the ground floor is
particularly eye-catching, with its
colourful décor of very pretty
Portuguese tiles.

Le Grand Louvre

Le Louvre 75001. **Map** 12 F2.
[01 40 20 53 41. **□** noon–3pm,
7pm–10pm Wed–Mon. **🖬 🖬 ¶@¶**
🖨 AE, DC, MC, V, JCB. **€€**

It is rare to find such a good
restaurant in a museum and that is
only part of the attraction of this

establishment. It is situated under the Louvre's glass pyramid entrance, and the sober wood and metal decor perfectly complements the glass structure. The menu draws much inspiration from southwest France – stuffed goose neck, *foie gras, boeuf en daube* (beef stew), prune ice cream with Armagnac – and was originally developed by André Daguin, one of the region's gastronomic stars.

L'Espadon

15 Rue Vendôme 75001. **Map** 6 D5.
【 *01 43 16 30 80.* ◯ *7am–11am, noon–3pm, 7.30pm–11pm daily.* 🍽
🏃 🕭 🆃 🔀 🖥 ★ 🖊 *AE, DC, MC, V, JCB.* €€€€€

Part of the Ritz *(see p281)*, this two Michelin-starred restaurant is well-worth the expense of the meal: its many merits include handsome decor, an idyllic garden, perfectly-executed service and modern classic cuisine from the chef M.Guillouët.

Goumard

9 Rue Duphot 75001. **Map** 5 C5.
【 *01 42 60 36 07.* ◯ *12.15pm–2.30pm, 7pm–10.30pm Tue–Sat.* 🆃 🖥
🍽 *lunch only.* 🖊 *AE, DC, MC, V, JCB.* €€€€

Formerly Prunier – a name still almost synonymous with seafood – this 19th-century restaurant was restored in lavish good taste by Monsieur Goumard. No expense has been spared in the handsome kitchen, fabulous Lalique light fixtures and sculptures, which harmonize well with the remaining original 1900s and 1930s elements. The fish is always fresh and there is a selection of excellent desserts.

Les Ambassadeurs

10 Pl de la Concorde 75008. **Map** 11 C1. 【 *01 44 71 16 16.* ◯ *7am–10.30am, noon–2.30pm, 7pm–10.30pm daily.* 🍽 🕭 🆃 🖥 ★ 🖊 *AE, DC, MC, V, JCB.* €€€€€

Part of the Hôtel de Crillon *(see p280)*, this is one of only two hotel restaurants in Paris with two Michelin stars. Chef Dominique Bouchet maintains high standards of creative cooking while intro-ducing his own particular brand of classical French food with a modern touch and a meticulous attention to detail. Bouchet changes his menu with the seasons, but look out for such delights as bacon-wrapped scallops with basil and tomato and crisp potato pancakes with whipped cream, smoked salmon and caviar. The service is superb and the all-marble dining room, overlooking the Place de la Concorde, is quite stunning.

Le Carré des Feuillants

14 Rue de Castiglione 75001.
Map 12 D1. 【 *01 42 86 82 82.*
◯ *noon–2pm, 7.30pm–10.30pm Mon–Fri, 7.30pm–10.30pm Sat.*
🖥 *Aug.* 🍽 🕭 🖥 ★ 🖊 *AE, DC, MC, V, JCB.* €€€€€

This is the showcase for star chef Alain Dutournier and the best products of his native southwest, including specially-ordered lamb, beef, *foie gras* and poultry. The Venetian glass and illusionistic painted ceilings give the restaurant a rural touch. The wine list is exceptional.

Le Grand Véfour

17 Rue de Beaujolais 75001.
Map 12 F1. 【 *01 42 96 56 27.*
◯ *12.30pm–2pm, 8pm–10pm Mon–Fri.* 🖥 *Aug.* 🍽 🆃 🖥 ★
🖊 *AE, DC, MC, V, JCB.*
€€€€€

This 18th-century restaurant with its ornate listed decor is considered by many to be the most attractive in Paris. The chef Guy Martin apparently effortlessly maintains his third Michelin star with dishes such as scallops with Beaufort cheese, cabbage ravioli with a truffle cream and endive *galette* (pancake). Ask to be seated at Colette's favourite table (or Victor Hugo's or Napoleon's). This is very much a place for celebrations.

ST-GERMAIN-DES-PRÉS

Aux Charpentiers

10 Rue Mabillon 75006. **Map** 12 E4.
【 *01 43 26 30 05.* ◯ *noon–3pm, 7pm–11.30pm daily.* 🍽 🔀 *AE, DC, MC, V, JCB.* €

There are no culinary surprises at this old-established bistro, eternally popular with students and St-Germain-des-Prés locals. The menu changes daily but you can count on well-prepared bistro stand-bys such as veal marengo, *boeuf à la mode* and homely pastries, served at reasonable prices in the big, noisy dining room.

Rôtisserie d'en Face

2 Rue Christine 75006. **Map** 12 F4.
【 *01 43 26 40 98.* ◯ *noon–2.30pm, 7.30pm–11pm Mon–Thu, 7pm–11.30pm Fri, Sat.* 🍽 🖊 *AE, DC, MC, V, JCB.* €

This elegant, bistro-style restaurant is one of four establishments belonging to two-star chef Jacques

Cagna. Even the wealthy appreciate a bargain and a smart crowd continues to come here for the reasonable fixed-price formula. Farm chicken from the rôtisserie with mashed potatoes, grilled salmon with fresh spinach, and profiteroles with chocolate sauce are among the favourite dishes on offer.

Le Petit St-Benoît

4 Rue St-Benoît 75006. **Map** 12 E3.
【 *01 42 60 27 92.* ◯ *noon–2.30pm, 7pm–10.30pm Mon–Sat.* 🕭 €

This is the place for anyone on a budget or just wanting to mix with the locals; the waitresses speak their mind and you might be seated at a table with others. Not much has been done to the decor over the years, but the good-value food is simple and homely.

Alcazar

62 Rue Mazarine 75006. **Map** 12 F4.
【 *01 53 10 19 99.* ◯ *noon–3pm, 7pm–1am daily.* 🍽 *lunch only* 🕭
🆅 🕭 🖊 *AE, DC, MC, V, JCB.* €

A fashionable club in the 1970's, l'Alcazar was bought by Sir Terence Conran in 1999. He converted it into a new brasserie-bar, and the result is this huge, elegant and thoroughly modern establishment which serves simple but well-made cuisine.

Le Procope

13 Rue de l'Ancienne Comédie 75006. **Map** 12 F4. 【 *01 40 46 79 00.* ◯ *11am–1am daily.* 🍽 🖊 *AE, MC, V.* €€

While the cuisine here may be sound but unexceptional, this is nonetheless a place you will want to visit if you like the idea of having some of the great names of Parisian history as your ghostly dining companions. Since its founding in 1686 (making it the longest-surviving restaurant in the city) it has been the gathering place of choice for writers, artists, politicians and philosophers, from Diderot to Danton, Beaumarchais to Balzac. It still cherishes its role as an artists' and writers' café and its 3-course menu for about 20€ (served until 8pm) seems made for impoverished intellectuals.

Yugaraj

14 Rue Dauphine 75006. **Map** 12 F3.
【 *01 43 26 44 91.* ◯ *noon–2.15pm Tue–Sun, 7pm–11pm daily.* 🍽 🆅
🖊 *AE, DC, MC, V.* €€

Recently redecorated, this is still considered by many to be the best

Indian restaurant in Paris. The chef emphasizes dishes from his native northern India, and key spices are bought in directly from the sub-continent. The wine list is perhaps surprisingly good too.

Aux Fins Gourmets

213 Blvd St-Germain 75007.
Map 11 C3. **[** 01 42 22 06 57.
○ noon–2.15pm, 7.30pm–10pm
Tue–Sat, 7.30pm–10pm Mon.
€€€

Situated at the far end of the Boulevard St-Germain near the Assemblée Nationale, this friendly neighbourhood place offers hearty, unpretentious cuisine. This features specialities from the southwest, including a good *cassoulet* (white bean and meat stew). Pastries come from the excellent pâtisserie Peltier.

Brasserie Lipp

151 Blvd St Germain 75006.
Map 12 E4. **[** 01 45 48 53 91.
○ noon–1am daily. 🔥
🖭 AE, DC, MC, V. €€€

This is the brasserie that everyone loves to hate. Yet its clientele, which includes entertainers and politicians, keeps returning for the straightforward brasserie food. The dishes include good herring in cream and a monumental *millefeuille* pastry. Ask to be seated downstairs if you want to be with the "in" crowd: the first floor is referred to as Siberia.

Tan Dinh

60 Rue de Verneuil 75007. **Map** 12 D3.
[01 45 44 04 84. ○ noon–2pm,
7.30pm–11pm Mon–Sat. ● Aug. 🖤
€€€€

The relatively high prices in this Franco-Vietnamese restaurant run by the discreet Vifian family are due to a combination of the very good quality cuisine and an out-standing wine list with one of the biggest collections of Pomerols in the city. There are no Oriental lanterns here – the interior decor is suitably sober and does not need to rely on flamboyance to create a pleasant atmosphere for eating.

Lapérouse

51 Quai des Grands Augustins 75006.
Map 12 F4. **[** 01 43 26 68 04.
○ noon–2.30pm Mon–Fri, 8pm–
10pm Sat. 🍷❶ 🔥 🖭 🖤
🖭 AE, DC, MC, V. €€€€€

This famous establishment from the 19th century was once one of the glories of Paris. Under the impeccable management of owner-chef Alain Hacquard, this is

still the case. The series of salons have kept their 1850s decor. The best tables are by the window.

Restaurant Jacques Cagna

14 Rue des Grands Augustins 75006.
Map 12 F4. **[** 01 43 26 49 39.
○ noon–2pm Tue–Fri, 7.30pm–
10.30pm Mon–Sat. 🍷❶ 🖭 🖤 🖤 ★
🖭 AE, DC, MC, V, JCB. €€€€€

This elegant 17th-century townhouse in the heart of old Paris is a showcase for the expensive trinkets and excellent classic-cum-contemporary cuisine of chef-owner Jacques Cagna. Occasional Oriental touches to the food show his love of the East. Possible dishes are red mullet salad with *foie gras*, pigeon *confit* (cooked and potted) with turnips, and a classic Paris-Brest (choux pastry filled with praline-flavoured cream). The wine list is admirable.

LATIN QUARTER

Restaurant Perraudin

157 Rue St-Jacques 75005. **Map** 16 F1.
[01 46 33 15 75. ○ noon–10.15pm
Tue–Fri, 7–10.15pm Mon & Sat.
● Aug. 🍷❶ 🔥 🖭 🖤 DC, MC, V. €

Close to the Pantheon, this tiny restaurant is not ashamed to serve oldies but goodies such as *oeuf-cocotte* and preserved duck. It is usually packed at lunchtime thanks to its friendly atmosphere.

Loubnane

29 Rue Galande 75005. **Map** 9 A4.
[01 43 26 70 60. ○ noon–3pm,
7pm–midnight Tue–Sun. 🍷❶ 🖤 🎵
🖭 🖭 AE, DC, MC, V. €€

A Lebanese restaurant where specialities include delicious and generous *mezzes*, served under the watchful eye of a *patron* whose main aim in life seems to be the happiness of his customers. Live Lebanese music is often performed in the basement.

Le Balzar

49 Rue des Ecoles 75005. **Map** 13 A5.
[01 43 54 13 67. ○ noon– midnight daily. 🖭 🖭 AE, MC, V. €€

There's a fair choice of brasserie food at this venue but the main attraction is the ambience. It is typically Left Bank in atmosphere: traditionally-dressed waiters weave their way amongst the bustle providing express service, with archetypal brasserie decor to match: large mirrors and comfortable leather seats.

Restaurant Moissonnier

28 Rue des Fossés St-Bernard 75005.
Map 13 B5. **[** 01 43 29 87 65.
○ noon–2pm, 7.30pm–10.30pm
Tue–Sat. ● Aug. 🍷❶ 🖭 MC, V.
€€€

This family-run bistro gives a taste of the provinces in Paris. It serves standard favourites which have Lyonnais overtones, such as *saladiers* (assorted salads), *gras-double* (tripe), *tablier de sapeur* (ox tripe), *quenelles de brochet* (pike dumplings) and chocolate cake. The wine list features Beaujolais wines traditionally served in a small bottle known as a *pot*. Ask to be seated downstairs.

Rôtisserie du Beaujolais

19 Quai de la Tournelle 75005.
Map 13 B5. **[** 01 43 54 17 47.
○ noon–2.15pm, 7.30pm–11pm
Tue–Sun. 🔥 🖭 V. €€€

Facing the Seine and owned by Claude Terrail of the Tour d'Argent next door, the restaurant has a large rôtisserie for roasting poultry and meats. Many of the meats and cheeses are ordered specially from the best suppliers in Lyon. A Beaujolais is, of course, the wine to order here.

La Tour d'Argent

15–17 Quai de la Tournelle 75005.
Map 13 B5. **[** 01 43 54 23 31.
○ noon–1.30pm, 7.30pm– 9pm
Tue–Sun. 🍷❶ 🖭 🔥 🖭 🖤 🖭 ★
🖭 AE, DC, MC, V. €€€€€

Established in 1582, the Tour appears to be eternal, but it is not moribund. Patrician owner Claude Terrail has hired a series of young chefs who have rejuvenated the classic menu. The ground-floor bar is also a gastronomic museum; from here there is a lift to the panoramic restaurant and its unbridled luxury. The wine cellar must be one of the finest on earth.

JARDIN DES PLANTES QUARTER

Au Petit Marguéry

9 Blvd de Port-Royal 75013.
Map 17 B3. **[** 01 43 31 58 59.
○ noon–2.15pm, 7.30pm–10.15pm
Tue–Sat. 🍷❶ 🖭 🔥 🖭 AE, DC,
MC, V. €€

This comfortable, reliable bistro is run by three brothers who create many dishes not found on classic bistro menus: mushroom salad with *foie gras*, cold lobster consommé with caviar, cod with spices and chocolate cake with a mocha sabayon sauce. It is also known for its pheasant and wild duck dishes.

MONTPARNASSE

La Coupole

102 Blvd du Montparnasse 75014. **Map** 16 D2. 01 43 20 14 20. 7.30am–1am (2am Fri–Sat) Sun–Thu. 24 Dec eve. AE, DC, MC, V, JCB.

This famous brasserie has been popular with the fashion crowd and with artists and thinkers since its creation in 1927. Under the same ownership as Brasserie Flo, La Coupole has a similar menu: good shellfish, smoked salmon, *choucroute* (sauerkraut) and many good desserts. Lamb curry is a speciality. The remarkable, semi-monumental decor was successfully restored in the late 1980's; this is a boisterous and lively place all through the day, from breakfast to 2am. *(See p178.)*

La Cagouille

10–12 Pl Constantin Brancusi 75014. **Map** 15 C3. 01 43 22 09 01. noon–2.30pm, 7.30pm–10.30pm daily. ★ AE, MC, V.

Situated on the stark new Place Brancusi in the rebuilt Montparnasse district, this large modern venue has a nautical atmosphere and is one of the best fish restaurants in Paris. Big fish are served simply with few sauces or adornments, and you might also find unusual seasonal ingredients like black bay scallops and *vendangeurs* – tiny red mullet.

Contre-Allée

83 Ave Denfert-Rochereau 75014. **Map** 16 E3. 01 43 54 99 86. noon–2pm Mon–Fri, 8pm–10pm Mon–Sat. AE, MC, V.

This restaurant off the Place Denfert-Rochereau is popular with professors from the Sorbonne as well as with the iconoclastic locals. Michel Inizian (former chef of Le Procope) conjurs up a cuisine which is a mix of good pasta dishes, cod with Parmesan, *hachis parmentier* (a kind of shepherd's pie) with *foie gras* and duck, delicious calves' liver and orange gratin. The decor is minimalist with striking black and white photographs and the service is young and energetic.

INVALIDES AND EIFFEL TOWER QUARTER

L'Oeillade

10 Rue de St-Simon 75007. **Map** 11 C3. 01 42 22 01 60. 12.30pm–2pm Tue–Fri, 7.30pm–11pm Mon–Sat. MC, V.

Abroad, major articles featuring this welcoming restaurant have turned it into a place for tourists. But it has a good-value, varied set menu that includes deep-fried smelt, *pipérade* (stewed sweet peppers, tomatoes and garlic) with poached egg, *sole meunière*, cod *brandade* (salt cod and garlic purée), roast lamb with cumin and *oeufs à la neige* (meringue in vanilla custard).

La Serre

29 Rue de l'Exposition 75007. **Map** 10 F3. 01 45 55 20 96. noon–3pm Tue–Sat, 7pm–11pm Tue–Sun. MC, V.

This small, cosy restaurant on a quiet street near the Eiffel Tower has a warm atmosphere. Owners Mary-Alice and Philippe Beraud offer good home-cooking, using the freshest ingredients, at reasonable prices. The cooking is tasty, with specialities from the southwest such as *gésiers confit* (preserved gizzards) *sur salade, cuisse de canard confite* (preserved leg of duck) with sauteed potatoes and a cooked-to-perfection pot-roasted calves' liver served with a *confiture d'onions*.

Thoumieux

79 Rue St-Dominique 75007. **Map** 11 A2. 01 47 05 49 75. noon–3.30pm, 6.30pm–midnight daily. AE, MC, V.

This well-run restaurant is good value for money. Ingredients are fresh and almost everything is made on the premises, including *foie gras*, duck *rillettes* (similar to pâté), *cassoulet* (white bean and meat stew) and chocolate mousse.

Vin sur Vin

20 Rue de Monttessuy 75007. **Map** 10 E2. 01 47 05 14 20. noon–2pm Tue–Sun, 8pm–10pm Mon–Sat. MC, V.

Owner Patrice Vidal is justly proud of his eight-table restaurant close to the Eiffel Tower. The menu is seasonal and original, the wine list fabulous with interesting wines at reasonable prices. Dishes might include *galette* (pancake) of squid, snail turnover, *blanquette* of whiting (with white sauce) and duck with peaches.

L'Arpège

84 Rue de Varenne 75007. **Map** 11 B3. 01 45 51 47 33. 12.30pm–2.30pm, 7.30pm–10.30pm Mon–Fri. ★ AE, DC, MC, V.

Chef owner Alain Passard's three-star restaurant near the Musée Rodin is one of the most highly regarded in Paris. It has striking pale-wood decor and sprightly young service as well as good food. Passard's lobster and turnip vinaigrette and duck Louise Passard are classics. Dishes are completed in the dining room. Don't miss the apple tart.

Le Jules Verne

2nd platform, Eiffel Tower 75007. **Map** 10 D3. 01 45 55 61 44. 12.15pm–1.30pm, 7.15pm–9.30pm daily. AE, DC, MC, V.

This is no tourist trap: the Jules Verne on the second platform of the Eiffel Tower is now one of the hardest dinner reservations to obtain in Paris. The sleek, all-black decor suits the monument perfectly and the pretty, flavourful cuisine is very good indeed. Ask for the dining room facing east or west.

CHAILLOT QUARTER PORTE MAILLOT

La Plage

Port Javel 75015. **Map** 9 B5. 01 40 59 41 00. 12.30pm–2.30pm, 7.30pm–10.30pm Mon–Fri. AE, DC, MC, V.

Facing the Statue of Liberty on the Ile aux Cignes, and in the heart of media land, the site alone is worth a look. The huge terrace is *the* place to be seen at lunchtime, as well as an idyllic place for a romantic candlelit dinner on a balmy summer's eve. The decor is an attractive mix of wood and pastel tones.

L'Huîtrier

16 Rue Saussier Leroy 75017. **Map** 4 E2. 01 40 54 83 44. noon–2.30pm, 7pm–10.30pm Tue–Sat, noon–2.30pm Sun. mid-Jul–Aug. AE, MC, V.

This freshly-decorated restaurant specializes in shellfish, especially oysters which you order by the half-dozen or dozen. It also serves several hot fish dishes and makes a good restorative stop before or after visiting the animated market in the nearby Rue Poncelet.

For key to symbols *see p289*

La Butte Chaillot

110 bis Ave Kléber 75116. **Map** 4 D5.
(01 47 27 88 88. 🕐 noon–
2.30pm, 7pm–midnight daily. **¶◯¶**
🚇 📧 *AE, MC, V, JCB.* €€€

This is the most recent boutique
restaurant of the renowned chef Guy
Savoy. It is also the most modern
with polished wood floors, glazed
ochre and beige walls, and a
massive steel and glass-sided staircase leading to tables on a lower
floor. The sophisticated country/
bistro cuisine includes snail salad,
oysters with a cream mousse, roast
breast of veal with rosemary and
apple tart. The clientele are smart.

Chez Géraud

31 Rue Vital 75016. **Map** 9 B3.
(01 45 20 33 00. 🕐 noon–2pm,
7.30pm–10pm Mon–Fri. ● Aug. **¶◯¶**
📧 *AE, MC, V.* €€€

Géraud Rongier, this bistro's jovial,
cherubic owner, welcomes you like
a friend and obviously wants you to
enjoy your meal. His is a scrupulous
cuisine du marché using what's best
at the market that day to create
dishes like shoulder of lamb
cooked on a spit, *sabodet* sausage
in red wine sauce, skate with
mustard, roast pigeon with port
sauce and bitter chocolate cake.
The pretty tile mural was created
specially for the restaurant.

Oum El Banine

16 bis Rue Dufrenoy 75016. **Map** 9 A1.
(01 45 04 91 22. 🕐 noon–
2pm, 8pm–10.30pm, 8pm–10.30pm
Tue–Sat. 📧 *AE, MC, V.* €€€

The owner of this small restaurant
in the chic residential quarter
learned her art from her mother in
Morocco and here prepares her
favourite dishes. There is good
harira soup (a thick, spicy soup),
pastilla (a savoury puff-pastry tart)
and *brik* (stuffed pastry triangle).
The couscous served with the five
choices of ragoût is exemplary. The
tagines (braised stews) are very
flavourful. This is a low-key,
authentic restaurant.

Le Timgad

21 Rue Brunel 75017. **Map** 3 C3.
(01 45 74 23 70. 🕐 noon–
2.30pm, 7.30pm–11pm daily. 📧
AE, DC, MC, V. €€€

This has been Paris's best-known,
most elegant Maghrebian restaurant
for years, hence the need to
reserve. The menu is extensive
with many different *briks* (stuffed
pastry triangles), *tagines* (braised
stews) and couscous dishes as
well as specialities like grilled
pigeon, *pastilla* (a savoury puff-

pastry tart) and *méchoui* (whole
roast lamb) if ordered in advance.
The elaborate stuccoed interior, the
waiters in dinner jackets and an
international clientele all add to the
atmosphere of opulence.

L'Astrance

4 Rue de Beethoven 75016. **Map** 9 C3.
(01 40 50 84 40. 🕐 12.15pm–
1.45pm, 7.45pm–9.45pm Tue pm–Sun.
¶◯¶ 📧 *AE, DC, MC, V.* €€€

The vigorous cuisine of L'Astrance's
two young chefs, both formerly at
L'Arpège, have made it so popular
that you have to book at least a
month ahead. Their skilfully
inventive dishes include sautéed
pigeon with a caramelised hazelnut
sauce, grilled lamb with a mint,
cinnamon and yoghourt sauce, and
apple and celery minestrone with
roasted spice ice cream. The excellent Menu Surprise is as unexpected
as the mountain flower from which
this restaurant draws its name.

Alain Ducasse

59 Ave Raymond Poincaré 75116.
Map 9 C1. **(** 01 47 27 12 27.
🕐 noon–2pm, 7.45pm–10pm
Mon–Fri. ● public hols, mid-Jul–mid-
Aug, 25 Dec–1st wk Jan. **¶◯¶** 🚇
🍴 ★ 🏠 📧 *AE, DC, MC, V, JCB.*
€€€€€

In this historic town house with its
'Belle Époque' façade, Alain
Ducasse creates the great 'classic'
dishes of France with exceptional
devotion to the quality of the
ingredients. The menu features
meticulously-chosen produce from
every culinary region of France
with particular influences from his
native southwest. The stylish dining
room, decorated with *trompe l'oeil*
and sculptures, is the perfect
setting for this wonderfully elegant
cuisine. Dishes include *turbot de
Bretagne, chevreuil* (venison)
d'Alsace, lamb in Pauillac wine and
fois gras de canard des Landes.
There is an enviable wine list with
some great treasures from Bordeaux.

Amphyclès

78 Ave des Ternes 75017. **Map** 3 C2.
(01 40 68 01 01. 🕐 noon–2.30pm
Mon–Fri, 8pm–10.30pm Mon–Sat.
¶◯¶ 🚇 🍴 ★ 📧 *AE, DC, MC, V,
JCB.* €€€€€

This small place with a fresh,
garden-like feel is the showcase
for Philippe Groult who made it
one of the finest restaurants in
Paris within months of the opening
night. House classics include a
soup of morel mushrooms, lobster
risotto with girolle mushrooms,
and duckling with orange and
coriander. Other creations include

steamed *foie gras* with beans, fillet
of sea bass with sesame, and pigeon
in a seaweed crust. Desserts are
served from a well-stocked trolley.

CHAMPS-ELYSÉES

La Fermette Marbeuf 1900

5 Rue Marbeuf 75008. **Map** 4 F5.
(01 53 23 08 00. 🕐 noon–3pm,
7pm–11.30pm daily. **¶◯¶** 🚇 📧
AE, DC, MC, V. €€€

Fabulous Belle Époque mosaics,
tiles and ironwork were
discovered beneath the formica
walls of this Champs-Elysées
bistro, putting it on the map.
Aside from the beautiful
surroundings, La Fermette
Marbeuf serves good brasserie-
style food including a
commendable set menu with
many *appellations contrôlées*
wines – a measure of their
quality. It is very Parisian and
very noisy late in the evening.

Savy

23 Rue Bayard 75008. **Map** 10 F1.
(01 47 23 46 98. 🕐 noon–3pm,
7.30pm–11pm Mon–Fri. ● Aug.
¶◯¶ 📧 *AE, MC, V.* €€

Although just up the street from
Dior and other such renowned
addresses, Savy has somehow
remained an unpretentious local
bistro. The Art Deco interior is
rustic, and the hearty cuisine
inspired by Monsieur Savy's native
Auvergne is flavourful, with dishes
such as stuffed cabbage, cod
fishcakes, roast shoulder of lamb,
roast guinea fowl and prune tart.

Sébillon

66 Rue Pierre Charron 75008. **Map** 4
F5. **(** 01 43 59 28 15. 🕐
noon–3pm, 7pm–midnight daily. **¶◯¶**
📧 *AE, DC, MC, V.* €€€

Situated just off the Champs-
Elysées, the present restaurant is
an offshoot of the original
Sébillon which has been
nurturing residents of the
bourgeois suburb of Neuilly since
1913. The menu is the same with
lots of shellfish, lobster salad,
scallops *à la provençale,* rib roast
of beef and gigantic *éclairs.* The
great speciality here is leg of
lamb – as much as you want,
sliced before you, in the pretty,
polished dining room.

Le Cercle Ledoyen

1 Ave Dutuit 75008. **Map** 11 B1. **(**
01 53 05 10 02. 🕐 noon–2.30pm,
7pm–11pm Mon–Sat. 🚇 📧 *AE,
DC, MC, V, JCB.* €€€

The cuisine here is quite refined with grilled brill and wild mushrooms and pheasant with quince or a more simple dish of smoked salmon (prepared by the owners) and scrambled eggs. There is a wonderful selection of chocolate desserts. The handsome curved dining room creates the atmosphere of an 1890's grill room with ceiling and wall panels decorated with scenes of Paris. Alternatively, have a heavenly meal outside on the stunning terrace.

Spoon

14 Rue de Marignan 75008. **Map** 4 F5. **[** 01 40 76 34 44. ◯ noon–2.30pm, 7pm–11pm Mon–Fri. **⛆ Ⓥ** ⊘ AE, MC, V, JCB. €€€

Owned by international superstar chef Alain Ducasse, this restaurant not only became an outrageously trendy place to eat within months of opening, it also proved that fusion food could be French. You have to book several weeks in advance, but the sublime steamed dishes, succulent wok-sautéed vegetables, and fondant chocolate tarts are well worth waiting for. The seating is comfortable and the décor a mixture of exotic woods.

L'Avenue

41 Ave Montaigne 75008. **Map** 10 F1. **[** 01 40 70 14 91. ◯ 8am–midnight daily. ⊘ AE, DC, MC, V. €€€€

Located at the intersection of the Avenues Montaigne and François-1er – the hub of couture fashion – L'Avenue attracts an expectedly elegant crowd. The unusual Neo-1950s decor is fresh and full of colour. Service can get somewhat hectic at peak lunch and dinner times, but then L'Avenue is a brasserie. The cuisine is good, there is something for all tastes and appetites and late-night supper is served.

La Maison Blanche/ 15 Avenue Montaigne

15 Ave Montaigne 75008. **Map** 10 F1. **[** 01 47 23 55 99. ◯ noon–2pm Tue–Fri, 8pm–11pm Mon–Sat. ● Aug. **⛆** **🖻** 🖥 ⊘ AE, MC, V, JCB. €€€€

The popular Maison Blanche restaurant affixed 15 Avenue Montaigne to its name when it moved here, on top of the Théâtre des Champs-Elysées. Although the decor is severely modern, the restaurant is almost opulently vast. The cuisine, with its Provençale and southwestern influences, is full of flavour and colour and is the main attraction for the worldly clientele that flocks here.

Lasserre

17 Ave Franklin D Roosevelt 75008. **Map** 11 A1. **[** 01 43 59 53 43, 01 43 59 67 45 ◯ 12.30pm–2.30pm Tue–Sat, 7.30pm–10.30pm Mon–Sat. **🍽 ⛆ 🖻** ⊘ AE, MC, V. €€€€€

This discreet restaurant opposite the Grand Palais is one of the finest in Paris. Charismatic owner René Lasserre has for over 50 years continued to create an opulent yet friendly ambience. The menu rests with the classic and fine. Chef Michel Roth offers cuisine of irreproachable quality such as canard (duck) de Chaillans à l'orange which is reputably the best of its kind. Other favourites include Mesclagne Landais Mère Irma (a dish of foie gras and chicken named after Lasserre's mother), pigeon André Malraux and sole rôtie aux Crustacés, sauce Noilly. The beautifully sculpted desserts are sublime; the wine list is exceptional. Enjoy watching the stars in the summer when the rooftop opens up to reveal the night sky.

Taillevent

15 Rue Lamennais 75008. **Map** 4 F4. **[** 01 44 95 15 01. ◯ 12.30pm–2pm, 7.30pm–10.30pm Mon–Fri. **⛆ 🍽 🖻 ★** ⊘ AE, DC, MC, V, JCB. €€€€€

Taillevent is the most elegant and patrician of Paris's three-starred restaurants. The quiet, dignified ambience doesn't suit everyone, but the sincere welcome of owner Jean-Claude Vrinat, impeccable service, extraordinary wine list and tempered neo-classic cuisine of the young chef Michel Del Burgo make for memorable meals. Other dishes on the Taillevent menu include celeriac turnover with morels and truffles, Pyrenees lamb with cabbage and a moelleux (cream) of lobster with bell pepper. The pastry chef is one of the finest in Paris. Not surprisingly, you need to book months ahead for dinner.

Guy Savoy

18 Rue Troyon 75017. **Map** 4 D3. **[** 01 43 80 40 61. ◯ 12.30pm–2.30pm Mon–Fri, 7.30pm–10.30pm Mon–Sat. ● 3 weeks Aug. **🍽 🖻 ★** ⊘ AE, DC, MC, V, JCB. €€€€€

Guy Savoy has the best of everything: a large, handsome dining room and professional service, and the remarkable cuisine of Guy Savoy himself which looks as good as it tastes. Choose between dishes such as

cold oysters in aspic, mussels with mushrooms, Bresse chicken with a sherry vinegar glaze and poached or grilled pigeon with lentils, then from the extraordinary desserts.

Laurent

41 Ave Gabriel 75008. **Map** 5 B5. **[** 01 42 25 00 39. ◯ 12.30pm–2.30pm Mon–Fri, 7.30pm–11pm Mon–Sat (Jun–Aug daily). ● public hols. **🍽 ⛆ 🖻 🖥 ★** ⊘ AE, DC, MC, V. €€€€€

This pretty, slightly pink-coloured 19th-century building is situated in the gardens of the Champs-Elysées. Laurent is where the rich and powerful eat out. The dining room is opulently decorated and outside a marvellous terrace is screened by thick hedges. The hors d'oeuvres arrive on a trolley and the lobster salad is prepared at the table. Dishes such as cannelloni of vegetables with squid, an excellent rack of lamb and a selection of wonderful pastries are typical.

OPÉRA QUARTER

Chartier

7 Rue du Faubourg Montmartre 75009. **Map** 6 F4. **[** 01 47 70 86 29. ◯ 11.30am–3pm, 6pm–10pm daily. **🍽** ⊘ MC, V. €

Despite the impressive, listed 1900s decor of this cavernous restaurant, it caters today, as it always has, to people on a budget. These are now mostly students and tourists, but some of the old habitués still come here for the basic cuisine (hard-boiled eggs with mayonnaise, house pâté, roast chicken and pepper steak). Expect to wait awhile for your meal, as waiters are often rushed off their feet.

La Ferme St-Hubert

21 Rue Vignon 75008. **Map** 6 D5. **[** 01 42 79 20. ◯ noon–3.30pm, 7pm–11pm (11.30 Fri, Sat) Mon–Thu. **Ⓥ** ⊘ AE, MC, V. €

This, the simple restaurant of the well-known fromagerie (cheese delicatessen) of the same name next door, is mobbed at lunch and busy at dinner. The cheese-based cuisine is good: the best croque-monsieur in Paris, raclette (all you can eat of this Swiss cheese dish), two styles of cheese fondue, salads with cheese and just plain cheese. Happily situated for all gourmets, it is very convenient for the fine food shops on the Place de la Madeleine.

Chez Clément

17 blvd des Capucines 75002.
Map 6 E5. **C** 01 53 43 82 00.
🕐 7am–1am daily. 🍴 🛇 *MC, V.* €

Just two minutes walk from the
Opéra, this comfortable bistro
(part of a chain of establishments)
serves its signature dishes of roast
meats until well after midnight
every day of the year. The dish of
the day is always good value and
unusually, is available for both
lunch and dinner.

Au Petit Riche

25 Rue le Peletier 75009. **Map** 6 F4.
C 01 47 70 68 68. 🕐 noon–
2.15pm, 7pm–midnight Mon–Sat.
🍴 🛇 *AE, DC, MC, V, JCB.* €€

Surrounded by theatres, this bistro
does not lack atmosphere. The
small rooms, resplendent in
polished copper, mirrors and
woodwork, are popular at lunch
with the Drouot auction house
crowd and at dinner with a
Parisian clientele. The Loire region
is reflected in the Vouvray-style
rillettes (meat paste, similar to
pâté), *boudin* (black or white
pudding), *andouillette* (tripe
sausage) and regional wines.

Café Runtz

16 Rue Favart 75002. **Map** 6 F5.
C 01 42 96 69 86. 🕐 10am–11pm
Mon–Fri; 6–11.30pm Sat. ● public
hols. 🛇 *AE, MC, V, DC.* €€

One of the few genuine Alsatian
weinstub (wine bars) in Paris, Café
Runtz has been doing business
since the turn of the century.
Photos of entertainment stars
remind you that the Salle Favart
(the former Opéra Comique) is
next door. Regional specialities
include Gruyère salad, onion tart,
choucroute (sauerkraut),
jambonneau and fruit tarts. The
service is friendly.

Le Vaudeville

29 Rue Vivienne 75002. **Map** 6 F5.
C 01 40 20 04 62. 🕐 noon–3pm,
7pm–1am daily. 🍴 V 🛇 🖼
🛇 *AE, DC, MC, V, JCB.* €€

This is one of seven brasseries
belonging to Paris's brasserie king,
Jean-Paul Bucher. The bright,
attractive Art Deco interior
provides an appealing backdrop
to the food: good shellfish, Bucher's
famous smoked salmon, many
different fish dishes as well as
classic brasserie standbys like
pig's trotters and *andouillette*
(tripe sausage). The speedy,
friendly service and noisy
atmosphere make it lots of fun,
and it's always full.

Les Noces de Jeannette

14 Rue Favart 75002. **Map** 6 F5.
C 01 42 96 36 89. 🕐 noon–2pm,
7pm–9.30pm daily. 🍴 🛇 🛇 *AE,
DC, MC, V.* €€

This is a typical Parisian bistro,
named for the one-act curtain-
raising opera which is performed
at the Opera Comique just across
the street. A rather ornate interior
belies the cosy, welcoming
atmosphere. The fixed-price menu
is good value, offering a wide
choice of classic bistro dishes. Try
the Vichyssoise or *terrine de
crustacés à la crème d'Oseille.*

Café Drouant

18 Rue Gaillon 75002. **Map** 6 E5.
C 01 42 65 15 16. 🕐 noon–3pm,
7pm–midnight daily. ● Aug. 🍴
🛇 🛇 *AE, DC, MC, V.* €€

Founded in the 19th century,
Drouant is one of Paris's most
historic restaurants. The café, not
to be confused with the much
more expensive restaurant, serves
excellent food until late and has
an extremely good value menu at
dinner. The interior includes a
famous shellfish-motif ceiling.

Le Grand Colbert

2 Rue Vivienne 75002. **Map** 6 F5.
C 01 42 86 87 88. 🕐 noon–
3.30pm, 7pm–1am daily. 🍴
🛇 *AE, DC, MC, V.* €€€

Situated in the restored Galérie
Colbert owned by the Bibliothèque
Nationale, Le Grand Colbert must
be one of the prettiest brasseries
in Paris. Its one, long dining area
is divided by frosted glass panels
and decorated with paintings and
mirrors. The menu offers classic
brasserie fare – herring fillets with
potatoes or cream, snails, onion
soup, classic whiting Colbert (in
breadcrumbs) and grilled meats.

A.G. Le Poète

27 Rue Pasquier 75008. **Map** 5 C4.
C 01 47 42 00 64. 🕐 noon–
2.30pm Mon–Fri, 7pm–10.30pm
Mon–Sat. ● 3 weeks Aug. 🍴
🛇 *AE, MC, V, JCB.* €€€

Situated near the Place de la
Madeleine, this romantically styled
restaurant with its red velvet decor
and soft lighting has some interesting dishes. Poet and chef
Antoine Gayet's passion for
cooking is evident, with a menu
that is not only a delight to read
but also to choose from. It includes
dishes such as red mullet and
baby scallops served with creamed
wild nettles and roast langoustines
with fried pig's trotters.

Chez Georges

1 Rue du Mail 75002. **Map** 12 F1.
C 01 42 60 07 11. 🕐 noon–
2.30pm, 7.15pm–9.30pm Mon–Sat.
● public hols, 3 weeks Aug.
🛇 *AE, MC, V.* €€€€

Most of the authentic local
restaurants around the Place des
Victoires have been turned into
trendy clothes boutiques, but Chez
Georges is one of the few that has
resisted. With its eclectic decor
and no-nonsense waitresses, it
attracts Parisians who enjoy the
bistro cuisine of chicken liver
terrine, sole *meunière* (coated with
flour, sautéed and served in hot
melted butter with sliced lemon)
and rum babas.

Lucas Carton

9 Pl de la Madeleine 75008. **Map** 5 C5.
C 01 42 65 22 90. 🕐 noon–
2.30pm Tue–Fri, 7.45pm–10.30pm
Mon–Sat. ● Aug. 🍴 lunch only.
🔇 🔇 ★ 🛇 *AE, DC, MC, V.*
€€€€€

The audacious three-Michelin-
starred cuisine of super-chef Alain
Senderens is something you will
either love or hate. His legendary
creations include *foie gras* with
cabbage, spicy duck Apicius and a
mango *tarte tatin*. The restaurant's
Belle Époque decor is stunning, the
service crisp and efficient and the
crowd glamourous.

MONTMARTRE

La Table d'Anvers

2 Pl d'Anvers 75009. **Map** 7 A2.
C 01 48 78 35 21. 🕐 12.15pm–
2.15pm Mon–Fri, 7.15pm–10.15pm
Mon–Sat. 🍴 🔇 🛇 *AE, MC,
V, JCB.* €€€

Near the Butte Montmartre, this
serious restaurant is run by a
father and two sons. The menu
has many Italian and Provençal
touches such as gnocchi of
langoustines and wild mushrooms,
rabbit with polenta, and sea bass
with thyme and lemon. The
pastries and desserts are excellent.

Beauvilliers

52 Rue Lamarck 75018. **Map** 2 E5.
C 01 42 54 54 42. 🕐 12.30–2pm
Tue–Sat, 7.30pm–10.30pm Mon–Sat.
🍴 🔇 🛇 🛇 *AE, DC, MC, V, JCB.*
€€€€

This joyful place is the best in
Montmartre and one of the most
festive in Paris. Flower-filled
rooms are animated by the
effusive chef Edouard Carlier. The

renowned chef Paul Bocuse dines here, and the restaurant is also popular with entertainment stars. Carlier delves into old cookbooks for ideas: *escabèche* of red mullet (the fish is cooked and marinated), veal *rognonnade* (part of a loin of veal with the kidney included), stuffed beef fillet and a very lemony lemon tart are among the choices. There is a delightful covered terrace.

FURTHER AFIELD

Dao Vien

82 Rue Baudricourt 75013. **Map** 18D5.
(01 45 85 20 70. ◻ noon–3pm,
7pm–11.30pm daily. ¶●¶ & €

There are many Oriental restaurants in the original Paris Chinatown, but this friendly Vietnamese place is especially pleasant. *Soupe Saïgonnaise* is a speciality, along with egg-stuffed crêpes, chicken with ginger, and jasmine tea.

Le Volant

13 Rue Beatrix Dussane 75015. **Map** 10D5. **(** 01 45 75 70 04.
◻ noon–2pm, 8pm–11pm Mon–Fri, 8pm–11pm Sat. ● Sat lunch, Sun & 1-15 Aug. ¶●¶ ᗑ AE, MC, V. €

The owner of Le Volant (The Steering Wheel) is fanatical about motorcar racing, as the décor of this small restaurant testifies, with its photo-lined walls of racing stars. There's nothing racy, however, about the cooking: it is simple, traditional French cuisine at its best: *boeuf bourguignon*, mouth-watering home-made fruit tarts and the never-to-be-forgotten chocolate mousse.

Astier

44 Rue Jean-Pierre Timbaud 75011.
Map 14 E1. **(** 01 43 57 16 35.
◻ noon–2pm, 8pm–11pm Mon–Fri.
● Aug & public hols. ¶●¶
ᗑ MC, V. €

Quality here is among the best for the price in Paris, and the dining rooms are always full. The food is very good, including mussel soup with saffron, rabbit in mustard sauce, duck breast with honey, and good cheeses and wines.

Chez Fernand

7–9 Rue de la Fontaine au Roi 75011.
Map 8 E5. **(** 01 43 57 46 25.
◻ noon–2.30pm, 8pm–11.30pm
Tue–Sat. ● Aug. ¶●¶ ᗑ MC, V. €

The banal decor of this small restaurant near the Place de la République is no reflection of the good Normandy-based cuisine

with a touch of creativity: mackerel *rillettes* (similar to pâté), skate with Camembert, duck, *tarte Normande* (apple tart) flambéed with Calvados. The prices are modest, as they are in the chef's other restaurant next door.

Brasserie Flo

7 Cour des Petites-Ecuries 75010.
Map 7 B4. **(** 01 47 70 13 59.
◻ noon–3pm, 7pm–1am daily. ¶●¶
ᗑ AE, DC, MC, V. €

This authentic Alsatian brasserie is situated in a passageway in a slightly unsavoury neighbourhood. But it is worth the effort to find it: the rich wood and stained-glass decor is unique and very pretty and the straightforward brasserie menu includes good shellfish and *choucroute* (sauerkraut). Alsatian wine is sold by the jug.

Julien

16 Rue du Faubourg St-Denis 75010.
Map 7 B5. **(** 01 47 70 12 06.
◻ noon–3pm, 7pm–1.30am daily.
ᗑ AE, DC, MC, V. €

With its superb 1880s decor, Julien sets an upmarket scene at reasonable prices. Under the same ownership as Brasserie Flo, it has the same friendly service and wide variety of desserts. The brasserie cuisine shows imagination and includes hot *foie gras* with lentils, breaded pig's trotter, grilled sole and Julien's version of *cassoulet* (white bean and meat stew).

Le Baron Rouge

1 Rue Théophile Roussel 75012.
Map 14 F5. **(** 01 43 42 54 65.
◻ 10am–2pm & 5.30–9.30pm
Tue–Sun lunch. ᗑ V ¶●¶ €

This bistro is not quite like others! Right next to the lively Marché d'Aligre (*see p233*), Parisians rush here at weekends to sample the exquisite oysters, brought straight from Cap Ferret (on the far side of the Bassin d'Arcachon on the Atlantic coast). These are eaten half out on the pavement, standing round large wine barrels. The proprietor touts his wares with gusto, but don't expect to linger; he'll move you on when he sees fit! During the week, it's also a good wine bar.

Le Petit Keller

13 bis Rue Keller 75011. **Map** 14 F4.
(01 47 00 12 97. ◻ 7pm–2am
Mon–Sat. ᗑ ᗑ DC, MC, V. €

Far removed from the tourist traps of La Bastille, this chic and elegant brasserie is good value, and does a fabulous sautéed pork dish with olives.

Pause Café Bastille

41 Rue Charonne 75011. **Map** 14 F4.
(01 48 06 80 33. ◻ noon–midnight Mon–Sat. ☑ ᗑ ▦
ᗑ AE, MC, V. €

Since the shooting of *Chacun cherche son chat*, this has been an 'in' place to be seen. Luckily this has not ruined the friendly ambience nor the cuisine: light dishes such as steak tartar, tarts with salads and excellent home-made pastries.

L'Occitanie

96 Rue Oberkampf 75011.
Map 14 F1. **(** 01 48 06 46 98.
◻ noon–2pm, 7.30pm–11pm
Mon–Fri & Sat pm. ● Aug. ¶●¶
(lunch). ᗑ ᗑ DC, MC, V. €

As the name indicates, the cuisine here is deeply rooted in the owner's native south-west, as is the welcome from this Occitan-speaking *bon-viveur*. *Cassoulet, confit* or *potage à rouzole* (soup with sausage-meat and herb dumplings) are some of the typical dishes served here, and helpings are generous.

Favela Chic

18 Rue Fbg du Temple 75011.
Map 8 D5. **(** 01 40 21 38 14.
◻ 7pm–2am Mon–Sat. ☑
ᗑ AE, MC, V. €

Not much of Brazil is missing from this sleepy yet lively haven, run by Jerome and Roseanne. The *caipirinha* (fresh lime, cane-sugar alcohol and lots of crushed ice) has lost none of its buzz, and the *feijoada* tastes just as it does in back in Salvador Bahia. The place can get a bit noisy as the evening progresses, so come early and grab a table near the door!

Les Allobroges

71 Rue des Grands-Champs 75020.
(01 43 73 40 00. ◻ noon– 2pm, 8pm–10pm Tue–Sat. ● Aug. ¶●¶
ᗑ AE, MC, V. €€

It's worth the trip out into the 20th *arrondissement* to taste the fresh and innovative cooking of chef Olivier Pateyron. Especially good is the lobster soup which arrives as a complementary *amuse-gueule*, and the lightly-cooked tuna steak wrapped in bacon and served with a delicately-flavoured, emerald green cabbage *coulis*. Both service and ambience are rather lack-lustre – this is not the venue to impress a hot date – but for delicious food which won't break the bank, this is a great place to choose.

For key to symbols *see p289*

Le Bistro des Deux Théâtres

18 Rue Blanche 75009. **Map** 6 D3.
 01 45 26 41 43. noon–
2.30pm, 7pm–12.30am daily.
 MC, V. €€

If you are on a strict budget this
formula restaurant in the theatre
district is a real find, and even if
you have a good few francs left to
invest in an enjoyable meal, it is
still very much worth considering.
The reasonable set menu includes
apéritif, a choice of first and main
courses, cheese or dessert and a
half bottle of wine. The food is
good, including duck *foie gras*
and smoked salmon with *blinis*
(small savoury pancakes).

La Perle des Antilles

36 Ave Jean-Moulin 75014.
Map 16 D5. 01 45 42 91 25.
 noon–2.30pm, 7.45pm–11pm
daily.   MC, V.
€€

This pretty white restaurant with
green and yellow speckled walls
is like a bit of the Antilles in Paris.
Haïtian specialities are lovingly
prepared by a winning Haïtian
couple: vegetable *acras* (savoury
fritters), gratin of mirliton (a kind
of squash), various crab dishes
and chicken creole. Spices are
used with discretion and all the
ingredients are fresh. Come here
on a weekend evening for some
uptempo live music, order a
punch, knock it back, relax and
pretend you are in the islands.

Les Amognes

243 Rue du Faubourg St-Antoine
75011. 01 43 72 73 05.
 noon–2pm Tue–Fri,
7.30pm–11pm Mon–Sat. Aug.
  MC, V. €€

Chef Thierry Coué has worked
under Alain Senderens of Lucas
Carton *(see page 306)*, quite a
recommendation, and an
indication of the fare on offer. His
small restaurant, between the
Bastille and Nation, is not pretty,
but the food is very good and
original. It includes sardine tart,
cod fritters with tomatoes and
basil, tuna with artichokes and
bell pepper, sea bream with a
chilli-oil and pineapple soup with
Pina Colada. It's worth the trip.

L'Oulette

15 Pl Lachambeaudie 75012.
 01 40 02 02 12. noon–
2.15pm, 8pm–10.15pm Mon–Fri,
8pm–10.15pm Sat.
 AE, DC, MC, V. €€

The success of L'Oulette allowed it
to move to much larger quarters in
the new Bercy district. Its current
large, very modern decor lacks the
intimacy of the former restaurant.
However, the cuisine of chef
Marcel Baudis, reflecting his native
Quercy, remains excellent – it is
pretty visually and rich in flavours.
Dishes include *croustillant* of
cèpes (wild mushrooms wrapped
in a pastry parcel and baked in the
oven), salmon in bacon, braised
ox-tail, and *pain d'épices* (a kind
of spice cake).

La Marine

55 Quai Valmy 75010. **Map** 8 D5.
 01 42 39 69 81. noon–3pm,
8pm–11.30pm Mon–Sat.
 AE, DC, MC, V. €€

Don't look for the sailors on the
banks of the canal, the last ones
are here at La Marine. For several
years now this establishment has
been the headquarters of the
Internet trade, and as such, is
usually packed, so book ahead.
The main courses are good and
mainly fishy, such as red mullet in
puff pastry, fish steak with a
creamy nettle sauce, or fish stew.
The desserts are not so highly
recommended.

Aux Senteurs de Provence

295 Rue Lecourbe 75015. **Map** just W
of 15 A4. 01 45 57 11 98.
 12.15pm–2pm Mon–Fri, 7.30pm–
10.30pm Mon–Sat. 1–21 Aug.
    AE, DC, MC, V. €€

Tuscany meets Provence in the
cuisine of this Italian-owned quiet
restaurant. Tuna ravioli, cod with
sorrel, *daube* (stew) of lamb,
bouillabaisse and *bourride* (garlicky
fish soup) are among the better
dishes. The *assiette de gourmandise*
is a tasty plate of different desserts.

La Maison du Cantal

1 Pl Falguière 75015. **Map** 15 A3.
 01 47 34 12 24. noon–2pm
Tue–Sat, 7pm–10.30pm Mon–Sat.
  AE, MC, V. €€

This is the place to come on a
chilly evening for the hearty
country dishes of the Auvergne.
Fresh trout fried in butter with
crispy *lardons* makes a delicious
first course, followed perhaps by a
tender rump steak with *bleu
d'Auvergne* cheese sauce.

Le Clos Morillons

50 Rue des Morillons 75015. **Map** W
of 15 A4. 01 48 28 04 37. noon
–2pm, Tue–Fri, 7.30pm–10.30pm
Mon–Sat.   AE, MC, V. €€

This discreet family-run restaurant
has a constantly-evolving menu.
The Far eastern travels of chef,
Philippe Delacourcelle, are evident
in specialities such as cod roasted
with cinnamon, pigeon with
sesame and monkfish and lobster
with ginger. Other dishes on the
menu are more typically French –
the terrine of potatoes and *foie
gras* are especially delicious. Many
respectable Loire wines are included in the good-value set menu.

Le Bistrot d'à Côté Flaubert

10 Rue Gustave Flaubert 75017.
Map 4 E2. 01 42 67 05 81.
 12.30pm–2.30pm, 7.30pm–11pm
daily.   AE, MC, V. €€

This was the first and remains the
most appealing of star-chef Michel
Rostang's boutique bistros. The tiny
dining room with *de rigueur*
moleskin banquettes gives the
appearance of having been
furnished from grandmother's
attic. Many Lyonnais dishes are
served including lentil salad,
cervelas or *sabodet* sausage,
andouillette (tripe sausage), and
macaroni gratin. It is popular at
lunch with local executives and in
the evening with the bourgeoisie.

L'Auberge du Bonheur

Allée de Longchamps, Bois de
Boulogne 75016. **Map** 3 A3.
 01 42 24 10 17. May–Oct:
noon–3pm, 7pm–10pm daily;
Oct–Apr: noon–3pm Sun–Fri.
  AE, MC, V, JCB. €€€

This is probably the only affordable
restaurant in the Bois de Boulogne.
In summer you can sit on the
gravel terrace at tables under
chestnut and plane trees,
surrounded by wisteria and
bamboo. It is also delightful in cool
weather inside the cosy chalet.
The simple service complements
cuisine that emphasizes grilled
meats.

Le Chardenoux

1 Rue Jules Vallés 75011. 01 43
71 49 52. noon–2pm, 8pm–
10.30pm Mon–Fri, 8pm–10.30pm
Sat. public hols, Aug.
 AE, MC, V. €€€

This classic bistro needs sprucing
up but is still one of the prettiest
in Paris with its wood panelling,
frosted cut glass and impressive
marble bar. There is a wide choice
of salads and egg dishes, charcuterie and some rare regional dishes
like *aligot* (a cheese, garlic and
potato mixture) and *gigot
brayaude* (leg of lamb pierced
with cloves of garlic and braised
in white wine with potatoes). Loire

and Bordeaux wines are emphasized. The atmosphere is pleasant and relaxed.

Le Pavillon Montsouris

20 Rue Gazan 75014. **☎** *01 45 88 38 52.* ☐ *12.15pm–2.30pm, 7.30pm–10.30pm daily.* **†●‖ ⚹ ▦** ☷ *MC, V.* €€€

This restored building on the edge of the pretty Parc Montsouris has had a long history and once counted Trotsky, Mata Hari and Lenin among its customers. Today the attractive pastel interior and terrace under the trees make beguiling surroundings for a set menu that is excellent value for money. Dishes include mussel soup, duck *carpaccio* (in thin raw, cured slices), *galette* (pancake) of pigeon and mango *clafoutis* (a type of batter pudding). Service can be slow when the restaurant is full.

La Table de Pierre

116 Blvd Pereire 75017. **Map** 4 E1. **☎** *01 43 80 88 68.* ☐ *noon–2.30pm, 8pm–10.30pm Mon–Fri, 8pm–10.30pm Sat.* **⚹ ▦ ⅋** ☷ *AE, MC, V.* €€€

The Louis XVI decor inherited from the previous restaurant does not suit this Basque establishment, but is more than made up for by the jovial owner and interesting menu. A smart crowd enjoys regional specialities like *pipérade* (stewed sweet peppers, tomatoes and garlic), sweet peppers stuffed with cod *brandade* (salt cod and garlic purée), cod fillet with green sauce, stuffed duck's leg and *gâteau Basque* (sponge cake with *crème pâtissière*).

Au Trou Gascon

40 Rue Taine 75012. **☎** *01 43 44 34 26.* ☐ *noon–2pm, 7.30pm–10pm Mon–Fri, 7.30pm–10pm Sat.* ● *Aug, Xmas–New Year.* **†●‖** ☷ *AE, DC, MC, V, JCB.* €€€

This authentic 1900s bistro owned by star-chef Alain Dutournier (of Carré des Feuillants) is consistently one of the most popular places in Paris. The delicious Gascon food includes ham from the Chalosse region, top *foie gras*, lamb from the Pyrenees and local poultry. Dutournier's white chocolate mousse is now a classic.

Le Train Bleu

20 Blvd Diderot 75012. **Map** 18 E1. **☎** *01 43 43 09 06.* ☐ *11.30am–3pm, 7pm–11pm daily.* **†●‖ ⚹ ⅋** ☷ *AE, DC, MC, V.* €€€

Train station restaurants were once grand places for a meal.

Today this is not usually so, but the Train Bleu (named after the fast train that once took the élite down to the Riviera) in the Gare de Lyon is a pleasant exception. The food is upmarket brasserie cuisine such as hot Lyonnais sausage, with excellent pastries. The fabulous Belle Époque decor makes the place a landmark.

Augusta

98 Rue de Tocqueville 75017. **Map** 5 A1. **☎** *01 47 63 39 97.* ☐ *noon–2pm, 7.30pm–10pm Mon–Fri.* **⚹ ⅋** ☷ *MC, V.* €€€

This reliable, restaurant serves excellent fish and a few meat dishes. The *salade Augusta* is generously garnished with shellfish and the house speciality of *bouillabaisse* with potatoes must be one of the best in Paris. An unusual dish is lobster lasagne with Parmesan. The wine list is popular with well-off local regulars.

Pavillon Puebla

Parc des Buttes-Chaumont 75019. **☎** *01 42 08 92 62.* ☐ *noon–2pm, 7.30pm–10pm Tue–Sat.* **†●‖ ⓥ ⚹** ☷ *AE, MC, V.* €€€

This elegant, floral building, built under Napoleon III as an adornment for his new Parc des Buttes-Chaumont, is a delight both inside and outside on the terrace in fine weather. Chef Vergès prepares flavourful cuisine with a Catalan influence, which includes oyster ravioli with curry, squid in its ink with spices, veal tournedos with truffle juice and *crème Catalane* (crème brûlée). The entrance is on Rue Botzaris.

Le Villaret

13 Rue Ternaux 75011. **Map** 14 E2. **☎** *01 43 57 89 76.* ☐ *noon–2pm Tue–Sat (Sun in summer),* **⚹ ⅋ ★** **†●‖** ☷ *AE, DC, MC, V.* €€€

Tucked away on the northern fringes of the fast-developing Oberkampf district, it is well worth venturing out for. Run by some of the former staff from Astier just round the corner, it is renowned for its "cuisine du marché" (using the very freshest ingredients from the day's market), its meat carefully chosen and prepared. It also has a huge selection of cheeses. Not surprisingly, it is usually packed at weekends.

Au Pressoir

257 Ave Daumesnil 75012. **☎** *01 43 44 38 21.* ☐ *noon–2.30pm, 7.30pm–10.30pm Mon–Fri.* ● *Aug.* **†●‖ ⚹** ☷ *AE, MC, V, JCB.* €€€

Chef Séguin and his wife are passionate about quality. Dishes are often unusual, such as monkfish with bacon and split peas, *foie gras* with Jerusalem artichokes, pigeon with aubergine *blinis* (small savoury pancakes) and chocolate soup with *brioche*. The service is excellent, as is the wine list, and the surroundings are very comfortable.

Le Pré Catelan

Route de Suresnes, Bois de Boulogne 75016. **☎** *01 44 14 41 14.* ☐ *noon–2pm Tue–Sat (Sun in summer), 7.30pm–10pm Tue–Sat.* **⚹ ▦ ⅋ †●‖** ☷ *AE, DC, MC, V.* €€€€

This very elegant Belle Époque restaurant in the Bois de Boulogne is a delight, either in midsummer, after a stroll, when you can dine out on the idyllic terrace, or in mid-winter, when the lights and decoration inside are magical and inviting. The menu is luxurious, with huge langoustines, special Duclair duck with spices and sea urchin soufflé. Desserts are fabulous.

Faucher

123 Ave de Wagram 75017. **Map** 4 E2. **☎** *01 42 27 61 50.* ☐ *noon–2pm, 8pm–10pm Mon–Fri.* **†●‖ ⚹ ⅋** ☷ *AE, MC, V, JCB.* €€€€

Monsieur and Mme Faucher take a great interest in their restaurant and guests. The big beige dining room with large windows is very pretty and the terrace is a delight in fine weather. The food has original touches and includes *millefeuille* of spinach and sliced raw beef, truffle-stuffed egg, turbot with caviar cream and a very good selection of interesting desserts.

Apicius

122 Ave de Villiers 75017. **Map** 4 D1. **☎** *01 43 80 19 66.* ☐ *noon–2pm, 8pm–10pm Mon–Fri.* **⅋ ★** ☷ *AE, DC, MC, V, JCB.* €€€€€

Chef owner Jean-Pierre Vigato looks more like a model than a chef. Despite this, his cuisine has its hearty side – he enjoys preparing offal and treating fish almost like meat. Dishes include pig's trotters roasted *en crépinette* (with small sausages), roast turbot with bacon, roast sweetbreads, all-caramel or all-chocolate desserts. Service in two airy dining rooms is professionally and personally supervised by Madame Vigato.

Light Meals and Snacks

GOOD FOOD AND DRINK is so much a part of everyday life in Paris that you can eat and drink well without ever going to a restaurant. Whether you want to enjoy a meal or casual drink at a café, wine bar or tea room, buy a crêpe, quiche or a pizza from a street stand or bakery, or put together a picnic from cheeses, breads, salads and pâtés, informal eating is one of the great gastronomic strengths of the city.

Paris is also a wonderful city for drinking. Wine bars in every quarter offer many different wines by the glass. Beer bars have astounding selections, and Paris's Irish pubs serve Guinness in a relaxed, sometimes rowdy atmosphere. Alternatively choose from hotel bars or late-night bars. *(See also* What to Drink in Paris *pp292–3.)*

CAFÉS

YOU CAN'T WALK far in Paris without passing a café. They range in size from tiny to huge, some with pinball machines, some with elegant Belle Epoque decorations. Most will serve you light food and drink at any time of day.

Breakfast is one of the busiest times and fresh croissants and *pains au chocolat* (chocolate-filled pastries) sell fast. The French often eat these dipped in a bowl or large cup of milky coffee or hot chocolate.

The café lunch usually includes *plats du jour* (daily specials) and in the smaller cafés is one of the great Parisian bargains, rarely costing more than 12€ for two courses with wine. The specials are often substantial meat dishes such as *sauté d'agneau* (sautéed lamb) or *blanquette de veau* (veal with a white sauce), with fruit tarts for dessert. For a simpler lunch, salads, sandwiches and omelettes are usually available at any time of day. One of the best places for this kind of food is the **Bar du Marché** in St-Germain-des-Prés.

Most museums have reliable cafés, but those at the Pompidou Centre *(see pp110–11)* and the Musée d'Orsay *(see pp144–5)* are especially good. Should you find yourself in the department store La Samaritaine *(see p313)*, it's worth going to the café for the view over Paris.

Cafés in the main tourist and nightlife areas (Boulevard St-Germain, Avenue des Champs-Elysées, Boulevard Montparnasse, Opéra and Bastille) generally stay open late – some until 2am.

Some tea salons also offer light lunches, as well as breakfast and afternoon tea, including Bernardaud, the porcelain manufacturers, where you can choose which tea service to eat off *(see p311)*.

WINE BARS

MOST PARISIAN wine bars are small, convivial neighbourhood places. They open early, many doubling as cafés for breakfast, and offer a small, good-quality lunch menu. It's best to get there early or after 1.30pm if you want to avoid the crowd. Most wine bars have closed by 9pm.

Wine bar owners tend to be passionate about wine, most of them buying directly from producers. Young Bordeaux wines and those from the Loire, Rhône and the Jura can be surprisingly good, and wine bar owners have a knack for finding good ones. The **L'Ecluse** chain specializes in Bordeaux but for the most part you will find delicious lesser-known wines at very reasonable prices.

BEER BARS AND PUBS

PARIS HAS BOTH pubs and beer bars. Whereas pubs are simply for drinking, beer bars also serve a particular style of food and are larger. *Moules-frites* (a generous bowl of steamed mussels served with French fries), *tarte aux poireaux* (leek tart) and *tarte aux oignons* (onion tart) are classic examples of the food they serve. The chief reason for going to a beer bar, however, is for the beer. The lists are often vast: some specialize in Belgian *gueuze* (heavy, malty, very alcoholic beer), others have beers from all around the world.

Some beer bars are open from noon, whereas pubs open later in the afternoon. Pubs are usually open every day, often until 1am or 2am.

BARS

PARIS HAS ITS share of cocktail and smoky late-night bars too. Some pretty Paris brasseries, such as **La Coupole** and **Le Boeuf sur le Toit**, have long wooden or zinc bars and accomplished bartenders. The most elegant hotel bar in Paris (and possibly the most expensive) is the main bar at the **Hôtel Ritz** *(see p281)*. The **Hemingway Bar** at the Ritz is darker and less elegant, but full of nostalgia. It's only open for special occasions.

One of the most fun late-night bars in Paris is **Le Delmas**, while **Le Rosebud** and the **China Club** are young and trendy. Funkier still is **Le Piano Vache**, and **Birdland** has a great jazz jukebox.

TAKE-AWAY FOOD

CREPES ARE THE traditional Parisian street food. Although there are fewer good crêpe stands than there used to be, they still exist. Sandwich bars provide baguettes with a wide range of fillings, but the best fast food in Paris is freshly-baked flat *focaccia* bread sprinkled with savoury flavourings. It is sold fresh from a wood-burning oven and filled with one or more fillings of your choice. You can buy it at **Cosi** in Rue de Seine.

Ice-cream stands open around noon, and stay open late in summer. It's worth queuing for the city's best ice-cream at **Maison Berthillon**.

DIRECTORY

ILE DE LA CITÉ AND ILE ST-LOUIS

Wine Bars
Au Franc Pinot
1 Quai de Bourbon
75004. **Map** 13 C4.

Tea Salons
Le Flore en l'Ile
42 Quai d'Orléans
75004. **Map** 13 B4.

Ice-Cream Parlours
Maison Berthillon
31 Rue St-Louis-en-l'Ile
75004. **Map** 13 C4.

TUILERIES QUARTER

Wine Bars
La Cloche des Halles
28 Rue Coquillière
75001. **Map** 12 F1.

Juvenile's
47 Rue de Richelieu
75001. **Map** 12 E1.

Tea Salons
Angélina
226 Rue de Rivoli
75001. **Map** 12 D1.

Bernardaud
11 Rue Royale 75008.
Map 5 C5.

Ladurée
16 Rue Royale 75008.
Map 5 C5.

Bars
Bars du Ritz
15 Pl Vendôme 75001.
Map 6 D5.

THE MARAIS

Cafés
Ma Bourgogne
19 Pl des Vosges 75004.
Map 14 D3.

Tea Salons
Le Loir dans la Théière
3 Rue des Rosiers 75004.
Map 13 C3.

Mariage Frères
30–32 Rue du Bourg-
Tibourg 75004.
Map 13 C3.

Bars
China Club
50 Rue de Charenton
75012. **Map** 14 F5. .

L'Apparement Café
18 Rue des Coutures St-
Gervais 75004. **Map** 14 D2

Beer Bars
Café des Musées
49 Rue de Turenne 75003.
Map 14 D3.

Wine Bars
Le Coude Fou
12 Rue du Bourg-Tibourg
75004. **Map** 13 C3

Le Passage
18 Passage de la Bonne-
Graine 75011. **Map** 14 F4.

La Tartine
24 Rue de Rivoli 75004.
Map 13 C3.

BEAUBOURG AND LES HALLES

Cafés
Bistrot d'Eustache
(See p109.)

Café Beaubourg
100 rue St Martin 75004.
Map 13 B2. (See p108.)

Pubs
Flann O'Brien
6 Rue Bailleul 75001.
Map 12 F2.

ST-GERMAIN-DES-PRÉS

Cafés
Café de Flore
(See p139.)

Les Deux Magots
(See p138.)

Sandwich Bars
Cosi
54 Rue de Seine
75006.
Map 12 E4.

Wine Bars
Bistro des Augustins
39 Quai des Grands-
Augustins 75006.
Map 12 F4.

Au Sauvignon
80 Rue des Sts-Pères
75007. **Map** 12 D4.

Bars
Birdland
8 Rue Guisarde 75006.
Map 12 E4.

Le Bar du Marché
75 Rue de Seine 75007.
Map 11 B2.

Chez Georges
11 Rue des Canettes
75006. **Map** 16 D2

LATIN QUARTER

Wine Bars
Les Pipos
2 Rue de l'Ecole
Polytechnique 75005.
Map 13 A5.

Bars
Le Piano-Vache
8 Rue Laplace 75005.
Map 13 A5.

Beer Bars
La Gueuze
19 Rue Soufflot 75005.
Map 12 F5.

JARDIN DES PLANTES

Cafés
Le Moule à Gâteau
111 Rue Mouffetard
75005. **Map** 17 B2.

Le Delmas
Place de la Contrescarpe
75005. **Map** 17 B2.

Pubs
Finnegan's
9 Rue des Boulangers
75005. **Map** 17 B1.

Ice-Cream Parlours
Häagen-Dazs
3 Pl de la Contrescarpe
75005.
Map 17 A1.

LUXEMBOURG QUARTER

Beer Bars
L'Académie de la Bière
88 Blvd de Port-Royal
75005.
Map 17 B3.

MONTPARNASSE

Cafés
Café de la Place
23 Rue d'Odessa 75014.
Map 15 C2.

La Rotonde
7 Pl 25 Août 1944
75014. **Map** 16 D2.

Le Sélect Montparnasse
99 Blvd du Montparnasse
75006.
Map 16 D2.

Wine Bars
Le Rallye' Peret
6 Rue Daguerre 75014.
Map 16 D4.

Tea Salons
Max Poilâne
29 Rue de l'Ouest
75014.
Map 15 C3.

Bars
La Coupole (café bar)
102 Blvd du
Montparnasse 75014.
Map 16 D2 (See p178).

Le Rosebud
11 bis Rue Delambre
75014. **Map** 16 D2.

Cubana Café
45 Rue Vavin 75006.
Map 12 F5.

CHAMPS-ELYSÉES

Wine Bars
L'Ecluse
64 rue François Premier
75008. **Map** 4 F5.

Ma Bourgogne
133 Blvd Haussmann
75008. **Map** 5 B4.

Sandwich Bars
Bars
Le Boeuf sur le Toit
34 Rue du Colisée
75008. **Map** 5 A5.

OPÉRA QUARTER

Cafés
Café de la Paix
12 Blvd des Capucines
75009. **Map** 6 E5.
(See p213.)

Wine Bars
Bistro du Sommelier
97 Blvd Haussmann
75008. **Map** 5 C4.

FURTHER AFIELD

Wine Bars
Le Verre Volé
67 Rue de Lancry 75010.
Map 8 D4.

Bars
L'Ancienne Menuiserie
27 Rue des Trois-Bornes
75011. **Map** 14 E1.

L'Autre Café
62 Rue Jean-Pierre
Timbaud 75011.
Map 8 F5.

SHOPS AND MARKETS

Paris seems to be the very definition of luxury and good living. Beautifully dressed men and women sip wine by the banks of the Seine against a backdrop of splendid French architecture, or shop from small specialist shops. The least expensive way of joining the chic set is to create French style with accessories or costume jewellery. Alternatively buy the world-famous fashion, or the wonderful food and related items from kitchen gadgets to tableware.

Remember too that Parisian shops and markets are the ideal place to indulge in the French custom of strolling through the streets, seeing and being seen. For high fashion, the Rue du Faubourg-St-Honoré has many exquisite couture house window displays, or browse around the the bookstalls along the Seine. A survey of some of the best and most famous places to shop follows.

OPENING HOURS

Shops are usually open from 9.30am to 7pm, Monday to Saturday, but hours can vary considerably. Boutiques may shut for an hour or two at midday and markets and local neighbourhood shops close on Mondays. Some places shut for the summer, usually in August, but those selling essentials may well leave a note on the door with the name of an open equivalent nearby.

HOW TO PAY

Cash is readily available from the ATMs in most banks, which accept both credit cards and bank debit cards. Visa is the most widely accepted credit card, but some shops may accept others.

VAT EXEMPTION

A sales tax (TVA) from 5.5–19.6% is imposed on most goods and services in EU countries. Non-EU residents shopping in France are entitled to a refund of this if they spend a minimum of 175€ in one shop in one day. You must have been resident in France for less than six months with either carry the goods with you out of the country within three months of purchase or get the shop to forward them to you . If a group of you are shopping, you can usually buy goods together in order to reach the minimum.

Larger shops will generally supply a form (*bordereau de détaxe* or *bordereau de vente*) and help you to fill it in. When you leave France or the EU you present the form to Customs, who either permit you to be reimbursed straightaway, or forward your claim to the place where you bought the goods; the shop eventually sends you a refund. If you know someone in Paris it may be quicker if they can

Shopping in Avenue Montaigne

pick up the refund for you at the shop. Alternatively at large airports like Orly and Roissy some banks may have the facilities to refund you on the spot. Though the process involves a lot of paperwork, it can be worth it. There is no refund on food, drink, tobacco, cars and motorbikes. Bicycles, however, can be reimbursed.

SALES

The best sales (*soldes*) are in January and July, although you can sometimes find sale items before Christmas – a treat that used to be unheard of. If you see goods labelled *Stock*, it means that they are stock items. *Dégriffé* means designer labels marked down, frequently from the previous year's collections. *Fripes* means that the clothes are second-hand. The sales tend to occupy prime floor space for the first month and are then relegated to the back of the store.

La Samaritaine department store in Beaubourg and Les Halles

DEPARTMENT STORES

MUCH OF THE pleasure of shopping in Paris is derived from going to the specialist shops. But if time is short and you want to get all your purchases under one roof, then try the *grands magasins* (department stores).

Most department stores still operate a ticket system for selling goods. The shop assistant writes up a ticket for goods from their own boutique which you take to one of the cashiers. You then return with your validated ticket to pick up your purchase. This can be frustrating and time-consuming, so to avoid harassment go early in the morning and don't shop on Saturdays. The French don't pay much attention to queues, so be assertive!

Though the city's department stores are generally stocked with similar merchandise, they have different emphases. All have somewhere to eat. **Au Printemps** is noted for its exciting and innovative household goods, and large clothes departments for men, women and children. Fashion shows are held at 10am on Tuesdays (and Fridays from April to October: by invitation only –

Lionel Poilâne's bread bearing his trademark – a square (see pp322–3)

Kenzo designerwear in the Place des Victoires (see pp316–17)

Snails from the *charcuterie*

invitations are distributed to certain overseas travel agencies, airlines and hotels). The beauty department has one of the world's largest perfume selections and the domed restaurant in the cupola is one of the best.

BHV (Le Bazar de l'Hôtel de Ville) is a DIY enthusiast's paradise. Shop here for household basics and visit the restaurant for Seine views.

Designed by Gustave Eiffel, the Left Bank **Le Bon Marché** was the first department store in Paris and is the most chic, with a good food hall. **Galeries Lafayette** has a wide range of clothes at all price levels. Fashion shows are held at 11am on Wednesdays (and Fridays in summer). Open late on Wednesdays, **La Samaritaine** is one of the oldest shops in Paris. It is full of bargains and often carries the same merchandise as Galeries Lafayette at lower prices. It includes a shop devoted to sportswear and equipment and there are good sales on household goods and furnishings. There is a panoramic view of the Seine from the restaurant (closed late-Nov–early Apr). **Virgin Megastore** is open until late and has a wide selection of records and a good book section. **FNAC** specializes in records, books (foreign editions at Les Halles) and electronic equipment. **FNAC Microinformatique** sells computer-related material.

ADDRESSES

Au Printemps
64 Blvd Haussman 75009.
Map 6 D4. [01 42 82 50 00.

BHV
52–64 Rue de Rivoli 75004.
Map 13 B3. [01 42 74 90 00.

Le Bon Marché
22 Rue de Sèvres 75007.
Map 11 C5. [01 44 39 80 00.

Bookstall, Vanves market (see p327)

FNAC
Forum Les Halles, 1 Rue Pierre Lescot 75001. **Map** 13 A2. [01 40 41 40 00.
One of five branches.

FNAC Microinformatique
71 Blvd St–Germain 75005.
Map 13 A5. [01 44 41 31 50.

Galeries Lafayette
40 Blvd Haussmann 75009.
Map 6 E4. [01 42 82 34 56.
One of two branches.

La Samaritaine
19 Rue de la Monnaie 75001.
Map 12 F2. [01 40 41 20 20.

Virgin Megastore
52–60 Ave des Champs-Elysées 75008. **Map** 4 F5. [01 49 53 50 00.

Paris's Best: Shops and Markets

Old-fashioned and conservative yet full of surprises, Paris is a treasure trove of quality shops and boutiques. Time-honoured emporia mix with modern precincts in a city that buzzes with life in its inner quarters, not least in the markets. Here you can buy everything from exotic fruit and vegetables to fine china and antiques. Whether you're shopping for handmade shoes, perfectly-cut clothes or traditionally-made cheeses, or simply soaking in the atmosphere, you won't be disappointed.

Place de la Madeleine
Top-class groceries and delicacies are sold on the north side of this square. (See p214.)

THE CENTRE OF PARIS COUTURE

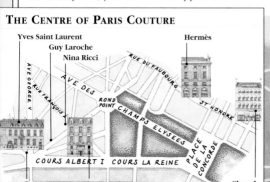

Yves Saint Laurent
Guy Laroche
Nina Ricci
RUE DU FAUBOURG
Hermès
AVE GEORGE V
AVE DES
RUE FRANÇOIS I
ROND POINT
CHAMPS ELYSEES
ST HONORE
COURS ALBERT I   COURS LA REINE
PLACE DE LA CONCORDE
Givenchy   Christian Dior
Chanel
RIVER

See inset map

Champs-Elysées

Chanel
Coco Chanel (1883–1971) reigned over the fashion world from No. 31 Rue Cambon. The main boutique is in the Avenue Montaigne. (See p317.)

Invalides and Eiffel Tower Quarter

Rue de Rivoli
Inexpensive mementos like this Paris snow shaker can be found in the shops on the Rue de Rivoli. (See p130.)

Marché de la Porte de Vanves
This charming and relaxed market sells old books, linen, postcards, china and musical instruments. (weekends only – see p327.)

Kenzo
The Japanese designer has colourful apparel for men, women and children in his clothes shops. (See p317.)

Cartier
The early Cartier jewellery designs with their beautifully-cut stones are still highly sought after. This shop in the Rue de la Paix sells all the Cartier lines. (See p319.)

Rue de Paradis
You can buy porcelain and crystal at reduced prices at the company showrooms on this street. Look out for Porcelainor, Baccarat and Lumicristal. (See pp320–21.)

Passage des Panoramas
This once-prosperous arcade at Les Galeries has an old engraving house. (See p216.)

Opéra Quarter

0 kilometres   1

0 miles   0.5

N

eries Quarter

Beaubourg and Les Halles

The Marais

St-Germain-des-Prés

Ile de la Cité

Ile St-Louis

Latin Quarter

Rue des Francs-Bourgeois
A L'Image du Grenier sur L'Eau sells old postcards, posters and prints. (See p324–5.)

Luxembourg Quarter

Jardin des Plantes Quarter

tparnasse

Rue Mouffetard
The market sells cheeses and other quality foods. (See p327.)

Forum des Halles
This modern glass arcade has many shops. (See p109.)

Clothes and Accessories

For many people Paris is synonymous with fashion and Parisian style is the ultimate in chic. More than anywhere else in the world, women in Paris seem to be in tune with current trends and when a new season arrives appear, as one, to don the look. Though less trend-conscious generally, Parisian men are aware of style and mix and match patterns and colours with élan.

Finding the right clothes at the right price means knowing where to shop. For every luxury boutique on the Avenue Montaigne, there are ten young designers' shops waiting to become the next Jean-Paul Gaultier – and hundreds more selling imitations.

Haute Couture

Paris is the home of *haute couture*. The original *haute couture* garments, as opposed to the imitations and adaptations, are one-off creations, designed by one of the 23 *couture* houses listed with the Fédération Française de la Couture. The rules for being classified *haute couture* are fairly strict, and many of the top designers such as Claude Montana and Karl Lagerfeld are not included. Astronomical prices put *haute couture* beyond the reach of most pockets, but it's still the lifeblood of the fashion industry providing inspiration for the mass market.

The fashion seasons are launched with the *haute couture* shows in January and July. Most shows are held in the Carrousel du Louvre *(see p123)*. If you want to see a show, you stand a better chance of getting a seat at the private *couture* shows (the main shows are for buyers and the press). Call the press office of the *haute couture* houses a month in advance. You can only be sure you have a place when you receive the ticket. For the private shows, telephone the fashion house or, if you're in Paris, try going to the boutique and asking if there's a show – and remember to dress the part.

Most *couture* houses make *prêt-à-porter* clothes as well – ready-to-wear clothes fitted on a standard model. They're still not cheap, but give you some of the designer elegance and creativity at a fraction of the *haute couture* cost.

Women's Clothes

The highest concentration of *couture* houses is on the Right Bank. Most are on or near the Rue du Faubourg-St-Honoré and the classier Avenue Montaigne: **Chanel**, **Ungaro**, **Christian Lacroix**, **Nina Ricci**, **Louis Féraud**, **Yves Saint Laurent**, **Pierre Cardin**, **Gianni Versace**, **Christian Dior**, **Guy Laroche**, **Jean-Louis Scherrer**, the list is almost endless. This is where you will rub shoulders with the rich and famous.

Hermès has classic country chic. **MaxMara's** Italian elegance is quite popular in France and no one can resist a **Giorgio Armani** suit. **Karl Lagerfeld**, despite designing for Chanel, has also created his own sleek line.

The theatrical **Paco Rabanne** is the only official *haute couturier* on the Left Bank, but it is surrounded by many fine fashion houses. Try **Sonia Rykiel** for knitwear, **Junko Shimada** for sporty casuals and **Barbara Bui** for soft, feminine clothes.

Many designers have a Left Bank branch in addition to their Right Bank bastions, and they all have ready-to-wear shops here. For sheer quality there's **Georges Rech**, but don't forget **Yves Saint Laurent** or **Jil Sander** for their exquisite tailoring. Try **Armani's** St-Germain temple of fashion, or **Prada's** affordable boutique, Miu Miu, in the Rue du Cherche-Midi. **Kashiyama** has its cult following for some imaginative clothes, and **Irié** is the place for reasonably-priced clothes

which are trendy but will stand the test of time.

Ready-to-wear shops blanket Paris, and in the beautiful Place des Victoires they thrive off shoppers visiting the Rue du Faubourg-St-Honoré. The **Victoire** boutique offers one of the best collections of current designer labels with Michael Klein, Helmut Lang and Thierry Mugler among many others. **Kenzo** is here, along with fellow Japanese designers **Comme des Garçons**, with its avant-garde, quirky fashion for both sexes, and **Yohji Yamamoto** just down the street, near **Ventilo**. The nearby Rue Jean-Jacques-Rousseau has also recently become one of the city's prime shopping stops.

Moving east to the Rue du Jour, **Diapositive's** body-hugging clothes are popular, while **Agnès B** and **Claudie Pierlot's** clothes have timeless elegance. There are also shops selling inexpensive copies of new designs in the centre.

The Marais is a haven for up-and-coming designers and is always busy on Saturdays. One of the best streets is the Rue des Rosiers, which includes Issey Miyake's **Pleats Please**, **L'Eclaireur** and a branch of **Tehen** for clothes. **Nina Jacob** is on the neighbouring Rue des Francs-Bourgeois, and daring designer **Azzedine Alaïa's** shop is just around the corner.

The Bastille area has many trendy boutiques, as well as some more established names. Eccentric designer **Jean-Paul Gaultier** has a boutique in the Rue du Faubourg St-Antoine. His "senior" and "junior" collections reflect price and attitude rather than age. *The* swimsuit store is **Eres**, while for leather, there's **Mac Douglas**.

Young designers' clothes are found at **Colette** and **Zadig & Voltaire**, while **Zucca** (Akira Onozuka's designs) now has several boutiques. **Réciproque** has some of the best nearly-new designer garb in Paris.

For fabulous, if pricey, clothes from the 1920s to the 1950s, try **Rag Time**.

DIRECTORY

WOMEN'S CLOTHES

Agnès B
6 Rue du Jour 75001.
Map 13 A1.
01 45 08 56 56.
One of several branches.

Azzedine Alaïa
7 Rue de Moussy 75004.
Map 13 C3.
01 40 27 85 58.

Barbara Bui
23 Rue Etienne-Marcel
75001. **Map** 13 A1.
01 40 26 43 65.
One of two branches.

Chanel
42 Ave Montaigne 75008.
Map 5 A5.
01 47 24 74 12.
One of several branches.

Christian Dior
30 Avenue Montaigne
75008. **Map** 10 F1.
01 40 73 54 44.

Christian Lacroix
73 Rue du Faubourg-St-
Honoré 75008. **Map** 5 B5.
01 42 68 79 00.

Claudie Pierlot
1 Rue Montmartre 75001.
Map 13 A1.
01 42 21 38 38.
One of two branches.

**Comme des
Garçons**
40–42 Rue Etienne-Marcel
75002. **Map** 13 A1.
01 42 33 05 21.

Colette
213 Rue St-Honoré 75001.
Map 12 D1.
01 55 35 33 90.

Diapositive
12 Rue du Jour 75001.
Map 13 A1.
01 42 21 34 41.
One of several branches.

L'Eclaireur
3 ter Rue des Rosiers
75004. **Map** 13 C3.
01 48 87 10 22.

Eres
2 Rue Tronchet 75008.
Map 5 C5.
01 47 42 24 55.
One of two branches.

Georges Rech
273 Rue St-Honoré 75008.
Map 12 D1.
01 42 61 41 14.
One of several branches.

Gianni Versace
62 Rue du Faubourg-St-
Honoré 75008.
Map 5 C5.
01 47 42 88 02.
One of two branches.

Giorgio Armani
6 Pl Vendôme 75001.
Map 6 D5.
01 42 61 55 09.
and
149 Blvd St-Germain
75006. **Map** 12 E4.
01 53 63 33 51.

Guy Laroche
30 Rue du Faubourg-St-
Honoré 75008.
Map 5 C5.
01 40 06 01 70.
One of several branches.

Hermès
24 Rue du Faubourg-St-
Honoré 75008.
Map 5 C5.
01 40 17 47 17.
One of several branches.

Irié
8 Rue du Pré-aux-Clercs
75007. **Map** 12 D3.
01 42 61 18 28.

**Jean-Louis
Scherrer**
51 Ave Montaigne
75008. **Map** 5 A5.
01 56 59 98 41.

**Jean-Paul
Gaultier**
6 Rue Vivienne 75002.
Map 12 F1.
01 42 86 05 05.
One of two branches.

Jil Sander
52 Avenue Montaigne
75008. **Map** 10 F1.
01 44 95 06 70.

Junko Shimada
54 Rue Etienne-Marcel
75002. **Map** 12 F1.
01 42 36 36 97.
One of two branches.

Kashiyama
147 Blvd St-Germain
75006. **Map** 12 E4.
01 55 42 77 55.

Kenzo
3 Pl des Victoires 75001.
Map 12 F1.
01 40 39 72 03.

Lolita Lempicka
18 Rue du Faubourg St-
Honoré 78008. **Map** 5C5.
01 49 24 94 01.

Louis Féraud
253 Rue St-Honoré 75008.
Map 5C5.
01 42 61 03 90.

Mac Douglas
9 Rue de Sèvres 75006.
Map 12 D4.
01 45 48 14 09.
One of several branches.

MaxMara
37 Rue du Four 75006.
Map 12 D4.
01 43 29 91 10.
One of two branches.

Miu Miu
23 Rue du Cherche-Midi
75006. **Map** 12 D5.
01 45 48 63 33.

Nina Jacob
23 Rue des Francs-
Bourgeois 75004
Map 14 D3.
01 42 77 41 20.

Nina Ricci
39 Avenue Montaigne
75008.**Map** 10 F1
01 49 52 56 00

Paco Rabanne
83 Rue des Sts-Pères
75006.
Map 12 D4.
01 45 48 82 26.

Pierre Cardin
27 Ave de Marigny 75008
Map 5 B5.
01 42 66 68 98.
One of two branches.

Pleats Please
3bis Rue des Rosiers 75004
Map 13C3.
01 40 29 99 66.
One of two branches.

Rag Time
23 Rue de l'Echaudé
75006. **Map** 12 E4.
01 56 24 00 36.

Réciproque
95 Rue de la Pompe
75016. **Map** 9 A1.
01 47 04 30 28.

Sonia Rykiel
175 Blvd St-Germain
75006. **Map** 12 D4.
01 49 54 60 60.
One of two branches.

Tehen
5 bis Rue des Rosiers
75004. **Map** 13 C3.
01 40 27 97 37.
One of several branches.

Ungaro
2 Ave Montaigne 75008.
Map 10 F1.
01 53 57 00 00.

Ventilo
27 bis Rue du Louvre
75002. **Map** 12 F2.
01 44 76 82 95.
One of six branches.

Victoire
12 Pl des Victoires 75002.
Map 12 F1.
01 42 61 09 02.
One of several branches.

Yohji Yamamoto
25 Rue du Louvre 75001.
Map 12 F1.
01 42 21 42 93.

**Yves Saint
Laurent**
38 Rue du Faubourg-St-
Honoré 75008. **Map** 5 C5.
01 42 65 74 59.
One of several branches.

Zadig & Voltaire
15 Rue du Jour 75001.
Map 13 A1.
01 42 21 88 70.

Zucca
8 Rue St-Roch 75001.
Map 12 E1.
01 44 58 98 88.

CHILDREN'S CLOTHES

Options for children exist in all styles and price ranges. Many designers of adult clothes have boutiques for children, including **Kenzo**, **Baby Dior**, **Agnès B**, **Sonia Rykiel** and **Teddies**. The latter carries a range of designers' children's lines.

Ready-to-wear chains like **Benetton** and **Bonpoint** (which sells chic, expensive, well-made clothes) are serviceable and wide-ranging; and **Tartine et Chocolat's** best-selling garments are overalls.

For little feet, **Froment-Leroyer** probably offers the best all-round classics. **Six Pieds Trois Pouces** has a vast choice of styles.

MEN'S CLOTHES

Men don't have the luxury of *haute couture* dressing: their choice is limited to ready-to-wear. Some men's clothes, mostly by womenswear designers, are very expensive. On the Right Bank, there's **Giorgio Armani**, **Pierre Cardin**, **Kenzo**, **Lanvin** (also good for accessories) and **Yves Saint Laurent**. On the Left Bank, **Michel Axel** and **Jean-Charles de Castelbajac** are known for their ties and **Francesco Smalto's** elegant creations are worn by cinema stars. **Yohji Yamamoto's** clothes are for those who want to make a serious fashion statement, while **Gianni Versace** is classic Italian in style, **APC** and **Paul Smith** garments are more contemporary, and **Olivier Strelli** and **Polo by Ralph Lauren** are chic without being overtly trendy.

JEWELLERY

The couture houses probably sell some of the best jewellery and scarves. **Chanel's** jewels are classics and **Christian Lacroix's** are fun. **Boutique YSL** is a great place for accessories.

Among the main expensive Paris jewellery outlets are **Boucheron** and **Mauboussin**. They are for the serious jewellery buyer. Two other top retailers are **Harry Winston** and **Cartier**. For a range of unusual jewellery and accessories, try the **Daniel Swarovski Boutique**, owned by the Swarovksi crystal family.

Trends and imitations can be found around the Marais, the Bastille and Les Halles, in that order for quality. Those of note include **Gian Paolo Maria** for its flamboyant jewellery, **Scooter** where chic young Parisians shop and **Agatha** for copies of Chanel designs and basics.

SHOES, BAGS AND BELTS

For sheer luxury **Harel** has a wide range of exotic leather footwear. Go to **Charles Jourdan** for a big selection of colours or to **Sidonie Larizzi** who will make up shoes from one of numerous leather swatches. **Carel** stocks smart basics.

Bowen has a selection of traditional men's shoes and **Fenestrier** makes chic versions of classics. **Christian Lacroix** and **Sepcoeur** make wonderful handbags and belts. Beautifully made leather goods in inviting colour ranges can also be found at **Longchamp**, **Gucci** and **Hermès**. For a great range of young and stylish shoes, boots and bags at reasonable prices, try **Jet-Set**.

HATS

One of Paris's favourite milliners is **Marie Mercié**. **Toni Pato** now creates men's hats at her old shop in Rue Tiquetonne. **Manon Martin** is offbeat and imaginative and **Philippe Model** is one of Paris's most creative and stylish hatmakers.

LINGERIE

For flattering, expensive lingerie go to **Capucine Puerari** whose tiny shop is filled with beautiful underwear. **La Boîte à Bas** sells fine French stockings while **Bas et Haut** offers a selection of stylish and serviceable items.

SIZE CHART

For Australian sizes follow the British and American conversions.

Children's clothing

French	2-3	4-5	6-7	8-9	10-11	12	14	14+ (years)
British	2-3	4-5	6-7	8-9	10-11	12	14	14+ (years)
American	2-3	4-5	6-6x	7-8	10	12	14	16 (size)

Children's shoes

French	24	25½	27	28	29	30	32	33	34
British	7	8	9	10	11	12	13	1	2
American	7½	8½	9½	10½	11½	12½	13½	1½	2½

Women's dresses coats and skirts

French	34	36	38	40	42	44	46
British	8	10	12	14	16	18	20
American	6	8	10	12	14	16	18

Women's blouses and sweaters

French	81	84	87	90	93	96	99 (cms)
British	31	32	34	36	38	40	42 (inches)
American	6	8	10	12	14	16	18 (size)

Women's shoes

French	36	37	38	39	40	41
British	3	4	5	6	7	8
American	5	6	7	8	9	10

Men's suits

French	44	46	48	50	52	54	56	58
British	34	36	38	40	42	44	46	48
American	34	36	38	40	42	44	46	48

Men's shirts

French	36	38	39	41	42	43	44	45
British	14	15	15½	16	16½	17	17½	18
American	14	15	15½	16	16½	17	17½	18

Men's shoes

French	39	40	41	42	43	44	45	46
British	6	7	7½	8	9	10	11	12
American	7	7½	8	8½	9½	10½	11	11½

DIRECTORY

CHILDREN'S CLOTHES

Agnès B
(See p317.)

Baby Dior
(See p317 Christian Dior.)

Benetton
113 Rue St-Dominique
75007. **Map** 10 F2-3.
[01 45 55 00 33.
One of several branches.

Bonpoint
15 Rue Royale 75008.
Map 5 C5.
[01 47 42 52 63.
One of several branches.

Teddies
38 Rue François-1er
75008. **Map** 10 F1.
[01 47 20 79 79.

Froment-Leroyer
7 Rue Vavin 75006.
Map 16 E1.
[01 43 54 33 15.
One of several branches.

Kenzo
(See p317.)

Six Pieds Trois Pouces
78 Ave de Wagram 75017.
Map 4 E2.
[01 46 22 81 64.
One of several branches.

Sonia Rykiel
(See p317.)

Tartine et Chocolat
105 Rue du Faubourg-St-
Honoré 75008. **Map** 5 B5.
[01 45 62 44 04.
One of several branches.

MEN'S CLOTHES

APC
39 Rue Madame 75006.
Map 12 E5.
[01 44 39 87 87.

Jean-Charles de Castelbajac
26 Rue Madame 75006.
Map 12 E5.
[01 45 48 40 55.

Francesco Smalto
44 Rue François-1er
75008. **Map** 4 F5.
[01 47 20 70 63.

Gianni Versace
(See p317.)

Giorgio Armani
(See p317.)

Kenzo
(See p317.)

Lanvin
32 Rue Marbeuf 75008.
Map 4 F5.
[01 53 75 02 20.
One of two branches.

Michel Axel
121 Blvd St-Germain
75006. **Map** 12 E4.
[01 43 26 01 96.

Olivier Strelli
7 Blvd Raspail 75007.
Map 12 D4.
[01 45 44 77 17.
One of two branches.

Paul Smith
22 Blvd Raspail 75007.
Map 12 D4.
[01 42 84 15 30.

Pierre Cardin
59 Rue du Faubourg St-
Honoré 75008. **Map** 5C5.
[01 42 66 64 74.

Yohji Yamamoto
69 Rue des Sts-Pères
75006. **Map** 12 E4.
[01 45 48 22 56.

Yves Saint Laurent
6 Pl St-Sulpice 75006.
Map 12 D4.
[01 43 26 84 40.

JEWELLERY

Agatha
97 Rue de Rennes 75006.
Map 12 D5.
[01 45 48 81 30.
One of several branches.

Boucheron
26 Pl Vendôme 75001.
Map 6 D5.
[01 42 61 58 16.

Boutique YSL
32 Rue du Faubourg-St-
Honoré 75008. **Map** 5 C5.
[01 42 65 01 15.

Cartier
13 Rue de la Paix 75002.
Map 6 D5.
[01 42 61 58 56.
One of several branches.

Chanel
(See p317.)

Christian Lacroix
(See p317.)

Daniel Swarovski Boutique
7 Rue Royale 75008.
Map 5 C5.
[01 40 17 07 40.

Gian Paolo Maria
12 Rue St-Paul 75004.
Map 14 D4.
[01 40 27 00 12.

Harry Winston
29 Ave Montaigne 75008.
Map 10 F1.
[01 47 20 03 09.

Mauboussin
20 Pl Vendôme 75001.
Map 6 D5.
[01 44 55 10 00.

Scooter
10 Rue de Turbigo 75001.
Map 13 A1.
[01 45 08 50 54.
One of several branches.

SHOES, BAGS AND BELTS

Bowen
5 Pl des Ternes 75017.
Map 4 E3.
[01 42 27 09 23.
One of several branches.

Carel
4 Rue Tronchet 75008.
Map 6 D4.
[01 42 66 21 58.
One of several branches.

Charles Jourdan
86 Ave de Champs-Elysées
75008. **Map** 4 F5.
[01 45 62 29 28.
One of several branches.

Fenestrier
23 Rue du Cherche-Midi
75006. **Map** 12 D5.
[01 42 22 66 02.

Gucci
350 Rue St-Honoré
75001. **Map** 5 C5.
[01 42 96 83 27.
One of two branches.

Harel
8 Ave Montaigne 75008.
Map 10 F1.
[01 47 23 83 03.
One of two branches.

Hermès
(See p317.)

Jet-Set
85 Rue de Passy 75016.
Map 9 B3.
[01 42 88 21 59.
One of two branches.

Longchamp
404 Rue St-Honoré
75001. **Map** 5 C5.
[01 43 16 00 16.

Sepcoeur
3 Rue Chambiges
75008.
Map 10 F1.
[01 47 20 98 24.

Sidonie Larizzi
8 Rue de Marignan
75008. **Map** 4 F5.
[01 43 59 38 87.

HATS

Marie Mercié
23 Rue St-Sulpice 75006.
Map 12 E4.
[01 43 26 45 83.

Manon Martin
19 Rue de Turenne 75004.
Map 14 D3.
[01 48 04 00 84.

Toni Pato
56 Rue Tiquetonne
75002. **Map** 13 A1.
[01 40 26 60 68.

Philippe Model
33 Pl du Marché St-
Honoré 75001.
Map 12 D1.
[01 42 96 89 02.

LINGERIE

Bas et Haut
182 Blvd St-Germain
75006. **Map** 11 C3.
[01 45 48 15 88.

La Boîte à Bas
27 Rue Boissy-d'Anglas
75008. **Map** 5 C5.
[01 42 66 26 85.
One of several branches.

Capucine Puerari
63 bis Rue des Sts-Pères
75006.
Map 12 D4.
[01 42 22 14 09.

Gifts and Souvenirs

Paris has a wealth of stylish gifts and typical souvenirs, from designer accessories and perfume to French delicacies and Eiffel Tower paperweights. Shops on the Rue de Rivoli offer a range of cheap holiday paraphernalia, or go to some of the souvenir shops such as **Les Drapeaux de France**. Mementos can often be found in museum shops, including reproductions, and creations by young designers. Try **Le Musée** or **Le Musée du Louvre**, **Musée d'Orsay** or **Musée Carnavalet**.

PERFUME

Many shops advertise discounted perfume and cosmetics. Some even offer duty-free perfume to shoppers outside the EC, with discounts on the marked prices when you show your passport. They include **Eiffel Shopping** near the Eiffel Tower. The **Sephora** chain has a big selection, or try the department stores for a range of designers' perfumes.

Among the traditional perfumeries is the old-fashioned store **Détaille**. **Parfums Caron** has many scents created at the turn of the century and which are unavailable elsewhere, while beautifully packaged perfumes made from natural essences are available from **Annick Goutal**. **Guerlain** has the ultimate in beauty care and **L'Artisan Parfumeur** specializes in making scents which evoke specific memories and has reissued favourites from the past, including perfume worn at the court of Versailles.

HOUSEHOLD GOODS

Though it's rather delicate to carry home, France produces some very elegant tableware. Many shops will arrange to ship crockery overseas. Luxury household goods can be found on the Rue Royale, where many of the best shops are located. They sell items such as rustic china and reproduction and modern silverware. **Lalique**'s Art Nouveau and Art Deco glass sculptures are collected all over the world.

Many of the brand names have showrooms on the Rue de Paradis and here you may make significant savings on porcelain and crystal. Try **Lumicristal**, which stocks Baccarat, Daum and Limoges crystal, or go to **Baccarat** itself. Baccarat also has a boutique on the Place de la Madeleine. For a unique knife, go to **Peter** and choose a handle made from wood or precious stones. And set the atmosphere for dinner with candles from **Point à la Ligne**'s huge selection.

For fabrics, try **Agnès Comar**. Alternatively the interior designers **Pierre et Patrick Frey** have an upstairs showroom displaying fabulous fabrics which have been made into cushions, bedspreads and tablecloths. **La Chaise Longue** has a selection of well-designed *objets* for the home, along with fun gift ideas. **Home Autour du Monde** is contemporary, while **La Tuile à Loup** carries more traditional French handicrafts.

BOOKS, MAGAZINES AND NEWSPAPERS

Many English and American publications can be found at large magazine stands or at some of the bookshops listed. If French is no obstacle the weeklies *Pariscope*, *L'Officiel des Spectacles* and *7 à Paris* have the most comprehensive listings of what's going on around town.

The *International Herald Tribune*, an English-language daily newspaper, is published in Paris and contains good American news coverage. Two periodicals, *Paris Free Voice* and the bi-weekly *France–US Contacts*, are also published in English.

Some of the large department stores have a book section *(see Department Stores p313)*. There is a large and helpful branch of **WH Smith** on the Rue de Rivoli, or try **Brentano**'s. A small, somewhat disorganized, but cosy and convivial bookshop is **Shakespeare and Co**. The American-influenced **Village Voice** has a good literary and intellectual selection of new books and **The Abbey Bookshop** does the same for second-hand books. **Tea and Tattered Pages** is a British second-hand bookshop.

French-language bookshops include **La Hune**, specializing in art, design, architecture, literature, photography, fashion, theatre and cinema; **Gibert Joseph**, selling general and educational books; and **Le Divan** which has strong social science, psychology, literature and poetry sections. After designer perfume comes the designer bookshop: Karl Lagerfeld's **7L** for design, fashion and contemporary art.

FLOWERS

Some Parisian florists such as **Christian Tortu** are very well known, competing for headlines with politicians and fashion designers. **Aquarelle** offers a good selection at reasonable prices; and **Mille Feuilles** is the place to go to in the Marais. *(See also Specialist Markets p326.)*

SPECIALIST SHOPS

For cigars, **A La Civette** is perhaps the most beautiful tobacconists in Paris and has humidified shop windows to preserve the merchandise perfectly.

Go to **A l'Olivier** for a selection of exotic oils and vinegar. Or if honey is a favourite condiment, try **La Maison du Miel** where you can buy all sorts of fine honeys including those made from the flowers of lavender and acacia. You can also buy beeswax soap and candles. **Mariage Frères** has become a cult favourite for its 350 varieties of tea, and also sells teapots.

Couture fabrics can be purchased from a range at **Wolff et Descourtis**, while at **Vassilev** you can pick up violins old and new, cheap and expensive. For an unusual gift of traditional French card games or tarot cards go to **Jeux Descartes**. One of the world's most famous toyshops is **Au Nain Bleu** while the name **Casse-grain** is synonymous with high-quality stationery and paper products. **Calligrane** sells a range of designer desk accessories and paper products.

DIRECTORY

SOUVENIR AND MUSEUM SHOPS

Les Drapeaux de France
13 Galerie Montpensier 75001. **Map** 12 E1.
☎ 01 42 97 55 40.

Le Musée
(Official National Museum reproductions.) Niveau 2, Forum des Halles, Porte Berger 75001. **Map** 13 A2.
☎ 01 40 39 97 91.

Musée Carnavalet
(See p97.)

Musée du Louvre
(See p123.)

Musée d'Orsay
(See p145.)

PERFUME

Annick Goutal
16 Rue de Bellechasse 75007. **Map** 11 C3.
☎ 01 45 51 36 13.
One of several branches.

L'Artisan Parfumeur
24 Blvd Raspail 75007.
Map 16 D1.
☎ 01 42 22 23 32.
One of several branches.

Détaille
10 Rue St-Lazare 75009.
Map 6 D3.
☎ 01 48 78 68 50.

Eiffel Shopping
9 Ave de Suffren 75007.
Map 10 D3.
☎ 01 45 66 55 30.

Guerlain
68 Ave des Champs-Elysées 75008. **Map** 4 F5.
☎ 01 45 62 11 21.
One of several branches.

Parfums Caron
34 Ave Montaigne 75008.
Map 10 F1.
☎ 01 47 23 40 82.

Sephora
Forum des Halles 75001.
Map 13 A2.
☎ 01 40 13 72 25.
One of several branches.

HOUSEHOLD GOODS

Agnès Comar
10 Ave George V 75008.
Map 10 E1.
☎ 01 47 23 33 85.

Baccarat
11 Pl de la Madeleine 75008. **Map** 5 C5.
☎ 01 42 65 36 26.
(See also p231.)

La Chaise Longue
30 Rue Croix-des-Petits-Champs 75001. **Map** 12 F1.
☎ 01 42 96 32 14.
One of several branches.

Home Autour du Monde
8 Rue des Francs Bourgeois 75003. **Map** 14 D3.
☎ 01 42 77 06 08.

Lalique
11 Rue Royale 75008.
Map 5 C5.
☎ 01 53 05 12 12.

Lumicristal
22 bis Rue de Paradis 75010. **Map** 7 B4.
☎ 01 47 70 27 97.

Peter
8bis Rue Boissy d'Anglas 75008. **Map** 5 C5.
☎ 01 40 07 05 28.

Pierre et Patrick Frey
7 Rue Jacob 75116.
Map 12 E3.
☎ 01 43 26 82 61.

Point à la Ligne
67 Ave Victor Hugo 75116. **Map** 3 B5.
☎ 01 45 00 87 01.

La Tuile à Loup
35 Rue Daubenton 75005.
Map 17 B2.
☎ 01 47 07 28 90.

BOOKS, MAGAZINES AND NEWSPAPERS

Abbey Bookshop
29 Rue de la Parcheminerie 75005. **Map** 13 A4.
☎ 01 46 33 16 24.

Brentano
37 Ave de l'Opéra 75002.
Map 6 E5.
☎ 01 42 61 52 50.

Le Divan
203 Rue de la Convention 75015. **Map** 12 E3.
☎ 01 53 68 90 68.

Gibert Joseph
26 Blvd St-Michel 75006.
Map 12 F5.
☎ 01 44 41 88 88.

La Hune
170 Blvd St-Germain 75006. **Map** 12 D4.
☎ 01 45 48 35 85.

7L
7 Rue de Lille 75007.
Map 12E3.
☎ 01 42 92 03 58

Shakespeare & Co
37 Rue de la Bûcherie 75005. **Map** 13 A4.
☎ 01 43 26 96 50

Tea and Tattered Pages
24 Rue Mayet 75006. **Map** 15 B1. ☎ 01 40 65 94 35.

Village Voice
6 Rue Princesse 75006.
Map 12 E4.
☎ 01 46 33 36 47.

W H Smith
248 Rue de Rivoli 75001.
Map 11 C1.
☎ 01 44 77 88 99.

FLOWERS

Aquarelle
15 Rue de Rivoli 75004.
Map 13 C3.
☎ 01 40 27 99 10.

Christian Tortu
6 Carrefour de l'Odéon 75006. **Map** 12 F4.
☎ 01 43 26 02 56.

Mille Feuilles
2 Rue Rambuteau 75003.
Map 13 C2.
☎ 01 42 78 32 93.

SPECIALIST SHOPS

A la Civette
157 Rue St-Honoré 75001.
Map 12 F2.
☎ 01 42 96 04 99.

A L'Olivier
23 Rue de Rivoli 75004.
Map 13 C3.
☎ 01 48 04 86 59.

Au Nain Bleu
408 Rue St-Honoré 75008.
Map 5 C5.
☎ 01 42 60 39 01.

Calligrane
4–6 Rue du Pont-Louis-Philippe 75004.
Map 13 B4.
☎ 01 48 04 31 89.

Cassegrain
422 Rue St-Honoré 75008.
Map 5 C5.
☎ 01 42 60 20 08.
One of two branches.

Jeux Descartes
52 Rue des Écoles 75005.
Map 13 A5.
☎ 01 43 26 79 83.
One of three branches.

La Maison du Miel
24 Rue Vignon 75009.
Map 6 D5.
☎ 01 47 42 26 70.

Mariage Frères
(See p286.)

Vassilev
45 Rue de Rome 75008.
Map 5 C3.
☎ 01 45 22 69 03.

Wolff et Descourtis
18 Galerie Vivienne 75002. **Map** 12 F1.
☎ 01 42 61 80 84.

Food and Drink

Paris is as famous for food as it is for fashion. Gastronomic treats include *foie gras*, cold meats from the *charcuterie*, cheese and wine. Certain streets are so overflowing with food shops that you can collect a picnic for 20 in no time: try the Rue Montorgueil (*see p327*). The Rue Rambuteau, running on either side of the Pompidou Centre, has a marvellous row of fishmongers, cheese delicatessens and shops selling prepared foods. (*See also* What to Eat and Drink in Paris *pp290–93 and* Light Meals and Snacks *pp310–11.*)

BREAD AND CAKES

There is a vast range of breads and pastries in France's capital. The *baguette* is often translated "French bread"; a *bâtard* is similar but thicker, while a *ficelle* is thinner. A *fougasse* is a crusty, flat loaf made from *baguette* dough, often filled with onions, herbs or spices. Since most French bread contains no fat it goes stale quickly: the sooner you eat it, the better.

The croissant can be bought *ordinaire* or *au beurre* – the latter is flakier and more buttery. *Pain au chocolat* is a chocolate-filled pastry eaten for breakfast and *chausson aux pommes* is filled with apples. There are also pear, plum and rhubarb variations.

L'établissement Poilâne sells perhaps the only bread in Paris known by the name of its baker and his excellent, hearty wholewheat loaves are tremendously popular. There are big queues at the weekend and around 4pm when a fresh batch comes out of the oven.

Many think **Ganachaud** bakes the best bread in Paris. Thirty different kinds of breads including ingredients such as walnuts and fruit are made in the old-fashioned ovens.

Although **Les Panetons** is part of a larger chain, it is one of the best of its kind with a broad range of breads. Favourites includes five-grain bread, sesame rolls, and *mouchoir aux pommes*, a variation on the traditional *chausson*.

Many of the Jewish delicatessens have the best ryes and the only pumpernickels in town. **Jo Goldenberg's** is the best known. **Stohrer** was founded by the pastry makers to Louis XV in 1730 and still makes some of the capital's best croissants.

Le Moulin de la Vierge uses a wood fire to make organic breads and rich pound cakes. **Maison Meli** is second only to **Max Poilâne** in the Montparnasse area with *baguettes*, *fougasses*, cakes and pastries. **J L Poujauran** is known for his black olive bread and nut-and-raisin wholegrain breads.

CHOCOLATE

Like all food in France, chocolate is to be savoured. **Christian Constant's** low-sugar creations are made with pure cocoa and are known to connoisseurs. **Dalloyau** makes all types of chocolate and is not too expensive (it's also known for its pâtisserie and cold meats). **Fauchon** is world famous for its luxury food products. Its chocolates are excellent, as is the pâtisserie. **Lenôtre** makes classic truffles and pralines. Robert Linxe at **La Maison du Chocolat** is constantly inventing fresh, rich chocolates with mouth-watering exotic ingredients. **Richart** boasts beautifully presented and hugely expensive chocolates, which are usually coated with dark chocolate or liqueur-filled.

CHARCUTERIE AND FOIE GRAS

Charcuteries often sell cheese, snails, truffles, smoked salmon, caviar and wine as well as cold meats. **Fauchon** has a good grocery, as does the basement of the department store **Le Bon**

Marché. **Hédiard** is a luxury shop similar to Fauchon, and **Maison de la Truffe** sells *foie gras* and sausages as well as truffles. For Beluga caviar, Georgian tea and Russian vodka go to **Petrossian**.

The Lyon and Auvergne regions of France are the best known for their *charcuterie*. Examples can be bought from **Terrier**. **Aux Vrais Produits d'Auvergne** has a number of outlets where you can stock up on dried and fresh sausages and delicious Cantal cheese (rather like Cheddar). **Pou** is a sparklingly clean and popular shop selling *pâté en croute* (pâté baked in pastry), *boudins* (black and white puddings), Lyonnais sausages, ham and *foie gras*. Just off the Champs-Elysées, **Vignon** has superb *foie gras* and Lyonnais sausages as well as popular prepared foods.

Together with truffles and caviar, *foie gras* is the ultimate in gourmet food. The quality (and price) depends upon the percentage of liver used. Though most specialist food shops sell *foie gras*, you can be sure of quality at **Comtesse du Barry** which has six outlets in Paris. **Divay** is relatively inexpensive and will ship overseas. **Labeyrie** has a range of beautifully-packaged *foie gras* suitable for giving as presents.

CHEESE

Although Camembert is undoubtedly a favourite, there is an overwhelming range of cheeses available. A friendly *fromager* will help you choose. **Marie-Anne Cantin** is one of the leading figures in the fight to protect traditional production methods, and her fine cheeses are available from the shop that she inherited from her father. Some say that **Alléosse** is the best cheese delicatessen in Paris: the facade may be in need of renovation, but all the cheeses are made using traditional methods. **Maison du Fromage** sells farm-made cheeses, many of which are in danger of becoming extinct, including a rare and delicious truffle Brie (when in season). **Boursault** is one of the best shops in Paris for all types of cheese: the *chèvre* (goat's cheese) is particularly good, and outside on the pavement the daily specials are offered at remarkably reasonable prices. **Barthelemy** in the Rue de Grenelle offer a truly exceptional Roquefort.

WINE

THE CHAIN store which has practically cornered the market is **Nicolas**: there's a branch in every neighbourhood with a range of wines for all pockets. As a rule the salespeople are knowledgeable and helpful. The stars shop at **L'Arbre à Vin, Caves Retrou**, or try the charming **Legrand** for a carefully chosen

selection. **Caves Taillevent** is worth a sightseeing tour. It is an enormous, overwhelming cellar with some of the most expensive wine. **Bernard Péret** has a vast selection and can advise you on all of it. The beautiful **Ryst-Dupeyron** displays ports, whiskies, wines and Monsieur Ryst's own Armagnac. He will even personalize a bottle for that special occasion.

Art and Antiques

IN PARIS YOU CAN EITHER BUY art and antiques from shops and galleries with established reputations, or from flea markets and avant-garde galleries. Many of the prestigious antiques shops and galleries are located around the Rue du Faubourg-St-Honoré and are worth a visit even if you can't afford to buy. On the Left Bank is the Carré Rive Gauche, an organization of 30 antiques dealers. You will need a certificate of authenticity to export designated *objets d'art* over 20 years old and any goods over a century old worth more than F1,000,000 in order to avoid paying duty. Seek professional advice from one of the large antique shops and declare the item at customs if you are in any doubt.

EXPORTING

THE MINISTRY of Culture designates *objets d'art*. Export licences are available from the **Centre Français du Commerce Extérieur**. The **Centre des Renseignements des Douanes** has a booklet, *Bulletin Officiel des Douanes*, with all the details.

MODERN CRAFTS AND FURNITURE

ONE OF THE BEST places for furniture and *objets d'art* by up-and-coming designers is **Avant-Scène** in the Latin Quarter. If you enjoy beautifully-designed modern furniture for the office, then **Havvorth** is well worth a visit. **Le Viaduc des Arts** is a railway viaduct, each arch of which has been transformed into a shop front and workshop space. Stroll along this street for a great show of contemporary metal-work, tapestry, sculpture, ceramics and more.

ANTIQUES/OBJETS D'ART

IF YOU WISH to buy antiques, you might like to stroll around the areas that boast many galleries: in Le Carré Rive Gauche around Quai Malaquais, try **L'Arc en Seine** and **Anne-Sophie Duval** for Art Nouveau and Art Deco. Rue Jacob is still one of the best places to seek beautiful objects, antique or modern. Close to the Louvre, the Louvre des Antiquaires *(see p120)* sells expensive, quality furniture. On the Rue du

Faubourg-St-Honoré you will find **Didier Aaron**, expert on furniture of the 17th and 18th centuries. **Village St-Paul** is the most charming group of antiques shops and is open on Sundays.

La Calinière has an excellent range of *objets d'art* and old lighting fixtures. European glassware from the 19th century to the 1960s is sold at **Verreglass**.

REPRODUCTIONS, POSTERS AND PRINTS

A BEAUTIFUL, contemporary art gallery called **Artcurial** has one of the best selections of international art periodicals, books and prints. On the Boulevard St-Germain, **La Hune** is a popular bookshop, particularly for art publications. The museum bookshops, especially those in the Musée d'Art Moderne *(see p201)*, Louvre *(see p123)*, Musée d'Orsay *(see p145)* and Pompidou Centre *(see p111)* are good places for recent art books and posters.

Galerie Documents sells original antique posters of all sorts. **A l'Image du Grenier sur l'Eau** is a place you can easily spend an entire afternoon browsing through a vast number of old postcards as well as posters and prints. Alternatively walk along the Seine and leaf through the secondhand books sold at the stalls along its banks.

ART GALLERIES

ESTABLISHED art galleries are located on or around the Avenue Montaigne. The **Louise Leiris** gallery was founded by D H Kahnweiler, the dealer who "discovered" both Pablo Picasso and Georges Braque. The gallery still shows Cubist masterpieces.

Artcurial holds many exhibitions and has an impressive permanent collection of 20th-century works, including works by Joan Miró, Max Ernst, Picasso and Alberto Giacometti. **Lelong** is devoted to contemporary artists.

On the Left Bank **Adrian Maeght** has a tremendous stock of paintings; he also publishes fine art books. **Galerie 1900–2000** organizes very good retrospective exhibitions and **Daniel Gervis** has a wide selection of abstract prints, engravings and lithographs. **Dina Vierny** is a bastion of Modernism, founded by one of the sculptor Aristide Maillol's models.

Some of the newest additions to the art gallery world are in the Marais and the Bastille and display mainly avant-garde, contemporary works. In the Marais try **Yvon Lambert, Daniel Templon** (specializing in American art), **Zabriskie** and **Alain Blondel,** and in the Bastille, **Levignes-Bastille** and **L et M Durand-Dessert,** also a fashionable place to buy catalogues on new artists.

AUCTIONS AND AUCTION HOUSES

THE GREAT Paris auction centre, in operation since 1858, is **Drouot-Richelieu** *(see p216)*. Bidding can be intimidating since most of it is done by dealers. If your French is not fluent then take a French friend – the high-speed auctioneer's patter is not easy to decipher in a foreign language. *La Gazette de L'Hôtel Drouot* tells you what auctions are coming up when. Drouot-Richelieu has its own auction catalogue available as well.

The house only accepts cash and French cheques but there is an exchange desk in house. A 10–15% commission to the house is charged, so add it on to any price you hear. You may view from 11am to 6pm on the day before the sale, and from 11am to noon on the morning of the sale. Items considered not good enough for the main house are sold at **Drouot-Nord**. Here auctions take place from 9am to noon and viewing is just 5 minutes before the sales begin. The most prestigious auctions are held at **Drouot-Montaigne**.

The **Crédit Municipal** holds around 12 auctions a month, and almost all the items on sale are small objects and furs off-loaded by rich Parisians. The rules follow those at Drouot. Information about these auctions can also be found in *La Gazette de L'Hôtel Drouot*.

Service des Domaines sells all sorts of odds and ends, and here you can still find bargains. Many of the wares come from bailiffs and from Customs and Excise confiscations. Viewing is from 10am to 11.30am on the day of the sale.

DIRECTORY

EXPORTING

Centre Français du Commerce Extérieur
10 Ave d'Iéna 75016.
Map 10 D1.
01 40 73 30 00.

Centre des Renseignements des Douanes
84 Rue d'Hauteville 75010.
01 53 24 68 24.

MODERN CRAFTS AND FURNITURE
Avant-Scène
4 Pl de l'Odéon 75006.
Map 12 F5.
01 46 33 12 40.

Havvorth
166 Rue du Faubourg-St-Honoré 75008. **Map** 5 A4.
01 56 88 55 10.

Le Viaduc des Arts
29 Ave Daumesnil
750012. **Map** 14 F5.
01 46 28 11 11.

ANTIQUES AND OBJETS D'ART

Anne-Sophie Duval
5 Quai Malaquais 75006.
Map 12 E3.
01 43 54 51 16.

L'Arc en Seine
31 Rue de Seine 75006.
Map 12 E3.
01 43 29 11 02.

Didier Aaron
118 Rue du Faubourg-St-Honoré 75008.
Map 5 C5.
01 47 42 47 34.

Village St-Paul
Between the Quai des Célestins, the Rue St-Paul and the Rue Charlemagne 75004.
Map 13 C4.

La Calinière
68 Rue Vieille-du-Temple 75003.
Map 13 C3.
01 42 77 40 46.

Verreglass
32 Rue de Charonne 75011. **Map** 14 F4
01 48 05 78 43.

REPRODUCTIONS, POSTERS, PRINTS

A l'Image du Grenier sur l'Eau
45 Rue des Francs-Bourgeois 75004.
Map 13 C3.
01 42 71 02 31.

Artcurial
61 Ave Montaigne 75008.
Map 5 A5.
01 42 99 16 16.

Galerie Documents
53 Rue de Seine 75006.
Map 12 E4.
01 43 54 50 68.

La Hune
170 Blvd St-Germain
75006. **Map** 12 D4.
01 45 48 35 85.

L et M Durand-Dessert
28 Rue de Lappe 75011.
Map 14 F4.
01 48 06 92 23.

ART GALLERIES

Adrian Maeght
42 Rue du Bac 75007.
Map 12 D3.
01 45 48 45 15.

Alain Blondel
4 Rue Aubry-Le-Boucher
75004. **Map** 13 B2.
01 42 78 66 67.
One of two galleries.

Daniel Gervis
14 Rue de Grenelle 75007.
Map 12 D4.
01 45 44 41 90.
(open by appt only)

Daniel Templon
30 Rue Beaubourg 75003.
Map 13 B1.
01 42 72 14 10.
(open by appt only)

Dina Vierny
36 Rue Jacob 75006.
Map 12 E3.
01 42 60 23 18.

Galerie 1900–2000
8 Rue Bonaparte 75006.
Map 12 E3.
01 43 25 84 20.

Lelong
13 Rue de Téhéran
75008. **Map** 5 A3.
01 45 63 13 19.

Levignes-Bastille
27 Rue de Charonne
75011. **Map** 14 F4
01 47 00 88 18.

Louise Leiris
47 Rue de Monceau
75008. **Map** 5 A3.
01 45 63 28 85.

Yvon Lambert
108 Rue Vieille-du-Temple
75003. **Map** 14 D2.
01 42 71 09 33.

Zabriskie
37 Rue Quincampoix
75004. **Map** 13 B2.
01 42 72 35 47.
(open by appt only)

AUCTION HOUSES
Crédit Municipal
55 Rue des Francs-Bourgeois
75004. **Map** 13 C3.
01 44 61 64 00.

Drouot-Montaigne
15 Ave Montaigne 75008.
Map 10 F1.
01 48 00 20 80.

Drouot-Nord
64 Rue Doudeauville
75018. 01 48 00 20 99.

Drouot-Richelieu
9 Rue Drouot 75009.
Map 6 F4.
01 48 00 20 20.

Service des Domaines
15–17 Rue Scribe 75009.
Map 6 D4.
01 44 94 78 78.

Markets

FOR EYE-CATCHING displays of wonderful food or a lively shopping atmosphere, there is no better place than a Paris market. There are large covered food markets; markets where stalls change regularly; and permanent street markets with a mixture of shops and stalls which are open on a daily basis. Each has its own personality reflecting the area in which it is located. Following is a list of some of the more famous markets, with approximate opening times. For a complete list of markets contact the Paris Office du Tourisme (see p274). And while you're enjoying browsing round the stalls remember to keep an eye on your money – and be prepared to bargain.

FRUIT AND VEGETABLE MARKETS

THE FRENCH treat food with the kind of reverence usually reserved for religion. Most still shop on a daily basis to be sure of buying the freshest produce possible, so food markets tend to be busy. The majority of fruit and vegetable markets are open from around 8am to 1pm and from 4pm to 7pm Tuesday to Saturday, and from 9am to 1pm Sunday.

Watch what you buy in the food markets or you may find you purchase a kilo of fruit or vegetables from a marvellous display only to discover later that all the produce hidden underneath is rotten. To avoid this, try to buy produce loose rather than in boxes. Most outdoor stalls prefer to serve you rather than allow you to help yourself, but you can point to the individual fruit and vegetables of your choice. A little language is useful for specifying *pas trop mûr* (not too ripe), or *pour manger ce soir* (to be eaten tonight). If you go to the same market every day you'll become familiar with the stall holders and are far less likely to be cheated. You will also get to know the stalls worth buying from and the produce worth buying. Seasonal fruit and vegetables are, of course, usually a good buy, tending to be fresher and cheaper than at other times of the year. Finally, it's best to go early in the day when the food is freshest and the queues are shortest.

FLEA MARKETS

IT'S OFTEN SAID that you can no longer find bargains at the Paris flea markets. Though for the most part this is true, it's still worth going to flea markets for the sheer fun of browsing. And bear in mind that the price quoted is probably not the price that you are expected to pay – it's generally assumed that you will bargain. Most flea markets are located on the boundaries of the city. Whether you pick up any real bargains probably has as much to do with luck as with judgement. Often the sellers themselves have little or no idea of the true value of the goods they are selling – which can work either for or against you. The biggest and most famous Paris flea market, incorporating a number of smaller markets, is the Marché aux Puces de St-Ouen.

SPECIALIST MARKETS

Try the Marché aux Fleurs Madeleine in the Opéra, the Marché aux Fleurs on the Ile de la Cité (see p81) or the Marché aux Fleurs Ternes in the Champs-Elysées district for fresh flowers. On the Ile de la Cité on Sundays the Marché aux Oiseaux bird market replaces the flower market. Stamp collectors will enjoy the permanent Marché aux Timbres where you can also buy old post-cards. In Montmartre the Marché St-Pierre, famous for cheap fabrics, is patronized by professional designers.

Marché d'Aligre

(See p233.)

Reminiscent of a Moroccan bazaar, this must be the cheapest and liveliest market in the city. Here traders hawk ingredients such as North African olives, groundnuts and hot peppers and there are even a few halal butchers. The noise reaches a crescendo at weekends when the cries of the market boys mingle with those of militants of all political persuasions as the latter petition and protest in the Place d'Aligre. The stalls on the square sell mostly second-hand clothes and bric-à-brac. This is a less affluent area of town with few tourists and many Parisians. There is also a covered market with a good cheese delicatessen, Maison du Fromage-Radenac (see pp322–3).

Rue Cler

(See p190.)

This high-class, pedestrianized food market is patronized mainly by the politicians and captains of industry who live and work in the vicinity. The produce is excellent: there's a Breton delicatessen and some good cheese delicatessens.

Marché Enfant Rouges

39 Rue de Bretagne 75003. **Map** 14 D2.
M *Temple, Filles-du-Calvaire.*
🕐 *8am–1pm, 4pm–8pm Tue–Fri, 8am–8pm Sat, 9am–1pm Sun.*

This long-established, charming fruit and vegetable market on the Rue de Bretagne is part covered, part outdoors and dates from 1620. On Sunday mornings street singers and accordionists sometimes enliven the proceedings.

Marché aux Fleurs Madeleine

Pl de la Madeleine 75008.
Map 5 C5. **M** *Madeleine.*
🕐 *8am–7.30pm Tue–Sun.*

Marché aux Fleurs Ternes

Pl des Ternes 75008. **Map** 4 E3.
M *Ternes.* 🕐 *8am–7.30pm Tue–Sun.*

Marché St-Pierre

Pl St-Pierre 75018. **Map** 6 F1. **M** *Anvers.* 🕐 *2–7pm Mon, 9.30am–7pm Tue–Sat.*

Marché aux Timbres

Cour Marigny 75008. **Map** 5 B5.
M *Champs-Elysées.* 🕐 *9am–7pm Thu, Sun & public hols.*

Marché St-Germain

Rue Mabillon and Rue Lobineau
75005. **Map** 12 E4. **M** *Mabillon.*
◑ *8am–1pm, 4pm–7.30pm Tue–Sat,
8.30am–1pm Sun.*

St-Germain is one of the few
covered markets left in Paris and
has been enhanced by renovation.
Here you can buy Italian, Mexican,
Greek, Asian and organic produce
and other goods.

Rue Lepic

75018. **Map** 6 F1. **M** *Blanche,
Lamarck-Caulaincourt.*
◑ *8am–1pm Tue–Sun.*

The Rue Lepic fruit and vegetable
market is situated conveniently
close to the sights of Montmartre
in this refreshingly unspoilt
winding old quarry road. The
market is at its liveliest at weekends.

Rue de Lévis

Blvd des Batignolles 75017. **Map** 5 B2.
M *Villiers.* **◑** *8am–1pm, 4pm–7pm
Tue–Sat, 9am–1pm Sun.*

Rue de Lévis is a bustling, popular
food market near the Parc
Monceau with a number of good
pâtisseries, an excellent cheese
delicatessen and a charcuterie
which is known for its savoury
pies. The part of the street that
leads to the Rue Cardinet sells
haberdashery and fabrics.

Rue Montorgueil

75001 & 75002. **Map** 13 A1.
M *Les Halles.* **◑** *8am–1pm,
4pm–7pm Tue–Sat, 9am–1pm Sun.*

The Rue Montorgueil is what
remains of the old Les Halles
market. The street has now been
repaved and restored to its former
glory. Here you can buy exotic
fruit and vegetables like green
bananas and yams from the
market gardeners' stalls, or sample
offerings from the delicatessens or
from the Stohrer pastry shop *(see
pp322–3).* Alternatively pick up
some of the pretty Moroccan
pottery for sale.

Rue Mouffetard

(See p166.)

Rue Mouffetard is one of the oldest
market streets in Paris. Although it
has become touristy and somewhat
overpriced, it's still a charming
winding street full of quality food
products. It's worth queueing for
the freshly-made bread at Les
Panetons bakery at No. 113 *(see
pp322–3).* There is also a lively
African market down the nearby
side street of Rue Daubenton.

Rue Poncelet

75017. **Map** 4 E3. **M** *Ternes.*
◑ *8am–12.30pm, 4pm–7.30pm
Tue–Sat, 8am–12.30pm Sun.*

The Rue Poncelet food market is
situated away from the main
tourist areas of Paris but is worth
visiting for its authentic French
atmosphere. Choose from the
many bakeries, pâtisseries and
charcuteries or enjoy authentic
Auvergne specialities from Aux
Fermes d'Auvergnes.

Marché de la Porte de Vanves

Ave Georges-Lafenestre & Ave Marc-
Sangnier 75014. **M** *Porte-de-Vanves.*
◑ *8am– 7pm Sat & Sun.*

Porte de Vanves is a small market
selling good-quality bric-à-brac
and junk as well as some second-
hand furniture. It's best to get to
the market early on Saturday
morning for the best choice of
wares. Artists exhibit nearby in
the Place des Artistes.

Marché Président-Wilson

Situated in Ave du Président-Wilson,
between Pl d'Iéna & Rue Debrousse
75016. **Map** 10 D1. **M** *Alma-Marceau.*
◑ *7am–1pm Wed & Sat.*

This very chic food market on
Avenue Président-Wilson is close
to the Musée d'Art Moderne and
the Palais Galliera fashion museum.
It has become important because
there are no other food shops
nearby. It is best for meat.

Marché aux Puces de Montreuil

Porte de Montreuil, 93 Montreuil
75020. **M** *Porte-de-Montreuil.*
◑ *8am–6pm Sat, Sun & Mon.*

Go early to the Porte de Montreuil
flea market, where you'll have a
better chance of picking up a
bargain. The substantial second-
hand clothes section attracts many
young people. There's also a wide
variety of items including used
bicycles, bric-à-brac and an exotic
spices stand.

Marché aux Puces de St-Ouen

(See p231.)

This is the most well-known, the
most crowded and the most
expensive of all the flea markets,
situated on the northern outskirts
of the city. Here you'll find a
range of markets, locals dealing
from their car boots and a number
of extremely large buildings

packed with stalls. Some of them
are very upmarket, others sell
junk. The flea market is a 10–15
minute walk from Clignancourt
metro – don't be put off by the
somewhat sleazy Marché Malik
which you have to pass through
on your way from the metro. A
Guide des Puces (guide to the flea
markets) can be obtained from the
information kiosk in the Marché
Biron on the Rue des Rosiers. The
more exclusive markets will take
credit cards and arrange for goods
to be shipped home. New stock
arrives on Friday, the day when pro-
fessionals come from all over the
world to sweep up the best buys.

Among the markets here the
Marché Jules Vallès is good for
turn-of-the-century *objets d'art.*
Marché Paul-Bert is more
expensive, but charming. Items on
sale include furniture, books and
prints. Both markets deal in second-
hand goods rather than antiques.

In a different league, Marché
Biron sells elegant, expensive
antique furniture of very high
quality. Marché Vernaison is the
oldest and biggest market, good
for collectables such as jewellery
as well as lamps and clothes. No
information about the Marché aux
Puces is complete without
mentioning Chez Louisette in the
Vernaison market. This café is
always full of locals enjoying the
home cooking and the well-
intentioned renditions of Edith
Piaf songs. Marché Cambo is a
fairly small market with beautifully-
displayed antique furniture.
Marché Serpette is popular with
the dealers: everything sold here is
in mint condition.

Marché Raspail

Situated on Blvd Raspail between Rue
du Cherche-Midi & Rue de Rennes
75006. **Map** 12 D5. **M** *Rennes
(closed Suns, use Sevres Babylone).*
◑ *7am–1pm Tue, Fri & Sun.*

The Raspail market sells typical
French groceries as well as
Portuguese produce on Tuesdays
and Fridays. But Sunday is the day
for which it's famous, when health-
conscious Parisians turn up in
droves for the organically-grown
produce. Marché Raspail is not a
cheap market, but it is very good.

Rue de Seine and Rue de Buci

75006. **Map** 12 E4. **M** *Odéon.*
◑ *8am– 1pm, 4pm–7pm Tue–Sat,
9am–1pm Sun.*

The stalls here are expensive and
crowded but sell quality fruit and
vegetables. There is also a large
florist's and two excellent
pâtisseries.

ENTERTAINMENT IN PARIS

WHETHER YOUR preference is for classical drama or cabaret, leggy show-girls or ballet, opera or jazz, cinema or dancing the night away, Paris has it all. There is plenty of free entertainment as well, from the street performers outside the Pompidou Centre to musicians busking in the metros and all over town.

Parisians themselves like nothing better than strolling along the boulevards or sitting at a pavement café and nursing a drink as they watch the world go by. If, however, you're looking for the ultimate "Gay Paree" experience, there are always the showgirls at the celebrated night-clubs.

For fans of spectator sports there is tennis, the Tour de France or horse racing. Recreation centres and gyms cater to the more active. And for those disposed either way, there's always the popular type of bowls played in Paris: *pétanque.*

PRACTICAL INFORMATION

FOR THE VISITOR in Paris there is no shortage of information about what's on offer in the city.

The **Office du Tourisme et des Congrés de Paris** is the city's main tourism distribution point for leaflets and schedules of events. There is a branch at the Gare de Lyon and at the Eiffel Tower. It has a recorded information telephone service giving details of free concerts and exhibitions along with information on transport to the venues. Its website is also useful. Your hotel reception desk or concierge should also be able to help. They usually keep a range of brochures and leaflets for guests and may even be happy to make reservations for you.

BOOKING TICKETS

DEPENDING ON the event, tickets can often be bought at the door, but for blockbuster concerts it is wiser, and often necessary, to book in advance. For most major events, including some classical music concerts and museum shows, tickets can be purchased at the **FNAC** chain or **Virgin Megastore**.

For dance, opera and theatre performances, very inexpensive tickets are often available up to the last minute. If they are marked *sans visibilité* you will be able to see the stage only partially, or perhaps not at all. Often, obliging ushers will put you in a better seat, depending on

Nightclubbing in Paris

availability, but don't forget to tip them a euro or two.

Theatre box offices are open daily from approximately 11am – 7pm (times vary). Most box offices accept credit card bookings made by telephone or in person. But you may have to arrive early to pick up your tickets if you booked by telephone, as they may be sold to someone else at the last minute.

Ballerina of the Ballet de l'Opéra

A concert at the Opéra de Paris Garnier (see p335)

LISTINGS MAGAZINES

Paris has several good listings magazines. Among them are *Pariscope,* the simplest to use, *L'Officiel des Spectacles* and *Sept à Paris.* They are published every Wednesday and are widely available. *Le Figaro* also has a good listings section on Wednesdays. Two English publications, *Paris Free Voice* and the quarterly *The City,* are both available at newsstands or **W H Smith** (see p329).

Buying tickets at the box office of a comedy club

You can always turn up at the box office just before the performance in case there are unclaimed or returned tickets.

TICKET TOUTS

IF YOU MUST HAVE a ticket to a sold-out performance, do as the French do: stand at the entrance with a sign that says *cherche une place* (or *deux*, etc). Many people have an extra ticket to sell. However, make sure you don't buy a counterfeit or overpriced one.

CUT-PRICE TICKETS

HALF-PRICE TICKETS to current plays are sold on the day of performance at Kiosque Théâtre. Credit cards are not accepted and a small commission is charged per ticket.

Pétanque players *(see p342)*

There is a booth on the Place de la Madeleine *(see p214)*, open from 12.30pm–8pm, Tuesday–Saturday, 12.30pm–4pm Sunday, and in the Parvis de la Gare Monparnasse 12.30–6pm Tuesday–Saturday.

DISABLED VISITORS' FACILITIES

WHERE FACILITIES do exist, they are either very good indeed or dreadful. Many venues have wheelchair space, but always phone in advance to make sure it is properly equipped. As far as public transport is concerned, the metro, with its long stairways, is completely inaccessible to wheelchairs, as are the buses.

LATE-NIGHT TRANSPORT

THE PARIS METRO *(see pp 368–9)* stops running at 1am. The last train leaves the end station at 12.45am, but to be sure of making any connections, be at the station by 12.30am at the latest.

From 1am–5.30am the choice is between night buses, Noctambus, which run once an hour and cover most of the city and the suburbs, or taxis. Taxis can be hailed on the street or found at a taxi rank, but at peak hours (and at 2am, when many bars close), they can be difficult or almost impossible to find.

USEFUL ADDRESSES

FNAC
Forum des Halles, 1 Rue Pierre-Lescot 75001. **Map** 13 A2. 🅒 *01 40 41 40 00.*

The Grand Rex cinema *(see p340)*

FNAC
26 Ave des Ternes 75017.
Map 4 D3. 🅒 *01 44 09 18 00.*
Plus other branches.

Office du Tourisme et des Congrès de Paris
127 Ave des Champs-Elysées 75008.
Map 4 E4. 🅵 *08 36 68 31 12.*
Ⓦ www.paris-touristoffice.com

Virgin Megastore
52–60 Ave des Champs-Elysées 75008. **Map** 4 F5.
🅒 *01 49 53 50 00.*

W H Smith
248 Rue de Rivoli 75001.
Map 11 C1.
🅒 *01 44 77 88 99.*

Theatre

FROM THE GRANDEUR OF the Comédie Française to slap-stick farce and avant-garde drama, theatre is flourishing in Paris. The city also has a long tradition of playing host to visiting companies, and today it attracts many foreign productions, often in the original languages.

Theatres are scattered at a multiplicity of locations throughout the city and the theatre season runs from September to July; national theatres close during August but many commercial ones stay open. For complete listings of what's on during your stay read *Pariscope* or *L'Officiel des Spectacles (see p328)*.

NATIONAL THEATRES

FOUNDED IN 1680 by royal decree, the **Comédie Française** *(see p120)*, with its strict conventions regarding the style of acting and interpretation, is the bastion of French theatre. Its aim is to keep classical drama in the public eye and also to per-form works by the best modern playwrights.

The Comédie Française is the oldest national theatre in the world and one of the few institutions of *ancien-régime* France to have survived the Revolution. It settled into its present home after players occupied the Palais-Royal next door during the Revo-lution. It was completely refurbished in the 1970s and now the traditionally-styled red velvet auditorium has a vast stage equipped with the latest technology.

The majority of the reper-toire is classical, dominated by Corneille, Racine and Molière, followed by second strings Marivaux, Alfred de Musset and Victor Hugo. The company also performs modern plays by French and foreign playwrights.

The **Odéon Théâtre de l'Europe**, also known as the Théâtre National de l'Odéon *(see p140)*, was at one time the second theatre of the Comédie Française. It now specializes in performing plays from other countries in their original languages.

Next door the **Petit Odéon** features new plays and those in foreign languages.

The **Théâtre National de Chaillot** is a huge under-ground auditorium in the Art Deco Palais de Chaillot *(see p198)*. It stages lively productions of mainstream European classics and, occasionally, musical revues. The theatre also contains a studio, the **Salle Gémier**, for more experimental work.

The **Théâtre National de la Colline** has two perfor-mance spaces and specializes in contemporary dramas.

FURTHER AFIELD

A THRIVING multi-theatre complex in the Bois de Vincennes, the **Cartoucherie** houses five separate avant-garde theatres including the internationally famous **Théâtre du Soleil.**

INDEPENDENT THEATRES

AMONG THE most important of the serious indepen-dents are the **Comédie des Champs-Elysées**, the **Hébertot** and the **Atelier**, which aims to be experi-mental. Other notable venues include the **Oeuvre**, for excellent modern French drama, the **Montparnasse** and the **Antoine-Simone Berriau** which pioneered the use of realism on stage. The **Madeleine** maintains consistently high standards and the **Huchette** specializes in Ionesco plays. The avant-garde producer/director Peter Brook has a loyal following at the **Bouffes-du-Nord**.

For over a hundred years the **Palais Royal** has been the temple of risqué farce. With fewer French Feydeau-style farce writers these days, translations of English and American sex comedies are filling the gap. Other notable venues include the **Bouffes-Parisiens**, **La Bruyère**, the **Michel** and the **St-Georges**. The **Gymnase-Marie Bell** presents popular one-man comedy shows.

CAFÉ-THEATRES AND CHANSONNIERS

THERE IS A LONG tradition of entertainment in cafés, but the café-theatres of today have nothing in common with the "café-concerts" of the turn of the century. These modern entertainments have originated because young actors and new playwrights could not find work, while drama students were unable to pay to hire out established theatres. Café-theatres rose to prominence during the 1960s and 1970s, when unknowns such as Coluche, Gérard Depardieu and Miou-Miou made their debut at the **Café de la Gare** before going on to success on the screen.

Good venues for seeing new talent include the **Café d'Edgar** and **Au Bec Fin**, while the **Lucernaire** stages more conventional fare. Traditional *chansonniers* – cabarets where ballads, folk songs and humour abound – include **Au Lapin Agile** *(see p233)*. Political satire is on offer at the **Caveau de la République** and the **Deux Anes** in Montmartre.

CHILDREN'S THEATRE

SOME PARIS THEATRES, such as the **Gymnase-Marie Bell**, the **Porte St-Martin** and the **Café d'Edgar**, have children's matinees on Wednesdays and weekends. In the city parks there are tiny puppet theatres (marionnettes), which are sure to delight children and adults alike. *(See Independent Theatres p331.)*

OPEN-AIR THEATRE

DURING THE summer, weather permitting, open-air performances of Shakespeare in French and classic French plays are given in the Shakespeare Garden in the Bois de Boulogne *(see p254)*.

ENGLISH-LANGUAGE THEATRE IN PARIS

THE ON STAGE Theatre Company and The Dear Conjunction Theatre are both Paris-based companies who perform in English (details in English pages of *Pariscope*).

STREET THEATRE

STREET THEATRE thrives during the summer. Jugglers, mime artists, fire-eaters and musicians can be seen mainly in tourist areas such as the Pompidou Centre *(see pp110–11)*, St-Germain-des-Prés and Les Halles.

BOOKING TICKETS

TICKETS CAN BE bought at the box office, by telephone or through theatre agencies. Box offices are open daily from about 11am–7pm; some accept credit card bookings by telephone or in person.

TICKET PRICES

TICKET PRICES range from 7€–30€ for the national theatres and 8€–38€ for the independents. Reduced-price tickets and student stand-bys are available in some theatres 15 minutes before curtain-up.

The Kiosque Théâtre offers half-price tickets on the day-of-performance: credit cards are not accepted and a small commission is charged for each ticket sold. There is a ticket booth in the Place de la Madeleine and one in the metro-RER station at Châtelet-Les Halles *(see p105)*.

DRESS

EVENING CLOTHES are now only worn to gala events at the Opéra de Paris Garnier, the Comédie Française or the grand premiere of an up-market play.

DIRECTORY

NATIONAL THEATRES

Comédie Française
Salle Richelieu, 2 Rue de Richelieu 75001. **Map** 12 E1. *01 44 58 15 15.*

Odéon Théâtre de l'Europe
(includes Petit Odéon)
Pl de l'Odéon 75006. **Map** 12 F5. *01 44 41 36 36.*

Théâtre National de Chaillot
(includes Salle Gémier)
Pl du Trocadéro 75016. **Map** 9 C2. *01 53 65 30 00.*

Théâtre National de la Colline
15 Rue Malte-Brun 75020. *01 44 62 52 52.*

FURTHER AFIELD

Cartoucherie
Route du Champ-de-Manoeuvre 75012.
Théâtre du Soleil *01 43 74 24 08.*

Théâtre de l'Aquarium *01 43 74 99 61*

Théâtre de l'Epee de Bois *01 48 08 39 74.*

Théâtre de la Tempete *01 43 28 36 36.*

Théâtre du Chaudron *01 43 28 97 04.*

INDEPENDENT THEATRES

Antoine-Simone Berriau
14 Blvd de Strasbourg 75010. **Map** 7 B5. *01 42 08 77 71 & 01 42 08 76 58.*

Atelier
Pl Charles Dullin 75018. **Map** 6 F2. *01 46 06 49 24.*

Bouffes-du-Nord
37 bis Blvd de la Chapelle 75010. **Map** 7 C1. *01 46 07 34 50.*

Bouffes-Parisiens
4 Rue Monsigny 75002. **Map** 6 E5. *01 42 96 92 42.*

La Bruyère
5 Rue La Bruyère 75009. **Map** 6 E3. *01 48 74 76 99.*

Comédie des Champs-Elysées
15 Ave Montaigne 75008. **Map** 10 F1. *01 53 23 99 19.*

Gymnase-Marie Bell
38 Blvd Bonne-Nouvelle 75010. **Map** 7 A5. *01 42 46 79 79.*

Hébertot
78 bis Blvd des Batignolles 75017. **Map** 5 B2. *01 43 87 23 23.*

Huchette
23 Rue de la Huchette 75005. **Map** 13 A4. *01 43 26 38 99.*

Madeleine
19 Rue de Surène 75008. **Map** 5 C5. *01 42 65 07 09.*

Michel
38 Rue des Mathurins 75008. **Map** 5 C4. *01 42 65 35 02.*

Montparnasse
31 Rue de la Gaîté 75014. **Map** 15 C2. *01 43 22 77 74.*

Oeuvre
55 Rue de Clichy 75009. **Map** 6 D2. *01 44 53 88 80.*

Palais Royal
38 Rue Montpensier 75001. **Map** 12 E1. *01 42 97 59 81 & 01 42 97 59 85.*

Porte St-Martin
16 Blvd St-Martin 75010. **Map** 7 C5. *01 42 08 00 32.*

St-Georges
51 Rue St-Georges 75009. Map 6 E3. *01 48 78 63 47.*

CAFÉ-THEATRES AND CHANSONNIERS

Au Bec Fin
6 Rue Thérèse 75001. **Map** 12 E1. *01 42 96 29 35.*

Au Lapin Agile
22 Rue des Saules 75018. **Map** 2 F5. *01 46 06 85 87.*

Café d'Edgar
58 Blvd Edgar-Quinet 75014. **Map** 16 D2. *01 42 79 97 97.*

Café de la Gare
41 Rue du Temple 75004. **Map** 13 B2. *01 42 78 52 51.*

Caveau de la République
1 Blvd St-Martin 75003. **Map** 8 D5. *01 42 78 44 45.*

Deux Anes
100 Blvd de Clichy 75018. **Map** 6 D1. *01 46 06 10 26.*

Lucernaire
53 Rue Notre-Dame-des-Champs 75006. **Map** 16 D1. *01 45 44 57 34.*

Classical Music

THE MUSIC SCENE in Paris has never been so busy. Government spending has ensured that there are many first-class venues with an excellent range of opera, and classical and contemporary music productions. There are also numerous concerts in churches and many music festivals.

Information about what's on is listed in *Pariscope*, *Zurban* and *L'Officiel des Spectacles*. A free monthly listing of musical events is given out at most concert halls. Also, try the Office du Tourisme et des Congrès de Paris *(see pp328–9)* for details of many free and open-air classical music performances.

OPERA

OPERA LOVERS will find themselves well catered for, with many productions mounted at the Bastille and the beautifully renovated **Opéra Garnier**. Opera is also an important part of the programming at the Théâtre du Châtelet, as well as being produced intermittently by a variety of small organizations, and there are occasional large-scale lavish productions at the Palais d'Omnisports de Bercy (POB – *see p343*).

The Opéra de Paris's ultra-modern home is the **Opéra de Paris Bastille** *(see p98)*, where performances have finally begun to make full use of the house's mind-boggling array of high-tech stage mechanisms. There are 2,700 seats, all with a good view of the stage, and the accoustics are excellent.

Productions feature classic and modern operas, and its interpretations are often avant-garde: Philippe Mamoury's *K...*; Bob Wilson's production of *The Magic Flute,* done in the style of Japanese Noh, with some of the cast delivering their lines while balancing on one leg; Messiaen's *St Francis of Assisi*, with video screens and neon added to bring the story up to date.

There are also occasional dance performances, when the Bastille plays host to the ballet company from the Opéra de Paris Garnier *(see p215)*. The house includes two smaller spaces, the **Auditorium** (500 seats) and the **Studio** (200 seats) for smaller-scale events connected to the current

productions on the main stages here and at the Opera Garnier.

The **Opéra Comique** (also known as the Salle Favart) sadly no longer has any opera. It is now run by Jérôme Savary, and stages a wide range of eccentric, lightweight productions, including some popular music-hall-style work.

CONCERTS

PARIS IS THE HOME of three major symphony orchestras, and a good half-dozen other orchestras; it is also a major venue for European and American orchestras on tour. Chamber music is also flourishing, either as part of the programming of the major venues, or in smaller halls and churches.

The **Salle Pleyel** is Paris's principal concert hall, with 2,300 seats, and was, until recently, the home of the Orchestre de Paris (now at the Théâtre Mogador). Its season runs from October to June, with an average of two concerts a week. The Salle Pleyel is also the main base of the Ensemble Orchestral de Paris and such reputable orchestral associations as the Lamoureux, the Pasdeloup and the Colonne, which organize concert seasons from October to Easter. The building also includes two smaller halls for chamber music, the Salle Chopin (470 seats) and the Salle Debussy (120 seats).

Over the last few years the **Théâtre du Châtelet** has become one of the city's principal venues for all kinds of concerts, opera and dance.

The high-quality programme includes opera classics from Mozart's *Così fan tutte* to Verdi's *La Traviata*, and more modern works, such as Boessman's *Contes d'Hiver*, and occasional concerts by international opera stars. Great attention is also devoted to 20th-century music here, and throughout the season there are lunchtime concerts and recitals in the foyer.

The beautiful Art Deco **Théâtre des Champs-Elysées** is a celebrated classical music venue which also produces some opera and dance. Radio-France is part-owner of the theatre, and its Orchestre National de France gives concerts here, as do many touring orchestras and soloists. The Orchestre de Champs-Elysées, directed by Philippe Herreweghe, is in residence here, and gives period-instrument performances. There are also other concerts ranging from Baroque to 20th-century music, and the Concerts du Dimanche Matin organization stages excellent concerts, mostly chamber music, on Sundays at 11am.

Radio-France is the biggest single concert organizer in Paris, with a musical force that includes two major symphony orchestras: the Orchestre National de France and the Orchestre Philharmonique. Many of its concerts are given in Paris's other concert halls, but the **Maison de Radio-France** has a large hall and several smaller studios that are used for concerts and broadcasts open to the public *(see p200, Musée de Radio France)*.

The **Salle Gaveau** is a medium-sized concert hall with a busy schedule of chamber music and recitals.

The **Auditorium du Louvre** was built as part of the ongoing expansion of the Louvre *(see pp122–9)* and it is used mostly for chamber music recitals.

The **Auditorium du Musée d'Orsay** is a medium-sized auditorium, with an active concert programme, at the Musée d'Orsay *(see pp144–7)*. Lunchtime concerts are free with museum tickets; evening concerts have varying prices.

Other museums often stage concerts as part of an exhibition theme – such as troubadours at the Musée de Cluny *(see p154–7)* – so check the listings magazines to see what's on.

The Musique à la Sorbonne organization puts on a concert series in the **Grand Amphithéâtre de la Sorbonne** and the **Amphithéâtre Richelieu de la Sorbonne**. Productions have included the Slavonic Music festival, featuring the works of East European composers.

Occasionally concerts are given in the **Conservatoire d'Art Dramatique**, where Ludwig van Beethoven was introduced to Paris audiences in 1828 and where Hector Berlioz's major work, *La Symphonie Fantastique*, was first performed. Otherwise, it is not usually open to the general public.

For something slightly different, the **New Opus Café** is a stylish cocktail bar where string quartets play classical music – see *Pariscope* for details of its current schedule.

CONTEMPORARY MUSIC

CONTEMPORARY MUSIC in Paris has a high profile and is definitely alive and kicking. Although no longer at the head of any orchestra, Pierre Boulez remains a major figure in the capital's contemporary music scene. Jonathan Nott now directs the experimental Ensemble InterContemporain, which continues to be lavishly supported by the French state in its home at the Cité de la Musique *(see pp234–5)*.

IRCAM, the vast laboratory of 'digital signal processing' underneath the Pompidou Centre, is still the envy of the world.

Other bright stars among the host of talented composers include Pascal Dusapin, Philippe Fénelon, George Benjamin and Philippe Manoury, as well as

Georges Aperghis, who specializes in musical theatre.

The newly-completed and fabulously-designed **Cité de la Musique** complex at Parc de la Villette includes both a spectacularly-domed *salle de concerts* surrounded by a glass-roofed arcade, and the **Conservatoire National de Musique** with its opera theatre and two small concert halls. The Chamber Orchestra of Europe is in residence here. Both venues are used for regular performances of all sorts of music, including jazz, ethnic and contemporary music, as well as *chansons* and early music.

For concert details either phone the venue concerned or consult the usual listings magazines. For those with a serious interest in contemporary music, the quarterly magazine *Résonance* is published by IRCAM at the Pompidou Centre.

FESTIVALS

SOME OF THE MOST important music festivals come about as a result of the work of the **Festival d'Automne à Paris**, which is not so much a series of performances as a behind the scenes simulator: commissioning new works, subsidizing others and in general enlivening the Parisian musical, dance and theatrical scene from September to December.

The **Festival St-Denis** running throughout June and July holds concerts, with an emphasis on large-scale choral works. Most performances are given in the Basilique St-Denis.

The **Musique Baroque au Château de Versailles** begins around the middle of September and runs through to the middle of October. It is an offshoot of the Baroque Music Centre, founded in Versailles in 1988. Operas, concerts, recitals, chamber music, dance and theatre are on offer in the fabulous surroundings of Versailles *(see pp248–53)*.

For tickets it is usually necessary to go to the box office of the theatre or

venue concerned, though some festivals may run an advance postal booking service.

CHURCHES

MUSIC IS everywhere in Paris's churches, in the form of classical concerts, organ recitals or religious services. Among the most outstanding of all the churches which hold regular concerts are **La Madeleine** *(see p214)*, **St-Germain-des-Prés** *(see p138)*, **St-Julien-le-Pauvre** *(see p152)* and **St-Roch** *(see p121)*. Music is also performed in the **Eglise des Billettes**, **St-Sulpice** *(see p172)*, **St-Gervais–St-Protais** *(see p99)*, **Notre-Dame** *(see pp82–5)*, **St-Louis-en-l'Ile** *(see p87)* and **Sainte-Chapelle** *(see pp88–9)*.

Some, but not all, of these concerts are free. If you have difficulty contacting the church in question, try the Office du Tourisme et des Congrès de Paris for information *(see pp328–9)*.

EARLY MUSIC

A NUMBER OF early-music ensembles have taken up residence in Paris. The Chapelle Royale give a concert series at the **Théâtre des Champs-Elysées** with programmes ranging from Renaissance vocal music to Mozart. Their sacred music concerts (look out for Bach cantatas) take place in the **Notre-Dame des Blancs Manteaux** *(see p102)*.

Baroque opera is more the domain of Les Arts Florissants, founded and directed by American-born William Christie, who perform French and Italian operas from Rossi to Rameau, and Les Musiciens du Louvre, directed by Marc Minkowski. Both companies perform regularly at the Théâtre du Châtelet and the Opera Garnier.

The **Théâtre de la Ville** and the charming rococo 1900's **Théâtre du Musée Grévin** *(see p216)*, are both venues for Baroque chamber music.

BOOKING TICKETS

For tickets, dealing directly with the relevant box office is almost always the best bet. Booking tickets at the main venues is possible by post up to two months before the performance and by telephone two weeks to one month in advance. If you want to be assured of a good seat, it is always best to book in advance as tickets tend to sell quickly.

Last-minute tickets may also be available at the box office, and certain venues, such as the Opéra de Paris Bastille,

keep a certain number of tickets for the cheaper seats aside for the purpose.

Ticket agents, notably in the FNAC stores (see p329), and a good hotel concierge may also be able to help. These agencies will accept credit card bookings – a useful service as not all venues are guaranteed to accept them.

Half-price tickets on the day of performance can be bought at the Kiosque Théâtre (see p329) which is found in the Place de la Madeleine and also at the RER station at Parvis de la Gare Montparnasse. However,

these agencies usually only deal for performances taking place at private theatres.

Note, however, that many theatres and concert halls may be closed during the holiday season in August, so inquire first to avoid disappointment.

TICKET PRICES

Ticket prices can range from 8€–85€ for the Opéra de Paris Bastille and the principal classical music venues, and from 5€–25€ for the smaller halls and concerts in churches, such as Sainte-Chapelle.

CLASSICAL MUSIC VENUES

Amphithéâtre Richelieu de la Sorbonne
17 Rue de la Sorbonne 75005. Map 12 F5.
01 42 62 71 71.

Auditorium
See Opéra de Paris Bastille.

Auditorium du Louvre
Musée du Louvre, Rue de Rivoli 75001. Map 12 E2.
01 40 20 52 29.

Auditorium du Musée d'Orsay
102 Rue de Lille 75007. Map 12 D2.
01 40 49 49 66.

Cité de la Musique
Parc de La Villette, 221 Ave Jean-Jaurès 75019. 01 44 84 44 84
w www.cite-musique.fr

Conservatoire d'Art Dramatique
2 bis Rue du Conservatoire 75009. Map 7 A4.
01 42 46 12 91.

Eglise des Billettes
24 Rue des Archives 75004. Map 13 C2.
01 42 72 38 79.

Festival d'Automne à Paris
156 Rue de Rivoli 75001. Map 12 F2.5
01 53 45 17 00.

Festival de St-Denis
6 Pl Legion d'Honneur 93200 St-Denis. Map 15 C3. 01 48 13 12 12.

Grand Amphithéâtre de la Sorbonne
47 Rue des Ecoles 75005. Map 13 A5.
01 42 62 71 71.

IRCAM
1 Pl Igor Stravinsky 75004. Map 13 B2.
01 44 78 48 43.

La Madeleine
14 Rue Surène 75008. Map 5 C5.
01 44 51 69 00.

Maison de Radio-France
116 Ave du Président-Kennedy 75016. Map 9 B4.
01 56 40 15 16.

Musique Baroque au Château de Versailles
Château de Versailles, Chapelle Royal, 78000 Versailles 01 30 83 78 00.

Notre-Dame
Pl du Parvis-Notre-Dame. Map 13 A4.
01 42 34 56 10.

Notre-Dame-des Blancs-Manteaux
12 Rue des Blancs-Manteaux 75004. Map 13 A4.
01 42 72 09 37.

Opéra Comique
(Salle Favart)
5 Rue Favart 75002. Map 6 F5.
01 42 44 45 46.

Opéra de Paris Bastille
120 Rue de Lyon 75012. Map 14 E4.
08 36 69 78 68.
w www.opera-de-paris.fr

Opéra de Paris Garnier
Place de l'Opéra 75009. Map 6 E4.
01 40 01 22 63.

Opus Café
167 Quai de Valmy 75010. Map 8 D3.
01 40 34 70 00

Pompidou Centre
Plateau Beaubourg 75004. Map 13 B2.
01 44 78 12 33.

Sainte-Chapelle
4 Blvd du Palais. Map 13 A3.
01 53 73 78 50.

St-Germain-des-Prés
Pl St-Germain-des-Prés 75006. Map 12 E4.
01 43 25 41 71.

St-Gervais–St-Protais
Pl St-Gervais 75004. Map 13 B3.
01 48 87 32 02.

St-Julien-le-Pauvre
1 Rue St-Julien-le-Pauvre 75005. Map 13 A4.
01 42 26 00 00.

St-Louis-en-l'Ile
19 bis Rue St-Louis-en-l'Ile 75004. Map 13 C5.
01 46 34 11 60.

St-Roch
296 Rue St-Honoré 75001. Map 12 D1.
01 42 44 13 20.

St-Sulpice
Pl St-Sulpice 75006. Map 12 E4.
01 46 33 21 78.

Salle Gaveau
45 Rue La Boétie 75008. Map 5 B4.
01 49 53 05 07.

Salle Pleyel
252 Rue du Faubourg St-Honoré 75008. Map 4 E3.
01 45 61 53 00.

Studio
See Opéra de Paris Bastille.

Théâtre de la Ville
2 Pl du Châtelet 75004. Map 13 A3.
01 42 74 22 77.

Théâtre des Champs-Élysées
15 Ave Montaigne 75008. Map 10 F1.
01 49 52 50 50

Théâtre du Châtelet
Pl du Châtelet 75001. Map 13 A3.
01 40 28 28 40.

Théâtre du Musée Grévin
10 Blvd Montmartre 75009. Map 6 F4.
01 47 70 85 05.

Dance

WHEN IT COMES to dance, Paris is more a cultural crossroads than a cultural centre. Due to a deliberate government policy of decentralization, many of the top French dance companies are based in the provinces, but they frequently visit the capital. In addition, the greatest dance companies from all over the world perform here. The French are very vocal in their appreciation or dislike of dance performances, and those who fail to please are subjected to boos, hisses and mass walk-outs in mid-performance.

CLASSICAL BALLET

THE OPULENT **Opéra de Paris Garnier** *(see p215)* is the home of the Ballet de l'Opéra de Paris, which is earning a reputation as one of the world's best classical dance companies.

Since the Opéra de Paris Bastille opened in 1989, the Opéra de Paris Garnier has been used almost exclusively for dance. It is one of the largest theatres in Europe, with performance space for 450 artists and a seating capacity of 2,200.

Modern dance companies such as the Martha Graham Company, Paul Taylor, Merce Cunningham, Alvin Ailey, Jerome Robbins and Roland Petit's Ballet de Marseille also regularly perform here.

The Opéra de Paris Garnier, extensively restored both inside and out, now shares operatic productions with the **Opera de Paris Bastille**.

MODERN DANCE

GOVERNMENT SUPPORT has helped the **Théâtre de la Ville** (once run by Sarah Bernhardt) to become Paris's most important venue for modern dance, with subsidies keeping ticket costs relatively low. Through performances at the Théâtre de la Ville, modern choreographers such as Jean-Claude Gallotta, Regine Chopinot, Maguy Marin and Anne Teresa de Keersmaeker have gained international recognition. Here you may also see troupes such as Pina Bausch's Wuppertal Dance Theatre, whose tormented, existential choreography may not be to everyone's taste, but is always popular with Parisian audiences.

Music performances also run throughout the season and include chamber music, recitals, world music and jazz.

The **Maison des Arts de Créteil** presents some of the most interesting dance works in Paris. It is located in the Paris suburb of Créteil, where the local council gives strong support to dance. Créteil's company choreographer, Maguy Marin, has won consistent praise for her darkly expressive work.

The Maison des Arts also brings in such innovative companies as the Sydney Ballet, and the Kirov from St Petersburg which is more inclined towards the classical.

Set amid the opulent couture shops and embassies, the elegant Art Deco **Théâtre des Champs-Élysées** has 1,900 seats. It is frequented by an upmarket audience who watch major international companies perform here. It was here that Nijinsky first danced Stravinsky's iconoclastic *The Rite Of Spring*, which led to rioting among the audience.

The theatre is more famous as a classical music venue, but recent visitors have included the Harlem Dance Company and London's Royal Ballet, and it is here that Mikhail Baryshnikov and American choreographer Mark Morris perform when they are in Paris. It also sponsors the popular *Géants de la Danse* series, an evening-length sampling of international ballet.

The lovely old **Théâtre du Châtelet** is a renowned opera and classical music venue, but it is also host to international contemporary dance companies such as the Tokyo Ballet and the Birmingham Royal Ballet.

Experimental dance companies perform in the **Théâtre de la Bastille**, where innovative theatre is also staged. Many directors and companies start here, then go on to international fame.

New companies to look out for include La P'tit Cie and L'Esquisse, but they have no fixed venue.

EVENTS LISTINGS

TO FIND OUT what's on, read the inexpensive weekly entertainment guides *Pariscope* and *L'Officiel des Spectacles*. Posters advertising dance performances are widely displayed in the metros and on the streets, especially on the green advertisement columns, the *colonnes Morris*.

TICKET PRICES

EXPECT TO PAY 10€–100€ for tickets to an opera at the Opéra de Paris Garnier (5€–60€ for a ballet), 6€–75€ for the Théâtre des Champs-Élysées, and anything from 9€–27€ for other venues.

DANCE VENUES

Maison des Arts et de la Culture de Créteil
Pl Salvador Allende 94000 Créteil.
📞 01 45 13 19 19.

Opéra de Paris Palais Garnier
See pp214–5.

Opéra de Paris Bastille
See p98.

Théâtre de la Bastille
76 Rue de la Roquette 75011.
Map 14 F3.
📞 01 43 57 42 14.

Théâtre de la Ville
See p334.

Théâtre des Champs-Elysées
See p334.

Théâtre du Châtelet
See p334.

Rock, Jazz and World Music

Music lovers will find every imaginable form of music in Paris and the surrounding areas, from international pop stars in major venues to talented buskers in the metro. There's a huge variety of styles on offer, with reggae, hip-hop, world music, blues, folk, rock and jazz – Paris is said to be second only to New York in the number of jazz clubs and jazz recordings and there is always an excellent selection of bands and solo performers.

On the summer solstice (21 June) each year, the *Fête de la Musique* takes place. This is the one day of the year when anyone can play any form of music, anywhere in Paris, without a licence. Ears may be assailed by a heavy metal rock band or lulled by an accordionist playing traditional French songs.

For complete listings of what's happening during your visit, buy *Pariscope* (published every Wednesday) at any kiosk. Jazz aficionados should read the monthly *Jazz* magazine for lists of schedules and in-depth reviews.

MAJOR VENUES

The top international acts are often at the enormous arenas: **Palais d'Omnisports** at Bercy, **Stade de France** at St-Denis (*see Directory p343*) or the **Zénith**. Other venues like the legendary *chanson* centre of the universe, the **Olympia**, or the **Grand Rex** (also a cinema), have assigned seating and a more intimate atmosphere. They host everyone from bewigged and cosmetically enhanced iconic first ladies of country to acid jazz stars.

ROCK AND POP

Paris's indigenous rock groups like Les Negresses Vertes, Noir Désir and Mano Negra have enjoyed some international popularity. They play raucous French pop, a cross between rock and street music. Multi-ethnic youngsters from the *banlieue* (suburbs) are forming French-language rap groups, including Alliance Ethnique, NTM and MC Solaar. Although they strive for hard-edged rebelliousness, few have emerged from a ghetto and they seem very innocent when compared with their authentic American counterparts.

Some of the best French pop singers are Françis Cabrel, Michel Jonasz, the beautiful and gifted Vanessa Paradis, Julien Clerc and blues man Paul Personne. Local group Rita Mitsouko still gathers acclaim with her curious musical hybrid of rock, electro, *chanson*, Latin and scratch. Visitors might want to catch the many foreign groups passing through town. The young frequent the converted cinema of **La Cigale**, **Elysée-Montmartre**.

For rock, rhythm and blues, go to the **Cithéa**. The pagoda-fronted **Bataclan** and the **Rex Club** are the best venues for hearing an eclectic selection of acts. Ever since the Beatles blew the roof off the **Olympia** in 1964, the major names on both the British and the American pop scenes have customarily regarded Paris as a must-play city, so it is always worth checking out who's in town. Many Paris nightclubs also double up as live music venues (*see pp338–9*).

JAZZ

Jazz-crazy Paris has innumerable packed clubs where the best talent can be heard any evening. Many American musicians have made the French capital their home because of the receptive atmosphere here. All styles, from free-form to Dixieland and swing, and even hiphop-jazz crossover, are on offer. Clubs range from quasi-concert halls to piano bars and pub-like venues. One of the most popular places, though more for the quality of the talent it attracts than for its comfortable ambience, is the **New Morning**. It's hot and smoky, and the table service is dreadful, but all the great jazz musicians have performed here. Arrive early to ensure a good seat. **Le Duc des Lombards** is a lively jazz club in Les Halles which also features salsa.

Many jazz clubs are also cafés, bars or restaurants. The latter includes the intimate **Bilboquet**, with its Belle Epoque interior. This is a stylish place favoured by film stars; downstairs is the disco **Club St-Germain**. Dining might not be a requirement, but check first.

Other jazz hotspots are **Le Petit Journal Montparnasse** for modern jazz, **Le Petit Journal St-Michel** for Dixieland and the **Sunset**. **Le Petit Opportun** is a tiny club (only 60 seats) with an excellent reputation. The **Café de la Plage** in the Bastille plays a variety of music to a trendy crowd. **Caveau de la Huchette** looks like the archetypal jazz joint but is no longer the leader of the jazz scene. Nowadays it favours swing and big-band music, and is popular with students.

For a change from smoke-filled basement clubs, try the local talent at small, friendly bars like the **Eustache**, which is less expensive than most, or the trendy **China Club**, with its 1940s *film noir* decor. The **Jazz-Club Lionel Hampton** in the Méridien hotel is a well-respected venue which features Sunday jazz brunch.

If you're in Paris in July, don't miss the annual JVC Halle That Jazz festival at the **Grande Halle de la Villette** where jazz stars, such as Grover Washington Jr, Fats Domino and B B King play. There are also films on jazz and *boeufs* (jam sessions) with all the top musicians taking part. The Paris Jazz Festival (May–July) also draws major international musicians to the Parc Floral.

The **Slow Club**, with its rocking couple neon sign, features swinging jazz and a dance-happy crowd showing off their talents.

WORLD MUSIC

Paris, with its large populations from West Africa and the countries of the Maghreb, the Antilles and Latin America, is a natural centre for world music. The excellent **Chapelle des Lombards** has played host to top acts; it also has jazz, salsa and Brazilian music with dancing until dawn. **Aux Trois Mailletz** is a medieval cellar with everything from blues to tango and rock and roll covers.

Many jazz clubs also intersperse their programmes with ethnic music. **New Morning** has African, Brazilian and other sounds, **Café de la Plage** mixes reggae and salsa and **Baiser Salé** has everything from blues to Brazilian music. Popular acts to catch include Makossa, Kassav, Malavoi and Manu Dibango.

TICKET PRICES

Prices at paris jazz clubs can be steep, and there may be a cover charge of over 15€ at the door, which usually pays for the first drink. If there is no cover charge, it is likely that drinks will be expensive and at least one must be bought.

BUYING TICKETS

Tickets to most events can be bought from FNAC outlets and Virgin Megastore *(see p329)*, or directly from venue box offices and at the door of the clubs themselves.

DIRECTORY

MAJOR VENUES

Grand Rex
5 Blvd Poissonnière
75002. **Map** 7 A5.
☎ 01 45 08 93 89.

Olympia
28 Blvd des Capucines
75009. **Map** 6 D5.
☎ 01 55 27 10 00.

Palais d'Omnisports de Paris-Bercy
8 Blvd de Bercy 75012.
Map 18 F2.
☎ 08 03 03 00 31.

Zénith
211 Ave de Jean-Jaurès
75019.
☎ 01 42 08 60 00.

ROCK AND POP

Bataclan
50 Blvd Voltaire 75011.
Map 14 E1.
☎ 01 43 14 35 35.

La Cigale
120 Blvd Rochechouart
75018. **Map** 6 F2.
☎ 01 42 23 15 15.

Cithéa
114 Rue Oberkampf
75011. **Map** 14 E1.
☎ 01 40 21 70 95.

Elysée-Montmartre
72 Blvd Rochechouart
75018. **Map** 6 F2.
☎ 01 44 92 45 45.

Rex Club
5 Blvd Poissonnière
75002.
Map 7 A5.
☎ 01 42 36 83 98.

JAZZ

Baiser Salé
58 Rue des Lombards
75001.
Map 13 A2.
☎ 01 42 33 37 71.

Bilboquet
13 Rue St-Benoît 75006.
Map 12 E3.
☎ 01 45 48 81 84.

Café de la Plage
47 Rue de Charonne
75011.
Map 14 F4.
☎ 01 47 00 04 81.

Caveau de la Huchette
5 Rue de la Huchette
75005.
Map 13 A4.
☎ 01 43 26 65 05.

China Club
50 Rue de Charenton
75012.
Map 14 F5.
☎ 01 43 43 82 02.

Club St-Germain
See Bilboquet.

Le Duc des Lombards
42 Rue des Lombards
75001.
Map 13 A2.
☎ 01 42 33 22 88.

Eustache
37 Rue Berger, Carré des
Halles 75001.
Map 13 A2.
☎ 01 40 26 23 20.

La Grande Halle de la Villette
211 Ave Jean-Jaurès 75019.
Map 8 F1
☎ 01 40 03 75 03.

Jazz-Club Lionel Hampton
Hôtel Méridien, 81 Blvd
Gouvion-St-Cyr 75017.
Map 3 C3.
☎ 01 40 68 30 42.

New Morning
7–9 Rue des Petites-
Écuries 75010.
Map 7 B4.
☎ 01 45 23 51 41.

Le Petit Journal Montparnasse
13 Rue du Commandant-
Mouchotte 75014.
Map 15 C2.
☎ 01 43 21 56 70.

Le Petit Journal St-Michel
71 Blvd St-Michel 75005.
Map 16 F1.
☎ 01 43 26 28 59.

Le Petit Opportun
15 Rue des Lavandières-
Ste-Opportune 75001.
Map 13 A3.
☎ 01 42 36 01 36.

Slow Club
130 Rue de Rivoli 75001.
Map 13 A2.
☎ 01 42 33 84 30.

Sunset
60 Rue des Lombards
75001. **Map** 13 A2.
☎ 01 40 26 46 60.

WORLD MUSIC

Aux Trois Mailletz
56 Rue Galande 75005.
Map 13 A4.
☎ 01 43 54 42 94.

Baiser Salé
See Jazz.

Café de la Plage
See Jazz.

Chapelle des Lombards
19 Rue de Lappe 75011.
Map 14 F4.
☎ 01 43 57 24 24.

New Morning
See Jazz.

Sunset
60 Rue des Lombards
75001. **Map** 13 A2.
☎ 01 40 26 46 60.

Discotheques and Nightclubs

MUSIC IN PARIS CLUBS TENDS to follow trends set in America and Britain. In Paris the locals dance *le rock*, a well-studied version of the classic 1950s rock and roll dance. Only a few clubs such as **Balajo** and **Folies Pigalle** are genuinely up-to-the-minute. Clubs in Paris tend to be fairly well established: places like **Les Bains** have been around for years, riding the rollercoaster of popularity but managing to keep a faithful clientele.

Le Figaro's weekly entertainment supplement, *7 à Paris* and *Pariscope* list up-to-the-minute information, with opening times and brief descriptions of club nights. Alternatively, read the posters at the Bastille metro station or listen to Radio NOVA 101.5 FM, which gives details of the night's best raves.

Other popular night-time options include ballroom dancing and piano bars. If you're wondering about what to wear, remember that most Parisians tend to dress up when going out on the town.

MAINSTREAM

A VAST YET CONVIVIAL venue, **Le Bataclan** is a showcase for current bands. After the show on Saturday nights, it becomes the trendiest nightclub in Paris, legendary for its mouth-watering choice of funk, soul and new jack swing.

Club 79 is lively and a "retro"-orientated disco; the inexpensive **La Scala** attracts a large, young crowd, while adventurous whirling hedonists roller skate to rap and rock at **La Main Jaune**.

Les Bains, one-time Turkish bath, is the "glamma" nightspot for fashion and show business people; its upstairs restaurant, now serving Thai food, is a popular place for private dinner parties. The dance floor is tiny and music is mainly house, with 70s and 80s disco on Mondays, and R&B on Wednesdays. Gay night is *Café con Leche* on Sundays.

Advertising executives and film-makers frequent the **Rex Club**. Music on different nights ranges from glam rock and house to "exotique": funk, reggae and world music. Sounds are mainly rock and roll at the smart and non-ageist **Zed Club**. The vast **La Locomotive** caters to mainstream tastes most nights, with rock, house, groove and dance music each occupying a different floor.

EXCLUSIVE

B EING RICH, BEAUTIFUL and famous may not be enough to get you into **Castel's**, but it could help. It is a strictly private club and the happy few who make it, dine in one of two very good restaurants before heading down to the dance floor.

Regine's is mostly full of be-suited executives and wealthy foreigners who dine and dance to the easy-listening music.

The wood-panelled, cosy **Ritz Club** in the legendary Ritz hotel is open only to members and hotel guests, though the chic and elegant are welcome. The ambience is upmarket and the music is easy listening.

TRENDY

O NCE A WORKING-CLASS music hall frequented by famous Parisians Edith Piaf and Jean Gabin, **Balajo** has now gone upmarket but is still one of the best clubs in Paris for dancing, and one of the few open on Mondays. It also holds ballroom dancing nights.

An ultra-hip young crowd flock to the small and cosy **Folie's Clubbing**, one-time strip joint and present day venue for live music. Its original theme nights make for some of the best fun clubbing around. For a top dancing night out try the fortnightly *Bal* with live big band at the

Elysée Montmartre. Here too look out for *Return to the Source*, Goa-trance nights all the way from London's Fridge.

WORLD MUSIC

A STYLISH AND expensive African-Antillean club, **Keur Samba** is popular with the African jet-set. Things get going after 2am and last long into the night. **Le Casbah** is exclusive, jazzy and one of the best established venues on the Paris club scene. Its African-Middle Eastern decor has always been a magnet for models and trendies who, in between dances, do a little night shopping in the club's downstairs boutique. Le Casbah is currently enjoying something of a renaissance of its chicest of the chic reputation.

If your nervous system responds favourably to the heaving rhythms and throbbing beat of authentic Latin music, you should head for **La Java** which combines glorious sounds with the quaint appeal of a Belleville dance hall.

Other lively world music nights are held at **Trottoirs de Buenos-Aires**, **Chapelle des Lombards** and the cellar bar at **Aux Trois Mailletz** (*see Rock, Jazz and World Music pp336–7*).

GAY AND LESBIAN

A HUGE GAY CLUB, **Le Queen** boasts a great line-up of DJs. Monday is disco night, Friday and Saturday are garage and soul and the rest of the week is drum and bass and house. Some of the raunchier events are men-only. Girls should go with pretty boys. Sunday nights at **La Locomotive** are the *Gay Tea Dance* which has moved from the now bankrupt Le Palace. Wednesday is *Respect*, formally of Le Queen. Lesbian club **Christhom** is a re-named, glamorous version of what used to be L'Entreacte. *Lounge* on Wednesday is cocktails, easy-listening and cabaret, while Thursday is house and disco. *Scream* is the gay night at the **Elysée Montmartre**.

CABARET

T HE MUSIC HALL revue is the entertainment form most associated with turn-of-the-century Paris. It evokes images of bohemian artists and champagne-induced debauchery. Nowadays, most of the girls are likely to be American and the audience is made up mainly of foreign businessmen and tour groups.

When it comes to picking a cabaret the rule of thumb is simple: the better-known places are the best. Lesser-known cabaret shows resemble nothing so much as Grade-B strip shows. All of the cabarets listed here guarantee topless women sporting outrageous feather- and sequin-encrusted headpieces, an assortment of vaudeville acts and, depending on your point of view, a spectacularly entertaining evening or an exercise in high kitsch.

The **Lido** is the most Las Vegas-like of the cabarets and stars the legendary Bluebell Girls. The **Folies-Bergères** is renowned for lively entertainment. It is the oldest music hall in Paris and probably the most famous in the world.

The **Crazy Horse Saloon** features some of the more risqué costumes and performances, and dancers with names such as Betty Buttocks, Fila Volcana and Nouka Bazooka. It has been transformed from its Wild West bar-room into a jewel-box theatre with a champagne bucket fastened to each seat. Here the lowly strip-tease of burlesque shows has been refined into a vehicle for comedy sketches and international beauties.

Paradis Latin is the most "French" of all the city's cabaret shows. It has variety acts with remarkable special effects and scenery in a beautiful, old Left Bank theatre, partially designed by Gustave Eiffel.

The **Don Camillo Rive Gauche** has more elegant, less touristy shows, with excellent *chanson* singers, comedians and other variety acts. The **Moulin Rouge** *(see p226)*, once the haunt of Toulouse-Lautrec, is the birthplace of the cancan. Outrageously camp, transvestite parodies of these showgirl reviews can be seen at **Chez Madame Arthur**.

ADMISSION CHARGES

S OME CLUBS are strictly private, others have a more generous admission policy. Prices can range from about 12€ to 15€ or 30€, or more, and may be higher after midnight and on weekends. But quite often there are concessions for women.

You can have dinner with the show or just a drink – but neither is cheap. Expect to pay from 23€ to 60€ for a ticket; and 68€ to 105€ including dinner. In general, one drink *(la consommation)* is included in the entry price; thereafter it can become an extremely expensive evening.

DISCO AND CLUB VENUES

Les Bains
7 Rue du Bourg-L'Abbé
75003. **Map** 13 B1.
C 01 48 87 01 80.

Balajo
9 Rue de Lappe 75011.
Map 14 E4.
C 01 47 00 07 87.

Le Bataclan
50 blvd Voltaire 75011.
Map 13 E1.
C 01 43 14 35 35.

La Casbah
18-20 Rue de la Forge-Royale 75011.
C 01 43 71 04 39.

Castel's
15 Rue Princesse 75006.
Map 12 E4.
C 01 40 51 52 80.

Chez Madame Arthur
75 bis Rue des Martyrs
75018. **Map** 6 F2.
C 01 42 54 40 21.

Club 79
22 Rue Quentin Bauchard
75008.
Map 4 F5.
C 01 47 23 68 75.

Crazy Horse Saloon
12 Ave George V 75008.
Map 10 E1.
C 01 47 23 32 32.

Don Camillo Rive Gauche
10 Rue des Sts-Pères
75007.
Map 12 E3.
C 01 42 60 82 84.

Elysée Montmartre
72 Blvd Rochechouart
75018. **Map** 6 F2.
C 01 42 52 76 84.

Folies-Bergères
32 Rue Richer 75009.
Map 7 A4.
C 01 44 79 98 98.

Folie's Clubbing
11 Pl Pigalle 75009.
Map 6 E2.
C 01 48 78 55 25.

La Java
105 Rue du Faubourg du
Temple 75010. **Map** 8 E5.
C 01 42 02 20 52.

Keur Samba
79 Rue de la Boétie 75008.
Map 5 A4.
C 01 43 59 03 10.

Lido
116 bis Ave des Champs-
Elysées 75008. **Map** 4 E4.
C 01 40 76 56 10.

La Locomotive
90 Blvd de Clichy 75018.
Map 4 E4.
C 08 36 69 69 28.

La Main Jaune
Pl de la Porte-Champerret
75017. **Map** 3 C1.
C 01 47 63 26 47.

Moulin Rouge
82 Blvd de Clichy 75018.
Map 6 E1.
C 01 53 09 82 82.

Paradis Latin
28 Rue du Cardinal-Lemoine
75005. **Map** 13 B5.
C 01 43 25 28 28.

Christhom
25 Blvd Poissonière
75002. **Map** 7 A5.
C 01 40 26 01 50.

Le Queen
102 Ave des Champs-
Elysees 75008. **Map** 4 E4.
C 01 53 89 08 90.

Regine's
49–51 Rue Ponthieu
75008. **Map** 5 A5.
C 01 43 59 21 60.

Rex Club
5 Blvd Poissonière 75002.
Map 7 A5.
C 01 42 36 83 98.

Ritz Club
Hôtel Ritz, 15 Pl
Vendôme 75001.
Map 6 D5.
C 01 43 16 30 30.

La Scala
188 bis Rue de Rivoli
75001. **Map** 12 E2.
C 01 42 60 45 64.

Zed Club
2 Rue des Anglais 75005.
Map 13 A5.
C 01 43 54 93 78.

Cinema

Paris is the world's capital of film appreciation. It was the cradle of the cinematograph nearly 100 years ago, and the incubator of that very Parisian vanguard movement, the New Wave, when film directors such as Claude Chabrol, François Truffaut, Jean-Luc Godard and Eric Rohmer in the late 1950s and early 1960s revolutionized the way films were made and perceived.

There are more than 300 screens within the city limits, distributed among 100 cinemas and multiplexes, showing a fabulous cornucopia of films, both brand-new and classic. Although American movies dominate the market more than ever, virtually every film-making industry in the world has found a niche in the city's art houses.

Cinemas change their programmes on Wednesdays. The cheapest practical guides to what's on are *Pariscope* and *L'Officiel des Spectacles (see p328)* with complete cinema listings and timetables for some 300 films. For more substantial reviews and articles, there are the larger-format weeklies such as *Télérama* and *7 à Paris*, and, for the serious-minded film-goer, the monthly magazines *Les Cahiers du Cinéma* and *Positif*.

Films shown in subtitled original language versions are coded "VO" *(version originale)*; dubbed films are coded "VF" *(version française)*.

The Fête du Cinéma is held one day in June. You pay full price for one film and then every film seen subsequently in any cinema on that day costs 1€. Film buffs have been known to watch six screenings on the day.

CINEMA ZONES

Most paris cinemas are concentrated in several cinema belts, which enjoy the added appeal of nearby restaurants and shops.

The Champs-Elysées remains the densest cinema strip in town, where you can see the latest Hollywood smash or French *auteur* triumph, as well as some classic re-issues, in subtitled original language versions. Cinemas in the Grands Boulevards, in the vicinity of the Opéra de Paris Garnier, show films in both subtitled and dubbed versions. The Place de Clichy is the last Parisian stronghold of Pathé, which operates no less than 13 screens there, all showing dubbed versions. A major hub of Right Bank cinema activity is in the Forum des Halles shopping mall.

The Left Bank, historically associated with the city's intellectual life, remains the centre of the art and repertory cinemas, yet has equally as many of the latest blockbusters. Since the 1980s, many cinemas in the Latin Quarter have closed down and the main area for Left Bank theatres is now the Odéon-St-Germain-des-Prés area. The Rue Champollion is an exception. It has enjoyed a revival as a mini-district for art and repertory films.

Further to the south, Montparnasse remains a lively film-going district of new films in both dubbed and subtitled prints.

BIG SCREENS AND PICTURE PALACES

Among surviving landmark cinemas are two Grands Boulevards venues, the 2,800-seat **Le Grand Rex** with its Baroque decor, and the **Max Linder Panorama**, which was completely refurbished by a group of independent film buffs in the 1980s for both popular and art film programming.

Another popular site is the **Gaumont Kinopanorama** with its curved wide screen. Despite its far-flung location in Grenelle, it is one of the best attended houses in town. Equally important, with the largest screen in the country, is the **Gaumont** flagship in the Place d'Italie district.

In the Cité des Sciences et de l'Industrie at La Villette, scientific films are shown at **La Géode** *(see p235)*. This has the largest screen in the world and an "omnimax" projector which uses 70-mm film shot horizontally to project an image which is nine times larger than the standard 35-mm print.

REVIVAL AND REPERTORY HOUSES

Each week, more than 150 titles representing the best of world cinema can be seen. For old Hollywood films, the independent **Grand Action** mini-chain can't be beaten. Other active repertory and re-issue venues include the **Reflets Médicis Logos** screens in the Rue Champollion and the renovated **Diagonal Europa** cinema near the Jardin du Luxembourg, operated by distributor/exhibitor Acacias-Cinéaudience.

CINÉMATHÈQUE FRANÇAISE

The private "school" of the New Wave generation, this famous film archive and repertory cinema was created by Henri Langlois in 1936 *(see p199)*. It has lost its monopoly on classic film screenings, but it is still a must for buffs in search of that rare film no longer in theatrical circulation or recently restored. The **Cinémathèque Française** currently runs two cinemas, one in the Palais de Chaillot *(see p198)*, and the other in the 10th arrondissement *(see Directory p341)*. By 2003, the Maison du Cinéma in Rue de Bercy should house these and other cinemas. Tickets are priced at about 4€, and there are subscriptions and special rates as well.

NON-THEATRICAL VENUES

IN ADDITION TO the Cinémathèque Française, film programmes and festivals are integral parts of two highly popular Paris cultural institutions, the Musée d'Orsay (see pp144–5) and the Pompidou Centre (see pp110–11) with its **Salle Garance**. The Musée d'Orsay regularly schedules film programmes to complement current art exhibitions and is usually restricted to silent films. The Pompidou Centre organizes vast month-long retrospectives, devoted to national film industries and on occasion to some of the major companies.

Finally, the **Forum des Images** (see p109) in the heart of Les Halles is a hi-tech film and video library with a vast selection of films and documentaries featuring the city of Paris from the late 19th century to the present day. The Forum has three cinemas, all of which run daily screenings of feature films, beginning at 2.30pm. One ticket allows the visitor access to both the video library and to the cinema screenings.

TICKET PRICES

EXPECT TO pay around 7€ at first-run venues or even more for films of unusual length or special media attention. However, exhibitors practise a wide array of collective discount incentives, including cut-rate admissions for students, the unemployed, the elderly, old soldiers and large families. Wednesday is discount day for everybody at all the city's cinemas – prices are slashed to as low as 4€.

France's three exhibition giants, Gaumont, UGC and Pathé, also sell special discount cards and accept credit card reservations for their flagship houses, while repertory houses issue "fidelity" cards, offering a sixth admission free.

The traditional *pourboire*, or tip, given to the usherettes, or *ouvreuses*, has now been abolished by the major cinemas, though independent cinemas still continue the practice: it is polite to give about half a euro.

Shows usually begin at 2pm and the last *séance*, or programme, starts between 9pm and 10pm. There are midnight screenings on Fridays and Saturdays at most first-run cinemas.

Some complexes, notably those in the Forum des Halles (see p109), offer low-price late morning screenings. A complete programme is supposed to include a short film before the main feature, but most exhibitors have dropped this in order to increase revenue with more advertising time. If you don't want to sit through 20 minutes of commercials, check the exact starting time for the feature. However, for particularly popular films you'll have to turn up early to queue for tickets if you want to be sure of getting a seat.

FILMS WITH STRONG IMAGES OF PARIS

Historical Paris (studio-made)

An Italian Straw Hat
(René Clair, 1927)

Sous les toits de Paris
(René Clair, 1930)

Les Misérables
(Raymond Bernard, 1934)

Hôtel du Nord
(Marcel Carné, 1937)

Les Enfants du Paradis
(Marcel Carné, 1945)

Casque d'Or
(Jacques Becker, 1952)

La Traversée de Paris
(Claude Autant-Lara, 1956)

Playtime
(Jacques Tati, 1967)

New Wave Paris (location-made)

Breathless
(Jean-Luc Godard, 1959)

Les 400 coups
(François Truffaut, 1959)

Documentary Paris

Paris 1900
(Nicole Vedrès, 1948)

La Seine a rencontré Paris
(Joris Ivans, 1957)

Paris as seen by Hollywood

Seventh Heaven
(Frank Borzage, 1927)

Camille
(George Cukor, 1936)

An American in Paris
(Vincente Minnelli, 1951)

Gigi
(Vincente Minnelli, 1958)

Irma La Douce
(Billy Wilder, 1963)

CINEMA ADDRESSES

Cinémathèque Française Palais de Chaillot
42 Blvd de Bonne Nouvelle 75010. **Map** 7 A5.
📞 01 56 26 01 01.

Diagonal Europa
13 Rue Victor-Cousin 75005. **Map** 12 F5.
📞 01 40 46 01 21.

Gaumont Gobelins
58 & 73 Ave des Gobelins 75013. **Map** 17 B4.

📞 08 36 68 75 55.
Reservations 📞 01 40 30 30 31.

La Géode
26 Ave Corentin-Cariou 75019.
📞 01 40 05 12 12.

Grand Action
Action Rive Gauche, 5 Rue des Ecoles 75005.
Map 13 B5.
📞 01 43 29 44 40.

Le Grand Rex
1 Blvd Poissonnière 75002.

Map 7 A5.
📞 08 36 68 70 23.

Gaumont Kinopanorama
60 Ave de la Motte-Picquet 75015.
Map 10 E5.
📞 08 36 68 75 55.
Reservations 📞 01 40 30 30 31.

Max Linder Panorama
24 Blvd Poissonnière 75009. **Map** 7 A5.
📞 08 36 68 70 23.

Reflets Médicis Logos
3 Rue Champollion 75005.
Map 12 F5.
📞 01 43 54 42 34.

Salle Garance
Centre Georges Pompidou, 19 Rue Beaubourg 75004.
Map 13 B2.

Forum des Images
2 Grande Galérie, Forum des Halles 75001.
Map 13 A2.
📞 01 44 76 62 00.

Sport and Fitness

THERE IS NO END OF SPORTING activities in Paris. Certain events such as the Roland Garros tennis tournament and the Tour de France bicycle race are national institutions. The only drawback is that many of the facilities are on the outskirts of the city.

For details regarding all sporting events in and around Paris contact **Allô Sports**, which runs a free information service (Monday to Friday, daytime only). The weekly entertainment guides *L'Officiel des Spectacles*, *Pariscope* and the Wednesday edition of *Le Figaro* also have good listings of the week's sporting events *(see p328)*. For in-depth sports coverage there is the daily paper *L'Equipe*. See also *Children's Paris* on page 346.

OUTDOOR SPORTS

THE ANNUAL Tour de France bicycle race finishes in July in Paris to city-wide frenzy, when the French president awards the coveted *maillot jaune* (yellow jersey) to the winner.

For those brave enough to tackle cycling through the city traffic, bikes may be hired throughout Paris, including at **Paris Vélo** and **Maison Roue Libre** *(see p367)*. The French state railway, SNCF, offers day trips with a bicycle as part of a package. The **Fédération Française de Cyclotourisme** will give you information on over 300 cycling clubs in and around Paris.

Parisians enjoy Sunday afternoon boating in the Bois de Vincennes *(see p246)*, the Bois de Boulogne *(see p254)* and the Parc des Buttes-Chaumont *(see p232)*. Just queue up to hire a boat.

At weekends, amateur *pétanque* players stake out almost any available piece of gravel or earth to play the game that, in poll after poll, Parisians claim is their favourite sport. It is a game similar to bowls. Contact the **Fédération Française de Pétanque et de Jeux Provençales** for information.

All the golf courses are outside Paris. Many are private clubs, but some will admit non-members – for further information contact the **Fédération Française du Golf**. Otherwise try the **Golf de Chevry**, **Golf de St-Pierre du Perray**, **Golf de St-Quentin en Yvelines** or

the **Golf de Villennes**. Expect to pay at least 25€ each time you want to play. You can go horse-riding in both the Bois de Boulogne and the Bois de Vincennes. Contact the **Ligue Equestre de Paris** for further information.

Tennis can be played at municipal courts such as the **Tennis Luxembourg** in the Jardin du Luxembourg. Courts are available every day on a first-come first-served basis. **Tennis de la Faluère** in the Bois de Vincennes is one of the better courts, but must be booked 24 hours in advance.

INDOOR SPORTS

THERE ARE PLENTY of gyms in Paris which you can use with a day pass. Expect to pay 20€ or more, depending on the facilities.

Along with multi-gym and body-building rooms **Espace Vit'halles** also offers a sauna, a turkish bath and a solarium. **Gymnase Club** is a well-equipped, popular chain of gyms. **Jean de Beauvais** is a state-of-the-art gym with personalized fitness programmes.

In theory the **Ritz Gym**, with the finest indoor swimming pool in Paris, is for guests or members only, but if the hotel is not too full you can buy a day pass.

Skating is a cheap pastime and can be enjoyed year-round at the **Patinoire d'Asnières-sur-Seine**.

Squash can be played at **Squash Club Quartier Latin**, where options also include

billiards, gym and a sauna. Other good clubs include the **Squash Montmartre**, **Squash Rennes-Raspail** and the **Squash Front de Seine**.

SPECTATOR SPORTS

A DAY OUT at the races is a chance to see the rich in all their finery. The world-famous Prix de l'Arc de Triomphe is held at the **Hippodrome de Longchamp** on the first Sunday in October. More flat racing takes place at the **Hippodrome de St-Cloud** and **Maison Lafitte**, which are a short drive west of Paris. For steeplechasing go to the **Hippodrome d'Auteuil**. The **Hippodrome de Vincennes** hosts the trotting races. For information telephone the **Fédération des Sociétés des Courses de France**.

The 24-hour car race at Le Mans, 185 km (115 miles) southwest of Paris, is one of the best-known road races in the world. It takes place every year in mid-June. Contact the **Fédération Française de Sport Automobile** for details.

The **Palais d'Omnisports de Paris-Bercy** sports stadium is the venue for a vast range of events, including the Paris tennis open, the six-day cycling race, showjumping, world-class martial arts demonstrations and rock concerts.

Parc des Princes can hold 50,000 people. It is home to the main Paris football team, Paris St-Germain, and hosts the rugby internationals.

Despite its glorious baptism in 1998 with France's World Cup victory, the **Stade de France** has failed to win a home team; meanwhile, it makes do with the Six Nations Trophy, Tina Turner and Johnnie Halliday.

The **Stade Roland Garros** is famous for its international tennis tournament. From late May to mid-June everyone lives and breathes tennis. Business meetings are transferred from the conference room to the stadium. Write for tickets several months ahead.

SWIMMING

THERE IS a massive aquatic fun park, known as **Aquaboulevard**, in south Paris (see p346). Besides an exotic artificial beach, swimming pools, water toboggans and rapids, there are tennis and squash courts, golf, bowling, table tennis, billiards, a gym, bars and shops.

Of the many municipal swimming pools, one of the best is the **Piscine Nouveau** **Forum des Halles**, an Olympic-sized swimming pool in the underground shopping complex. For a lovely 1930s mosaic decor with two levels of private changing cabins, a whirlpool, sauna and water jets, go to the **Piscine Pontoise-Quartier Latin**. The **Piscine Henry de Montherlant** is part of a municipal sports complex that includes tennis courts and a gym. Swimming pools are also available in some hotels.

MISCELLANEOUS

BASEBALL, FENCING, jogging in the parks, volleyball, windsurfing at La Villette (see pp234–9) and bowling are just some of the other sporting activities that can be enjoyed during your stay.

Fishing on the Seine is fast becoming a popular pastime with Parisiens. Due to a cleaning up operation the Seine is now home to a variety of freshwater fish.

DIRECTORY

Allô Sports
25 Blvd Bourdon 75004.
Map 14 D5.
☎ 01 42 76 54 54.

Aquaboulevard
4 Rue Louis-Armand 75015.
☎ 01 40 60 10 00.

Espace Vit'halles
48 Rue Rambuteau
75003. **Map** 13 B2.
☎ 01 42 77 21 71.

Fédération Française du Golf
68 Rue Anatole France,
92300 Levallois Perret.
☎ 01 41 49 77 00.

Fédération Française de Cyclotourisme
8 Rue Jean-Marie Jégo
75013. **Map** 17 B5.
☎ 01 44 16 88 88.

Fédération Française de Pétanque
9 Rue Duperré 75009.
Map 6 E2.
☎ 01 48 74 61 63.

Fédération Française de Sport Automobile
17 Ave Général Mangin
75016. **Map** 9 B4.
☎ 01 44 30 24 00.

Fédération des Sociétés des Courses de France
10 Blvd Malesherbes
75008. **Map** 5 5C.
☎ 01 42 68 87 87.

Golf de Chevry
91190 Gif-sur-Yvette.
☎ 01 60 12 40 33.

Golf de St-Pierre du Perray
91380 St-Pierre du Perray.
☎ 01 60 75 17 47.

Golf de St-Quentin en Yvelines
78190 Trappes.
☎ 01 30 50 86 40.

Golf de Villennes
Route d'Orgeval, 78670
Villennes-sur-Seine.
☎ 01 39 08 18 18.

Gymnase Club
26 Rue Berri 75008.
Map 4 F4.
☎ 01 43 59 04 58.

Hippodrome d'Auteuil
Bois de Boulogne 75016.
☎ 01 40 71 47 47.

Hippodrome de Longchamp
Bois de Boulogne 75016.
☎ 01 44 30 75 00.

Hippodrome Maison Lafitte
1 Ave de la Pelouze, 78600
Maison Lafitte. **Map** 5 B2.
☎ 01 39 62 06 77.

Hippodrome de St-Cloud
1 Rue de Camp Canadien,
92210 St-Cloud.
☎ 01 47 71 69 26.

Hippodrome de Vincennes
2 Route de la Ferme,
75012 Vincennes.
☎ 01 49 77 17 17.

Club Jean de Beauvais
5 Rue Jean de Beauvais
75005. **Map** 13 A5.
☎ 01 46 33 16 80.

Ligue Equestre de Paris
69 Rue Laugier 75017
☎ 01 42 12 03 43.

Palais d'Omnisports de Paris-Bercy
8 Blvd Bercy 75012. **Map**
18 F2. ☎ 08 03 03 00 31.

Stade de France
93210 La Plaine St-Denis.
☎ 01 55 93 00 00.

Parc des Princes
24 Rue du Commandant-
Guilbaud 75016.
☎ 01 42 30 03 60.

Paris Vélo
2 Rue du Fer-à-Moulin
75005. **Map** 17 C2.
☎ 01 43 37 59 22.

Maison Roue Libre
95 bis Rue Rambuteau
75001. **Map** 13 B2.
☎ 01 53 46 43 77.

Patinoire d'Asnières-sur-Seine
Blvd Pierre de Coubertin,
92600 Asnières.
☎ 01 47 99 96 06.

Piscine Henry de Montherlant
32 Blvd de Lannes 75016.
☎ 01 40 72 28 30.

Piscine Nouveau Forum des Halles
10 Pl de la Rotonde,
Niveau 3, Entrance Porte St
Eustache, Les Halles
75001. **Map** 13 A2.
☎ 01 42 36 98 44.

Piscine Pontoise-Quartier Latin
19 Rue de Pontoise
75005. **Map** 13 B5.
☎ 01 55 42 77 88.

Ritz Gym
Ritz Hotel, Pl Vendôme
75001. **Map** 6 D5.
☎ 01 43 16 30 30.

Stade Roland Garros
2 Ave Gordon-Bennett
75016.
☎ 01 47 43 48 00.

Squash Club Quartier Latin
19 Rue de Pontoise
75005. **Map** 13 B5.
☎ 01 55 42 77 88.

Squash Front de Seine
21 Rue Gaston-de-
Caillavet 75015. **Map** 9 B5.
☎ 01 45 75 35 37.

Squash Montmartre
14 Rue Achille-Martinet
75018. **Map** 2 E4.
☎ 01 42 55 38 30.

Squash Rennes-Raspail
149 Rue des Rennes
75006. **Map** 16 D1.
☎ 01 44 39 03 30.

Tennis de la Faluère
Route de la Pyramide
Bois de Vincennes 75012.
☎ 01 43 74 40 93.

Tennis Luxembourg
Jardins du Luxembourg
Blvd St-Michel 75006.
Map 12 E5.
☎ 01 43 25 79 18.

CHILDREN'S PARIS

It's never too early to instill a lifelong taste for this magical city in your children. A trip to Disneyland Paris *(see pp242–5)* or down the Seine *(see pp72–3)*, the dizzy heights of the Eiffel Tower *(see pp192–3)* or a visit to Notre-Dame *(see pp82–5)* are fun at any age, and with children in tow you will see old haunts through new eyes. The orderly and historic parks are probably best appreciated by older children and adults, but everyone will love the technological wizardry of the Disneyland Paris theme park. During the summer, funfairs, circuses and all sorts of impromptu events are staged in gardens and parks, notably in the Bois de Boulogne *(see p254)*. Or, take children to an entertainment centre, museum or adventure playground, or to a show at one of the café theatres.

La Cité des Enfants at La Villette

PRACTICAL ADVICE

Paris welcomes young families in hotels *(see p272)* and most restaurants *(see p289)*. Many sights and attractions offer child reductions, while infants under three or four enter free. The upper age limit for reductions is usually about 12 but can vary considerably. Many museums are free on Sundays; others allow children under 18 in free at any time. Ask at the Office du Tourisme *(see p274)* for full details of child reductions, or check in the weekly entertainment guides such as *Pariscope*. *Paris Selection* (free from the Office du Tourisme) has a list of events and attractions.

A lot of the children's activities are geared to end-of-school times, including Wednesday afternoons when French children have time off. For information on museum workshops, contact the **Ministère de la Culture**. The **Centre d'Information et de Documentation Jeunesse** has a list of activities for children under 15.

Cots and baby-buggies can be hired from major baby-sitting agencies like **Home Service**. **Ababa** is another specialist baby-sitting organization.

MUSEUMS

Top of the museum list for children is undoubtedly the Cité des Sciences et de l'Industrie *(see pp234–9)* at Parc de la Villette. Hands-on activities and changing exhibitions illuminate many aspects of science and modern technology in this immense complex. Highlights include the sound and light shows, the Odorama, the Flight Simulator and the high-tech La Géode cinema screen *(see p235)*. There is also a new section for young children called La Cité des Enfants. In central Paris the Palais de la Découverte *(see p206)* is an old-fashioned but lively science museum where staff adopt the role of mad inventors.

Other enjoyable museums for children include the Musée de la Marine *(see p199)* and the Musée de la Poupée *(see p114)*. The Musée de la Marine covers the history of the French maritime tradition and includes scale models. The Musée de la Poupée displays hand-made dolls dating from the mid-19th century. It also offers doll-making classes for both adults and children.

USEFUL CONTACTS

Ababa
☎ 01 45 49 46 46.

Centre d'Information et de Documentation Jeunesse
101 Quai Branly 75015.
Map 10 D3.
☎ 01 44 49 12 00.
FAX 01 40 65 02 61.

Home Service
☎ 01 42 82 05 04.

Ministère de la Culture
3 Rue de Valois 75001.
Map 12 F1.
☎ 01 40 15 80 00.

The Café d'Edgar theatre

The Guignol marionettes

PARKS, ZOOS AND ADVENTURE PLAYGROUNDS

THE BEST CHILDREN'S park within Paris is the Jardin d'Acclimatation *(see p254)* in the Bois de Boulogne. It is, however, quite expensive. During term-time it's best to go on Wednesday afternoon or at the weekend, or else you may find some attractions are un-manned. The Musée en Herbe *(see p254)* offers educ-ational, entertaining activities; you can leave children with supervisors in the Jardin des Halles in the Forum des Halles *(see p109)*. In the Bois de Vincennes, the inexpensive

Pony rides, Jardin d'Acclimatation

Parc Floral *(see p246)* has simple amusements for child-ren. The Bois de Vincennes also houses Paris's largest zoo *(see p246)*. Perhaps the most appealing zoo is the small Ménagerie *(see p164)*.

ENTERTAINMENT CENTRES

THERE ARE MANY supervised children's activity centres in Paris. The Atelier des Enfants in the Pompidou Centre *(see pp110–11)* has a workshop on Wednesday and Saturday afternoons from 2.30 to 4pm. The medium of instruction is French but the circuses, mime-shows, marionnettes and craft or museum workshops focus on actions rather than words.

Several café-theatres, including Café d'Edgar *(see p331)* and Au Bec Fin *(see p331)*, offer children's shows where mime, dance or music form part of the con-tent. Children's television programmes are generally shown from 7am to 8am and 5pm to 6pm. The most spectacular cinema-tic experience is in La Géode at the Cité des Sciences et de l'Industrie (see p235). The cinema **Le Saint Lambert**

Lion in the Bois de Vincennes zoo

specializes in French children's films and comic strips. Cinema tickets are generally cheaper on Wednesdays, with no child reductions at weekends.

A more unusual outing is a day at the circus. The **Cirque de Paris** offers children a day's entertainment when they can meet the animals, put on clown make-up or practise tightrope walking. Shows are held in the afternoon following lunch with the *artistes*.

The Guignol marionnette puppet shows are a summer tradition in Paris. The themes are similar to the traditional English Punch and Judy shows with a dominant wife battering a husband with the interven-tion of a policeman. Most of the main parks hold Guignol shows during the summer on Wednesday afternoons and at weekends. One or two shows are free. Consult the entertain-ment guides such as L'Officiel des Spectacles and Pariscope.

ADDRESSES

Cirque de Paris
115 Blvd Charles de Gaulle 92390. Ville-neuve la Garenne. ☎ *01 47 99 40 40.*

Le Saint Lambert
6 Rue Peclet 75015. ☎ *01 45 32 91 68.*

Circus acrobats training at the Cirque de Paris

Fireworks over Sleeping Beauty's Castle, Disneyland Paris

THEME PARKS

THE TWO PARKS of Disney-land Paris *(see pp242–5)* are the biggest and most spectacular of the Paris theme parks. Six hotels, each with a different, imaginative theme, and a campsite provide on-site accommodation. The complex also includes a golf course, shops and restaurants.

Parc Asterix is a French theme park centring around the legendary world of Asterix the Gaul. Here six themed "worlds" feature gladiators, slave auctions and rides among the many attractions. The park is situated 38 km (24 miles) northeast of Paris. Take the RER line B to Charles de Gaulle Airport then take the shuttle bus to Parc Asterix.

Donald Duck

SPORTS AND RECREATION

THE GIANT waterpark **Aqua-boulevard** is one of the best places to take energetic youngsters. Another good swimming pool in Paris is the indoor pool at **Nouveau Forum**. The weekly entertainment guide *Pariscope* has details of all swimming pools in and around Paris.

Accomplished roller-skaters and skate-boarders practise outside the Palais de Chaillot *(see p198)*. There is an official roller-skating rink in the Parc Monceau *(see pp258–9)*, and the Parc des Buttes-Chaumont *(see p232)* and Disneyland Paris *(see pp242–5)* have ice-skating rinks. Disneyland Paris also has a wide range of other sports facilities.

Old-fashioned fairground carousels are situated near Sacré-Coeur *(see pp224–5)* and Forum Les Halles *(see p109)*. Great fun too, is a boat trip. Several companies compete. The oldest is **Bateaux Mouches** *(see pp72–3)*, whose crafts depart from the Pont de l'Alma and pass a host of waterfront sites including Notre-Dame, the Louvre, and the Musée d'Orsay. Boats departing from La Villette travel along the Paris canal system. Radio-controlled model boats are popular on the ponds of the Jardin du Luxembourg *(see p172)*. Or, take the family boating on the lakes of the Bois de Boulogne *(see p254)* or the Bois de Vincennes *(see p246)*. Riding is also popular in these parks *(see p343 Directory)*.

ADDRESSES

Aquaboulevard
4 Rue Louis Armand 75015.
☎ *01 40 60 10 00.* ☐ *9am–11pm Mon–Thu, 9am– midnight Fri, 8am–midnight Sat, 8am–11pm Sun.*

Bateaux Mouches
Pont de l'Alma. **Map** 10 F1.
☎ *01 42 25 96 10.*
For departures, see p73.

La Piscine des Halles
Nouveau Forum, 10 Pl de la Rotonde, Les Halles 75001. **Map** 12 F2. ☎ *01 42 36 98 44.* ☐ *11.30am–10pm Mon–Fri, 9am–7pm Sat–Sun.*

Parc Asterix
Plailly 60128. ☎ *08 36 68 30 10.*
☐ *Apr–mid-Oct: 10am–6pm Mon–Fri, 9am–7pm w/e & hols.*

Roller-skaters near the Eiffel Tower

CHILDREN'S SHOPS

There is no shortage of chic children's fashion in Paris. A good place to start is the Rue du Jour in Beaubourg and Les Halles which has a number of children's boutiques such as Un Après-Midi de Chien at No. 10 and Claude Vell at No. 8. The city has many appealing toy shops but, like the clothes shops, they can be prohibitively expensive. *(See also Children's Clothes p318.)*

Characters from the book *Tintin*, in Au Nain Bleu toy shop *(see p321)*

Carousel near Sacré-Coeur

STREET LIFE AND MARKETS

O UTSIDE THE Pompidou Centre *(see pp110–11)* street entertainers draw the crowds on sunny afternoons. Musicians, conjurors, fire-eaters and artists of all kinds perform here. In Montmartre there is a tradition of street-painting, predominantly in the Place du Tertre *(see p222)*.

Model boats for hire in the Jardin du Luxembourg

where someone will always be willing to draw your child's portrait. It's also fun to take the funicular up the hill to Sacré-Coeur *(see pp224–5)*, then walk down through the pretty streets.

Parisian markets are colour-ful and animated. Try taking children to the Marché aux Fleurs on the Ile de la Cité *(see p81)* or to the food mar-kets on the Rue Mouffetard, in the Jardin des Plantes Quarter *(see p166 and p327)*, or the Rue de Buci in St-Germain-des-Prés. The biggest flea market, Marché aux Puces de St-Ouen is at weekends in Place Clignan-court *(see p231 and p327)*.

Alternatively take children to the quiet Ile de la Cité or Ile St-Louis on the Seine.

VIEWPOINTS AND SIGHTSEEING

T OP OF THE sightseeing list for children is a trip up the Eiffel Tower *(see pp192–3)*. On a clear day spectacular views over Paris will enable you to point out a number of sights, and at night the city is magically lit up. Lifts run until 11pm and queues are much shorter in the evenings. If you are pushing a baby buggy, bear in mind that the ascent is in three stages, using two separate lifts.

Other interesting sights for children include Sacré-Coeur *(see pp224–5)* with its ovoid dome – the second highest point in Paris after the Eiffel Tower – and Notre-Dame cathedral *(see pp82–3)* on the Ile de la Cité. Children will enjoy feeding the pigeons in the cathedral square, counting the 28 kings of Judah on the West Front and listening to you recount the story of the hunchback of Notre-Dame. There are incomparable views from the towers. Children and adults alike will appreciate the enchanting Sainte-Chapelle *(see pp88–9)*, also on the Ile de la Cité. There are reductions for children under the age of 17.

Contrast ancient and modern Paris with a visit to the Pom-pidou Centre *(see pp110–11)* and enjoy a ride on the caterpillar-like escalators outside, or go to the café on the roof terrace for the views. There is also the 56-storey Montparnasse Tower *(see p178)* with some spectacular telescopic views from the top terrace; and there is the huge arch at La Défense *(see p255)* which has lifts to exhibition platforms where visitors can overlook the whole complex.

OTHER INTERESTS

C HILDREN are quick to see the funny side of unusual spectacles. Les Egouts, Paris's sewers, now welcome apprehensive visitors for a

Escalators at the Pompidou Centre

short tour of the city's sewer-age system *(see p190)*. Display boards in several languages explain the processes.

The Catacombs *(see p179)* are a long series of quarry tunnels built in Roman times, now lined with ancient skulls.

On the Ile de la Cité is the Conciergerie *(see p81)*, a turreted prison where many hapless aristocrats spent their final days. The Musée Grévin waxworks are in Boulevard Montmartre *(see p216)*. The museum's Revolution rooms will especially appeal to older children, with gruesome scenes and grisly sound effects, demonstrating the reality of social upheaval.

EMERGENCIES

T HE FREE 24-hour child helpline is Enfance et Partage, which can also be for adults. One of the largest children's hospitals in Paris is Hôpital Necker.

Enfance et Partage
[C] 08 00 05 12 34.

Hôpital Necker 149 Rue de Sèvres 75015. **Map** 15 B1. [C] 01 44 49 40 00.

A young visitor to Paris

SURVIVAL
GUIDE

PRACTICAL INFORMATION

As in most large cities, it's easy to waste your limited sightseeing time in Paris on transport and in queues. A little forward planning can minimize this. Ring in advance to confirm the sight is open, and isn't closed for refurbishment or holidays – a phonecard, or *télécarte*, is a wise investment *(see p356)*. Purchase a *carnet* or travel pass to economize and simplify transport on the buses and metro *(see pp368–71)*. Buying a *Paris Carte-Musées-Monuments* will give unlimited access to museums and monuments, and cuts down on queues. Beware the Paris lunch break (around 1–3pm), as many essential services shut down, as well as some museums. Guided tours are often the best way to see the essential sights before you get your bearings. If you're on a tight budget, admission prices are sometimes lower at certain times of day, or on Sundays; card-carrying students can obtain discounts on some tickets and admissions *(see p358)*.

MUSEUMS AND MONUMENTS

There are 172 museums and monuments open to the public in Paris. Most are open Monday (or Tuesday) to Sunday, and from 10am to 5.40pm. Some offer evening visits. The national museums are closed on Tuesdays, except Versailles and the Musée d'Orsay, which are closed on Mondays. The municipal museums, such as those run by the city of Paris (Ville de Paris) are usually closed on Mondays.

An admission fee is usually charged, or a donation is expected. The entrance fee to national museums is reduced by half on Sundays, and totally waived on the first Sunday of each month. Those under 18 are admitted free and those 18–25 and over 60 pay half-price. The municipal museums, and some other museums, do not charge a fee to see their permanent collections on Sundays. Those under 7 and over 60 are admitted free at all times. To obtain the discounts you will have to provide absolute proof of who you are, what

Paris museum passes, for saving time and money

Train station sign for information services

you do and how old you are. It is worth buying the pass known as *Paris Carte-Musées-Monuments*. This gives the bearer access to 70 museums and monuments for 1, 3 or 5 days. The user is also entitled to an unlimited number of visits and does not have to queue, a significant advantage in the Paris high season, when crowds can become a highly frustrating problem. The pass can be purchased at any of the city's museums and monuments, main metro stations, Batobus stops, FNAC ticket counters and also at the head-quarters of the **Paris Convention and Visitors Bureau**.

OPENING HOURS

This guide lists opening times for each sight individually. Most Paris shops and businesses are open from 9am to 7pm. While many stay open all day, others close for an hour or two from noon or 12.30. Some smaller shops open earlier, around 7am, and take a longer midday break. Almost all business is closed on Sunday, and many shops close Monday too. Some rest-

Tourist Office logo

aurants close at least one day a week. Banks are open from around 9am to 4.30–5.15pm Mon–Fri, and 9am–noon Sat. Some close noon–2pm. The day before a public holiday they close at noon.

TOURIST INFORMATION

There are three tourist offices in Paris: the head-quarters on the Champs-Elysées *(see p351)*, one at the Gare de Lyon, and one at the Eiffel Tower (seasonal). All provide maps, information and brochures. They also offer last-minute hotel reservation services. At the Gare de Lyon office, which is particularly useful for incoming travellers, the service is slow in summer, when backpackers arrive in droves. Expect to wait.

ENTERTAINMENT

The main listings magazines in Paris, available at all newsagents, are *Pariscope* and *L'Officiel des Spectacles (see p328)*. Each Wednesday they present, in a clear fashion, full information on the week's current theatre, cinema and exhibits, as well

Paris sightseeing tour bus

as on cabarets, dinner clubs and some restaurants.

FNAC ticket agencies book all the entertainment venues, including temporary museum shows. There are FNAC branches throughout Paris. For more information call one of their central branches *(see p329)*.

For booking the theatre only, the Kiosque Théâtre sells same-day tickets at 50% discount. The two locations are Place de la Madeleine and the Parvis de la Gare Montparnasse *(see p329)*.

Visitors should be aware that smoking is not allowed in theatres, cinemas or other public places.

Kiosque Théâtre booking kiosk

GUIDED TOURS

THERE ARE double-decker bus tours with comment-aries in English, Italian, Japanese and German. These are organized by major companies **Cityrama** and **Paris Vision**. The tours begin from the city centre and take about two hours. They pass the main sights but do not stop at all of them. Because departure times vary, visitors should phone the bus operators for details. Another operator, **Cars Rouges**, runs British double-decker bus tours stopping at many of the sights in Paris, which allow you to leave the bus at any of the stops and to continue the tour later (ticket valid 2 days).

The Caisse Nationale des Mon-uments Historiques *(see p95)* offers guided walking tours.

DISABLED ACCESS

SERVICES FOR disabled people in Paris are still limited. Although most pavements have now been contoured to allow wheelchairs an easier passage, many restaurants, hotels, and even museums and monuments are poorly equipped. However, better facilities are being incorporated into all renovated and new buildings. For up-to-date information on public facilities for the disabled, contact the **Comité National pour la Réadaption des Handicapés (CNRH)** and request the pamphlet *Paris, Ile de France pour vous*.

DISABILITY INFORMATION

Les Compagnons du Voyage
17 Quai d'Austerlitz 75013.
Map 18 E2.
📞 01 45 83 67 77.
🕐 *9am–5pm Mon–Fri*. Seven day escort services on all transport. Costs vary. 🖥 www.compagnons.com

Association des Paralysés de France
17 Blvd August Blanqui 75013.
Map 17 B5
📞 01 40 78 69 00.
📠 01 45 89 40 57.
🖥 www.apf-asso.com

CNRH
236 bis rue Tolbiac 75013.
📞 01 53 80 66 66.
📠 01 53 80 66 67.

Voyages Asa
148-150 Blvd de la Villette 75019
📞 01 40 33 12 70.
📠 01 40 33 12 52.

Personal Security and Health

PARIS IS AS SAFE or as dangerous as you make it – common sense is usually sufficient to stay out of trouble. If, on the other hand, you fall sick during your visit, pharmacists are an excellent source of advice. In France pharmacists can diagnose many health problems and suggest appropriate treatment. For more serious medical help, someone at the emergency numbers below will be able to deal with most enquiries. There are many specialist services available, including a general advice line for English-speakers in crisis, an English-speaking Alcoholics Anonymous group, and a phoneline for psychiatric help.

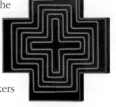
French pharmacy sign

Emergency button at metro stations

EMERGENCY NUMBERS

SAMU (ambulance)
[15 *(freecall)*.

Police [17 *(freecall)*.

Pompiers (fire department) [18 *(freecall)*.

European Emergency Call [112 *(freecall)*.

SOS Medecin (doctor, house calls)
[01 47 07 77 77.

SOS Dentaire (dentist)
[01 43 37 51 00.

Burn Specialists
[01 58 41 41 41.

SOS Help (English language crisis line)
[01 47 23 80 80.
○ 3pm–11pm daily.

SOS Dépression (for psychiatric help)
[01 45 22 44 44.

Sexual Disease Centre
[01 40 78 26 00.

Family Planning Centre
[01 48 88 07 28.
○ 9am–5pm Mon–Fri.

PERSONAL SECURITY

FOR A CITY of 2.2 million people, Paris is surprisingly safe. The centre of the city in particular has little violent crime. Muggings and brawls do occur, but they are rare compared to many other world capitals. However, do try to avoid poorly lit or isolated places. Beware of pickpockets, especially on the metro during the rush hour. Keep all valuables securely concealed and if you carry a handbag or case, never let it out of your sight.

When travelling late at night, it is a good idea, for women especially, to avoid long transfers in metro stations, such as Montparnasse and Châtelet-Les Halles. Generally, areas around RER train stations tend to attract groups of youths from outlying areas who come to Paris for entertainment, and

may become unruly. The last runs each night of RER trains to and from outlying areas should also be avoided. In an emergency in the metro, call the station agent by using the yellow telephone marked *Chef de Station* on all metro and RER platforms, or go to the ticket booth at the entrance. Most metro stations also have emergency buttons. Carriages also have alarm pulls. If there is a problem outside stations, or at bus stops, telephone the police by dialling 17.

PERSONAL PROPERTY

TAKE GREAT CARE with your personal property at all times. Make sure you insure your possessions before arrival. On sightseeing or entertainment trips do not carry valuables with you. Also, only take as much cash as you think you will need. Traveller's cheques are the

Paris fireman

Policewoman

Policeman

Typical Paris police car

Paris fire engine

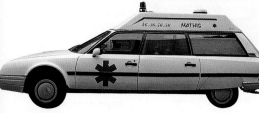

Paris ambulance

safest method of carrying large sums of money. You should never leave your luggage unattended in metro or train stations – it may be stolen. For missing persons, or in the case of robbery or assault, call the police or go to the nearest police station (*Commissariat de Police*). For lost or stolen passports call your consulate (*see p359*).

MEDICAL TREATMENT

A LL EUROPEAN community nationals are entitled to French Social Security coverage. However, treatment must be paid for, and hospital rates vary widely. Reimbursements may be obtained if you are carrying Form E111 (available free to EU citizens), but the process is long and involved. All travellers should consider purchasing travel insurance, and obtain a Form E111 in

case of emergencies. Non-EU nationals must carry their own medical insurance.

In the case of a medical emergency, call **SAMU** (*see box on facing page*) or the **Pompiers** (fire department). Fire department ambulances are often the quickest to arrive at an emergency. First-aid and emergency treatment is provided at all fire stations.

Hospitals with casualty departments are shown on the Street Finder (*see p374*). For English-language visitors there are two hospitals with English-speaking staff and doctors: the **American Hospital** and the **British Hospital**.

There are many pharmacies and a short list is provided here. Pharmacies are recognized by the green crosses on the shop front. At night and on Sundays, pharmacies hang in their doorway the address of the nearest one open.

(*see box on facing page*)
(*see p374*)
(*see p359*)

DIRECTORY

LOST PROPERTY BUREAU

Service des Objets Trouvés, 36 Rue des Morillons 75015.
⏰ 8.30am–5pm Mon, Wed, 8.30am–8pm Tue, Thu (Jul–Aug: 5pm), 8.30am–5.30pm Fri.
📞 01 55 76 20 20.

MEDICAL CENTRES

American Hospital
63 Blvd Victor-Hugo, 92200 Neuilly. **Map** 1 B2.
📞 01 46 41 25 25. Private hospital. Enquire about insurance and costs.

British Hospital
3 Rue Barbés 92300 Levallois-Perret. 📞 01 46 39 22 22.
A private hospital.

Centre Médical Europe
44 Rue d'Amsterdam 75009.
Map 6 D3. 📞 01 42 81 93 33.
For dentists 📞 01 42 81 80 00.
⏰ 8am–8pm Mon–Sat.
An inexpensive private clinic. Appointments, or walk-in.

PHARMACIES

British and American Pharmacy
1 Rue Auber 75009. **Map** 6 D4.
📞 01 42 65 88 29.
⏰ 8.30am– 8pm Mon–Fri, 10am–8pm Sat.

Pharmacie Subra
12 Rue St-Michel 75006. **Map** 12 F5. 📞 01 43 26 92 66.
⏰ 9am –9pm daily.

Pharmacie Anglo-Americaine
6 Rue Castiglione 75001.
Map 12 D1. 📞 01 42 60 72 96.
⏰ 8.30am–7.30pm Mon–Sat.

Pharmacie des Halles
10 Blvd Sebastopol 75004.
📞 01 42 72 03 23.
⏰ 9am – midnight Mon–Sat, 9am–10pm Sun.

Pharmacie Dhery
84 Ave des Champs-Elysées 75008. **Map** 4 F5. 📞 01 45 62 02 41. ⏰ 24 hours daily.

Pharmacie Matignon
2 Rue Jean-Mermoz 75008.
Map 5 A5. 📞 01 43 59 86 55.
⏰ 8.30am–2am Mon –Sat, 10am– 2am Sun.

Banking and Local Currency

VISITORS TO PARIS will find that the banks usually offer them the best rates of exchange. Privately owned bureaux de change, on the other hand, have variable rates, and care should be taken to check small print details relating to commission and minimum charges before any transaction is completed.

BANKING

THERE IS NO restriction on the amount of money or currency you may bring into France. It is wise to carry large sums in the form of travellers' cheques. To exchange travellers' cheques or cash, bureaux de change are located at airports, large railway stations, and in some hotels and shops.

Many bank branches in central Paris have their own bureaux de change. They generally offer the best exchange rates but also charge a commission for doing the exchange.

Many independent, non-bank exchange offices do not charge commission, but they offer poorer rates of exchange. Central Paris non-bank exchanges are usually open 9am–6pm Mon–Sat, and are found along the Champs-Elysées, around the Opéra and Madeleine, and near some tourist attractions and monuments. They can also be found at all main railway stations, open 8am–9pm daily. Note that the bureaux located at Gare St-Lazare and Gare d'Austerlitz are closed on Sunday. Airport offices are open 7am–11pm daily.

CHANGE
CAMBIO-WECHSEL

Sign at bureau de change

CARDS AND CHEQUES

TRAVELLERS' CHEQUES can be obtained from **American Express**, **Thomas Cook** or from your bank. If you know that you will spend most of them, it is best to have them issued in Euros. American

Express cheques are widely accepted in France and, if the cheques are exchanged at an Amex office, no commission will be charged. In the case of theft, your cheques will be replaced at once.

Because of the high commissions charged, many French businesses do not accept the American Express credit card. The most commonly used credit card is Carte Bleue/Visa. Eurocard/Mastercard is also widely accepted.

Credit card cash dispenser

French credit cards are now "smart cards", with a *puce* (a microchip capable of storing data) instead of a magnetic strip on the back. Many retailers have machines designed to read both smart cards and magnetic strips. Conventional non-French cards cannot be read in the smart card slot. Ask the cashier to swipe the card through the magnetic reader (*bande magnétique*). You may also be asked to tap in your PIN code (*code confidentiel*) and press the green key (*validez*) on a small keypad by the cash desk.

CONVERSION CHART

THE FOLLOWING is a rough guide to equivalent currency values, rounded up or down for ease of use.

EUROS	FRANCS
1	6.5
5	33
20	130
50	330
100	650

DIRECTORY

AFTER-HOURS BUREAUX DE CHANGE

Ancienne Comédie
5 Rue Ancienne-Comédie 75006.
Map 12 F4.
(01 43 26 33 30.
○ 9am–11pm daily.

CCF
103 Ave des Champs-Elysées 75008.
Map 4 E4.
(01 40 70 27 22.
○ 8.45am–8pm Mon–Sat.

Global Change
134 Blvd St-Germain 75006
Map 12 F4.
(01 40 46 87 75.
○ 9am–10.30pm daily.

Europullman
10 Rue Alger 75001.
Map 12 D1.
(01 42 60 55 58.
○ 9am–7pm Mon–Sat.

FOREIGN BANKS

American Express
11 Rue Scribe 75009.
Map 6 D5.
(01 47 14 50 00.

Barclays
45 Blvd Haussman 75009.
Map 6 F4.
(01 55 27 55 27.

HSBC
20 bis Avenue Rapp 75007.
Map 3 C4.
(01 44 42 70 00.

Thomas Cook
8 Place de l'Opéra 75009.
(01 47 42 46 52.

LOST CARDS AND TRAVELLERS' CHEQUES

American Express
Cards (01 47 77 70 00.
Cheques (08 00 90 86 00

Mastercard
Cards (01 45 67 53 53.

Visa/Carte Bleue
Cards (08 36 69 08 80.

THE EURO

THE EURO (€), the single European currency, is now operational in 12 of the 15 member states of the EU. Austria, Belgium, Finland, France, Germany, Greece, Ireland, Italy, Luxembourg, Netherlands, Portugal and Spain all chose to join the new currency; the UK, Denmark and Sweden chose to stay out, with an option to review their decision.

Euro notes and coins came into circulation on 1 January 2002. There is a transition period during which euros and francs may be used concurrently, but the franc cease to be legal tender on 17 February 2002. Franc notes and coins may, however, still be exchanged at banks until 30 June 2002, after which time they become worthless.

Bank Notes

Euro bank notes have seven denominations. The 5-euro note (grey in colour) is the smallest, followed by the 10-euro note (pink), 20-euro note (blue), 50-euro note (orange), 100-euro note (green), 200-euro note (yellow) and 500-euro note (purple). All notes show the stars of the European Union.

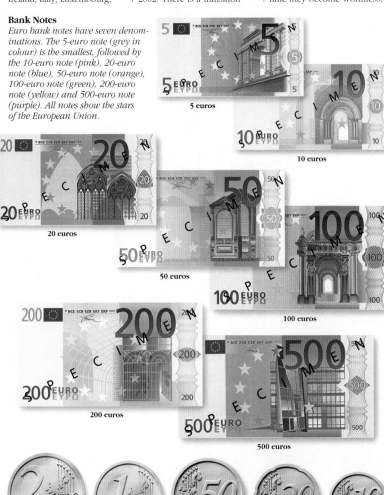

5 euros

10 euros

20 euros

50 euros

100 euros

200 euros

500 euros

2 euros

1 euro

50 cents

20 cents

10 cents

Coins

The euro has eight coin denominations: 1 euro and 2 euros; 50 cents, 20 cents, 10 cents, 5 cents, 2 cents and 1 cent. The 2- and 1-euro coins are both silver and gold in colour. The 50-, 20- and 10-cent coins are gold. The 5-, 2- and 1-cent coins are bronze.

5 cents

2 cents

1 cent

Telephone and Postal Service

THE FRENCH TELECOMMUNICATIONS agency is called France Télécom, the postal service is La Poste. Both work efficiently, though the customer services of the post offices may not. So, be prepared to wait in queues. There are many *bureaux des postes* scattered throughout the city. These are identified by the blue-on-

yellow La Poste sign *(see p357)*. Public telephones are located in most public places, including on the streets and in railway and metro stations. If you are dialling abroad from Paris, the best way is to purchase a telephone card *(télécarte)*, then find a quiet location to call from.

Telephone Boxes

Coin-operated telephone boxes are now rare. Card-operated telephones are cheap and easy to use, but you must buy a télécarte *first.*

Modern, card-
operated phonebox

Older-style
phonebox

USING THE TELEPHONE

MOST FRENCH telephones have push-buttons, but some older dial telephones are still found in cafés and restaurants. Telephone directories *(annuaires)* are found in post offices, cafés and restaurants, but not in telephone booths *(cabines)*.

To use a Paris payphone, you generally need a phone card *(télécarte)*. Sold in *tabacs*, post offices and some news-agents, these are available in 50 or 120 telephone units, and are simple to use. Remember to buy a new card before the old one runs out! Coin telephones have virtually disappeared from the streets of Paris. They can still be found in cafés but they are reserved for the use of customers. Reverse charge calls are known as *PCV* in France. Most telephone boxes can be rung from anywhere. The telephone box number is displayed above the telephone unit.

All French telephone numbers have ten digits. The first two digits indicate the region: 01 indicates Paris and the Ile de France; 02, the northwest; 03, the northeast; 04, the southeast; and 05, the southwest. Do not dial the initial zero when phoning from abroad.

Most new mobile phones brought from another European or Mediterranean country can be used in France. Alert your network that you plan to use the phone abroad so that they can enable it. However, US-based mobiles need to be "triple band" to be used in France. Remember that making and receiving international mobile calls can be very expensive. Mobile phones can easily be hired.

USING A PHONECARD (TÉLÉCARTE) TELEPHONE

1 Lift the receiver and wait for a dialling tone.

2 Holding the *télécarte* with the arrow side up, insert it into the slot in the direction that the arrow is pointing.

3 Wait for the display screen to indicate how many units are stored on the card. The screen will then tell you to dial.

4 Dial the number and wait to be connected.

5 If you want to make another call do not replace the receiver, simply press the green follow-on call button.

6 When you have finished the call, replace the receiver. The card will emerge from the slot. Remove it.

FRANCE TELECOM
600 AGENCES
PARTOUT
EN FRANCE
TELECARTE 50

Télécarte phonecard

Reaching The Right Number

- **In the case of emergencies, dial 17.**

- **Directory enquiries** dial 12.

- **International directory enquiries**, for all countries, dial 32 12.

- **International telegrams** dial 0800 33 44 11.

- **Home Direct** calls, dial 0800 99, then the country code (preceded by 00 in most cases).

- To make direct international calls, dial 00, wait for the tone, then dial the country code, area code (omit the intital 0) and the number.

- The country codes for the following are: **Australia**: 61; **Canada and USA**: 1; **Eire**: 353; **New Zealand**: 64; **UK**: 44.

- **Low-rate period** (for most places): 7pm–8am Mon–Fri, all day Sun and public hols.

- The middle pages of the telephone directory give the cost of calls per minute for each country and list their country codes, Home Direct codes, etc.

- To telephone **France** from your home country, dial: from the UK and US: 00 33; from Australia: 00 11 33. Omit the first 0 of the French area code.

Mail and Postal Services – Using La Poste

LA POSTE

Post office sign

I N ADDITION TO ALL NORMAL services – telegrams, postage stamps, registered letters, special delivery, delivery of packages and books – the post office also sells collectors' stamps, and will cash or send international money orders. Fax and telex services, as well as public telephones and Minitel, are available in all main offices.

Paris-Champs Elysées
71 Ave des Champs Elysées 75008.
Map 4 F5.
☎ 01 53 89 05 80.
FAX 01 42 56 13 71.
◷ 9am–7.30pm Mon–Fri,
10am–7pm Sat.

Sending a Letter

C OMMON postage stamps *(timbres)* **are** sold singly or in *carnets* of ten. These are valid for letters and postcards up to 20 g (approximately an ounce) to most EU countries. Stamps can often be bought in *tabacs*.

Paris post office hours are 8am–7pm Mon–Fri, 8am–noon Sat. At post offices you can consult the phone book *(annuaire)*, buy phonecards *(télécartes)*, send or receive money orders *(mandats)* and call anywhere in the world.

Letters are dropped into yellow mail boxes.

For poste restante (mail holding), the sender should write the recipient's name in block letters, then "Poste Restante", then the address of the Paris-Louvre post office.

When sending a letter poste restante, it is wise to underline the surname, as French officials otherwise sometimes assume the first name is the family name.

Main Post Offices

Paris-Louvre
52 Rue de Louvre 75001. **Map** 12 F1.
☎ 01 40 28 76 00. FAX 01 45 08 12 82. ◷ 24 hours daily.

Paris-Forum des Halles
Forum des Halles 75001. **Map** 13 A2.
☎ 01 44 76 84 60. ◷ 8am–6pm
Mon–Fri, 8am– noon Sat .

Destinations

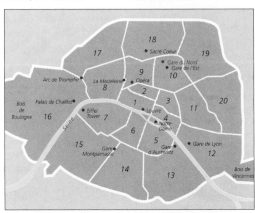

Paris letter box

Paris Arrondissements

The districts or arrondissements *of Paris* are numbered *from 1 to 20 (see p374). The first three numbers of the postcode – 750 (sometimes 751) – indicate Paris; the last two give the arrondissement number. The first arrondissement's postcode is 75001.*

CUSTOMS AND IMMIGRATION

FOR TRAVELLERS coming from with the EU's "Schengen" zone (ie. those that agreed to the Schengen Treaty), no documentation at all is needed to enter France. For "non-Schengen" nationals, including the UK, a passport (or similar) is required. Visitors from the US or New Zealand do not need a visa if staying under 3 months. After this, all visitors (including EU citizens), must acquire a *Carte de Séjour*, which involves a fair bit of paperwork. Visitors from Canada, Australia and other countries should request information from the French consulate in their own country before leaving.

TAX-FREE GOODS

THE PURCHASE OF goods "Duty Free" for export to another EU country is no longer possible. Visitors resident outside the European Union can reclaim the sales tax (TVA, or VAT; *see p312*) they pay on French goods if they spend more than 175€ in the same shop in one day and take the goods out of France.

Détaxe receipts can be issued on purchase to reclaim the tax paid, and reimbursements are collected when exiting the country, within three months of purchase. There are some goods you cannot claim a rebate on, namely food and drink, medicines, tobacco, cars and motorbikes.

DUTY-PAID AND DUTY-FREE GOODS

THERE ARE NO longer any restrictions on the quantities of duty-paid and VAT-paid goods you can take from one EU country to another, as long as they are for your own use and not for resale. You may be asked to prove the goods are for your own use if they exceed the EU suggested quantities. If you cannot do so, the entire amount of the goods (not just the deemed excess) may be confiscated and destroyed. The suggested limits are: 10 litres of spirits (i.e. drinks over 22° proof), 90 litres of wine, 110 litres of beer and 800 cigarettes. Some dangerous goods are illegal. Visitors under the age of 17 are not allowed to import duty-paid tobacco or alcohol.

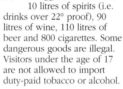

Bottle of scent

IMPORTING OTHER GOODS

IN GENERAL, all personal goods (eg. car or bicycle) may be imported to France if they are obviously for personal use and not for sale. The brochure *Voyagez en toute liberté* clarifies this. It is available from the **Centre** below, which also gives advice on import regulations, but this is usually in French.

CUSTOMS INFORMATION

Centre des Renseignements des Douanes
84 rue d'Hauteville 75010.
📞 01 53 24 68 24.
FAX 01 53 24 68 30.
🕐 9am–5pm Mon–Fri.

ELECTRICAL ADAPTORS

THE VOLTAGE in France is 220 volts. Plugs have two small round pins; heavier-duty installations have two large round pins. Better hotels offer built-in adaptors for shavers only. Adaptors can be bought at department stores, such as BHV *(see p313)*.

French two-pin electrical plug

STUDENT INFORMATION

STUDENTS WITH VALID ID cards benefit from discounts of 25–50% at theatres, museums, cinemas and many public monuments. Students may purchase an ISIC card (the International Student ID card) from Office de Tourisme de l'Université offices (**OTU**), other main travel agencies and the Centre d'Information et de Documentation Jeunesse (**CIDJ**). CIDJ provides information on student life in Paris and can furnish a list of inexpensive accommodation. They do not provide a hostel service, however, the Bureau Voyage Jeunesse (**BVJ**) has double rooms and dormitory accommodation *(see pp273–4 and 359)* at reasonable prices.

PUBLIC TOILETS IN PARIS

Most old-fashioned urinals and toilets have been replaced by modern pay toilets. They are found on pavements all over the city. In some units, classical music is played. It is crucial that children under 10 are not allowed into these toilets on their own. They have an automatic cleaning function which can be a danger to small children.

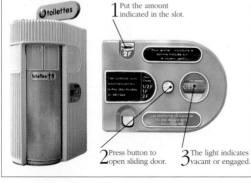

1 Put the amount indicated in the slot.

2 Press button to open sliding door.

3 The light indicates vacant or engaged.

International Bookshops

Brentano's
37 Ave de l'Opéra 75002.
Map 6 E5. 📞 *01 42 61 52 50.*
◯ *10am–7.30pm Mon–Sat.*

Gibert Jeune
5 Place St-Michel 75005.
Map 13 A4. 📞 *01 56 81 22 22.*
◯ *9.30am–7.30pm Mon–Sat.*

W H Smith
248 Rue de Rivoli 75001. **Map** 11 C1.
📞 *01 44 77 88 99.* ◯ *9am–7.30pm
Mon–Sat; 1–7.30pm Sun.*

TV, Radio, Press

Bᴿɪᴛɪsʜ ᴀɴᴅ ᴏᴛʜᴇʀ European
papers can be bought on
the day of publication at
maisons de la presse (news-

Foreign newspapers from kiosks

agents) or *kiosques* (news-
stands) throughout the city.
Some are European or
international editions, such as
Financial Times Europe, *The
Guardian Europe* and the
Guardian International, *The
Weekly Telegraph*, *USA Today*,
The Economist, and *The
International Herald Tribune*.

The main French national
dailies are – from right to left
on the political spectrum – *Le
Figaro*, *France Soir*, *Le Monde*,
Libération and *L'Humanité*.
The weeklies include satirical
Le Canard Enchaîné, news
magazines *Marianne*, *Le
Nouvel Observateur* and
L'Express, and numerous titles
devoted to fashion, gossip
and gastronomy.

The French TV channels
are *TF1* and *France 2*, both
with a lightweight mix, *France
3*, with documentaries, debate
and classic films, *5ᵉ* ("La
Cinquième") and the Franco-
German high-culture *ARTE*,
which share a channel special-
ising in arts, classical music
and films, and *M6* which
devotes a lot of time to pop
and rock. Cable and satellite
channels include CNN and Sky.

BBC Radio 4 can be picked
up during the day, while at
night, *BBC World Service* uses
the same channel (648AM or

198 Long Wave). *Voice of
America* is on at 90.5, 98.8
and 102.4FM. *Radio France
International* (738AM) gives
daily news in English from
3–4pm.

Paris Time

Pᴀʀɪs ɪs ᴏɴᴇ hour ahead of
Greenwich Mean Time
(GMT) in winter and two
hours ahead in summer. The
French use the 24-hour clock,
therefore, 9am is 09.00, 9pm
is 21.00. New York is 6 hours
behind Paris, Los Angeles 9
hours behind and Auckland
11 hours ahead.

Conversion Chart

Imperial to metric
1 inch = 2.54 centimetres
1 foot = 30 centimetres
1 mile = 1.6 kilometres
1 ounce = 28 grams
1 pound = 454 grams
1 pint = 0.6 litre
1 gallon = 4.6 litres

Metric to imperial
1 millimetre = 0.04 inch
1 centimetre = 0.4 inch
1 metre = 3 feet 3 inches
1 kilometre = 0.6 mile
1 gram = 0.04 ounce
1 kilogram = 2.2 pounds
1 litre = 1.8 pints

DIRECTORY

STUDENT INFO

OTU Offices
119 Rue St-Martin 75004.
Map 13 B2.

2 Rue Malus 75005.
Map 17 B1.

39 Ave Georges Bernanos
75005. **Map** 16 F2.
📞 *01 40 29 12 12*
(for all 3).

CIDJ
101 Quai Branly 75015.
Map 10 E2.
📞 *01 44 49 12 00.*
◯ *9.30am–6pm Mon–
Fri, 9.30am– 1pm Sat.*

BVJ
44 Rue des Bernardins
75015. **Map** 13 B5.
📞 *01 53 00 90 90.*

EMBASSIES

Australia
4 Rue Jean Rey 75015.
Map 10 D3.
📞 *01 40 59 33 00.*

Canada
35 Ave Montaigne 75008.
Map 10 F1.
📞 *01 44 43 29 00.*

Great Britain
35 Rue du Faubourg St-
Honoré 75008.
Map 5 C5. **Consulate**
(visas) 18bis Rue d'Anjou
75008. 📞 *01 44 51 31 00.*

Ireland (Eire)
4 Rue Rude 75116. **Map**
4 D4. 📞 *01 44 17 67 00.*

New Zealand
7 ter, Rue Léonard de
Vinci 75116. **Map** 3 C5.
📞 *01 45 01 43 43.*

USA
2 Ave Gabriel 75008.
Map 5 B5.
📞 *01 43 12 22 22.*

RELIGIOUS SERVICES

**PROTESTANT
American Church**
65 Quai d'Orsay 75007.
Map 10 F2.
📞 *01 40 62 05 00.*

**Church of
Scotland**
17 Rue Bayard 75008.
Map 10 F1.
📠 *01 48 78 47 94.*

**St George's
Anglican Church**
7 Rue Auguste Vacquerie
75116. **Map** 4 E5.
📞 *01 47 20 22 51.*

**CATHOLIC
Basilique du
Sacré-Coeur**
35 Rue du Chevalier de la
Barre 75018.
Map 6 F1.
📞 *01 53 41 89 00.*

**Cathédrale de
Notre-Dame**
Pl du Parvis Notre-Dame
75004. **Map** 13 A4.
📞 *01 42 34 56 10.*

**JEWISH
Synagogue
Nazareth**
15 Rue Notre Dame de
Nazareth 75003. **Map**
7 C5. 📞 *01 42 78 00 30.*

**MOSLEM
Grande Mosquée
de Paris**
Place du Puits de l'Ermite
75005. **Map** 17 B2.
📞 *01 45 35 97 33.*

GETTING TO PARIS

Paris is a major hub of European air, road and rail travel. Direct flights from around the world, though not yet from Australia and New Zealand, serve the French capital's international airports. Paris is also the centre of Europe's growing high-speed rail network, with arrivals throughout the day of Eurostar from London, Thalys from Brussels, Amsterdam and Cologne, and TGVs from Geneva and the Mediterranean port of Marseille. Approaching by road, *autoroutes* (motorways) converge on Paris from all directions, including – via Eurotunnel's Channel rail shuttle – the UK.

Boeing 737 passenger jet

ARRIVING BY AIR

The main British airlines with regular flights to Paris are **British Airways** and **British Midland**, and the main French airline is **Air France**. From the United States there are regular flights direct to Paris from about 30 cities, mainly on **American, United, Northwest, Continental, Delta, Virgin** and **British Airlines**. From Canada, **Air France** and **Air Canada** fly direct to Paris. **Qantas** is one of the few carriers providing connecting flights from Australia and New Zealand.

High airport charges have generally deterred Europe's no-frills low-cost airlines from flying to Paris, though **buzz** does offer a very inexpensive London-Paris CDG service, while **Ryanair** flies from Dublin and Glasgow (Prestwick) to Beauvais, an hour or more's bus journey west of Paris. For airline offices in Paris, see page 363.

The peak summer season in Paris is from July to September. Airline fares are at their highest during this time. Different airlines, however, may have slightly different high summer season periods, so check with the airlines or an agent as to which months are covered by these fares.

If you are prepared to look around for the best deals, there are very good ones on offer from reputable discount agents. If you book a cheap deal with a discount agent, check whether you will get a refund if the agent or operator ceases trading, and don't part with the full fare until you actually see the ticket.

Addresses of reputable discount agencies with offices in Paris are listed on page 363. These offer charters and regular scheduled flights at competitive prices. Many of them have representatives in other countries. Note that children can travel more cheaply than adults.

Flight Times
Here are some flight times from cities in different parts of the world: London 1 hour; Dublin 90 minutes; Montreal 7.5 hours; New York 8 hours; Los Angeles 12 hours; Sydney 23 hours.

CHARLES DE GAULLE AIRPORT

The terminals CDG1, CDG2 and T9 are linked by shuttle buses. The main transport services to Paris are shown below, but it is advisable to check door numbers as they are subject to change.

CDG1 is used for international flights, except those of Air France (see CDG2).

The airport complex

CDG2 is used for all Air France flights and for international flights by other carriers.

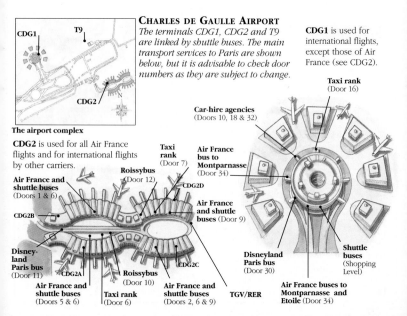

Car-hire agencies (Doors 10, 18 & 32)

Taxi rank (Door 16)

Taxi rank (Door 7)

Air France bus to Montparnasse (Door 34)

Roissybus (Door 12)

CDG2D

Air France and shuttle buses (Doors 1 & 6)

Air France and shuttle buses (Door 9)

CDG2B

Disneyland Paris bus (Door 11)

CDG2A

Roissybus (Door 10)

CDG2C

Disneyland Paris bus (Door 30)

Shuttle buses (Shopping Level)

Air France and shuttle buses (Doors 5 & 6)

Taxi rank (Door 6)

Air France and shuttle buses (Doors 2, 6 & 9)

TGV/RER

Air France buses to Montparnasse and Etoile (Door 34)

ORLY AIRPORT

The two terminals Orly Sud and Orly Ouest are linked by shuttle bus, but they are within walking distance of one another.

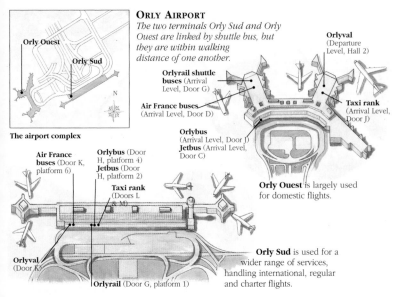

Orly Ouest

Orly Sud

N

The airport complex

Orlyval
(Departure Level, Hall 2)

Orlyrail shuttle buses (Arrival Level, Door G)

Air France buses (Arrival Level, Door D)

Taxi rank (Arrival Level, Door J)

Orlybus (Arrival Level, Door J)
Jetbus (Arrival Level, Door C)

Orly Ouest is largely used for domestic flights.

Air France buses (Door K, platform 6)

Orlybus (Door H, platform 4)
Jetbus (Door H, platform 2)

Taxi rank (Doors L & M)

Orlyval (Door K)

Orlyrail (Door G, platform 1)

Orly Sud is used for a wider range of services, handling international, regular and charter flights.

CHARLES DE GAULLE (CDG) AIRPORT

THIS IS PARIS'S main airport, lying 30 km (19 miles) north of the city. It has two main terminals, CDG1 and CDG2, and a charter flight terminal, T9. CDG2 straddles the TGV-RER station and comprises five linked halls, referred to as CDG2A, CDG2B, CDG2C, CDG2D and CDG2F

Getting into Town
Buses, trains and taxis all run to central Paris. Air France operates two services: one to Porte Maillot and Charles de Gaulle-Etoile, which leaves about every 10 minutes and takes about 40 minutes; the other goes to the Gare de Lyon and the Montparnasse TGV train station, leaving every 30 minutes and taking about 50 minutes. The Roissybus service, run by the RATP, takes travellers to Opéra. This journeys take about 50 minutes and the buses leave every 15 minutes or so.

All three services connect up in central Paris with the metro, the RER and the RATP bus network.

A Disneyland Paris bus service operates every 30–45 minutes.

The nearby Roissy Rail RER train service is linked by shuttle bus service from the terminals. Trains leave every 15 minutes and take about 35 minutes to reach the city centre, at the Gare du Nord, where there is a link to the metro and to other RER lines.

Airport Shuttle provides door to door service in a small minibus for both airports, for 18€ for one person, or 14€ each for two or more (must book 48 hours ahead). Normal taxis to the centre run between 38€ and 45€, often with long queues.

ORLY AIRPORT (ORY)

THIS IS PARIS'S second airport, located 15 km (9 miles) south of the capital. It has two terminals, Orly Sud and Orly Ouest.

Getting into Town
Transport services take travellers to the southern part of the city and a special bus links the airport with Disney-land Paris, leaving every 45 minutes.

Travellers arriving at Orly can take a taxi, bus or train to central Paris. The bus services are run by Air France and RATP (Orlybus). Air France buses take about 30 minutes to reach the city centre,

stopping at Les Invalides and Montparnasse. The Orlybus, also leaving every 12 minutes, takes about 25 minutes to reach the city centre at Denfert-Rochereau. The recent Jet Bus service takes travellers from the airport to Villejuif-Louis Aragon metro station every 15 minutes.

Shuttle buses link the airport with the RER Orlyrail services at nearby Rungis. Trains leave every 15 minutes (every 30 minutes after 9pm), taking 35 minutes to reach the Gare d'Austerlitz. A train service, Orlyval, links up with the Roissy Rail RER line B at Antony station nearby, with trains leaving every 4–8 minutes.

Taxis take 25–45 minutes to reach the city centre depending on how heavy the traffic is, and cost 23€–30€.

Orlyval train leaving Orly Airport

CROSSING THE CHANNEL

TRAVELLERS COMING to Paris from Britain by road will need to cross the English Channel. The simplest and most popular way is on the vehicle-carrying train shuttles through the Channel Tunnel. Operated by **Eurotunnel**, these run between the terminals at Folkestone and Calais. You are directed onto the trains and remain with your vehicle, though you may get out of your car and walk about inside the train. The journey through the Tunnel takes about 30 minutes, is unaffected by sea conditions or weather, and trains depart every 15-30 minutes, depending on demand. On both the English and the French side, the Tunnel terminal has direct motorway access.

There are also several ship or catamaran car ferries across the Channel. On the short Dover-Calais route, there are up to 100 crosssings per day, operated by several operators running frequent, fast services. **P&O Stena** ships make this crossing in 75-90 minutes, **SeaFrance** take 90 minutes, while **Hoverspeed** Super Seacat catamarans cross in 45 minutes. Hoverspeed's Super Seacat also travels between Newhaven and Dieppe in 2 hours. **Transmanche Ferries**, part of Corsica Ferries, also run this route, but take nearly 4 hours. **Norfolkline** runs a 2-hour Dover to Dunkerque crossing.

A long-haul coach

Two companies ply the longer western routes across the Channel. **Brittany Ferries** crossings from Plymouth to Roscoff take 6 hours, and from Poole to Cherbourg they take 4¼ hours on conventional ferry, or 2¼ hours on fast ferry. From Portsmouth, Brittany take 6 hours to Caen, and 8¾ hours overnight to St-Malo, while **P&O Portsmouth** take 6½ hours to Le Havre, and 5-6 hours to Cherbourg. When choosing a cross-Channel route, look carefully at total journey times. Driving to Paris from Cherbourg takes 4-5 hours; from Dieppe or Le Havre, about 2½-3 hours; from Calais, 2 hours.

ARRIVING BY COACH

THE MAIN COACH operator to Paris is **Eurolines**, based at the Gare Routière Internationale in eastern Paris. Its coaches travel to Belgium, Holland, Ireland, Germany, Scandinavia, United Kingdom, Italy and Portugal.

Their terminus in London is Victoria Coach Station, from where there are between three and five daily departures for Paris, depending on the season. The journey from London to Paris takes between 8 and 9 hours.

USEFUL CONTACTS

Eurostar
London Waterloo International.
☎ 08705-186 186.
W www.eurostar.com

Eurotunnel
☎ 08705 35 35 35.

Brittany Ferries
☎ 02 33 88 44 88.

Hoverspeed/Seacat
☎ 08 20 00 35 55.

Norfolkline
☎ 03 28 59 01 01.

P&O Stena/Portsmouth
☎ 03 21 46 10 10.

SeaFrance
☎ 03 21 34 55 00.

Eurolines
Ave de Général de Gaulle, Bagnolet.
☎ 08 36 69 52 52.
Victoria Coach station, London SW1.
☎ 08705-143 219.
W www.eurolines.co.uk

ARRIVING BY RAIL

EUROSTAR TRAINS travel directly from central London (Waterloo) to central Paris (Gare du Nord) in exactly 3 hours. There are up to 24 departures daily. Other high-speed rail services into Paris

The high-speed TGV train

THE TGV

Trains à Grande Vitesse, or TGV high-speed trains, travel at speeds up to 300 km/h (186mph). TGVs for northern France leave from the Gare du Nord, for the Atlantic Coast and Brittany from Gare Montparnasse, and for Provence and the southeast from Gare de Lyon. The network serves a large number of stations on routes to these destinations, and the number of stations served is growing all the time, making this an ever-more convenient form of transport *(see pp364–5).*

include **Thalys**, from Brussels, Amsterdam and Cologne, and **TGVs** from throughout France. Travel on all these services must be pre-booked, though reservations can be made up to the last moment. Prices are much cheaper booked ahead.

As the railway hub of France and the Continent, Paris has five major international railway stations operated by the French state railways, known as SNCF *(see p372)*. The Gare de Lyon in eastern Paris is the city's main station, serving the south of France, the Alps, Italy, Switzerland and Greece. The Gare de l'Est serves eastern France, Austria, Switzerland and Germany.

Arriving at the Gare du Nord are trains from Holland, Belgium and Scandinavia. Trains from some Channel ports arrive at the Gare St-Lazare. The terminus for trains from Spain, as well as from the Brittany ports, is the Gare Montparnasse. The other main stations are Massy-Palaiseau (SW of the city), Marne-la-Vallée for Disney-land Paris (E), and Aeroport Charles-de-Gaulle (NE).

There is a tourist office at the Gare de Lyon where you can book accommodation *(see p351)*. All the railway stations are served by city buses, the metro and RER trains. Directional signs show where to make connections to the city transport system.

ARRIVING BY CAR

PARIS IS AN oval-shaped city. It is surrounded by an outer ring road called the Boulevard Périphérique. All motorways leading to the capital link in to the Périphér-ique, which separates the city from the suburbs. Each former city gate, called a *porte*, now corresponds to an exit from (or entrance to) the Périphérique. Arriving motorists should check their destination address and consult a map of central Paris to find the closest correspond-ing *porte*. For example, a motorist who wants to get to the Arc de Triomphe should exit at Porte Maillot.

DIRECTORY

MAIN AIRLINES SERVING PARIS

Aer Lingus
52–4 Rue Belle Feuille 92100.
☎ 01 55 38 38 55.
W www.aerlingus.ie

Air Canada
10 Rue de la Paix 75002.
Map 6 D5.
☎ 08 25 880 881.
W www.aircanada.ca

Air France
119 Ave des Champs-Elysées 75008. **Map** 4 E4.
☎ 0802 802 802.
W www.airfrance.com

American Airlines
109 Rue du Faubourg-St-Honoré 75008.**Map** 5 B5.
☎ 08 01 872 872.
W www.aa.com

British Airways
13–15 Blvd de la Madeleine 75001. **Map** 6 D5. ☎ 08 25 825 400.
W www.british-airways.com

British Midland
4 Place de Londres, Roissy-en-France 95700.
☎ 01 41 91 87 04.
W www.iflybritish midland.com

buzz
☎ 01 55 17 42 42
W www.buzzaway.com

Delta Airlines
119 Ave de Champs-Elysées 75008. **Map** 4 E4.
☎ 08 00 35 40 80.
W www.delta-air.com

Qantas Airlines
13–15 Blvd de la Madeleine 75001. **Map** 6 D5. ☎ 0803 846 846.
W www.qantas.com

Ryanair
☎ 08 25 07 16 26 (France).
W www.ryanair.com

DISCOUNT TRAVEL AGENCIES

Directours
90 Ave des Champs-Elysées 75008. **Map** 4 E4.
☎ 01 45 62 62 62.
W www.directours.fr

Forum Voyages
1 Rue Cassette 75006.
Map 12 D5.
☎ 01 45 44 38 61.

Jet Tours
29 Ave de la Motte Picquet 75007. **Map** 10 F4.
☎ 01 47 05 01 95.
W www.jettours.com

Nouvelles Frontières
87 Blvd de Grenelle 75008.
Map 10 D4. ☎ 08 10 20 10 20. W www.nouvelles-frontieres.fr

USIT Voyages
6 Rue Vaugirard 75006.
☎ 01 42 34 56 90.
52 Grosvenor Gardens London SW1W OAG.
☎ 0870 240 1010.

AIRPORT INFORMATION

W www.adp.fr

Air France Buses
☎ 01 41 56 89 00.

Disabled Assistance
☎ 01 48 62 28 24 (CDG 1) & 01 48 62 59 00 (CDG 2).
☎ 01 49 75 30 70/25 (Orly Sud/Orly Ouest).

Paging Travellers
☎ 01 48 62 22 80 (CDG).
01 49 75 15 15 (Orly).

Travel Information
☎ 01 48 62 22 80 (CDG).
01 49 75 15 15 (Orly).

Orlyrail
☎ 01 53 90 20 20.

RATP Bus
☎ 08 36 68 77 14 (French) or 08 36 68 41 14 (English).
W www.ratp.fr

RER Train
☎ Ile de France: 01 53 90 20 20; TGV: 08 36 35 35 35.
W www.sncf.fr

Airport Shuttle
☎ 01 30 11 11 90 or 1 888 426 2705 (from US).
W www.airportshuttle.fr

CDG AIRPORT HOTELS

Ibis
☎ 01 49 19 19 20.
@ h1404-@accor-hotels.com

Eliance Cocoon
☎ 01 48 62 06 16.

Holiday Inn
☎ 01 34 29 30 00.
@ hircdg@club-internet.fr

Novotel
☎ 01 49 19 27 27.
@ h1014@accor-hotels.com

Sofitel
☎ 01 49 19 29 29.
@ hotel.sofitel @wanadoo.fr

ORLY SUD AIRPORT HOTELS

Ibis
☎ 01 56 70 50 50.
@ h1413@accor-hotels.com.

Hilton Hotel
☎ 01 45 12 45 12.
@ oryhitwrm @oryhitw.com

Mercure
☎ 01 46 87 23 37.
@ h1246@accor-hotels.com.

Arriving in Paris

THIS MAP DEPICTS the bus and rail services between the two main airports and the city. It shows the ferry-rail links from the UK, the main railway links from other parts of France and Europe, and the long-haul coach services from other European countries. It also shows the main city railway and coach termini, the airport shuttle connections and the airport bus and rail stops. The frequency of services and journey times from the airport are provided, as are the approximate times of rail journeys from other cities. Metro and RER line connections to other parts of Paris are indicated at the termini and route stops.

CALAIS
Ferry and Eurotunnel links with Dover and Folkestone. Eurostar train from London to Paris Gare du Nord (3 hrs) passes through here but cannot be boarded at Calais.
SNCF train to Gare du Nord (3 hrs).

LE HAVRE
Ferry links with Portsmouth.
SNCF train to Gare St-Lazare (2 hrs).

DIEPPE
Ferry links with Newhaven (summer). SNCF train to Gare St-Lazare (2 hrs 20 mins).

CAEN
Ferry links with Portsmouth.
SNCF train to Gare St-Lazare (1 hrs 45 mins).

CHERBOURG
Ferry links with Portsmouth and Poole.
SNCF train to Gare St-Lazare (4 hrs).

Porte Maillot
M (1)
RER (A) (C)

Charles de Gaulle-Etoile
M (1) (2) (6)
RER (A)

Champs-Elysées

Chaillot Quarter

Gare S
M (3)

Invalides
M (8) (13)
RER (C)

Invalides and Eiffel Tower Quarter

GARE ST-LAZARE
Rouen (1 hr 10 mins).

Montparnasse

GARE MONTPARNASSE
Bordeaux (3 hrs)
Brest (4 hrs 30 mins)
Lisbon (24 hrs)
Madrid (16 hrs)
Nantes (2 hrs)
Rennes (2 hrs 5 mins)

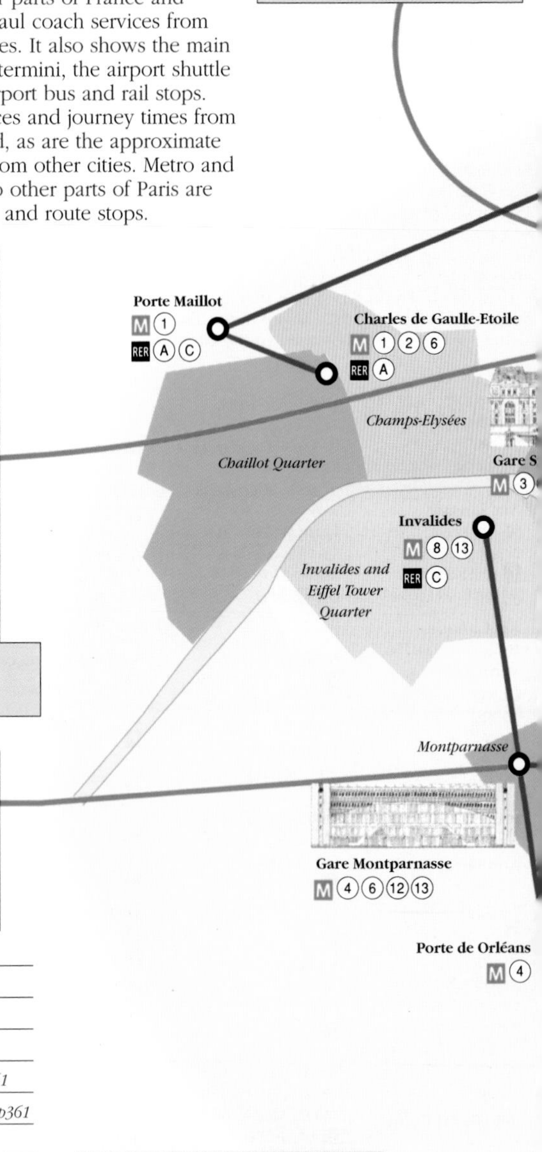

Gare Montparnasse
M (4) (6) (12) (13)

Porte de Orléans
M (4)

KEY

▬▬▬	SNCF see pp362–3
▬▬▬	Coaches see p362
▬▬▬	RATP bus see p361
▬▬▬	Air France bus see p361
▬▬▬	RER B-Roissy Rail see p361
▬▬▬	Orlyrail see p361
▬▬▬	Orlyval see p361
▬▬▬	Orlybus see p361
▬▬▬	Jet Bus see p361
M	Metro station
RER	RER station

GARE TGV DE MASSY-PALAISEAU
Bordeaux (3 hrs 20 mins)
Lille (1 hr 40 mins)
London (3 hrs 40 mins)
Lyon (2 hrs 20 mins)
Nantes (2 hrs 10 mins)
Rennes (2 hrs 5 mins)
Rouen (1 hr 10 mins)

Antony

365

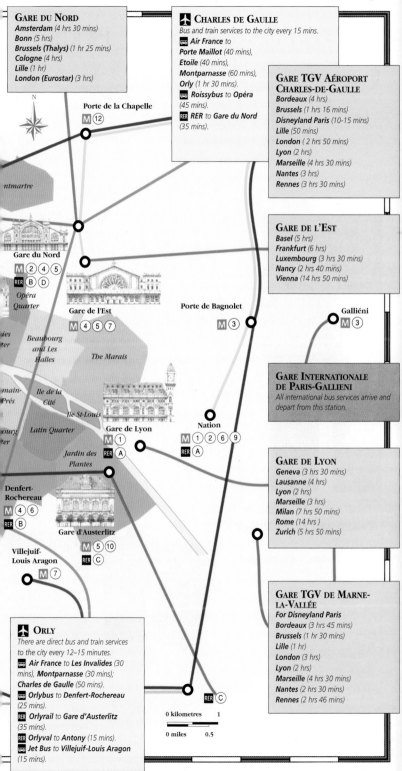

GARE DU NORD
Amsterdam *(4 hrs 30 mins)*
Bonn *(5 hrs)*
Brussels (Thalys) *(1 hr 25 mins)*
Cologne *(4 hrs)*
Lille *(1 hr)*
London (Eurostar) *(3 hrs)*

✈ CHARLES DE GAULLE
Bus and train services to the city every 15 mins.
🚌 **Air France** to
Porte Maillot *(40 mins)*,
Etoile *(40 mins)*,
Montparnasse *(60 mins)*,
Orly *(1 hr 30 mins)*.
🚌 **Roissybus** to **Opéra** *(45 mins)*.
RER **RER** to **Gare du Nord** *(35 mins)*.

GARE TGV AÉROPORT CHARLES-DE-GAULLE
Bordeaux *(4 hrs)*
Brussels *(1 hrs 16 mins)*
Disneyland Paris *(10-15 mins)*
Lille *(50 mins)*
London *(2 hrs 50 mins)*
Lyon *(2 hrs)*
Marseille *(4 hrs 30 mins)*
Nantes *(3 hrs)*
Rennes *(3 hrs 30 mins)*

Porte de la Chapelle
M ⑫

ntmartre

Gare du Nord
M ② ④ ⑤
RER Ⓑ Ⓓ

Opéra
Quarter

Gare de l'Est
M ④ ⑤ ⑦

GARE DE L'EST
Basel *(5 hrs)*
Frankfurt *(6 hrs)*
Luxembourg *(3 hrs 30 mins)*
Nancy *(2 hrs 40 mins)*
Vienna *(14 hrs 50 mins)*

Porte de Bagnolet
M ③

Galliéni
M ③

Beaubourg
and Les
Halles

The Marais

GARE INTERNATIONALE DE PARIS-GALLIENI
All international bus services arrive and depart from this station.

main-
Prés

Ile de la
Cité

Ile St-Louis

Latin Quarter

Gare de Lyon
M ①
RER Ⓐ

Nation
M ① ② ⑥ ⑨
RER Ⓐ

Jardin des
Plantes

ourg
er

Denfert-
Rochereau
M ④ ⑥
RER Ⓑ

GARE DE LYON
Geneva *(3 hrs 30 mins)*
Lausanne *(4 hrs)*
Lyon *(2 hrs)*
Marseille *(3 hrs)*
Milan *(7 hrs 50 mins)*
Rome *(14 hrs)*
Zurich *(5 hrs 50 mins)*

Gare d'Austerlitz
M ⑤ ⑩
RER Ⓒ

Villejuif-
Louis Aragon
M ⑦

GARE TGV DE MARNE-LA-VALLÉE
For Disneyland Paris
Bordeaux *(3 hrs 45 mins)*
Brussels *(1 hr 30 mins)*
Lille *(1 hr)*
London *(3 hrs)*
Lyon *(2 hrs)*
Marseille *(4 hrs 30 mins)*
Nantes *(2 hrs 30 mins)*
Rennes *(2 hrs 46 mins)*

✈ ORLY
There are direct bus and train services to the city every 12–15 minutes.
🚌 **Air France** to **Les Invalides** *(30 mins)*, **Montparnasse** *(30 mins)*;
Charles de Gaulle *(50 mins)*.
🚌 **Orlybus** to **Denfert-Rochereau** *(25 mins)*.
RER **Orlyrail** to **Gare d'Austerlitz** *(35 mins)*.
RER **Orlyval** to **Antony** *(15 mins)*.
🚌 **Jet Bus** to **Villejuif-Louis Aragon** *(15 mins)*.

RER Ⓒ

| 0 kilometres | 1 |
| 0 miles | 0.5 |

GETTING AROUND PARIS

ENTRAL PARIS is compact. The best way to get around is to walk. However, visitors unfamiliar with the motoring code and undisciplined French driving need to take care. Cycling, too, can be dangerous, due to traffic conditions and aggressive drivers. Bike lanes are often not respected. Driving a car in the city centre is not recommended. Traffic is often heavy, there are many one-way streets, and parking is difficult and expensive. However, a bus, metro and RER train system operated by the RATP makes getting around cheap and easy. The city is divided into five travel zones: zones 1 and 2 corresponding to the centre and zones 3, 4 and 5 to the suburbs and the airport. The city is also divided into 20 arrondissements, which will help visitors in their search for addresses (see p357).

Parisian drivers do not always respect pedestrian crossings.

Stop sign   **Walk sign**

WALKING IN PARIS

AUSTRALIAN, BRITISH, Irish and New Zealand visitors need to remember that cars drive on the right-hand side of the road. There are many two-stage road crossings where pedestrians wait on an island in the centre of the road before proceeding. These are marked *piétons traversez en deux temps*.

CYCLING IN PARIS

PARIS IS AN EXCELLENT city for cyclists. It's reasonably flat, manageably small, has many backstreets where car traffic is restricted, and about 150 km (103 miles) of cycle lanes (*pistes cyclables*). Parisian motorists are increasingly respectful of cyclists as more and more of their fellow citizens turn to two wheels. The RATP's own cycling centre,

the **Maison Roue Libre**, in the heart of Paris, is most helpful for rental and organised tours, as well as for repairs and storage (brochures available in most RATP metro, RER and bus stations). Bicycles may be taken on SNCF trains, and some suburban train stations rent bicycles. For the energetic, **Bullfrog Bike Tours** offer inexpensive tours in English, departing from near the Eiffel Tower (see p367).

A Parisian cyclist

TICKETS AND TRAVEL PASSES

A wide variety of tickets and passes can be purchased at all main metro and RER stations, at the airports and several tourist offices. Among the most useful for tourists are: individual tickets, or a block of ten (*carnet*) at a discount; a one-day *Mobilis* card for selected zones; *Carte Orange*, giving unlimited travel for a week or month for selected zones, a Monday–Sunday weekly ticket (*hebdomadaire*) for two zones; and the *Paris Visite* pass for one, two, three or five days, which includes discounted entry to some sights but is comparatively expensive unless you intend to travel fairly extensively.

Paris Visite pass and one-day ticket

Mobilis card

Carte Orange

Tickets for use on metro, RER or bus

An Hebdomadaire ticket

Carte Orange one-month travel ticket for zones 1 and 2

DRIVING IN PARIS

THOUGH DRIVING and parking can be difficult in central Paris, a hire car can be useful for visiting outlying areas. To hire a car, a valid driving licence and passport are required (most firms also require one major credit card). For payment by cheque or cash, additional ID may be required (including air tickets and credit cards). International driving licences are not needed for drivers from EU countries, Scandinavia, North America, Australia and New Zealand.

Cars drive on the right-hand side of the road and must yield to traffic merging from the right, even on thoroughfares, unless marked by a *priorité* sign, which indicates right of way. Cars on a roundabout usually have right of way, though one exception is the Arc de Triomphe, where cars yield to traffic from the right.

PARKING

PARKING IN Paris is difficult and expensive. Park only in areas with a large "P" or a *Parking Payant* sign on the pavement or on the road, and pay at the *horodateur* machine nearby. Never park where there are *Parking Interdit* or *Stationnement Interdit* signs.

No entry sign

INTERDIT SUR TOUTE LA LONGUEUR DE LA VOIE

Parking Interdit (no parking)

30

Speed limit sign in km/h

ARRÊT GÊNANT
ARTICLE A 301 DU CODE DE LA ROUTE

Tow-away zone

For towed or clamped cars, phone or go to the nearest police station *(Commissariat de Police)*. For towing away there is a fine, plus a fee for each day the car is held. There are seven car pounds *(perfourrières)* in Paris. Cars are taken to different ones depending on which area they were towed away from, and kept there for 48 hours, then sent to outlying long-term garages *(fourrières)*.

Les Relais Parking is a useful parking service available at twenty sites (kiosques) in central Paris, from where professional chauffeurs park and oversee your vehicle until your return.

BICYCLE HIRE/REPAIR & TOURS

Maison Roue Libre
95 bis Rue Rambuteau 75001.
Map 13 B2. ☎ 01 53 46 43 77.
Bicycle rental, storage, repair.

Bullfrog Bike Tours
Ave Gustave Eiffel 75007.
Map 10 D3. ☎ 01 47 42 00 01.
English language bicycle tours.

Bicloune
7 Rue Froment 75011.
Map 14 E3. ☎ 01 48 05 47 75.
Bicycle sales and repairs only.

Paris à vélo c'est sympa!
37 Blvd Bourdon 75004.
Map 14 D5. ☎ 01 48 87 60 01.
Bicycle rental

Paris Vélo
2 Rue du Fer-à-Moulin 75005.
Map 17 C2. ☎ 01 43 37 59 22.
Bicycle rental

RATP Information
☎ 08 36 68 77 14.
W www.ratp.fr

SNCF Information
☎ 08 36 35 35 35.
W www.sncf.fr

CAR HIRE AGENCIES

CAR HIRE AGENCIES abound in Paris. Here is a list of major firms with agencies at Charles de Gaulle and Orly airports, main railway stations and city-centre locations. Telephone for reservations and pick-up and drop-off information.

ADA
☎ 08 36 68 40 02.

Avis
☎ 01 49 75 44 91.

Budget
☎ 08 00 10 00 01.

Europcar
☎ 01 45 00 08 06,

Hertz
☎ 08 03 86 18 61.

National Citer
☎ 01 44 38 61 61.

Les Relais Parking
☎ 08 25 82 50 08
W www.relaisparking.com

USING AN HORODATEUR MACHINE

Horodateurs (parking meters) operate from 9am–7pm Mon–Fri. Unless otherwise indicated, parking is free Sat–Sun, public holidays and in August.

Card-only machine

1 If using coins, insert according to the tariff shown. If using a card, see step 2.

Parking card

2 If using a card, insert and press blue button for each 15 minutes required.

3 Press green button for ticket.

4 Remove ticket and place inside car windscreen.

Travelling by Metro

THE RATP (Paris transport company) operates 14 metro lines, referred to by their number and terminus names, criss-crossing Paris and its suburbs. This is often the fastest and cheapest way to get across the capital, as there are dozens of stations scattered around the city. Metro stations are easily identified by their logo, a large circled "M", and sometimes their elegant Art Nouveau entrances. Neighbourhood maps are found in all stations, near the exits. The metro and RER (Paris rail network) systems operate in much the same way, though RER carriages are slightly larger. The first trains leave their termini at 5.30am and the last return at 1.15am.

RATP logo

Art Nouveau metro sign

Modern metro sign

Reading the Metro Map

Metro and RER lines are shown in various colours on the metro map. Metro lines are identified by a number, which is located on the map at either end of a line. Some metro stations serve only one line, others serve more than one. There are stations sharing both metro and RER lines and some are linked to one another by interconnecting passages.

Metro and RER stations with inter-connecting passage

RER and metro station serving the same lines

Metro line

Metro station serving one line

Metro station serving two lines

RER line

Metro line identification number

USING THE RER

THE RER is a system of commuter trains, travelling underground in central Paris and above ground in outlying areas. Both metro tickets and passes are valid on it. There are five lines, known by their letters: A, B, C, D and E. Each line forks. For example, Line C has six forks, labelled C1, C2 etc. All RER trains bear names (for example, ALEX or VERA) to make it easier to read RER timetables in the station halls and on platforms. Digital panels on all RER platforms indicate train name, direction of travel (terminus) and upcoming stations.

RER stations are identified by a large circled logo. The main city stations are: Charles de Gaulle-Etoile, Châtelet-Les-Halles, Gare de Lyon, Nation, St-Michel-Notre-Dame, Auber-Haussmann St-Lazare and the Gare du Nord-Magenta.

The RER and metro systems overlap in central Paris. It is often quicker to take an RER train to a station served by both, as in the case of La Défense and Nation. However, getting into the RER stations, which are often linked to the metro by a maze of corridors, can be very time-consuming.

The RER is particularly useful for getting to Paris airports and to many of the outlying towns and tourist attractions. Line B3 serves Charles de Gaulle airport; Lines B4 and C2 serve Orly airport; Line A4 goes to the Disneyland Paris; and Line C5 runs to Versailles.

RER logo

BUYING A TICKET

ORDINARY METRO and RER tickets can be bought either singly or as a *carnet* of 10, from ticket booths or ticket machines in the booking halls (carry some 1 and 2 Euro coins). The useful **Paris Visite** bus, metro and RER pass (*see p366*) is widely available, and you can also buy it in advance at certain travel agencies and rail ticket agents abroad (eg. Rail Europe in London).

One metro ticket "section urbaine" entitles you to travel anywhere on the metro, and on RER trains in central Paris. RER trips outside the centre (such as to airports) require special tickets. Fares to suburbs and nearby towns vary. Consult the fare charts posted in all RER stations. Passengers on all city transport must retain their tickets during the trip, as regular inspections are made and fines can be imposed for not having a ticket.

MAKING A JOURNEY BY METRO

1 To determine which metro line to take, travellers should first find their destination on a metro map. (Maps can be found inside stations and also on the inside back cover of this book.) Trace the metro line by following the colour coding and the number of the line. At the end of the line you will see the number of the terminus – remember this, as it will help you to find the correct train.

Insert the train ticket in the first barrier.

Remove the ticket from the second barrier.

2 Metro tickets are sold at all stations. Some stations are equipped with coin-operated automatic machines. All metro tickets are second class. One ticket allows the bearer travel for one journey and any transfers on the metro system.

← DIRECTION
Ⓜ ① CHÂTEAU DE VINCENNES

CORRESPONDANCES

GARE DE LYON
REUILLY-DIDEROT
NATION
PORTE DE VINCENNES
SAINT-MANDÉ-TOURELLE
BÉRAULT
CHÂTEAU DE VINCENNES

3 To enter the platform area, insert the metro ticket, with the magnetic strip facing down, into the first barrier slot. Remove the ticket from the second slot, then push through the turnstyle, or step through the barrier if automatic.

4 At the entrance to each station platform, or in the station corridors, there is a list of upcoming stations corresponding to a given terminus. Terminus names are also indicated on the platform and should be checked before boarding the train.

DIRECTION
Ⓜ ①
CHÂTEAU DE VINCENNES

5 To change lines, get off at the appropriate transfer station and follow the *correspondance* (connections) signs on the platform indicating the appropriate direction.

6 On older trains there are door handles which have to be lifted to open the door. On more modern trains there is a release button which you press to open the door. Before the doors open and close, a single tone will sound.

7 Inside the trains are charts of the line being served by the train. The station stops are plotted on the chart, so travellers can track their journeys.

← SORTIE

8 The "Sortie" sign indicates the way out. At all metro exits there are neighbourhood maps.

Travelling by Bus

T HE BUS IS AN EXCELLENT way to see the great sights of Paris. The bus system is run by the RATP, as is the metro, so you can use the same tickets for both. There are 60 bus lines in Paris and over 2,000 buses in daily circulation. This is often the fastest way to travel short distances. However, buses can get caught up in heavy traffic and are often crowded during peak hours. Visitors should check the times for the first and last buses as they vary widely, depending on the line. Most buses run from Monday to Saturday, from early morning to mid-evening (6am–8.30pm).

Bus Stop Signs
Signs at bus stops display route numbers. A white background indicates a service every day all year; a black one means no service on Sundays or public holidays.

Bus terminus sign

Bus stop   **Night bus sign**

Ticket-cancelling machine

Bus ticket

Cancelling a Bus Ticket
Insert the ticket into the machine in the direction of the arrow, then withdraw it.

TICKETS AND PASSES

A SINGLE BUS ticket entitles the bearer to a single journey on a single line. If you want to make a change, you'll need another ticket. (Exceptions to this rule are the buses Balabus, Noctambus,

Orlybus and Roissybus, and lines 221, 297, 299 350 and 351.) Children under four are allowed to travel for free, and those aged between four and ten may travel at half price. You can purchase a *carnet* of 10 tickets, each of them valid for a single bus or metro journey. However, a *carnet* can only be obtained at the metro stations, not on the buses. Metro tickets may be used for bus travel. Bus-only tickets are purchased on board the bus, from the driver, and these must be cancelled to be valid. To do this insert the ticket into the cancelling machine inside the main doors of the

Red exit button

bus. Be sure to hold on your ticket until the end of the journey. Inspectors do make random checks and are empowered to levy on-the-spot fines if you cannot produce a valid cancelled ticket for your journey. Travel passes are a useful and economical idea if you want the freedom of unlimited travel on Paris buses (*see p366*). Never cancel these as it will render them invalid. They should be shown to the bus driver when ever you board a bus, and to a ticket inspector on request.

Paris's Buses
Passengers can identify the route and destination of a bus from the information on the panels at the front. Some buses have open rear platforms, however these are becoming more rare.

Bus route number

Bus destination

Bus route number on rear of bus

Passengers enter the bus at the front door

Bus front displaying information

Open rear platform

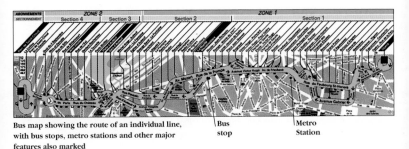

Bus map showing the route of an individual line, with bus stops, metro stations and other major features also marked / **Bus stop** / **Metro Station**

USING THE BUSES

Bus stops and shelters are identified by the number shields of the buses that stop at them, and by the distinctive RATP logo. Route maps at bus stops indicate transfers and nearby metro and RER stops. Bus stops also display timetables, and show first and last buses. Neighbourhood maps are also displayed at most bus shelters.

Most buses must be flagged down. Some new models have multiple doors which must be opened by pressing a red button inside the bus to exit, or outside the bus to enter. All buses have buttons and bells to signal for a stop. Some buses do not go all the way to their terminus; in that case, there will be a slash through the name of the destination on the front panel.

Buses do not have special facilities for the handicapped, but some seats are reserved for disabled and elderly persons, war veterans and pregnant women. These seats are identified by a sign and must be given up on request.

NIGHT AND SUMMER BUSES

There are 18 night bus lines, called Noctambus, for Paris and its suburbs (running 1.00–5.30am daily). The terminus for most of the lines is Châtelet, at Avenue Victoria or Rue St-Martin. Noctambus stops are clearly identified by a shield bearing an owl and a yellow moon. Noctambus must be flagged down. Travel passes are valid, but the normal metro tickets are not. Fares vary according to destination. Travellers may buy tickets on board the bus.

The RATP also operates buses in the Bois de Vincennes and Bois de Boulogne during the summer. The **RATP Information** is extremely helpful on these services, on the best ways to get around the city, and about tickets and passes in general.

RATP Information
53 Quai des Grands Augustins
75006. 📞 08 36 68 77 14
🖥 www.ratp.fr

USEFUL BUS ROUTES

Here is a selection of the best sightseeing bus routes around the centre of Paris, taking in some of the great sights of the city. The routes show the major bus stops, the nearest metro stations and locations of some of the notable sights.

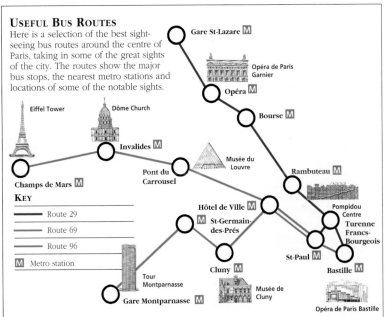

KEY

Route 29
Route 69
Route 96
Ⓜ Metro station

Using the SNCF Trains

T HE FRENCH STATE railway, Société Nationale des Chemins de Fer (**SNCF**), has two kinds of service in Paris: the Banlieue suburban service and the Grandes Lignes, or long-distance service. The suburban services all operate within the five-zone network (*see p366*). The long-distance services operate throughout France. These services allow visitors to visit parts of France close to Paris in a day round trip. The TGV high-speed service is particularly useful for such journeys, as it is capable of travelling about twice as fast as the normal trains (*see pp362–3*).

Gare de l'Est railway station in 1920

RAILWAY STATIONS

A S THE RAILWAY hub of France and the Continent, Paris boasts six major international railway stations operated by the SNCF. The railway stations are the Gare du Nord, Gare de l'Est, Gare de Lyon, Gare d'Austerlitz, Gare St-Lazare and Gare Montparnasse.

All the main train stations have long-distance and suburban destinations. Some of the main suburban locations, such as Versailles and Chantilly, are served by both long-distance and suburban trains.

The stations have departures and arrivals boards showing the train number, departure and arrival time, delay, platform number or letter, provenance, and main stops along the route. For those with heavy luggage,

Rail traveller with luggage trolley

there are trolleys, requiring a 1 Euro coin (refunded when the trolley is returned).

TICKETS

T ICKETS TO suburban destinations can often be purchased at coin-operated automatic machines located inside station halls, so it is useful to carry coins (the machines give change).

Otherwise you can buy tickets at the ticket counters.

Before boarding a train, travellers must time-punch their tickets and reservations in a *composteur* machine. Inspectors do check travellers' tickets and anyone who fails to time-punch their ticket can be fined.

Ticket booths are usually marked with panels indicating the kind of tickets (*billets*) sold: *Banlieue* for suburban tickets, *Grandes Lignes* for mainline tickets, and *Internationale* for international tickets.

Substantial fare discounts of 25-50% are offered to over 60s (*Découverte Senior*),

Composteur Machine

The composteur *machines are located in station halls and at the head of each platform. Tickets and reservations must be inserted face up.*

A time-punched ticket

under 26s (*Découverte 12-25*), up to four adults travelling with a child under 12 (*Découverte Enfant Plus*), or anyone booking more than 30 days or more than 8 days in advance (*Découverte J30* or *J8*).

STUDENT AND YOUTH DISCOUNT TICKETS

Nouvelles Frontières
87 Blvd de Grenelle 75015. **Map** 10D4.
[C] 08 25 00 08 25/ 01 45 68 70 00.
[W] www.nouvelles-frontieres.fr

Wasteels
12 Rue La Fayette 75009. **Map** 6 E4.
[C] 01 42 47 82 77.

SUBURBAN TRAINS

S UBURBAN LINES are found at all main Paris train stations and are clearly marked Banlieue. Tickets for city

A double-decker Banlieue train

transport cannot be used on Banlieue trains, with the exception of some RER tickets to stations with both SNCF and RER lines. Several tourist destinations are served by Banlieue trains, including Chantilly, Chartres, Fontainebleau, Giverny and Versailles (*see pp248–53*). Telephone the SNCF for details on 08 36 35 35 35 or try their website:
[W] www.sncf.fr

Travelling by Taxi

TAXIS ARE MORE EXPENSIVE than trains or buses, but they are an advantage after 1am, when the metro has stopped running. There are taxi ranks throughout the city; a list of some of these is provided below.

A Paris taxi rank sign

CATCHING A TAXI

THERE ARE over 10,000 taxis operating in central Paris. Yet there never seem to be enough of them to meet demand, particularly during rush hours and on Friday and Saturday nights.

Taxis can be hailed in the street, but not within 50 m (165 ft) of a taxi rank. Since ranks always take priority over street stops, the easiest way to get a cab is to find a rank and join the queue. Ranks are found at many busy crossroads, at main metro and RER stations, and at all hospitals, train stations and airports. An illuminated

white light on the roof shows that the taxi is available. A small light lit below means that the taxi is occupied. If the white light is covered the taxi is off duty. Taxis on their last run can refuse to take passengers.

The meter should have a specified initial amount showing at the taxi rank, or when it is hailed. Initial charges on radio taxis vary widely, depending on the distance the taxi covers to arrive at the pick-up point. No cheques or credit cards are accepted as payment.

Rates vary with the part of the city and the time of day. Rate A, in the city centre, is charged per kilometre. The higher rate B applies in the city centre on Sundays, holidays and at night (7pm–7am), or daytime in the suburbs or airports. Even higher rate C applies to the suburbs and airports at night. Taxis charge for each piece of luggage. There's no need to give a tip.

Fare · **Tariff rate**

PRIX A PAYER · TARIF

The taxi fare is recorded on the meter in the cab

TAXI PARISIEN

Taxi roof sign

The light indicates tariff rate and that the taxi is occupied

A typical Paris taxi

DIRECTORY

TAXI RANKS

Charles de Gaulle-Etoile
1 Ave Wagram 75017.
Map 4 D4.
☎ 01 43 80 01 99.

Eiffel Tower
Quai Branly 75007.
Map 10 D3.
☎ 01 45 55 85 41.

Metro Concorde
252 Rue de Rivoli 75001.
Map 11 C1.
☎ 01 42 61 67 60.

Place de Clichy
Pl de Clichy 75009.
Map 6 D1.
☎ 01 42 85 00 00.

Place Denfert-Rochereau
297 Blvd Raspail 75014.
Map 16 E3.
☎ 01 43 35 00 00.

Place de la Madeleine
8 Blvd Malesherbes 75008.
Map 5 C5.
☎ 01 42 65 00 00.

Place de la République
1 Ave de la République 75011.
Map 14 D1.
☎ 01 43 55 92 64.

Place St-Michel
29 Quai St-Michel 75005.
Map 13 A4.
☎ 01 43 29 63 66.

Place du Trocadéro
1 Ave D'Eylau 75016.
Map 9 C1.
☎ 01 47 27 00 00.

Rond Point des Champs-Elysées
7 Ave Matignon 75008.
Map 5 A5.
☎ 01 42 56 29 00.

St-Paul
Ⓜ St-Paul.
Map 13 C3.
☎ 01 48 87 49 39.

TAXIS BOOKED BY TELEPHONE

Alpha
☎ 01 45 85 85 85.

Artaxi
☎ 01 42 03 50 50.

G7
☎ 01 47 39 47 39.

Les Taxis Bleus
☎ 01 49 36 10 10.

SNCF INFORMATION

General Information and Ticket Reservations
☎ 08 36 35 35 35.
🖥 www.sncf.fr

TAA (Car trains)
☎ 01 53 33 60 11
(Paris Bercy).or
01 56 33 06 00 (CRNI,
for international trains).

STREET FINDER

THE MAP REFERENCES given with all sights, hotels, restaurants, shops and entertainment venues described in this book refer to the maps in this section (*see* How Map References Work *opposite*). A complete index of street names and all the places of interest marked on the maps can be found on the following pages. The key map shows the area of Paris covered by the *Street Finder*, with the arrondissement numbers for the various districts. The maps include not only the sightseeing areas (which are colour-coded), but the whole of central Paris with all the districts important for hotels, restaurants, shopping and entertainment venues. The symbols used to represent sights and features on the *Street Finder* maps are listed opposite.

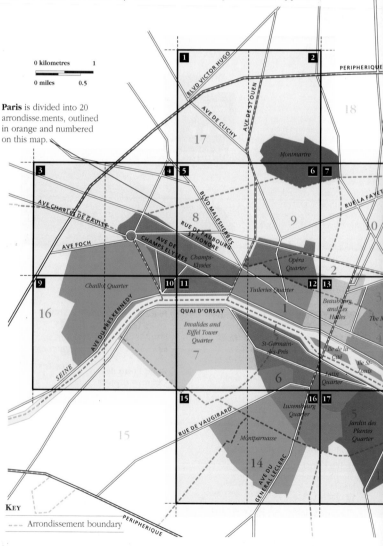

0 kilometres   1

0 miles   0.5

Paris is divided into 20 arrondisse.ments, outlined in orange and numbered on this map.

PERIPHERIQUE

BLVD VICTOR HUGO

AVE DE ST OUEN

AVE DE CLICHY

17

18

Montmartre

AVE CHARLES DE GAULLE

BLVD MALESHERBES

RUE DE FAUBOURG ST HONORE

RUE LA FAYE

AVE FOCH

AVE DES CHAMPS ELYSEES

8

9

Champs-Elysées

Opéra Quarter

16

Chaillot Quarter

AVE DU PRES KENNEDY

QUAI D'ORSAY

Invalides and Eiffel Tower Quarter

7

Tuileries Quarter

1

St-Germain-des-Prés

6

Beaubourg and les Halles

Île de la Cité

Île St-Louis

Latin Quarter

SEINE

15

RUE DE VAUGIRARD

Montparnasse

14

AVE DU GENERAL LECLERC

Luxembourg Quarter

5

Jardin des Plantes Quarter

KEY

- - - Arrondissement boundary

PERIPHERIQUE

HOW THE MAP REFERENCES WORK

The first figure tells you which *Street Finder* map to turn to.

Hôtel de Ville ⑲

4 Pl de l'Hôtel-de-Ville 75004.
Map 13 B3. ☎ 01 42 76 50 49.
Ⓜ *Hôtel de Ville.* ◯ 10.30am
Mon for tour, phone to check.
⬤ *public hols, official
functions* ♿ ✔

The letter and number give the grid reference. Letters go across the map's top and bottom; figures on its sides.

The map continues on page 17 of the *Street Finder*.

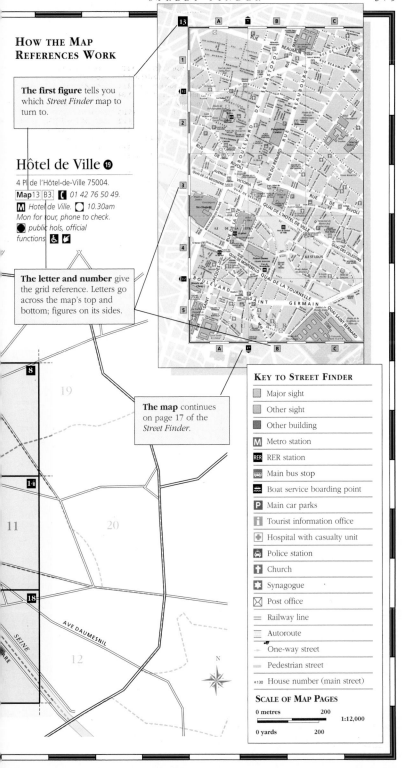

KEY TO STREET FINDER

▢	Major sight
▢	Other sight
▢	Other building
Ⓜ	Metro station
RER	RER station
🚏	Main bus stop
⛴	Boat service boarding point
P	Main car parks
ℹ	Tourist information office
✚	Hospital with casualty unit
🚓	Police station
✚	Church
✡	Synagogue
⊠	Post office
=	Railway line
▭	Autoroute
→	One-way street
▬	Pedestrian street
«130	House number (main street)

SCALE OF MAP PAGES

0 metres	200	
		1:12,000
0 yards	200	

Street Finder Index

Each place name is followed by its arrondissement number, and then by its Street Finder reference.

Each place name is followed by its arrondissement number, and then by its Street Finder reference.

Each place name is followed by its arrondissement number, and then by its Street Finder reference.

H

I

J

Each place name is followed by its arrondissement number, and then by its Street Finder reference.

Each place name is followed by its arrondissement number, and then by its Street Finder reference.

Each place name is followed by its arrondissement number, and then by its Street Finder reference.

Each place name is followed by its arrondissement number, and then by its Street Finder reference.

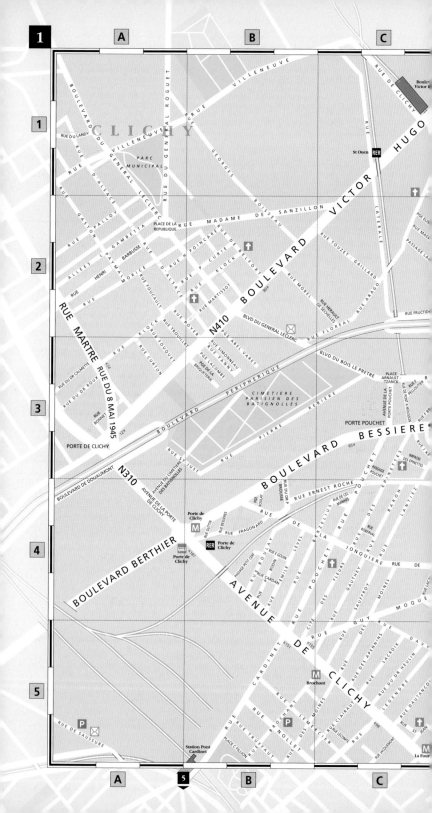

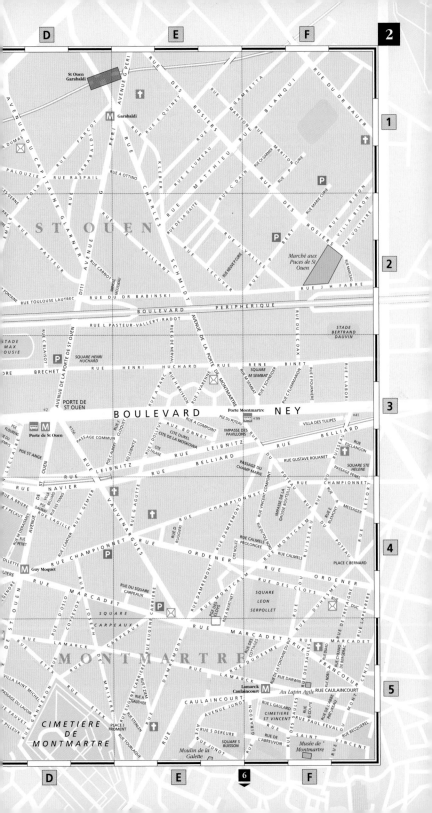

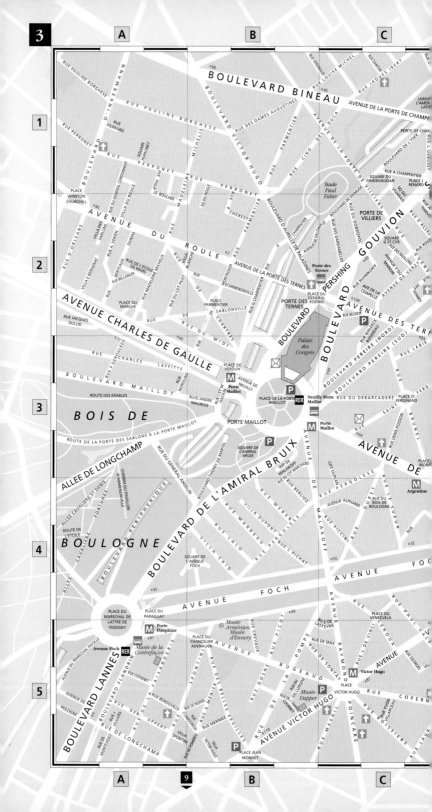

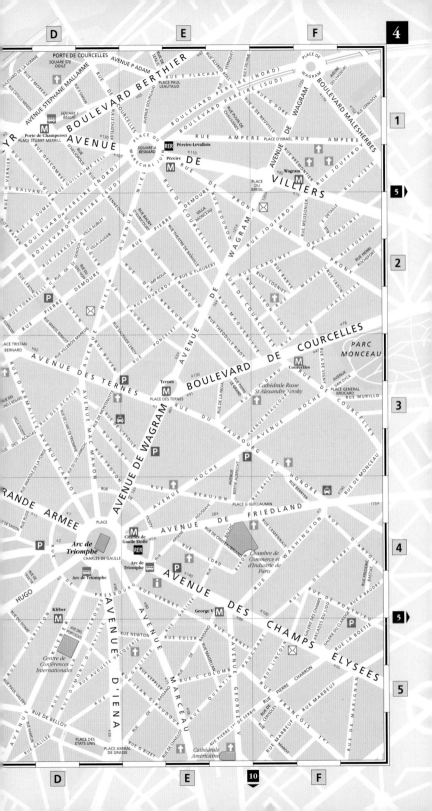

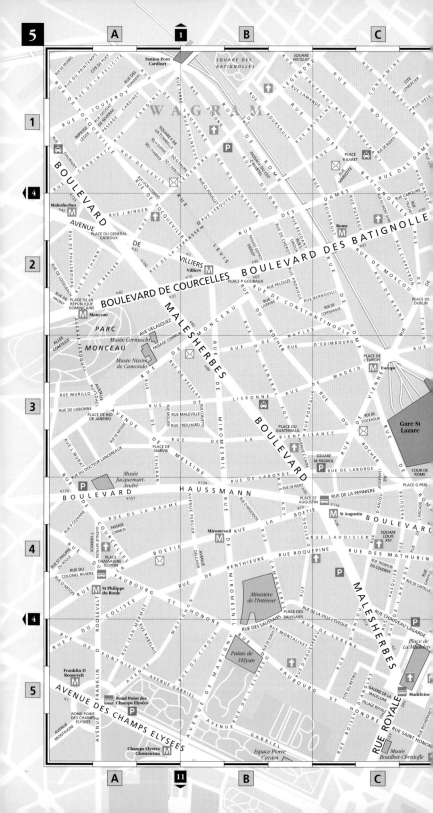

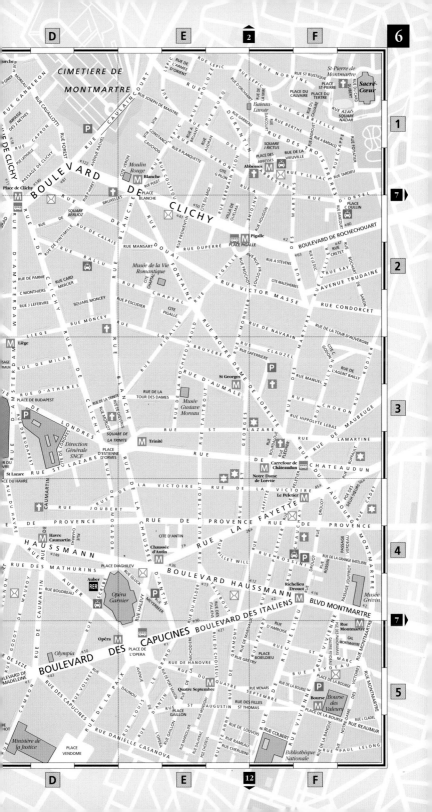

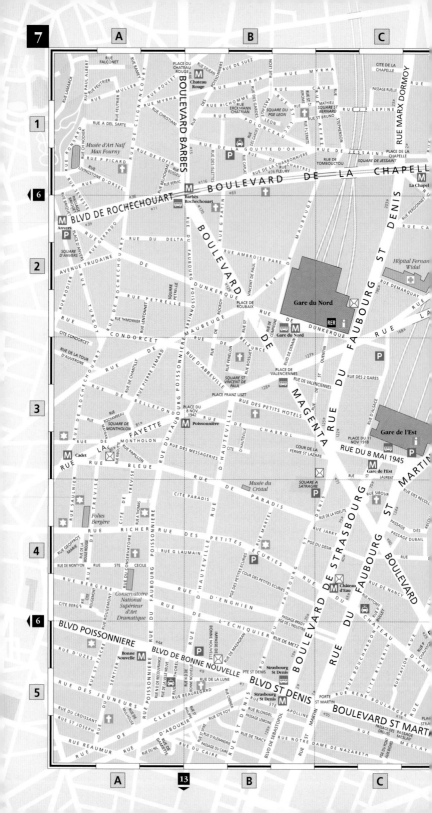

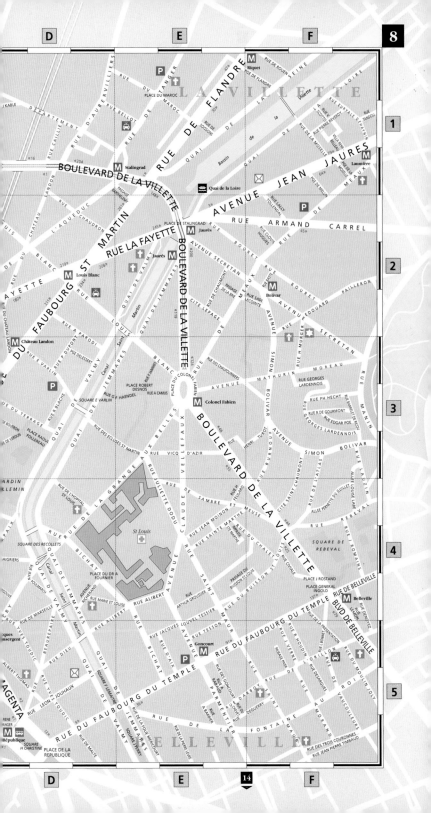

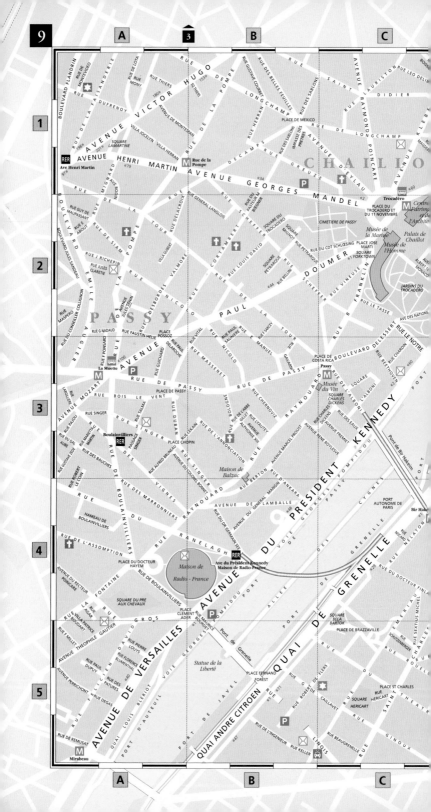

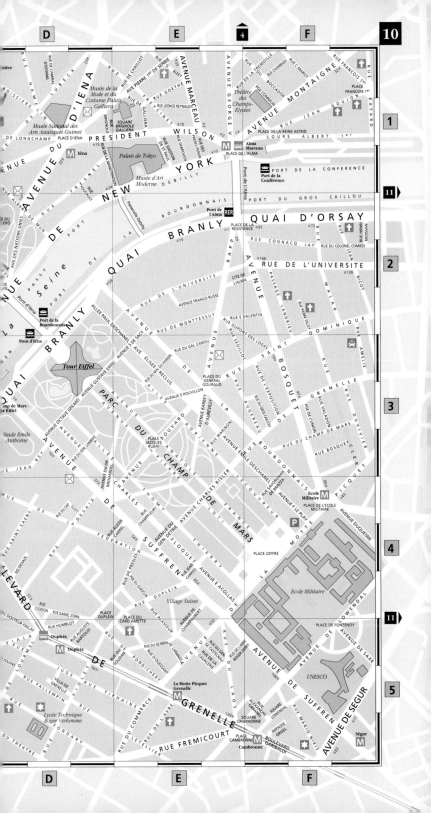

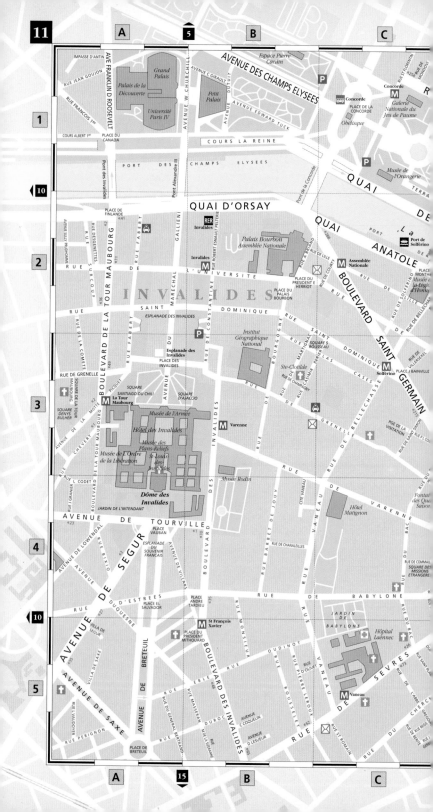

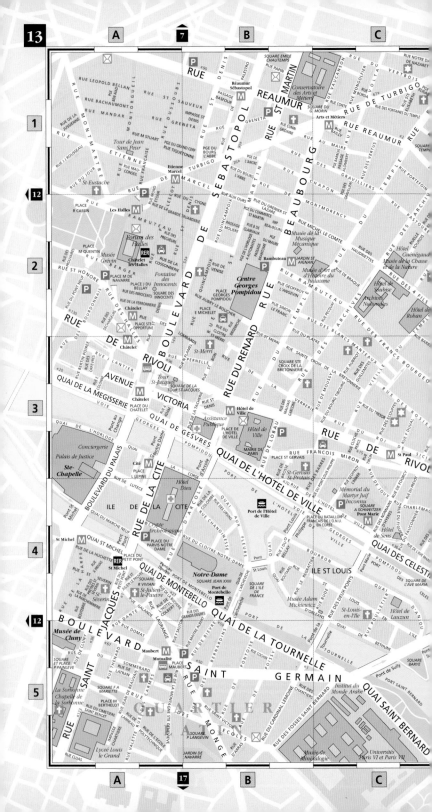

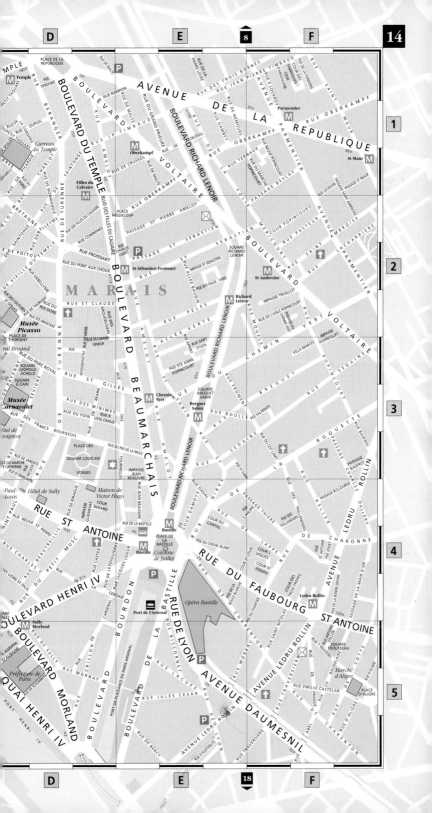

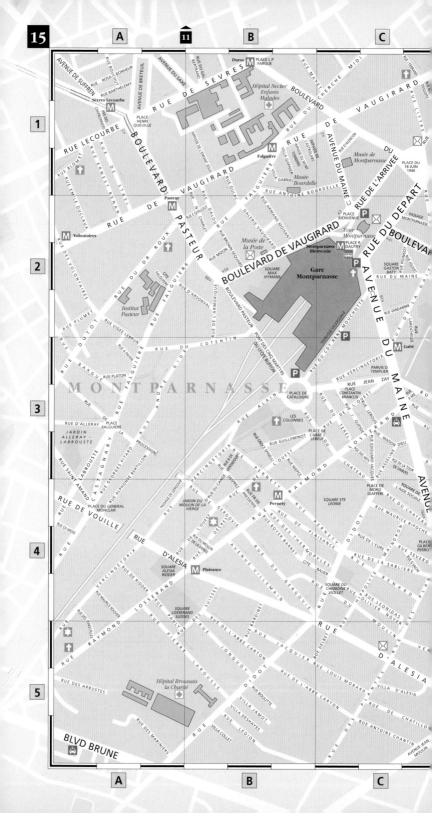

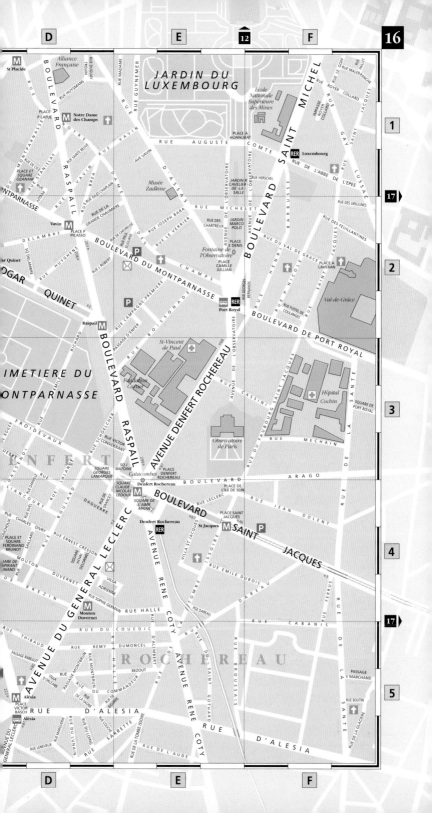

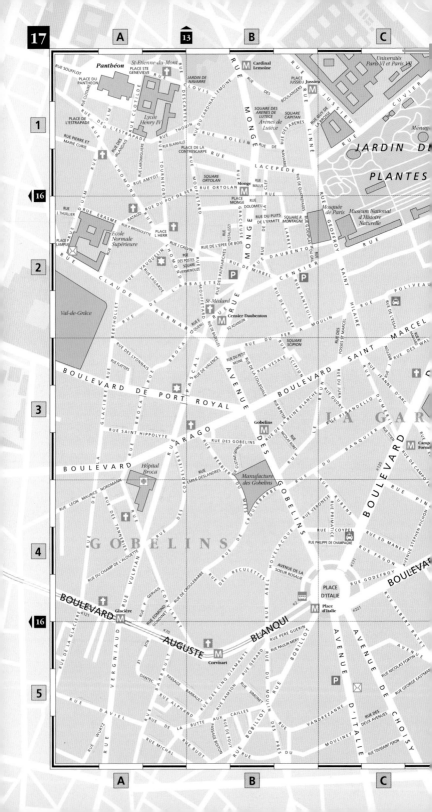

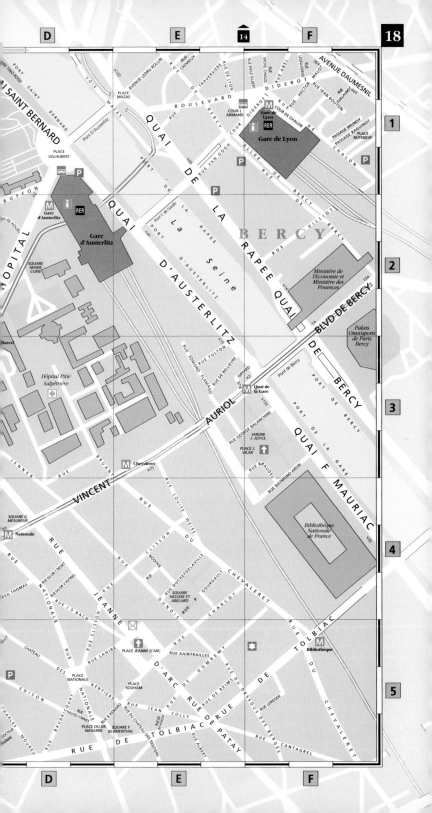

General Index

Acknowledgments

DORLING KINDERSLEY would like to thank the many people whose help and assistance contributed to the preparation of this book.

MAIN CONTRIBUTOR
Alan Tillier has lived in all the main areas of Paris for 25 years, during which time he has been Paris correspondent for several journals including *Newsweek*, *The Times* and the *International Herald Tribune*. He is the author of several *Herald Tribune* guides for business travellers to Europe.

CONTRIBUTORS
Lenny Borger, Karen Burshtein, Thomas Quinn Curtiss, David Downie, Fiona Dunlop, Heidi Ellison, Alexandre Lazareff, Robert Noah, Andrew Sanger, Martha Rose Shulman, David Stevens, Ian Williams, Jude Welton.

DORLING KINDERSLEY wishes to thank the following editors and researchers at Websters International Publishers: Sandy Carr, Siobhan Bremner, Valeria Fabbri, Gemma Hancock, Sara Harper, Annie Hubert, Celia Woolfrey.

ADDITIONAL PHOTOGRAPHY
Andy Crawford, Michael Crockett, Lucy Davies, Mike Dunning, Philip Gatward, Steve Gorton, Alison Harris, Chas Howson, Dave King, Ranald MacKechnie, Eric Meacher, Neil Mersh, Stephen Oliver, Poppy, Susannah Price, Tim Ridley, Philippe Sebert, Steve Shott, Peter Wilson, Steven Wooster.

ADDITIONAL ILLUSTRATIONS
John Fox, Nick Gibbard, David Harris, Kevin Jones Associates, John Woodcock.

CARTOGRAPHY
Andrew Heritage, James Mills-Hicks, John Plumer, Chez Picthall (DK Cartography). Advanced Illustration (Cheshire), Contour Publishing (Derby), Euromap Limited (Berkshire). Street Finder maps: ERA-Maptec Ltd (Dublin) adapted with permission from original survey and mapping by Shobunsha (Japan).

CARTOGRAPHIC RESEARCH
Roger Bullen, Tony Chambers, Paul Dempsey, Ruth Duxbury, Ailsa Heritage, Margeret Hynes, Jayne Parsons, Donna Rispoli, Andrew Thompson.

DESIGN AND EDITORIAL
MANAGING EDITOR Douglas Amrine
MANAGING ART EDITOR Geoff Manders
SENIOR EDITOR Georgina Matthews
SERIES DESIGN CONSULTANT Peter Luff
EDITORIAL DIRECTOR David Lamb

ART DIRECTOR Anne-Marie Bulat
PRODUCTION CONTROLLER Hilary Stephens
PICTURE RESEARCH Naomi Peck
DTP DESIGNER Andy Wilkinson
Janet Abbott, Emma Ainsworth, Hilary Bird, Vanessa Courtier, Maggie Crowley, Lisa Davidson, Guy Dimond, Elizabeth Eyre, Simon Farbrother, Fay Franklin, Eric Gibory, Paul Hines, Fiona Holman, Gail Jones, Nancy Jones, Stephen Knowlden, Chris Lascelles, Rebecca Milner, Fiona Morgan, Lyn Parry, Shirin Patel, Philippa Richmond, Philippe Rouin, Andrew Szudek.

SPECIAL ASSISTANCE
Miranda Dewer at Bridgeman Art Library, Editions Gallimard, Lindsay Hunt, Emma Hutton at Cooling Brown, Janet Todd at DACS.

PHOTOGRAPHIC REFERENCE
Musée Carnavalet, Thomas d'Hoste.

PHOTOGRAPHY PERMISSIONS
DORLING KINDERSLEY would like to thank the following for their kind permission to photograph at their establishments:
Aéroports de Paris, Basilique du Sacré-Coeur de Montmartre, Beauvilliers, Benoit, Bibliothèque Historique de la Ville de Paris, Bibliothèque Polonaise, Bofinger, Brasserie Lipp, Café de Flore, Caisse Nationale des Monuments Historiques et des Sites, Les Catacombes, Centre National d'Art et de Culture Georges Pompidou, Chartier, Chiberta, La Cité des Sciences et de l'Industrie and L'EPPV, La Coupole, Les Deux Magots, Fondation Cousteau, Le Grand Colbert, Hôtel Atala, Hôtel Liberal Bruand, Hôtel Meurice, Hôtel Relais Christine, Kenzo, Lucas-Carton, La Madeleine, Mariage Frères, Memorial du Martyr Juif Inconnu, Thierry Mugler, Musée Armenien de France, Musée de l'Art Juif, Musée Bourdelle, Musée du Cabinet des Medailles, Musée Carnavalet, Musée Cernuschi: Ville de Paris, Musée du Cinema Henri Langlois, Musée Cognacq-Jay, Musée de Cristal de Baccarat, Musée d'Ennery, Musée Grévin, Musée Jacquemart-André, Musée de la Musique Méchanique, Musée National des Châteaux de Malmaison et Bois-Préau, Collections du Musée National de la Légion d'Honneur, Musée National du Moyen Age-Thermes de Cluny, Musée de Notre-Dame de Paris, Musée de l'Opéra, Musée de l'Ordre de la Libération, Musée d'Orsay, Musée de la Préfecture de la Police, Musée de Radio France, Musée Rodin, Musée des Transports Urbains, Musée du Vin, Musée Zadkine, Notre-Dame du Travail, A l'Olivier,

Palais de la Découverte, Palais de Luxembourg, Pharamond, Pied de Cochon, Lionel Poilaîne, St Germain-des-Prés, St Louis en l'Ile, St Médard, St Merry, St-Paul– St-Louis, St-Roch, St-Sulpice, La Société Nouvelle d'Exploitation de La Tour Eiffel, La Tour Montparnasse, UNESCO, and all the other museums, churches, hotels, restaurants, shops, galleries and sights too numerous to thank individually.

PICTURE CREDITS

t=top; tc=top centre; tr=top right; cla=centre left above; ca=centre above; cra=centre right above; cl=centre left; c=centre; cr=centre right; clb=centre left below; cb=centre below; crb=centre right below; bl=bottom left; bc=bottom centre; br=bottom right.

Works of art have been reproduced with the permission of the following copyright holders: © SUCCESSION H MATISSE/DACS 1993: 111ca; © ADAGP/SPADEM, Paris and DACS, London 1993: 44cl; © ADAGP, Paris and DACS, London 1993: 61br, 61tr, 105tc, 107cb, 109b, 111tc, 111cb, 112bl, 112t, 112br, 113bl, 113br, 119c, 120b, 179tl, 180bc, 181cr, 211tc; © DACS 1993: 13cra, 36tl, 43cra, 45cr, 50br, 55cr, 57tl, 100t, 100br, 100clb, 100cl, 100ca, 101t, 101ca, 101cr, 101bl, 104, 107cra, 113c, 137tl, 178cl, 178ca, 208br.

CHRISTO–THE PONT NEUF WRAPPED, Paris, 1975-85: 38cla; © CHRISTO 1985, by kind permission of the artist. Photos achieved with the assistance of the EPPV and the CSI pp 234-9; Courtesy of ERBEN OTTO DIX: 110bl; Photos of DISNEYLAND ® PARIS: 242tr, 243bl, 243cr. The characters, architectural works and trademarks are the property of THE WALT DISNEY COMPANY. All rights reserved; FONDATION LE CORBUSIER: 59t, 254bl; Courtesy of THE ESTATE OF JOAN MITCHELL: 113t; © HENRY MOORE FOUNDATION 1993: 191b. Reproduced by kind permission of the Henry Moore Foundation; BETH LIPKIN: 241t; Courtesy of the MAISON VICTOR HUGO, VILLE DE PARIS: 95cl; Courtesy of the MUSÉE D'ART NAIF MAX FOURNY PARIS: 221b, 223b; MUSÉE CARNAVALET: 212b; MUSÉE DE L'HISTOIRE CONTEMPORAINE (BDIC), PARIS: 208br; MUSÉE DE L'ORANGERIE: 130tr; MUSÉE DU LOUVRE: 125br, 128c; MUSÉE NATIONAL DES CHÂTEAUX DE MALMAISON ET BOIS-PRÉAU: 255cr; MUSÉE MARMOTTAN: 58c, 58cb, 59c, 60tl, 131tr; MUSÉE DE LA MODE ET DU COSTUME PALAIS GALLIERA: 57br; MUSÉE DE MONTMARTRE, PARIS: 221t; MUSÉE DES MONUMENTS FRANÇAIS: 197tc, 198cr; MUSÉE NATIONAL DE LA LÉGION D'HONNEUR: 30bc, 143bl; MUSÉE DE LA VILLE DE PARIS: MUSÉE DU

PETIT PALAIS: 54cl, 205cb; © SUNDANCER: 346bl.

The Publishers are grateful to the following individuals, companies and picture libraries for permission to reproduce their photographs:

ADP: 361b; ALLSPORT UK: Sean Botterill 39br; ALLVEY & TOWERS: 362bl; THE ANCIENT ART AND ARCHITECTURE COLLECTION: 20clb; JAMES AUSTIN: 88t.

BANQUE DE FRANCE: 133t; NELLY BARIAND: 165c; GÉRARD BOULLAY: 84tl, 84tr, 84bl, 84br, 85t, 85cra, 85crb, 85br, 85bl; BRIDGEMAN ART LIBRARY, LONDON: (detail) 19br, 20cr, 21cl, 28cr–29cl, (detail) 33br; British Library, London (detail) 16br, (detail) 21bl, (detail) 22tl, (detail) 29tl; B N, Paris 17bl, (detail) 21tc, (detail) 21cr; Château de Versailles, France 17tr, 17bc, (detail) 17br, (detail) 28br, (detail) 155b; Christie's, London 8–9, (detail) 22cb, 32cla, 34tl, 44c; Delomosne, London 30clb; Detroit Institute of Art, Michigan 43ca; Giraudon 14, (detail) 24bl, (detail) 24clb, (detail) 25br, (detail) 28bl, (detail) 28cla, (detail) 29bl, 31cb, 58br, (detail) 60bl, 60ca, 60c; Lauros– Giraudon 21tr; Louvre, Paris 56t, 60br, 61bl, 61tl; Roy Miles Gallery 25tr; Musée de L'Armée, Paris (detail) 83br; Musée Condé, Chantilly (detail) 4tr, 16bl, 17tcl, (detail) 17tcr, 17c, (detail) 20tl, (detail) 24bc; Musée Crozatier, Le Puy en Velay, France (detail) 23bl; Musée Gustave Moreau, Paris 56b, 231t; National Gallery (detail) 27tl, (detail) 44b; Musée d'Orsay, Paris 43br; Musée de la Ville de Paris, Musée Carnavalet (detail) 28bc, (detail) 29tr, 29crb; Collection Painton Cowen 38cla; Palais du Tokyo, Paris 59b; Philadelphia Museum of Modern Art, Pennsylvania 43cra; Temples Newsham House, Leeds 23cr; Uffizi Gallery, Florence (detail) 22br; © THE BRITISH MUSEUM: 29tc.

CITÉ DE LA MUSIQUE: Eric Mahondieu 235br; CITÉ DES SCIENCES ET DE L'INDUSTRIE: Michel Lamoureux 236cb, 236b, 238t; Michel Virad 237tl, 238br; CORBIS: Burnstein Collection 227b; CSI: Pascal Prieur 238cl, 238cb.

R Doisneau: RAPHO 143t.
ESPACE MONTMARTRE: 220bl; EUROPEAN COMMISSION 355; MARY EVANS PICTURE LIBRARY: 36bl, 42br, 81br, 89tl, 94b, 130b, 141cl, 191c, 192cr, 193crb, 209b, 224bl, 247br, 251t, 253b, 372t.

GIRAUDON: (detail) 20bl, (detail) 21crb; Lauros–Giraudon (detail) 31bl; Musée de la Ville de Paris: Musée Carnavalet (detail) 211t; LE GRAND VÉFOUR: 287t.

ROBERT HARDING PICTURE LIBRARY: 20br, 24tl, 27ca, 27br, 34cla, 36tl, 39br, 45cr, 65br,

240cb, 365cr; B M 25ca; B N 191tr, 208bc; Biblioteco Reale, Turin 127t; Bulloz 208cb; P Craven 364b; R Francis 82clb; I Griffiths 360t; H Josse 208br; Musée National des Châteaux de Malmaison et Bois-Préau 31tc; Musée de Versailles 24cl; R Poinot 345b; P Tetrel 251crb; Explorer 10bl; F. Chazot 329b; Girard 65c; P Gleizes 62bl; F Jalain 362b; J Moatti 328bl, 328cl; Walter Rawlings 41bc; A Wolf 123br, 123tl; ALISON HARRIS: Musée de Montparnasse 179cl; Pavillon des Arts 108br; Le Village Royale 132tl; JOHN HESELTINE PHOTOGRAPHY: 12br, 174; HULTON GETTY: 42cl, 43bl, 43cr, 43t, 45cl, 101br, 181tc, 231bl, 232c; Charles Hewitt 38clb; Lancaster 181tc.

© IGN PARIS 1990 Authorisation Nº 90–2067: 11b; INSTITUT DU MONDE ARABE: Georges Fessey 165tr.

THE KOBAL COLLECTION: 42t, 44t, 140b; Columbia Pictures 181br; Société Générale de Films 36tc; Paramount Studios 42bl; Les Films du Carrosse 109t; Montsouris 197cra; Georges Méliès 198bl.

THE LEBRECHT COLLECTION: 227br; FRANÇOIS LEQUEUX 194cl.

MAGNUM: Bruno Barbey 64b; Philippe Halsmann 45b; MINISTERE DE L'ECONOMIE ET DES FINANCES: 355c; MINISTERE DE L'INTÉRIEUR SGAP DE PARIS: 352bc, 352br, 353t; COLLECTIONS DU MOBILIER NATIONAL-CLICHÉ DU MOBILIER NATIONAL: 167cr; © photo MUSÉE DE L'ARMÉE: 189cr; MUSÉE DES ARTS DÉCORATIFS, PARIS: L Sully Jaulmes 54t; MUSÉE DES ARTS DE LA MODE–Collection UCAD–UFAC: 121b; MUSÉE BOUILHET-CHRISTOFLE: 57tr, 132t; MUSÉE CANTONAL DES BEAUX-ARTS, LAUSANNE: 115b; MUSÉE CARNAVALET: Dac Karin Maucotel 97b; MUSÉE D'ART ET D'HISTOIRE DU JUDAISME/Christophe Fouin 103br; MUSÉE NATIONAL DE L'HISTOIRE NATURELLE: D Serrette 167cl; MUSÉE DE L'HOLOGRAPHIE: 109cl; © MUSÉE DE L'HOMME, PARIS: D Ponsard 199c, 199cl; © PHOTO MUSÉE DE LA MARINE, PARIS: 30bl, 196cl; MUSÉE NATIONAL D'ART MODERN–CENTRE GEORGES POMPIDOU, PARIS: 61tr, 110br, 110bl, 111t, 111ca, 111cb, 112t, 112bl, 112br, 113t, 113c, 113bl, 113br;

MUSÉE DES PLANS-RELIEFS, PARIS: 186crb; MUSÉE DE LA POSTE, PARIS: 179tl; MUSÉE DE LA SEITA, PARIS: D Dado 190t.

PHILIPPE PERDEREAU: 132b, 133b; CLICHÉ PHOTOTHÈQUE DES MUSÉES DE LA VILLE DE PARIS – © DACS 1993: 19ca, 19crb, 26cr–27cl, 96tr; POPPERFOTO: 227t.

PAUL RAFERTY 246b; RATP.SG/G.I.E. TOTHEME 54; 370; REDFERNS: W Gottlieb 36clb; © PHOTO RÉUNION DES MUSÉES NATIONAUX: Grand Trianon 24crb; Musée Guimet 54cb, 200tr; Musée du Louvre: 25cb, (detail) 30cr–31cl, 55tl, 123bl, 124t, 124c, 124b, 125t, 125c, 126c, 126bl, 126br, 127b, 128t, 128b, 129t, 129c; Musée Nationaux d'Art Moderne © DACS/ADAGP 111crb; Musée Picasso 55cr, 100t, 100c, 100cl, 100clb, 100br, 101bl, 101cr, 101ca, 101t; ROGER-VIOLLET: (detail) 22clb, (detail) 37bl, (detail) 192bc, (detail) 209t; ANN RONAN PICTURE LIBRARY: 173cr; PHILIPPE RUAULT: Fondation Cartier 179bl.

LA SAMARITAINE, PARIS: 115c; SEALINK PLC: 362cl; SIPAPRESS: 222c; FRANK SPOONER PICTURES: F Reglain 64ca; P Renault 64c; SYGMA: 33crb, 240cl; F Poincet 38tl; Keystone 38bc, 241cra; J Langevin 39br; Keler 39crb; J Van Hasselt 39tr; P. Habans 62c; A Gyori 63cr; P Vauthey 65bl; Y Forestier 188t; Sunset Boulevard 241br; Water Carone 328t.

TALLANDIER: 23cb, 23tl, 26cl, 26clb, 26bl, 27bl, 28tl, 29cr, 29ca, 30tl, 30cb, 30br, 36cla, 37ca, 37br, 38cb, 52cla; B N 26br, 30crb, 36bc; Brigaud 37crb; Brimeur 32bl; Charmet 34cb; Dubout 15b, 18br, 22ca, 23br, 24br, 28c, 31cr, 31tr, 32br, 33bl, 34clb, 34bl, 34br, 35bl, 35br, 35clb, 35tl, 36crb; Josse 18cla, 18tc, 18c, 18clb, 19tl, 34bc; Josse-B N 18bl; Joubert 36c; Tildier 35ca; Vigne 32clb; LE TRAIN BLEU: 289t.

VIDÉOTHÈQUE DE PARIS: Hoi Pham Dinh 106llb

AGENCE VU: Didier Lefèvre 328cr.

Front Endpaper: RÉUNION DES MUSÉES NATIONAUX: Musée Picasso cr.Back endpaper: RATP CML AGENCE CARTOGRAPHIQUE.

All other pictures: © DORLING KINDERSLEY.

Phrase Book

In Emergency

Help!	**Au secours!**	*oh sekoor*
Stop!	**Arrêtez!**	*aret-ay*
Call a doctor!	**Appelez un médecin!**	*apuh-lay uñ medsañ*
Call an ambulance!	**Appelez une ambulance!**	*apuh-lay oon oñboo-loñs*
Call the police!	**Appelez la police!**	*apuh-lay lah pob-lees*
Call the fire brigade!	**Appelez les pompiers!**	*apuh-lay leh poñ-peevay*
Where is the nearest telephone?	**Où est le téléphone le plus proche?**	*oo ay luh teblehfon luh ploo prosh*
Where is the nearest hospital?	**Où est l'hôpital le plus proche?**	*oo ay l'opeetal luh ploo prosh*

Communication Essentials

Yes	**Oui**	*wee*
No	**Non**	*noñ*
Please	**S'il vous plaît**	*seel voo play*
Thank you	**Merci**	*mer-see*
Excuse me	**Excusez-moi**	*exkoo-zay mwah*
Hello	**Bonjour**	*boñzhoor*
Goodbye	**Au revoir**	*oh ruh-vwar*
Good night	**Bonsoir**	*boñ-swar*
Morning	**Le matin**	*matañ*
Afternoon	**L'après-midi**	*l'apreb-meedee*
Evening	**Le soir**	*swar*
Yesterday	**Hier**	*eeyehr*
Today	**Aujourd'hui**	*oh-zhoor-dwee*
Tomorrow	**Demain**	*dubmañ*
Here	**Ici**	*ee-see*
There	**Là**	*lah*
What?	**Quel, quelle?**	*kel, kel*
When?	**Quand?**	*koñ*
Why?	**Pourquoi?**	*poor-kwah*
Where?	**Où?**	*oo*

Useful Phrases

How are you?	**Comment allez-vous?**	*kom-moñ talay voo*
Very well, thank you.	**Très bien, merci.**	*treb byañ, mer-see*
Pleased to meet you.	**Enchanté de faire votre connaissance.**	*oñshoñ-tay dub febr votr kon-ay-sans*
See you soon.	**A bientôt.**	*byañ-tob*
That's fine.	**Voilà qui est parfait**	*vwalah kee ay par-fay*
Where is/are...?	**Où est/sont...?**	*oo ay/soñ*
How far is it to...?	**Combien de kilometres d'ici à...?**	*kom-byañ dub keelo-metr d'ee-see ah*
Which way to...?	**Quelle est la direction pour...?**	*kel ay lah deer-ek-syoñ poor*
Do you speak English?	**Parlez-vous anglais?**	*par-lay voo oñg-lay*
I don't understand.	**Je ne comprends pas.**	*zhuh nub kom-proñ pah*
Could you speak slowly please?	**Pouvez-vous parler moins vite s'il vous plaît?**	*poo-vay voo par-lay mwañ veet seel voo play*
I'm sorry.	**Excusez-moi.**	*exkoo-zay mwah*

Useful Words

big	**grand**	*groñ*
small	**petit**	*pub-tee*
hot	**chaud**	*show*
cold	**froid**	*frwah*
good	**bon**	*boñ*
bad	**mauvais**	*mob-veh*
enough	**assez**	*assay*
well	**bien**	*byañ*
open	**ouvert**	*oo-ver*
closed	**fermé**	*fer-meh*
left	**gauche**	*gobsh*
right	**droit**	*drwah*
straight on	**tout droit**	*too drwah*
near	**près**	*preb*
far	**loin**	*lwañ*
up	**en haut**	*oñ ob*
down	**en bas**	*oñ bab*
early	**de bonne heure**	*dub bon urr*
late	**en retard**	*oñ rub-tar*
entrance	**l'entrée**	*l'on-tray*
exit	**la sortie**	*sor-tee*
toilet	**les toilettes, le WC**	*twab-let, vay-see*
free, unoccupied	**libre**	*leebr*
free, no charge	**gratuit**	*grab-twee*

Making a Telephone Call

I'd like to place a long-distance call.	**Je voudrais faire un interurbain.**	*zhub voo-dreb febr uñ añter-oorbañ*
I'd like to make a reverse charge call.	**Je voudrais faire une communication avec PCV.**	*zhub voo-dreb febr oon komoonikah-syoñavek peb-seb-veh*
I'll try again later.	**Je rappelerai plus tard.**	*zhub rapel-eray ploo tar*
Can I leave a message?	**Est-ce que je peux laisser un message?**	*es-keb zhub pub leb-say uñ mebsazh*
Hold on.	**Ne quittez pas, s'il vous plaît.**	*nub kee-tay pab seel voo play*
Could you speak up a little please?	**Pouvez-vous parler un peu plus fort?**	*poo-vay voo par-lay uñ pub ploo for*
local call	**la communication locale**	*komoonikah-syoñ low-kal*

Shopping

How much does this cost?	**C'est combien s'il vous plaît?**	*say kom-byañ seel voo play*
I would like ...	**je voudrais...**	*zhub voo-dray*
Do you have?	**Est-ce que vous avez?**	*es-kuh voo zavay*
I'm just looking.	**Je regarde seulement.**	*zhub rubgar sublmoñ*
Do you take credit cards?	**Est-ce que vous acceptez les cartes de crédit?**	*es-kuh voo zaksept-ay leh kart dub kreb-dee*
Do you take traveller's cheques?	**Est-ce que vous acceptez les cheques de voyages?**	*es-kuh voo zaksept-ay leh shek dub vwayazb*
What time do you open?	**A quelle heure vous êtes ouvert?**	*ab kel urr voo zet oo-ver*
What time do you close?	**A quelle heure vous êtes fermé?**	*ab kel urr voo zet fer-may*
This one.	**Celui-ci.**	*subl-wee-see*
That one.	**Celui-là.**	*subl-wee-lab*
expensive	**cher**	*shebr*
cheap	**pas cher, bon marché**	*pab shebr, boñ mar-shay*
size, clothes	**la taille**	*tye*
size, shoes	**la pointure**	*pwañ-tur*
white	**blanc**	*bloñ*
black	**noir**	*nwabr*
red	**rouge**	*roozb*
yellow	**jaune**	*zhobwn*
green	**vert**	*vebr*
blue	**bleu**	*blub*

Types of Shop

antique shop	**le magasin d'antiquités**	*maga-zañ d'oñteekee-tay*
bakery	**la boulangerie**	*booloñ-zhuree*
bank	**la banque**	*boñk*
book shop	**la librairie**	*lee-brebree*
butcher	**la boucherie**	*boo-sbebree*
cake shop	**la pâtisserie**	*patee-sree*
cheese shop	**la fromagerie**	*fromazb-ree*
chemist	**la pharmacie**	*farmab-see*
dairy	**la crémerie**	*krem-ree*
department store	**le grand magasin**	*groñ maga-zañ*
delicatessen	**la charcuterie**	*sbarkoot-ree*
fishmonger	**la poissonnerie**	*pwasson-ree*
gift shop	**le magasin de cadeaux**	*maga-zañ dub kadoh*
greengrocer	**le marchand de légumes**	*mar-sboñ dub lay-goom*
grocery	**l'alimentation**	*alee-moñta-syoñ*
hairdresser	**le coiffeur**	*kwafubr*
market	**le marché**	*marsb-ay*
newsagent	**le magasin de journaux**	*maga-zañ dub zhoor-no*
post office	**la poste, le bureau de poste, le PTT**	*pobst, boorob dub pobst, peb-teb-teb*
shoe shop	**le magasin de chaussures**	*maga-zañ dub show-soor*
supermarket	**le supermarché**	*soo pebr-marshay*
tobacconist	**le tabac**	*tabab*
travel agent	**l'agence de voyages**	*l'azboñs dub vwayazb*

Sightseeing

abbey	**l'abbaye**	*l'abay-ee*
art gallery	**la galerie d'art**	*galer-ee dart*
bus station	**la gare routière**	*gabr roo-tee-yebr*

English	French	Pronunciation
cathedral	la cathédrale	katay-dral
church	l'église	l'aygleez
garden	le jardin	zhar-dañ
library	la bibliothèque	beebleeo-tek
museum	le musée	moo-zay
railway station	la gare (SNCF)	gabr (es-en-say-ef)
tourist	les renseignements	roñsayn-moñ
information	touristiques, le	toorees-teek, sandee-
office	syndicat d'initiative	ka d'eenee-syateev
town hall	l'hôtel de ville	l'obtel duh veel
closed for	fermeture	febrmeb-tur
public holiday	jour férié	zhoor febree-ay

STAYING IN A HOTEL

English	French	Pronunciation
Do you have a	Est-ce que vous	es-kuh voo-zavay
vacant room?	avez une chambre?	oon shambr
double room,	la chambre à deux	shambr ah dub
with double bed	personnes, avec	pebr-son avek un
	un grand lit	gronñ lee
twin room	la chambre à	shambr ah
	deux lits	dub lee
single room	la chambre à	shambr ah
	une personne	oon pebr-son
room with a	la chambre avec	shambr avek
bath, shower	salle de bains,	sal dub bañ,
	une douche	oon doosb
porter	le garçon	gar-soñ
key	la clef	klay
I have a	J'ai fait une	zhay fay oon
reservation.	réservation.	rayzehrva-syoñ

EATING OUT

English	French	Pronunciation
Have you	Avez-vous une	avay-voo oon
got a table?	table de libre?	tabbl duh leebr
I want to	Je voudrais	zhub voo-dray
reserve	réserver	rayzehr-vay
a table.	une table.	oon tabbl
The bill	L'addition s'il	l'adee-syoñ seel
please.	vous plaît.	voo play
I am a	Je suis	zhub swee
vegetarian.	végétarien.	vezhay-tebryañ
Waitress/	Madame,	mah-dam,
waiter	Mademoiselle/	mab-demwahzel/
	Monsieur	mub-syub
menu	le menu, la carte	men-oo, kart
fixed-price	le menu à	men-oo ab
menu	prix fixe	pree feeks
cover charge	le couvert	koo-vebr
wine list	la carte des vins	kart-deb vañ
glass	le verre	vebr
bottle	la bouteille	boo-tay
knife	le couteau	koo-tob
fork	la forchette	for-shet
spoon	la cuillère	kwee-yebr
breakfast	le petit	pub-tee
	déjeuner	deb-zhuh-nay
lunch	le déjeuner	deb-zhuh-nay
dinner	le dîner	dee-nay
main course	le plat principal	plab prañsee-pal
starter, first	l'entrée, le hors	l'oñ-tray, or-
course	d'oeuvre	dubvr
dish of the day	le plat du jour	plab doo zhoor
wine bar	le bar à vin	bar ah vañ
café	le café	ka-fay
rare	saignant	say-noñ
medium	à point	ah pwañ
well done	bien cuit	byañ kwee

MENU DECODER

English	French	Pronunciation
apple	la pomme	pom
baked	cuit au four	kweet ob foor
banana	la banane	banan
beef	le boeuf	bubf
beer, draught	la bière, bière	bee-yebr, bee-yebr
beer	à la pression	ab lab pres-syoñ
boiled	bouilli	boo-yee
bread	le pain	pan
butter	le beurre	burr
cake	le gâteau	gab-tob
cheese	le fromage	from-azh
chicken	le poulet	poo-lay
chips	les frites	freet
chocolate	le chocolat	sboko-lab
cocktail	le cocktail	cocktail
coffee	le café	kab-fay
dessert	le dessert	deb-ser
dry	sec	sek
duck	le canard	kanar

English	French	Pronunciation
egg	l'oeuf	l'uf
fish	le poisson	pwah-ssoñ
fresh fruit	le fruit frais	fruee freb
garlic	l'ail	l'eye
grilled	grillé	gree-yay
ham	le jambon	zhoñ-boñ
ice, ice cream	la glace	glas
lamb	l'agneau	l'anyob
lemon	le citron	see-troñ
lobster	le homard	omabr
meat	la viande	vee-yand
milk	le lait	leb
mineral water	l'eau minérale	l'ob meeney-ral
mustard	la moutarde	moo-tard
oil	l'huile	l'weel
olives	les olives	leb zoleev
onions	les oignons	leb zonyoñ
orange	l'orange	l'oroñzb
fresh orange juice	l'orange pressée	l'oroñzb press-eb
fresh lemon juice	le citron pressé	see-troñ press-eb
pepper	le poivre	pwavr
poached	poché	posh-ay
pork	le porc	por
potatoes	les pommes de terre	pom-dub tebr
prawns	les crevettes	krub-vet
rice	le riz	ree
roast	rôti	row-tee
roll	le petit pain	pub-tee pañ
salt	le sel	sel
sauce	la sauce	sobs
sausage, fresh	la saucisse	sobsees
seafood	les fruits de mer	fruee dub mer
shellfish	les crustaces	kroos-tas
snails	les escargots	leb zes-kar-gob
soup	la soupe, le potage	soop, pob-tazb
steak	le bifteck, le steack	beef-tek, stek
sugar	le sucre	sookr
tea	le thé	tay
toast	le toast	toast
vegetables	les légumes	lay-goom
vinegar	le vinaigre	veenaygr
water	l'eau	l'ob
red wine	le vin rouge	vañ roozb
white wine	le vin blanc	vañ bloñ

NUMBERS

	French	Pronunciation
0	zéro	zeb-rob
1	un, une	uñ, oon
2	deux	dub
3	trois	truab
4	quatre	katr
5	cinq	sañk
6	six	sees
7	sept	set
8	huit	weet
9	neuf	nerf
10	dix	dees
11	onze	oñz
12	douze	dooz
13	treize	trebz
14	quatorze	katorz
15	quinze	kañz
16	seize	sebz
17	dix-sept	dees-set
18	dix-huit	dees-weet
19	dix-neuf	dees-nerf
20	vingt	vañ
30	trente	tront
40	quarante	karoñt
50	cinquante	sañkoñt
60	soixante	swasoñt
70	soixante-dix	swasoñt-dees
80	quatre-vingts	katr-vañ
90	quatre-vingts-dix	katr-vañ-dees
100	cent	soñ
1,000	mille	meel

TIME

English	French	Pronunciation
one minute	une minute	oon mee-noot
one hour	une heure	oon urr
half an hour	une demi-heure	oon dub-mee urr
Monday	lundi	luñ-dee
Tuesday	mardi	mar-dee
Wednesday	mercredi	mehrkrub-dee
Thursday	jeudi	zhub-dee
Friday	vendredi	voñdrub-dee
Saturday	samedi	sam-dee
Sunday	dimanche	dee-moñsh

COUNTRY GUIDES

AUSTRALIA • CANADA • CRUISE GUIDE TO EUROPE AND THE
MEDITERRANEAN • EGYPT • FRANCE • GERMANY • GREAT BRITAIN
GREECE: ATHENS & THE MAINLAND • THE GREEK ISLANDS
IRELAND • ITALY • JAPAN • MEXICO • POLAND
PORTUGAL • SCOTLAND • SINGAPORE
SOUTH AFRICA • SPAIN • THAILAND
GREAT PLACES TO STAY IN EUROPE
A TASTE OF SCOTLAND

REGIONAL GUIDES

BALI & LOMBOK • BARCELONA & CATALONIA • CALIFORNIA
EUROPE • FLORENCE & TUSCANY • FLORIDA • HAWAII
JERUSALEM & THE HOLY LAND • LOIRE VALLEY
MILAN & THE LAKES • NAPLES WITH POMPEII & THE AMALFI
COAST • NEW ENGLAND • NEW ZEALAND
PROVENCE & THE COTE D'AZUR • SARDINIA
SEVILLE & ANDALUSIA • SICILY • SOUTHWEST USA & LAS VEGAS
A TASTE OF TUSCANY • VENICE & THE VENETO

CITY GUIDES

AMSTERDAM • BERLIN • BOSTON • BRUSSELS • BUDAPEST
CHICAGO • CRACOW • DELHI, AGRA & JAIPUR • DUBLIN
ISTANBUL • LISBON • LONDON • MADRID
MOSCOW • NEW YORK • PARIS • PRAGUE • ROME
SAN FRANCISCO • STOCKHOLM • ST PETERSBURG
SYDNEY • VIENNA • WARSAW • WASHINGTON, DC

NEW FOR SPRING 2002

CUBA • INDIA • MUNICH & THE BAVARIAN ALPS
NEW ORLEANS • TURKEY

FOR UPDATES TO OUR GUIDES, AND INFORMATION ON
<u>DK TRAVEL MAPS</u> & <u>PHRASEBOOKS</u>

VISIT US AT
eyewitnesstravel.dk.com

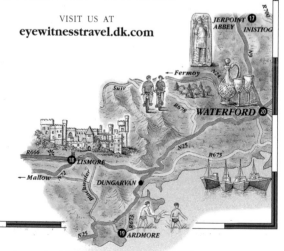

Paris Metro and Regional Express Railway (RER)

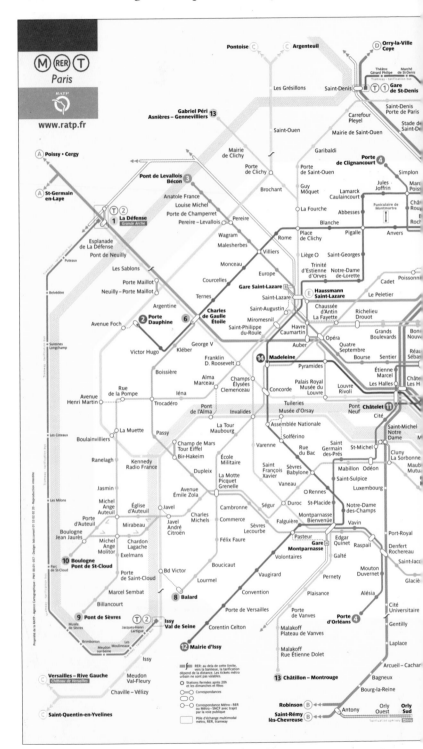